The Collected Works of St. John of the Cross

CHRIST CRUCIFIED
A DRAWING BY ST. JOHN OF THE CROSS

THE COLLECTED WORKS

of

ST. JOHN OF THE CROSS

Translated by
Kieran Kavanaugh, O.C.D.
and
Otilio Rodriguez, O.C.D.

with Introductions by
Kieran Kavanaugh, O.C.D.

ICS PUBLICATIONS
INSTITUTE OF CARMELITE STUDIES
WASHINGTON, D.C.
1973

Imprimi potest: Christopher Latimer, O.C.D.
Provincial

Nihil obstat: Kevin Culligan, O.C.D. and Jerome Flynn, O.C.D.
Censores Deputati

Imprimatur: Patrick A. O'Boyle
Archbishop of Washington

October 23, 1963

First paperback edition 1973

ICS Publications

INSTITUTE OF CARMELITE STUDIES
2131 Lincoln Road, Northeast
Washington, D. C. 20002

CONTENTS

Frontispiece
Foreword 13
General Introduction 15
Note on Drawing of Christ on the Cross 39
Introduction to *The Ascent of Mount Carmel-The Dark Night* 43

THE ASCENT OF MOUNT CARMEL

Sketch of the Mount 66
Theme 68
Stanzas 68
Prologue 69

BOOK ONE

Chapter

1 Some remarks about the two different nights through which spiritual persons pass in both the lower and higher part of their nature. A commentary on the first stanza. 73

2 The nature of the dark night through which a soul journeys to divine union. 74

3 The first cause of this night—the privation of the appetite in all things. Reason for the use of the expression "night." 76

4 The necessity of truly traversing this dark night of sense (mortification of the appetites) in journeying toward union with God. 77

5 Continuation of the same matter. Proofs from passages of Sacred Scripture for the necessity of journeying to God through this dark night, the mortification of the appetites. 81

6 The harm, privative as well as positive, that appetites engender in the soul. 84

7 How the appetites torment a man. Proofs through comparisons and passages from Sacred Scripture. 87

8 The appetites darken and blind a man. 89

9 The appetites defile a man. Proofs through comparisons and passages from Sacred Scripture. 91

10 The appetites weaken a soul and make it lukewarm in the practice of virtue. 94

11 Proofs of how freedom from all appetites, even the smallest, is necessary to attain divine union. 95

12 The answer to another question. An explanation of the kinds of appetites which can bring this harm upon a soul. 99

13 The manner and method of entering this night of sense. 101
14 An explanation of verse 2 of the first stanza. 104
15 An exposition of the remaining verses of the first stanza. 105

BOOK TWO

Chapter

1 The Second Stanza. 107
2 Faith, the second cause or part of this night. Two proofs of why it is darker than the first and third. 109
3 Arguments, passages, and figures from Scripture in proof that faith is a dark night for the soul. 110
4 A general discussion of the darkness of soul required for the effective guidance through faith to supreme contemplation. 112
5 Explanation of the nature of union with God. An illustration. 115
6 The theological virtues perfect the faculties of the soul and produce emptiness and darkness in them. 119
7 The extreme narrowness of the path leading to eternal life. The denudation and freedom required of those who tread it. The nakedness of the intellect. 121
8 No creature or knowledge comprehensible to the intellect can serve it as a proximate means for the divine union with God. 125
9 Faith is the proximate and proportionate means to the intellect for the attainment of the divine union of love. Proofs from passages and figures of sacred Scripture. 129
10 A division of all apprehensions and ideas comprehensible to the intellect. 130
11 The impediment and harm caused by intellectual apprehensions arising from objects supernaturally represented to the exterior senses. The proper conduct of the soul in their regard. 131
12 The nature of natural imaginative apprehensions. Proofs that they are inadequate means for the attainment of union with God. The harm caused from attachment to them. 136
13 The signs for recognizing in spiritual persons when they should discontinue discursive meditation and pass on to the state of contemplation. 140
14 A demonstration of the need for these three signs in order to advance. 142
15 Proficients, at the beginning of their entry into this general knowledge of contemplation, must at times practice discursive meditation and work with the natural faculties. 148
16 The imaginative apprehensions represented supernaturally to the phantasy are incapable of serving as a proximate means to union with God. 150
17 An answer to the proposed question. God's procedure and purpose in communicating spiritual goods by means of the senses. 155

18   The harm caused by some spiritual directors in not giving souls adequate guidance with regard to visions. An explanation of how both can be misled even by visions having a divine origin.   160

19   Visions and locutions, even though from God, can mislead us. Proofs from divine Scripture.   163

20   Proofs from Scripture of how God's words, although always true, are not always certain. This certitude of outcome depends on the causes of the pronouncements.   169

21   God's displeasure at the quest for revelations and locutions, even though He sometimes answers them. Proofs of how He is frequently angered in spite of His condescension and response.   172

22   The answer to a question concerning the reason for the illicitness in the Law of Grace of a practice permissible in the Old Law, that of petitioning God through supernatural means. Proof from St. Paul.   178

23   A discussion of spiritual, intellectual apprehensions.   187

24   Two kinds of supernatural, spiritual visions.   189

25   The nature and kinds of revelation.   193

26   The two kinds of knowledge of naked truths. The proper conduct of the soul in their regard.   193

27   The second kind of revelation: the disclosure of secrets and hidden mysteries. The ways in which this knowledge can be either a contribution or a hindrance toward union with God. The devil's power of seriously deceiving souls in this matter.   200

28   The nature and kinds of supernatural locutions received by the spirit.   202

29   The first kind of locution the recollected spirit sometimes forms. A discussion of its origin and of the profit or harm it may occasion.   203

30   Interior words formally and supernaturally produced in the spirit. A warning about their danger and a necessary precaution against delusion.   208

31   Substantial locutions produced in the spirit. How these differ from formal locutions, the profit they cause, and the resignation and respect that should be had concerning them.   210

32   The intellectual apprehensions of the spiritual feelings supernaturally imparted to the soul. The cause of these interior feelings and the attitude necessary for the avoidance of impediments in the journey toward union with God.   211

BOOK THREE

Chapter

1   The theme of this book.   213

2   The natural apprehensions of the memory. The emptiness required for union with God according to this faculty.   214

3   Three kinds of harm resulting from not darkening the memory of its knowledge and discursive reflection. A discussion of the first kind.   219

4   The second kind of harm, that which comes from the devil through the natural apprehensions of the memory.   221

5   The third kind of harm which follows from the natural, distinct knowledge of the memory.   222

6   The benefits derived from forgetting the natural thoughts and knowledge of the memory.   223

7   The second kind of apprehension, which is of supernatural imaginative knowledge.   224

8   The harm caused from reflection upon this supernatural knowledge. Tells how many kinds of harm there are.   225

9   The second kind of harm—the danger of falling into self-esteem and vain presumption.   226

10   The third kind of harm that comes from the devil through the imaginative apprehensions of the memory.   227

11   An impediment to union with God, the fourth kind of harm resulting from the distinct supernatural apprehensions of the memory.   229

12   Base and improper judgments of God, the fifth kind of harm arising from supernatural imaginative forms and apprehensions.   229

13   The benefits obtained through the rejection of the apprehensions of the imagination. Answers certain objections and explains the difference between the natural and the supernatural imaginative apprehensions.   230

14   Spiritual knowledge in the memory.   234

15   A general rule of conduct for spiritual persons in their use of the memory.   235

16   The beginning of the treatise on the dark night of the will. A division of the emotions of the will.   237

17   The first emotion of the will. The nature of joy and a division of the objects of joy.   239

18   Joy in temporal goods. How the soul should direct it to God.   240

19   The harm caused from joy in temporal goods.   242

20   Benefits derived through the withdrawal of joy from temporal goods.   246

21   The vanity of joy in natural goods, and the method of directing joy through them to God.   248

22   The harm resulting from joy of will in natural goods.   249

23   The benefits the soul acquires from not rejoicing in natural goods.   252

24   Sensory goods, the third kind that can be the object of the feeling of joy. An exposition of their nature and number and of how the will should be directed to God through the purgation of this joy.   254

25   The harm incurred by the desire for joy of will in sensory
     goods.   256
26   The spiritual and temporal benefits resulting from the denial
     of joy in sensory goods.   258
27   The nature of moral goods, the fourth kind, and the permis-
     sible manner of rejoicing in them.   260
28   Seven kinds of harm which can result from joy of the will
     in moral goods.   262
29   Benefits derived through the removal of joy from moral goods. 265
30   Supernatural goods, the fifth class in which the will can re-
     joice. Their nature, the factors distinguishing them from spir-
     itual goods, and how joy in them must be directed to God.   266
31   Harm incurred from rejoicing in this class of goods.   268
32   The two benefits acquired through the negation of joy in
     supernatural goods.   271
33   The nature and division of the sixth kind of good which is a
     possible object of joy for the will.   272
34   The proper conduct of the will as to joy in the distinct spir-
     itual goods communicable to the intellect and memory.   273
35   Delightful spiritual goods. A division.   274
36   A continued discussion of statues; the ignorance of some in
     their use of them.   276
37   The direction of joy of the will to God in order to avoid errors
     and obstacles arising from images.   278
38   A continued discussion of motivating goods. Oratories and
     dedicated places of prayer.   280
39   How a person should use oratories and churches and direct
     his spirit to God through them.   282
40   The continuation of this topic on the direction of the spirit
     toward interior recollection.   283
41   Some harm resulting from the surrender to sensible grati-
     fication in the use of devotional objects and places.   284
42   The proper conduct of the will in the use of three different
     kinds of devotional places.   285
43   The large variety of ceremonies as another motivating means
     which many people use for prayer.   287
44   The manner of directing the joy and strength of the will to
     God in these devotions.   288
45   The second kind of distinct goods in which the will can
     vainly rejoice.   290

THE DARK NIGHT

Prologue for the Reader   295
Stanzas of the Soul   295

BOOK ONE

Chapter

1   Quotes the first verse and begins to discuss the imperfections of beginners.   297
2   Some of the imperfections of pride possessed by beginners.   299
3   Some imperfections of spiritual avarice commonly found in beginners.   302
4   The imperfections of lust, the third capital vice, usually found in beginners.   303
5   The imperfections of the capital vice of anger into which beginners fall.   306
6   The imperfections of spiritual gluttony.   307
7   The imperfections of spiritual envy and sloth.   310
8   The beginning of the exposition of this dark night. An explanation of verse 1 of the first stanza.   311
9   Signs for discerning whether a spiritual person is treading the path of this sensory night and purgation.   313
10 The conduct required of souls in this dark night.   316
11 Explains three verses of the stanza.   318
12 The benefits this night causes in the soul.   320
13 Other benefits of this night of senses.   324
14 An explanation of the last verse of the first stanza.   327

BOOK TWO

Chapter

1   The beginning of the treatise on the dark night of the spirit. Explains when this night commences.   329
2   Other imperfections of these proficients.   331
3   An explanation for what is to follow.   332
4   First Stanza—Explanation.   334
5   Begins to explain how this dark contemplation is not only night for the soul but also affliction and torment.   335
6   Other kinds of affliction suffered in this night.   337
7   A continuation of the same subject; other afflictions and straits of the will.   340
8   Other afflictions that trouble the soul in this state.   343
9   Although this night darkens the spirit, it does so to give light.   346
10 Explains this purgation thoroughly by means of a comparison. 350
11 The beginning of an explanation of verse 2 of the first stanza. Tells how the fruit of these dark straits is a vehement passion of divine love.   352

12   The resemblance of this frightful night to purgatory. How the divine wisdom illumines men who suffer this night on earth by the same illumination with which He illumines and purges the angels in heaven.   355

13   Other delightful effects of this dark night of contemplation in the soul.   357

14   An explanation of the three last verses of the first stanza.   361

15   Second Stanza—Explanation.   362

16   An explanation of how the soul is secure when it walks in darkness.   363

17   An explanation of the secrecy of this dark contemplation.   368

18   An explanation of how this secret wisdom is also a ladder.   371

19   An explanation of the first five of the ten steps on the mystical ladder of divine love.   373

20   The remaining five steps of love.   376

21   An explanation of the term "disguised" and a description of the colors of the disguise the soul wears in this night.   378

22   An explanation of verse 3 of the second stanza.   381

23   An explanation of the fourth verse. Tells of the soul's wondrous hiding place during this night and how, though the devil enters other very high ones, he is unable to gain entry to this one.   382

24   The concluding explanation of this second stanza.   387

25   A brief explanation of the third stanza.   388

THE SPIRITUAL CANTICLE

Introduction to The Spiritual Canticle   393
Prologue   408
Poem   410
Theme   415
Stanzas   416
    1   Where have You hidden   416
    2   Shepherds, you that go   424
    3   Seeking my Love   427
    4   O woods and thickets   432
    5   Pouring out a thousand graces   434
    6   Ah, who has the power to heal me   435
    7   All who are free   437
    8   How do you endure   440
    9   Why, since You wounded   442
    10   Extinguish these miseries   445
    11   Reveal Your presence   448
    12   O spring like crystal   453
    13   Withdraw them, Beloved   457
    14   My Beloved is the mountains   462
    15   The tranquil night   462
    16   Catch us the foxes   474

17   Be still, deadening north wind   478
18   You girls of Judea   482
19   Hide Yourself, my Love   485
20   Swift-winged birds   487
21   By the pleasant lyres   487
22   The bride has entered   495
23   Beneath the apple tree   499
24   Our bed is in flower   501
25   Following Your footprints   506
26   In the inner wine cellar   510
27   There He gave me His breast   517
28   Now I occupy my soul   520
29   If, then, I am no longer   523
30   With flowers and emeralds   526
31   You considered   531
32   When You looked at me   534
33   Do not despise me   537
34   The small white dove   540
35   She lived in solitude   543
36   Let us rejoice, Beloved   545
37   And then we will go on   549
38   There You will show me   553
39   The breathing of the air   557
40   No one looked at her   563

THE LIVING FLAME OF LOVE

Introduction to *The Living Flame of Love*   569
Prologue   577
Stanzas Which the Soul Recites   578
Stanza 1   579
Stanza 2   595
Stanza 3   610
Stanza 4   643

THE MINOR WORKS

Introduction to the Minor Works   653
The Precautions   656
Counsels to a Religious on How to Reach Perfection 662
Sayings of Light and Love   666
Maxims and Counsels   674
*Censure and Opinion on the Spirit and the Attitude in Prayer
of a Discalced Carmelite Nun*   683
Letters   685

POETRY

Introduction to the Poetry 709

The Dark Night 711

The Spiritual Canticle 712

The Living Flame of Love 717

Stanzas Concerning an Ecstasy Experienced in High Contemplation 718

Stanzas of the Soul That Suffers with Longing to See God 720

More Stanzas Applied to Spiritual Things 721

More Stanzas Applied to Spiritual Things on Christ and the Soul 722

Song of the Soul That Rejoices in Knowing God through Faith 723

Romances—First Romance: On the Gospel 724

Romance 2—On the communication among the three Persons 725

Romance 3—On Creation 726

Romance 4—Creation (continued) 727

Romance 5—Creation (continued) 729

Romance 6—Creation (continued) 730

Romance 7—The Incarnation 730

Romance 8—The Incarnation (continued) 731

Romance 9—The Birth 732

A Romance on the Psalm "By the Waters of Babylon" 733

Commentary Applied to Spiritual Things—
"Without support and with support" 734

Commentary Applied to Spiritual Things—"Not for all of beauty" 735

Del Verbo Divino 737

The Sum of Perfection 737

Note on the Introductions 739

FOREWORD

It is a privilege to introduce this translation of St. John of the Cross's complete works. Father Kieran Kavanaugh, O.C.D., Professor of Spiritual Theology at the College of Theology of the Discalced Carmelites, Washington, D.C., and Father Otilio Rodriguez, O.C.D., Carmelite historian from Burgos, Spain, have spent years in translating and in editing these writings. Readers seeking a deeper understanding and appreciation of the teachings of the Mystical Doctor will welcome this translation.

St. John of the Cross wrote with the intention of teaching souls the dynamics of growth in union with God. He charted the course they must follow to achieve divine intimacy, beginning with the first feeble steps and eventually reaching a perfect union. The Oriental imagery and analytical skill of the medieval scholar combine in an intense style which reflects not only the magnificence of the Saint's spiritual vision but the full flowering of Spanish poetic genius.

Interest in St. John of the Cross's writings was never greater than in our day; but until now there has been the need of an English translation which would be both more precise and more readable. In every age the classics are translated anew, for our idiom is constantly evolving; but the spiritual needs of man are always basically the same. In response to these needs, the vitality of the Saint's message will live on with that freshness of a true classic, reflecting the spiritual genius of the "Little Seneca."

Father Kieran and Father Otilio have had the advantage of being able to interpret the meaning of the Saint against the background of Carmelite tradition, with which they are both eminently familiar. Only those who have analyzed the Saint's Spanish prose can fully appreciate the exacting dedication of these two Carmelites. They selected the best reading of each passage and, where necessary, interpreted the meaning in the light of the entire work.

The reader will find in this book not only the results of a scholarly effort to preserve true meaning and present it as clearly as possible, but the doctrinal and historical information which leads to a deeper understanding of the Saint and his words.

> *Very Rev. Christopher Latimer, O.C.D.*
> PROVINCIAL
> Immaculate heart of Mary Province
> of the Discalced Carmelites
> Washington, D.C.

GENERAL INTRODUCTION

I. Biographical Sketch

St. John of the Cross was doubtless a profound contemplative, theologian, and poet, but in an unusual combination he was at the same time a co-founder, reformer, and busy administrator. Although we do not possess as many facts as we should like concerning the events of his life, we do have enough to fashion some idea of his education as well as of the bizarre sixteenth-century complexities in which he became involved as a founder, with St. Teresa, of the Discalced Carmelites. St. John of the Cross could hardly have gained the title of Mystical Doctor if he himself had not been one of the Church's greatest mystics, but a great saint and mystic he would never have been without severe purifying trials, many of which were occasioned by his mission to assist St. Teresa in the work of her Reform. Out of his own experience in life, one of his several sources, he gathered materials for deep reflection and the ultimate construction of his doctrinal synthesis. His poetry, too, was partly the fruit of his darknesses. Knowledge of his life, then, is a necessary background for the reading of his works. With this in mind we are presenting a brief sketch of his life and of a few of the intricate problems in the history of the Reform which left their mark on him. Complete studies can be found in Father Bruno's *St. John of the Cross* and Father Crisogono's *The Life of St. John of the Cross*.

Juan de Yepes y Alvarez was born in 1542 at Fontiveros, Spain, a small town located in the central plateau of Old Castile, some twenty-four miles northwest of Avila, the birthplace of St. Teresa. His birth date was probably June 24, the feast of the Nativity of St. John the Baptist, and in honor of this saint he received the name Juan. His father, Gonzalo de Yepes, belonged to a wealthy family of silk merchants from Toledo. On one of his business trips to Medina del Campo, Gonzalo met, in Fontiveros, Catalina Alvarez, a weaver of poor and humble background. Gonzalo married Catalina in 1529 in spite of bitter opposition from the members of his family, who dismissed and disowned him because of their proud persuasion that marriage to a girl of low position was shameful. Deprived of financial security, he was forced to adapt to his wife's surroundings of poverty and hard work and to learn her lowly trade of silk weaving. Three sons were born of this marriage.

Shortly after the birth of John, who was the youngest son, Gonzalo died of a painful and costly illness which had lasted two years. Reduced to extreme poverty, his young, courageous widow made a hard, tiring journey to Toledo, Torrijos, Gálvez, and Arévalo, visiting members of her husband's family with hopes of receiving assistance in her dire need, but she was mercilessly repulsed by each of them. The burden of responsibility was thus left to her alone. She settled in Medina del Campo, where she returned to her work of weaving the twill.

Here John began to attend the Catechism School, an institution resembling an orphanage in which the children of the poor were fed and clothed and given an elementary education. While at this school he was chosen to serve as an acolyte at the Convent of the Augustinian Nuns; this meant duties in the sacristy for four hours in the morning, and in the afternoons whenever the Superior, the Chaplain, or the Sacristan needed him. In addition to his elementary studies, he also received the opportunity to learn something of carpentry, tailoring, sculpturing, and painting through apprenticeships to local craftsmen. When he was about seventeen years of age, he began to work at the Plague Hospital de la Concepcion, and the founder of the hospital, Don Alonso Alvarez, allowed him to enroll in the recently established Jesuit College in Medina del Campo, provided of course that he also fulfill his duties at the hospital.

John attended the Jesuit College during the years 1559–63, and there received a solid formation in the humanities. Six hours a day, three in the morning and three in the afternoon, were devoted to classes in grammar, rhetoric, Greek, Latin, and religion. The grammar and rhetoric courses in both Latin and Spanish were taught by the great humanist Padre Juan Bonifacio, S.J. In his Spanish course, this renowned Jesuit followed the text of Nebrija, who was the foremost Spanish grammarian of the times, and supplemented the text with readings from the classics. He required his students to write compositions in prose and verse, in both Latin and native Castilian. In Padre Bonifacio's own words about his teaching we have an enlightening report concerning the extent of the humanistic training he gave to his students: "I lecture without any difficulty on Valerius Maximianus, Suetonius, Aliciatus; I explain some passages from Ammianus Marcelinus, Pliny, and Pomponius Mela; I translate some difficult passages from the Breviary including some of the hymns, also the Catechism, the letters of St. Jerome, and the proceedings of the Council of Trent. To my non-clerical pupils I lecture on Cicero, Virgil, and sometimes Seneca's tragedies, Horace and Martial expurgated, Caesar, Sallust, Livy, and Curtius, that they might have examples and models of everything: speeches, poetry, and history."

His professors of the Greek language and culture were Fathers Juan Guerra and Miguel de Anda. Although we do not know the methods they used, we can surmise that they were not much different from those used by Father Juan Bonifacio. John's professor in religion was Padre Gaspar Astete, who later became famous for his Catechism, one of the most popular in the Spanish language. It is uncertain whether or not John studied philosophy while he was at this college, but we can affirm with certainty that he left the Jesuit College "well trained in Latin and rhetoric," and that "he learned to read and write very well," and that "to these years must be assigned his first contact with the Latin and Spanish classics and the beginning of his love for humanism . . . on the basis of an abundance of exercises, reading, and composition."

After John had completed his four years of study in the humanities, Don Alonso offered to defray the cost of his education for the priesthood, if John so desired. In this way, too, once ordained, John could become Chaplain to the hospital, a post which would have provided him with the means to assist his mother and eldest brother in their material needs (his other brother had died early in life). But John believed that God was calling him to a Religious Order. In 1563, at the age of twenty, he entered the Carmelite Order at the Monastery of Santa Ana in Medina del Campo; he received the habit of Our Lady of Mount Carmel February 24, 1563, changing his name to Juan de Santo Matía.

Little is known about his life in the Novitiate, but after his profession of vows he was sent for studies to his Order's College of San Andrés at Salamanca, a journey of fifty miles. Besides attending classes at the Carmelite College, he studied at the University of Salamanca, which at the time ranked with the great universities of Bologna, Paris, and Oxford. The name of Fray Juan de Santo Matía appears on the matriculation record for the first time during the school year of 1564-65. His name is found again on the records of the School of Arts for the years 1565-66, and 1566-67. We do not know exactly which courses he followed as an Arts student, but we do know the courses that were taught and the names of the eminent men who held professorships. Master Enrique Hernández, the author of a treatise on Philosophy, taught the classes in Natural Philosophy; Francisco Navarro held the Chair of Ethics; Hernando de Aguilera, who had worked out an astrolabe, held the Chair of Astronomy; Francisco Sanchez, known as El Brocense, taught grammar and even today is considered an authority on the subject; Master Martín de Peralta explained the *Summulas* (an introduction to Logic), and Juan de Ubredo held the Chair of Music. The statutes of the university prescribed the works of Aristotle for the Arts course, but this merely meant that a prescribed text from the philosopher was to be read at the beginning of the lecture; the professor could then go on to interpret it with full liberty, if not leave it aside entirely.

Fray John registered in the theological course at the University of Salamanca only during the school year of 1567-68. It seems that he did most of his theological studies at the College of San Andrés and complemented these with some courses taken at the University. Again, we possess no record of which classes in theology he attended. Probably he assisted at the Prime Lecture, which lasted an hour and a half and began at eight o'clock in the morning in the winter and at seven in the morning from Easter until the end of the term. This Chair of Theology, the most important one at the University, was held by a Dominican Father, Mancio de Corpus Christi, who explained the *Summa Theologica* of St. Thomas Aquinas. In addition, Juan probably attended the lectures in Sacred Scripture given by Gaspar Grajal. At this particular time the University was troubled by a lively struggle of ideas concerning the interpretation of Sacred Scripture. The "scholastics," tenacious partisans of fidelity to the biblical tradition of the preceding centuries, opposed the "scripturists," who sought the literal sense of Scripture through a development of scientific methods and the study of languages. Grajal, Fray John's probable teacher, was a prominent figure among the "scripturists," and was later on account of his ideas imprisoned for a time by the Inquisition.

While still a student, John was appointed Prefect of Studies. This office, conferred only on the most outstanding of students, obliged him to teach class daily, defend public theses, and assist the Regent Master in resolving those objections which were raised.

Fray John was ordained to the priesthood in the spring of 1567, but not until the beginning of September did he sing his first Mass in his home town, Medina del Campo. This visit to Medina was the occasion for his fateful meeting with Madre Teresa of Jesus, who was in the city arranging the final details of her second foundation of a community of nuns professing the Carmelite life in the Reform which she had begun. She was at the time considering the extension of her strict Reform to the friars. When a young student from the University of Salamanca suggested Fray John as a possible prospect to help her in this new field of endeavor, she immediately arranged for an interview with him. She was fifty-two at this time, and he was twenty-five. Fray Juan told her in confidence about his longing to transfer to the Carthusian Order for the sake of embracing a life of deeper solitude and prayer. The holy Madre pointed out to him that he could find this without leaving "Our Lady's Order," and spoke of her plan to restore the Primitive Rule for the friars of the Mitigation. Showing interest, Fray John promised to adopt this life within the Order, but only on the condition that he would not have too long a wait.

The following summer, after finishing his studies in theology, he was appointed assistant professor at the Monastery of Santa Ana in Medina. By that time the Madre had returned to the city and was able to tell him about the small farmhouse in Duruelo which had been offered her and which might prove adequate for the first monastery of the Reform among the Friars. Fray John had long interviews with Madre Teresa to learn about the new form of life he had decided to take up. In order that he familiarize himself further with details of the Reform by observing firsthand the daily routine of the nuns, it was decided that he accompany Madre Teresa to the new foundation in Valladolid as confessor and chaplain to the new community. He remained in Valladolid from August 10 until October 1, when Madre Teresa, fully satisfied with the training of her *novice*, sent him to Duruelo to adapt the farmhouse according to her plan and direction. Fray John made the journey to Duruelo with a young man aspiring to be a lay brother in the new Reform. By the end of November they had converted this little house with its porch, main room, alcove, and small kitchen into the first monastery of the friars of the Reform. Besides Fray John and the prospective lay brother, three others decided to embrace this new mode of life within the Carmelite Order; one of these was sixty-year-old Fray Antonio de Heredia, the former Prior of the monastery in Medina. On the first Sunday of Advent, November 28, 1568, the Father Provincial said Mass and then received the renunciation of the Mitigated Rule from the little community and their profession of the Primitive Rule. Fray Juan de Santo Matía at that time changed his name to Fray John of the Cross.

The new life they undertook in keeping with the Primitive Rule was predominantly contemplative, but the active apostolate was by no means absent. The contemplative element comprised the recitation of the Divine Office in common, with Matins recited at the hour of midnight; two hours of mental prayer daily; and conventual Mass. The Rule and Constitutions called likewise for fasts and total abstinence from flesh meat; poverty in the type of dwelling, clothing, and food; enclosure and withdrawal from the world. They were also to go barefoot, and thus were soon referred to as the *Discalced* Carmelites. Their active work consisted mainly of preaching and of hearing confessions.

In the spring of 1569, the Father Provincial raised the status of the new foundation to the rank of a Priory with the authorization to receive novices. Fray Antonio was appointed Prior, and Fray John of the Cross, Subprior and novice master. With the arrival of two postulants in September or October of 1569, the small converted farmhouse was decidedly overcrowded. Thus in June of 1570, the community moved to Mancera de Abajo, where Fray John continued his office as novice master.

Through the efforts of the untiring Madre Teresa, another novitiate was founded at Pastrana. This novitiate, which was to become one of the most important in the Reform, was located not far from the university city of Alcalá, and the life that was led by the reformed friars attracted many young vocations from among the students attending the University of Alcalá, which at the time was a center of Spanish culture. The need to provide for the further education of these young Discalced friars prompted the founding of a house of studies in Alcalá in 1570. Fray John of the Cross was appointed Rector of the newly established house, and he guided the students in their studies and spiritual development.

Meanwhile, in the spring of 1571, Madre Teresa was ordered to return to the Convent of the Incarnation to govern and reform its 130 nuns. A reform was necessary since the existing state of poverty had reduced the community and religious life to a mere semblance. The nuns were spending most of their time outside the convent seeking sustenance for life, or they were in the parlors entertaining those benefactors who brought them food. With no meals served in a common refectory, each nun had to look after herself. When they heard of Teresa's appointment, they bitterly opposed it, even to the extent of refusing her entrance. They were fearful that she would impose the Discalced Reform on them. After an odd struggle, the tactful Madre took charge as Prioress and at once began to remedy this unfortunate situation. She realized, however, that she needed the help of a prudent, learned, and holy confessor to assist her in this reform, and, seemingly without concern for the vital loss this would mean for the Discalced friars in their crucial beginnings, obtained permission from the Apostolic Visitor for Fray John of the Cross to assume the responsibility as Vicar and confessor. He arrived to take this position toward the end of May 1572. His new work as spiritual director at the Incarnation included the guidance of Madre Teresa herself, and under his expert direction she reached the highest state of intimacy with God possible on this earth, the spiritual marriage. According to her testimony, she received this favor on November 18, 1572.

During the time that Fray John of the Cross remained at the Convent of the Incarnation, the attitude of the Calced toward the Reform began to change. How and why this understandable change came about is worth noting. In 1566, Father Rubeo, the General of the Order, began a visitation of all the monasteries in Spain. A year later, King Philip II, anxious to execute the decrees of the Council of Trent, which called for a reform of all religious Orders, received permission from the Holy See to appoint Apostolic Visitors to investigate these same monasteries with almost the same powers as the General, but independently of him. When news of this Brief so apt to embroil the work he had been achieving reached Father Rubeo in 1568, he sought to have it canceled. But the following year, the King named two Dominican priests as Visitors, Francisco Vargas and Pedro Fernández. One of these Fathers, Pedro Fernández, acted in wise accordance with the desires of the General, but the other showed no concern and acted in complete independence of him; he gave to the Discalced a monastery belonging to the Calced, and authorized foundations of Discalced monasteries in Seville, Granada, and Peñuela. These acts were in direct opposition to the express wishes of Father Rubeo. Amid these irksome developments, the Spanish Provincials met in 1574 and decided to request the Holy See to replace the Dominicans with members of the Order as Visitors. Their desires were granted the same year in a Brief of Gregory XIII, dated August 3. But when Nicolás Ormaneto, the Papal Nuncio, learned of this, he used his own powers as Pontifical Legate and appointed the same Dominicans as "Reformers," giving them the office they had had before and the same, if not greater, authority. He likewise appointed Fray Jerónimo Gracián, a Discalced Carmelite, as Provincial of the Discalced and Visitor of the Calced in Andalusia. He commanded the reluctant Fray Jerónimo to accept this office and to fulfill his duties under the penalty of excommunication. Ormaneto's appointments were confirmed by the Pope, December 27, 1574.

Convening in Chapter at Piacenza, Italy, in May 1575, the Calced, without full information concerning all the bewildering activities and apparent disobedience of the Discalced in Spain, resolved to suppress the houses which had been founded without the General's permission; they forbade any new Discalced foundation; they ordered Madre Teresa to choose some convent of the Reform as her permanent place of residence; and they prohibited the Discalced nuns to move from one house to another. To carry out these resolutions, they would seek the help of secular arms, if necessary. These measures were taken to bring a halt to the expansion of the Reform, and even to suppress it, since its rapid and uncontrolled development threatened the existence of the Order. Padre Jerónimo Tostado was appointed General Visitor with the assignment of enforcing these decrees. When, however, halfway through the year 1576, he arrived in Spain with all his documents and a strong determination to carry out the decisions of this Chapter, the King and the Nuncio were unimpressed and did not find the documents to be in agreement with the pontifical powers given to the Nuncio, and thus they prevented him from taking immediate action.

In September of 1576, the Discalced friars convened at Almodóvar in a Chapter presided over by Fray Jerónimo Gracián, the Provincial designated by Ormaneto. Among other things it was decided that Fray John of the Cross relinquish his office at the Incarnation and return it to the Calced, who coveted the position. For he had not gone unharassed while there, and the Calced at the beginning of 1576 had already, a first time, carried him off by force to Medina. Only through the intervention of Ormaneto did they restore him to his post at the Incarnation, but the situation was obviously strained, and the frail young confessor had suffered much. However, the nuns at the Incarnation, regardless of the decision of the Chapter, wanted Fray John, and at their request the Nuncio ordered that he stay in that office.

In June of 1577, Ormaneto, the Nuncio who had been so friendly toward the Discalced, died. His death, together with the disturbing news that the Discalced had convened the Chapter at Almodóvar, prompted the Calced to executed the resolutions of Piacenza. Thus during the night of December 2, 1577 a group of Calced Fathers, men-at-arms, and some seculars, seized Fray Juan and his companion to bring them to a Calced monastery. Fray John of the Cross was taken to Toledo where the acts of the Chapter of Piacenza were read to him and a complete renunciation of the Reform was demanded. If he refused to renounce the Reform, he would be declared a rebel. But Fray John of the Cross did not renounce it. He was keen-minded enough to distinguish properly in this maze of conflicting jurisdiction and conclude that the proscriptions of the Chapter were directed against the friars of Granada, Seville, and Peñuela, and not against him, and that he had been at his post at the Incarnation by the orders of the Nuncio, which were still in effect. However, the tribunal called him both rebellious and contumacious and prescribed imprisonment.

Fray John was led to his prison cell, a little room originally intended as a closet, six feet wide and ten feet long. It had no window; the only opening was a slit high up in the wall. It was frightfully cold there in winter, and suffocating in summer. They deprived him of his hood and scapular as a token of punishment for his rebellion. His food was bread, sardines, and water. Three evenings a week he had to eat kneeling on the floor in the middle of the refectory. Then when the friars were finished their supper, his shoulders were bared and each member of the community struck him with a lash, some very vigorously, for the wounds he received would not heal properly for years. This scourging lasted for the time it takes to recite the Psalm *Miserere*. Since he continued in his refusal to renounce the Reform, they would then conduct him back to his bleak prison. No compassion could be shown him, for the Constitutions under the most severe penalties forbade one to show favor to a prisoner. After six months of prison life, the Saint was assigned a new warder. This one did manifest some elements of compassion; for instance, he gave him a change of clothes, and also furnished him with paper and ink, thus enabling him in these sad surroundings to write down the great lyric poems which, as a means of passing the time, he had been composing in his mind.

Taking advantage of the leniency of his new jailer, Fray John familiarized himself with every aspect of the monastery during his daily reprieves from the prison cell. On the night of August 16, 1578, in a manner some declare was miraculous, he managed to escape and find his way to the Discalced nuns in Toledo, who hid him from the search party. Eventually he was able to journey to El Calvario in the south of Spain, where he was safer and had the opportunity to restore his health.

In October of that year, the Discalced Fathers convened another Chapter at Almodóvar, in spite of some doubts about the legality of such a procedure. At this Chapter Fray John of the Cross was elected Prior of the monastery of El Calvario. After the meeting the new Provincial, Fray Antonio, and some of the Chapter Fathers went to Madrid to explain to the new Nuncio, Felipe Sega, the resolutions this Chapter had taken and to ask for his approval and blessing. Sega's reaction was almost violent. He declared the resolutions null and void, placed the Discalced under the jurisdiction of the Calced, sent the Fathers present to prison, and excommunicated all who had taken part, which included Fray John of the Cross. But probably Fray John did not hear of this censure; he was making his way to El Calvario in Andalusia to take over his new office.

In addition to his duties as Prior, he acted as confessor and spiritual director of the nuns at Beas. Madre Ana de Jesús, the Prioress, did not immediately recognize either his holiness or his talents. She wrote to Madre Teresa lamenting the lack of a suitable confessor. Mother Teresa was quick and decisive in her reply:

"I am really surprised, daughter, at your complaining so unreasonably, when you have Padre Fray John of the Cross with you, who is a divine, heavenly man. I can tell you, daughter, that since he went away I have found no one like him in all Castile, nor anyone who inspires people with so much fervor on the way to heaven. You would not believe how lonely his absence makes me feel. You should reflect that you have a great treasure in that holy man, and all those in the convent should see him and open their souls to him, when they will see what great good they get and will find themselves to have made great progress in spirituality and perfection, for our Lord has given him a special grace for this.

"I can assure you I should very much like to have Fray John of the Cross here, for he is indeed the father of my soul, and one of those whom it does me most good to have dealings with. I hope you and your daughters will talk to him with the utmost frankness, for I assure you, that you can talk to him as you would to me, and you and they will find great satisfaction, for he is very spiritual and of great experience and learning. Those who were brought up on his teaching miss him greatly. Give thanks to God who has arranged that he should be near you. I am writing to tell him to look after you and I know that in his great kindness he will do so whenever the need arises."

Madre Ana soon discovered for herself that she had an uncommon spiritual treasure in the person of Fray John of the Cross. It was for her that he later wrote his commentary on the *Spiritual Canticle*.

From Calvario, Fray John was assigned in June of 1579 to found and become rector of a college for the education of students of the Reform in the southern part of Spain, near the University of Baeza. Although this University of Baeza could not compete with Salamanca or Alcalá, it had nonetheless acquired a certain prestige and was making important contributions to studies in Sacred Scripture. While rector of the Carmelite college, Fray John guided his own students in their studies, and records reveal, too, that professors of the University of Baeza, impressed by his knowledge of the Bible, frequently consulted him and held long conversations with him concerning difficult scriptural passages.

While Fray John of the Cross was Rector of the Carmelite college in Baeza, the Discalced, through the personal intervention of King Philip II, finally obtained their independence of jurisdiction. The Holy See, in 1580, allowed them to erect an autonomous Province which was to be governed by a Discalced Provincial, but under the higher jurisdiction of the Calced General. (Complete juridic independence did not come until December 20, 1593, when Pope Clement VIII accorded them the same rights and privileges as other religious orders.)

The years that followed all the stormy conflicts in the establishing and securing of the Reform were for Fray John of the Cross busy years, but comparatively calm ones. Most of his activity was devoted to carrying out the duties of the responsible positions he held in the Reform. At Alcalá, in March, 1581, in the first Chapter of the Reform, which he attended in his capacity as Rector of Baeza, he was elected Third Definitor. One year later, the Fathers of Granada elected him Prior. At the Chapter of Lisbon, March 1585, he was elected Vicar Provincial of Andalusia, a position which made him responsible for the monasteries of the friars in Granada, El Calvario, La Peñuela, Málaga, Caravaca, Seville, and Guadalcázar. He also had in his charge all the houses of nuns in that part of Spain, for they were under the direct and total jurisdiction of the Order. At the Chapter of Valladolid, April, 1587, he was elected again Prior of Granada. In June, 1588, at the Chapter of Madrid, he was elected Major Definitor and Third Counselor; it was thus his duty likewise to act as Prior of Segovia. Besides his work in administration, he gave much time to prayer. We can surmise the high character of his contemplation and absorption in God from a perusal of his writings on the state of perfect union with God. It was, in fact, during these years that he also did most of his writing. Furthermore, as always throughout his priestly life, he was much sought out as a spiritual director, and was liberal with his time in guiding his own friars, the nuns, and the many lay persons who came to him.

But toward the end of Fray John of the Cross's life, the outward calm was disturbed by a new clash, one this time within the Reform. Father Nicolás Doria, Vicar General of the Discalced, called an extraordinary Chapter in June, 1590 for the purpose of undertaking two controvertible moves. First he desired to abandon jurisdiction over the nuns.

This was a reprisal against Madre Ana de Jesús. She had somewhat shrewdly obtained a Brief from the Holy See prohibiting any change in the Constitutions of St. Teresa and ordaining that the nuns be governed by only one Father of the Reform, to be chosen by the Vícar General from among the superiors, but not, as Father Doria wished, by the governing body which he had set up, known as the Consulta. Second, Father Doria proposed the expulsion of Padre Jerónimo Gracián from the Reform. Fray John of the Cross, when asked for his opinion, firmly opposed the Vicar General in both matters. In the Chapter of the following year, as was to be expected considering the power wielded by Father Doria, Fray John of the Cross for the first time was not elected to any office. When news of the unfortunate situation reached the monasteries and convents where he was known and so much esteemed, vigorous protests were raised. But it seems that Fray John's spiritual view of the whole affair left him with a feeling of happiness at being free at last of an office. With words conveying his mind, he wrote to Madre Ana de Jesús:

". . . If things did not turn out as you desired, you ought rather to be consoled and thank God profusely. Since His Majesty has so arranged matters, it is what most suits everyone . . . And it is obvious that this is not evil or harmful, neither for me nor for anyone. It is in my favor since, being freed and relieved from the care of souls, I can, if I want and with God's help, enjoy peace, solitude, and the delightful fruit of forgetfulness of self and of all things. It is also good for others that I be separated from them, for thus they will be freed of the faults they would have committed on account of my misery . . . Now, until God gives us this good in heaven, pass the time in the virtues of mortification and patience, desiring to resemble somewhat in suffering this great God of ours, humbled and crucified. This life is not good if it is not an imitation of His life."

Father John of the Cross was sent to the solitude of La Peñuela in Andalusia and arrived there with a joyful heart, August 10, 1591. Yet the awesome silence of Peñuela was soon shattered by incredible and shocking news. Efforts were being made to expel Fray John of the Cross from the Reform. Fray Diego, a former but resentful subject of Fray John, was seeking to gather information against him by means of intrigue and defamation of character. This hateful process was never completed, however, for Fray John died in the meantime.

In mid-September he noticed a slight fever which was caused by an inflammation of the leg. At first he thought it was nothing serious, but since it persisted he was ordered by his Superior to seek further medical attention, which was not available at La Peñuela. He was given the choice of one of two places, Baeza or Ubeda. "I will go to Ubeda, for at Baeza they know me very well and in Ubeda, nobody knows me." He left

Peñuela on September 28, 1591; this was to be his last journey in life. The Prior of Ubeda, Fray Francisco Crisóstomo, did not welcome the sick man. Even though learned and a famous preacher, Fray Crisóstomo possessed a mean and rigid temperament and completely lacked the qualities of a good superior. He was unfriendly toward Fray John. His cold lack of consideration was evident in the fact that he assigned him the worst cell in the monastery and voiced his vexation at the expenses incurred by him. He felt a particular aversion to Fray John precisely because of his reputation for holiness.

Fray John's sickness grew worse; his legs were already ulcerated, and the disease spread to his back where a new tumor appeared, larger than the size of a fist. On December 13, realizing that time was running out, he called for the Prior and begged his pardon for all of the trouble and expenses he had caused him. Fray Crisóstomo, in turn, begged for forgiveness and left the cell in tears. This circumstance profoundly changed him, for he was later to die in the odor of sanctity. That same night, without agony, without struggle, at the age of forty-nine, Fray John of the Cross died, repeating the words of the Psalmist: "Into your hands, O Lord, I commend my spirit." The favors he had asked for in his declining years he had now received: Not to die as a superior; to die in a place where he was unknown; and to die after having suffered much.

St. John of the Cross was beatified by Clement X in 1675, canonized by Benedict XIII in 1726, and declared a Doctor of the Church by Pius XI in 1926.

II. A Portrait of the Saint

These, then, were the main events in the short life of St. John of the Cross. But the picture would be left incomplete if no description were given of his character and personal spiritual life. His early privations, the misunderstanding, imprisonment, and final persecution which he suffered might easily, instead of a purified and enlightened man, have produced a bitter cynic. In reality these sad events brought about a transformation in Fray John of the Cross and occasioned in him a great love of others, a deep understanding of and compassion for the sufferer, an uncommonly clear vision of the beauty of God's creation, and an intimacy with the Blessed Trinity which he found describable only through comparison to the properties of the Beatific Vision.

But, first, in regard to the physical appearance of St. John of the Cross, he was a small man, about five feet. St. Teresa refers with relative frequency to his smallness of stature. She calls him "little Seneca"; "the holy little Fray John"; or the half friar in saying, "I now have a friar and a half." In telling of his imprisonment, she writes: "All the nine months he was in a small prison, where, little as he is, there was not enough room for him to move." Besides being small he was also thin. His face was oval and lean, his forehead was broad and receded into a baldness which gave him a venerable appearance. He had a slightly aquiline nose and large, dark eyes. This humble figure of Fray John was completed by an old, rough, brown habit and a white cloak so coarse that it seemed to be made of goat hair.

John was deeply impressed by the pains of poverty which he suffered as a child and also again as a friar. He could not forget them, and his severe experiences doubtless urged him to bring relief to others afflicted by the misfortune of material need. He did not restrict himself to seeking the spiritual good of his penitents but sought as well to aid them when they were in want. Sometimes he gave them alms from the small funds of the monastery, and sometimes he begged alms from devout people to help them. Once, it is told, Fray John, noticing that a priest who came to confession to him had only an old, worn-out cassock, asked some benefactors for money to buy this priest a new cassock. He grieved over the poverty of the nuns of the Incarnation and went about begging alms to be able to give them what they needed. One day, entering the convent to exercise his priestly ministery, he saw that a nun was sweeping the cloister barefooted, not out of penance but because she had no shoes. He left the convent, went up to the city and asked some charitable persons for money which he afterwards handed to the nun to buy a pair of shoes. Then there was the year 1584, a year of barrenness and hunger in Andalusia. Padre John of the Cross, Prior of Los Martires in Granada, tried to help with either food or money all the needy who came to the monastery door. He went out of his way also to assist secretly those of good position who, though in want, were ashamed to beg openly at the monastery.

Accompanying this compassion for the poor was his pity and special concern for the sick. Certainly his early experience in the hospital at Medina bore the good effect of bestowing on him an intense sympathy for the ever-present sufferings and needs of the sick. If any of his friars were ill, he made it a point to spend time at their bedside and would often himself prepare special food for them. Nor did the question of money ever interfere with his desire to give his sick the best possible care, not even when it was a matter of medicine capable of no more than alleviating pain. Once, for example, he asked the doctor if there was any efficacious remedy for an illness which was causing one of his lay brothers extraordinary suffering. The doctor replied that he knew only of a medicine that would relieve the suffering somewhat and that it was very expensive. Despite the poverty of the monastery, John sent for the medicine immediately and gave it to the sick brother himself; he was happy to offer any little relief he could to the suffering brother.

It was also noted and remembered that if the nuns of the Incarnation, who were so poor, served him any special dishes of food while he was confessor there, he sent these dishes back to the convent with the explicit and kind instructions that they be given to the sick. His special charity toward the sick was also evident in his custom upon arriving at a monastery of first visiting the sick after his visit to the Blessed Sacrament.

Another affliction which John was quick to notice in his neighbor and which he sought always to relieve was sadness and depression. He did not like to see someone downcast and made every effort to console anyone who he knew was sad. On this account, though he was naturally serious, he enjoyed making others laugh, and several of his contemporaries have told of his special gift for humor and how the other Religious looked forward to having Fray John of the Cross present with them at recreation.

When as a superior it was necessary for him to correct his subjects, he was cautious lest through impatience or anger he would succeed only in saddening or discouraging them. "He made his corrections with much gentleness and charity and always saw to it that the one being corrected would not leave his presence sad." His method of governing was not one of harshness. "Who has ever seen men persuaded to love God by harshness?" he used to ask. And he said that when Religious are brought up with such irrational severity, they become pusillanimous in undertaking things of great virtue. Another characteristic of his "wonderfully gracious" manners was his custom of asking his subjects for their opinions in various matters or problems which arose. All of this created a holy environment of serenity and joy in the relationship of the friars to their superior.

The needs of man are not only material and psychological; he has as well distinctively spiritual needs. St. John of the Cross was apostolic, ardent in his zeal for the spread of God's kingdom. He used to teach that the more the soul loves God the more it desires that God be loved and honored by all men; that the greater this desire becomes the more the soul labors toward that end, both in prayer and in all other possible and necessary works. John's preferred apostolate was spiritual direction, by which he could help to free souls from their spiritual sicknesses. In this zealous endeavor he spared himself neither time nor energy. Doubtless it was his singular awareness of the importance and high destination of the individual which made spiritual direction his preferred field of apostolic labor. Nor did he limit himself to any particular class of people; he had time for and showed interest in everyone.

To his confessional in Baeza came every type, from the Rector and the professors of the University to humble and unlettered shepherds' wives. He was willing to give the simple and the unlearned as much time as he gave to others. The ease which the humble lay sister, Catalina de la

Cruz, felt in his presence is evident in the kind of candid questions she asked the holy doctor. Once she inquired why when she went near the pond in the garden the frogs that were on the brink leapt into the water, almost before they could hear the sound of her footsteps, and hid themselves in the depths of the pool. Fray John, a master of the spiritual application, answered that it was because they felt safe in the depth of the pool and that "that is what you must do, flee from creatures and hide yourself in God." Sinners, too, found it easy to manifest their conscience to him. "The holier a confessor," he said, "the less fear one should have of him."

In directing others he stressed the life of faith, hope, and charity, understanding that man's good consists especially in interior acts, not in exterior acts. Thus he was known as a moderator of penances, and in different monasteries of the Reform he ordered that the practices of penance (so severe in those times) be kept within bounds lest they degenerate into the "penance of beasts."

But his deepest concern was for those who in their spiritual life were suffering. The needs of souls undergoing interior trials prompted him to write *The Ascent of Mount Carmel* and *The Dark Night*. If his vehement portrayal of the afflictions of the dark night proves frightening to some, it is only because he wished to describe these sufferings in their most intense form and thereby exclude no one. Everyone could then take comfort in the thought that no matter how severe the purification, it is still the work of God's gentle hand, clearing away the debris of inordinate affection and making room for the divine light.

Finally, St. John of the Cross could not for long stand by watching others bear the burdens of manual labor without sharing in them himself. He on no account adhered to the pernicious teaching of the Illuminists prevalent in his day, that manual labor should not be undertaken by the servants of God. Both at Granada and at Segovia, when these monasteries were in the course of erection, he went out to help the workmen in quarrying stone for the construction. The time that his office of spiritual director for the nuns left him free at Beas he often spent doing manual work for them, setting up partition walls, laying bricks, working in the garden, and so on. His love of cleanliness prompted him, even as superior, to take part in the more humble tasks such as sweeping and scrubbing the monastery floors. He endeavored as well to keep the altars in the Church spotless and tastefully decorated.

Fray John taught that creatures bring harm to a man only insofar as man's love of them is disordered. He insisted upon the need of a purgation wrought through mortification and deprival that a man may be freed from what is inordinate in his love and able to love God and His creatures with well-ordered charity. The clearness of vision which sprang from Fray John's detached heart empowered him to uncover in a striking manner the beauties of God's creatures. He beheld in them some trace of who God is, of His beauty, grandeur, might, wisdom, and other attributes. According to the Mystical Doctor's own teaching, a man through detachment from creatures acquires a clearer knowledge of them, a better understanding of both natural and supernatural truths concerning them. He taught that the joy a detached man receives from creatures is far different from the joy of the man who is attached to them. The detached man enjoys them according to their truth and what is best in them, whereas the attached man enjoys them according to their falseness and what is worst in them, for he fails to live by the principle that "there is nothing worthy of a man's joy save the service of God and the procurement of His honor and glory in all things."

St. John of the Cross was thus a lover of nature. For this reason he greatly preferred the country to the city and missed the lyric country solitude of *El Calvario* after founding the Carmelite College in the city of Baeza. In fact, at this time he bought some property in the country so that he as well as others in the community could escape from time to time the bustling and clamor of the city. He often took his friars out to the mountains, sometimes for the sake of recreation and relaxation—"to prevent their wanting to leave the monastery through spending too much time in it," as he once remarked—sometimes that each one might pass the day alone in the mountains "in solitary prayer and in speaking to our Lord from his heart." At Segovia, too, there was his favorite grotto which nature had hollowed out of rock and which overlooked a great stretch of sky, river, and landscape. John loved this silent grotto and used to spend there all the time he could spare.

Besides his love of nature and the exquisite charity and compassion he showed toward others, there was the special love he bore for his eldest brother, Francisco. He used to introduce Francisco, saying: "May I introduce you to my brother, who is the treasure I most value in the world." St. Teresa, too, was an object of his particular esteem, though not much is known of St. John's close ties with her since the correspondence between them unfortunately has not been preserved. It is a fact, however, that Fray John of the Cross had a high regard for and love of Madre Teresa, so much so that he carried her portrait about with him. There is the oft-told account of how one feast of the Blessed Trinity John of the Cross was speaking to Teresa about the sublime mystery of the day when suddenly both of them were seized by the ardor of the Spirit and raised aloft. "One cannot speak of God to Padre John of the Cross because he at once goes into an ecstasy and causes others to do the same," Teresa afterwards exclaimed.

Accompanying all the external, evangelical simplicity of his manner, then, was a soul on fire in its relations with God. This is evident in the splendor of the descriptions of *The Spiritual Canticle* and of *The Living*

Flame of Love. Concerning his intimacy with God, he once admitted in Granada: "God communicates the mystery of the Trinity to this sinner in such a way that if His Majesty did not strengthen my weakness by a special help, it would be impossible for me to live." He was not infrequently overwhelmed with an awareness of God's goodness and heard to exclaim: "O what a good God we have!" He did not need much sleep and spent a notable part of the night in prayer, sometimes kneeling at the altar steps before the Blessed Sacrament; at other times beneath the trees in the garden; and sometimes at the window of his cell, from which he could see the heavens and all the countryside. In the latter years of his relatively brief life his absorption in God sometimes became so great that he found it difficult to attend to ordinary affairs and is known to have secretly hit his knuckles against the wall when in the company of others so as not to lose the trend of conversation.

The height of the holy doctor's contemplation did not lessen his appreciation for the public prayer of the Church. The contemplation of St. John of the Cross was a contemplation within the Church, nourished by the Sacraments and the liturgical life. All who were witnesses of his life spoke of the particular devotion with which he celebrated Mass. The Mass was the center of his contemplation and often proved to be the occasion of special graces. At his first Mass he prayed for the grace never to commit a mortal sin, and the Lord promised to hear his prayer. There were times during the celebration of the Holy Sacrifice when he became so lost in God that he no longer had consciousness of where he was. His greatest suffering in the prison of Toledo was being deprived of Mass. The Blessed Sacrament was "all his glory, all his happiness, and for him far surpassed all the things of the earth." The only privilege he sought when major superior in Segovia was the cell closest to the Blessed Sacrament.

Nor did he limit his efforts to spiritual persons in administering the Sacrament of penance; hardened sinners, the worldly, the scrupulous whom other confessors did not want to bother with also sought him out.

Conjoined to his esteem for the Sacraments and the liturgical prayer of the Church was his love for the liturgical seasons. They were something more than just a commemoration; they were the occasion of a veritable interior transformation in the spirit of the mystery being celebrated. On the day before Christmas he organized a kind of paraliturgical procession with his friars to recall how Mary and Joseph went in search of lodging for the divine Infant. At Christmas time above all he felt his heart enkindled with love for the Child Jesus. One Christmas seeing a statue of the Infant lying on a cushion, he cried out: "Lord, if love is to slay me, the hour has now come." Another Christmas, taken with love, he grasped the statue of the Infant in his arms and began to dance with joy.

His aspect, in fact, and visage corresponded with the Church's liturgy. At Passiontide one could notice the pain he felt, and during Holy Week he once suffered so intensely from the Passion of Christ our Lord that he was unable to leave the monastery to hear the nuns' confessions. Among his favorite feasts, besides those of Corpus Christi and the Blessed Trinity, were the feasts of the Blessed Virgin. In his prison cell, on the Vigil of the Assumption, after nine months of bitter privation, he was asked what he was thinking of, and he replied: "I was thinking that tomorrow is the feast of our Lady and that it would give me great joy to say Mass." The countless favors which the Mother of God bestowed on him were such that the mere sight of her image gave him new life and brought love and brightness to his soul. Once, upon seeing an image of our Lady while he was preaching to the nuns in Caravaca, he could not conceal his love for her and exclaimed: "How happy I would be to live alone in a desert with that image."

The Bible was the book he cherished most of all; he loved to withdraw to hidden parts of the monastery with his Bible. The Gospels, chiefly, helped him to enter into intimacy with the three Persons of the Trinity. He so fully understood that in His Son the Father had spoken and revealed everything and that hidden in Christ were all the treasures of the wisdom and knowledge of God. There was no need for him, therefore, when he was in Lisbon to accompany a group of friars on a visit to the famed stigmatic who lived in that city; he had his Bible, and he remained reading and reflecting upon it along the shore of the sea while his companions went off to satisfy their curiosity.

Finally, his nearness to God filled him with confidence and freed him in a remarkable way from all worry and anxiety. Some of the monasteries where he was Prior were very poor, and this frequently caused his religious no little concern. But Fray John's confidence in God was so great during the times of want that he even hesitated to allow the procurator of the monastery to go out and beg for food. This complete trust in Providence, this habit of seeing the hand of God in all things, contributed to an air of peace and calm in the monastery. One feast day the brother cook let a pot of rice boil over and burn. Far from becoming angry, Fray John quietly consoled the brother: "Don't worry, my son; we can have whatever else you've got. Our Lord does not mean us to have rice today." This was his way, too, in persecution. He saw the hand of God there and exhorted others not to speak uncharitably or to grow disturbed about his persecutors, but to think "only that God ordains all." He taught that trust in God should be o great that even if the whole world were to collapse and come to an end one should not become disturbed. The endurance of all with peaceful equanimity, he wrote, not only reaps many blessings but helps a man in the midst of his adversity to make the proper judgment and apply the right remedy. This complete trust in

God left him perfectly at peace in his final illness, and when someone reminded him of all he had suffered, he replied with these remarkable words: "Padre, this is not the time to be thinking of that; it is by the merits of the blood of our Lord Jesus Christ that I hope to be saved."

III. THE WRITINGS

In considering the doctrinal-literary production of St. John of the Cross, it is at once obvious that it is not comparable in quantity and thematic variety to the works of many of the other doctors of the Church, of St. Augustine, for example, or St. Gregory, or St. Thomas Aquinas. Leaving aside those writings attributed to him without adequate foundation, and those which have never been found but of which there is testimony, we number only three major treatises: *The Ascent of Mount Carmel-The Dark Night; The Spiritual Canticle;* and *The Living Flame of Love.* The remainder of his writings comprise relatively few letters, various maxims and counsels, and his poems. All his works that have come down to us were written during the last fourteen years of his life, between the age of thirty-six and forty-nine, after he had attained an intellectual and spiritual maturity. A study of his doctrine discloses that his synthesis of the spirtual life was substantially complete in his mind once he began to write, and thus there is no essential change of thought in his teaching. A study of his writings does not reveal, as is the case with other writers, ideas representing an earlier period of thought which can then be contrasted with those of a later period. The themes with which he mainly deals are also constant: the way leading to union with God, and the life itself of divine union.

The table following gives a general picture of the authentic works as well as of the places and dates of composition.

Num.	Year	Title	Place of Composition
1.	1578	The Spiritual Canticle—Poem (st. 1–31 incl.)	Toledo—Prison
2.	"	For I Know Well the Spring—Poem	" "
3.	"	The Romances—Poem	" "
4.	"	On the Psalm: "By the Waters of Babylon"—Poem	" "
5.	1579–81	The dark night—Poem	Calvario-Baeza
6.	1579	The Sketch of the Mount	Calvario-Beas
7.	"	Sayings of Light and Love	" "
8.	"	Precautions	" "
9.	?	Maxims on Love	?
10.	?	Degrees of Perfection	?
11.	1579–85	The Ascent of Mount Carmel	Calvario-Baeza-Granada
12.	1581	Del Verbo Divino—Poem	Granada

Num.	Year	Title	Place of Composition
13.	1581–91	Letters	Various Places
14.	1582	The Spiritual Canticle—Poem (st. 32–34)	Granada
15.	1582–85	The Dark Night—Commentary	"
16.	"	The Spiritual Canticle—Poem (st. 35–39)	"
17.	"	The Living Flame of Love—Poem	"
18.	"	I Entered into Unknowing—Poem	"
19.	"	I Live, but Not in Myself—Poem	"
20.	"	I Went Out Seeking Love—Poem	"
21.	"	A Lone Young Shepherd—Poem	"
22.	1584	The Spiritual Canticle—Commentary (1st redaction)	"
23.	1585–87	The Living Flame of Love—Commentary (1st redaction)	"
24.	"	Counsels to a Religious	"
25.	1586	The Spiritual Canticle (st. 11 of 2nd redaction)	Segovia?
26.	1586?	The Sum of Perfection	Segovia
27.	1586–88	Not for All of Beauty—Poem	Granada-Segovia?
28.	"	Without Support and with Support—Poem	"
29.	1586–91	The Spiritual Canticle—Commentary (2nd redaction)	Granada-Segovia-Peñuela
30.	"	The Living Flame of Love—Commentary (2nd redaction)	"

With the exception of the *Sayings of Light and Love* and some of his letters—whose autographs are conserved—St. John of the Cross's original writings have been lost, and thus his works have reached us only through numerous codices containing more or less faithful copies. This has created the critical problem concerning the original reading and the selection of that codex which most accurately reproduces this reading. In the special introductions we shall indicate the codex we have followed, which is always the one held by specialists to be most trustworthy.

In the field of Spanish literature, St. John of the Cross has won a prominent place, particularly for his poetry. As a poet he is ranked among the greatest in the history of Spain. Such eminent critics as Menéndez Pelayo and Dámaso Alonso have confessed to a religious terror they felt before the beauty and the burning passion of his verses.

His prose style, on the other hand, has not gained such certain praise. It is in the main didactic and often discursive, especially in the *Ascent*. Concerned with the practical goals of teaching, of pointing out the way that leads to perfection, St. John obviously made no particular effort to phrase his ideas in graceful, stylish, and impeccable prose. We find it quite unpolished (he himself complained of his style), cluttered with repetitions, redundancies, ambiguities, split constructions that are often complicated and obscure, Latinisms, and so on. His long, labyrinthine sentences have not infrequently proved a challenge to his editors seeking clear punctuation. We have the fantastic example in a recent Spanish edition of his works in which one sentence has been buttressed with fifty commas, four semicolons, two uses of parentheses, and a use of the dash. In spite of all, however, there are not lacking prose passages in which the Mystical Doctor shows plainly his literary genius for expressing a thought in phrases of beauty, originality, and power.

In doctrine, there is no longer any doubt concerning the mark he has left in the area of ascetical and mystical theology. Manuals in spiritual theology more and more reflect the theologian's dependence upon St. John of the Cross in the arrangement of the subject-matter and the resolution of thorny problems. But wonderfully combining both the practical and the theoretical, his works, while appealing to psychologists, philosophers, and theologians, have never failed to appeal as well to a large number of the devout who are not specialists.

In the bull proclaiming St. John of the Cross a Doctor of the Church, placing the Church's highest approval upon his writings, Pius XI declared:

"Although they treat of difficult and profound matters, *The Ascent of Mount Carmel, The Dark Night of the Soul, The Living Flame of Love,* and several other shorter works and letters written by him, are nevertheless full of such sound spiritual doctrine and are so well suited to the reader's understanding, that they are rightly looked upon as a code and guide for the faithful soul endeavoring to embrace a more perfect life."

Subsequent to this declaration of Pius XI, Jacques Maritain, in his introduction to Pere Bruno's life of the Saint, has perhaps summed up as well as any scholar the significance of the Mystical Doctor in our age:

"The doctrine of St. John of the Cross is the pure Catholic doctrine of the mystical life. We may well believe that, if he has been proclaimed in our own days a Doctor of the Church, it is because, like Thomas Aquinas, he meets a special need of the age. At the present day, Naturalism has so ruined and subverted Nature that there is no possible healing for Nature itself, no possible return to the stable order of reason, save by a full and complete recognition of the rights of the supernatural, the absolute, the demands of the Gospel and of living faith."

A New Translation

For many years the Carmelites have received requests from priests, religious, and lay people for a new English translation of the works of St. John of the Cross, a rendering that would prove clearer, more readable, and better suited to the character of the English language. These desires were prompted by the zealous wish to see the profitable, sound, and inspiring doctrine of this saint presented other than in an archaic, obscure, and forbidding fashion. Being assigned to this task, we have kept the motives behind these requests foremost in mind; they provided us with the understandable and legitimate goals worth seeking in a new version and edition.

To lay bare the true meanings hidden in the sixteenth-century Spanish of St. John of the Cross as well as in his own personal way with words and expressions, we found it necessary first of all to prepare a complete lexicon, recording every word and usage found (and as often as found) in his writings so that the authentic sense could be determined in each difficult case through comparison, and thus with sound basis and all possible precision. In addition we noted the advantage and even necessity in this translation of often shortening and simplifying the sentences, of substituting the suitable noun for many misleading pronouns, and avoiding where possible Latinisms and redundancy. (The pleonasm is usually worth preserving because of the help it affords in establishing the different meanings he attributes to a word.) Because of its importance, though, in the field of spiritual theology, we have attempted to preserve the terminology of St. John, usually referred to as sanjuanist terminology, which at times is original and at other times borrowed from the scholastic sciences. Thus we have for example: the dark night, the passive nights, the accidents of knowledge, the substance of knowledge, the senses, the spirit, the substantial touch, forms, images, mode, suppositum, appetites, the supreme principle, first movements, spiritual exercises, annihilation, and so on.

Since we are still awaiting a definitive Spanish critical edition of the works of St. John of the Cross (and since those comparatively few scholars who would want to consult the usually insignificant readings of other manuscripts ordinarily have sufficient knowledge of Spanish), we have omitted all critical references to variant readings. This, together with the omission of the first redactions of The Spiritual Canticle and The Living Flame of Love, has enabled us to present a one-volume edition more in keeping with the requirements of the general reader.

For these reasons we have not translated any of the existing critical editions but have used as our source those codices which in the judgment of the experts are the most trustworthy. When—and these instances were rare—there were omissions in the codex selected or the expressions proved unintelligible or excessively obscure, we chose the complete or clearer rendering of another reliable codex. Since we do not possess the autographs of the Saint it would be pointless to adhere so slavishly to one manuscript as to attempt the translation of meaningless statements.

Since St. John of the Cross often, and perhaps always, made his own translations of Scriptural passages from the Latin, we have translated from his quite literal rendering rather than use one of the new English translations of the Bible. This, moreover, was frequently necessary because the Saint commonly develops his thought in line with the words he uses in translating the sacred text.

Recent Spanish editions have contrived to present the works in a chronological order. Since the dates are not always certain and since he worked on different projects during the same years, we have followed the arrangement which has been traditional, placing the major works first, then the minor works, the letters, and finally the poems.

In the numbering of chapters and paragraphs we have adopted that introduced in the edition of Padre Silverio. This facilitates references for the sanjuanist student and enables him to confer readily the citations of articles in his own as well as foreign languages, for most editions follow this enumeration. We use the following signs in referring to the major works: A=*The Ascent of Mount Carmel;* N=*The Dark Night;* C=*The Spiritual Canticle;* F=*The Living Flame of Love.* Following these identifying letters, we give the number of the book and chapter, or of the stanza, and then the number of the paragraph.

NOTE ON DRAWING OF
CHRIST ON THE CROSS

One day St. John of the Cross handed Ana María de Jesús, a holy nun at the Incarnation, a small piece of paper on which he had drawn in pen and ink a picture of Christ on the cross. It represented a vision he had recently had. Fortunately the small drawing has not been lost, but is still preserved in a reliquary at the Convent of the Incarnation in Avila. This is an enlarged photo of the original.

René Huyghe, Conservator in Chief of the paintings in the Museum of the Louvre, wrote concerning this drawing:

"Some people imagine that seeing is merely a matter of opening one's eyes. Seeing is a technique, a science which makes slow progress from century to century. There is a technique in vision just as much as in execution . . . Saint John of the Cross escapes right out of those visual habits by which all artists form a part of their period. He knows nothing of the rules and limitations of contemporary vision; he is not dependent on the manner of seeing current in his century; he is dependent on nothing but the object of his contemplation. It is an eminently mystical attitude: penetrated by it, flooded with it, submerged in it, Saint John submits himself to it as to a revealed vision; he accepts it as completely as the stigmata; he can only set down the divine vision, however inexpressible and inconceivable in the visual terms of the period it may be, just as at other times his interior life received and lived what is inconceivable and inexpressible for the contemporary intellect. This is precisely the mark of the mystic and of his superhuman powers. The vertical perspective—bold, almost violent, emphasized by light and shade—in which he caught his Christ on the cross cannot be matched in contemporary art; in the context of that art it is hardly imaginable.

"Perhaps this drawing is even more astonishing than it seems at first sight. It is always our instinct to refer the unknown to the known, to make anything which contradicts our habits conform to them. Thus it is usual to set this crucified Christ upright, as we are accustomed to see Him. When Bernard Champigneulle showed the drawing to our old and deeply regretted friend, the painter José Maria Sert, he, without a moment's hesitation, turned it sideways. Its power and originality are then redoubled: the cross is leaning forward like a crucifix pressed to the lips of a dying man. This is why Christ is dragging away from it, His arms stretched almost to the breaking-point, His head bent; He is falling forward by His own weight. Perhaps Saint John of the Cross, remembering this ritual act of presenting the crucifix, had this corporeal vision of the crucified Christ, coming to him, leaning over him, in one shattering gift. . ." Father Bruno de J. M., O.C.D., editor, *Three Mystics*, pp. 96–98 (London: Sheed & Ward, 1952).

The Ascent of Mount Carmel

AND

The Dark Night

INTRODUCTION TO
THE ASCENT OF MOUNT CARMEL-THE DARK NIGHT

The entire work of the Ascent-Night comprises four integral parts: the sketch of the Mount; the poem consisting of eight stanzas; the first part of the commentary and treatise entitled *The Ascent of Mount Carmel;* the second part of the commentary and treatise entitled *The Dark Night.*

THE SKETCH OF THE MOUNT

St. John of the Cross made many copies of his drawing of *The Mount* (see p. 66), first for the Carmelite nuns in Beas and later for his own friars in Baeza and Granada. Besides the copies he made for these religious, he also, according to his explicit testimony, placed one at the beginning of the *Ascent* to serve as a summary of the doctrine contained in the treatise. Doubtless there were differences in the copies he made. According to the testimony of Madre Magdalena del Espíritu Santo, he gave each nun a copy to keep in her breviary, but later added and changed some things. None of the autograph copies has been found, but we are reproducing here a faithful and authenticated replica of an autograph that was preserved in the monastery of Nuestra Señora de las Nieves in Málaga. In this way we are certain of having *The Mount* as St. John of the Cross sketched it, for many of the later editors of his works, unimpressed by the rough primitive appearance of his sketches, had their own more elaborate drawings made, but without taking pains in many instances to preserve pure the doctrine contained in St. John's drawing. Since the drawing was meant to serve as a summary of the saint's teaching, the doctrine contained in *The Ascent of Mount Carmel* and *The Dark Night* provides the best means of understanding this drawing.

THE POEM

The poem was probably written while the Saint was confessor to the nuns in Beas—sometime, then, between 1579–81. It consists of eight stanzas, each having five verses. It is an allegory in which the lover sings of her good fortune in having gone out one dark night to be united with her Beloved (st. 1–5), and then of the wonderful effects of this union (st. 6–8).

THE TREATISE

The Ascent of Mount Carmel was probably begun in El Calvario and continued in Baeza and Granada, and covering the years 1579–85. *The Dark Night* was no doubt composed in Granada during the years 1582–84. Of this we have a very clear assertion from Padre Juan Evangelista, the saint's companion.

The codex we have followed in our translation of the *Ascent* is that made by Fray Juan Evangelista in Granada and which is preserved in the Silverian Archives in Burgos. It bears that title *The Codex of Alcaudete,* and being a transcript of the original is the most valuable and trustworthy copy of the *Ascent.* Other important copies of the *Ascent* are: *The Codex of Alba de Tormes,* conserved in the archives of the Carmelite Fathers in Salamanca; *The Codex of Burgos,* conserved in the National Library of Madrid; and *The Codex of Calatayud,* conserved also in the National Library of Madrid.

The Dark Night is the sanjuanist work of which we possess the most copies. But unfortunately none of them has value as a transcript from the original. The best codex from the critical viewpoint, and one we have followed, is that known as *Hispalense* and which is conserved in the National Library of Madrid.

To aid the reader in the understanding of many difficult matters encountered in the treatise and in order to share with him some of the good fruits of recent research, we shall discuss in greater detail certain points concerning the character, themes, structure, doctrine, and destination of the *Ascent-Dark Night.*

General Theme and Character

On the opening page of *The Ascent of Mount Carmel* St. John of the Cross indicates the nature of his treatise by declaring his intention to explain how one reaches the "high state of perfection." This assertion at the outset plainly marks the practical character of his book. It is a work which describes the path to be followed in order to reach perfection, which he chooses to call union with God. Yet, though his book, having such a purpose, is necessarily practical, we cannot conclude that it is nothing but a collection of workable rules and techniques. We discover in fact that, in addition to setting down rules, the *Ascent* gives a keen analysis of the principles which support them. It provides us with a systematic presentation of both the theory and the practical norms governing the development of the spiritual life and can be placed among those works belonging to that branch of the sacred science called spiritual (or ascetical-mystical) theology.

In the prologue, answering the question, which was bound to arise, concerning the sources of his teaching, St. John of the Cross indicates three founts from which he intends to draw his doctrine: the sciences; experience; and Sacred Scripture. But experience and the sciences are not his chief sources, for he states explicitly that the principal fount of his teaching is Sacred Scripture, which a study of his writing confirms.

The reason he attributes so prominent a place to Sacred Scripture is his firm belief that the "Holy Spirit speaks to us through it," and that by study and reflection upon the revealed word, and submission to "Our Holy Mother the Catholic Church," a man can reach some understanding of "the abundant meanings of the Holy Spirit" contained in Scripture.

It is worthwhile noting that St. John of the Cross wrote his work, just as he composed the stanzas of the poem *The Dark Night,* after he had personally journeyed the way of the active and passive purifications of the nights and had attained the state of perfection, union with the divine Bridegroom. He consequently views the narrow path ascending without deviation to the height of the mount of perfection from that very height, as one who has already trod it and who, looking down, can mark its peculiarities with a clearness of view unobtainable by those who have still much ground to cover. The excellent view, afforded at the summit, of the snares which lay along the slope of this mount to hinder anyone striving to reach perfection, prompted him to write *The Ascent of Mount Carmel,* by which he could encourage spiritual persons and point out to them the safe path.

Union with God

The aim of the spiritual life, as the Mystical Doctor envisioned it, is the state of perfect union with God through love; this is the summit of Mount Carmel. Before analyzing the structure of this work, we ought to examine the concept of union with God which appears in it, for through an understanding of the goal, an explanation of the path reaching up to it is more intelligible, since every way acquires its authentic meaning from the goal to which it leads.

The Saint dedicated Chapter 5 of Book Two of the *Ascent* to his conception of union with God. He tells us that he is referring to a supernatural union and not the natural or essential union by which God is always present in creatures preserving them in being. This supernatural union is "the total and permanent union according to the substance of the soul and its faculties." It is "the obscure habit of union." In other words, it is a habitual union distinguishable from the more intense actual unions which, though supernatural and total, are transient, incapable of being permanent here on earth.

The shorter term for the habitual state of supernatural and total union is "the union of likeness." It is a union produced by love, a habitual, perfect love of God which makes the soul resemble Him in all its activity—to the extent that the soul and God "seem to be one."

To illustrate this union of likeness he adopts the example of the sun shining upon a window. We could summarize his illustration with the following points:

1. God (compared to the sun) is ever present in the soul (compared to the window) communicating and preserving its natural being, just as the sun shines on the window.

2. When the window is wholly smeared with dirt, the sun does not illumine it, as it does when the window is unstained; likewise a soul utterly smeared with inordinate affection for creatures is unprepared to receive the communication of God's supernatural being.

3. In the measure that the window is clean, the sun illumines it; as the soul through love wipes away everything unconformed to the divine will, God communicates Himself supernaturally, or through grace.

4. When the window is entirely clean, the sunlight so illumines it that it makes it appear to be the light. Yet, regardless of its total resemblance to the light, the window in its nature remains distinct from the nature of the sunlight. Similarly, when the soul in its activity is completely purified of everything unlike God, when it is entirely conformed with God's will through love, God will so communicate His supernatural being that it will be like God and seem to be God. Yet in its nature it will be as distinct from God as before. A soul that has reached such perfect conformity and likeness has attained the high state of perfection, union with God, or transformation in God.

From the standpoint of the soul the comparison is basically negative: that the divine light may transform it, the soul must purify itself. "To love," declares the saint, "is to labor to divest and deprive oneself for God of all that is not God." But the positive factor cannot be absent, for the effort to purify is an effort of love; love's very function calls for this purification by conforming the human will to the divine will and directing all the soul's activity toward God.

Elsewhere the saint gives us a positive picture of this love. If a man is to reach God by union of the will through charity, he must "employ all the faculties, appetites, operations, and emotions of his soul in God so that he may avoid the use of his strength and ability for anything else . . . When the will directs these faculties, passions, and appetites toward God, turning them away from all that is not God, the soul preserves its strength for God and comes to love Him with all its might." (A3, 16, 1–2)

Love is the force which purifies by centering the soul's faculties, appetites, operations, and passions in God. Failure to employ all this "strength" in God is the disorder of which one must be purged.

The Soul

Since St. John of the Cross's notion of the soul plays a decisive role in the structure of his treatise, a word about this notion is also in order before analyzing the work itself. He divides the soul into two main parts: the sensory, and the spiritual. Each of these parts has its own powers or faculties. The sensory part, which has to do with sensible or corporal objects, possesses exterior sense faculties of sight, hearing, smell, taste, and touch; it also claims inner sense faculties, which he reduces to the phantasy and the imagination. (A2, 11, 1; 12, 1, 3; C28, 4–5) The spiritual part of the soul, which is concerned with spiritual or incorporeal objects, numbers three faculties: intellect, memory, and will. The sensory faculties as well as the spirtual faculties of intellect and memory are cognitive; they involve the perception, or as the Saint terms it, apprehension and cognition of objects. The will on the other hand is an appetitive faculty. It inclines toward the good; to it, consequently, are related the appetites and the emotions or passions of joy, hope, fear, and sorrow. (A2, 6, 1, 4–5; A3, 16, 2)

The General Divison of The Ascent of Mount Carmel

The poetic figure "dark night" provided St. John of the Cross with a mysterious-sounding metaphor to designate the entire way leading to union with God. The path, then, in the center of the mount of perfection, and which alone leads to the summit, is a dark night. In Chapter 2 of Book One of the *Ascent,* he lists three reasons for calling this path to union a dark night. These reasons are inspired by the three terms found in all change: the *terminus a quo,* the *mean,* and the *terminus ad quem.* In passing from the initial stages of the spiritual life to perfect union with God, the soul must leave all things by denying its appetites for them, and advance by means of faith to God, its end.

Without exploring in this limited introduction St. John's many-faceted use of the figure "night," we can affirm from this chapter that basically there are three reasons for calling the path to union with God a dark night. They are: the mortification of the appetites; the journey in faith; and God's communication to the soul. At the end of the chapter he states his planned method of procedure: to discuss these reasons separately, beginning with an exposition of the first, the mortification of the appetites.

This proposal comes as quite a surprise since he presents the main division of his work in Chapter 1. There he asserts that in order to attain union with God the soul "must ordinarily pass through two principal kinds of night (which spiritual persons call purgations or purifications of the soul) in order to reach the state of perfection." These nights are the purifications of the two main parts of the soul and are wrought in a double manner: actively, through the soul's own efforts; and passively, through God's work in it. He informs us that he will deal with the active night or purification of the sensory part in the first section of his work, with the active night of the spiritual part in the second and third, and with the passive night in the fourth part.

To determine the relation, if any, these separate divisions have to each other, it is necessary to analyze the work itself, mark the various parts, record the themes of each, and note whether the three reasons given in Chapter 2 for calling the path toward union with God a dark night have any relationship to the various purifications listed in Chapter 1.

The Mortification of the Appetites

A perusal of the first book of the *Ascent* reveals that its main theme is the mortification of the appetites, or the first reason for the adoption of the literary figure "dark night." In beginning to treat of this mortification, St. John indicates that the use in his treatise of the image "night" is metaphorical, based on the negative idea of privation. "Just as night is nothing but the privation of light and, consequently, of all objects visible by means of the light . . . the mortification of the appetites can be called a night for the soul. To deprive oneself of the gratification of the appetites in all things is like living in darkness and in a void." (A1, 3, 1)

Since St. John of the Cross expresses his ideas in a variety of ways, it is important that we take care not to attribute meanings which he never intended to his frequent vigorous statements and uses of hyperbole; nor must the effort to avoid such distortions result in diluting the austere demands of his doctrine on love of God. Without contradicting himself, or even changing his thought in any point of his synthesis, he often defines an object in different ways and uses various words to express it.

With this in mind we must ascertain what he intends by the mortification of the appetites. Some of the other terms he substitutes for the word "appetite" are: attachment, affection, the love of creatures, the will for something, inclination, and desire. Manifestly from the expressions used, these appetites belong to the affective or appetitive function of the soul; we could specify them as affective tendencies toward some object.

Not until Chapter 11, however, does St. John pose the question as to which appetites must be mortified. The first factor he underscores in his answer is that he means voluntary appetites, for the involuntary appetites "do not so hinder a man as to prevent him from attaining divine union."

Secondly, he remarks that these voluntary appetites of which he speaks involve either mortal sin, and these are the "most serious," or venial sin, which are "less grave," or imperfections, which are the "least serious." (A1, 11, 2; 9, 7; 12, 3) And in no. 4 of Chapter 11 he gives some examples of these imperfections, or "least serious." The appetites, then, which must be mortified are in different degrees inordinate, unordained at least in some way toward rendering pure honor and glory to God.

Finally, he points out that the habitual appetites are what he particularly has in mind; these inordinate, voluntary habitual tendencies not only spur one on to sinful or imperfect acts, but they embody a certain stability uncharacteristic of an act. "I am referring here to habitual appetites, because certain scattered acts of different desires are not such a hindrance to union, since they are not a determined habit." (A1, 11, 3)

To mortify the voluntary, inordinate appetites is to put them to death, to destroy their voluntariness by holding back consent and rejecting them. And if a man is courageous and constant in resisting involuntary appetites, refusing to allow them to become voluntary, in spite of their continuing assault upon him, "he wins strength, purity, light, comfort, and many blessings." That he grows strong thereby is true even though these appetites and temptations seem at the time of their disturbance to breed harmful effects and hinder union with God. (A1, 12, 6) In conjunction with this truth, the Saint makes the explicit observation that in the measure that one renounces the inordinate appetites one practices virtue and matures in it. (A1, 5, 6)

From these points flows the principle that creatures in themselves do not thwart union with God; it is the voluntary inordinate appetite for creatures that interferes with this union. "We are not discussing the mere lack of things; this lack will not divest the soul if it craves for all these objects. We are dealing with the denudation of the soul's appetites . . . Since the things of the world cannot enter the soul, they are not in themselves an encumbrance or harm to it; rather, it is the will and appetite dwelling within it that causes the damage." (A1, 3, 4)

Further analysis discloses that the denial of one's consent must be the work of supernatural love. St. John of the Cross often reminds us that the appetites must be ordered or directed to God through love, employed in loving God. (A1, 9, 2; A3, 16, 1; 35, 8; N2, 11, 3-5)

When charity is perfect, all the appetites of the sensory and spiritual part of the soul "move in and through love." (C28, 8; A1, 5, 8; 10, 1) When all a man's activity lies under the rule of charity, the use of creatures is not motivated by the search for personal satisfaction, but solely by this supernatural love which in its benevolence toward God seeks only His honor and glory in the use of things. (A3, 16, 2; 17, 2) Through the high degree of charity present in the soul that has reached union, the affective tendency toward God is habitual and deep-rooted. Thus we read of this state: ". . . the affections, senses, desires, appetites, hope, joy, and all the energy from the first instant incline toward God, although, as I say, the soul may not advert to the fact that she is working for Him." (C28, 5) We read also of the appetites which are wholly under the dominion of love as being divine. The reason he calls them divine is that they no longer flow from natural motives or ends, for charity has only God as its origin and its end. (cf. N2, 11, 3–5; F2, 33–34; F3, 74)

Toward the close of this first book, St. John of the Cross directs our attention to Christ, Who is the sublime model upon Whom each man must pattern his life. Christ had only one desire: to do the will of His heavenly Father. Thus, the Saint counsels, anything which is not purely for the honor and glory of God should be renounced. (A1, 13, 3–4)

The mortification of the appetites, therefore, which St. John of the Cross deals with is the renunciation of all affective tendency contrary to the love of God and to the quest for His honor and glory alone in all things. The total mortification of all the inordinate appetites is not wrought until a soul reaches perfect union with God. Since this is true, the task placed before us in Book One of the Ascent extends far beyond the active purification of the senses. Still, the author in all likelihood adverts frequently to that initial period of the spiritual life, the active purification of the senses, because mortification must be one of the chief concerns of beginners. (C22, 3)

Book One of the Ascent accordingly treats of both the mortification of the appetites and the active night of the senses. These two themes are not identical, but neither are they entirely exclusive of one another. Without being unmindful of the other legitimate ways of summing up the subject matter of this book, we might phrase it thus: To reach union with God, the soul must mortify within itself all voluntary, inordinate appetites for creatures, since these appetites are contrary to the perfect love of God and consequently to union with God. In the active night of the senses a person must struggle particularly for the habit of seeking only God's honor and glory in the use of his senses, in imitation of Christ and out of love for Him.

The Journey in Faith

The road of faith along which one advances toward God is the second reason for naming the path to divine union a dark night. It is the theological virtue of faith taken in its strict sense which undoubtedly prompted St. John of the Cross to term the entire path, or life, of faith a dark night. Laying stress on the doctrine of theologians that the virtue of faith is an obscure habit, he teaches that "it brings us to believe truths revealed by God which transcend every natural light and infinitely exceed all human understanding." (A2, 3, 1) But in his ponderous underscoring of how the light of faith "suppresses" and "overwhelms" and "nullifies" the natural light of the intellect, he sometimes leaves one with the cold impression that faith simply does away with all knowledge. Reflecting upon some of his strong statements on the obscurity of faith, we must not, however, overlook other texts in which he definitely declares that faith gives us knowledge of God. (A2, 9, 1; C12, 3–6) The Saint's wish, obviously, is to turn our attention to the obscurity of faith and impress upon our minds the inability of the intellect to acquire by its own power the knowledge which faith affords of the strictly supernatural mysteries of God, or even to understand them fully once they have been revealed.

In speaking of faith, St. John of the Cross has especially in mind that obscure encounter with God which it affords us. It is the only "proximate and proportionate means" to union with God in the cognitive order. To advance toward God, a man "must lean on dark faith, take it for his guide and light, and rest on nothing of what he understands, tastes, feels, or imagines." (A2, 4, 2) To journey to union with God in faith a man "is decidedly hindered . . . when he is attached to any understanding, feeling, imagining, opinion, will, or way of his own, or to any other of his works or affairs." (A2, 4, 4) The reason for this hindrance lies in the truth that none of this particular knowledge or feeling constitutes a proximate means toward union with God, for God infinitely transcends all of this.

In discussing faith as the proximate means to union with God, the Mystical Doctor addresses particularly those "whom God has favored with the state of contemplation" (A2, 6, 8; 7, 13; A3, 2, 2), those in whom the theological virtues have more fully matured, who "bring to prayer no other support than faith, hope, and love." This results in a special treatment of the active purification of the spiritual faculties. "As we outlined for the sensory night a method of emptying the sense faculties of desire for their objects that the soul might leave the point of departure for the mean, which is faith, so for this spiritual night we will present, with the divine help, a method of emptying and purifying the spiritual faculties of all that is not God. By this method these faculties can abide in the darkness of these three virtues which are the means and preparation for the soul's union with God." (A2, 6, 6)

The beginner, unable to be occupied in the obscure, general, loving knowledge which is communicated through faith, must employ the remote means to God, which is meditation. He must reflect upon particular ideas and images for the purpose of acquiring some knowledge and love of God. (A2, 14, 2; 13, 2; 12, 3–4; 17, 3) In the initial stages of the spiritual life the soul is still attached to the senses and is unable to advance without their support. God respects this weakness; it is by means of the senses that He draws beginners to Himself. (A2, 17, 3; F3, 32) The holy images formed in meditation gradually replace worldly thoughts and assist the beginner in directing his affection to a spiritual object. (A3, 39, 1; A1, 14, 2)

But as a person is freed from his dependence upon the senses, he enters the way of faith; not a faith, however, which excludes charity and hope. Journeying by faith, a man advances also in hope and love, since it is through each of the theological virtues purifying its respective faculty that he darkens and blinds himself as to all that he understands, tastes, feels, and imagines. "Faith causes darkness and a void of understanding in the intellect, hope begets an emptiness of possessions in the memory, and charity produces the nakedness and emptiness of affection and joy in all that is not God." (A2, 6, 2)

The object of faith, on the other hand, is not limited to God alone; faith also gives us knowledge of how we must act in order to reach Him. The journey in faith then embraces supernatural prudence, and full adherence to the objective content of faith means likewise that a person through prudence in the cognitive order must employ all his powers in entire conformity with the demands the truths of faith make upon him. By acting contrary to these requirements, he deviates from the road of faith and ceases to journey to God in faith. Thus to make progress along the path of faith he must be guided "in all by the law of Christ the man and that of His Church and His ministers." (A2, 22, 7) One must not violate the limits God has set by one's seeking knowledge in extraordinary ways, "since a person can be sufficiently guided by natural reason and the law and doctrine of the Gospel . . . There is no difficulty or necessity unsolvable or irremediable by these means." (A2, 21, 4) "Since the Christian has the light of faith . . . through his good customs and virtues he should fix his eyes only upon the service and honor of God." (A3, 27, 4)

In Books Two and Three of the *Ascent,* consequently, St. John of the Cross explains how the intellect and the memory must turn away from all the particular knowledge and remembrances that do not help one render greater honor and glory to God, and how the will must not set its joys, hopes, fears, or sorrows upon goods that do not serve for God's greater honor and glory. Through the life of faith, hope, and charity the soul uproots every ungodly thing and unites itself to God, all of which would be wholly impossible without these virtues. In their inner dynamism they grow by purifying and purify by growing; to the extent that they unite with God they empty of what is not God, and to the extent that they empty a soul of every godless thing they unite it with God.

Obviously the second reason for calling the path to divine union a dark night is not restricted to the active purification of the spirit. For instance, the beginner must also live by faith in the active night of the senses, and, in fact, that part dealing with the journey in faith has many references relating to the active purification of the senses. (A3, 18–26; 35–44)

Yet, since in his exposition on the journey in faith, St. John keeps in mind those especially "who have begun to enter the state of contemplation," he emphasizes the necessity of turning in prayer from all particular knowledge to a general attentiveness to God through faith, since it is through faith that the general loving, dark knowledge called contemplation is infused. The Holy Spirit "illumines the intellect according to the mode of its recollection, and the intellect can find no better recollection than in faith, and thus the Holy Spirit will not illumine it in any other recollection more than in faith." (A2, 29, 6; 24, 4, 8)

We find a good practical summary of St. John of the Cross's teaching concerning the proper attitude toward images (exterior as well as interior) and particular knowledge in Chapter 15 of Book Three.

". . . as often as distinct ideas, forms, and images occur to him, he should immediately without resting in them turn to God with loving affection, in emptiness of everything rememberable. He should not think or look upon these things for a longer time than is sufficient for the understanding and fulfillment of his obligations, if they refer to this. And then he should consider these ideas without becoming attached or seeking gratification in them, lest they leave their effects in the soul. Thus a man is not required to cease recalling and thinking about what he must do and know, for, since he is not attached to the possession of these thoughts, he will not be harmed . . . Yet it must be noted here that by our doctrine we are not in agreement, nor do we desire to be, with that of those pestiferous men, who, persuaded by the pride and envy of Satan, have sought to remove from the eyes of the faithful the holy and necessary use and the renowned cult of the images of God and His saints . . . But when a person uses and dwells upon the means more than he ought, his excessive use of them becomes as much an impediment as anything else. This is even truer in the case of supernatural visions and images, with which I am especially dealing here and which are the cause of many delusions and dangers . . . Images will always help a person toward union with God, provided that he does not pay more attention to them than is necessary, and that he allows himself to soar—when God bestows the favor—from the painted image to the living God, in forgetfulness of all creatures and things pertaining to creatures." (A3, 15, 1-2)

In view of all these factors concerning Books Two and Three of the *Ascent*, we might summarize its content as follows: In these books St. John of the Cross deals with the journey in faith and likewise with the active purification of the spirit, themes which are unidentical, but not exclusive of each other. To reach union with God a person must journey in faith, depriving himself of everything in contradiction with full adherence to God and to the law of Christ and of His Church. In the active purification of the spirit he must contrive to purify his spiritual faculties through the theological virtues, each virtue emptying the faculty in which it resides of all that is not purely for God's honor and glory and uniting it to God. Those "who have begun to enter the state of contemplation" must turn aside in prayer from particular knowledge that they may receive through a general loving attentiveness in faith the general loving knowledge God infuses.

The Ascent of Mount Carmel ends abruptly—in the middle of a sentence—with the Saint dealing with provocative spiritual goods. He had yet to discuss according to his explicit plan the directive and perfective spiritual goods, and then continue with an exposition of the other three passions: hope, fear, and sorrow. His intention had been to bring Book Three of the *Ascent* to a close after discussing these passions. (A3, 1, 3) Besides what is lacking to Book Three, there is likewise his promise to explain the passive purifications in Part 4 of the *Ascent*. (A1, 1, 2) Or again, from another view, he has yet to expound the third reason for calling the way leading to union with God a dark night.

The Dark Night *and The Communication of God*

Another treatise of St. John of the Cross, which has come down to us and exists in the greater number of known manuscripts independently of the *Ascent*, bears the title *The Dark Night*. In this work the Mystical Doctor expounds the passive purifications of the soul; first the purification of the senses, and then the purification of the spirit. He fulfills, in effect, with all precision his promise concerning the matter to be explained in Part 4 of the *Ascent*. The question which comes spontaneously to the fore is: Did St. John of the Cross intend the work always known, insofar as can be determined, under the title of *The Dark Night* to constitute a part of the *Ascent*?

The above question definitely differs from another regarding the necessity of the passive nights in order to reach that union which is the goal of the *Ascent*. That St. John considered the passive purifications necessary to attain union with God is manifest from the very first chapter of the *Ascent* where he proposes to treat both the active and passive aspects of these nights. He firmly declares in several places that the active purification is alone insufficient for the attainment of the perfection, or union with God, set before us in the *Ascent*. "We shall not discuss in this active night and purgation the divine effects that the union, when perfect, produces in the intellect, memory, and will, because the divine union is not perfected by this night alone. But we will speak of them in the passive night, for it is by means of this passive night that union with God is wrought." (A3, 2, 14; *cf.* A1, 1, 2; 13, 1; A2, 2, 3)

As for our question, the lack of adequate external evidence to support an assertion that *The Dark Night* is a major part of *The Ascent of Mount Carmel* in no way signifies the lack of convincing internal evidence. In *The Living Flame of Love*, St. John plainly refers to *The Dark Night* as belonging to the *Ascent*: ". . . of this we treated in *The Dark Night* of *The Ascent of Mount Carmel*." (F1, 25) In Book Two of *The Dark Night* he says: ". . . the reason I undertook this task was to explain this night to many souls who in passing through it do not understand it, as is pointed out in the prologue." (N2, 22, 2) Yet, it is in the prologue of the *Ascent* that he laments the failure of many souls to understand the sufferings encountered in the passive nights, and accents the dire need for knowledge of this night. The short prologue of the *Night*, however, mentions nothing at all of this difficulty and need. Clearly, he considers the prologue of the *Ascent* to be a prologue for the *Night* as well.

Again, he promises several times in the *Ascent* to discuss points which he does manifestly treat in *The Dark Night*. In A1, 13, 1, for example, he discloses his intention to speak of the imperfections of beginners; this he does from Chapters 1 to 7 in the first book of the *Night*. In A2, 11, 7, he tells of his plan to explain something of spiritual gluttony, which he does in Chapter 6 of the first book of the *Night*. In A2, 18, 4, he reveals his design to deal with material which he also handles subsequently in Book One of the *Night*.

Given this decided evidence, it is commonly admitted today that the treatise entitled *The Dark Night* was in St. John of the Cross's mind a part of *The Ascent of Mount Carmel*, that part which discusses the passive purgation. (A1, 1, 2)

The *Ascent*, in short, is an explanation of how, in order to reach perfection, a soul must through "the mortification of the appetites" and "the journey in faith" seek to purify the sensory and spiritual faculties of everything contrary to a life of perfect faith and love. The *Night*, on the other hand, describes how God purifies the soul passively and brings its faith and love to the perfection delineated in the *Ascent*. The far-reaching demands of the *Ascent* are not fully met without the passive purifications explained in the *Night*.

Returning to the reasons for calling the path to divine union a dark night, we recall that the third reason is God's communication to the soul. This communication is an essential topic of *The Dark Night*. We have already noted how God's communication is gauged by one's conformity to His will through love. (A2, 5, 4) Growth in the spiritual life is not effected sharply. Chapter 17 of Book Two of the *Ascent* explains how God leads the soul forward step by step, first communicating His life to it through the senses and through images and gradually preparing it thereby to receive His more spiritual communications without the aid of the senses. The saint often designates this communication of God to the soul by other terms, such as: "inflow," "infusion," "manifestation," "illumination," "illustration," and so on.

In meditation, by which the soul works with the senses and with images, the communication of God is received in "morsels." In contemplation, it is not received through the senses but directly in the spiritual part of the soul, and thus the inflow of God can be more abundant. (F3, 32–34)

In the initial stages of contemplation the soul's "sensory part is left in dryness." But the dryness, the emptiness, the solicitude caused by the purificative contemplation of the passive night of the senses is not as keen and profound as in the night of the spirit. Yet, regardless of the difference in intensity, there is a certain similarity in the contemplative knowledge received, as the Mystical Doctor observes: "Hence the dark night with its aridities and voids is the means to the knowledge of God and self, although the knowledge given in this night is not as plenteous and abundant as that of the other night of spirit, for the knowledge of this night is as it were the foundation of the other." (N1, 12, 6)

It does not fall within the scope of *The Dark Night* to treat of God's communication to the soul as it exists in all the periods of the spiritual life, but only insofar as this communication is received in the passive purifications.

In the passive nights God communicates "a general and obscure knowledge," "contemplation, which is imparted through faith." (A2, 11, 4) This contemplation of the passive purifications is not "delightful" but "painful" to the soul. (A3, 33, 3–5) Accordingly, God's communication in the passive purgations is a night not merely because it is infused through faith, but also because it is painful to the soul. (N2, 5, 2)

It is in expounding the passive night of the spirit that St. John of the Cross explores more fully the manner in which God purifies the soul. In discussing the night of the senses, he explains particularly the defects of beginners, the signs of initial contemplation, and the benefits which result from the purification. But in St. John's own words "the purgation of the senses is only the gate to and beginning of the contemplation which leads to the purgation of the spirit," and it "serves more for the accommodation of the senses to the spirit than for the union of the spirit with God." (N2, 2, 1)

It should be more beneficial, then, to sketch briefly the manner in which God purifies the soul in the passive night of the spirit, for the Mystical Doctor gives us a vivid painting and thorough analysis of this most intense form of God's purgative communication, which can, with the proper applications and restrictions, serve to illustrate the passive purification of the senses as well. In addition, it is worthy of note that the force of the purification depends upon the imperfections of the soul and the degree of union to which it is destined. (N1, 14, 5)

Here then, outlined briefly, are the main aspects involved in the passive purification of the spirit:

1. Through the light of contemplation, God illumines the soul in regard to its own wretchedness and, at the same time, increases this awareness by enlightening it as well in regard to His own purity and transcendence. (N2, 5, 5)

2. The knowledge this contemplation accords generates the feeling of being abandoned both by God and by creatures and deprives the soul of the connatural satisfaction it ordinarily obtains in the actuation of its faculties. (N2, 8, 1; 16, 1; 3, 3)

3. The want of satisfaction in the activity of the faculties inclines the soul in its prayer to forsake this activity; it then "resembles one who is imprisoned in a dark dungeon, bound hands and feet, and able neither to move, nor see, nor feel any favor from heaven or earth." (N2, 7, 3) Through this kind of inactivity the soul is liberated from its imperfect tendencies or habits (which are sustained by the satisfaction found in the acts of the faculties), for these tendencies gradually die away through this lack of actuation. The faculties are thus fully prepared for the supernatural or divine mode of operation. (N2, 16, 2-4)

4. On the other hand, this feeling of being abandoned by God—which is only intensified by the soul's inability to act with the faculties—occasions a veritable torment for the soul, since in its intense love of God, by which it vehemently longs for Him with all its force, it now feels frustrated. (N2, 13, 5)

5. The contemplation, besides illumining the intellect, also communicates love to the will, which intensifies the soul's hunger and thirst for perfection and makes it search solicitously for ways of pleasing God and winning back His favor. Through this love, all the appetites and the faculties, unable to derive satisfaction in any other object, are withdrawn from everything and concentrated intensely upon God:

"This happens very particularly in this dark purgation, as was said, since God so weans and recollects the appetites that they cannot find satisfaction in any of their objects. God proceeds thus so that by withdrawing the appetites from other objects and recollecting them in Himself, He strengthens the soul and gives it the capacity for this strong union of love, which He begins to accord by means of this purgation." (N2, 11, 3)

"The touch of this divine love and fire so dries up the spirit and so enkindles the soul's longings to slake its thirst for this love that a person will go over these longings in his mind a thousand times and pine for God in a thousand ways . . . In all its thoughts and in all its business and in all events, it loves in many ways and desires and also suffers in its desire in many ways, and at all times and in many places." (N2, 11, 5–6; 11, 7; 13, 9)

"That dark love enkindles in the soul a remarkably vigilant care and interior solicitude about what to do or omit in order to please God. A man will ponder whether or not he may have angered God and go over this in his mind a thousand times . . . In this dark contemplation the soul's appetites, strength, and faculties are withdrawn from all other things, and its effort and strength is expended only in paying homage to God." (N2, 16, 14)

Evidently, the soul is not inactive in the passive purifications in such a way that it ceases to love God or to render Him service or to live by faith. Were it to fail to respond through its own efforts to live by faith and love, God would lack the very means by which He purifies it. Through the theological virtues the soul is purified and through them it lives transformed in God; they are the warp and woof of the life of one wholly united to God. (N2, 21)

When a soul makes creatures the object of its activity, it lives the life of the world, a natural life, the life of the "old man." When it centers its operation on God, it lives the life of God, a divine life, the life of the "new man." (F2, 32–34)

That which is perfect in an act is the work of virtue, of centering one's activity on God, together with the motion of grace enabling this achievement. That which is imperfect, inordinate, and mingled with the act of virtue is the operation of the soul turned partly toward the creature: its own satisfaction; vainglory; self-interest; human respect; and so on. This defective portion of an act is subtracted from the influence of God's supernatural motion.

The more a man turns from what is imperfect in his activity—the more he directs this activity to God—the greater becomes his capacity for the supernatural motion of God. When he has withdrawn entirely from all imperfection in his operations, he will be wholly empty of creatures, fully purified, and completely capable of receiving the light, warmth, strength, and plenitude of God's grace.

We can conclude, consequently, that *The Dark Night* deals with the communication of God, not considered in all its extension, but insofar as it is the contemplation which purifies and perfects the soul in the passive nights or purifications of the senses and of the spirit.

If in the *Ascent-Night* St. John of the Cross accents the necessity of the privation, purification, eradication, annihilation of everything contrary to perfect union with God through the full exercise of the theological virtues, it is doubtless because in the passive nights God's method of purifying and perfecting the soul is one of privation. The entire structure underlying the sanjuanist synthesis owes its origin to a keen analysis of the manner in which God purifies the soul. In spite of the stark negative tone of some of the saint's assertions, there is no possibility according to his teaching of complete negation or an utter void of both God and creatures—although in the passive night of the spirit a similar void may be felt. In the measure that the soul has one, it is empty of the other.

The path to union with God, this dark night, is the "narrow way which leads to life"; on it a man "denies himself," "takes up his cross," and "loses his soul"; this path is the "hating of one's own life," "the chalice" of Christ, His "yoke" and "burden"; it is Christ, "the door," by which one enters; it is the imitation of Christ, which means death in Christ, for to imitate Christ is to die; it is the "renouncing of all one's possessions," the "stripping self of the old man." This path culminates in "life," "the saving of one's soul," "the sweetness of Christ," "the kingdom of God," "poverty and purity of spirit," "the new man," "resurrection in Christ," "evangelical perfection," being the "sons of God."

The Purpose and the Destination of the Ascent-Night

It has sometimes been alleged that St. John of the Cross wrote for contemplatives and that consequently his doctrine applies only to those who have entered upon the mystical way. But the saint's clearly stated intention of explaining the path which leads to union with God does not allow such a restriction. In point of fact we have in the prologue explicit remarks concerning the universal character of his doctrine.

"Our goal will be, with God's help, to explain all these points, so that everyone who reads this book will in some way discover the road that he is walking along, and the one he ought to follow if he wants to reach the summit of this mount . . . But if some people still find difficulty in understanding this doctrine, it will be due to my deficient knowledge and awkward style, for the doctrine itself is good and very necessary." (Prologue of the *Ascent*, 7–8)

The earnest reader of the *Ascent-Night* should discover the path he must take to reach perfection. Even if one may encounter difficulties in understanding or practicing the doctrine, it still remains good and necessary for all who desire to attain union with God through love.

The assertion that a teaching is good for all is quite different from the assertion that *all* the doctrine applies at all times to everyone's particular situation and stage. Thus, each reader should uncover in this treatise the instructions that are necessary for him in his particular situation and stage, the road he must follow in order to reach the summit of the mount. Sometimes the rules and instructions are exclusively suited to those who have begun to receive contemplation. At other times they apply to those who still commune with God by way of meditation. (*cf.*, for example: A3, 18–26; 35–44; N1, 1–7)

Not everyone, however, will find to his liking the rugged demands of following Christ:

"But I am inclined to believe that even if it were presented with greater accuracy and polish, only a few would find profit in it, because we are not writing on pleasing and delightful themes addressed to the kind of spiritual people who like to approach God along sweet and satisfying paths. We are presenting a substantial and solid doctrine for all those who desire to reach this nakedness of spirit." (Prologue of the *Ascent*, 8)

To this thought St. John adds that his main intention is to address "some of the persons of our holy Order of the Primitive Observance of Mount Carmel, both friars and nuns." The reason he wished to write for *some* of these Carmelites was not specifically because they were contemplatives, but because in their eagerness to know more about how to reach perfection they begged him to write for them a work of this kind.

Doubtless, knowing these Carmelites personally, St. John of the Cross was aware of their having already acquired a good measure of detachment and thus felt confident that they would have less difficulty with his doctrine. "Because they are already detached to a great extent from the temporal things of this world, they will more easily grasp this doctrine on the nakedness of spirit."

One ought to reflect upon his teaching in the *Ascent* should one wonder why detachment facilitates the understanding of his teaching.

"By the very fact that a spiritual person rejoices in something and gives reign to the appetite in trifles, his rapport with God is darkened and his intellect clouded . . . joy in these trifles and concupiscence for them is alone sufficient to produce the first degree of this harm: dullness of mind and darkness of judgment in understanding truth and judging well of each thing as it is in itself." (A3, 19, 3)

The doctrine of the *Ascent-Night* will be more meaningful to those who sincerely seek to know the way to union with God and who are already to some extent detached from the things of the world. But if at the outset the doctrine seems obscure, the reader "should not be surprised . . . as he reads on he will understand it better since the latter parts will explain the former. Then, if he reads this work a second time, the matter will seem clearer and the doctrine sounder." (Prologue of the *Ascent*, 8)

The Commentary on the Poem

In declaring the theme at the beginning of the *Ascent*, St. John of the Cross informs us of his design to comment upon the verses of his poem *The Dark Night*. We have shown that the poetic figure "dark night" of the first verse of the poem provides the basis for the three notions which form the fundamental structure of the *Ascent-Night*. The work as a whole is a logical presentation and development of these three ideas: the mortification of the appetites; the journey in faith; and God's communication to the soul.

In the first book of the *Ascent* he gives no commentary on the verses of the poem until the last two chapters, where he briefly explains the remaining four lines of the first stanza, assigning them to the active night of the senses.

In Book Two of the *Ascent* the Saint opens with the second stanza of the poem, noting that this stanza alludes to the journey in faith, but then he continues to discuss in logical order the soul's advance in faith without ever returning to comment upon the second stanza of the poem.

In Book One of *The Dark Night* he reverts once more to the first stanza, but here again the opening line serves only as an incentive to treat of the imperfections which weigh upon beginners and of the transition, through initial contemplation, from the state of beginners to the state of proficients. But in Chapter 11 he resumes his commentary on the poem, interpreting the remaining lines of the stanza from the viewpoint of the passive night of the senses.

In beginning his explanation of the passive night of the spirit, the saint does not take up his commentary where he left off, as might have been expected, but commences to explain stanza 1 for the third time. Yet here we mark a stricter adherence to the lines of the poem. The poetry itself supplies the order in which the matter is expounded and by its figurative character greatly influences the literary style of the exposition. This style of the second book of the *Night* bears closer resemblance to *The Spiritual Canticle* and *The Living Flame of Love* than to the other sections of the *Ascent-Night*. Greater caution is necessary in interpreting doctrine presented in this manner, lest the imagery borrowed from the lyric poetry obstruct a clear vision of the essential elements constituting the doctrine.

The passive night of the spirit comments line by line upon the first two stanzas of the poem. In beginning his commentary upon the third stanza, St. John of the Cross draws his study to a close, for he had indeed amply discussed all he had intended to expound, in short: "the dark night through which a soul journeys toward the divine light of perfect union with God." (Prologue of the *Ascent*, 1)

The poem itself refers in all likelihood to that particular period of the spiritual life in which a soul undergoes its final purification and passes from the state of proficients to that of the perfect.

A Brief Outline of the Ascent-Night

I. Introduction
   A. Theme
   B. Prologue
   C. A twofold division of the matter proposed for discussion based on both the first stanza and the first verse (A1, Chs. 1–2)

II. The Mortification of the Appetites—The Active Night of the Senses (Book One of the *Ascent*)
   A. Why the mortification of the appetites is called a night (Ch. 3)
   B. The necessity of this mortification to reach union with God
     1. From the nature of the union (Ch. 4); from Sacred Scripture (Ch. 5); from the privative and positive harm the appetites cause (Chs. 6–10)
     2. The kind of appetites which must be mortified (Ch. 11)
     3. The degree of harm caused by the various kinds of appetites (Ch. 12)
   C. Rules for practicing this mortification (Ch. 13)
   D. Commentary on the remaining four verses of the first stanza (Chs. 14–15)

III. The Journey in Faith—The Active Night of the Spirit (Books Two and Three of the *Ascent*)
   A. A general explanation of the second stanza from the viewpoint of the journey in faith (Chs. 1–2)
   B. Why the journey in faith is called a night (Chs. 3–4)
   C. The necessity of the journey in faith (and of the denial this involves) in order to reach union with God
     1. A general explanation (Chs. 4–6), with a parenthetical discussion of the nature of union with God (Ch. 5)
     2. General proofs from Scripture (Ch. 7)
     3. Particular explanations and proofs
       a. The intellect—faith (Book Two)
         (1) No creature serves the intellect as a proximate means to union (Ch. 8); faith is the proximate means (Ch. 9)

      (2) The natural and supernatural apprehensions of which the intellect must be purified through faith (Ch. 10)

         (a) apprehensions through exterior bodily senses: natural (Ch. 11); supernatural (Ch. 11)

         (b) apprehensions through interior bodily senses
           —natural: meditation (Ch. 12); transition from meditation to contemplation (Chs. 13–15)
           —supernatural: imaginative visions (Chs. 16–22)

         (c) spiritual apprehensions: supernatural and distinct (Ch. 23)
           —visions (Ch. 24)
           —revelations (Chs. 25–27)
           —locutions (Chs. 28–31)
           —spiritual feelings (Ch. 32)

   b. The memory—hope (Book Three, Chs. 1–15)

      (1) The three kinds of apprehensions of which the memory must be purified in order to reach union with God through hope (Ch. 15)

         (a) natural (Chs. 2–6)
         (b) supernatural imaginative (Chs. 7–13)
         (c) spiritual (Ch. 14)

      (2) General rules for governing this faculty (Ch. 15)

   c. The will—charity (Book Three, Chs. 16–45)

      (1) The purification of the will of all inordinate feelings or passions of joy, hope, fear, and sorrow (Ch. 16)

         (a) joy (Ch. 17)
           —the different kinds of goods and the basic norm for directing joy to God amid these goods (Ch. 17)
           —temporal goods (Chs. 18–20); natural goods (Chs. 21–23); sensory goods (Chs. 24–26); moral goods (Chs. 27–29); supernatural goods (Chs. 30–32); spiritual goods: notion and division (Ch. 33), in intellect and memory (Ch. 34), motivating (Chs. 35–42), provocative (Ch. 45)

Note: In Chapter 45 he discontinues his treatise, leaving this section unfinished.

IV. The Communication of God in the Passive Nights

   A. The Passive Night of the Senses (Book One of *The Dark Night*)

     1. A general commentary on the first stanza

     2. A commentary on each verse of stanza 1 under the general theme announced in the first verse, "One dark night,"

        a. Characteristics and imperfections of beginners (Chs. 1–7)

        b. An explanation of the passive night of the senses (Ch. 8)

        c. The signs for recognizing this night (Ch. 9)

        d. The conduct required of souls in this night (Ch. 10)

       e. Commentary on the remaining verses of the first stanza (Chs. 11–14)

       f. The trials accompanying this night (Ch. 14, 1–4)

       g. The duration of this night (Ch. 14, 5–6)

B. The Passive Night of the Spirit (Book Two of *The Dark Night*)

    1. A description of the proficient's state of soul; the time in which God places one in this night (Chs. 1–3)

    2. A general commentary on the first stanza giving a summary explanation of the passive night of the spirit (Ch. 4)

    3. A commentary on each verse of stanza 1 under the general theme announced in the first verse, "One dark night"

       a. Why this inflow of God into the soul (the communication of God) is called a night

         (1) It is darkness to the soul (Ch. 5, 2–3)

         (2) It is painful to the soul (Ch. 5, 2, 4–6; Ch. 6, 1–4; Ch. 7, 2–3)

       b. Duration and intensity of the purification (Ch. 7, 3–6); comparisons (Ch. 7, 7; Ch. 8, 3–5)

       c. Necessity of the passive night of the spirit

         (1) A general demonstration (Ch. 9)

         (2) A comparison: fire and the log of wood (Ch. 10)

       d. "Fired with love's urgent longings": Love in the passive night of the spirit (Chs. 11–13)

       e. "Ah, the sheer grace!—I went out unseen, My house being now all stilled" (Ch. 14)

       f. Commentary on the second stanza

         (1) "In darkness, and secure" (Ch. 16)

         (2) "By the secret ladder, disguised"

           (*a*) "secret" (Ch. 17, 2–8)

           (*b*) "ladder" (Chs. 18–20)

           (*c*) "disguised" (Ch. 21)

         (3) "Ah, the sheer grace" (Ch. 22)

         (4) "In darkness and concealment" (Ch. 23)

         (5) "My house being now all stilled" (Ch. 24)

       g. The third stanza: a summary explanation (Ch. 25)

Here the treatise ends, remaining incomplete.

The Ascent of Mount Carmel

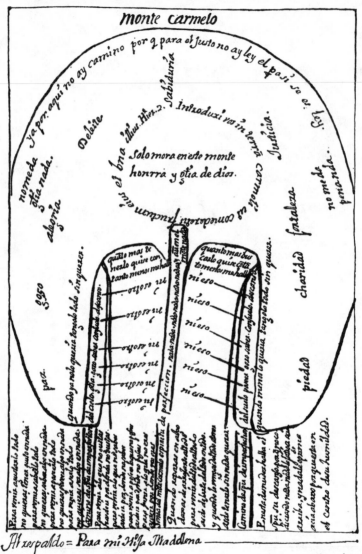

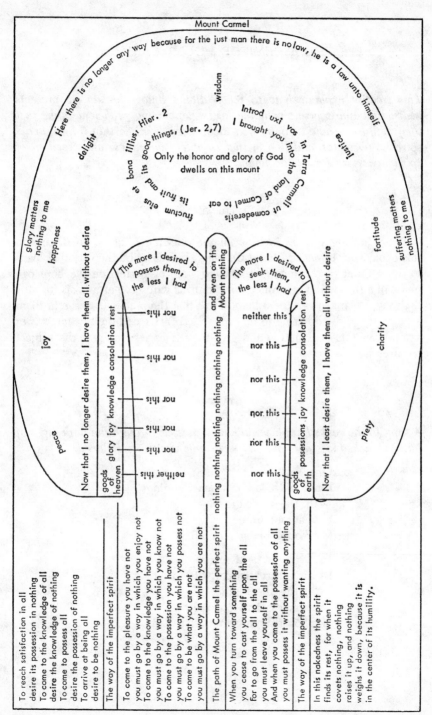

THE ASCENT OF MOUNT CARMEL

This treatise explains how to reach divine union quickly. It presents instruction and doctrine valuable for beginners and proficients alike that they may learn how to unburden themselves of all earthly things, avoid spiritual obstacles, and live in that complete nakedness and freedom of spirit necessary for divine union.

THEME

The following stanzas include all the doctrine I intend to discuss in this book, *The Ascent of Mount Carmel*. They describe the way that leads to the summit of the mount—that high state of perfection we here call union of a soul with God. Since these stanzas will serve as a basis for all I shall say, I want to cite them here in full that the reader may see in them a summary of doctrine to be expounded. Yet I will quote each stanza again before its explanation and give the verses separately if the subject requires it.

STANZAS

A song of the soul's happiness in having passed through the dark night of faith, in nakedness and purgation, to union with its Beloved.

1. One dark night,
   Fired with love's urgent longings
   —Ah, the sheer grace!—
   I went out unseen,
   My house being now all stilled;

2. In darkness, and secure,
   By the secret ladder, disguised,
   —Ah, the sheer grace!—
   In darkness and concealment,
   My house being now all stilled;

3. On that glad night,
In secret, for no one saw me,
Nor did I look at anything,
With no other light or guide
Than the one that burned in my heart;

4. This guided me
More surely than the light of noon
To where He waited for me
—Him I knew so well—
In a place where no one else appeared.

5. O guiding night!
O night more lovely than the dawn!
O night that has united
The Lover with His beloved,
Transforming the beloved in her Lover.

6. Upon my flowering breast
Which I kept wholly for Him alone,
There He lay sleeping,
And I caressing Him
There in a breeze from the fanning cedars.

7. When the breeze blew from the turret
Parting His hair,
He wounded my neck
With His gentle hand,
Suspending all my senses.

8. I abandoned and forgot myself,
Laying my face on my Beloved;
All things ceased; I went out from myself,
Leaving my cares
Forgotten among the lilies.

PROLOGUE

1. A deeper enlightenment and wider experience than mine is necessary to explain the dark night through which a soul journeys toward that divine light of perfect union with God which is achieved, insofar as possible in this life, through love. The darknesses and trials, spiritual and temporal, that fortunate souls ordinarily encounter on their way to the high state of perfection are so numerous and profound that human science cannot understand them adequately; nor does experience of

them equip one to explain them. He who suffers them will know what this experience is like, but he will find himself unable to describe it.

2. In discussing this dark night, therefore, I shall not rely on experience or knowledge, for these can fail and deceive us. Although I shall not neglect whatever possible use I can make of them, my help in all that, with God's favor, I shall say, will be Sacred Scripture, at least in the most important matters, or those which are difficult to understand. Taking Scripture as our guide we do not err, since the Holy Ghost speaks to us through it. If I should misunderstand or be mistaken on some point, whether I deduce it from Scripture or not, my intention will not be to deviate from the true meaning of Sacred Scripture or from the doctrine of our Holy Mother the Catholic Church. If this should happen, I submit entirely to the Church, or even to anyone who judges more competently about the matter than I.

3. I am not undertaking this arduous task because of any particular confidence in my own abilities. Rather, I am confident that the Lord will help me explain this matter, because it is extremely necessary to so many souls. Even though these souls have begun to walk along the road of virtue, and our Lord desires to place them in the dark night so they may move on to the divine union, they do not advance. Sometimes, the reason is, they do not want to enter the dark night or allow themselves to be placed in it, and sometimes they misunderstand themselves and are without suitable and alert directors who will show them the way to the summit. God gives many souls the talent and grace for advancing, and should they desire to make the effort they would arrive at this high state. And so it is sad to see them continue in their lowly method of communion with God because they do not want or know how to advance, or because they receive no direction on breaking away from the methods of beginners. Even if our Lord finally comes to their aid to the extent of making them advance without these helps, they reach the summit much later, expend more effort, and gain less merit, because they do not willingly adapt themselves to God's work of placing them on the pure and reliable road leading to union. Although God does lead them—since He can do so without their cooperation—they do not accept His guidance. In resisting God who is conducting them, they make little progress, and their merit is lessened, because they do not apply their wills, and as a result they must endure greater suffering. Some souls, instead of abandoning themselves to God and cooperating with Him, hamper Him by their indiscreet activity or resistance. They resemble children who kick and cry, and struggle to walk by themselves when their mothers want to carry them; in walking by themselves they make no headway, or if they do, it is at a child's pace.

4. With God's help, then, we shall propose doctrine and counsel for beginners and proficients that they may understand or at least know how to practice abandonment to God's guidance when He wants them to advance.

For some spiritual directors are likely to be a hindrance and harm rather than a help to these souls that journey on this road. Such directors have neither enlightenment nor experience of these ways. They are like the builders of the tower of Babel. [Gn. 11:1–9] When these builders were supposed to provide the proper materials for the project, they brought entirely different supplies, because they failed to understand the language. And thus nothing was accomplished. Hence, it is arduous and difficult for a soul in these periods of the spiritual life when it cannot understand itself nor find anyone else who understands it.

It will happen that while an individual is being conducted by God along a sublime path of dark contemplation and aridity, in which he feels lost, he will encounter in the midst of the fullness of his darknesses, trials, conflicts, and temptations someone who, in the style of Job's comforters [Jb. 4:8–11], will proclaim that all of this is due to melancholia, or depression, or temperament, or to some hidden wickedness, and that as a result God has forsaken him. Therefore the usual verdict is that, since such trials afflict this person, he must have lived an evil life.

5. Others will tell him that he is falling back, since he finds no satisfaction or consolation as he previously did in the things of God. Such talk only doubles the trial of the poor soul, because its greatest suffering is caused by the knowledge of its own miseries; that it is full of evil and sin is as clear as day, and even clearer, for, as we shall say presently, God is the author of this enlightenment in the night of contemplation. And when this soul finds someone who agrees with what it feels (that these trials are 'all its own fault), its suffering and distress grow without bounds. And this suffering usually becomes worse than death. Such a confessor is not satisfied with this but, in judging these trials to be the result of sin, he urges souls who endure them to go over their past and make many general confessions—which is another crucifixion. The director does not understand that now perhaps is not the time for such activity. Indeed, it is a period for leaving these persons alone in the purgation God is working in them, a time to give comfort and encouragement that they may desire to endure this suffering as long as God wills, for until then, no remedy—whatever the soul does, or the confessor says—is adequate.

6. We shall discuss all this with the divine help: how the individual should behave; what method the confessor should use in dealing with him; the signs for the recognition of this purification of the soul (which we call the *dark night*), whether it is the purification of the sense or of

the spirit; how we can determine if this affliction is caused by melancholia or any other deficiency of sense or spirit.

Some souls—or their confessors—may think that God is leading them along this road of the dark night of spiritual purgation, but perhaps this is not the case. What they suffer will owe its origin to one of these deficiencies. Likewise, many individuals think they are not praying, when, indeed their prayer is intense. Others place high value on their prayer, while it is little more than nonexistent.

7. Some people—and it is sad to see them—work and tire themselves greatly, and yet go backwards; they look for perfection in exercises that are of no profit to them, but rather a hindrance. Others continue to make fine progress in peace and tranquillity.

Some individuals encounter an encumbrance in the very consolations and favors God bestows on them for the sake of their advancement, and they advance not at all.

We will also discuss many other experiences of those who walk along this road: joys, afflictions, hopes, and sorrows—some of these originating from the spirit of perfection, others from the spirit of imperfection.

Our goal will be, with God's help, to explain all these points, so that everyone who reads this book will in some way discover the road that he is walking along, and the one he ought to follow if he wants to reach the summit of this mount.

8. The reader should not be surprised if this doctrine on the dark night (through which a soul advances toward God) appears somewhat obscure. This, I believe, will be the case as he begins to read, but as he reads on he will understand it better, since the latter parts will explain the former. Then, if he reads this work a second time, the matter will seem clearer and the doctrine sounder.

But if some people still find difficulty in understanding this doctrine, it will be due to my deficient knowledge and awkward style, for the doctrine itself is good and very necessary. But I am inclined to believe that even if it were presented with greater accuracy and polish, only a few would find profit in it, because we are not writing on pleasing and delightful themes addressed to the kind of spiritual people who like to approach God along sweet and satisfying paths. We are presenting a substantial and solid doctrine for all those who desire to reach this nakedness of spirit.

9. My main intention is not to address everyone, but only some of the persons of our holy Order of the Primitive Observance of Mount Carmel, both friars and nuns, whom God favors by putting them on the path leading up this mount, since they are the ones who asked me to write this

work. Because they are already detached to a great extent from the temporal things of this world, they will more easily grasp this doctrine on the nakedness of spirit.

BOOK ONE

CHAPTER 1

Some remarks about the two different nights through which spiritual persons pass in both the lower and higher part of their nature. A commentary on the first stanza.

First Stanza

> One dark night,
> Fired with love's urgent longings
> —Ah, the sheer grace!—
> I went out unseen,
> My house being now all stilled;

1. The soul sings in this first stanza of its good luck and the grace it had in departing from its inordinate appetites and imperfections.

To understand this departure one should know that a soul must ordinarily pass through two principal kinds of night (which spiritual persons call purgations or purifications of the soul) in order to reach the state of perfection. Here we shall term these purgations nights, because in both of them the soul journeys in darkness as though by night.

2. The first night, or purgation, which this stanza refers to, and which will be under discussion in the first part of this book, concerns the sensory part of man's nature. The second stanza refers to the night of the spiritual part of man's soul, with which we shall deal, insofar as the purgation is active, in the second and third parts of our book. In Book Four we shall discuss the passive purgation.

3. This first night is the lot of beginners, at the time God commences to introduce them into the state of contemplation; it is a night in which the spirit of man also participates, as we shall explain in due time. The second night or purification takes place in those who are already proficients, at the time God desires to lead them into the state of divine union. This purgation, of course, is more obscure, dark, and dreadful, as we shall subsequently point out.

Explanation of the Stanza

4. In this stanza the soul desires to declare in summary fashion that it departed on a dark night, attracted by God and enkindled with love for Him alone. This dark night is a privation and purgation of all sensible appetites for the external things of the world, the delights of the flesh, and the gratifications of the will. All this deprivation is wrought in the purgation of sense. That is why the poem proclaims that the soul departed when its house was stilled, for the appetites of the sensory part were stilled and asleep in the soul, and the soul was stilled in them. One is not freed from the sufferings and anguish of the appetites until they are tempered and put to sleep. So it was a sheer grace, the soul declares, to have gone out unseen, without encumbrance from the appetites of the flesh, or from anything else. It was also fortunate the departure was at night; that is, that God took from the soul all these things through a privation that was a night to it.

5. It was a sheer grace to be placed by God in this night that occasioned so much good. The soul would not have succeeded in entering it, because nobody is able alone to empty himself of all his appetites in order to reach God.

6. Summarily, then, we have an explanation of the first stanza. Now we shall expound upon it verse by verse and explain whatever pertains to our subject. We shall follow the method mentioned in the prologue: first cite each stanza, and then the individual verses.

CHAPTER 2

The nature of the dark night through which a soul journeys to divine union.

One dark night

1. We can offer three reasons for calling this journey toward union with God a night.

The first has to do with the point of departure, because the individual must deprive himself of his appetite for worldly possessions. This denial and privation is like a night for all his senses.

The second reason refers to the means or the road along which a person travels to this union. Now this road is faith, and for the intellect faith is also like a dark night.

The third reason pertains to the point of arrival, namely, God. And God is also a dark night to man in this life. These three nights pass through a soul, or better, the soul passes through them in order to reach divine union with God.

2. They are symbolized in the Book of Tobias [Tb. 6:18–22], where we read that the angel ordered the young Tobias to wait three nights before any union with his bride.

On the first night he was to burn the fish heart in the fire. That heart symbolized the human heart that is attached to worldly things. To undertake the journey to God the heart must be burned and purified of all creatures with the fire of divine love. Such a purgation puts the devil to flight, for he has power over a man attached to temporal and bodily things.

3. Tobias, on the second night, as the angel told him, was to be admitted into the society of the holy patriarchs, the fathers of the faith. After passing through the first night (the privation of all sensible objects), a man soon enters the second night by living in faith alone, not a faith that is exclusive of charity, but a faith that excludes other intellectual knowledge, as we shall explain later. For faith does not fall into the province of the senses.

4. The angel told him that on the third night he would obtain that blessing, which is God. God, by means of faith, which is the second night, communicates Himself so secretly and intimately that He becomes another night for the soul. While this communication of God is in progress, the night, as we shall soon point out, becomes far darker than those other two nights. When this third night (God's communication to the spirit, which usually occurs in extreme darkness of soul) has passed, a union with the Spouse, who is the Wisdom of God, then follows. The angel also told Tobias that, after the third night had come to an end, he would be joined to his bride in the fear of the Lord. Now when the fear of God is perfect, love is also perfect, and love is perfect when the transformation of the soul in God is achieved.

5. In actuality these three nights comprise only one night, a night divided into three parts, just as the natural night. The first part, the night of the senses, resembles early evening, that time of twilight when things begin to fade from sight. The second part, faith, is completely dark, like midnight. The third part, representing God, is like the very early dawn just before the break of day.

To provide further enlightenment about all this, we shall discuss each of these causes of night separately.

CHAPTER 3

The first cause of this night—the privation of the appetite in all things. Reason for the use of the expression "night."

1. We are using the expression "night" to signify a deprival of the gratification of man's appetite in all things. Just as night is nothing but the privation of light and, consequently, of all objects visible by means of the light—darkness and emptiness, then, for the faculty of sight—the mortification of the appetites can be called a night for the soul. To deprive oneself of the gratification of the appetites in all things is like living in darkness and in a void. The eye feeds upon its objects by means of light in such a way that when the light is extinguished the eye no longer sees them. Similarly does a man by means of his appetite feed and pasture on worldly things that gratify his faculties. When the appetites are extinguished—or mortified—he no longer feeds upon the pleasure of these things, but lives in a void and in darkness with respect to his appetites.

2. Let us draw an example from each of the faculties.

An individual, by depriving himself of his appetites for the delights of hearing, lives in darkness and emptiness in this sense faculty.

And depriving himself of the pleasure of seeing things, he lives in darkness and poverty in the faculty of sight.

And denying himself the fragrances pleasing to the sense of smell, he abides in emptiness and darkness in this sense faculty.

Then too by denying the palate the pleasures of delicious foods, he is also in the void and in darkness in the sense of taste.

Finally, by mortifying himself of all the delights and satisfactions of the sense of touch, he likewise dwells in darkness and in a void in this faculty.

The conclusion is that any individual who may have denied and rejected the gratification that all things afford him, by mortifying his appetite for them, lives as though in the night—in darkness, which is nothing else than a void within him of all things.

3. The cause of this darkness is attributable to the fact that—as the scholastic philosophers say—the soul is like a *tabula rasa* (a clean slate) when God infuses it into the body, so that it would be ignorant without the knowledge it receives through its senses, because no knowledge is communicated to it from any other source. Accordingly, the presence of the soul in the body resembles the presence of a prisoner in a dark dungeon, who knows no more than what he manages to behold through

the windows of his prison and has nowhere else to turn if he sees nothing through them. For the soul, naturally speaking, possesses no means other than the senses (the windows of its prison) of perceiving what is communicated to it.

4. We can easily affirm that if a man denies whatever is perceptible through the senses, he lives in darkness and in a void, since light can enter by no other natural means than these five senses. Now it is true that the sensory perceptions of hearing, sight, smell, taste, and touch are unavoidable; yet they will no more hinder a man—if he denies them —than if they were not experienced. It is true also that anyone desiring to keep his eyes closed will live in darkness just like a blind man.

David says on this subject: *Pauper sum ego, et in laboribus a juventute mea* (I am poor and in labors from my youth). [Ps. 87:16] Even though he was manifestly rich, he says he was poor because his will was not fixed on riches; and he thereby lived as though really poor. On the other hand, had he been actually poor, without his will being so, there would have been no true poverty, because the appetite of his soul would have been rich and full.

Hence, we call this nakedness a night for the soul. For we are not discussing the mere lack of things; this lack will not divest the soul, if it craves for all these objects. We are dealing with the denudation of the soul's appetites and gratifications; this is what leaves it free and empty of all things, even though it possesses them. Since the things of the world cannot enter the soul, they are not in themselves an encumbrance or harm to it; rather, it is the will and appetite dwelling within it that causes the damage.

5. This first kind of night refers to the sensory part of the soul, and it is one of the two nights mentioned above through which a person passes on his journey toward union with God.

6. It is time to explain how fitting it is that a person leave his house, and journey through this dark night toward union with God.

CHAPTER 4

The necessity of truly traversing this dark night of sense (mortification of the appetites) in journeying toward union with God.

1. The necessity of passing through this dark night (the mortification of the appetites and the denial of pleasure in all things) for the attainment of the divine union with God arises from the fact that all of man's attachments to creatures are pure darkness in God's sight. Clothed in these affections, a person will be incapable of the enlightenment and

dominating fullness of God's pure and simple light, unless he rejects them. There can be no concordance between light and darkness; as St. John says: *Tenebrae eam non comprehenderunt* (The darkness could not receive the light). [Jn. 1:5]

2. The reason, as we learn in philosophy, is that two contraries cannot coexist in the same subject. Darkness, an attachment to creatures, and light, which is God, are contraries and bear no likeness toward each other, as St. Paul teaches in his letter to the Corinthians: *Quae conventio luci ad tenebras?* (What conformity is there between light and darkness?). [2 Cor. 6:14] Consequently, the light of divine union cannot be established in the soul until these affections are eradicated.

3. For a better proof of this, it ought to be kept in mind that an attachment to a creature makes a person equal to that creature; the firmer the attachment, the closer is the likeness to the creature, and the greater the equality. For love effects a likeness between the lover and the object loved. As a result David said of those who set their hearts upon their idols: *Similes illis fiant qui faciunt ea, et omnes qui confidunt in eis* (Let all who set their hearts on them become like them). [Ps. 113:8] He who loves a creature, then, is as low as that creature, and in some way even lower, because love not only equates, but even subjects the lover to the loved object.

By the mere fact, then, that a man loves something, his soul becomes incapable of pure union and transformation in God; for the baseness of a creature is far less capable of the sublimity of the Creator than is darkness of light.

All the creatures of heaven and earth are nothing when compared to God, as Jeremias points out: *Aspexi terram, et ecce vacua erat et nihil; et caelos, et non erat lux in eis* (I looked at the earth, and it was empty and nothing; and at the heavens, and I saw they had no light). [Jer. 4:23] By saying that he saw an empty earth, he meant that all its creatures were nothing and that the earth too was nothing. In stating that he looked up to the heavens and beheld no light, meant that all the heavenly luminaries were pure darkness in comparison with God. All creatures in contrast to God are nothing, and a man's attachments to them are less than nothing, since these attachments are an impediment to and deprive the soul of transformation in God—just as darkness is nothing, and less than nothing, since it is a privation of light. A man who is in darkness does not comprehend the light, so neither will a person attached to creatures be able to comprehend God. Until a man is purged of his attachments he will not be equipped to possess God, neither here below through the pure transformation of love, nor in heaven through the beatific vision.

For the sake of greater clarity we shall be more specific.

4. We just asserted that all the being of creatures compared with the infinite being of God is nothing, and that, therefore, a man attached to creatures is nothing in the sight of God, and even less than nothing, because love causes equality and likeness and even brings the lover lower than the object of his love. In no way, then, is such a man capable of union with the infinite being of God. There is no likeness between what is not and what is.

To be particular, here are some examples:

All the beauty of creatures compared with the infinite Beauty of God is supreme ugliness. As Solomon says in Proverbs: *Fallax gratia, et vana est pulchritudo* (Comeliness is deceiving and beauty vain). [Prv. 31:30] So a person attached to the beauty of any creature is extremely ugly in God's sight. A soul so unsightly is incapable of transformation into the beauty which is God, because ugliness does not attain to beauty.

All the grace and elegance of creatures compared with God's grace is utter coarseness and crudity. That is why a person captivated by this grace and elegance of creatures becomes quite coarse and crude in God's sight. Accordingly, he is incapable of the infinite grace and beauty of God because of the extreme difference between the coarse and the infinitely elegant.

Now all the goodness of creatures in the world compared with the infinite goodness of God can be called evil, since nothing is good, save God only. [Lk. 18:19] A man, then, who sets his heart on the good things of the world becomes extremely evil in the sight of God. Since evil does not comprehend goodness, this person will be incapable of union with God, Who is supreme goodness.

5. All of the world's wisdom and human ability contrasted with the infinite wisdom of God is pure and utter ignorance, as St. Paul writes to the Corinthians: *Sapientia hujus mundi stultitia est apud Deum* (The wisdom of this world is foolishness in God's sight). [1 Cor. 3:19] Anyone, therefore, who values his knowledge and ability as a means of reaching union with the wisdom of God is highly ignorant in God's sight and will be left behind, far away from this wisdom. Ignorance does not grasp what wisdom is; and in God's sight those who think they have some wisdom are very ignorant. For the Apostle says of them in writing to the Romans: *Dicentes enim se esse sapientes, stulti facti sunt* (Taking themselves for wise men, they became fools). [Rom. 1:22]

Only those who set aside their own knowledge and walk in God's service like unlearned children receive wisdom from God. This is the wisdom about which St. Paul taught the Corinthians: *Si quis videtur inter vos sapiens esse in hoc saeculo, stultus fiat ut sit sapiens. Sapientia enim hujus mundi stultitia est apud Deum* (If anyone among you thinks he is wise, let him become ignorant so as to be wise. For the wisdom of this world is foolishness with God). [1 Cor. 3:18–19] Accordingly, a man must advance to union with God's wisdom by unknowing rather than by knowing.

6. All the sovereignty and freedom of the world compared with the freedom and sovereignty of the Spirit of God is utter slavery, anguish, and captivity.

A person, then, because he is attached to prelacies, or other such dignities, and to freedom of his appetites, and because he finds unacceptable God's holy teaching, that whoever wants to be the greater will be the least, and that whoever wants to be the least will become the greater [Lk. 22: 26], is considered and treated by God as a base slave and prisoner, not as a son. For such a one, the royal freedom of spirit attained in divine union is impossible, because freedom has nothing to do with slavery. And freedom cannot abide in a heart dominated by the appetites—in a slave's heart; it dwells in a liberated heart, which is a son's heart. This is why Sara told her husband Abraham to cast out the bondwoman and her son, declaring that the bondwoman's son should not be an heir together with the free son. [Gn. 21:10]

7. All the delights and satisfactions of the will in the things of the world in contrast to all the delight that is God is intense suffering, torment, and bitterness. He who links his heart to these delights, then, deserves in God's eyes intense suffering, torment, and bitterness. He will not be capable of attaining the delights of the embrace of union with God, since he merits suffering and bitterness.

All the wealth and glory of creation compared with the wealth that is God is utter poverty and misery in the Lord's sight. The person who loves and possesses these things is completely poor and miserable before God, and will be unable to attain the richness and glory of the state of transformation in God; the miserable and poor is extremely distant from the supremely rich and glorious.

8. Divine Wisdom, with pity for these souls that become ugly, abject, miserable, and poor on account of their love for worldly things which in their opinion are rich and beautiful, exclaims in Proverbs: *O viri, ad vos clamito, et vox mea ad filios hominum. Intelligite, parvuli, astutiam, et insipientes, animadvertite. Audite quia de rebus magnis locutura sum.* And further on: *Mecum sunt divitiae et gloria opes superbae et justitia. Melior est fructus meus auro et lapide pretioso, et genimina mea argento electo. In viis justitiae ambulo, in medio semitarum judicii, ut ditem diligentes me, et thesauros eorum repleam.* The meaning of this passage is: O men, I cry to you, my voice is directed to the sons of men. Be attentive, little ones, to cunning and sagacity; and you ignorant, be careful. Listen, because I want to speak of great things.

Riches and glory are mine, high riches and justice. The fruit you will find in me is better than gold and precious stones; and my generations (what will be engendered of Me in your souls) are better than choice silver. I walk along the ways of justice, in the midst of the paths of judgment, to enrich those who love me and fill their treasures completely. [Prv. 8:4–6; 18–21]

God speaks, here, to all those who are attached to the things of the world. He calls them little ones because they become as little as the things they love. He tells them, accordingly, to be cunning and careful, that He is dealing with great things, not small things, as they are; and that the riches and glory they love are with Him and in Him, not where they think; and that lofty riches and justice are present in Him. Although in their opinion the things of this world are riches, He tells them to bear in mind that His riches are more precious, that the fruit found in them will be better than gold and precious stones, and that what He begets in souls has greater value than cherished silver, which signifies every kind of affection possible in this life.

CHAPTER 5

Continuation of the same matter. Proofs from passages and figures of Sacred Scripture for the necessity of journeying to God through this dark night, the mortification of the appetites.

1. We have some idea, from what was said, of the distance which lies between what creatures are in themselves, and what God is in Himself, and, since love produces equality and likeness, of how souls attached to any of these creatures are just as distant from God. With a clear realization of this distance, St. Augustine addressed God in the *Soliloquies: Miserable man that I am, when will my pusillanimity and imperfection be able to conform with your righteousness? You indeed are good, and I, evil; You merciful, and I, wicked; You are holy, and I, miserable; You are just, and I am unjust; You are light, and I, blindness; You are life, and I am death; You are medicine, I am sickness; You are supreme truth, and I, utter vanity* [Pseudo-Augustine, *Soliloquiorum animae ad Deum liber unus*, c. 2: PL 40, 866]. These are the words of the Saint.

2. A person is indeed ignorant if he thinks it is possible to reach this high state of union with God without first emptying his appetite of all the natural and supernatural things which can be a hindrance to him. For there is an extreme distance between such appetites and that which is given in this state, which is nothing less than transformation in God. Our Lord, instructing us about this way, stated according to St. Luke: *Qui non renuntiat omnibus quae possidet, non potest meus esse discipulus*

(He who does not renounce all that he possesses with his will cannot be My disciple). [Lk. 14:33] This statement is clear, for the doctrine the Son of Man came to teach is contempt of all things, that we may receive the gift of God's Spirit. As long as an individual fails to rid himself of these possessions, he is incapable of receiving God's Spirit in pure transformation.

3. This is symbolized in Exodus where we read that God did not give the children of Israel the heavenly manna until they exhausted the flour brought from Egypt. [Ex. 16:3-4, 15] The meaning here is that first a total renunciation is needed, for this bread of angels is disagreeable to the palate of anyone desirous of tasting the food of men. Persons feeding upon other strange tastes not only become incapable of the divine Spirit, but even greatly anger His divine Majesty, because in their aspirations for spiritual food they are not satisfied with God alone, but intermingle with these aspirations a desire and affection for other things. This is likewise apparent in Sacred Scripture where it states that the people, discontented with that simple food, requested and craved for meat, and seriously angered our Lord because of their desire to commingle a food so base and coarse with one so high and simple, which, even though simple, contained the savor and substance of all foods. [Nm. 11:4, 6, 10] Consequently, while morsels of manna were yet in their mouths, the wrath of God descended upon them (as David also says: *Ira Dei descendit super eos* [Ps. 77:31]), spouting fire from heaven and reducing thousands of them to ashes. [Nm. 11:1] For God thought it shameful for them to crave other food while He was giving them heavenly food.

4. Oh, if people knew how much spiritual good and abundance they lose by not attempting to raise their appetites above childish things, and if they knew to what extent, by not desiring the taste of these trifles, they would discover in this simple spiritual food the savor of them all! The Israelites did not perceive the taste, contained in the manna, of every other food, because their appetite was not restricted to this manna. They were unsuccessful in deriving from the manna all the taste and strength they were looking for because of their craving for other foods. Similarly, he who loves something together with God undoubtedly makes little of God, for he weighs in the balance with God an object far distant from God.

5. It is the common knowledge of experience that when the will is attached to an object, it esteems that object higher than any other, even though another, not as pleasing, may deserve higher admiration. And if a man desires pleasure from both objects, he is necessarily offensive to the more deserving, because through his desire for both he equates

the two. Since nothing equals God, a person who loves and is attached to something other than God, or together with Him, offends God exceedingly. If this be true, what would happen if he loved something more than God?

6. This was also indicated when God ordered Moses to climb to the top of the mountain. He did this that Moses might be able to speak to Him. He commanded Moses not only to ascend alone, and leave the children of Israel below, but to rule against the pasturing of beasts on the mountainside. [Ex. 34:3] The meaning is that a person ascending this mount of perfection to converse with God must not only renounce all things, by leaving them at the bottom, but also restrict his appetites (the beasts) from pasturing on the mountainside, on things which are not purely God. For in God, or in the state of perfection, all appetites cease.

The road and ascent to God, then, necessarily demands a habitual effort to renounce and mortify the appetites; the sooner this mortification is achieved, the sooner the soul reaches the top. But until the appetites are eliminated, a person will not arrive, no matter how much virtue he practices. For he will fail to acquire perfect virtue, which lies in keeping the soul empty, naked, and purified of every appetite.

We also have a striking figure of this in Genesis. When the patriarch Jacob desired to ascend Mount Bethel to build an altar for the offering of sacrifice to God, he first ordered his people to do three things: to destroy all strange gods; to purify themselves; and to change their garments. [Gn. 35:2]

7. Anyone desiring to climb to the summit of the mount in order to become an altar for the offering of a sacrifice of pure love and praise and reverence to God, must first accomplish these three tasks perfectly.

First, he must cast out the strange gods, all alien affections and attachments.

Second, through a habitual denial and repentance of these appetites —by the dark night of the senses—he must purify himself of their residue.

The third requisite for reaching the top of this high mount is the change of garments. God, by means of the first two conditions, will substitute new vestments for the old. The soul will be clothed in God, in a new understanding of God (through the removal of the understanding of the old man), and in a new love of God in God—once the will is stripped of all the cravings and satisfactions of the old man. And God vests the soul with new knowledge when the other old ideas and images are cast aside. He causes all that is of the old man, the abilities of the natural being, to cease, and attires all the faculties with new supernatural abilities. As a result a man's activities, once human, now become divine. This is achieved in the state of union where the soul in which God alone dwells has no other function than that of an altar, on which God is adored in praise and love.

God commanded that the altar of the Ark of the Covenant be empty and hollow [Ex. 27:8] to remind the soul how void of all things God wishes it, if it is to serve as His worthy dwelling. It was forbidden that the altar have any strange fire, or that its own go out; so much so that when Nadab and Abiu, the sons of the high priest, offered strange fire on our Lord's altar, God became angry and slew them there in front of the altar. [Lv. 10:1–2] The lesson we derive here is that a man's love for God must never fail, nor be mixed with alien loves, if he wants to be a worthy altar of sacrifice.

8. God allows nothing else to dwell together with Him. We read, consequently, in the First Book of Kings that when the Philistines put the Ark of the Covenant in a temple with their idol, the idol was hurled to the ground at the dawn of each day and broken in pieces. [1 Kgs. 5:2–4] The only appetite God permits and wants in His dwelling place is the desire for the perfect fulfillment of His law and the carrying of His cross. Scripture does not teach that God ordered anything else to be placed in the Ark where the manna was; He wanted only the Law and the rod of Moses (signifying the cross) to be placed there. [Dt. 31: 26; Nm. 17:10] A person who has no other goal than the perfect observance of God's law and the carrying of the cross of Christ will be a true ark, and he will bear within himself the real manna (which signifies God) when he possesses perfectly, without anything else, this law and this rod.

CHAPTER 6

The harm, privative as well as positive, that appetites engender in the soul.

1. For the sake of a clearer and fuller understanding of our assertions, it will be beneficial to explain here how these appetites cause two main areas of harm within the person in whom they dwell: they deprive him of God's Spirit; and they weary, torment, darken, defile, and weaken him. Jeremiah mentions this in Chapter 2: *Duo mala fecit populus meus: dereliquerunt fontem aquae vivae, et foderunt sibi cisternas dissipatas, quae continere non valent aquas* (They have forsaken Me, the fountain of living water, and dug for themselves leaking cisterns that hold no water). [Jer. 2:13]

Any inordinate act of the appetite causes both this privative and positive damage.

To begin with, it is clear in speaking of the privative harm, that a person by mere attachment to a created thing is less capable of God, according to the degree of the entity of that appetite. For two contraries cannot coexist in the same subject, as the philosophers say, and as we also mentioned in Chapter 4. Since love of God and attachment to creatures are contraries, they cannot coexist in the same will. What has creature to do with Creator, sensory with spiritual, visible with invisible, temporal with eternal, heavenly food that is pure and spiritual with food that is entirely sensory, the nakedness of Christ with attachment to something?

2. In natural generation a new form cannot be introduced into a subject without expulsion of the form already there, which is an impediment to the new form because of the existing contrariety. Similarly, insofar as a person is subject to a sensory form, an entirely spiritual one cannot enter him. This is why our Lord said in St. Matthew's Gospel: *Non est bonum sumere panem filiorum et mittere canibus* (It is unbecoming to take the children's bread and give it to the dogs). [Mt. 15:26] Also in another part He says through this same Evangelist: *Nolite sanctum dare canibus* (Do not give what is holy to the dogs). [Mt. 7:6] Our Lord compares to the children of God all those who dispose themselves for the pure reception of God's Spirit through the denial of their appetites for creatures; and He compares to the dogs all those who desire to feed their appetites on creatures. It is the privilege of children to eat at table with their father and from his dish, thereby symbolizing their share in His Spirit, but the dogs must eat the crumbs that fall from the table. [Mt. 15:26-27]

3. Our lesson here is that all creatures are like crumbs which have fallen from God's table; and that they who go about feeding upon creatures are rightly designated as dogs, and are deprived of the children's bread, because they refuse to rise from the crumbs of creatures to the uncreated Spirit of their Father. This is precisely why they wander about hungry as dogs. For the crumbs serve more to whet their appetite than to satisfy their hunger. David says of them: *Famem patientur ut canes, et circuibunt civitatem. Si vero non fuerint saturati, et murmurabunt* (They will suffer hunger like dogs, and wander around the city. And if they are not filled, they will murmur). [Ps. 58:15-16] Here is a peculiarity of a man with appetites: he is always dissatisfied and bitter, like someone who is hungry.

What, then, in common has the hunger caused by creatures with the fullness fostered by the Spirit of God? This uncreated fullness cannot find entry to a soul until this other hunger caused by the desires is expelled. Since hunger and fullness are contraries they cannot coexist in the same person.

4. It will be evident from our explanation that God accomplishes more in cleansing and purging a person of these contraries than He does in creating him from nothing. These impediments of contrary attachments and appetites are more opposed and resistant to God than nothingness, for nothingness raises no opposition.

Since we have already said a good deal about this first kind of harm (resistance to God's Spirit) caused by the appetites, our comments here should be sufficient.

5. Let us now deal with the second effect, the numerous kinds of impairment wrought in the soul. For the appetites weary, torment, darken, defile, and weaken it. We shall discuss these five effects separately.

6. As for the first, it is plain that the appetites are wearisome and tiring for a man. They resemble little children, restless and hard to please, always whining to their mother for this thing or that, and never satisfied. Just as a man who digs covetously for a treasure grows tired and exhausted, so does he who strives to acquire the demands of his appetites become wearied and fatigued. And even if he does finally obtain them, he is still always weary because he is never satisfied. For, after all, he digs leaking cisterns which cannot contain the water that slakes thirst. As Isaias says: *Lassus adhuc sitit, et anima ejus vacua est,* which means: He is yet faint with thirst and his soul is empty. [Is. 29:8]

A man with desires wearies himself, because he is like someone with a fever whose thirst increases by the minute, and who feels ill until the fever leaves. It is said in the Book of Job: *Cum satiatus fuerit, arctabitur, aestuabit, et omnis dolor irruet super eum* (When he has satisfied his appetite, he will be more burdened and oppressed; the heat of appetite will have increased and every sorrow will fall upon him). [Jb. 20:22]

The appetites are wearisome and tiring to a man, because they agitate and disturb him just as wind does with water. And they so upset him that they do not let him rest in any place or thing. Isaias declares of such a soul: *Cor impii quasi mare fervens* (The heart of a wicked man is like a stormy sea). [Is. 57:20] And the man who does not conquer his desires is evil.

The man seeking the satisfaction of his desires grows tired, because he is like a famished person who opens his mouth to satisfy himself with air, only to find that instead of being filled his mouth drys up more, since air is not his proper food. With this in mind Jeremias says: *In desiderio animae suae attraxit ventum amoris sui* (In the appetite of his will he drew in the air of his attachment). [Jer. 2:24] To comment on the dryness in which the soul is left, he immediately adds the advice: *Prohibe pedem tuum a nuditate, et guttur tuum a siti.* This means: Hold back your foot (that is, your mind) from nakedness, and your throat from thirst (that is, your will from satisfying its desire, which only causes greater thirst). [Jer. 2:25]

Just as a lover is wearied and depressed when on a longed-for day his opportunity is frustrated, so is a man wearied and tired by all his appetites and their fulfillment, because the fulfillment only causes more hunger and emptiness. An appetite, as they say, is like a fire that blazes up when wood is thrown on it, but necessarily dies out when the wood is consumed.

7. In regard to the appetites, things are even worse. The fire dwindles as the wood is consumed, but the intensity of the appetite does not diminish when the appetite is satisfied, even though the object is gone. Instead of waning like the fire after the wood is burned, the appetite faints with fatigue, because its hunger has increased and its food diminished. Isaias refers to this: *Declinabit ad dexteram, et esuriet; et comedet ad sinistram, et non saturabitur* (He will turn to the right and be hungry, and eat toward the left and not be filled). [Is. 9:20] When those who do not mortify their appetites turn to the right, they naturally see the abundance of the sweet spirit which is the lot of those who are at the right hand of God, but which is not granted to them. When they eat at the left (satisfy their appetite with some creature) they are of course discontent because in turning from what alone satisfies, they feed on what augments their hunger. It is clear, then, that the appetites weary and fatigue a man.

CHAPTER 7

How the appetites torment a man. Proofs through comparisons and passages from Sacred Scripture.

1. Torment and affliction is the second kind of damage the appetites cause in an individual. The affliction they engender is similar to the torture of the rack, where a person has no relief until freed from the torment of being bound by these cords. David says of this torture: *Funes peccatorum circumplexi sunt me* (The cords of my sins—my appetites—have tightened around me). [Ps. 118:61]

A person is tormented and afflicted when he reclines on his appetites as is a man lying naked on thorns and nails. Like thorns, the appetites wound and hurt, stick to a person and cause him pain. David says of them: *Circumdederunt me sicut apes, et exarserunt sicut ignis in spinis* (They circled around me like bees, stung me, and burned me like fire among thorns). [Ps. 117:12] For among the appetites, symbolized by the thorns, the fire of anguish and torment increases.

Just as a peasant, covetous of the desired harvest, goads and torments the ox that pulls the plow, so concupiscence, in order to attain the object of its longing, afflicts the man who lives under the yoke of his appetites. This is evident in Dalila's desire to know where Samson acquired such strength. Scripture states that the desire was such a fatigue and torment to her that she fainted away and almost died: *Defecit anima ejus, et ad mortem usque lassata est.*[1] [Jgs. 16:15-16]

2. The intensity of the torment is commensurate with the intensity of the appetite. As a result the torment is as great as the appetite, and the more numerous the appetites that possess a person the greater in number are his torments. In the person possessed by his appetites we find fulfilled even in this life what is said of Babylon in the Apocalypse: *Quantum glorificavit se, et in deliciis fuit, tantum date illi tormentum et luctum* (In the measure of her desire for self-exaltation and fulfillment of her appetites, give her torment and anguish). [Ap. 18:7]

A man who lets his desires capture him suffers torture and affliction like an enemy held prisoner. The Book of Judges contains a figure of this in that passage which narrates how the enemies captured mighty Samson who was once the free, strong judge of Israel and weakened him, pulled out his eyes, and chained him to grind at the millstone, where he was grievously tortured and tormented. [Jgs. 16:21] This same thing happens to a man in whom the enemy appetites reside and triumph. First they weaken and blind him, as we shall point out below, then they afflict and torment him by chaining him to the mill of concupiscence, for they are the chains by which he is bound.

3. God, then, with compassion for all those who through such labor and cost to themselves strive to satisfy the thirst and hunger of their desires for creatures, proclaims through Isaias: *Omnes sitientes, venite ad aquas et qui non habetis argentum, properate, emite, et comedite: venite, emite absque argento vinum et lac. Quare appenditis argentum non in panibus, et laborem vestrum non in saturitate?* [Is. 55:1-2] This is interpreted: Come to the waters all you who experience the thirst of your appetites; and you who have not the silver of your own will and desires, make haste; buy from me and eat; come and buy wine and milk (peace and spiritual sweetness) from me without the silver of your own will, without paying with labor as you do for the satisfaction of your appetites. Why do you offer the silver of your will for what is not bread (the bread of the divine Spirit) and waste the efforts of your appetites on what cannot satisfy them? Come, listen to me, and you will have the food you desire, and your soul will delight in abundance.

4. This movement toward abundance is a departure from the pleasures of creatures, because the creature torments, while the Spirit of God

[1] His soul fainted, and was wearied even until death.

refreshes. Accordingly, God calls us through St. Matthew: *Venite ad me, omnes qui laboratis et onerati estis, et ego reficiam vos, et invenietis requiem animabus vestris,* as though He were to say: All you going about tormented, afflicted, and weighed down by your cares and appetites, depart from them, come to me and I will refresh you; and you will find the rest for your souls that the desires take away from you. [Mt. 11:28–29] They are indeed a heavy burden, because David says of them: *Sicut onus grave gravatae sunt super me.*[2] [Ps. 37:5]

CHAPTER 8

The appetites darken and blind a man.

1. The third kind of harm the appetites bring upon a person is blindness and darkness. Vapors make the air murky and are a hindrance to the bright sunshine; a cloudy mirror does not clearly reflect a person's countenance; so too muddy water reflects only a hazy image of his features. In just this way a man's intellect, clouded by the appetites, becomes dark and impedes the sun of either natural reason or supernatural wisdom from shining within and completely illumining it. As a result David says when speaking of this: *Comprehenderunt me iniquitates meae, et non potui ut viderem* (My iniquities surrounded me and I was unable to see). [Ps. 39:13]

2. And due to the darkening of the intellect, the will becomes weak and the memory dull and disordered in its proper operation. Since these faculties depend upon the intellect in their operations, they are manifestly disordered and troubled when the intellect is hindered. Thus David says: *Anima mea turbata est valde* (My soul is exceedingly troubled). [Ps. 6:4] This is like saying the faculties of my soul are disordered. For the intellect (as the murky air in relation to the sun's light) is incapable of receiving the illumination of God's wisdom; and the will is incapable of an embrace of pure love of God (just as the mirror clouded with vapors has not the capacity for clearly reflecting the countenance before it); and the memory obscured by the darkness of appetite has still less capacity for the impression of the serenity of God's image upon it (as muddy water cannot clearly reflect the features of one who looks for his image in it).

3. The appetite blinds and darkens the soul because the appetite as such is blind. It is blind because of itself it has no intellect. Reason always acts as a blind man's guide for the appetite. Consequently, every time a man's appetite leads him, he is blinded, just as we might say that

---

[2] As a heavy burden they weigh upon me.

when a blind man guides someone who has good eyesight both are blind. The logical outcome is what our Lord proclaims in St. Matthew: *Si caecus caeco ducatum praestet, ambo in foveam cadunt* (If a blind man leads a blind man, both will fall into the ditch). [Mt. 15:14]

A moth is not helped much by its eyes, because, blinded in its desire for the beauty of light, it will fly directly into a bonfire.

The man who feeds on his appetites is comparable to a fish dazzled by a light that so darkens it that it cannot see the fishermen's snares. David describes this blindness well: *Supercecidit ignis, et non viderunt solem* (Fire, that gives off heat and dazzles by its light, came upon them). [Ps. 57:9] The appetite causes this in the soul: it enkindles concupiscence and overwhelms the intellect so that it cannot see its light. The reason is that a new light set directly in front of the visual faculty blinds this faculty so that it fails to see the light farther away. And since the appetite is so close to a man as to be actually within him, he is impeded by this interior light, feeds upon it, and is unable to see the clear light of his intellect; nor will he see it until he extinguishes this blinding light of his appetite.

4. The ignorance of some is extremely lamentable; they burden themselves with extraordinary penances and many other exercises, thinking these are sufficient for the attainment of union with the divine wisdom. But these practices are insufficient if a person does not diligently strive to deny his appetites. If these people would attempt to devote only a half of that energy to the renunciation of their desires, they would profit more in a month than in years with all these other exercises. As the tilling of soil is necessary for its fruitfulness—untilled soil produces only weeds—mortification of the appetites is a requisite for man's spiritual fruitfulness. I venture to say that without this mortification all a man does for the sake of advancement in perfection, and in knowledge of God and of himself, is no more profitable than seed sown on uncultivated ground. Accordingly, darkness and coarseness will always be with a soul until its appetites are extinguished. The appetites are like a cataract on the eye or specks of dust in it; until removed they obstruct vision.

5. David, observing the blindness of such people, how impeded their souls are from seeing truth clearly, and the extent of God's anger with them, warns: *Priusquam intelligerent spinae vestrae rhamnum: sicut viventes, sic in ira absorbet eos,* as though to say: before your thorns (that is, your appetites) understand, He will absorb them in His wrath as He would the living. [Ps. 57:10] Before the appetites living in the soul come to an understanding of God, He will absorb them in this life, or in the next, by chastisement and correction, that is, through purgation. He says God will absorb them in wrath, because the suffering

caused by the mortification of the appetites is a chastisement for the havoc they produce in man.

6. Oh, if men but knew what a treasure of divine light this blindness caused by their affections and appetites deprives them of, and the number of misfortunes and evils these appetites occasion each day when left unmortified!

They must not so rely on their sharp intellects nor upon the gifts received from God as to believe that their attachments or appetites will not blind, darken, and cause them to grow gradually worse. Who would have thought that a man as perfect in the wisdom and gifts of God as Solomon could, when he was old, have sunk into such blindness and torpor of will as to construct altars to countless idols, and then worship them himself? Yet this was caused by nothing else than his affection for women and his neglect to deny the appetites and delights of his heart. [3 Kgs. 3:12–13; 11:1–4] He says in Ecclesiastes that he did not deny his heart what it asked of him. [Eccl. 2:10] Although in the beginning he was truly restrained, this rush after his desires, and failure to deny them, gradually blinded and darkened his intellect so that finally the powerful light of God's wisdom was extinguished. Consequently, in his old age, Solomon abandoned God.

7. If the unmortified appetites could do this in a man who possessed such lofty knowledge of the distance between good and evil, what terrible damage can they cause in us who are ignorant. For as God said to Jonas about the Ninivites: We do not know the difference between our right hand and our left. [Jon. 4:11] At every step we mistake evil for good and good for evil. This is peculiar to our nature. But what will happen if appetite is added to our natural darkness? Nothing else than what Isaias says: *Palpavimus sicut coeci parietem et quasi absque oculis attrectavimus: impegimus meridie quasi in tenebris.* [Is. 59:10] The prophet is speaking with those who love to pursue their appetites, as though to say: We have felt our way along the wall as though blind, we have groped as if without eyes, and our blindness has reached the point that we stumble along in broad daylight as though walking in the dark.

CHAPTER 9

The appetites defile a man. Proofs through comparisons and passages from Sacred Scripture.

1. The fourth way the appetites harm the soul is by defiling and staining it. The Book of Ecclesiasticus teaches: *Qui tetigerit picem,*

inquinabitur ab ea (He who touches pitch will be defiled by it). [Ecclus. 13:1] And a person handles pitch when he satisfies the appetite of his will for some creature. It is noteworthy that the Wise Man compares creatures to pitch, for the difference between the excellence of the soul and the best in creatures is greater than between gold, or a bright diamond, and pitch. The gold, or the diamond, when placed upon pitch becomes more stained and unsightly as the heat melting the pitch increases. Similarly, a man, fired by his appetite for some creature, is stained and blackened by that creature because of the heat of his desire.

There is as much difference between the soul and other corporal creatures as there is between a transparent liquid and the filthiest mire. This liquid would be polluted if mud were mixed with it; so too attachment to creature defiles a soul, because this attachment makes it similar to the creature. Strokes of soot would ruin a perfect and extraordinarily beautiful portrait, so too inordinate appetites would defile and dirty the soul, in itself a perfect and extremely beautiful image of God.

2. Jeremiah, weeping over the ravages of unsightliness these inordinate appetites cause in a soul, first lists the soul's beauty and then its ugliness: *Candidiores sunt nazarei ejus nive, nitidiores lacte, rubicundiores ebore antiquo, sapphiro pulchriores. Denigrata est super carbones facies eorum, et non sunt cogniti in plateis* (Its hair—that is, of the soul—is whiter than snow, more resplendent than milk, ruddier than ancient ivory, more beautiful than sapphire stone. Its surface became blacker than coal and went unrecognized in the public squares). [Lam. 4:7–8]

The hair refers to a man's affections and thoughts; when ordered to the end intended by God—which is God Himself—it is whiter than snow, clearer than milk, ruddier than ancient ivory, and more beautiful than sapphire. These four objects of comparison indicate every kind of beauty and excellence in corporal creatures; yet the beauty and excellence of the soul's operations, which are symbolized by the Nazarites or hair, is, he says, greater. If these operations of the soul are inordinate and occupied in an end not intended by God—that is, in creatures—their surface, says Jeremiah, will become blacker than coal.

3. Inordinate appetites for the things of the world do all this damage to the beauty of the soul, and even more. So great is the harm that if we try to express how ugly and dirty is the imprint the appetites leave in the soul we find nothing comparable to it—neither a place full of cobwebs and lizards, nor the unsightliness of a dead body, nor the filthiest thing imaginable in this life.

Although it is true that the disordered soul possesses in its natural being the perfection that God bestowed when creating it, nevertheless in its rational being it is ugly, abominable, dirty, dark, and full of all the evils here described, and many more besides. One inordinate appetite alone, as we shall explain, suffices to make a soul so captive, dirty, and unsightly that until the appetite is purified the soul is incapable of conformity with God in union. This is true even though there may be no matter for mortal sin in the appetite. What then will be the ugliness of a soul entirely disordered in its passions and surrendered to its appetites? How far it will be from God and His purity!

4. The variety of filth caused in the soul is both inexplicable and unintelligible! For were it comprehensible it would be surprising and also distressing to see how in the measure of its quantity and quality each appetite leaves a deposit of filth and an unsightly mark in the soul. It would be a surprise and a pity to observe how only one inordinate act can in its own way occasion innumerable kinds and various degrees of filth. The well-ordered soul of the just man in a single perfect act possesses countless rich gifts and beautiful virtues. Each of these gifts and virtues is different and pleasing in its own way according to the multitude and diversity of the affections the soul has had for God. Similarly, in an inordinate soul there is a deposit of as miserable a variety of filth and degradation as the variety of its appetites for creatures.

5. We have an excellent figure of these varied appetites in Ezechiel. It is written that God showed this prophet all kinds of crawling reptiles and all the abomination of unclean animals painted on the interior walls of the temple. God then said to Ezechiel: Son of man, have you not seen indeed the abominations that each of these accomplishes in the secrecy of his chamber? And when God commanded the prophet to enter further and behold greater abominations, Ezechiel says he saw women seated there and weeping for Adonis, the god of love. Being commanded by God to penetrate still further for the sight of even greater abominations, he beheld there twenty-five old men whose backs were turned on the temple. [Ez. 8:10–16]

6. The many reptiles and unclean animals painted on the walls of the first room in the temple represent intellectual thoughts of abject earthly things and of all creatures. These creatures are painted just as they are in the temple of the soul if it allows its intellect, the first chamber, to be encumbered with them.

The women further within, in the second chamber, weeping for the god Adonis, represent the appetites residing in the second faculty of the soul which is the will. These appetites weep as it were by coveting what the will is attached to, that is, they covet the reptiles painted in the intellect.

The men in the third room are a representation of the images of creatures which the third part of the soul, the memory, preserves and reflects upon. The passage states that these men turned their backs on the temple, for when the soul is wholly joined with an earthly object through an embrace of these three faculties, we can say that it has turned its back on the temple of God. And the temple of God represents the soul's right reason, which admits nothing of creatures.

7. What we have said is sufficient at present for some understanding of the unsightly disorder of the soul caused by its appetites. We would never finish if we tried to discuss in particular the lesser degree of ugliness, and its variety, that imperfections cause in the soul, or the still greater degree, and its variety, produced by venial sins, or that of total ugliness caused by mortally sinful appetites. The variety of the total ugliness corresponds to the extensive diversity of all three degrees. Not even the angelic intellect could have an adequate understanding of all this unsightliness. The point I am making and desire to make is that any appetite, even one that is but slightly imperfect, stains and defiles the soul.

CHAPTER 10

The appetites weaken a soul and make it lukewarm in the practice of virtue.

1. Weakness and tepidity is the fifth kind of harm the appetites produce in a man. For the appetites sap the strength needed for perseverance in the practice of virtue. Because the force of the desire is divided, it becomes weaker than if it were completely fixed on one object. The more objects there are dividing an appetite, the weaker becomes this appetite for each. This is why the philosophers say that virtue when united is stronger than when scattered. It is therefore clear that if the desire of the will extends to something other than virtue, it grows weaker in the practice of virtue. A man whose will is divided among trifles is like water which, due to some leakage, will not rise higher and consequently becomes useless. This is why the patriarch Jacob compared his son Ruben, who had given rein to his appetites in a certain sin, to spilled water: *You are poured out like water, grow not.* [Gn. 49:4] This was like saying: Because according to the appetites you are poured out like water, you will not grow in virtue.

Hot water quickly loses its heat if left uncovered, and aromatic spices when unwrapped eventually lose the strength and pungency of their scent. So the soul that is not recollected in one appetite alone, the desire for God, loses heat and strength in the practice of virtue. Clearly understanding this, David said to God: *Fortitudinem meam ad te custodiam* (I will keep my strength for you). [Ps. 58:10] I will do this by concentrating the strength of my appetites on You alone.

2. The appetites weaken a person's virtue, because they are like shoots burgeoning about a tree, sapping its strength, and causing it fruitlessness. The Lord says of such people: *Vae praegnantibus et nutrientibus in illis diebus!* (Woe to them who will be with child in those days, and to them who will be nursing!). [Mt. 24:19] Being with child and nursing refer to the appetites which, if not cut off, gradually grow. Their growth will be costly, like the growth of sprouts around the tree, for they debilitate the soul's strength. Our Lord consequently advises us: *Let your loins be girt.* [Lk. 12:35] The loins here indicate the appetites. The desires are indeed like leeches, always sucking blood from one's veins. This is what the Wise Man calls them: *The daughters* (the appetites) *are leeches always calling: give! give!* [Prv. 30:15]

3. Manifestly, then, the appetites do not bring any good to a man. Rather they rob him of what he already has. And if he does not mortify them, they will not cease until they accomplish what it is said the offspring of vipers do within the mother: while growing within her they eat away at her entrails and finally kill her to remain alive at her expense. So the unmortified appetites result in killing a man in his relationship with God, and thus, because he did not put them to death first, they alone live in him. This is why it says in the Book of Ecclesiasticus: *Aufer a me Domine ventris concupiscentias et concubitus concupscentiae ne apprehendant me.*[3] [Ecclus. 23:6]

4. Even though they do not go to this extent, it is sad to consider the condition of the poor person in whom they dwell. How unhappy he is with himself, how cold toward his neighbors, how sluggish and slothful in the things of God! No illness makes walking as burdensome, or eating as distasteful, as do the appetites for creatures render the practice of virtue burdensome and saddening to a man. Ordinarily, the reason many people do not have diligence and eagerness for the acquisition of virtue is that their appetites and affections are not fixed purely on God.

CHAPTER 11

Proofs of how freedom from all appetites, even the smallest, is necessary to attain divine union.

1. The reader has apparently desired for quite a while to ask if the total mortification of all the appetites, large and small, is a requirement for the attainment of this high state of perfection, or if it is sufficient to mortify just some of them and leave the others, at least those that seem

[3] Take away from me, O Lord, lustful cravings, let not the desires of the flesh lay hold of me.

trifling. For it seems to be an extremely arduous task for a person to attain such purity and nakedness that he has no affection for anything.

2. First of all, in answer to this query, it is true that not all the appetites are equally detrimental, nor are all equally a hindrance to the soul. I am speaking of the voluntary appetites, because the natural ones are little or no hindrance at all to the attainment of union, provided they do not receive one's consent nor pass beyond the first movements in which the rational will plays no role. For to eradicate the natural appetites, that is, to mortify them entirely, is impossible in this life. Even though they are not entirely mortified, as I say, they do not so hinder a man as to prevent him from attaining divine union. A man can easily experience them in his sensitive nature and yet be free of them in the rational part of his being. It will even happen that while a person is experiencing an intense union of will in the prayer of quiet these appetites will be actually dwelling in his sensory part—yet the superior part of his soul will be paying no attention to them. But all the other voluntary appetites, whether they are the most serious, which involve mortal sin, or less grave in that they concern venial sin, or whether they be the least serious of all in that they only involve imperfections, must be mortified. A person must be liberated of them all, however slight they be, in order to arrive at this complete union.

The reason is that in the state of divine union a man's will is so completely transformed in God's will that it excludes anything contrary to God's will, and in all and through all is motivated by the will of God.

3. Here we have the reason for stating that two wills become one. And this one will is God's will which becomes also the soul's. If a man should desire an imperfection unwanted by God, this one will of God would be destroyed because of the desire for what God does not will.

If anyone is to reach perfect union with God through his will and love, he must obviously first be freed from every appetite however slight. That is, he must not give the consent of his will knowingly to an imperfection, and he must have the power and freedom to be able, upon advertence, to refuse this consent.

I say "knowingly," because he will fall into imperfections, venial sins, and the above-mentioned natural appetites without having advertence or knowledge or control in the matter. It is written of these semivoluntary and inadvertent sins that the just man will fall seven times a day and rise up again. [Prv. 24:16] But any one of the voluntary appetites, even if trifling, is sufficient to impede the union, as I have said, if it is not mortified. I am referring here to habitual appetites, because certain scattered acts of different desires are not such a hindrance to union, since they are not a determined habit. Yet the soul must be liberated of these acts too, since they also proceed from habitual imperfection. Yet some habitual voluntary imperfections that are never completely mortified are not only an impediment to divine union but to spiritual progress as well.

4. Some examples of these habitual imperfections are: the common habit of loquacity; a small attachment one never really desires to conquer, for example, to a person, to clothing, to a book or a cell, or to the way food is prepared, and to other trifling conversations and little satisfactions in tasting, knowing, and hearing things, etc. Any of these habitual imperfections, and attachment to them, causes as much harm to an individual as would the daily commission of many other imperfections. Sporadic venial sins and imperfections that do not result from habitual practice having evil dimensions will not hinder a man as much as his attachment to something. As long as he continues this attachment, it is impossible for him to make progress in perfection, even though the imperfection may be very small.

It makes little difference whether a bird is tied by a thin thread or by a cord. For even if tied by thread, the bird will be prevented from taking off just as surely as if it were tied by cord—that is, it will be impeded from flight as long as it does not break the thread. Admittedly the thread is easier to rend, but no matter how easily this may be done, the bird will not fly away without first doing so. This is the lot of a man who is attached to something; no matter how much virtue he has he will not reach the freedom of the divine union.

An individual's appetite and attachment resemble the remora, which if successful in clinging to a ship will hold it back and prevent it from reaching port, or even from sailing, despite the fact that this fish is exceptionally small. It is regrettable, then, to behold some souls, laden as rich vessels with wealth, deeds, spiritual exercises, virtues, and favors from God, never advancing because they lack the courage to make a complete break with some little satisfaction, attachment, or affection (which are all about the same), and thereby never reaching the port of perfection, which requires no more than a sudden flap of one's wings to tear the thread of attachment, or the rejection of the clinging remora.

5. It is a matter for deep sorrow that, while God has bestowed on them the power to break other stronger cords of attachment to sins and vanities, they fail to attain so much good because they do not become detached from some childish thing which God has requested them to conquer out of love for Him and which amounts to no more than a thread or hair. What is worse, they not only fail to advance but they turn back because of their small attachment, losing what they have gained in their journey at the expense of so much time and effort. Everyone knows that not to go forward on this road is to turn back, and not to gain ground is to lose. This is what our Lord wanted to teach when He said:

He who is not with Me is against Me, and he who does not gather with Me scatters. [Mt. 12:30]

If one small crack in a pitcher goes unrepaired, it alone can cause the leakage of all the liquid. The Book of Ecclesiasticus gives clear teaching of this when it says: *He that despises small things will fall little by little.* [Ecclus. 19:1] For as it teaches elsewhere: *A great fire is occasioned by a tiny spark.* [Ecclus. 11:34] Accordingly one imperfection leads to another, and these to still more. You will scarcely ever find a person negligent in the mortification of one appetite who will not have many others flowing from the identical weakness and imperfection caused by this one appetite. Such persons, consequently, are ever faltering along the road.

We have witnessed many persons, whom God favored with progress in detachment and freedom, fall from happiness and firmness in their spiritual exercises and end up by losing everything merely because they began to indulge in some slight attachment to conversation and friendship under the color of good. For by this attachment they gradually emptied themselves of both holy solitude and the spirit and joy of God. All this happened because they did not put a stop to their initial satisfaction and sensitive pleasure, and preserve themselves for God in solitude.

6. The attainment of our goal demands that we never stop on this road, which means we must continually mortify our appetites rather than indulge them. For if we do not mortify them all completely, we will not wholly reach our goal. A log of wood cannot be transformed into the fire if even a single degree of heat is lacking to its preparation for this. The soul, similarly, will not be transformed in God even if it has only one imperfection. A man, as we shall explain in speaking of the night of faith, has only one will, which, if encumbered or occupied by anything, will not possess the freedom, solitude, and purity requisite for the divine transformation.

7. We have a figure of this in the Book of Judges. It narrates that the angel announced to the children of Israel that because they had not completely destroyed their enemies but made a pact with some of them, these enemies would be left in their midst as an occasion of their fall and perdition. [Jgs. 2:1–3] God does precisely this with some souls. He has withdrawn them from the world, slain the giants which are their sins, and destroyed the multitude of their enemies (the occasions of sin encountered in the world) for the sole purpose of their entering with greater freedom into the promised land of divine union. Nevertheless, in spite of all this, they will fraternize and make pacts with the insignificant people of their imperfections by not mortifying them completely. And God in His anger allows them to go from bad to worse in their appetites.

8. We find another figure of this in the Book of Josue. There we read that God commanded Josue, when he was about to enter into possession of the promised land, to destroy everything in the city of Jericho without leaving anything alive, neither men nor women, young nor old, nor any animals. And He ordered him not to covet or seize any of the booty. [Jos. 6:18, 19, 21] The lesson here is that all objects living in the soul—whether they be many or few, large or small—must die in order that the soul enter divine union, and it must bear no desire for them but remain detached as though they were nonexistent to it, and it to them.

St. Paul teaches this clearly in Corinthians: *What I tell you, brothers, is that the time is short; what remains and suits you is that those with wives should act as though they had none, and those who weep for the things of this world as though they were not weeping, and those who rejoice as though not rejoicing, and the buyers as though they did not possess, and the users of the world should behave as though they made no use of it.* [1 Cor. 7:29–31] In this text St. Paul explains, in view of a soul's going to God, the extent which detachment from all things must reach.

CHAPTER 12

The answer to another question. An explanation of the kinds of appetites which can bring this harm upon a soul.

1. We could explain this night of sense at greater length by mentioning everything relevant to the kind of damage the appetites cause, for they injure not merely in the ways described but in many others as well. What we have explained, however, is sufficient for our purpose. It has probably been understood how the mortification of the appetites can be called night and how suitable it is for a person to enter this night in his approach to God. The only point which remains before we treat, in conclusion, the method of entering this night is a response to a doubt which may bother the reader concerning this matter.

2. First, can any appetite produce and cause the two evils mentioned above, namely: the privative, which removes the grace of God from the soul; and the positive, which causes the five cardinal kinds of harm we explained?

Second, is any appetite, however slight or of whatever kind, enough to produce all these types of damage together, or does each cause only a particular kind, in that one may produce torment, another weariness, and another darkness, etc.?

3. To the first query, I answer that relevant to the privative evil, the loss of grace, only the voluntary appetites whose object may involve mortal sin can do this completely. For they deprive the soul of grace in this life and of glory, the possession of God, in the next.

To the second, my answer is that all these positive evils are together occasioned in the soul by each of these appetites. This is true whether the appetites concern mortal sin, venial sin, or imperfection. We call these evils positive, though in a certain fashion they are privative, because they are related to a conversion toward the creature, just as the privative evils correspond to the aversion from God.

Yet there is this difference: the appetites for mortal sin produce total blindness, torment, filth, and weakness, etc., whereas the others do not cause these kinds of harm in a complete and absolute degree. For they do not deprive the soul of grace—a privation that would give them full possession, since the death of grace means life for the appetites. But these smaller appetites do cause this damage in a lesser degree according to the loss of grace they occasion. The extent of the torment, blindness, and weakness will correspond to the weakening of grace brought on by the appetites.

4. It is noteworthy, however, that, though each appetite causes all these kinds of positive harm, it will cause one kind principally and directly, and the others indirectly.

For though it is true that a sensual appetite breeds all these kinds of evil, it principally and properly defiles the soul and body.

And an appetite of avarice produces them all too, yet principally and directly it causes afflictions.

And one of vainglory similarly causes them all, yet principally and directly it darkens and blinds.

And whereas an appetite of gluttony begets all the evils, it chiefly produces lukewarmness in virtue.

And so on with the others.

5. The reason any act of a voluntary appetite gives rise to all these evils together is that it directly opposes the acts of virtue, which generate the contrary effects. An act of virtue produces in a man mildness, peace, comfort, light, purity, and strength, just as an inordinate appetite brings about torment, fatigue, weariness, blindness, and weakness. Through the practice of one virtue all the virtues grow, and similarly, through an increase of one vice, all the vices and their effects grow.

These evils do not unmask themselves at the moment the appetite is being satisfied, since the pleasure of the moment is an obstacle to this. Yet sooner or later the harmful effects will certainly be felt. A good illustration of this is found in the Apocalypse. An angel commanded St. John to eat the book which was sweet to the mouth, but in the belly sour. [Ap. 10:9] For the appetite when satisfied seems sweet and pleasant, but eventually the sour effect is felt. This truth will certainly be clear to anyone who allows himself to be carried away by his appetites. I am aware, however, that there are some so blind and insensible that they do not experience this bitter effect. Since they do not walk in God, they do not perceive what keeps them from Him.

6. I am not speaking here of the other natural, involuntary appetites, nor of thoughts that do not pass beyond the first movements, nor of other temptations in which there is no consent. These temptations do not give rise to any of the evils previously mentioned. Though the passion and disturbance they momentarily cause make it seem to a person that he is being defiled and blinded, such is not the case; rather, they occasion the opposite good effects. Insofar as a person resists them, he wins strength, purity, light, comfort, and many blessings, as our Lord told St. Paul: Virtue is made perfect in weakness. [2 Cor. 12:9]

But the voluntary appetites bring on all these evils, and even more. That is why the chief concern of spiritual directors with their penitents is the immediate mortification of every appetite. The directors should make them remain empty of what they desire so as to liberate them from so much misery.

CHAPTER 13

The manner and method of entering this night of sense.

1. Some counsels are in order now that the individual may both know the way of entering this night and be able to do so. It should be understood, consequently, that a man ordinarily enters this night of sense in two ways: active and passive.

The active manner of entry, which will be the subject of the following counsels, comprises what a man can do and does by himself to enter this night.

In the passive way an individual does nothing, for God accomplishes the work in him, while he acts as the recipient. This will be the subject of the fourth book where we shall discuss beginners. Since, with God's help, I will there give counsels pertinent to the numerous imperfections beginners ordinarily possess on this road, I shall not take the time to offer many here. Nor is this the proper place to give them, since presently we are dealing only with the reasons for calling this journey a night, and with the nature and divisions of this night.

Nevertheless, if we do not offer some immediate remedy or counsel, this part would seem very short and less helpful. Therefore I want to set down the following abridged method. And I will do the same at the end of my discussion of each of the next two parts (or reasons for the use of the term night) which, with God's help, will follow.

2. Though these counsels for the conquering of appetites are brief and few in number, I believe they are as profitable and efficacious as they are concise. He who sincerely wants to practice them will need no others, since all the others are included in these.

3. First, have a habitual desire to imitate Christ in all your deeds by bringing your life into conformity with His. You must then study His life in order to know how to imitate Him and behave in all events as He would.

4. Second, in order to be successful in this imitation, renounce and remain empty of any sensory satisfaction that is not purely for the honor and glory of God. Do this out of love for Jesus Christ. In His life He had no other gratification, nor desired any other, than the fulfillment of His Father's will, which He called His meat and food. [Jn. 4:34]

For example, if you are offered the satisfaction of hearing things that have no relation to the service and glory of God, do not desire this pleasure or the hearing of these things.

When you have an opportunity for the gratification of looking upon objects that will not help you come any closer to God, do not desire this gratification or sight.

And if in speaking there is a similar opportunity, act in the same way.

And so on with all the senses insofar as you can duly avoid this pleasure. If you cannot escape the experience of this satisfaction, it will be sufficient to have no desire for it.

By this method you should endeavor, then, to leave the senses as though in darkness, mortified, and empty of pleasure. With such vigilance you will gain a great deal in a short time.

5. Many blessings flow from the harmony and tranquillity of the four natural passions—joy, hope, fear, and sorrow. The following maxims contain a complete remedy for mortifying and pacifying the passions. If put into practice these maxims will give rise to abundant merit and great virtues.

6. Endeavor to be inclined always:
 not to the easiest, but to the most difficult;
 not to the most delightful, but to the harshest;
 not to the most gratifying, but to the less pleasant;
 not to what means rest for you, but to hard work;
 not to the consoling, but to the unconsoling;
 not to the most, but to the least;

not to the highest and most precious, but to the lowest and most despised;

not to wanting something, but to wanting nothing;

do not go about looking for the best of temporal things, but for the worst,

and desire to enter into complete nudity, emptiness, and poverty in everything in the world.

7. You should embrace these practices earnestly and try to overcome the repugnance of your will toward them. If you sincerely put them into practice with order and discretion, you will discover in them great delight and consolation.

8. These counsels if truly carried out are sufficient for entry into the night of senses. But that we give abundant enough counsel, here is another exercise which teaches the mortification of the concupiscence of the flesh, the concupiscence of the eyes, and the pride of life, which, as St. John says, reign in the world and give rise to all the other appetites. [1 Jn. 2:16]

9. First, try to act with contempt for yourself and desire that all others do likewise.

Second, endeavor to speak in contempt of yourself and desire all others to do so.

Third, try to think lowly and contemptuously of yourself and desire that all others do the same.

10. As a conclusion to these counsels and rules it would be appropriate to repeat the verses presented in *The Ascent of Mount Carmel* (the drawing at the beginning of the book), which are instructions for climbing to the summit, the high state of union. Although in the drawing we admittedly refer to the spiritual and interior aspect we also deal with the spirit of imperfection existent in the sensory and exterior part of the soul, as is evident by the two roads, one on each side of that path which leads to perfection. Consequently, these verses will here bear reference to the sensory part. Afterwards, in the second division of this night, they may be interpreted in relationship to the spiritual part.

11. The verses are as follows:

To reach satisfaction in all
desire its possession in nothing.
To come to possess all
desire the possession of nothing.
To arrive at being all
desire to be nothing.
To come to the knowledge of all

desire the knowledge of nothing.
To come to the pleasure you have not
you must go by a way in which you enjoy not.
To come to the knowledge you have not
you must go by a way in which you know not.
To come to the possession you have not
you must go by a way in which you possess not.
To come to be what you are not
you must go by a way in which you are not.
When you turn toward something
you cease to cast yourself upon the all.
For to go from all to the all
you must deny yourself of all in all.
And when you come to the possession of the all
you must possess it without wanting anything.
Because if you desire to have something in all
your treasure in God is not purely your all.
In this nakedness the spirit finds
its quietude and rest.
For in coveting nothing,
nothing raises it up
and nothing weighs it down,
because it is in the center of its humility.
When it covets something
in this very desire it is wearied.

Chapter 14

An explanation of verse 2 of the first stanza.

Fired with love's urgent longings

1. Now that we have explained the night of sense, to which the first verse of this stanza refers, and have discussed the nature of this night, the reason for calling it night, and the method of actively entering it, we should logically continue with an explanation of the admirable properties and effects contained in the remaining stanzas. I shall explain these verses, as promised in the prologue, by merely touching upon them, and then proceed to Book Two, a treatise on the remaining, or spiritual, part of this night.

2. The soul then states that "fired with love's urgent longings" it passed through this dark night of sense to union with the Beloved.

A love of pleasure, and attachment to it, usually fires the will toward the enjoyment of things that give pleasure. A more intense enkindling of another, better love (love of one's heavenly Bridegroom) is necessary for the vanquishing of the appetites and the denial of this pleasure. By finding his satisfaction and strength in this love, a man will have the courage and constancy to deny readily all other appetites. The love of one's Spouse is not the only requisite for conquering the strength of the sensitive appetites; an enkindling with longings of love is also necessary. For the sensory appetites are moved and attracted toward sensory objects with such cravings that if the spiritual part of the soul is not fired with other more urgent longings for spiritual things, the soul will neither be able to overcome the yoke of nature nor enter the night of sense; nor will it have the courage to live in the darkness of all things by denying its appetites for them.

3. This is not the appropriate section for a description—nor would it be possible—of the nature of these longings of love or of the numerous ways they occur at the outset of the journey to union. Neither is it the place for a discussion of the diligence and ingenuity of persons in departing from their house—self-will—into the night of the mortification of their senses, nor of how easy, sweet, and delightful these longings for their Spouse make all the trials and dangers of this night seem. It is better to experience all of this and meditate upon it than to write of it. We shall proceed, consequently, to the next chapter and explain the remaining verses.

CHAPTER 15

An exposition of the remaining verses of the first stanza.

> —Ah, the sheer grace!—
> I went out unseen,
> My house being now all stilled;

1. The soul uses as a metaphor the wretched state of captivity. It is a sheer grace to be released from this prison without hindrance from the jailers. The soul, through original sin, is a captive in the mortal body, subject to passions and natural appetites; when liberated from this bondage and submission, it considers its escape, which is unnoticed, unimpeded, and unapprehended by its passions and appetites, a sheer grace.

2. To achieve this liberation it was advantageous for the soul to depart in the dark night, that is, in the privation of all satisfactions and in the mortification of all appetites, as we mentioned. "My house being now

all stilled" means that the house of all the appetites, the sensitive part of the soul, is now stilled, and the desires conquered and lulled to sleep. Until slumber comes to the appetites through the mortification of sensuality, and until this very sensuality is stilled in such a way that the appetites do not war against the spirit, the soul will not walk out to genuine freedom, to the enjoyment of union with its Beloved.

END OF THE FIRST BOOK

BOOK TWO

This book is a treatise on faith, the proximate means of ascent to union with God. It consequently considers the second part of this night, the night of spirit to which the following stanza refers.

CHAPTER 1

The Second Stanza

In darkness, and secure,
By the secret ladder, disguised,
—Ah, the sheer grace!—
In darkness and concealment,
My house being now all stilled;

1. This second stanza tells in song of the sheer grace that was the soul's in divesting the spirit of all its imperfections and appetites for spiritual possessions. This grace is far greater here because of the greater hardship involved in quieting the house of man's spiritual nature and entering this interior darkness (the spiritual nudity of all sensory and immaterial things), leaning on pure faith alone, in an ascent by it to God.

The "secret ladder" represents faith, because all the rungs or articles of faith are secret to and hidden from both the senses and the intellect. Accordingly the soul lived in darkness, without the light of the senses and intellect, and went out beyond every natural and rational boundary to climb the divine ladder of faith that leads up to and penetrates the deep things of God. [1 Cor. 2:10]

The soul declares it was disguised, because in the ascent through faith its garments, apparel, and capacities were changed from natural to divine. Because of this disguise, neither the devil, temporal, nor rational things recognized or detained it. None of these can do harm to the man who walks in faith.

The soul's advance, moreover, was so concealed, hidden, and withdrawn from all the wiles of the devil that it indeed involved darkness and concealment. That is, the soul was hidden from the devil, to whom the light of faith is worse than darkness. We can say as a result that a man who walks in faith is concealed and hidden from the devil; this will be more evident as we proceed.

2. The soul, consequently, affirms that it departed "in darkness, and secure." For anyone fortunate enough to possess the ability to journey in the obscurity of faith, as a blind man with his guide, and depart from all natural phantasms and intellectual reasonings, walks securely.

The soul also asserts that it departed in this spiritual night because its house was now all stilled. That is, the spiritual and rational part of the soul was stilled, because once the soul attains union with God the natural faculties and the impulses and anxieties of the spiritual part remain at rest. The poem does not proclaim that the soul went out with urgent longings, as it does of the first night of sense. To enter the night of sense and denude itself of sensible things, the soul needed the longings of sensitive love. But all that is required for a complete pacification of the spiritual house is the negation through pure faith of all the spiritual faculties and gratifications and appetites. This achieved, the soul will be joined with the Beloved in a union of simplicity and purity and love and likeness.

3. It is noteworthy that, in considering the senses, the poem asserts that the soul departed on a dark night, and, in speaking of the spirit, it says that the soul went out in darkness. The obscurity of the spirit is far more intense, just as "in darkness" indicates thicker obscurity than "dark night." For, however dark a night may be, some objects are still visible, but in total darkness nothing at all can be seen. In the night of sense there is yet some light, because the intellect and reason remain and suffer no blindness. But this spiritual night of faith removes everything, both in the intellect and in the senses.

As a result the soul declares in this stanza that it departed in darkness and secure, which it did not affirm in the former. For the less a soul works with its own abilities, the more securely it proceeds, because its progress in faith is greater.

This will be the subject matter of Book Two, and we shall discuss it at length. The devout reader, consequently, must proceed thoughtfully, because our exposition will be most important for persons of genuine spirituality. Though these truths are somewhat obscure, they so shed light on one another that I believe they will all be clearly understood.

CHAPTER 2

Faith, the second cause or part of this night. Two proofs of why it is darker than the first and third.

1. Faith, the second part of this night, is our next subject for discussion. Faith is that admirable means of advancing to God, our goal. And God, we said, is also for the soul a part, or the third cause, of this night.

Faith, the means, is comparable to midnight. We can affirm, then, that it is darker for a man than the first part of the night and, in a certain way, darker than the third.

The first part, pertinent to the senses, resembles twilight, the time sensible objects begin to fade from sight. Accordingly, it is not a time so far removed from all light as is midnight.

The third part, that period before the dawn, approximates the light of day. The darkness is not like that of midnight, since in this third period of the night we approach the illumination of day. And this daylight we compare to God. Although naturally speaking God is indeed as dark a night to the soul as is faith, it can be affirmed that He is less dark. For when these three parts of the night—which are night to the soul from a natural viewpoint—have passed, God supernaturally illumines the soul with the ray of His divine light. This light is the principle of the perfect union which follows after the third night.

2. The first night pertains to the lower, sensory part of man's nature and is consequently more external. As a result the second night is darker. The second, darker night of faith belongs to the rational, superior part; it is darker and more interior because it deprives this part of its rational light, or better, blinds it. Accordingly, it is indeed comparable to midnight, the innermost and darkest period of night.

3. We must prove, now, how this second part, faith, is night to the spirit just as the first is to the senses. Then we shall also discuss the factors in opposition to this night and how a person prepares actively for entering it. In its proper place we shall speak of passivity, that is, of God's work—without the soul—in effecting this night. I plan to discuss this matter in the third book.

CHAPTER 3

Arguments, passages, and figures from Scripture in proof that faith is a dark night for the soul.

1. Faith, the theologians say, is a certain and obscure habit of soul. It is an obscure habit because it brings us to believe divinely revealed truths which transcend every natural light and infinitely exceed all human understanding. As a result the excessive light of faith bestowed on man is darkness for him, because a brighter light will eclipse and suppress a dimmer one. The sun so obscures all other lights that they do not seem to be lights at all when it is shining, and instead of affording vision to the eyes it overwhelms, blinds, and deprives them of vision, since its light is excessive and unproportioned to the visual faculty. Similarly the light of faith in its abundance suppresses and overwhelms that of the intellect. For the intellect, by its own power, comprehends only natural knowledge, though it has the potency to be raised to a supernatural act whenever our Lord wishes.

2. A man of himself knows only in the natural way, that is, by means of the senses. If he is to know in this natural way, the phantasms and species of objects will have to be present either in themselves or in their likenesses; otherwise he will be incapable of knowing naturally. As the scholastic philosophers say: *Ab objecto et potentia paritur notitia* (Knowledge arises in the soul from both the faculty and the object at hand). If a person were told of objects he had never known or seen resemblances of, he would in the end have no more knowledge than before.

For example, if a man were informed that on a certain island there was an animal whose like or kind he had never seen, he would then have no more idea or image of that animal in his mind than previously, no matter how much he was told.

Another clearer example will shed more light on this subject: If a man born blind were told about the nature of the color white or yellow, he would understand absolutely nothing no matter how much instruction he received. Since he never saw these colors, nor their like, he would not have the means to form a judgment about them. Only their names would be grasped since the names are perceptible through hearing; but never their form or image, because these colors were never seen by him.

3. Such is faith to the soul—it informs us of matters we have never seen or known, either in themselves or in their likenesses; in fact nothing like them exists. The light of natural knowledge does not show us the

object of faith, since this object is unproportioned to any of the senses. Yet, we come to know it through hearing, by believing what faith teaches us, blinding our natural light and bringing it into submission. St. Paul states: *Fides ex auditu.*[1] [Rom. 10:17] This amounts to saying that faith is not a knowledge derived from the senses, but an assent of the soul to what enters through hearing.

4. Faith, moreover, far exceeds what these examples teach us. Not only does it fail to produce knowledge and science, but, as we said, it deprives and blinds a person of any other knowledge or science by which he may judge it. Other knowledge is acquired by the light of the intellect, but not the knowledge that faith gives. Faith nullifies the light of the intellect, and if this light is not darkened, the knowledge of faith is lost. Accordingly, Isaias said: *Si non credideritis, non intelligetis* (If you do not believe, you will not understand). [Is. 7:9]

Faith, manifestly, is a dark night for man, but in this very way it gives him light. The more darkness it brings upon him, the more light it sheds. For by blinding it illumines him, according to those words of Isaias that if you do not believe you will not understand, that is, you will not have light. [Is. 7:9]

Faith was foreshadowed in that cloud which separated the children of Israel, just before their entry into the Red Sea, from the Egyptians. [Ex. 14:19–20] Scripture says of the cloud: *Erat nubes tenebrosa et illuminans noctem* (The cloud was dark, and illuminative in the night). [Ex. 14:20]

5. How wonderful it was—a cloud, dark in itself, could illumine the night! This was related to illustrate how faith, a dark and obscure cloud to man (also a night in that it blinds and deprives him of his natural light), illumines and pours light into the darkness of his soul by means of its own darkness. This is fitting that the disciple be like the master.

A man in darkness does not receive adequate enlightenment save by another darkness, according to David's teaching: *Dies diei eructat verbum et nox nocti indicat scientiam* (The day brims over and breathes speech to the day, and the night manifests knowledge to the night). [Ps. 18:3] Expressed more clearly, this means: The day, which is God (in bliss where it is day), communicates and pronounces the Word, His Son, to the angels and blessed souls, who are now day; and this He does that they may have knowledge and enjoyment of Him. And the night, which is the faith present in the Church Militant, where it is still night, manifests knowledge to the Church and, consequently, to every soul. This knowledge is night to a man because he does not yet possess the clear, beatific wisdom, and because faith blinds him as to his own natural light.

[1] Faith depends on hearing.

6. Our deduction is that since faith is a dark night, it illumines the soul that is in darkness. We verify, then, David's assertion on this matter: *Et nox illuminatio in deliciis meis* (Night will be my illumination in the midst of my delights). [Ps. 138:11] This amounts to saying: The night of faith will be my guide in the delights of my pure contemplation and union with God. By this passage David clearly informs us of the darkness demanded on this road if a soul is to receive light.

CHAPTER 4

A general discussion of the darkness of soul required for the effective guidance through faith to supreme contemplation.

1. I believe you are learning how faith is a dark night for the soul, and how the soul as well must be dark—or in darkness as to its own light—that it may allow itself to be guided by faith to this high goal of union. But for knowledge of how to do this, a somewhat more detailed explanation of the darkness required for entering this abyss of faith will be beneficial. In this chapter I will deal with this darkness generally. Further on, with God's help, I will present a more detailed explanation of the behavior necessary for obviating error in faith and any encumbrance to its guidance.

2. I affirm, then, that if a person takes faith as a good guide to this state, he must not only live in darkness in the sensory and lower part of his nature (concerning creatures and temporal things), which we have already discussed, but he must also darken and blind himself in that part of his nature which bears relation to God and spiritual things. This latter part, which we are now discussing, is the rational and higher portion of his nature.

The attainment of supernatural transformation manifestly demands a darkening of the soul and an elevation above all the sensory and rational parts of nature. For the word "supernatural" indicates that which is above nature; nature, consequently, remains beneath.

Since this transformation and union is something that falls beyond the reach of the senses and of human capability, the soul must empty itself perfectly and voluntarily—I mean in its affection and will—of all the earthly and heavenly things it can grasp. It must through its own efforts empty itself insofar as it can. As for God, who will stop Him from accomplishing His desires in the soul that is resigned, annihilated, and despoiled?

Insofar as he is capable, a person must void himself of all, so that, however many supernatural communications he receives, he will continually live as though denuded of them and in darkness. Like a blind man he must lean on dark faith, accept it for his guide and light, and rest on nothing of what he understands, tastes, feels, or imagines. All these perceptions are a darkness that will lead him astray. Faith lies beyond all this understanding, taste, feeling, and imagining.

If he does not blind himself in these things and abide in total darkness, he will not reach what is greater—the teaching of faith.

3. A man who is not yet entirely blind will not allow a good guide to lead him. Still able to perceive a little, he thinks that road he sees is the best, for he is unable to see other and better ones. And because he is the one giving the orders, he will consequently lead astray his young guide who has better vision. Similarly, if the soul in traveling this road leans upon any elements of its own knowledge or experience of God, it will easily go astray or be detained for not having desired to abide in complete blindness, in faith which is its guide. For, however impressive may be one's knowledge or feeling of God, that knowledge or feeling will have no resemblance to God and amount to very little.

4. St. Paul implied this in his assertion: *Accedentem ad Deum oportet credere quod est* (He who would approach union with God should believe in His existence). [Heb. 11:6] This is like saying: To attain union with God, a person should advance neither by understanding, nor by the support of his own experience, nor by feeling or imagination, but by belief in God's being. For God's being cannot be grasped by the intellect, appetite, imagination, or any other sense, nor can it be known in this life. The most that can be felt and tasted of God in this life is infinitely distant from God and the pure possession of Him. Isaias and St. Paul affirm: *Nec oculus videt, nec auris audivit, nec in cor hominis ascendit quae praeparavit Deus iis qui diligunt illum* (No eye has ever seen, nor ear heard, nor has the heart or thought of man ever grasped what God has prepared for those who love Him). [Is. 64:4; 1 Cor. 2:9]

Now a man may be striving for a perfect union in this life through grace with that to which through glory he will be united in the next (with what St. Paul says eye has not seen, nor ear heard, nor the heart of carnal man grasped). But, manifestly, the perfect union in this life through grace and love demands that he live in darkness to all the objects of sight, hearing, imagination, and everything comprehensible to the heart, that is, to the soul.

A man, then, is decidedly hindered from the attainment of this high state of union with God when he is attached to any understanding, feeling, imagining, opinion, desire, or way of his own, or to any other of his works or affairs, and knows not how to detach and denude himself of these impediments. His goal transcends all of this, even the loftiest object that can be known or experienced. Consequently, he must pass beyond everything to unknowing.

5. As regards this road to union, entering on the road means leaving one's own road, or better, moving on to the goal; and turning from one's own mode implies entry into what has no mode, that is, God. A person who reaches this state no longer has any modes or methods, still less is he—nor can he be—attached to them. I am referring to modes of understanding, taste, and feeling. Within himself, though, he possesses all methods, like one who though having nothing yet possesses all things. [2 Cor. 6:10] By being courageous enough to pass beyond the interior and exterior limits of his nature, he enters within supernatural bounds— bounds that have no mode, yet in substance possess all modes. To reach the supernatural bounds a person must depart from his natural bounds and leave self far off in respect to his interior and exterior limits in order to mount from a low state to the highest.

6. Passing beyond all that is naturally and spiritually intelligible or comprehensible, a person ought to desire with all his might to attain what in this life is unknowable and unimaginable. And parting company with all he can, or does, taste and feel, temporally and spiritually, he must ardently long to acquire what surpasses all taste and feeling. To be empty and free for the achievement of this, he should by no means seize upon what he receives spiritually or sensitively (as we shall explain in our particular discussion of this matter), but consider it of little import. The higher rank and esteem a man gives to all his knowledge, experience, and imagining (whether spiritual or not), the more he subtracts from the Supreme Good and the more he delays in his journey toward Him. And the less he esteems what he can possess relative to the Supreme Good—however estimable it may be—the more he values and prizes Him, and, consequently, the closer he comes to Him. In this way, in obscurity, a man swiftly approaches union by means of faith, which is also dark. And in this way faith gives him wondrous light. Obviously, if a person should desire to see, he would be in darkness as regards God more quickly than if he opened his eyes to the blinding brightness of the sun.

7. By blinding his faculties along this road, a man will see light, as the Saviour proclaims in the Gospel: *In judicium veni in hunc mundum: ut qui non vident, videant, et qui vident caeci fiant* (I have come into this world for judgment, that they who see not, may see, and that they who see may become blind). [Jn. 9:39] Literally, these words should be understood in reference to the spiritual road, that is: Anyone who lives in darkness and blinds himself of all his natural lights will have supernatural

vision, and anyone who wants to lean on some light of his own will become blind and be held back on this road leading to union.

8. That we may continue less confusedly, I believe it will be necessary in the following chapter to explain this reality we call union with God. Since an understanding of the nature of union will shed more light on the subsequent doctrine, I think this is the suitable place for a discussion of it. Although our thread of thought will be interrupted, we will not be digressing, because an explanation of this union will serve in illustration of the matter we are treating. The following chapter will be like a parenthesis within the same enthymeme, since in this second night we plan to treat of the relationship of the three faculties of the soul to the three theological virtues.

CHAPTER 5

Explanation of the nature of union with God. An illustration.

1. In our previous discussion, we have already given some indication of the meaning of the phrase "union of the soul with God." Thus our teaching here about the nature of this union will be more understandable.

It is not my intention now to discuss the divisions and parts of this union. Indeed, I would never finish were I to begin explaining the union of the intellect, or that of the will, or of the memory, or to try to expound the nature of the transitory and the permanent union in each of these faculties, or the significance of the total, the transitory, or the permanent union wrought in these three faculties together. We shall discuss all this frequently in the course of our treatise. But such an exposition is unnecessary for an understanding of what we now wish to state about these different unions. A better explanation of them will be given in sections dealing with the subject, and then we shall have a concrete example to go with the actual teaching. In those sections the reader will note and understand the union being discussed and will form a better judgment of it.

2. Here I only intend to discuss this total and permanent union in the substance and faculties of the soul. And I shall be speaking of the obscure habit of union, for we will explain later, with God's help, how a permanent actual union of the faculties in this life is impossible; such a union can only be transient.

3. To understand the nature of this union, one should first know that God sustains every soul and dwells in it substantially, even though it may be that of the greatest sinner in the world. This union between God and creatures always exists. By it He conserves their being so that if the

union would end they would immediately be annihilated and cease to exist.

Consequently, in discussing union with God, we are not discussing the substantial union which is always existing, but the union and transformation of the soul in God. This union is not always existing, but we find it only where there is likeness of love. We will call it "the union of likeness," and the former "the essential or substantial union." The union of likeness is supernatural, the other natural. The supernatural union exists when God's will and the soul's are in conformity, so that nothing in the one is repugnant to the other. When the soul completely rids itself of what is repugnant and unconformed to the divine will, it rests transformed in God through love.

4. The lack of conformity with God's will can be not only in one's acts, but in one's habits as well. Not only must actual voluntary imperfections cease, but habitual imperfections must be annihilated too.

No creature, none of its actions and abilities can reach or express God's nature. Consequently a man must strip himself of all creatures and of his actions and abilities (of his understanding, taste, and feeling) so that when everything unlike and unconformed to God is cast out, his soul may receive the likeness of God, since nothing contrary to the will of God will be left in him, and thus he will be transformed in God.

It is true that God is ever present in the soul, as we said, and thereby bestows and preserves its natural being by His sustaining presence. Yet He does not always communicate supernatural being to it. He communicates supernatural being only through love and grace, which not all souls possess. And those who do, do not have it in the same degree. Some have attained higher degrees of love, others remain in lower degrees. God communicates Himself more to the soul more advanced in love, that is, more conformed to His will. A person who has reached complete conformity and likeness of will has attained total supernatural union and transformation in God.

Manifestly, then, the more a person through attachment and habit is clothed with his own abilities and with creatures, the less disposed he is for this union. For he does not afford God full opportunity to transform his soul into the supernatural. As a result, a man has nothing more to do than strip his soul of these natural contrarieties and dissimilarities so that God who is naturally communicating Himself to it through nature may do so supernaturally through grace.

5. This is what St. John meant when he said: *Qui non ex sanguinibus, neque ex voluntate carnis, neque ex voluntate viri, sed ex Deo nati sunt* [Jn. 1:13], which can be interpreted: He gives power for becoming the children of God (for being transformed in God) only to those who are

born not of blood (not of natural complexion and humors), nor of the will of the flesh (the free will included in the natural aptitude and capacity), nor even less of the will of man (which includes every mode and manner by which the intellect judges and understands). To none of these has He conferred the power of becoming the children of God; only to those who are born of God (those who, in their rebirth through grace and death to everything of the old man, rise above themselves to the supernatural and receive from God this rebirth and sonship which transcends everything imaginable).

St. John affirms elsewhere: *Nisi quis renatus fuerit ex aqua et spiritu Sancto non potest videre regnum Dei* (He who is not reborn in the Holy Spirit will be unable to see the kingdom of God, which is the state of perfection). [Jn. 3:5] To be reborn in the Holy Spirit during this life is to become most like God in purity, without any mixture of imperfection. Accordingly, pure transformation can be effected—although not essentially—through the participation of union.

6. Here is an example that will provide a better understanding of this explanation. A ray of sunlight shining upon a smudgy window is unable to illumine that window completely and transform it into its own light. It could do this if the window were cleaned and polished. The less film and stain are wiped away, the less the window will be illumined; and the cleaner the window is, the brighter will be its illumination. The extent of illumination is not dependent upon the ray of sunlight but upon the window. If the window is totally clean and pure, the sunlight will so transform and illumine it that to all appearances the window will be identical with the ray of sunlight and shine just as the sun's ray. Although obviously the nature of the window is distinct from that of the sun's ray (even if the two seem identical), we can assert that the window is the ray or light of the sun by participation.

The soul upon which the divine light of God's being is ever shining, or better, in which it is always dwelling by nature, is like this window, as we have affirmed.

7. A man makes room for God by wiping away all the smudges and smears of creatures, by uniting his will perfectly to God's; for to love is to labor to divest and deprive oneself for God of all that is not God. When this is done the soul will be illumined by and transformed in God. And God will so communicate His supernatural being to it that it will appear to be God Himself and will possess all that God Himself has.

When God grants this supernatural favor to the soul, so great a union is caused that all the things of both God and the soul become one in participant transformation, and the soul appears to be God more than a soul. Indeed, it is God by participation. Yet truly, its being (even though transformed) is naturally as distinct from God's as it was before, just as the window, although illumined by the ray, has an existence distinct from the ray.

8. Consequently, we understand with greater clarity that the preparation for this union, as we said, is not an understanding by the soul, nor the taste, feeling, or imagining of God or any other object, but purity and love, which is the stripping off and perfect renunciation of all these experiences for God alone. Also we clearly see how perfect transformation is impossible without perfect purity, and how the illumination of the soul and its union with God corresponds to the measure of its purity. The illumination will not be perfect until the soul is entirely cleansed, clear, and perfect.

9. The following example will also shed light on the nature of this union. Let us imagine a perfect painting with many finely wrought details and delicate, subtle adornments, including some so delicate and subtle that they are not wholly discernible. Now one whose sense of sight is not too clear and refined will discover less detail and delicacy in the painting; he whose vision is somewhat purer will discover more details and perfections; and another with yet clearer vision will find still more perfection; finally, the one who possesses the clearest faculty will discern the greatest number of excellent qualities and perfections. There is so much to behold in the painting that no matter how much one sees in it, still more remains unseen.

10. We can make the same application to souls in their relationship with God in this illumination and transformation. Although a person may have truly reached union, this union will be proportioned to his lesser or greater capacity, for not all souls attain an identical degree of union. This depends on what the Lord wishes to grant each one. Here we have a resemblance to the saints' vision of God in heaven: some see more, others less, but all see Him and are happy owing to the satisfaction of their capacity.

11. In this life we may encounter individuals who are in the state of perfection and enjoying equal peace and tranquillity, and the capacity of each will be satisfied, yet one may be many degrees higher than the other. A person who does not reach purity in the measure of his capacity never achieves true peace and satisfaction, for he will not have attained in his faculties the nakedness and emptiness required for the simple union.

CHAPTER 6

The theological virtues perfect the faculties of the soul and produce emptiness and darkness in them.

1. We must discuss the method of leading the three faculties (intellect, memory, and will) into this spiritual night, the means to divine union. But we must first explain how the theological virtues (faith, hope, and charity, related to these faculties as their proper supernatural objects, and through which the soul is united with God) cause the same emptiness and darkness in their respective faculties: faith in the intellect, hope in the memory, and charity in the will. Then we shall explain how in order to journey to God the intellect must be perfected in the darkness of faith, the memory in the emptiness of hope, and the will in the nakedness and absence of every affection.

As a result, the necessity of the soul's journey through this dark night with the support of these three virtues will be manifest. They darken and empty it of all things that its advancement along this spiritual road may be more secure. As we said, the soul is not united with God in this life through understanding, nor through enjoyment, nor through imagination, nor through any other sense; but only faith, hope, and charity (according to the intellect, memory, and will) can unite the soul with God in this life.

2. These virtues, as we said, void the faculties: Faith causes darkness and a void of understanding in the intellect, hope begets an emptiness of possessions in the memory, and charity produces the nakedness and emptiness of affection and joy in all that is not God.

Faith, we know, affirms what cannot be understood by the intellect. St. Paul refers to it *ad Hebraeos* in this way: *Fides est sperandarum substantia rerum, argumentum non apparentium.* [Heb. 11:1] In relation to our discussion here, this means that faith is the substance of things to be hoped for and that these things are not manifest to the intellect, even though its consent to them is firm and certain. If they were manifest, there would be no faith. For though faith brings certitude to the intellect, it does not produce clarity, but only darkness.

3. Hope, also, undoubtedly puts the memory in darkness and emptiness as regards all earthly and heavenly objects. Hope always pertains to the unpossessed object. If something were possessed there could no longer be hope for it. St. Paul says *ad Romanos: Spes quae videtur, non est spes; nam quod videt quis, quid sperat?* (Hope that is seen is not hope, for how does a man hope for what he sees—that is, what he possesses?). [Rom.

8:24] As a result this virtue also occasions emptiness, since it is concerned with unpossessed things and not with the possessed object.

4. Charity, too, causes a void in the will regarding all things, since it obliges us to love God above everything. A man has to withdraw his affection from all in order to center it wholly upon God. Christ says through St. Luke: *Qui non renuntiat omnibus quae possidet, non potest meus esse discipulus* (He who does not renounce all that he possesses with his will cannot be my disciple). [Lk. 14:33]

Consequently, these three virtues place a soul in darkness and emptiness in respect to all things.

5. That parable our Redeemer told in the eleventh chapter of St. Luke is noteworthy here. [Lk. 11:5] He related that a man went to a friend at midnight to ask for three loaves (symbolizing these three virtues). And He asserted that the man asked for them at midnight to indicate that the soul must acquire these three virtues by a darkness in its faculties regarding all things, and must perfect itself in these virtues by means of this night.

In the sixth chapter of Isaias we read that the prophet saw one of the seraphim on each side of God, and that they each had six wings: with two wings they covered their feet, symbolizing the blinding and quenching of the affections of the will because of God; with two they covered their faces, symbolizing the darkness of the intellect in God's presence; and with the two remaining wings they flew, indicating both the flight of hope toward things that are not possessed and the elevation above all earthly or heavenly possessions that are not God. [Is. 6:2]

6. We must lead the faculties of the soul to these three virtues and inform each faculty with one of them by stripping and darkening it of everything which is not conformable to these virtues.

We termed this above the active spiritual night, because a person does what lies in his own power to enter this night. As we outlined for the sensory night a method of emptying the sense faculties of desire for their objects that the soul might leave the point of departure for the mean, which is faith, so for this spiritual night we will present, with the divine help, a method of emptying and purifying the spiritual faculties of all that is not God. By this method these faculties can abide in the darkness of these three virtues, which are the means and preparation for the soul's union with God.

7. This method provides complete security against the cunning of the devil and the power of self-love in all its ramifications. Usually self-love subtly deceives and hinders the journey of spiritual persons along this road, because they do not know how to denude and govern themselves by means of these three virtues. They have no success, therefore, in

finding the substance and purity of spiritual good; neither do they journey by as straight and short a road as they might.

8. Remember that I am now addressing those especially who have begun to enter the state of contemplation; with regard to beginners this journey should be discussed somewhat more completely. We will do this with God's help in the second book when we deal with the characteristics of beginners.

CHAPTER 7

The extreme narrowness of the path leading to eternal life. The denudation and freedom required of those who tread it. The nakedness of the intellect.

1. I would need greater knowledge and perfection than I possess to treat of the denudation and purity of the three faculties of the soul. For we would desire to give clear instructions to spiritual persons on the narrowness of the way leading to eternal life—that narrowness of which Our Saviour spoke—so that convinced of this they would not marvel at the emptiness and nakedness in which we must leave the faculties of the soul in this night.

2. We ought to record carefully the words Our Saviour, in Chapter 7 of St. Matthew's Gospel, spoke about this road: *Quam angusta porta et arcta via est quae ducit ad vitam! Et pauci sunt qui inveniunt eam* (How narrow is the gate and straight the way that leads to life! And few there are who find it). [Mt. 7:14]
We should note particularly in this passage the exaggeration and hyperbolism conveyed by the word *quam*. Considering the emphatic use of *quam*, the phrase could be reworded: Indeed the gate is very narrow, more so than you think.
We must also be mindful that first He says the gate is narrow to teach that entrance through this gate of Christ (the beginning of the journey) involves a divestment and narrowing of the will in relation to all sensible and temporal objects by loving God more than all of them. This task belongs to the night of sense, as we have said.
Next He asserts that the way (of perfection) is straight in order to teach that the journey along this way includes entry through the narrow gate, a void of sense objects, and also a "straitening" of oneself through the dispossession and removal of obstacles in matters relating to the spiritual part of the soul.

3. We can apply, then, what Christ says about the narrow gate to the sensitive portion of man, and what He says about the straight way to the

spiritual or rational part of his soul. Since He proclaims that few find it, we ought to note the cause: Few there are with the knowledge and desire for entering upon this supreme nakedness and emptiness of spirit. As this path on the high mount of perfection is narrow and steep, it demands travelers who are not weighed down by the lower part of their nature, nor burdened in the higher part. This is a venture in which God alone is sought and gained, thus only God ought to be sought and gained.

4. Obviously a man's journey must not only exclude the hindrance of creatures, but also embody a dispossession and annihilation in the spiritual part of his nature. Our Lord, for our instruction and guidance along this road, imparted that wonderful teaching—I think it is possible to affirm that the more necessary the doctrine the less it is practiced by spiritual persons—which I will quote fully and explain in its genuine and spiritual sense because of its importance and relevance to our subject. He states in the eighth chapter of St. Mark: *Si quis vult me sequi, deneget semetipsum et tollat crucem suam et sequatur me. Qui enim voluerit animam suam salvam facere, perdet eam; qui autem perdiderit animam suam propter me . . . salvam faciet eam* (If anyone wishes to follow My way, let him deny himself, take up his cross and follow Me. For he who would save his soul shall lose it, but he who loses it for Me shall gain it). [Mk. 8:34–35]

5. O, who can make this counsel of Our Saviour understandable, and practicable, and attractive that spiritual persons might become aware of the difference between the method many of them think is good and that which ought to be used in traveling this road!

They are of the opinion that any kind of withdrawal from the world or reformation of life suffices. Some are content with a certain degree of virtue, perseverance in prayer, and mortification, but never achieve the nakedness, poverty, selflessness, or spiritual purity (which are all the same) that the Lord counsels us here. For they still feed and clothe their natural selves with spiritual feelings and consolations rather than divesting and denying themselves of these for God's sake. They think a denial of self in worldly matters is sufficient without an annihilation and purification of spiritual possessions. It happens that, when some of this solid, perfect food (the annihilation of all sweetness in God—the pure spiritual cross and nakedness of Christ's poverty of spirit) is offered them in dryness, distaste, and trial, they run from it as from death and wander about in search only of sweetness and delightful communications from God. Such an attitude is not the hallmark of self-denial and nakedness of spirit, but the indication of a "spiritual sweet tooth."

Through this kind of conduct they become, spiritually speaking, enemies of the cross of Christ. [Phil. 3:18]

A genuine spirit seeks the distasteful in God rather than the delectable, leans more toward suffering than toward consolation, more toward going without everything for God rather than toward possession. It prefers dryness and affliction to sweet consolation. It knows that this is the significance of following Christ and denying self, that the other method is perhaps a seeking of self in God—something entirely contrary to love. Seeking oneself in God is the same as looking for the caresses and consolations of God. Seeking God in oneself entails not only the desire of doing without these consolations for God's sake, but also the inclination to choose for love of Christ all that is most distasteful whether in God or in the world—and such is the love of God.

6. O, who can explain the extent of the denial Our Lord wishes of us! This negation must be similar to a complete temporal, natural, and spiritual death, that is, in reference to esteem of the will which is the source of all denial.

Our Saviour referred to this when He declared: *He that wishes to save his life shall lose it* (if anyone wants to possess something, or seeks it for himself, he will lose it); *and he who loses his soul for My sake, the same shall gain it.* [Mt. 16:25; Lk. 9:24] The latter affirmation signifies: He who renounces for Christ all that his will can desire and enjoy by choosing what bears closer resemblance to the cross—which Our Lord in St. John terms hating one's own soul [Jn. 22:25]—the same will gain it.

His Majesty taught this to those two disciples who came to ask Him for places at His right and left. Without responding to their request for glory, He offered them the chalice He was about to drink as something safer and more precious on this earth than enjoyment. [Mt. 20:22]

7. This chalice symbolizes death to one's natural self through denudation and annihilation. As a result of this death a man is able to walk along the narrow path in the sensitive part of his soul, as we said, and in its spiritual part (in his understanding, joy, and feeling). Accordingly, one can attain to dispossession in both parts of the soul. Not only this, but even in his spirit a person will be unhindered in his journey on the narrow road, for on this road there is room only for self-denial (as Our Saviour asserts) and the cross. The cross is a supporting staff and greatly lightens and eases the journey.

Our Lord proclaimed through St. Matthew: *My yoke is sweet and my burden* (the cross) *light.* [Mt. 11:30] If a man resolutely submits to the carrying of this cross, if he decidedly wants to find and endure trial in all things for God, he will discover in all of them great relief and sweetness. This will be so because he journeys the road denuded of all and with no desire for anything. If he aims after the possession of something, from God or elsewhere, his journey will not be one of nakedness and detachment from all things, and consequently there will be no room for him on this narrow path nor will he be able to climb it.

8. I should like to persuade spiritual persons that the road leading to God does not entail a multiplicity of considerations, methods, manners, and experiences—though in their own way these may be a requirement for beginners—but demands only the one thing necessary: true self-denial, exterior and interior, through surrender of self both to suffering for Christ and to annihilation in all things. In the exercise of this self-denial everything else, and even more, is discovered and accomplished. If one fails in this exercise, the root and sum total of all the virtues, the other methods would amount to no more than going about in circles without any progress, even if they result in considerations and communications as lofty as those of the angels. A man makes progress only through imitation of Christ Who is the Way, the Truth, and the Life. No one goes to the Father but through Him, as He states Himself in St. John. [Jn. 14:6] Elsewhere He says: *I am the door, if any man enter by Me he shall be saved.* [Jn. 10:9] Accordingly, I should not consider any spirituality worthwhile that would walk in sweetness and ease and run from the imitation of Christ.

9. Because I have said that Christ is the way and that this way is a death to our natural selves in the sensory and spiritual parts of the soul, I would like to demonstrate how this death is patterned on Christ's. For He is our model and light.

10. First, during His life He died spiritually to the sensitive part, and at His death He died naturally. He proclaimed during His life that He had no place whereon to lay His head. [Mt. 8:20] And at His death He had less.

11. Second, at the moment of His death He was certainly annihilated in His soul, without any consolation or relief, since the Father left Him that way in innermost aridity in the lower part. He was thereby compelled to cry out: *My God, My God, why have You forsaken me?* [Mt. 27:46] This was the most extreme abandonment, sensitively, that He had suffered in His life. And by it He accomplished the most marvelous work of His whole life, surpassing all the works and deeds and miracles that He had ever performed on earth or in heaven. That is, He brought about the reconciliation and union of the human race with God through grace. The Lord achieved this, as I say, at the moment in which He was most annihilated in all things: in His reputation before men, since in beholding Him die they mocked Him instead of esteeming Him; in His human nature, by dying; and in spiritual help and consolation from His Father, for He was forsaken by His Father at that

time so as to pay the debt fully and bring man to union with God. David says of Him: *Ad nihilum redactus sum et nescivi*[2] [Ps. 72:22], that the true spiritual person might understand the mystery of the door and way (which is Christ) leading to union with God, and that he might realize that his union with God and the greatness of the work he accomplishes will be measured by his annihilation for God in the sensory and spiritual parts of his soul. When he is brought to nothing, the highest degree of humility, the spiritual union between his soul and God will be effected. This union is the most noble and sublime state attainable in this life. The journey, then, does not consist in recreations, experiences, and spiritual feelings, but in the living, sensory and spiritual, exterior and interior death of the cross.

12. I will not enlarge upon this, though I would like to continue discussing the matter, because from my observations Christ is to a great extent unknown by those who consider themselves His friends. Because of their extreme self-love they go about seeking in Him their own consolations and satisfactions. But they do not seek, out of great love for Him, His bitter trials and deaths.

I am referring to those who believe themselves His friends; not to those who live withdrawn and afar off from Him, men of extensive learning and high repute, and any others living yonder with the world, anxious about their pretensions and rank. These men, we can affirm, do not know Christ. However prosperous the end of their lives may seem, it will be in fact most bitter to them. On judgment day they will be spoken of, for they are the ones to whom we should first speak this word of God. [Acts 13:46] Because of their learning and higher state, they are the ones whom God intended as the target for this doctrine.

13. Let us address the intellect of the spiritual man, particularly of him whom God has favored with the state of contemplation, for, as I asserted, I am now speaking especially to these individuals. We shall discuss the direction of self to God through faith, and the purification of what is contrary to faith so that the soul by "straitening" itself may enter upon the narrow path of obscure contemplation.

CHAPTER 8

No creature or knowledge comprehensible to the intellect can serve it as a proximate means for the divine union with God.

1. Before dealing with faith, the proper and adequate means of union with God, we should prove how nothing created or imagined can serve

2 I was brought to nothing and did not understand.

the intellect as a proper means for union with God, and how all that can be grasped by the intellect would serve as an obstacle rather than a means, if a person were to become attached to it.

This chapter will contain a general proof of this; afterwards we shall discuss in particular the knowledge which the intellect can receive through the interior or exterior senses. We shall also deal with the difficulty and harm occasioned by these exterior and interior ideas, for due to them the intellect does not advance with the support of faith, which is the proper means.

2. Let it be recalled, then, that according to a philosophical axiom all means must be proportionate to their end. That is, they must manifest a certain accord with and likeness to the end—of such a degree that they would be sufficient for the attainment of the desired goal.

For example, if a man wants to reach a city, he must necessarily take the road, the means, that leads to the city.

As another example: If fire is to be united with a log of wood, it is necessary for heat, the means, to prepare the log first with a certain likeness and proportion to the fire. This is done by communicating to the wood a particular amount of heat. Now if anyone wanted to prepare the log by an inadequate means, such as air, water, or earth, there would be no possibility of union between the log and the fire, just as it would be impossible to reach the city without taking the proper road that connects with it.

If the intellect, then, is to reach union with God in this life, insofar as is possible, it must take that means which bears a proximate likeness to God and unites with Him.

3. It is noteworthy that among all creatures both superior and inferior none bears a likeness to God's being or unites proximately with Him. Though truly, as theologians say, all creatures carry with them a certain relationship to God and a trace of Him (greater or less according to the perfection of their being), yet God has no relation or essential likeness to them. Rather the difference which lies between His divine being and their being is infinite. Consequently, intellectual comprehension of God through heavenly or earthly creatures is impossible, since there is no proportion of likeness.

David proclaims in reference to heavenly creatures: *There is none among the gods like You, O Lord!* [Ps. 85:8], thereby calling the angels and saints gods. And elsewhere he declares: *O God, your way is in the holy place, what great God is there like our God?* [Ps. 76:14] This was equivalent to saying that the way of approach to You, O God, is a holy way, namely, purity of faith. For what god can be great enough (that is, what angel so elevated in being, or saint in glory) to serve as an adequate and sufficient approach to You?

David also proclaims of earthly and heavenly things: *The Lord is high up and looks at low things, and the high things He knows from afar.* [Ps. 137:6] In other words: High in His own being, He looks at the being of objects here below as exceedingly low in comparison with His high being; and the high things, the heavenly creatures, He knows to be far distant from His own being.

Thus, no creature can serve the intellect as a proportionate means to the attainment of God.

4. Nothing which could possibly be imagined or comprehended in this life can be a proximate means of union with God.

In our natural way of knowing, the intellect can only grasp an object through the forms and phantasms of things perceived by the bodily senses. Since these objects cannot serve as a means, the intellect cannot profit from its natural knowing.

As for the supernatural way of knowing, the intellect according to the possibilities of its ordinary power is neither capable nor prepared, while in the prison of the body, for the reception of the clear knowledge of God. Such knowledge does not belong to this state, since death is a necessary condition for possessing it.

God told Moses, who had asked for this clear knowledge, that no one would be able to see Him: *No man shall see Me and remain alive.* [Ex. 33:20] St. John exclaims: *No man has ever seen God nor anything like Him.* [Jn. 1:18] And St. Paul with Isaias says: *Eye has not seen, nor ear heard, nor has it entered into the heart of man.* [1 Cor. 2:9; Is. 64:4] This is why Moses, as affirmed in the Acts of the Apostles, dared not look at the bush while God was present, because, in conformity with his feelings about God, he thought his intellect was powerless to look fittingly upon Him. [Acts 7:30–32] It is told of our Father Elias that on the mount he covered his face (blinded his intellect) in the presence of God. [3 Kgs. 19:11–13] He did this because he did not dare, in his lowliness, to gaze on something so lofty, and he realized that anything he might behold or understand particularly would be far distant from God and most unlike Him.

5. In this mortal life no supernatural knowledge or apprehension can serve as a proximate means for the high union with God through love. Everything the intellect can understand, the will experience, and the imagination picture is most unlike and disproportioned to God, as we have said.

Isaias brought this out admirably in a noteworthy passage: *To what have you been able to liken God? Or what image will you fashion like to Him? Will the ironsmith by chance be able to cast a statue? Or will the goldsmith be able to mold Him out of gold, or the silversmith with plates of silver?* [Is. 40:18–19]

The ironsmith signifies the intellect whose work is to form the concept by removing the iron of sensible species and phantasms.

The goldsmith symbolizes the will which is capable of receiving the figure and form of delight caused by the gold of love.

The silversmith, who was unable to fashion Him from plates of silver, typifies both the memory and the imagination. The concepts and images which these powers mold and construct can easily be likened to plates of silver.

It is as if Isaias had said that the intellect will not be able through its ideas to understand anything like God, nor the will experience a delight and sweetness resembling Him, nor the memory place in the phantasy remembrances and images representing Him.

Manifestly, then, none of these ideas can serve the intellect as a proximate means leading to God. In order to draw nearer the divine ray the intellect must advance by unknowing rather than by the desire to know, and by blinding itself and remaining in darkness rather than by opening its eyes.

6. Contemplation, consequently, by which the intellect has a higher knowledge of God, is called mystical theology, meaning the secret wisdom of God. For this wisdom is secret to the very intellect that receives it. St. Dionysius on this account refers to contemplation as a ray of darkness. [Pseudo-Dionysius Areopagita, *De Mystica Theologia*, c.1 §1: PG 3, 999] The prophet Baruch declares of this wisdom: *There is no one who knows its way or can think of its paths.* [Bar. 3:23] To reach union with God the intellect must obviously blind itself to all the paths along which it can travel. Aristotle teaches that just as the sun is total darkness to the eyes of a bat, so the brightest light in God is complete darkness to our intellect. And he teaches in addition that the loftier and clearer the things of God are in themselves, the more unknown and obscure they are to us. [*Metaphys.*, lib. brevior, c.1, ed. Didot, II, 486] The Apostle also affirms this teaching: That which is highest in God is least known by men. [Rom. 11:33]

7. We would never finish if we continued to quote passages and present arguments as proof that there is no ladder among all created, knowable things by which the intellect can reach this high Lord. Rather, it should be known that if the intellect did desire to use all or any of these objects as a proximate means to this union, they would be not merely an encumbrance to it, but also an occasion of many errors and deceptions in the ascent of this mount.

CHAPTER 9

Faith is the proximate and proportionate means to the intellect for the attainment of the divine union of love. Proofs from passages and figures of sacred Scripture.

1. We can gather from what has been said that to be prepared for this divine union the intellect must be cleansed and emptied of everything relating to sense, divested and liberated of everything clearly apprehensible, inwardly pacified and silenced, and supported by faith alone, which is the only proximate and proportionate means to union with God. For the likeness between faith and God is so close that no other difference exists than that between believing in God and seeing Him. Just as God is infinite, faith proposes Him to us as infinite; as there are Three Persons in the One God, it presents Him to us in this way; and as God is darkness to our intellect, so does faith dazzle and blind us. Only by means of faith, in divine light exceeding all understanding, does God manifest Himself to the soul. The more intense a man's faith, the closer is his union with God.

St. Paul indicated this in the passage cited above: *He who would be united with God must believe.* [Heb. 11:6] This means that a man must walk by faith in his journey to God. The intellect must be blind and dark, and abide in faith alone, because it is joined with God under this cloud. And as David proclaims, God is hidden under the cloud: *He set darkness under His feet. And He rose above the cherubim and flew upon the wings of the wind. He made darkness and the dark water His hiding place.* [Ps. 17:10-12]

2. This darkness under God's feet and of His hiding place, and the dark water of His dwelling denote the obscurity of faith in which He is enclosed. The verse stating that He rose above the cherubim and flew upon the wings of the wind alludes to how God soars above all understanding. The cherubim typify those who understand or contemplate; the wings of the wind signify the subtle ideas and lofty concepts of the spirit; above these is His being, which no man can reach through his own efforts.

3. In Scripture we read figuratively of this that when Solomon had completed the Temple, God descended in darkness and filled it so that the children of Israel were unable to see; Solomon then said: *The Lord has promised to dwell in darkness.* [3 Kgs. 8:12] God was also covered with darkness when He appeared to Moses on the mount. [Ex. 24:16] And as often as God communicated at length with someone, He appeared

in darkness. This is evident in the Book of Job, where Scripture asserts that God spoke to Job from the dark air. [Jb. 38:1; 40:1]

All this darkness symbolizes the obscurity of faith with which the divinity is clothed while communicating itself to the soul. This darkness will be dispelled when, as St. Paul states, that which is in part (this darkness of faith) is taken away, and that which is perfect (the divine light) comes. [1 Cor. 13:10] We also find a fairly good figure of this obscurity of faith in the Scriptural narration about the militia of Gedeon. According to the account, all the soldiers held lamps in their hands, yet did not see the light because the lamps were hidden in darkness within earthenware jars. But when these jars were broken, the soldiers immediately beheld the shining light. [Jgs. 7:16-20] Faith, typified by those clay jars, contains the divine light. When faith has reached its end and is shattered by the ending and breaking of this mortal life, the glory and light of the divinity, the content of faith, will at once begin to shine.

4. Manifestly, then, union with God in this life, and direct communication with Him, demands that one be united with the darkness in which, as Solomon said [3 Kgs. 8:12], God promised to dwell, and that one approach the dark air in which God was pleased to reveal His secrets to Job. A man must take in darkness the earthenware jars of Gedeon and hold in his hands (the works of his will) the lamp (the union of love, though in the darkness of faith), so that when the clay jar of this life, which is all that impedes the light of faith, is broken, he may see God face to face in glory.

5. We must discuss now in particular all the concepts and apprehensions of the intellect, the hindrance and harm they cause along the road of faith, and the proper conduct of the soul. We do so that the soul may profit rather than suffer harm from either sensory or spiritual apprehensions.

CHAPTER 10

A division of all apprehensions and ideas comprehensible to the intellect.

1. To discuss in particular the advantage and the harm which intellectual concepts and apprehensions cause to the soul's faith, which is the means to divine union, we need to set up a division of all the natural and supernatural apprehensions of the intellect. Later, then, in a more logical order we shall be able to guide the intellect through them into the night and darkness of faith. Our division will be as concise as possible.

2. It is noteworthy that the intellect can get ideas and concepts in two ways, naturally and supernaturally.

Natural knowledge includes everything the intellect can understand by way of the bodily senses or through reflection.

Supernatural knowledge comprises everything imparted to the intellect in a way transcending its natural ability and capacity.

3. This supernatural knowledge is subdivided into corporal and spiritual.

The corporal is made up of two kinds: knowledge originating from the exterior bodily senses; and that received from the interior bodily senses, including all the imagination can apprehend, form, or fashion.

The spiritual is also made up of two kinds: distinct and particular knowledge; and vague, dark, and general knowledge.

4. The particular knowledge includes four kinds of distinct apprehensions communicated to the spirit without the means of bodily senses: visions, revelations, locutions, and spiritual feelings.

The dark and general knowledge (contemplation, which is imparted in faith) is of one kind only. We have to lead the soul to this contemplation by guiding it through all these other apprehensions, and, beginning with the first, divesting it of them.

CHAPTER 11

The impediment and harm caused by intellectual apprehensions arising from objects supernaturally represented to the exterior senses. The proper conduct of the soul in their regard.

1. The first kind of knowledge referred to in the preceding chapter is that which originates naturally. Since we already discussed this kind of knowledge in the first book where we guided the soul through the night of sense, we shall have nothing to say of it here. There we presented appropriate doctrine about this knowledge.

Our discussion in this chapter will deal only with the supernatural knowledge which reaches the intellect by way of the exterior bodily senses (sight, hearing, smell, taste, and touch). Through these senses, spiritual persons can, and usually do, perceive supernatural representations and objects.

As for sight, they are wont to have visions of images and persons from the other life: of saints, of the good and bad angels, and of unusual lights and splendors.

Through hearing they apprehend certain extraordinary words, sometimes from the envisioned persons, and at other times without seeing the one who speaks.

With the sense of smell they sometimes notice sensibly the sweetest fragrances without knowledge of their origin.

Also it happens in regard to taste that they experience very exquisite savors.

And concerning touch they feel extreme delight, at times so intense that all the bones and marrow rejoice, flourish, and bathe in it. This delight is usually termed spiritual unction, because in pure souls it passes from the spirit to the senses, and it is common with spiritual persons. It is an overflow from the affection and devotion of the sensible spirit, which each person receives in his own way.

2. It must be known that even though these apprehensions come to the bodily senses from God, one must never rely on them or accept them. A man should rather flee from them completely, and have no desire to determine whether they be good or bad. The more exterior and corporal they are, the less certain is their divine origin. God's communication is more commonly and appropriately given to the spirit, in which there is greater security and profit for the soul, than to the senses, where ordinarily there is extreme danger and room for deception. Thinking that these supernatural communications are identical with what is felt, the bodily senses usually set themselves up as arbiter and judge over them. But the communications are as different from what is felt as is the body from the soul, and sensibility from reason. The bodily sense is as ignorant of rational matters as a beast of burden. Indeed, it is more ignorant of them, and still more of spiritual matters.

3. He who esteems these apprehensions is in serious error and extreme danger of being deceived. Or at least he will hinder his spiritual growth because, as we mentioned, these corporal perceptions bear no proportion to what is spiritual. These manifestations ought always to be considered diabolical more certainly than divine. For the devil possesses greater leeway in influencing the exterior and corporal part of man. He can deceive the soul more readily through this action than through a more interior and spiritual kind.

4. The more exterior these corporal objects and forms, the less profitable they are to the interior and spiritual part of the soul. This is due to the extreme distance and disparity between the corporal and spiritual. Even though some spiritual nourishment results from these corporal communications—which is always the case when they have a divine origin—it is far less than when the communications are more spiritual and interior. As a result they are a ready occasion for the breeding of error, presumption, and vanity. Palpable, tangible, and material as they

are, they strongly affect the senses so that in one's judgment they seem more worthwhile. A man, then, forsaking faith, will follow after these communications believing that their light is the guide and means to his goal, which is union with God. But the more importance he gives to these communications the further he strays from faith, the way and means.

5. Furthermore, a person receiving these apprehensions often develops secretly a rather fine opinion of himself—that now he is someone in God's eyes. Such a view is contrary to humility.

The devil too is adept at suggesting to the individual a secret self-satisfaction which becomes truly obvious at times. He often purveys objects to the senses, affording to the sense of sight images of saints and most beautiful lights, and to the hearing, dissembled words, and to the sense of smell, fragrant odors; and he puts sweetness in one's mouth and delight in the sense of touch. He does all of this so that by enticing persons through these sensory objects he may induce them into many evils.

Such representations and feelings, consequently, must always be rejected. Even though some may be from God, this rejection is no affront to Him, neither will one upon voluntarily dismissing them cease to receive the fruit God wishes to produce through these communications.

6. The reason is that if the corporal vision or feeling of the senses has a divine origin it produces its effect in the spirit at the very moment of its perception, without allowing any deliberation about wanting or not wanting it. This is likewise so with the more interior communications. Since God grants these favors without the individual's own ability and effort, He causes the desired effect of these favors without this ability and effort, for this is an effect He produces passively in the spirit. The good effect, accordingly, does not depend upon wanting or not wanting the communication. Were fire to come into immediate contact with a person's flesh, that person's desire not to get burned would hardly be helpful, for the fire will produce its effect necessarily. So too with good visions and sensible communications: Even when a person dismisses them, they produce their effect first and foremost in the soul rather than in the body.

Those from the devil also, even though the soul does not desire them, cause in the spirit either agitation, dryness, and vanity or presumption. Yet diabolical communications are not as efficacious in doing harm as God's communications are in doing good. For the diabolical communications can only arouse the first movements without being able to move the will any further if it is unwilling to be moved. The unrest caused by them will not last long, unless the individual's lack of courage and circumspection occasion its endurance.

The divine communications, however, penetrate the soul, move the will to love, and leave their effect within. The soul, even if it wants to, can no more resist them than can a window withstand the sunlight shining on it.

7. A person should never dare accept these communications, even though, as I say, they have a divine origin. If he does, six kinds of harm will result.

First, faith will gradually diminish, for sensible experiences greatly detract from it. Faith, as we said, transcends all sense. By not closing the eyes of his soul to all these sensory apprehensions, a person strays from the means to union with God.

Second, if left unrejected they are an impediment to the spirit, because they detain it and prevent it from soaring to the invisible. This is why Our Lord told the disciples that it was fitting for Him to go that the Holy Spirit might come. [Jn. 16:7] And so that Mary Magdalen would be grounded in faith, He refused to allow her to touch His feet. [Jn. 20:17]

Third, the soul begins to develop a possessive attitude toward these communications and fails to continue on its journey to genuine renunciation and nakedness of spirit.

Fourth, a man gradually loses the effect of these communications and the interior spirituality they produce, because he sets his eyes upon their sensible aspect, which is the least part of them. As a consequence he does not acquire so copiously the spirituality they cause. This spirituality is preserved and more deeply impressed in the soul if the sensible element, which is far different from pure spirituality, is denied.

Fifth, a man gradually loses God's favors, because he receives them as if they belonged to himself, and does not profit well by them. Taking them as his own and failing to profit by them is the same as desiring to receive them. God does not bestow them so that the recipient may desire them, for a person must never decidedly believe that they are from God.

Sixth, through the desire of accepting them one opens the door to the devil. The devil can then deceive one by other communications expertly feigned and diguised as genuine. In the words of the Apostle, he can transform himself into an angel of light. [2 Cor. 11:14] We shall discuss this matter, with God's help, in the third book, in the chapter on spiritual gluttony.

8. Regardless of the cause of these apprehensions, it is always good for a man to reject them with closed eyes. If he fails to do so, he will make room for those having a diabolical origin and empower the devil to impose his communications. Not only this, but the diabolical representations will multiply while those from God will gradually cease, so that eventually all will come from the devil and none at all from God. This has occurred with many incautious and uninstructed people who in

their sureness concerning the reception of these communications encountered real difficulty in returning to God through purity of faith. Many have been unable to return because of the deep roots the devil has taken in them. Consequently, it is expedient to be closed to these communications and to deny them all, for in this way diabolical errors coming from the bad apprehensions are eliminated, the hindrance to faith occasioned by the good communications is avoided, and the spirit gathers the fruit.

If a person admits these communications, God will gradually withdraw them. For by considering them his own, he fails to receive due profit. The devil then inserts and increases his, since he finds an opening for them. So too, on the other hand, when a person renounces and opposes these representations, God will augment and meliorate His favors in this humble and dispossessed soul. He will set it over many things as in the case of the servant who was faithful in a few things. [Mt. 25:21]

9. If a man remains both faithful and retiring in the midst of these favors, the Lord will not cease raising him degree by degree until he reaches the divine union and transformation. Our Lord proves and elevates the soul by first bestowing graces that are exterior, lowly, and proportioned to the small capacity of sense. If the person reacts well by taking these first morsels with moderation for his own strength and nourishment, God will bestow a more abundant and higher quality of food. If the individual is victorious over the devil in the first degree, he will pass on to the second; and if so in the second, he will go to the third; and likewise through all the seven mansions (the seven degrees of love) until the Spouse puts him in the wine cellar of perfect charity. [Ct. 2:4]

10. Happy the man who knows how to carry on the fight against the beast of the Apocalypse and its seven heads, which are in opposition to these seven degrees of love. [Ap. 12:3; 13:1] With each of its heads, the beast wars against one of these degrees, and by so doing it wages battle with the soul in each of these mansions. And in every mansion the soul is exercising the love of God and winning another degree. Doubtless, if a man fights faithfully and conquers in each mansion, he will merit an advancement from degree to degree and from mansion to mansion unto the ultimate where he will have cut off the seven heads of the beast against which he fought the furious war. This is so full of violence that St. John says the beast was permitted to fight against the saints, and was victorious in each of these degrees of love by using arms and abundant munitions. [Ap. 13:7] It is most regrettable that many upon entering this battle against the beast are even incapable of severing the first head through denial of the sensible objects of the world. Some make the effort and cut it off, but then fail to sever the second, which

consists of the sensory visions we are discussing. What is most lamentable is that after some have cut off not only the first and second but the third also (in regard to the interior corporal senses), by passing out of the state of meditation and advancing further, they at the moment of their entrance into purity of spirit are conquered by this spiritual beast which returns to the assault and revives even unto the first head. In their fall the last state becomes worse than the first, since the beast takes with it seven other spirits worse than itself. [Lk. 11:26]

11. The spiritual person ought to deny all the apprehensions and temporal delights of the exterior senses, if he desires to cut off the first and second head of the beast by entering the first mansion of love and the second of living faith. One should not desire to clutch sensory communications nor suffer encumbrance from them, since they are what most derogates from faith.

12. Manifestly, these visions and sense apprehensions cannot serve as a means for union since they bear no proportion to God. This was one of the reasons for Christ's not wanting Mary Magdalen or St. Thomas to touch Him. [Jn. 20:17, 27–29]

The devil is most pleased when he sees that a man desires to admit revelations. For then he has an excellent opportunity to inject errors and disparage faith. As I have declared, a man desiring these apprehensions becomes coarse in his faith and even exposes himself to many temptations.

13. I have treated of these exterior apprehensions somewhat at length so as to shed more light on the others which we shall soon discuss. There is so much to say, however, on this subject that I believe I would never finish. And I think I was too brief in only explaining that a person should be careful never to accept them—unless in some rare case and with extremely competent advice, and then without any desire for them. But I think my exposition of this subject is sufficient.

CHAPTER 12

The nature of natural imaginative apprehensions. Proofs that they are inadequate means for the attainment of union with God. The harm caused from attachment to them.

1. Before discussing the imaginative visions, which are usually imparted supernaturally to the interior senses (imaginative power and phantasy), an exposition of the natural apprehensions of this interior corporal sense is in order. As a result we can proceed logically, and progress from the lesser to the greater and from the more exterior to

the more interior until reaching. the ultimate perfection in which the soul is united with God. We have been following this very method: first we discussed the divesting of the exterior senses of their natural apprehensions, and, consequently, of the natural strength of the appetites. This we did in Book One where we spoke of the night of sense. Then we began to divest these senses of the supernatural exterior apprehensions and to lead the soul into the night of the spirit, as in the preceding chapter.

2. The first point to consider in this second book concerns the interior corporal sense (the imaginative power and phantasy). We must also empty this sense of every imaginative form and apprehension that can be naturally grasped by it, and demonstrate the impossibility of union with God before the activity relating to these apprehensions ceases. Such apprehensions are incapable of being the proper and proximate means of this union.

3. We are speaking of two interior bodily senses: the imagination and the phantasy. They are of service to each other in due order, because the one is discursive and the other forms the images. For our discussion there will be no need of differentiating between them. This should be remembered if we do not mention them both explicitly.

All that these senses, then, can receive and construct are termed imaginations and phantasms. These are forms represented to the interior senses through material images and figures.

There are two kinds: supernatural and natural. The supernatural are represented passively without the work of the senses. These we call supernatural imaginative visions; we shall discuss them afterwards. The natural are those the soul can construct actively through forms, figures, and images.

Meditation is the work of these two faculties, since it is a discursive act built upon forms, figures, and images, imagined and fashioned by these senses. For example: the imagining of Christ crucified, or at the column, or in some other scene; or of God seated upon a throne with resplendent majesty; or the imagining and considering of glory as a beautiful light, etc.; or the picturing of any other human or divine object imaginable.

The soul will have to empty itself of these images and leave this sense in darkness if it is to reach divine union. For these images, just like the corporal objects of the exterior senses, cannot be an adequate, proximate mean to God.

4. The reason is that the imagination cannot fashion or imagine anything beyond what it has experienced through the exterior senses, that is, seen with the eyes, heard with the ears, etc. At the most it can compose

resemblances of these objects that are seen, heard, or felt. But such resemblances do not reach a greater entity nor even as much entity as that of other sense objects. Even though a person may imagine palaces of pearls and mountains of gold—for he has seen gold and pearls—all of this imagination will indeed be less than the essence of a little gold or of a pearl. And this, even though in the imagination there is a larger quantity and more excellent structure. Since all created things, as has been said, are unproportioned to God's being, all imaginings fashioned out of their similarities are incapable of serving as proximate means toward union with Him. Rather, as we said, they serve for much less.

5. Those who imagine God through some of these figures (as an imposing fire or as brightness, or through any other forms) and think that He is somewhat like them are very far from Him. These considerations, forms, and methods of meditation are necessary to beginners that the soul may be enamored and fed through the senses, as we shall point out later. They are suitable as the remote means to union with God, which beginners must ordinarily use for the attainment of their goal and the abode of spiritual repose. Yet these means must not be so used that a person always employs them and never advances, for then he would never achieve his goal, which is unlike the remote means and unproportioned to it—just as none of the steps on a flight of stairs has any resemblance to the goal at the top toward which they are the means. If a man in climbing them does not leave each one behind until there are no more, or if he should want to stay on one of them, he would never reach the level and peaceful room at the top.

Consequently, a man, who wants to arrive at union with the Supreme Repose and Good in this life, must climb all the steps, which are considerations, forms, and concepts, and leave them behind, since they are dissimilar and unproportioned to the goal toward which they lead. And this goal is God. Accordingly, St. Paul teaches in the Acts of the Apostles: *Non debemus aestimare auro vel argento, aut lapidi sculpturae argentis, et cogitationis hominis divinum esse simile* (We should not consider or esteem the divinity to be like gold or silver, or stone sculptured by the artist, nor like anything a man can fashion with his imagination). [Acts 17:29]

6. Many spiritual persons, after having exercised themselves in approaching God through images, forms, and meditations suitable for beginners, err greatly if they do not determine, dare, or know how to detach themselves from these palpable methods. For God then wishes to lead them to more spiritual, interior, and invisible graces by removing the gratification derived from discursive meditation. They even attempt to hold on to these methods, desiring to travel the road of consideration and meditation, using images as before. They believe such procedure is a

permanent requirement. They strive hard to meditate, but draw out little satisfaction, or none at all; rather their lot becomes aridity, fatigue, and restlessness of soul. This aridity augments as their strivings through meditation for that former sweetness, now unobtainable, increase. A person will no longer taste that sensible food, as we said, but rather enjoy another food, more delicate, interior, and spiritual. He will not acquire this spiritual nourishment through the labor of his imagination, but by pacifying his soul, by leaving it to its more spiritual quiet and repose.

The more spiritual a man is, the more he discontinues trying to make particular acts with his faculties, for he becomes more engrossed in one general, pure act. Once the faculties reach the end of their journey, they cease to work, just as a man ceases to walk when he reaches the end of his journey. If everything consisted of going, one would never arrive; and if everywhere we found means, when and where could one enjoy the end and goal?

7. It is sad to see many disturb their soul when it desires to abide in this calm and repose of interior quietude, where it is filled with the peace and refreshment of God. Desirous of making it retrace its steps and revert from the goal in which it now reposes, they draw it out to more exterior activity, to considerations which are the means. This they do not without strong repugnance and reluctance in the soul. The soul would want to remain in that unintelligible peace as in its right place. A man is deeply pained if, after intense effort to reach his place of rest, he is forced to return to his labor.

Since these individuals do not understand the mystery of that new experience, they imagine themselves to be idle and doing nothing. Thus, in their struggle with considerations and discursive meditations they disturb their quietude. They become filled with aridity and trial because of efforts to get satisfaction by means no longer apt. We can say that the more intense their efforts, the less will be their gain. The more they persist at meditation, the worse their state becomes, because they drag the soul further away from spiritual peace. They resemble one who abandons the greater for the lesser, turns back on a road already covered, and wants to redo what is already done.

8. The advice proper for these individuals is that they must learn to abide in that quietude with a loving attentiveness to God and pay no heed to the imagination and its work. At this stage, as we said, the faculties are at rest, and do not work actively but passively, by receiving what God is effecting in them. If at times they put the faculties to work, they should not make use of excessive efforts or studied reasonings, but do so with gentleness of love, moved more by God than by their own abilities, as we shall explain later.

This explanation is sufficient at present for those aspiring toward advancement. They will understand the suitability and necessity of detaching oneself at the required time and season from all these methods, ways, and uses of the imagination.

9. To explain just when this practice must be employed, we shall in the following chapter describe some signs which the spiritual person must notice in himself. These signs will indicate that the time and season has come when one can freely make use of that loving attentiveness, and discontinue his journey along the way of reasoning and imagination.

CHAPTER 13

The signs for recognizing in spiritual persons when they should discontinue discursive meditation and pass on to the state of contemplation.

1. To avoid obscurity in this doctrine it will be opportune to point out in this chapter when one ought to discontinue discursive meditation (a work through images, forms, and figures) so that the practice will not be abandoned sooner or later than required by the spirit. Just as it is fit to abandon it at the proper time that it may not be a hindrance in the journey to God, it is also necessary not to abandon this imaginative meditation before the due time so that there be no regression. For though the apprehensions of these faculties are not a proximate means toward union for proficients, they are a remote means for beginners. By these sensitive means beginners dispose their spirit and habituate it to spiritual things, and at the same time they void their senses of all other base, temporal, secular, and natural forms and images.

Hence we shall delineate some signs and indications by which one can judge whether or not it is the opportune time for the spiritual person to discontinue meditation.

2. The first is the realization that one cannot make discursive meditation nor receive satisfaction from it as before. Dryness is now the outcome of fixing the senses upon subjects which formerly provided satisfaction. As long as one can, however, make discursive meditation and draw out satisfaction, one must not abandon this method. Meditation must only be discontinued when the soul is placed in that peace and quietude to be spoken of in the third sign.

3. The second sign is an awareness of a disinclination to fix the imagination or sense faculties upon other particular objects, exterior or interior. I am not affirming that the imagination will cease to come and go (even in deep recollection it usually wanders freely), but that the person is disinclined to fix it purposely upon extraneous things.

4. The third and surest sign is that a person likes to remain alone in loving awareness of God, without particular considerations, in interior peace and quiet and repose, and without the acts and exercises (at least discursive, those in which one progresses from point to point) of the intellect, memory and will; and that he prefers to remain only in the general, loving awareness and knowledge we mentioned, without any particular knowledge or understanding.

5. To leave safely the state of meditation and sense and enter that of contemplation and spirit, the spiritual person must observe within himself at least these three signs together.

6. It is insufficient to possess the first without the second. It could be that the inability to imagine and meditate derives from one's dissipation and lack of diligence. The second sign, the disinclination and absence of desire to think about extraneous things, must be present. When this inability to concentrate the imagination and sense faculties upon the things of God proceeds from dissipation and tepidity, there is then a yearning to dwell upon other things and an inclination to give up the meditation.

Neither is the realization of the first and second sign sufficient, if the third sign is not observed together with them. When one is incapable of making discursive meditation upon the things of God and disinclined to consider subjects extraneous to God, the cause could be melancholia or some other kind of humor in the heart or brain capable of producing a certain stupefaction and suspension of the sense faculties. This anomaly would be the explanation for want of thought or of desire and inclination for thought. It would foster in a person the desire to remain in that delightful ravishment.

Because of this danger, the third sign, the loving knowledge and awareness in peace, etc., is necessary.

7. Actually, at the beginning of this state the loving knowledge is almost unnoticeable. There are two reasons for this: first, ordinarily the incipient loving knowledge is extremely subtle and delicate, and almost imperceptible; second, a person who is habituated to the exercise of meditation, which is wholly sensible, hardly perceives or feels this new insensible, purely spiritual experience. This is especially so when through failure to understand it he does not permit himself any quietude, but strives after the other more sensory experience. Although the interior peace is more abundant, the individual allows no room for its experience and enjoyment.

But the more habituated he becomes to this calm, the deeper his experience of the general, loving knowledge of God will grow. This knowledge is more enjoyable than all other things, because without the soul's labor it affords peace, rest, savor, and delight.

8. For greater clarity we shall expound in the following chapter some reasons showing the necessity for these three signs in order to journey on the road of spirit.

CHAPTER 14

A demonstration of the need for these three signs in order to advance.

1. As for the first sign it should be known that there are two reasons almost comprised in one for requiring the spiritual person to give up the imaginative way or sensory meditation when he is unable to meditate or derive satisfaction from it and enter the way of the spirit, which is the contemplative way.

First, because the person has been granted all the spiritual good obtainable through discursive meditation on the things of God. An indication of this is his inability to make discursive meditation as before, or derive from it any new satisfaction or pleasure. For previously he had not yet arrived at the spirituality which was in store for him.

Ordinarily, as often as an individual receives some profitable grace, he experiences—at least spiritually—gratification in the means through which the grace is obtained. If this is not received, there will rarely be profit, neither will he find in the cause of that former gratification the support and satisfaction he did before when he received grace through that means. This agrees with what the philosophers hold: *Quod sapit, nutrit* (What is savory, nourishes and fattens). Hence holy Job queries: *Numquid poterit comedi insulsum, quod non est sale conditum?* (Could one perchance eat the unsavory that is not seasoned with salt?). [Jb. 6:6]

Here we have the cause of the person's inability to consider and meditate as before: the lack of savor and benefit derived by the spirit from this exercise.

2. The second reason is that he has now acquired the substantial and habitual spirit of meditation. It should be known that the purpose of discursive meditation on divine subjects is the acquisition of some knowledge and love of God. Each time a person through meditation procures some of this knowledge and love he does so by an act. Many acts, in no matter what area, will engender a habit. Similarly, the repetition of many particular acts of this loving knowledge becomes so continuous that a habit is formed in the soul. God, too, effects this habit in many souls, without the precedence of at least many of these acts as means, by placing them at once in contemplation.

What the soul, therefore, was periodically acquiring through the labor of meditation on particular ideas has now, as we said, been converted into the habitual and substantial, general and loving knowledge. This knowledge is neither distinct nor particular, as the previous. Accordingly the moment prayer begins, the soul, as one with a store of water, drinks peaceably, without the labor and the need of fetching the water through the channels of past considerations, forms, and figures. At the moment it recollects itself in the presence of God, it enters upon an act of general, loving, peaceful, and tranquil knowledge, drinking wisdom and love and delight.

3. This is why a man experiences difficulty and displeasure when others, in spite of the calm he is enjoying, endeavor to force him to meditate and work with particular concepts. His experience resembles that of the suckling child which finds that the breast is taken away just when it is beginning to taste the milk that was gathered there for it, and as a result is forced to renew its efforts. Or like the experience of a man who, while enjoying the substance of the fruit, once the rind is peeled, is forced to stop and begin again to remove the rind from the fruit even though it has already been peeled. In such an instance he would fail to find the rind and cease to enjoy the substance of the fruit which he holds in his hands. Or this is like turning away from the captured prey to go hunting for another.

4. Many behave similarly at the beginning of this state. They are of the opinion that the whole matter consists in understanding particular ideas and reasoning through images and forms (the rind of the spirit). Since they do not encounter these images in that loving, substantial quietude, where nothing is understood particularly and in which they like to rest, they believe they are wasting time and straying from the right road; and they turn back to search for the rind of images and reasoning. They are unsuccessful in their search because the rind has already been removed. There is no enjoyment of the substance nor ability to meditate, and they become disturbed with the thought of backsliding and going astray. Indeed they are getting lost, but not in the way they imagine, for they are losing the exercise of their own senses and first mode of experience. This loss indicates they are approaching the spirit being imparted to them, in which the less they understand the further they penetrate into the night of the spirit—the subject of this book. They must pass through this night to a union with God beyond all knowing.

5. There is little to be said about the second sign, for it is obvious that a person at this time necessarily finds worldly images dissatisfying, since even those that concern God, which are more conformable to his state, fail to satisfy him, as we explained. Nevertheless, as we mentioned above, the imagination usually wanders back and forth during this recollection. But a person does not desire or find delight in this, rather

he is troubled about it due to the disturbance it brings to that gratifying peace.

6. Nor do I believe it is necessary to indicate here why the third sign (the loving, general knowledge or awareness of God) is a requirement for discontinuing meditation. Some doctrine has already been expounded about this sign in our explanation of the first one, and afterwards in the proper place we will have a special discussion of this when dealing with the general, obscure knowledge. This matter will be taken up after our treatise on the distinct, intellectual apprehensions. We shall, however, state one reason which manifests how this loving, general knowledge and awareness of God in the soul is required before discontinuing discursive meditation.

If a man did not have this knowledge or attentiveness to God, he would, as a consequence, be neither doing anything nor receiving anything. Having left the discursive meditation of the sensitive faculties and still lacking contemplation (the general knowledge in which the spiritual faculties—memory, intellect, and will—are actuated and united in this passive, prepared knowledge), he would have no activity whatsoever relative to God. For a person can neither conceive nor receive knowledge already prepared for him save through either the sensitive or spirtual faculties. With the sensory faculties, as we affirmed, a person can make discursive meditation, seek out and form knowledge from the objects; and with the spiritual faculties he can enjoy the knowledge received without any further activity of the senses.

7. The difference between the functions of these two groups of faculties resembles that existing between toil and the enjoyment of the fruits of this toil; between the drudgery of the journey and the rest and quiet gladdening its end; or again between cooking a meal and eating without effort what has already been cooked and prepared; or it is like the difference between receiving a gift and profiting by it.

If the sensitive faculties are idle as to their work of discursive meditation, and the spiritual faculties as to the contemplation and knowledge received and formed in them, there is no basis for asserting that the soul is occupied.

This knowledge is a requisite, then, in order to leave the way of discursive meditation.

8. It is noteworthy that this general knowledge is at times so recondite and delicate (especially when purer, simpler, and more perfect), spiritual, and interior that the soul does not perceive or feel it, even though employed with it.

This is especially so when, as we affirmed, this knowledge is clearer, simpler, and more perfect; and then this knowledge is still less perceptible when it shines upon a purer soul, one freer from the particular ideas and concepts apprehensible by the senses or intellect. Since the individual lacks the feelings of the sensitive part of the soul, by not possessing these particular ideas and concepts which the senses and intellect are accustomed to act upon, he does not perceive this knowledge.

For this reason the purer, simpler, and more perfect the general knowledge is, the darker it seems to be and the less the intellect perceives. On the other hand, the less pure and simple the knowledge is in itself, although it enlightens the intellect, the clearer and more important it appears to the individual, since it is clothed, wrapped, or commingled with some intelligible forms apprehensible to the intellect or the senses.

9. The following example is a clear illustration of this.

In observing a ray of sunlight stream through the window, we notice that the more it is pervaded with particles of dust, the clearer and more palpable and sensible it appears to the senses; yet obviously the sun ray in itself is less pure, clear, simple, and perfect in that it is full of so many specks of dust. We also notice that when it is more purified of these specks of dust it seems more obscure and impalpable to the material eye; and the purer it is, the more obscure and inapprehensible it seems to be. If the ray of sunlight should be entirely cleansed and purified of all dust particles, even the most minute, it would appear totally obscure and incomprehensible to the eye, since visible things, the object of the sense of sight, would be absent. Thus the eye would find no images on which to rest, because light is not the proper object of sight, but only the means through which visible things are seen. If there is nothing visible off which the ray of light can reflect, nothing will be seen. If the ray, then, were to enter through one window and go out another without striking any quantitative object, it would be invisible. Yet the ray of sunlight would be purer and cleaner than when, on account of being filled with visible objects, it is more manifestly perceived.

10. The spiritual light has a similar relationship to the intellect, the eye of the soul. This supernatural, general knowledge and light shines so purely and simply in the intellect and is so divested and freed of all intelligible forms (the objects of the intellect) that it is imperceptible to the soul. This knowledge, when purer, is even at times the cause of darkness, because it dispossesses the intellect of its customary lights, forms, and phantasies and effects a noticeable darkness.

When this divine light does not strike so forcibly, a person apprehends neither darkness, nor light, nor anything at all from heavenly or earthly sources. Thus he will sometimes remain in deep oblivion and afterwards will not realize where he was, nor what occurred, nor how the time passed. As a result it can and does happen that an individual will spend many hours in this oblivion, yet upon returning to self think that only a moment or no time at all has passed.

11. The purity and simplicity of the knowledge is the cause of this oblivion. While occupying a man's soul, it renders it simple, pure, and clear of all the apprehensions and forms through which the senses and memory were acting when conscious of time. And thus it leaves the soul in oblivion and unaware of time.

Although, as we asserted, this prayer lasts a long while, it seems of brief duration to the individual, since he has been united with pure knowledge which is independent of time. This is the short prayer which, it is said, pierces the heavens. [Ecclus. 35:21] It is short because it is not subject to time, and it penetrates the heavens because the soul is united with heavenly knowledge. When the individual returns to himself he observes the effects this knowledge produced in him without his having been aware of this. These effects are: an elevation of mind to heavenly knowledge, and a withdrawal and abstraction from all objects, forms, and figures as well as from the remembrance of them.

David declares that such was his experience upon returning to himself after this oblivion: *Vigilavi, et factus sum sicut passer solitarius in tecto* (I became conscious and discovered that I was like the solitary sparrow on the housetop). [Ps. 101:8] By solitary he refers to the withdrawal and abstraction from all things; by the housetop, to the mind elevated on high. The soul remains, in consequence, as though ignorant of all things, since it knows only God without knowing how it knows Him. For this reason the bride in the Canticle of Canticles, when she states that she went down to Him, numbers unknowing among the effects this sleep and oblivion produced in her, saying: *Nescivi* (I knew not). [Ct. 6:10–11]

As we mentioned, it seems to a person when occupied with this knowledge that he is idle because he is not at work with his senses or faculties. Nevertheless he must believe that he is not wasting time, for even though the harmonious interaction of his sensory and spiritual faculties ceases, his soul is occupied with knowledge in the way we explained. This is why, also in the Canticle of Canticles, the wise bride responded to one of her doubts: *Ego dormio et cor meum vigilat.* [Ct. 5:2] This was like saying: Though I (according to what I am) sleep, naturally, by ceasing to work, my heart watches, supernaturally, in its elevation to supernatural knowledge.

12. But one should not think this knowledge, if it is to be all we said it was, will necessarily cause oblivion. This forgetfulness occurs only when God abstracts the soul from the exercise of all the natural and spiritual

faculties. Because such knowledge does not always occupy the entire soul, this forgetfulness is less frequent. The knowledge we are discussing only requires abstraction of the intellect from any particular, temporal or spiritual knowledge and an unwillingness to think of either. For then we have a sign that the soul is occupied.

This sign is necessary for recognizing this knowledge when it is applied and communicated only to the intellect. For then sometimes it is imperceptible. When, however, there is also a communication to the will, as there almost always is, an individual will not fail to understand more or less his being occupied with this knowledge, if he wants to discern this, for he will be aware of the delight of love, without particular knowledge of what he loves. As a result he will call it a general, loving knowledge.

This communication, consequently, is called a general, loving knowledge, for just as it is imparted obscurely to the intellect, so too a vague delight and love is given to the will without distinct knowledge of the object loved.

13. This explanation is sufficient at present to understand the need for this knowledge before one leaves the way of discursive meditation and for the assurance that, despite the apparent idleness, the soul is well employed if these three signs are noticeable. It is also sufficient for an understanding of how the representation of this light in a more comprehensible and palpable way is not a sign of its greater purity, sublimity, and clarity, as was demonstrated through the example of the ray of sunlight permeated with dust particles and thereby perceptible to the eye. Evidently, as Aristotle [*Metaphys.* lib. brevior, c. 1, ed. Didot, II, 486] and the theologians assert, the higher and more sublime the divine light, the darker it is to our intellect.

14. A great deal can be said about this divine knowledge, both as to its nature and the effects it produces in the soul. We are reserving this discussion for its proper place. There was no reason for such a lengthy treatment of it here, except that we were undesirous of leaving this doctrine somewhat more vague than it is. Certainly, I admit that it is very obscure. To the fact that it is a subject seldom dealt with in this style, in word or in writing, since in itself it is supernatural and obscure, can be added that of my unpolished style and lack of knowledge. Doubtful of my ability to make myself understood, I am often aware of exceeding the limits required for a sufficient presentation of this doctrine. I confess that I sometimes do so intentionally, because what is not understandable with one reason may become so by others. Also I think that such procedure will give more clarification to later explanations.

15. In conclusion, I think a question concerning the duration of this knowledge should be answered. I shall do so briefly in the following chapter.

Chapter 15

Proficients, at the beginning of their entry into this general knowledge of contemplation, must at times practice discursive meditation and work with the natural faculties.

1. A question may arise about our teaching. Are proficients (those whom God begins to place in this supernatural knowledge of contemplation), because they are beginning to experience contemplation, never again to practice discursive meditation and work with natural forms?

We did not mean that those beginning to have this general loving knowledge should never again try to meditate. In the beginning of this state the habit of contemplation is not so perfect that one can at will enter into this act, neither is one so remote from discursive meditation as to be always incapable of it. One can meditate naturally through forms and scenes as before, and discover something new in it. Indeed, at the outset, upon judging through the signs mentioned above that his soul is not occupied in repose and knowledge, a person will need to make use of meditation. This need will continue until he acquires the habit of contemplation in a certain perfect degree. The indication of this will be that every time he intends to meditate, he will immediately notice this knowledge and peace as well as his own lack of power or desire to meditate, as we said. Until reaching this stage (of those already proficient in contemplation) a person will sometimes contemplate, and sometimes meditate.

2. He will often find that he is experiencing this loving or peaceful awareness passively without having first engaged in any active work (regarding particular acts) with his faculties. But on the other hand he will frequently find it necessary to aid himself gently and moderately with meditation in order to enter this state.

But once he has been placed in it, as we already pointed out, he does not work with the faculties. It is more exact to say that then the work is done in the soul and the knowledge and delight is already produced, than that the soul does anything, besides attentively loving God and refraining from the desire to feel or see anything. In this loving awareness the soul receives God's communication passively, just as a man, without doing anything else but keep his eyes open, receives light passively. This reception of the light infused supernaturally into the soul is a passive knowing. It is affirmed that the person does nothing, not because he fails to understand, but because he understands by dint of no effort other than the reception of what is bestowed. This process is similar to God's illuminations and inspirations, although here the person freely accepts this general, obscure knowledge.

3. One should not commingle other more palpable lights of forms, concepts, or figures of meditative discourse, if one wants to receive this divine light in greater simplicity and abundance. For none of these tangible lights are like that serene, limpid light. If an individual should desire to consider and understand particular things, however spiritual they may be, he would hinder the general, limpid, and simple light of the spirit; he would be interfering by his cloudy thoughts. When an obstruction is placed in front of a person's eyes, he is impeded from seeing the light and the view before him.

4. The manifest conclusion is that, when a person has finished purifying and voiding himself of all forms and apprehensible images, he will abide in this pure and simple light, and be perfectly transformed into it. This light is never lacking to the soul, but because of creature forms and veils weighing upon and covering it, the light is never infused. If a person will eliminate these impediments and veils, and live in pure nakedness and poverty of spirit, as we shall explain later, his soul in its simplicity and purity will then be immediately transformed into simple and pure Wisdom, the Son of God. As soon as natural things are driven out of the enamored soul, the divine are naturally and supernaturally infused, since there can be no void in nature.

5. When the spiritual person cannot meditate, he should learn to remain in God's presence with a loving attention and a tranquil intellect, even though he seems to himself to be idle. For little by little and very soon the divine calm and peace with a wondrous, sublime knowledge of God, enveloped in divine love, will be infused into his soul. He should not interfere with forms or discursive meditations and imaginings. Otherwise his soul will be disquieted and drawn out of its peaceful contentment to distaste and repugnance. And if, as we said, scruples about his inactivity arise, he should remember that pacification of soul (making it calm and peaceful, inactive and desireless) is no small accomplishment. This, indeed, is what our Lord asks of us through David: *Vacate et videte quoniam ego sum Deus.* [Ps. 45:11] This would be like saying: Learn to be empty of all things—interiorly and exteriorly—and you will behold that I am God.

CHAPTER 16

The imaginative apprehensions represented supernaturally to the phantasy are incapable of serving as a proximate means to union with God.

1. A discussion of the natural apprehensions which the phantasy and imagination receive and work with through discursive meditation should be followed by a discussion of the supernatural apprehensions, called imaginative visions. These visions pertain to the phantasy just as natural apprehensions do, because they belong to the category of image, form, and figure.

2. It is to be known that by this term "imaginative vision" we are referring to everything supernaturally represented to the imagination under the category of image, form, figure, and species. All the apprehensions and species represented naturally to the soul through the five bodily senses and impressed upon it can be represented to it supernaturally without the intervention of the exterior senses.

This interior sense, the phantasy coupled with the memory, is for the intellect the archives or receptacle in which all the intelligible forms and images are received. Like a mirror, this faculty contains them within itself, whether they come to it from the five bodily senses or supernaturally. It in turn presents them to the intellect, and the intellect considers and makes a judgment about them. Not only is the phantasy capable of this, but it can even compose and imagine other objects resembling those known.

3. It is noteworthy that as the five exterior senses send the images and species of their objects to these interior senses, so God and the devil can supernaturally represent to these faculties—without the exterior senses—the same images and species. In fact, they can effect this in a more beautiful and perfect way. God often represents many things to a person through these images, and teaches him great wisdom, as is obvious throughout Scripture. For example: Isaias beheld God in His glory under the form of smoke covering the temple and under the form of the seraphim covering their faces and feet with their wings [Is. 6:2, 4]; or Jeremias saw the rod keeping watch [Jer. 1:11], and Daniel a multitude of visions. [Dn. 7; 8; 10] The devil too attempts with his seemingly good visions to deceive a person. An example of this is found in the Book of Kings, where we read that he deceived all of Achab's prophets by representing to their imaginations the horns with which, he claimed, Achab was to destroy the Assyrians. And this was a lie.

[3 Kgs. 22:11, 12, 21, 22] And then there are the visions Pilate's wife had about not condemning Christ [Mt. 27:19]; and many others.

It is understandable, therefore, how in this mirror of the proficient's phantasy these imaginative visions are received more frequently than are the corporal visions in the exterior senses.

As far as image and species is concerned, these visions do not differ from those coming through the exterior senses. But as for their perfection and the effect produced, there is great difference, for being more interior they are more subtle and effective in the soul. Yet this does not mean that some of these exterior corporal visions may not be more effective, since after all God gives His communications as He pleases. But we are dealing with these visions insofar as they are in themselves more spiritual.

4. The devil ordinarily comes with his wiles, natural or supernatural, to this sense, the imagination and phantasy, for it is the gate and entry to the soul. Here the intellect comes as though to a seaport or market to buy and sell provisions. As a result, God—and the devil too—comes here with the jewels of images and supernatural forms to proffer them to the intellect. Yet God does not depend on this means alone for instructing the soul. He dwells in it substantially and can impart knowledge to it by Himself or by other means.

5. There is no reason to delay in giving signs for the discernment of good visions from bad ones, nor in enumerating the various kinds. My sole intention here is to instruct the intellect about them so that it may not be hindered and impeded by the true ones from union with divine wisdom, nor deceived by the false ones.

6. I affirm, then, that since these imaginative apprehensions, visions, and other forms or species are presented through some image or particular idea, a person must neither feed upon nor encumber himself with them. And this is true whether these visions be false and diabolical or whether they are recognized as authentic and of divine origin. Neither should a person desire to accept them or keep them, because with such an attitude he can not remain detached, divested, pure, and simple, and without any mode or method, as the union demands.

7. The reason is that in being apprehended these forms are always represented as we said in some limited mode or manner. But God's wisdom to which the intellect must be united has neither mode nor manner, neither does it have limits nor does it pertain to distinct and particular knowledge, because it is totally pure and simple. That the two extremes, the soul and the divine wisdom, may be united, they will have to come to accord by means of a certain likeness. As a result the soul must also be pure and simple, unlimited and unattached to any particular knowledge,

and unmodified by the boundaries of form, species, and image. Since God is unincluded in any image, form, or particular knowledge, the soul in order to be united with Him should not be limited by any particular form or knowledge.

8. The Holy Spirit in Deuteronomy clearly manifests that God has no form or likeness: *Vocem verborum ejus audistis, et formam penitus non vidistis* (You heard the voice of his words, and you saw absolutely no form in God). [Dt. 4:12] But He asserts that darkness, the cloud, and obscurity (that vague, dark knowledge in which the soul is united to God) were present. Then further on He adds: *Non vidistis aliquam similitudinem in die qua locutus est vobis Dominus in Horeb de medio ignis* (You did not see God in any image that day on Mt. Horeb when He spoke with you from the midst of the fire). [Dt. 4:15]

9. The Holy Spirit also asserts in the Book of Numbers that the soul cannot reach, insofar as possible in this life, God's height by means of any forms or figures. For God reproves Aaron and Mary for murmuring against their brother Moses and thus lets them know the high state of union and friendship in which He had placed Moses: *Si quis inter vos fuerit propheta Domini, in visione apparebo ei, vel per somnium loquar ad illum. At non talis servus meus Moyses, qui in omni domo mea fidelissimus est: ore enim ad os loquor ei, et palam, et non per aenigmata, et figuras Dominum videt* (If there is any prophet of the Lord among you, I will appear to him in some vision or form, or speak with him in his dreams. But no one is like my servant Moses, the most faithful one in all my house, and I speak with him mouth to mouth, and he does not see God through comparisons, likenesses, and figures). [Nm. 12:6–8]

Manifestly, in this high state of union God does not communicate Himself to the soul—nor is this possible—through the disguise of any imaginative vision, likeness, or figure, but mouth to mouth: the pure and naked essence of God (the mouth of God in love) with the pure and naked essence of the soul (the mouth of the soul in the love of God).

10. To reach this essential union of love of God, a person must be careful not to lean upon imaginative visions, forms, figures, or particular ideas, since they cannot serve as a proportionate and proximate means for such an effect—they would instead be a hindrance. As a result a person should renounce them and endeavor to avoid them. The only reason for admitting and valuing them would be the profit and good effect the genuine ones bring to the soul. But admitting them is unnecessary for the obtainment of this good effect; for the sake of progress, rather, one should always deny them.

As with the exterior corporal visions, the good these imaginative visions can communicate to the soul is either knowledge, or love, or sweetness. But that they do this, it is unnecessary for a person to have the desire of accepting them. As we pointed out, at the very moment they are present in the imagination, they are also in the soul, and infuse knowledge and love, or sweetness, or whatever God wants them to cause.

They are present to the imagination and the soul together, but their effects may not be simultaneous. They produce their main effect in the soul passively, with out its being able to hinder this, even though it may desire to do so. It was similarly powerless to know how to acquire the effect—although it did know how to become disposed. As a window is unable to hinder the ray of sunlight shining upon it and is disposed through its cleanness to be illumined passively without active effort, so too, however much a person wants to reject these visions, he cannot but receive the influences and communications of those figures. A negative will, humbly and lovingly resigned, cannot resist the supernatural infusions. Only imperfection and impurity of soul hinder these communications, just as stains on a window impede the bright sunlight.

11. Obviously, in the measure that a person divests himself from willful attachments to the apprehensions of those stain-like figures, forms, and images—the wrappings of spiritual communications—he will prepare himself for the goods and communications they cause. Having left aside all those apprehensions, which are like curtains and veils covering the spiritual goods contained in them, he will receive these goods in greater abundance, clarity, freedom of spirit, and simplicity. If the soul desires to feed upon them, the spirit and senses will be so occupied that a free and simple communication of spirituality will be impossible. For, obviously, if occupied with the rind, the intellect will have no freedom for the reception of those spiritual communications.

Should a person desire to admit and pay attention to them, he would be setting up an encumbrance and remaining content with the least important—the form, image, and particular knowledge, which is the only kind of knowledge he can get from these visions. For he is unable to apprehend or understand the more important factor, the spirituality infused in his soul; neither does he know the way he receives it nor how he may speak about it, since it is purely spiritual. According to his own way of knowing, the only knowledge he can have about these visions concerns the less important element, the forms apprehended through the senses. I affirm, consequently, that the unintelligible or unimaginable element in these visions is communicated to it passively, exclusive of any effort of the soul to understand. The soul would not even know how to go about making this effort.

12. The eyes of the soul, then, should be ever withdrawn from distinct, visible, and intelligible apprehensions. Such elements are pertinent

to sense and provide no security or foundation for faith. Its eyes should be fixed on the invisible, on what belongs not to sense but to spirit, and on what, as it is not contained in a sensible figure, brings the soul to union with God in faith, the proper means as was said. These visions will be substantially advantageous to the soul insofar as faith is concerned, if it knows clearly how to reject their sensible and intelligible aspect and make good use of the purpose for which God gives them. As we pointed out, God's purpose in bestowing corporal visions is not that a person desire and become attached to them.

13. A question, though, may arise concerning this subject: If it is true that God in giving supernatural visions does not want one thereby to desire, lean upon, or pay attention to them, why does He give them at all? Through them an individual can fall into numerous dangers and errors, or at least encounter the many impediments to further progress described here. Furthermore, why would God do this if He can communicate to the soul substantially and spiritually what He bestows upon it through the sensible communication of these visions and forms?

14. We shall explain our answer to this question in the following chapter. There we shall present for spiritual persons and their teachers doctrine that, in my opinion, is both important and necessary. We shall expound God's method and purpose—of which many are ignorant—in bestowing these visions. As a result of their ignorance about visions, many are unenlightened on how to behave and how to guide themselves or others through them to union. They think that, because of their awareness of the genuinity and divine origin of these visions, it is advantageous to admit and trust them. They do not reflect that, as with worldly goods, failure to deny them can be a hindrance, and cause attachment and possessiveness concerning them. They consider it beneficial to admit some visions as true and reject others as false. In this way they subject themselves and other souls to the considerable labor and danger of discerning the truth or falsity of these visions. God does not impose this task upon them, nor does He desire the exposure of simple and unlearned people to this dangerous endeavor, for these persons have faith, the sound and safe doctrine by which they can advance.

15. There is no advancing in faith without the closing of one's eyes to everything pertaining to the senses and to clear, particular knowledge. Though St. Peter was truly certain of his vision of Christ's glory in the transfiguration, yet, after relating the fact in his second canonical epistle [2 Pt. 1:16–18], he did not want anyone to take this as the chief testimony for certitude. But leading them on to faith, he declared: *Et habemus firmiorem propheticum sermonem: cui benefacitis attendentes, quasi lucernae lucenti in caliginoso loco, donec dies elucescat*

(We have a more certain testimony than this vision of Tabor: the sayings and words of the prophets bearing testimony to Christ which you must make good use of, as of a candle shining in a dark place). [2 Pt. 1:19]

Reflecting upon this comparison, we discover the doctrine taught here. Telling us to behold the faith spoken of by the prophets as we would a candle shining in a dark place, he asserts that we should live in darkness, with our eyes closed to all other lights, and that in this darkness faith alone—which is dark also—should be the light we use. If we want to employ these other bright lights of distinct knowledge, we cease to make use of faith, the dark light, and we cease to be enlightened in the dark place mentioned by St. Peter. This place (the intellect—the holder on which the candle of faith is placed) must remain in darkness until the day, in the next life, when the clear vision of God dawns upon the soul; and in this life, until the daybreak of transformation in and union with God, the goal of a person's journey.

CHAPTER 17

An answer to the proposed question. God's procedure and purpose in communicating spiritual goods by means of the senses.

1. A great deal may be said about God's intention (the elevation of a soul from its low state to divine union) and method of procedure in bestowing these goods. All spiritual books deal with these points, and in our explanation we will also consider them. Accordingly, in this chapter I shall do no more than offer a sufficient solution to our doubt. The question is: Since there is so much danger and hindrance to progress extant in these supernatural visions, as we said, why does God, Who is all wise and in favor of removing obstacles and snares, communicate them?

2. An answer to this requires the establishment of three fundamental principles.

The first is taken from St. Paul's Epistle to the Romans: *Quae autem sunt, a Deo ordinata sunt* (The works that are done by God are well-ordered). [Rm. 13:1]

The second comes from the Holy Spirit in the Book of Wisdom: *Disponit omnia suaviter.* This is similar to stating: God's wisdom, though it touches from one end to the other (from one extreme to the other), disposes all things gently. [Wis. 7:30; 8:1]

The third originates with the theologians who say: *omnia movet secundum modum eorum* [St. Thomas Aquinas, *De Veritate*, q. 12, a. 6] (God moves each thing according to its mode).

3. In order that God lift the soul from the extreme of its low state to the other extreme of the high state of divine union, He must obviously, in view of these fundamental principles, do so with order, gently, and according to the mode of the soul. Since the order followed in the process of knowing involves the forms and images of created things, and since knowledge is acquired through the senses, God, to achieve His work gently and to lift the soul to supreme knowledge, must begin by touching the low state and extreme of the senses. And from there He must gradually bring the soul after its own manner to the other end, His spiritual wisdom, which is incomprehensible to the senses. Thus, naturally or supernaturally, He brings a person to the supreme spirit of God by first instructing him through discursive meditation and through forms, images, and sensible means, according to the individual's own manner of acquiring knowledge.

4. This is the reason God gives a person visions, forms, images, and other sensitive and spiritual knowledge—not because He does not desire to give spiritual wisdom immediately, in the first act. He would do this if the two extremes (human and divine, sense and spirit) could through the ordinary process be united by only one act, and if He could exclude the many preparatory acts, which are so connected in gentle and orderly fashion that, as is the case with natural agents, each is the foundation and preparation for the next. The first preparative acts serve the second; the second, the third; and so on. Therefore God perfects man gradually according to his human nature, and proceeds from the lowest and most exterior to the highest and most interior.

He first perfects the corporal senses, moving one to make use of natural exterior objects that are good, such as: hearing sermons and masses, looking upon holy objects, mortifying the palate at meals, and disciplining the sense of touch through penance and holy rigor.

When these senses are somewhat disposed, He is wont to perfect them more by granting some supernatural favors and gifts to confirm them further in good. These supernatural communications are, for example: corporal visions of saints or holy things, very sweet odors, locutions, and extreme delight in the sense of touch. The senses are greatly confirmed in virtue through these communications and the appetites withdrawn from evil objects.

Besides this the interior bodily senses, such as the imagination and phantasy, are gradually perfected and accustomed to good through considerations, meditations, and holy reasonings, and the spirit is instructed.

When through this natural exercise they are prepared, God may enlighten and spiritualize them further with some supernatural imaginative visions from which the spirit, as we affirmed, at the same time profits notably. This natural and supernatural exercise of the interior sense gradually reforms and refines the spirit.

This is God's method of bringing a soul step by step to the innermost good, although it may not always be necessary for Him to keep so mathematically to this order, for sometimes God bestows one kind of communication without the other, or a less interior one by means of a more interior one, or both together. The process depends on what God judges expedient for the soul, or upon the favors He wants to confer. But His ordinary procedure conforms with our explanation.

5. By this method, then, God instructs a person and makes him spiritual. He begins by communicating spirituality, in accord with the person's littleness and small capacity, through elements that are exterior, palpable, and accommodated to sense. He does this so that by means of the rind of those sensible things, in themselves good, the spirit making progress in particular acts and receiving morsels of spiritual communication may form a habit in spiritual things and reach the actual substance of spirit, foreign to all sense. A person only obtains this little by little, after his own manner, and by means of the senses to which he has always been attached.

In the measure that a man approaches spirit in his dealings with God, he divests and empties himself of the ways of the senses, of discursive and imaginative meditation. When he has completely attained spiritual communion with God he will be voided of all sensory apprehensions concerning God. The more an object approaches one extreme, the further it retreats from the other; upon complete attainment of the one extreme, it will be wholly separated from the other. There is a frequently quoted spiritual axiom which runs: *Gustato spiritu, desipit omnis caro* (Once the taste and savor of the spirit is experienced, everything carnal is insipid). The ways of the flesh (which refer to the use of the senses in spiritual things) afford neither profit nor delight.

This is obvious; if something is spiritual, it is incomprehensible to the senses, but if the senses can grasp it, it is no longer purely spiritual. The more knowledge the senses and natural apprehensions have about it, the less spiritual and supernatural it will be, as we explained above.

6. As a result the perfect spirit pays no attention to the senses; it neither receives anything through them, nor uses them principally, nor judges them to be requisite in its relationship with God, as it did before its spiritual growth.

A passage from St. Paul's epistle to the Corinthians bears this meaning: *Cum essem parvulus, loquebar ut parvulus, sapiebam ut parvulus, cogitabam ut parvulus. Quando autem factus sum vir, evacuavi quae erant parvuli* (When I was a child, I spoke as a child, I knew as a child,

I thought as a child. But when I became a man, I put away childish things). [1 Cor. 13:11]

We have already explained how sensible things and the knowledge the spirit can abstract from them are the work of a child. Should a person always have attachment to them and never become detached, he would never stop being a little child, or speaking of God as a child, or knowing and thinking of God as a child. In his attachment to the rind of sense (the child), he will never reach the substance of spirit (the perfect man). For the sake of his own spiritual growth, therefore, a person should not admit these revelations, even though God is the author of them, just as a child must be weaned in order to accustom its palate to a hardier and more substantial diet.

7. Is it necessary, you may ask, for the soul while it is a child to accept these sensible things and then set them aside when grown, just as an infant must be nourished at the breast until when grown older it can be weaned?

I reply in regard to discursive meditation, in which an individual begins his quest for God, that it is true that he must not turn away from the breast of the senses for his nourishment until he arrives at the time and season suitable for so doing—that is, when God brings the soul to a more spiritual converse, to contemplation, of which we spoke in Chapter 11 of this book. [c. 13]

But when there is question of imaginative visions or other supernatural communications apprehensible by the senses and independent of a man's free will, I affirm that at whatever time or season (in the state of perfection or one less perfect) an individual must not desire to give them admittance, even though they come from God. And this for two reasons:

First, because God, as we said, produces His effect in the soul without its being able to hinder this, although it can impede the vision—which often happens. Consequently the effect to be communicated becomes more substantial even though it is given differently. As we said, a person cannot hinder the goods God desires to impart, nor in fact does he do so, except by some imperfection or possessiveness. And there is no imperfection or possessiveness if he renounces these apprehensions with humility and misgivings.

Second, by so doing a person frees himself from the task and danger of discerning the true visions from the false ones and deciding whether his visions come from an angel of light or of darkness. Such an effort is profitless, a waste of time, a hindrance to the soul, an occasion of many imperfections as well as of spiritual stagnancy, since the individual is not then employed with the more important things and disencumbered of the trifles of particular apprehensions and knowledge. This was mentioned regarding the corporal visions, and it will be asserted later in respect to imaginary visions.

8. One can be sure that if our Lord did not have to lead a soul according to its own manner of being, He would never communicate the abundance of His Spirit through these aqueducts of forms, figures, and particular knowledge by which He sustains the soul with crumbs.

This is why David said: *Mittit crystallum suam sicut bucellas* (He sent His wisdom in morsels). [Ps. 147:17] It is extremely regrettable that a soul having as it were an infinite capacity should be fed, because of its limited spirituality and sensory incapacity, with morsels for the senses.

St. Paul, too, when writing to the Corinthians grieved over this littleness and limited preparation for the reception of spirituality: *When I came to you brethren I could not speak as to spiritual persons, but only as to carnal, because you were unable to receive it, nor can you now. Tamquam parvulis in Christo lac potum vobis dedi, non escam* (As to infants in Christ I gave you milk to drink and not solid food to eat). [1 Cor. 3:1-2]

9. In conclusion, a person must not fix the eyes of his soul upon that rind of the figure and object supernaturally accorded to him, whether the object pertains to the exterior senses (locutions and words to the sense of hearing; visions of saints and beautifully resplendent lights to the sense of sight; fragrance to the sense of smell; delightful tastes to the palate; and to the sense of touch other pleasures derived from the spirit, as is more commonly the case with spiritual persons), or whether it is an interior imaginative vision. He must instead renounce them all.

He must fasten the eyes of his soul only upon the valuable spirituality they cause, and endeavor to preserve it by putting into practice and properly doing whatever is for the service of God, and pay no attention to those representations, nor desire any sensible gratification.

By this attitude a person takes from these apprehensions only what God wants him to take, that is, the spirit of devotion, since God gives them for no other principal reason. And he rejects the sensory element which would not have been imparted had he possessed the capacity for receiving spirituality without the apprehensions and exercises of the senses.

CHAPTER 18

The harm caused by some spiritual directors in not giving souls adequate guidance with regard to visions. An explanation of how both can be misled even by visions having a divine origin.

1. We are unable to be as brief on this subject of visions as we would like because of the amount of matter to be covered.

Although we have presented the substance of a suitable explanation of what a spiritual person should do about these visions and how his director should guide and deal with him, yet it will not be superfluous to particularize a little more on this doctrine and shed some light on the harm arising from these visions. Even if the visions are from God, this harm can come both to spiritual persons and to their directors if they are very credulous about them.

2. The reason motivating me to enlarge somewhat on this subject is the want of discretion—it seems to me—in some spiritual directors. Trusting these supernatural apprehensions, counting them to be authentic and of divine origin, these directors together with their penitents have gone astray and become bewildered, realizing in themselves the word of our Saviour: *Si caecus caeco ducatum praestet, ambo in foveam cadunt* (If a blind man leads a blind man, both fall into the pit). [Mt. 15:14]

He does not say they shall fall, but that they do fall. In order to take a fall it is not necessary for a blind man to wait until he falls into error, since, by the very fact that he dares to be guided by another blind man, he is already in error, and thereby has already taken his first, though less serious, fall. The method of some directors is sufficient to encumber souls receiving these visions, or even to lead them astray. They do not guide them along the paths of humility, and they give them a free hand in this matter, which causes a want of the true spirit of faith. Neither do these directors ground their penitents in faith, for they frequently make these visions a topic of conversation. Consequently, the individuals get the idea that their directors are setting store by their visions, and as a result they do the same and stay attached to them, instead of deepening their faith and becoming detached, emptied and divested of apprehensions so as to soar to the heights of dark faith.

All this arises from the attitude and language the individual remarks in his director. This is so true that—I know not how—this person with immeasurable ease and an inability to do otherwise begets a high esteem for these visions—even to the point of withdrawing his eyes from the abyss of faith.

3. The reason the soul becomes so readily engrossed in visions must be their sensible aspect toward which it has a natural bent. And since a person is already attracted and disposed through his distinct and sensible apprehensions, it is enough that he see in his director, or any other person, some esteem for these visions for him to acquire the same. His desire for them, however, is also stimulated, and he feeds upon them and becomes most intensely inclined and attached to them without being aware of the fact.

Numerous imperfections consequently arise, for the person loses humility. He thinks his visions are significant, that he possesses something profitable, and that he is prominent in God's eyes. He is pleased and somewhat satisfied with himself, which is against humility. Although this person is unaware of it, the devil then secretly augments this feeling and begins to suggest thoughts about others: whether they receive these visions or not, or whether their visions are authentic or not. Such thoughts are contrary to holy simplicity and spiritual solitude.

4. Let us bring to a close now our discussion of these kinds of harm and of how there is no growth in faith unless souls turn from these visions. Although they may not be as noticeable as these, other more subtle kinds of harm, more hateful in God's eyes, result from this attitude. Their source lies in a failure to walk wholly on the road of nakedness. We shall discuss them when dealing with spiritual gluttony and the other six vices. Then, God willing, we shall expound many points about these subtle and delicate stains which, because the director does not guide souls along the way of denudation, adhere to the spirit.

5. Let us now say something about the attitude of some directors who give their penitents poor instructions. Assuredly, I wish I knew how to speak of this, because I think it is difficult to explain how the spirit of the disciple is secretly fashioned after that of his spiritual father. This subject involves such prolixity that it is wearisome to me, for it seems one factor cannot be explained without an elucidation of another, since in these spiritual matters they are interrelated.

6. But to cover the matter sufficiently here, I might point out that it seems to me—and indeed it is so—that if the spiritual father has such a bent toward revelations that they produce in his soul some effect, pleasure, or complete satisfaction, he cannot avoid—even though unaware—affecting his disciple with this attitude and pleasure, if the disciple is not more advanced than he. And even if the penitent is more advanced, the director can bring serious harm to him by continuing to give him direction. From the inclination and gratification the spiritual father discovers in these visions there rises a certain esteem for them, and unless he is on his guard he will manifest indications of this to his penitent.

And if his penitent has the same inclination, there cannot be between them, as far as I can see, anything but a communication of esteem for these matters.

7. To be less demanding, let us speak of the confessor who, inclined or not toward these visions, does not use the necessary care to disencumber and divest his disciple of desire for them, but rather makes the vision a topic of conversation and the main theme of his spiritual colloquies, by giving instructions on the signs for the discernment of good visions from bad ones.

Although knowledge of these signs is worthwhile, there is no reason to burden the soul with this labor, solicitude, and danger; by refusing to pay attention to these visions, a person escapes all this effort of discernment and does what he ought. But these confessors do not stop here. Observing that their penitents receive these manifestations from God, they ask them to request of Him a revelation about some matter, and the foolish souls do so in the belief that this method of gaining knowledge is lawful. Merely because God, in the way or for the motive He wishes, grants a supernatural revelation, they think it is licit to desire that He grant it, and they even petition Him to do so.

8. If in response to their request God reveals the matter to them, they become more self-confident, thinking that God is pleased with their petition and desires it, whereas in reality He is displeased with such an entreaty and does not desire it. They often act or believe in accordance with the answer or revelation, for since they are attached to this manner of dealing with God, their will becomes adapted to these revelations and firmly rooted in them. They find natural satisfaction in them and fit them naturally into their own way of thinking. They often err exceedingly, and are then taken aback at the unexpected outcome. Then doubts come to the fore concerning the divine origin of these revelations, since events do not come to pass as they were led to believe.

They presupposed two factors: first, that the revelations were from God, since from the beginning they firmly adhered to them. Yet this adherence was probably due to their natural inclination toward them, as we asserted. Second, that, since the revelations were from God, events would occur according to their anticipations.

9. This belief was a gross delusion, for God's revelations or locutions do not always turn out according to man's expectations, nor according to the literal sense of the words. One should neither be sure of them nor believe them blindly, even though he knows they are God's revelations, responses, or words. Though they may in themselves contain certitude and truth, they do not always have it in their causes and in our way of understanding them.

We shall prove this in the next chapter, and also that, even though God answers questions supernaturally, He is not pleased to do so, but is even sometimes angered.

CHAPTER 19

Visions and locutions, even though from God, can mislead us. Proofs from divine Scripture.

1. We mentioned the two reasons why, although God's visions and locutions are true and certain in themselves, they are not always so for us. The first reason is because of our defective manner of understanding them, and the second because their basic causes are sometimes variable. We shall give proof for both with scriptural texts.

Clearly, in regard to the first, not all revelations turn out according to the literal meaning. The cause is that, since God is immense and profound, He usually embodies in His prophecies, locutions, and revelations other ways, concepts, and ideas remarkably different from the meaning we generally find in them. And the surer and more truthful they are, the less they seem so to us.

We behold this frequently in Scripture. With a number of the ancients, many of God's prophecies and locutions did not turn out as they had expected, because they interpreted them with their own different and extremely literal method. This is apparent in the following texts.

2. In Genesis, God told Abraham when He had brought him into the land of the Canaanites: *Tibi dabo terram hanc* (I will give you this land). [Gn. 15:7] And since God had promised this frequently, Abraham, already old and still receiving the promise, questioned God: *Domine unde scire possum quod possesurus sum eam?* (How, or by what sign, am I to know that I will possess it?). [Gn. 15:8] Then God revealed to him that he was not going to possess it at all, but that his offspring would four hundred years thence. [Gn. 15:13] Abraham, thus, finally understood the promise, which in itself was true because God, in bestowing it on his offspring out of love for him, gave it to him. Consequently Abraham was misled in his understanding of the prophecy. If he had acted according to his understanding he would have erred decidedly, since the possession of this land was not to come about during his life. And those who beheld him die without having received the promise of the prophecy, after having heard that God was going to grant it to him, would have been baffled and left with the notion that the prophecy was false.

3. While Abraham's grandson Jacob was on his journey to Egypt at the time Joseph, his son, had ordered him to come because of the famine in

Canaan, God appeared to him and said: *Jacob, Jacob, noli timere, descende in Aegyptum, quia in gentem magnam faciam te ibi. Ego descendam tecum illuc, et inde adducam te revertentem* (Jacob, do not fear, go down to Egypt and I will go with you; and when you depart from there, I will lead you out and be your guide). [Gn. 46:1–4]

These words were not fulfilled in their literal sense, for we know that the saintly old Jacob died in Egypt and never returned from there alive. [Gn. 49:32] But the prophecy was fulfilled in his offspring, whom God, acting Himself as guide along the way, delivered from Egypt years later. Manifestly, then, anyone knowing of God's promise to Jacob would have thought that Jacob, who through God's favor and command had entered Egypt in person and alive, would unquestionably make his exit alive and in person, since God had promised this and the help for achieving it. This individual would have been misled, and filled with wonder over Jacob's death in Egypt, because God would not have thereby fulfilled His promise as expected. Although God's promise in itself was true, there would have been utter delusion in its interpretation.

4. In the Book of Judges we also read that when all the tribes of Israel united for war to punish Benjamin's tribe for a certain iniquity, they were positive of victory because God had appointed them a captain of war. So certain were they that, when defeat came and twenty-two thousand of their men were slain, they were amazed and baffled before God and they wept the entire day, ignorant of the cause of their downfall, for they had understood that victory would be theirs.

And when they asked God if they should return to battle, He told them to return. Convinced that now victory was theirs, they set out with remarkable daring, and they were defeated the second time with a loss of eighteen thousand men. As a result they were extremely bewildered and puzzled about their next move, because God had commanded them to wage war and yet they were always vanquished, but especially because they surpassed their enemy in number and strength: four hundred thousand to twenty-five thousand seven hundred.

They were deluded in their interpretation of God's words, which in themselves were undeceptive. He did not say they would conquer but that they should fight, for in these defeats God wished to punish a certain neglect and presumption of theirs, and thus humble them. But when finally He replied that victory would be won, it was achieved, though not without much strategy and hardship. [Jgs. 20:11–48]

5. In this and many other ways souls are misled by imparting to God's locutions and revelations a literal interpretation, an interpretation according to the outer rind. As has been explained, God's chief objective in conferring these revelations is to express and impart the elusive,

spiritual meaning contained in the words. This spiritual meaning is richer and more plentiful than the literal meaning and transcends those limits.

Anyone bound to the letter, locution, form, or apprehensible figure cannot avoid serious error and will later become confused for having been led by the literal sense and not having allowed for the spiritual meaning which is divested of the literal sense. *Littera, enim, occidit, spiritus autem vivificat* (The letter kills and the spirit gives life). [2 Cor. 3:6] The soul should renounce, then, the literal sense and live in the darkness of faith, for faith is the spirit which is incomprehensible to the senses.

6. Because many of the children of Israel took the words of the prophets literally and because these prophecies did not come true as expected, they began to disregard and distrust them. Hence a saying was born, becoming almost a proverb among them, by which they scoffed at the prophets. Isaias complains of this in the following passage: *Quem docebit Dominus scientiam? Et quem intelligere faciet auditum? Ablacta- tos a lacte, avulsos ab uberibus. Quia manda remanda, manda remanda, expecta reexpecta, expecta reexpecta, modicum ibi, modicum ibi. In loquela enim labii, et lingua altera loquetur ad populum istum* (Whom will God instruct? And to whom will He explain His word and prophecy? Only to those who are weaned and fresh from their mother's breast. For everyone is saying—concerning the prophets—promise and promise again, wait and wait some more, wait and wait some more, a word with you here, a word with you there. For with words from His lips, but in another tongue, He will speak to this people). [Is. 28:9–11]

In this passage Isaias clearly demonstrates the mockery these people made of the prophets and the derision repeated in the proverb, "wait and wait some more." He indicates that the prophecies were never fulfilled because the people were bound to the letter (the milk of infants) and to the senses (the breasts), which run contrary to spiritual knowledge. Because of this he says: "To whom shall He teach the wisdom of His prophecies? And to whom shall He explain His doctrine, if not to those who are already weaned from the milk of the letter and the breasts of the senses? And because these people are not so weaned, they understand only according to the milk of the rind and letter, or to the breasts of the senses, for they exclaim: "promise and promise again, wait and wait some more, etc." God must speak doctrine to them from His mouth, and not theirs, and in a tongue other than theirs.

7. One should not interpret the prophecy literally, for God's spiritual meaning is difficult to understand and different from our literal interpretation. This is so true that even Jeremias, a prophet himself, observing that the ideas in God's words were so different from the meaning men would ordinarily derive from them, seems to waver and defend the people: *Heu, heu, heu, Domine Deus, ergone decipisti populum istum et Jerusalem,*

dicens: Pax erit vobis, et ecce pervenit gladius usque ad animam? (Alas, alas, alas, Lord God, have You perchance deceived this people and Jerusalem, saying: Peace will come to you; and behold the sword reaches even to the soul?). [Jer. 4:10]

The reason for the misunderstanding was that the promised peace was to be that effected between God and man through the coming Messiah, whereas they took the words to mean temporal peace. Consequently, when wars and trials came upon them, it seemed God was a deceiver because everything was turning out contrary to their expectations. Thus they proclaimed as Jeremias also did: *Expectavimus pacem, et non erat bonum* (We had hoped for peace, and there is no blessing of peace). [Jer. 8:15] Guiding themselves, then, according to the literal sense it was impossible to avoid deception.

Who will not be perplexed and misled if bound to the literal meaning of all David prophesies about Christ in the seventy-first psalm? *Et dominabitur a mari usque ad mare; et a flumine usque ad terminos orbis terrarum* (He shall reign from sea to sea; and from the river unto the ends of the earth) [Ps. 71:8], and also: *Liberabit pauperem a potente, et pauperem cui non erat adjutor* (He will liberate the poor man from the power of the mighty, and the poor man who has no helper). [Ps. 71:12] For afterwards, Christ is born in an humble state, lives in poverty, and dies in misery; and not only did He fail to reign temporally upon the earth, but He was subject to a lowly people and died under Pontius Pilate's rule. He did not merely fail to liberate His people from the hands of the temporally powerful, but allowed them to be persecuted and slain for His name's sake.

8. These prophecies about Christ should have been understood in their spiritual sense, in which they turned out to be true. Since Christ was God He was Lord not solely of the earth but of heaven too. And not merely was He to redeem the poor, who were His followers, and free them from the power of the devil (the mighty one against whom they had no helper), but He was also to make them heirs of the kingdom of heaven.

In prophesying about Christ and His followers, God was speaking of the more important factors (the eternal kingdom and eternal freedom), and in their interpretation of these words the people dwelt on matters of slight importance (temporal dominion and temporal freedom) to which God pays little heed, since in His eyes freedom and a temporal dominion are neither freedom nor a kingdom.

Blinded by the base literal sense and ignorant of the spiritual meaning, they killed their Lord and God, as St. Paul exclaimed: *Qui enim habitabant Jerusalem, et principes ejus, hunc ignorantes, et voces prophetarum, quae per omne Sabbatum leguntur, judicantes impleverunt* (The inhabitants of Jerusalem, and its rulers, ignorant of who He was, and misunderstanding the sayings of the prophets recited each Sabbath, after judging Him, killed Him). [Acts 13:27]

9. This difficulty in giving a suitable interpretation to God's words reached such a point that even His disciples, who went about with Him, were deceived. For example: those two who after His death were journeying to the town of Emmaus, sad and distrustful, saying: *Nos autem sperabamus quod ipse esset redempturus Israel* (We were expecting that He would redeem Israel). [Lk. 24:21] They also were of the opinion that His would be a temporal liberation and reign, but Christ, our Redeemer, appearing to them, reproved them for being foolish, dull, and heavy of heart in believing the things foretold by the prophets. [Lk. 24:25]

Even when He was about to ascend into heaven, some still maintained that dullness and queried of Him: *Domine, si in tempore hoc restitues regnum Israel* (Lord, let us know if at this time You will restore the kingdom of Israel). [Acts 1:6]

The Holy Spirit causes many pronouncements in which He has a meaning different from that understood by men. This is seen by what He brought Caiphas to say of Christ: *It is better that one man die than that the whole nation perish.* [Jn. 11:50] Caiphas did not enunciate these words on his own, and he expressed and understood them in one way while the Holy Spirit did so in another.

10. Evidently, then, even though the words and revelations be from God, we cannot find assurance in them, since in our understanding of them we can easily be deluded, and extremely so. They embody an abyss and depth of spiritual significance, and to want to limit them to our interpretation and sensory apprehensions is like wanting to grasp a handful of air, which will escape the hand entirely and leave only a particle of dust.

11. The spiritual director should try to see to it that his disciple is not detained by the desire of giving heed to supernatural apprehensions (which are no more than small particles of spirituality and the only thing he will be left with), and he should turn him away from all visions and locutions and teach him to remain in freedom and the darkness of faith, in which spiritual liberty and plenitude is obtained, and, consequently, the proper wisdom and understanding of God's pronouncements.

It is impossible for someone unspiritual to judge and understand the things of God correctly; and one is not spiritual if one judges them literally. And thus even though they are clothed in that literal meaning, they are not understood. This is what St. Paul really asserts: *Animalis autem homo non percipit ea quae sunt spiritus Dei; stultitia enim est illi, et non potest intelligere, quia de spiritualibus examinatur. Spiritualis autem judicat omnia* (The animal man fails to perceive the things that are of the Spirit of God, for they are foolishness to him, and he is unable to understand them because they are spiritual. Yet the spiritual man judges all things). [1 Cor. 2:14-15] "The animal man" refers to one who uses only the senses; "the spiritual man" to him who is neither bound to nor guided by the senses. It is temerarious, hence, to dare communicate with God by means of supernatural, sensory apprehension, or to allow anyone to do so.

12. For the sake of greater clarity here are some examples:

Suppose God says to a saintly man who is deeply afflicted because of persecution by his enemies: "I will free you from your enemies." This prophecy could be very true; nonetheless it will happen that his enemies prevail and kill him. Anyone who had given these words a temporal interpretation would have been deceived, because God had been speaking of the true and principal freedom and victory—salvation, in which the soul is free and victorious over its enemies much more truly and loftily than if liberated from them here below. This prophecy had greater truth and richness than was understandable through an interpretation which related the freedom to this life. By His words, God always refers to the more important and profitable meaning, whereas man will refer them to a less important sense, in his own way and for his own purpose, and thus be deceived.

We see this in David's messianic prophecy: *Reges eos in virga ferrea, et tamquam vas figuli confringes eos* (You shall rule all nations with an iron rod, and dash them to pieces like a vessel of clay). [Ps. 2:9] In this prophecy God referred to the more important, perfect, and eternal dominion, which did eventuate; not to the least important, temporal dominion, which did not come to pass during Christ's life on earth.

13. Here is another example: A soul has intense desires to be a martyr. God answers, "you shall be a martyr"; and He bestows deep interior consolation and confidence in the truth of this promise. Regardless of the promise, this person in the end does not die a martyr; yet the promise will have been true. Why, then, was there no literal fulfillment? Because the promise will be fulfilled in its chief, essential meaning: the bestowal of the essential love and reward of a martyr. God truly grants the soul the essence of both its desire and His promise, because the formal desire of the soul was not a manner of death, but the service of God through martyrdom and the exercise of a martyr's love for Him. The manner of death in itself is of no value without this love, and God bestows martyrdom's love and reward perfectly by other means. Even though the individual does not die a martyr, he is profoundly satisfied, since God has fulfilled his desire.

When these aspirations and other similar ones born of love are unful-filled in the way one expected, they are fulfilled in another, far better way, and render more honor to God than was thought of in making the request. David proclaims: *Desiderium pauperum exaudivit Dominus* (The Lord has granted the poor their desire). [Ps. 9:17] And in Prov-erbs, divine Wisdom affirms: *Desiderium suum justis dabitur* (The de-sire of the just shall be answered). [Prv. 10:24] Since numerous saints de-sired various particular favors from God, yet did not receive them in this life, it is of faith that as their desire was just and good it was fulfilled per-fectly in heaven. Consequently, if God makes the promise in this life, "your desire shall be fulfilled," it will come true, even though in a dif-ferent way.

14. God's words and visions in this and other ways may be true and certain, yet they may mislead us if we do not know how to understand them in their lofty meaning and according to God's purposes. The safest and most suitable method of procedure is to oblige souls to flee prudently from these supernatural occurrences, and to accustom them, as we pointed out, to purity of spirit in dark faith—the means toward union.

CHAPTER 20

Proofs from Scripture of how God's words, although always true, are not always certain. This certitude of outcome depends on the causes of the pronouncements.

1. We must prove now the second reason why God's visions and locu-tions, although always true in themselves, are not always certain for us. This uncertainty is due to the causes on which they are founded.

God's affirmations are frequently founded upon creatures and their effects, which are liable to change and failure, and, consequently, words based on these creatures can also change and fail. If one factor upon which another is dependent fails, the other fails too. For example, if God were to say that in a year He would send a plague upon a kingdom be-cause of an offense committed against Him there, and if the offense were to cease or change, the punishment could be withheld. Yet the warning would be true since it was based on the actual fault, and if the fault were to continue the threatened punishment would be executed.

2. This happened in the city of Ninive when God proclaimed: *Adhuc quadraginta dies et Ninive subvertetur* (Forty days from now Ninive will be razed). [Jon. 3:4] This did not happen because the cause of the threat, their sins, ceased on account of the penance that was done. [Jon. 3:5-10] But if they had not done penance the warning would have been

carried out. We also read in the Third Book of Kings that when King Achab had committed a very serious sin, God, through our holy father Elias, sent him a message threatening severe punishment on his person, his house, and his kingdom. [3 Kgs. 21:17–22] And because Achab rent his garments with grief, put on a hair shirt, fasted, slept in sackcloth, and went about sad and humbled, God once more sent this prophet to him with these words: *Quia igitur humiliatus est mei causa, non inducam malum in diebus ejus, sed in diebus filii sui* (Insofar as Achab has humbled himself for love of me I will not in his days send the evil I spoke of, but in those of his son). [3 Kgs. 21:27–29] Evidently, then, because Achab changed his conduct and disposition, God also altered His sentence.

3. We can thus deduce for our purpose here that, although God may have revealed or affirmed some fact to a person (whether it is good or bad, or concerns this person or another), it can become greater or less, or change, or be taken away entirely according to the variation of this person's tendency or of the cause upon which it is based. Thus the event may not turn out as expected, and frequently no one but God knows why.

God usually affirms, teaches, and promises many things, not so that there be an immediate understanding of them, but that afterwards at the proper time, or when the effect is produced, one may receive light about them. Christ acted this way with His disciples. He told them many parables and maxims which they did not understand until the time for preaching had come, when the Holy Spirit descended upon them. As Christ affirmed, the Holy Spirit was to explain to them all that He had taught them during His life. [Jn. 14:26] St. John, speaking of Christ's entrance into Jerusalem, states: *Haec non cognoverunt discipuli ejus primum: sed quando glorificatus est Jesus, tunc recordati sunt quia haec erant scripta de eo.*[3] [Jn. 12:16] As a result many particular works of God can come to pass in a soul, which neither the soul nor its director can understand until the opportune time.

4. In the First Book of Kings we also read that God, angered because Heli the priest of Israel failed to punish his sons for their sins, sent Samuel to him with, among other messages, the following one: *Loquens locutus sum, ut domus tua, et domus patris tui, ministraret in conspectu meo, usque in sempiternum. Verumtamen absit hoc a me* (Certainly I have said before that your house and the house of your father will continually minister to me in the priesthood and in my presence forever. Yet this proposal is very far from Me; I shall not bring it about). [1 Kgs. 2:30] Since the ministry of the priesthood is based on rendering honor and glory to God, God promised it to Heli's father forever. When Heli lacked

---

[3] These things His disciples did not at first understand. But when Jesus was glorified, then they remembered that these things were written about Him.

zeal for the honor of God, because, as God Himself complained, he gave more honor to his sons than to God, dissimulating their sins so as not to reprove them, the promise also failed. [1 Kgs. 3:13] It would have been kept forever if their good service and zeal had been enduring.

We should not think, therefore, that because revelations and locutions have a divine origin—and especially if they are dependent on human, changeable causes—they will infallibly eventuate according to their literal meaning.

5. Although God knows when these locutions and revelations are dependent on human causes, He does not always manifest it, but in His communication of the locution or revelation He will remain silent about the condition. Such was the case when He told the Ninivites definitely that they would be destroyed after forty days. [Jon. 3:4] At other times He declares, as He did to Roboam: *If you keep my commandments as my servant David did, I will also be with you as I was with him, and I will build you a house as I did my servant David.* [3 Kgs. 11:38]

Whether God discloses the conditional element or not, a person cannot find assurance in his own interpretation, because he is incapable of comprehending the secret truths and the diverse meanings of God's sayings. God is above the heavens and speaks from the depths of eternity; we on this earth are blind and understand only the ways of the flesh and of time. This, I believe, is why the Wise Man said: *God is above the heavens and you upon the earth; therefore do not be prolix or careless in speech.* [Eccl. 5:1]

6. You will perchance ask: If we are not to understand or meddle with them, why does God communicate them?

I have already mentioned that by order of Him who spoke, everything will be understood at the opportune time; and he whom God wills shall understand clearly that so it was fitting, since God does nothing without cause and truth. But, believe me, a person cannot completely grasp the meaning of God's locutions and deeds, nor can he determine this by appearances without extreme error and bewilderment.

The prophets, entrusted with the word of God, were well aware of this. Prophecy for them was a severe trial because, as we affirmed, the people observed that a good portion of the prophecy did not come true according to the literal meaning. As a result the people jibed and mocked the prophets excessively. It reached such a point that Jeremias exclaimed: *They mock me all day long, everyone scoffs at and despises me, because for a long time now I have cried out against iniquity and promised them destruction, and the Lord's word has become a reproach to me and a mockery all the time. And I said: I do not have to remember Him nor speak any more in His name.* [Jer. 20:7-9]

Although the holy prophet spoke with resignation and in the semblance of a weak man unable to suffer the changing ways of God, he teaches us the difference between the fulfillment of the divine locutions and their common literal sense. The prophets were considered seducers, and they endured such suffering because of their prophecies that Jeremias also proclaims in another place: *Formido et laqueus facta est nobis vaticinatio et contritio* (Prophecy has become for us fear, snares, and contradiction of spirit). [Lam. 3:47]

7. When God sent Jonas as the preacher of the destruction of Ninive, he fled because of his knowledge of the diverse meanings and causes of God's locutions. [Jon. 1:1–3] Lest the people should make fun of him when his prophecy was unfulfilled, he fled from prophesying and waited outside the city for the entire forty days to see if his prophecy would be fulfilled. [Jon. 4:5] Since it was not, he became extremely afflicted—to such an extent that he said to God: *Obsecro, Domine, numquid non hoc est verbum meum, cum adhuc essem in terra mea? Propter hoc praeoccupavi, ut fugerem in Tharsis* (I beseech You, Lord, was not this perhaps what I said when in my country? On this account I was contradictory and fled into Tharsis). [Jon. 4:2] And the saint became angry and petitioned God to take away his life. [Jon. 4:1, 3]

8. Why, then, should we be surprised if God's locutions and revelations do not materialize as expected? Suppose God affirms or represents to an individual some promise (good or bad, pertaining to the person himself or to another); if this promise is based on certain causes (devotion or service rendered to God, or offense committed against Him, now or in the future) and these causes remain, the promise will be accomplished. But since the duration of these causes is uncertain, the fulfillment of the promise is too. One should seek assurance, therefore, not in understanding but in faith.

CHAPTER 21

God's displeasure at the quest for revelations and locutions, even though He sometimes answers them. Proofs of how He is frequently angered in spite of His condescension and response.

1. Some spiritual persons, as we said, convince themselves that their curiosity to know of certain things through supernatural means is good because God sometimes answers these petitions. They think this conduct is good and pleasing to God because He responds to their urgent request. Yet the truth is that, regardless of God's reply, such behavior is neither

good nor pleasing to God. Rather He is displeased; not only displeased but frequently angered and deeply offended.

The reason lies in the illicitness of transcending the natural boundaries God has established for the governing of creatures. He has fixed natural and rational limits by which man is to be ruled. A desire to transcend them, hence, is unlawful, and to desire to investigate and arrive at knowledge in a supernatural way is to go beyond the natural limits. It is unlawful, consequently, and God who is offended by everything illicit is displeased.

King Achab knew this well. For although Isaias told him to ask in God's name for some sign, he was unwilling to do so: *Non petam, et non tentabo Dominum* (I will not ask for such a thing, nor shall I tempt God). [Is. 7:12] For to tempt God is to desire communication with Him in extraordinary, supernatural ways.

2. You will say: If it is true that God is displeased, why does He sometimes answer? I reply: Sometimes the devil answers; but when God responds, He does so because of the weakness of the individual who desires to advance in that way. This person could become sad and turn back, or imagine that God is unhappy with him, and become overly afflicted. Or there may be other motives known to God, prompted by that person's weakness and because of which God sees the appropriateness of condescending with such an answer.

God also does this in the extremely sensory communion that many weak and tender souls have with Him, as was mentioned above. But He does not act thus because He is desirous or pleased that communication with Him be carried on in such a manner. But God gives to each one according to each one's mode; He is like a fountain from which everyone draws as much water as the jug he carries will hold. Sometimes He lets souls draw water through these extraordinary spouts, but it does not follow that this is lawful, for it belongs only to God to bestow this when, how, and to whomever He wills, and for whatever reason He desires, and without any right on the part of the soul. Accordingly, as we asserted, He sometimes condescends to the petition of certain individuals, for since they are good and simple, He does not like to let them go unanswered, lest they become sad. But that He hears them does not mean He is pleased with this practice.

3. Here is an example to illustrate this truth. A father of a family provides at table many different kinds of food, some better than the other. One of his children will ask for a dish, not of the better food, but of the first that meets the eye, and the child will do so because it knows how to eat this kind of food better than the other. Now when the father observes that his child refuses to eat the food offered to it and wants and likes

only that first dish, he gives it to his child sadly so that it will not become unhappy and go without its meal.

This is the way God acted with the children of Israel when they asked Him for a king. He gave them one regretfully, because it was not good for them. Thus He said to Samuel: *Audi vocem populi in omnibus quae loquuntur tibi: non enim te objecerunt, sed me* (I heard the voice of this people and granted them the king they requested, for they have not rejected you but they have rejected Me, that I might not reign over them). [1 Kgs. 8:7]

God accordingly condescends to some souls by granting what is not the best for them, because they are ignorant of how to journey by any other way. Some souls obtain sensible or spiritual sweetness from God because they are incapable of eating the stronger and more solid food of the trials of the cross of His Son. He would desire them to take the cross more than any other thing.

4. I consider the desire for knowledge of things through supernatural means far worse than a desire for spiritual gratifications in the sensitive part of the soul. I fail to see how a person who tries to get knowledge in this supernatural way—as well as the one who commands this or gives consent—can help but sin, at least venially, no matter how excellent his motives or advanced in perfection he may be. There is no necessity for any of this kind of knowledge, since a person can get sufficient guidance from natural reason, and the law and doctrine of the Gospel. There is no difficulty or necessity unsolvable or irremediable by these means, which are very pleasing to God and profitable to souls.

We should make such use of reason and the law of the Gospel that, even though—whether we desire it or not—some supernatural truths are told to us, we accept only what is in harmony with reason and the Gospel law. And then we should receive this truth, not because it is privately revealed to us, but because it is reasonable, and we should brush aside all feeling pertinent to the revelation. We ought, in fact, to consider and examine the reasonableness of the truth when it is revealed even more than when it is not, since the devil in order to delude souls says much that is true, conformed to reason, and that will come to pass.

5. In all our necessities, trials, and difficulties, no better or safer aid exists for us than prayer and hope that God will provide for us by the means He desires. Scripture counsels this where we read that King Josaphat, deeply afflicted and surrounded by his enemies [2 Par. 20:1-4], began to pray to God: *Cum ignoremus quid facere debeamus, hoc solum habemus residue, ut oculos nostros dirigamus ad te* (When means are lacking and reason cannot find a way of providing for our necessities, we have only to raise our eyes to You that You may provide in the manner most pleasing to You). [2 Par. 20:12]

6. We have already pointed out that even though God sometimes responds to these requests, He is angered. Yet some proofs from Scripture will be helpful.

In the First Book of Kings we read that while King Saul was requesting a locution from the prophet Samuel, who was already dead, this prophet appeared; yet God was angered, because Samuel immediately reproved Saul for having made such a plea: *Quare inquietasti me, ut suscitarer?* (Why have you disturbed me by making me revive?). [1 Kgs. 28:15]

We are also well aware that, though God answered the children of Israel in providing the requested flesh meat, He was nonetheless seriously angered. According to the Pentateuch and David's account He immediately sent fire from heaven as a chastisement: *Adhuc escae eorum erant in ore ipsorum et ira Dei descendit super eos* (While the morsels were yet in their mouths, the anger of God descended upon them). [Ps. 77:30–31; Nm. 11:18–33]

We read too in the Book of Numbers that because the prophet Balaam went to the Madianites at the beckon of King Balac, God was extremely provoked with him. As a result of Balaam's request, God had told him to go; yet while he was on his way, an angel appeared carrying a sword, desirous of killing him, and saying: *Perversa est via tua mihique contraria* (Your way is perverse and contrary to Me). [Nm. 22:32] Because of this perversity the angel desired to kill Balaam.

7. God, though angered, condescends in this and many other ways to the desires of souls. Scripture affords many testimonies and examples of this fact, yet it is unnecessary to cite them, since our affirmation is so clear.

I only say that the desire to communicate with God in this way is extremely dangerous—more so than I can say. The man attached to such ways will go far astray and often become greatly bewildered. Anyone who has esteemed them will understand what I mean through his own experience.

Besides the hardship of avoiding any error resulting from God's locutions and visions, there is also the difficulty of discerning those communications which the devil causes. For his usually have resemblance to God's. He imparts facsimiles of God's communications so that, disguised among the flock like the wolf in sheep's clothing, his meddling may be hardly discernible. [Mt. 7:15] Since the devil through conjecture makes many reasonable manifestations that turn out to be true, people may be easily misled, thinking that the revelations must then be from God. These people do not realize the ease with which the devil with his clear natural light knows, through their causes, many past or future events. Since his light is so vivid, he can easily deduce a particular effect from a specific cause. Yet the effect does not always materialize according to his deduction, since all causes depend upon God's will.

8. Here is an example: The devil perceives that when the earth, air, and sun have reached a certain interrelationship, they will necessarily at that time become corrupted and thereby cause a pestilence. He is also cognizant of the areas in which the pestilence will be grave and those in which it will be mild. The example, then, is that of a pestilence known in its causes. Is it a wonder, then, that the devil's prediction about a pestilence, due within six months or a year, comes true? Yet it is a prophecy of the devil. Similarly, observing that the cavities of the earth are being filled with air, he can foresee earthquakes and predict that at a particular time there will be an earthquake. This is natural knowledge for which an intellect free of the passions is sufficient, as Boetius teaches: *Si vis claro lumine cernere verum, gaudia pelle, timorem, spemque fugato, nec dolor adsit* (If you want to know truths with natural clarity, cast aside joy, fear, hope, and sorrow). [*De Consolatione Philosophiae*, lib. 2, met. 7. PL 63, 656–58]

9. Supernatural events can also be known in their causes, since the divine Providence responds most certainly and justly to what the good or bad causes arising from the sons of men demand. One can know naturally that a particular person or city, or some other factor, will reach such a point that God in His providence and justice must respond in conformity with the punishment or reward that cause warrants. With this knowledge he can say: at this particular time God will certainly give this, or do that, or that some other event will ensue.

The holy Judith made Holofernes aware of this when, in order to persuade him that the children of Israel would be destroyed, she first related their numerous sins and evil conduct, and then added: *Et quoniam haec faciunt, certum est quod in perditionem dabuntur* (Because they do these things, it is certain they will be destroyed). [Jdt. 11:7–11; 12] This represents knowledge of the punishment through its causes. It is like saying: surely such sins must occasion certain punishments from the most just God. And divine Wisdom says: *Per quae quis peccat, per haec et torquetur* (Each one is punished in, or through, that by which he sins). [Wis. 11:17]

10. The devil knows this, not only in a natural way, but also from having observed God do these things, and he can conjecture and announce the outcome correctly.

The holy Tobias also knew through its cause the coming chastisement of the city of Ninive. He warned his son: Behold, son, when your mother and I are dead depart from this land because it will no longer remain. *Video enim quia iniquitas ejus finem dabit ei* (I see that its very evil will be the cause of its punishment, the end and destruction of everything). [Tb. 14:12–13] Tobias and the devil were able to come by this knowledge not merely through the wickedness of the city, but through experience, in observing that the Ninivites possessed the sins which occasioned the destruction of the world by the flood and of the Sodomites by fire. [Gn. 6:12–13; 13:13; 19:24] Tobias, however, also knew this through divine inspiration.

11. The devil can learn and foretell that Peter's life will naturally last only a certain number of years. And he can determine many other events through such various ways that we would never finish recounting them all, nor could we even begin to explain many because of their intricacy and the devil's craftiness in inserting lies. One cannot be liberated from him without fleeing from all revelations, visions, and supernatural communications.

God is rightly angered with anyone who admits them, for He sees the rashness of exposing oneself to this danger, presumption, curiosity, and pride, and to the root and foundation of vainglory, to contempt for the things of God, and to the beginning of the numerous evils into which many fall.

These individuals so stir God's wrath that, by giving full scope to their vanities and phantasies, He purposely allows them to go astray, suffer delusion and spiritual darkness, and abandon the established ways of life. Isaias affirms: *Dominus miscuit in medio ejus spiritum vertiginis.* [Is. 19:14] This is like saying: The Lord has mingled in their midst the spirit of dissension and confusion, which in plain words means the spirit of misunderstanding. Isaias manifestly says this in accord with our teaching, since he refers to those who were striving for supernatural knowledge of future events. [Is. 19:12] As a result he asserts that God mingled in their midst a spirit of misconstruing everything, not because He desired this, nor really gave them this spirit of error, but because they were desirous of knowing what was naturally unattainable. Provoked by this, God allowed them to go astray and gave no enlightenment concerning this matter in which He did not want them to meddle. Thus Isaias proclaims that negatively God commingled that spirit of dissension. Accordingly, God is the cause of that harm, that is, the privative cause, which consists in such a withdrawal of His light and favor that they necessarily fall into error.

12. In this way God permits the devil to blind and delude many, who merit this by their sins and audacities. The devil is able and successful to the extent that others believe what he says and consider him a good spirit. So firm is their belief that it is impossible, for anyone who tries, to persuade them of the diabolic origin. For with God's permission they

have already been affected by the spirit of misunderstanding. We read that this happened to the prophets of King Achab whom God allowed to be deluded by the spirit of prevarication. He permitted the devil to do this, saying: *Decipies, et praevalebis; egredere, et fac ita* (You shall prevail with your lie and deceive them; go out and do it thus). [3 Kgs. 22:22] The devil deceived the prophets and King so successfully that they were unwilling to believe the prophet Micheas who spoke the truth in contradiction to what the others had prophesied. That God allowed them to be blinded is the explanation of their unbelief, for in their attachment they wanted events to happen and God to answer according to their own desires and appetites. This was the surest means and preparation for God to abandon them to blindness and deception.

13. Ezechiel prophesied about this in God's name. He censures the curious one who in vanity of spirit desires knowledge in a divine way: *When this man asks the prophet to inquire of Me for him, I myself, the Lord, shall answer, and I will set my angry countenance upon that man. And when the prophet shall err in his reply, Ego Dominus decepi prophetam illum* (I the Lord have deceived that prophet). [Ez. 14:7–9] This signifies that God does not concur with His help to prevent that man's deception; such is the meaning of the words: I, the Lord, angered, will myself answer (withdraw My grace and favor from such a man). Deception necessarily follows when one is forsaken by God. The devil then intervenes, answering in harmony with that person's desire and pleasure; and since the devil's replies and communications are pleasing and satisfactory, the individual will let himself become seriously deluded.

14. We have seemingly wandered somewhat from the matter proposed in the title of this chapter: proofs that although God answers He sometimes becomes angry. Nonetheless, if everything we mentioned is thoroughly considered, it will contribute to the proof of our assertion. Our explanation points to the fact that God is displeased with desires for these visions, since as a consequence He permits souls to suffer diverse delusions.

CHAPTER 22

The answer to a question concerning the reason for the illicitness in the Law of Grace of a practice permissible in the Old Law, that of petitioning God through supernatural means. Proof from St. Paul.

1. Questions keep springing up so that we are unable to make the rapid progress we would like. Since we raise them, we necessarily have the obligation of answering them, that the truth of the doctrine will

remain clear and vigorous. These questions have this advantage that, although they slow up our progress, they are still an aid to greater clarity and to further explanations about our subject. Such is the case with this question.

2. In the last chapter we affirmed that God was unwilling that souls desire the supernatural communications of visions and locutions, etc. On the other hand, in the proofs from Scripture we saw that these communications with God were lawful and made use of in the Old Law. Not only was this licit, but God commanded it. When the people did not comply, God reproved them. An example of this is seen in Isaias when the children of Israel desired to descend into Egypt without first asking God; and He thus reprehended them: *Et os meum non interrogastis* (You did not first ask from My mouth what was suitable). [Is. 30:2] We also read in Josue that when the children of Israel were deceived by the Gabaonites, the Holy Spirit reminded them of this fault: *Susceperunt ergo de cibariis eorum, et os Domini non interrogaverunt* (They took their food without consulting the mouth of the Lord). [Jos. 9:2–14]

We observe in sacred Scripture that Moses, King David, the kings of Israel, in their wars and necessities, and the priests and ancients always questioned God, and that He replied and spoke to them without becoming angry. And they had done well if they questioned Him, but if they failed to do so, they were at fault. And if this is true, why, then, in the new Law of Grace is it different than it was previously?

3. In answer to this, the chief reason why in the Old Law the inquiries made of God were licit, and the prophets and priests appropriately desired visions and revelations from Him, was that at that time faith was not yet perfectly established, nor was the Gospel law inaugurated. It was necessary for them to question God, and that He respond, sometimes by words, sometimes through visions and revelations, now in figures and types, now through many other kinds of signs. All His answers, locutions, and revelations concerned mysteries of our faith or matters touching upon or leading up to it. Since the truths of faith are not derived from man but from the mouth of God (for He speaks them through His own mouth), it was required of them to seek an answer from the mouth of God. He therefore reproved them because in their affairs they did not seek counsel from His mouth, that He might answer and direct them toward the unknown and as yet unfounded faith.

But now that the faith is established through Christ, and the Gospel law made manifest in this era of grace, there is no reason for inquiring of Him in this way, or expecting Him to answer as before. In giving us His Son, His only Word (for He possesses no other), He spoke everything to us at once in this sole Word—and He has no more to say.

4. This is the meaning of that passage where St. Paul tries to persuade the Hebrews to turn from communion with God through the old ways of the Mosaic law and instead fix their eyes on Christ: *Multifariam multisque modis olim Deus loquens patribus in prophetis: novissime autem diebus istis locutus est nobis in Filio* (That which God formerly spoke to our fathers through the prophets in many ways and manners, now, finally, in these days He has spoken to us all at once in His Son). [Heb. 1:1–2] The Apostle indicates that God was as it were mute, with no more to say, because what He spoke before to the prophets in parts, He has now spoken all at once by giving us the All Who is His Son.

5. Any person questioning God or desiring some vision or revelation would not only be guilty of foolish behavior but also of offending Him, by not fixing his eyes entirely upon Christ and by living with the desire for some other novelty.

God could respond as follows: If I have already told you all things in My Word, My Son, and if I have no other word, what answer or revelation can I now make that would surpass this? Fasten your eyes on Him alone, because in Him I have spoken and revealed all, and in Him you shall discover even more than you ask for and desire. You are making an appeal for locutions and revelations that are incomplete, but if you turn your eyes to Him you will find them complete. For He is My entire locution and response, vision and revelation, which I have already spoken, answered, manifested, and revealed to you, by giving Him to you as a brother, companion, master, ransom, and reward. Since that day when I descended upon Him with My Spirit on Mount Tabor proclaiming: *Hic est filius meus dilectus in quo mihi bene complacui, ipsum audite* (This is my Beloved Son in Whom I am well pleased, hear Him) [Mt. 17:5], I have relinquished these methods of answering and teaching, and presented them to Him. Hear Him because I have no more faith to reveal nor truths to manifest. If I spoke before, it was to promise Christ; if they questioned Me, their inquiries were related to their petitions and longings for Christ in Whom they were to obtain every good (as is evidenced in all the doctrine of the Evangelists and Apostles). But now anyone asking Me in that way and desiring that I speak and reveal something to him would somehow be requesting Christ again, and more faith, yet he would be failing in faith, because Christ has already been given. Accordingly, he would offend My Beloved Son deeply, because he would not merely be lacking faith in Him, but obliging Him to become incarnate and undergo His life and death again. You shall not find anything to ask or desire through revelations and visions; behold Him well, for in Him you will uncover all these revelations already made, and many more.

6. If you desire Me to answer with a word of comfort, behold My Son, subject to Me and to others out of love for Me, and you will see how much He answers. If you desire Me to declare some secret truths or events to you, fix your eyes on Him, and you will discern hidden in Him the most secret mysteries, and wisdom, and the wonders of God, as My Apostle proclaims: *In quo sunt omnes thesauri sapientiae et scientiae Dei absconditi* (In the Son of God are hidden all the treasures of the wisdom and knowledge of God). [Col. 2:3] These treasures of wisdom and knowledge will be far more sublime, delightful, and advantageous than what you want to know. The Apostle, therefore, gloried, affirming that he had acted as though he knew no other than Jesus Christ and Him crucified. [1 Cor. 2:2] And if you should seek other divine or corporal visions and revelations, behold Him, become human, and you will encounter more than you imagine, because the Apostle also says: *In ipso habitat omnis plenitudo Divinitatis corporaliter* (In Christ all the fullness of the divinity dwells bodily). [Col. 2:9]

7. One should not, then, inquire of God in this manner, nor is it necessary for God to speak any more. For, since He has finished revealing the faith through Christ, there is no more faith to reveal, nor will there ever be. Anyone wanting to get something in a supernatural way, as we stated, would as it were be accusing God of not having given us in His Son all that is required. Although in such endeavors one presupposes the faith and believes in it, still, one's curiosity displays a lack of faith. Hence there is no reason to hope for doctrine or anything else through supernatural means.

When Christ dying on the cross exclaimed: *Consummatum est* (It is consummated) [Jn. 19:30], He consummated not these ways alone, but all the other ceremonies and rites of the Old Law. We must be guided humanly and visibly in all by the law of Christ the man and that of His Church and of His ministers. This is the method of remedying our spiritual ignorances and weaknesses; here we shall find abundant medicine for them all. Any departure from this road is not only curiosity, but extraordinary boldness. One should disbelieve anything coming in a supernatural way, and believe only the teaching of Christ, the man, as I say, and of His ministers who are men. So true is this that St. Paul insists: *Quod si angelus de coelo evangelizaverit, praeterquam quod evangelizavimus vobis, anathema sit* (If an angel from heaven should preach to you any gospel other than that which we men have preached, let him be accursed and excommunicated). [Gal. 1:8]

8. Since it is true that one must ever adhere to Christ's teaching, and that everything unconformed to it is nothing and worthy of disbelief, anyone who desires to commune with God after the manner of the Old Law is walking in vain.

We see even more how true this is when we recall that it was not lawful at that time for everyone to question God; nor did God give an answer to everyone, but only to the priests and prophets from whom the common people were to learn the law and doctrine. Anyone eager to know something from God did not ask by himself, but through a prophet or priest. If David sometimes asked of himself, it was because he was a prophet. But even then he did not do so without being clothed in priestly vestments, as is evident in the First Book of Kings when he said to Abimelech the priest: *Applica ad me Ephod.*[4] [1 Kgs. 23:9] The ephod was the most dignified of the priest's vestments, and the priest wore it for consultation with God. At other times he consulted God through the prophet Nathan or through other prophets. And the people were to believe that God spoke to them through the mouth of these prophets and priests and not through their own opinion.

9. What God said at that time did not have the authority or force to induce complete belief unless approved by the priests and prophets. God is so content that the rule and direction of man be through other men, and that a person be governed by natural reason, that He definitely does not want us to bestow entire credence upon His supernatural communications, nor be confirmed in their strength and security until they pass through this human channel of the mouth of man. As often as He reveals something to a person, He confers upon his soul a kind of inclination to manifest this to the appropriate person. Until a man does this, he usually goes without complete satisfaction, for he has not received it from another man like himself.

In Judges we see that this happened to the captain Gedeon. Though God had often told him that he would be conqueror of the Madianites, he nonetheless remained doubtful and cowardly, since God had left him in that weakness until through the mouth of men he had heard what God had revealed to him. Since God saw that he was weak, he declared: *Rise up and go down to the camp; . . . et cum audieris quid loquantur, tunc confortabuntur manus tuas, et securior ad hostium castra descendes* (when you hear what the men are saying there, you shall get strength from what I have told you, and you will descend more securely to the enemy host). [Jgs. 7:9–11] And it happened that when Gedeon heard of a Madianite's dream about the future victory, he was deeply strengthened; and full of gladness he prepared for the battle. [Jgs. 7:13–15] Evidently, then, God was undesirous that Gedeon receive assurance through supernatural means alone, for until Gedeon had certitude through natural means, God did not bestow upon him a feeling of security.

4 Bring here the Ephod.

10. And still more wondrous is what happened in a similar instance to Moses. In spite of the fact that God had commanded him with many persuasive arguments to go and bring about the liberation of the children of Israel, and had confirmed these arguments with signs from the rod, that was changed into a serpent, and from the leprous hand [Ex. 4:2-4, 6-10], he was so weak and doubtful about this mission that, in spite of God's anger [Ex. 4:14], he did not possess the courage to give strong credence to it until God heartened him through his brother Aaron: *Aaron frater tuus Levites, scio quod eloquens sit: ecce ipse egredietur in occursum tuum, vidensque te, laetabitur corde. Loquere ad eum, et pone verba mea in ore ejus, et ego ero in ore tuo, et in ore illius* (I know that your brother Aaron is an eloquent man: behold he will go to meet you and at sight of you sincerely rejoice. Speak and tell him all My words, and I will be in your mouth and in his so that each of you will receive certitude through the mouth of the other). [Ex. 4:14-15]

11. At these words Moses was immediately encouraged in the hope of the comfort he was to obtain from his brother's counsel. [Ex. 4:18] This is the trait of a humble person: he does not dare deal with God independently, nor can he be completely satisfied without human counsel and direction. God is desirous of this, for to declare and strengthen truth on the basis of natural reason, He draws near those who come together in an endeavor to know it. He indicated this by asserting that He would be in the mouth of both Aaron and Moses when they would come together for consultation.

This is why He also affirmed in the Gospel: *Ubi fuerint duo vel tres congregati in nomine meo, ibi sum ego in medio eorum* (Where two or three are gathered to consider what is for the greater honor and glory of My name, there I am in the midst of them—that is, clarifying and confirming divine truths in their hearts). [Mt. 18:20] It is noteworthy that He did not say: where there is one alone, there I am; rather He said: where there are at least two. Thus God announces that He does not want the soul to believe only by itself the communications it thinks are of divine origin, nor that anyone be assured or confirmed in them without the Church or her ministers. For God will not bring clarification and confirmation of the truth to the heart of one who is alone. Such a person would remain weak and cold in regard to truth.

12. This is what Ecclesiastes extols: *Vae soli, quia cum ceciderit, non habet sublevantem se. Si dormierint duo, favebuntur mutuo: unus quomodo calefiet? et si quispiam praevaluerit contra unum, duo resistent ei.* [Eccl. 4:10-12] The interpretation of this is: Woe to the one who is alone, for when he falls he has no one to lift him up. If two sleep together, the one shall give warmth (the warmth of God who is in their midst) to the other; how shall one alone be warm? how shall he stop

being cold in the things of God? And if one prevails and overcomes the other (that is, if the devil prevails and overcomes anyone who may desire to remain by himself in the things of God), two together will resist him—and these are the disciple and the master who come together to know the truth and practice it. Until consulting another, a man will usually experience only tepidity and weakness in the truth, no matter how much he may have heard from God. This is so true that after St. Paul had for a long time been preaching the gospel, which he heard not from man but from God [Gal. 1:12], he could not resist going and conferring about it with St. Peter and the Apostles: *ne forte in vacuum currerem aut cucurrissem* (lest he should run or might have run in vain). [Gal. 2:2] He did not feel secure until man had given him assurance. This, then, seems remarkable, O Paul! Could not He Who revealed the gospel to you also give security from any error you might make in preaching its truth?

13. This text clearly teaches that there is no assurance in God's revelations save through the means we are describing. Even though a person does have certitude that the revelation is of divine origin—as St. Paul had of his gospel, since he had already begun to preach it—he can still err in regard to the object of the revelation or its circumstances. For even though God reveals one factor, He does not always manifest the other; often He will reveal something without telling how to accomplish it. He usually does not effect or reveal to a person that which through human effort or counsel can be done, even though He may frequently and affably commune with him. St. Paul understood this clearly, since, as we stated, he went to confer about the gospel in spite of his knowledge that it was divinely revealed.

This is evident, too, in Exodus. Even though God conversed familiarly with Moses, He never gave him that salutary counsel which his father-in-law Jethro imparted: that he select other judges as helpers so that the people would not be waiting from morning till night. [Ex. 18: 13–23] God approved this advice, but He did not give it, because human reason and judgment were sufficient means for solving this problem. Usually God does not manifest such matters through visions, revelations, and locutions, because He is ever desirous that man insofar as possible take advantage of his own reasoning powers. All matters must be regulated by reason save those of faith, which though not contrary to reason transcend it.

14. Let no one imagine that just because God and the saints converse amiably with him on many subjects, they will tell him his particular faults, for he can come to the knowledge of these through other means. Hence there is no motive for assurance, for we read in the Acts of the Apostles what happened to St. Peter. Though he was a prince of the

Church and received immediate instruction from God, he was mistaken about a certain ceremony practiced among the Gentiles. And God was so silent that St. Paul reproved Peter: *Cum vidissem, quod non recte ad veritatem Evangelii ambularent, dixi coram omnibus: Si tu judaeus cum sis, gentiliter vivis, quomodo gentes cogis judaizare?* (As I noticed that the disciples were not walking rightly according to the truth of the gospel, I said to Peter in front of them all: If you being a Jew, as you are, live as a Gentile, why do you force the Gentiles to live as the Jews?). [Gal. 2:14] God did not Himself inform St. Peter of this fault, because that simulation was a rationally discernible fault.

15. On judgment day, God will punish the faults and sins of many with whom He communed familiarly here below and to whom He imparted much light and power. For they neglected their obligations and trusted in their converse with Him and the power He bestowed on them. As Christ declares in the Gospel, they will then be surprised and plead: *Domine, Domine, nonne in nomine tuo prophetavimus et in nomine tuo daemonia ejecimus, et in nomine tuo virtutes multas fecimus?* (Lord, Lord, did we not speak in Your name the prophecies You spoke to us, and did we not cast out devils in Your name and perform many miracles and prodigies?). [Mt. 7:22] And the Lord states that His reply will be: *Et tunc confitebor illis, quia numquam novi vos: discedite a me omnes qui operamini iniquitatem* (Depart from Me, workers of iniquity, for I have never known you). [Mt. 7:23]

Among the workers of iniquity were the prophet Balaam and others like him; though God spoke with them and bestowed favors on them, they were sinners. But the Lord will also in due proportion, because of their faults and neglects, reprove His friends and chosen ones with whom He conversed familiarly here on earth. It was unnecessary for God Himself to inform them of these faults, since He had already done so through the natural law and the reasoning powers He had bestowed on them.

16. I deduce in concluding this part that whatever is received through supernatural means (in whatever manner) should immediately be told clearly, integrally, and simply to one's spiritual director. It may appear that there is no reason for a manifestation to one's spiritual director, or that doing so would be a waste of time, since as we pointed out one is safe in being undesirous of these communications and in rejecting and paying no attention to them (especially in this matter of visions or revelations or other supernatural communications, since it would matter little if they were not clear). Yet it is always necessary to manifest the entire communication, even though there is no apparent reason for so doing. This requisite is based on three reasons:

First, the effect, light, strength, and security of many divine communications are not completely confirmed in a soul, as we stated, until it discusses them with one whom God has destined to be spiritual judge over it, who has power to bind, loose, approve, and reprove. We have established this principle through the texts cited above, and through experience we see it verified each day. We witness humble recipients of these experiences obtain new satisfaction, strength, light, and security after consulting about them with the proper person. This is so true that to some it seems that these communications neither take root nor belong to them until they confer about them, and that the communications are then seemingly imparted anew.

17. Second, a soul ordinarily needs instruction pertinent to its experiences in order to be guided through the dark night to spiritual denudation and poverty. Without this instruction a person would unknowingly become hardened in the way of the spirit and habituated to that of the senses, in which these communications are partly experienced.

18. Third, for the sake of humility, submission, and mortification, a person should give a complete account to his director, even if he disregards or disesteems these communications. Because these communications are seemingly of little importance, or because of concern about the director's possible reaction, some may dread to tell their director about them. This indicates a lack of humility, and for that very reason one should submit to the ordeal. Others feel abashed about manifesting these favors lest they appear to be saints on account of these experiences, and because of other difficulties they feel in speaking about them. They think that because they themselves pay no attention to these experiences, a manifestation of them to their director is unnecessary. But because of this very hardship they ought to mortify themselves and manifest it all to their director, and thereby become humble, simple, meek, and prompt in relating these communications. And from then on they will always do so easily.

19. It ought to be noted in this regard that not because we have greatly stressed the rejection of these communications and the duty of confessors to forbid souls from making them a topic of conversation should directors show severity, displeasure, or scorn in dealing with these souls. With such an attitude they would make them cower and shrink from a manifestation of these experiences, and close the door to them, which would occasion a multitude of difficulties. Since God is leading them by this means, there is no reason for opposing it, nor becoming frightened or scandalized over it; the director should instead be kind and peaceful. He should give these souls encouragement and the opportunity of speaking about their experiences, and, if necessary, oblige them

to do so, for at times everything is needful on account of the hardship some find in discussing these matters.

Spiritual directors should guide them in the way of faith, by giving them good instructions on how to turn their eyes from all these things and on their obligation to denude their appetite and spirit of these communications; they should explain how one act done in charity is more precious in God's sight than all the visions and communications possible —since they imply neither merit nor demerit—and how many who have not received these experiences are incomparably more advanced than others who have had many.

CHAPTER 23

A discussion of spiritual, intellectual apprehensions.

1. Though our doctrine on the intellectual apprehensions which are derived from the senses is somewhat brief in comparison with what it ought to be, I have been undesirous of presenting a lengthier exposition. I believe, rather, that our explanation has been longer than necessary in view of the goal I have in mind, which is to liberate the intellect from these apprehensions and direct it to the night of faith.

Now we shall embark upon a discussion of those other four kinds of intellectual apprehensions: visions, revelations, locutions, and spiritual feelings.

We call these apprehensions purely spiritual because they are not communicated to the intellect through the corporal senses as are imaginary corporal visions. They are clearly, distinctly, and supernaturally imparted to the intellect without the intervention of the exterior or interior bodily senses; and this is done passively, that is, the soul posits no act, at least through its own effort.

2. Let it be known that in a broad sense these four kinds of apprehension can all be titled visions of the soul, because as we say the understanding of a soul is its vision. And insofar as all these apprehensions are intelligible, they are called spiritually visible. Accordingly, the ideas formed from them in the intellect can be termed intellectual visions. The objects of the other senses (of sight, hearing, smell, taste, and touch) are objects of the intellect insofar as they bear relation to the notion of truth or falsehood; and all that is intelligible to the intellect, the spiritual eye of the soul, causes spiritual vision, just as all that is corporally visible to the material eye causes corporal vision. For as we said, understanding an object is seeing it. Thus, speaking generally, we can call these four apprehensions visions. This could not be done with the other senses, be-

cause none of them is capable of perceiving the object as such of any
of the others.

3. But since these apprehensions reach the soul in ways similar to
those of the other senses, we can, properly and specifically speaking,
apply the term vision to whatever the intellect receives in a manner
resembling sight, because the intellect can see objects spiritually just as
the eyes can corporally. And the new truth the intellect gains (just as
the ears in hearing what has never before been heard) as though by
learning and understanding, we call revelation. A locution signifies whatever is received in a way similar to that of hearing. And we apply the
term spiritual feelings to whatever is perceived after the manner of the
other senses, such as the supernaturally enjoyable experience of a sweet
spiritual fragrance, savor, or delight. The intellect derives knowledge or
spiritual vision from all these communications, without the apprehension
of any form, image, or figure of the imagination or natural phantasy.
For these experiences are bestowed immediately upon the soul through
a supernatural work and means.

4. As was the case with the imaginary corporal apprehensions, we
must disencumber the intellect of these spiritual apprehensions by guiding and directing it past them into the spiritual night of faith, to the
divine and substantial union with God, lest the solitude and denudation
concerning all things, which is a requisite for this union, be impeded by
the hindrance and weakness these apprehensions occasion. These apprehensions are nobler, safer, and more advantageous than the imaginative corporal visions, because they are already interior, purely spiritual,
and less exposed to the devil's meddlesomeness. They are more purely
and delicately communicated to the soul and involve none of its own
work—at least active. Nonetheless, through lack of caution and by treading such a path, the intellect might not merely be encumbered but
highly deceived.

5. As a general conclusion, we could give the same counsel for these
four kinds of apprehensions that we accorded for the others: that they
be the object of neither our aims nor our desires. Yet it would be worthwhile to discuss these apprehensions in particular in order to explain
some points about each of them and shed more light on the practice of
this counsel.

And thus we shall deal with the first kind, which are the spiritual
or intellectual visions.

CHAPTER 24

Two kinds of supernatural, spiritual visions.

1. Speaking properly, now, of spiritual visions (those which exclude the bodily senses), I find that there are two kinds relating to the intellect: those of corporal substances, and those of separate or incorporeal substances.

The corporal visions deal with the material things of heaven and earth. The soul, even while in the body, can see these objects by means of a certain supernatural light derived from God, which bestows the power of seeing all heavenly and earthly objects that are absent. We read of such a vision in Chapter 21 of the Apocalypse where St. John relates the description and excellence of the heavenly Jerusalem which he beheld as it descended from heaven. We also read that St. Benedict viewed the entire world in a spiritual vision. [St. Gregory the Great, *Vita S. Benedicti*. Dial., lib. 2, c. 35: PL 66, 198] St. Thomas in the first *Quodlibetum* affirms that this vision was received through a light derived from above, as we stated. [Quodl. 1, a. 1, ad 1.]

2. The visions of incorporeal substances cannot be seen by means of this light derived from God, but by another higher light, the light of glory. These visions of incorporeal substances (angels and souls) do not occur in this life, nor can we while in this mortal body view such substances. If God should desire to let the soul see these substances essentially (as they are in themselves), it would immediately depart from the body and be loosed from this mortal life.

God, when asked to show His essence, proclaimed to Moses: *Non videbit me homo, et vivet* (No man will see Me and be able to remain alive). [Ex. 33:20] When the children of Israel thought they were going to see God, or that they had seen Him or some angel, they were afraid of dying. We read of this in Exodus where they fearfully exclaimed: *Non loquatur nobis Dominus, ne forte moriamur* (May God not openly communicate Himself to us, lest we die). [Ex. 20:19] In the Book of Judges we read too that Manue, Samson's father, thinking that he and his wife had seen in its essence the angel that had appeared to them as a most handsome man, declared to his wife: *Morte moriemur, quia vidimus Dominum* (We shall die because we have seen the Lord). [Jgs. 13:22]

3. These visions do not occur in this life, unless in some rare case and in a transient way. In such an instance, through a dispensation of the natural law, God preserves the nature and life of the individual,

abstracts the spirit entirely, and by His own power supplies the natural functions of the soul toward the body.

When, as is the opinion, St. Paul saw them (the separated substances in the third heaven), he accordingly declared: *Sive in corpore, sive extra corpus nescio; Deus scit* (that he was carried up to them, and that he does not know whether he saw while in the body or out of the body that God knows). [2 Cor. 12:2, 4] Manifestly, he was transported above the ways of our natural life through the intervention of God. Also when God, as is believed, revealed His essence to Moses, He declared that He would place Moses in the cleft of the rock and protect him from death at the passing of the divine glory by covering him with His right hand. This "passing" indicates both God's transient manifestation of Himself and the concomitant preservation, with His right hand, of the natural life of Moses. [Ex. 33:22]

Such substantial visions as those of St. Paul, Moses, and our Father Elias (when he covered his face at the whistling of the gentle breeze of God) [3 Kgs. 19:13], even though transitory, occur rarely or hardly ever, and to only a few. For God imparts this kind of vision only to those who are very strong in the spirit of the Church and God's law, as were these three.

4. Though these spiritual substances cannot be unclothed and seen clearly in this life by the intellect, they can nonetheless be felt in the substance of the soul by the most delightful touches and conjunctions. These pertain to the category of spiritual feelings, which with God's help we shall discuss later.

For we are directing and guiding our pen toward these, that is, to the divine conjunction and union of the soul with the divine substance. We shall speak about this when dealing with the vague or dark mystical knowledge (yet to be expounded) and treating of how, by means of this loving and obscure knowledge, God joins Himself to the soul in a high and divine degree. In a way, this dark, loving knowledge, which is faith, serves as a means for the divine union in this life as does the light of glory for the clear vision of God in the next.

5. Let us discuss now the visions of corporal substances received spiritually in the soul in a way similar to that of bodily visions. As the eyes behold corporal objects by means of the natural light, so the intellect through a supernatural light, as we said, sees interiorly these same objects and others too according to God's wishes. The difference between the two kinds of vision lies in the mode and manner.

The spiritual and intellectual visions are far clearer and more delicate than the corporal ones. For when God desires to bestow this favor upon a soul, He communicates that supernatural light we mentioned so that through it the soul may behold with greater facility and clarity the earthly and heavenly objects He desires it to see. The absence or presence of these objects, then, is of no importance nor does it hinder the vision. To get some idea of this phenomena, suppose that a door were opened so that the soul could see as it would if a flash of lightning were to illumine the dark night and momentarily make objects clearly and distinctly visible, only to leave them all in darkness again—though the forms and images of these objects would remain in the phantasy. This illumination takes place far more perfectly in the soul, for the objects seen in that light are so impressed on it that as often as it adverts to them it beholds them as it did before, just as the forms reflected in a mirror are seen as often as one looks in it. And those objects of its vision are impressed on it so strongly that they are never entirely removed, although in the course of time they do become somewhat more remote.

6. The effects these visions produce in the soul are: quietude, illumination, gladness resembling that of glory, delight, purity, love, humility, and an elevation and inclination toward God. Sometimes these effects are more intense, sometimes less; sometimes one effect predominates, at other times another. This diversity is due to the spirit that receives them and to God's wishes.

7. Through spiritual suggestion and by means of a certain natural light, the devil can also cause these visions in the soul, whether the objects be present or absent. That account in St. Matthew which tells of the devil showing Christ *omnia regna mundi et gloriam eorum* (all the kingdoms of the world and their glory) [Mt. 4:8] is explained by some doctors as an example of spiritual suggestion by the devil, because it would have been impossible for him to make Christ see with His bodily eyes all the kingdoms of the world and their glory.

A great difference lies between diabolical and divine visions, for the effects of diabolical visions are unlike those produced by the divine. The devil's visions produce spiritual dryness in one's communion with God and an inclination to self-esteem, to admitting them and to considering them important. In no way do they cause the mildness of humility and the love of God. Neither are the forms of these diabolical visions impressed with a delicate clarity upon the soul, as are the others. These impressed forms are not lasting, but are soon obliterated from the soul, except when its esteem causes a natural remembrance of them. But the memory of them is considerably arid, and unproductive of the love and humility caused by the remembrance of the good visions.

8. These visions cannot serve the intellect as a proximate means for union with God because they deal with creatures that bear no proportion or essential conformity to God. Consequently, to advance by the proximate means, which is faith, a person should behave in a purely negative

way regarding them, as we have said. A person should not store up or treasure the forms of these visions impressed within him, neither should he have the desire of clinging to them. In doing so, he would impede himself by what dwells within him (those forms, images, and figures of persons), and he would not journey to God through the negation of all things. Though these forms remain impressed within his soul, they are not a great impediment if he is unwilling to pay heed to them. Even if the remembrance of these visions really does stir the soul to some contemplation and love of God, denudation, pure faith, and darkness regarding them will stir and elevate it much more, and without its knowing how or whence this elevation comes.

It will happen that a person will be enkindled with anxieties of very pure love without cognizance of their origin or foundation. The reason for this is that just as faith is infused and rooted more deeply in the soul by means of that emptiness, darkness, and nakedness regarding all things, or by that spiritual poverty (which are all the same), so too the charity of God is simultaneously infused and deeply rooted in the soul. The more one desires darkness and annihilation of himself regarding all visions, exteriorly or interiorly receivable, the greater will be the infusion of faith and consequently of love and hope, since these three theological virtues increase together.

9. But a person does not always grasp or feel this love, because it does not reside with tenderness in the senses, but in the soul, with properties of strength and of greater courage and daring than before, though at times it overflows into the senses imparting a gentle, tender feeling. Accordingly, to attain that love, happiness, and joy caused and produced in the soul by these visions, a person should possess fortitude, mortification, and love so as to remain in emptiness and darkness regarding all creatures; and he should base his love and joy upon what he neither sees nor feels (nor is capable of seeing or feeling), that is, upon God who is incomprehensible and transcendent. This is why our journey toward God must proceed through the negation of all. Even if a person is so shrewd, humble, and strong that the devil is unable to deceive him by these visions or make him (as he usually does) fall into any presumption, the visions will be an obstacle to his advancement if he fails to practice this denial, since they impede spiritual nudity, poverty, and emptiness in faith—the requisite for union with God.

10. Since the same doctrine we taught about supernatural sensory visions and apprehensions in Chapters 19 and 20 is valid also for these visions, we shall not waste any more time here in their discussion.

CHAPTER 25

The nature and kinds of revelation.

1. Logically, our next discussion should deal with the second kind of spiritual apprehensions, which are termed revelations and belong properly speaking to the spirit of prophecy.

First it should be understood that a revelation is nothing else than the disclosure of some hidden truth, or the manifestation of some secret or mystery, as when God imparts understanding of some truth to the intellect, or discloses one of His past, present, or future deeds.

2. We can affirm, therefore, the existence of two kinds of revelation: first, the disclosure of truths to the intellect (these are properly called intellectual notions or concepts); second, the manifestation of secrets. The term revelation is more properly applied to these latter than to the former. The first kind cannot strictly speaking be called revelations, since in them God bestows clear and manifest understanding of naked truths concerning not only temporal but also spiritual objects. I desire to discuss these under the heading of revelations because of their close alliance and affinity with them, and to avoid a multiplication of divisions.

3. As a result we can divide revelations into two classes of apprehensions: the one, we shall call intellectual knowledge, and the other, God's secrets and hidden mysteries. Beginning with intellectual knowledge, we shall deal with these as briefly as possible in the following two chapters.

CHAPTER 26

The two kinds of knowledge of naked truths. The proper conduct of the soul in their regard.

1. For an adequate exposition of this subject (the knowledge of naked truths), God would have to move my hand and pen. For you should know, beloved reader, that what they in themselves are for the soul is beyond words. Since, however, I intentionally speak of these only so as to impart instruction and guide the soul through them to the divine union, let me discuss them in a brief and restricted way, which will be sufficient for our purpose.

2. This kind of vision (knowledge of naked truths) is far different from the kind we dealt with in Chapter 24. This intellectual vision is not like

the vision of corporal objects, but rather refers to an intellectual understanding or vision of truths about God, or to a vision of present, past, or future events, which bears great resemblance to the spirit of prophecy, as we shall perhaps explain later.

3. This type of knowledge is divided into two kinds: the object of the one kind is the Creator; and that of the other is the creature, as we said. Both kinds bring intense delight to the soul. Yet those of God produce an incomparable delight; there are no words or terms to describe them, for* they occasion knowledge and delight of God Himself, and as David says: *there is nothing like unto Him.* [Ps. 39:6] God is the direct object of this knowledge in that one of His attributes (His omnipotence, fortitude, goodness and sweetness, etc.) is sublimely experienced. And as often as this experience occurs, it remains fixed in the soul. Since this communication is pure contemplation, the soul clearly understands that it is ineffable. A person is capable of describing it only through general expressions— expressions caused by the abundance and delight of these experiences. But he realizes the impossibility of explaining with these expressions what he tasted and felt in this communication.

4. David after receiving a similar experience spoke in these unprecise and general terms: *Judicia Domini vera, justificata in semetipsa. Desiderabilia super aurum et lapidem pretiosum multum, et dulciora super mel et favum* (God's judgments—the virtues and attributes we experience in God—are true, in themselves justified, more desirable than gold and extremely precious stone, and sweeter than the honey and the honeycomb). [Ps. 18:10–11].

We read that Moses spoke only in general terms of the lofty knowledge God, while passing by, gave him. And it happened that when the Lord passed before him in that knowledge, Moses quickly prostrated himself, crying: *Dominator Domine Deus, misericors et clemens, patiens, et multae miserationis, ac verax. Qui custodis misericordiam in millia,* etc. (Sovereign Lord God, merciful and clement, patient, and of great compassion, and true. You guard the mercy that you promise to thousands). [Ex. 34:6–7] Evidently, since Moses could not express with one concept what he knew in God, he did so through an overflow of words.

Although at times a person uses words in reference to this knowledge, he clearly realizes that he has said nothing of his experience, for no term can give adequate expression to it.

5. This divine knowledge of God never deals with particular things, since its object is the Supreme Principle. Consequently one cannot express it in particular terms, unless a truth about something less than God is seen together with this knowledge of Him. But in no way can anything be said of that divine knowledge.

This sublime knowledge can be received only by a person who has arrived at union with God, for it is itself that very union. It consists in a certain touch of the divinity produced in the soul, and thus it is God Himself who is experienced and tasted there. Although the touch of knowledge and delight that penetrates the substance of the soul is not manifest and clear, as in glory, it is so sublime and lofty that the devil is unable to meddle, nor produce anything similar (for there is no experience similar or comparable to it), nor infuse a savor and delight like it. This knowledge savors of the divine essence and of eternal life, and the devil cannot counterfeit anything so lofty.

6. He could, nevertheless, in his apery and in an effort to persuade the soul that its experience is from God, proffer to it a certain sensory feeling of grandeur and fulfillment. But this diabolical communication does not enter the substance of the soul and suddenly renew and enamor it as does a divine touch. Some of these divine touches produced in the substance of the soul are so enriching that one of them would be sufficient not only to remove definitively all the imperfections which the soul would have been unable to eradicate throughout its entire life, but also to fill it with virtues and blessings from God.

7. These touches engender such sweetness and intimate delight in the soul that one of them would more than compensate for all the trials suffered in life, even though innumerable. Through these touches a person becomes so courageous and so resolved to suffer many things for Christ that he finds it a special suffering to observe that he does not suffer.

8. A man is incapable of reaching this sublime knowledge through any comparison or imagining of his own, because it transcends what is naturally attainable. Thus God effects in the soul what it is incapable of acquiring. God usually grants these divine touches, which cause certain remembrances of Him, at times when the soul is least expecting or thinking of them. Sometimes they are produced suddenly through some remembrance which may only be of some slight detail. They are so sensible that they sometimes cause not only the soul but also the body to tremble. Yet at other times with a sudden feeling of spiritual delight and refreshment, and without any trembling, they occur very tranquilly in the spirit.

9. Or again they may occur upon uttering or hearing a word from Sacred Scripture or from some other source. These touches do not always have the same efficacy, nor are they always felt so forcefully, because they are often very weak. Yet no matter how weak they may be, one of these divine touches is worth more to the soul than numberless other thoughts and ideas about God's creatures and works.

Since this knowledge is imparted to the soul suddenly, without exercise of free will, a person does not have to be concerned about desiring it or not. He should simply remain humble and resigned about it, for God will do His work at the time and in the manner He wishes.

10. I do not affirm that a person should be negative about this knowledge as he should be with the other apprehensions, because this knowledge is an aspect of the union toward which we are directing the soul and which is the reason for our doctrine about the denudation and detachment from all other apprehensions. God's demands for granting such a grace are humility, suffering for love of Him, and resignation as to all recompense. God does not bestow these favors on a possessive soul, since He gives them out of a very special love for the recipient. For the individual receiving them is one who loves God with great detachment. The Son of God meant this when He stated: *Qui autem diligit me, diligetur a Patre meo, et ego diligam eum, et manifestabo ei me ipsum* (Anyone who loves Me will be loved by My Father, and I will love him and manifest Myself to him). [Jn. 14:21] This manifestation includes the knowledge and touches which God imparts to a person who has reached Him and truly loves Him.

11. The second kind of knowledge, or vision, of interior truths is far different from the type we just explained because it deals with things inferior to God. This class embodies knowledge of the truth of things in themselves and of the deeds and events of men. It is so embedded in the soul—without anyone telling it anything—that if someone were to assert the opposite, it would be unable to give interior assent even by force, for it has a spiritual knowledge of this truth which resembles clear vision. This knowledge pertains to the spirit of prophecy and to the grace St. Paul terms the discernment of spirits. [1 Cor. 12:10]

Although a man may consider his knowledge certain and true, as we pointed out, and be unable to cast off that passive interior assent, he must not, on account of this conviction, fail to believe and give the assent of reason to the instructions and commands of his spiritual director, even if they are extremely contrary to what he feels. In this way one will be led by faith to the divine union, for a soul must journey to it more by believing than by understanding.

12. We have clear testimonies in the Bible of both these kinds of knowledge. As for spiritual knowledge of things the Wise Man declares: *Ipse dedit mihi horum quae sunt scientiam veram, ut sciam dispositionem orbis terrarum, et virtutes elementorum, initium et consummationem temporum, vicissitudinum permutationes, et consummationes temporum, et morum mutationes, divisiones temporum, et anni cursus, et stellarum dispositiones, naturas animalium et iras bestiarum vim ventorum, et cogitationes hominum, differentias virgultorum, et virtutes radicum, et quaecumque sunt abscondita, et improvisa didici: omnium enim artifex docuit me*

sapientia (God gave me true knowledge of existing things: to know the
disposition of the earthly globe and the virtues of the elements, the beginning, ending, and midst of the times, the various vicissitudes and
changes of the seasons, the change of customs, the divisions of time, the
courses of the year, and the position of the stars, the natures of animals,
and the rages of beasts, the power and strength of the winds, the thoughts
of men, the diversities of plants and trees, and the healing power of
roots; and I learned all hidden and unforeseen things, for Wisdom, the
maker of all, taught me). [Wis. 7:17–21]

Although this knowledge of all things, which the Wise Man avows was
given to him by God, was infused and general, this passage offers sufficient proof about all the particular knowledge God infuses supernaturally in souls according to His desires. It does so not because God gives
souls the general habit of knowledge as He did to Solomon, but because
He sometimes reveals to them certain truths about the things enumerated
here by the Wise Man.

Indeed, our Lord infuses habits about different truths in many souls,
although never as general a habit as was Solomon's. These habits are
like those different kinds of divine gifts which St. Paul specifies; among
them he includes wisdom, knowledge, faith, prophecy, discernment or
understanding of spirits, knowledge of tongues, interpretation of words,
etc. [1 Cor. 12:8–10] All these kinds of knowledge are infused habits
which God grants naturally or supernaturally to whomsoever He wills:
naturally, as in the case of Balaam, other idolatrous prophets, and many
sybils, to whom He imparted the spirit of prophecy; and supernaturally,
as to the holy prophets, apostles, and other saints.

13. Yet prescinding from these habits or graces *gratis datae,* we affirm
that those who have reached perfection or are already close to it usually
do possess light and knowledge about events happening in their presence
or absence. This knowledge derives from their illumined and purified
spirits. That passage from Proverbs can be interpreted as referring to this
ability: *Quomodo in aquis resplendent vultus prospicientium, sic corda
hominum manifesta sunt prudentibus* (As the faces of those who look in
the water are reflected there, so are the hearts of men manifest to the
prudent). [Prv. 27:19] These prudent men are those who possess the
wisdom of the saints, which Sacred Scripture calls prudence. [Prv. 10:
23] Through this ability, these persons also come now and then to the
knowledge of other truths, although not whenever they desire, for such
facility would be proper only to those who have the habit. And even those
who possess the habit do not always have this ability in regard to everything, for that would depend on the assistance God wishes to give them.

14. It is worthy of note, though, that individuals whose spirit is purified
can naturally perceive—some more than others—the inclinations and tal-

ents of men and what lies in the heart or interior spirit. They derive this knowledge through exterior indications (even though extremely slight) such as words, gestures, and other signs. Just as the devil, because he is a spirit, is endowed with this skill, so is the spiritual person, according to the Apostle: *Spiritualis autem judicat omnia* (The spiritual man judges all things). [1 Cor. 2:15] And again he declares: *Spiritus enim omnia scrutatur, etiam profunda Dei* (The spirit searches all things, even the deep things of God). [1 Cor. 2:10]

Although spiritual persons cannot know naturally the thoughts of others, or their interior state, they can know this clearly through supernatural enlightenment or through indications. And though they can often be deceived in their knowledge deduced from these indications, they are more often correct in their surmise. But they must not put trust in knowledge acquired through either of these two ways, because, as we shall point out, the devil is a notorious and subtle meddler in this area. Consequently they should always renounce such knowledge.

15. We have an example and testimony in the Fourth Book of Kings of how spiritual persons, even when absent, can also possess knowledge of human deeds and events. When Giezi, the servant of our Father Elias, desired to hide the money received from Naaman, Elias said: *Nonne cor meum in praesenti erat, quando reversus est homo de curru suo in occursum tui?* (Was not my heart perchance present when Naaman turned from his chariot and went to meet you?) [4 Kgs. 5:25-26] Spiritually, this takes place in such a way that the soul beholds the event as if it were happening right before it. We find another proof of this in the same book where we read that Eliseus told the King of Israel everything that the King of Syria discussed with his counselors in his private chamber; and thus these meetings bore no fruit. When the King of Syria realized that their decisions were no longer secret, he complained to his counselors: *Why do you not tell me who among you is betraying me to the King of Israel?* And then one of his counselors exclaimed: *Nequaquam, domine mi rex, sed Eliseus propheta, qui est in Israel indicat regi Israel omnia verba quaecumque locutus fueris in conclavi tuo* (Not so, my lord king, but Eliseus the Prophet who is in Israel reveals to the king everything you say in your private chamber). [4 Kgs. 6:11-12]

16. These kinds of knowledge, as well as the others, come to the soul passively, and thereby exclude any active endeavor of the soul. For it will happen that, while a person is distracted and inattentive, a keen understanding of what he is hearing or reading will be implanted in his spirit, an understanding far clearer than that conveyed through the sound of the words. And although sometimes he fails to grasp the sense

of the words—as when expressed in Latin, a language unknown to him—this meaning is revealed without his understanding the words themselves.

17. We could expound a great deal upon the deceptions the devil can and does cause with regard to this kind of knowledge and understanding, for his deceits are gross and singularly concealed. He can through suggestion ingrain an abundance of knowledge so deeply in the soul that it will seem to be the truth; and if the soul is not humble and distrustful, he will doubtless bring it to believe a thousand lies.

At times the suggestion produces so strong an impression on a person—especially when his soul shares somewhat in the weakness of the senses—and imbeds the knowledge in him with such power, persuasion, and conviction that he then needs a great deal of prayer and strength in order to discard it. Sometimes the devil represents clearly, but falsely, the sins, evil consciences, and evil souls of others in order to defame them. And he is desirous that this be published abroad so that many sins may be committed, and he imparts zeal to the soul by convincing it that the reason for all of this is that prayer may be offered to God for these sinners. Now it is true that God sometimes shows holy souls the necessities of their neighbors so that through their prayer He may provide a remedy. We read, for example, that the affliction of the prophet Baruch was manifested to Jeremias so that he could instruct Baruch about it. [Jer. 45:3] Nevertheless, the devil does this very frequently so as to occasion defamations, sins, and distress; and of this we have much experience. And again at other times the devil will implant deeply in souls other convincing knowledge, and make them believe it.

18. Regardless of whether or not this knowledge is from God, it will be of little profit to a person in his advance toward union if he is attached to it. If he is careless about denying himself this knowledge, it will not only be an obstacle, but the occasion of serious harm and error. All the dangers and difficulties we have discussed up to this point, arising from supernatural apprehensions, and even more, can result from this knowledge.

I shall not enlarge on this subject any more, since we have given sufficient instruction in previous chapters. I shall only point out that a person should be extremely careful always to reject this knowledge, and he should desire to journey to God by unknowing, and always give an account of these revelations to his spiritual director and abide by his counsel. The director should allow the soul to relate this experience briefly, but should not make it the main factor in the soul's journey toward union with God. The effect God desires to produce through these passive communications will be fixed in the soul without its having need for efforts of its own.

As it seems to me, there is no reason, then, for a discussion of the different effects caused by the true and the false knowledge, for this would be wearisome and unending. These effects could not be condensed to a few words because the quantity and variety of this knowledge causes a quantity and variety of effects—the good knowledge causes good effects and the evil knowledge evil effects, etc. It was sufficient to insist upon the rejection of all this knowledge as a control against any error.

CHAPTER 27

The second kind of revelation: the disclosure of secrets and hidden mysteries. The ways in which this knowledge can be either a contribution or a hindrance toward union with God. The devil's power of seriously deceiving souls in this matter.

1. We stated that the second kind of revelation is the disclosure of secrets and hidden mysteries. It can be divided into two further categories:

The first concerns God Himself, which includes the revelation of the mystery of the three Persons in one God.

The second concerns God in His works; this comprises the remaining articles of our Catholic faith and the propositions of truths that can be explicitly formed about His works. These propositions embody a large number of revelatory prophecies, of promises and threats from God, and of other past and future events in regard to this matter of faith.

We can include in this second category many other particular facts revealed ordinarily by God about the universe in general, and, in particular, about kingdoms, provinces, states, families, and individuals.

We have numerous examples of these manifestations, both general and particular, in the divine Scriptures, especially in the writings of the prophets in which all these kinds of revelations are found. Since this assertion is clear and evident, I do not want to waste time here in quoting scriptural passages. I merely want to affirm that these revelations are not given by word only, for God bestows them in a variety of ways and manners: sometimes by word alone; at other times only by signs, figures, images, and likenesses; and sometimes by both together, as is seen in the writings of the prophets. This is particularly evident throughout the Apocalypse where we find examples of all these various kinds of revelations and also of the different ways they are imparted.

2. Even in our time God grants revelations of this second category to whom He wills. He will reveal to some the number of days they have to live, or the trials they will have to endure, or something that will befall

a particular person or kingdom, etc. He will uncover and declare to the spirit truths concerning the mysteries of our faith—although this properly speaking would not be a revelation since they are already revealed; it would be instead a manifestation or declaration of the already revealed.

3. The devil can be a great meddler with this kind of revelation. Since the truths are imparted through words, figures, and likenesses, etc., he can make counterfeits more easily than when the revelations are purely spiritual. If, in these two categories we mentioned, some new truth about our faith is revealed, or something at variance with it, we must by no means give assent, even though we may have the evidence that it was spoken by an angel from heaven. Thus St. Paul states: *Licet nos, aut angelus de coelo evangelizet vobis praeterquam quod evangelizavimus vobis, anathema sit* (Though we, or an angel from heaven, declare or preach something other than what we have preached, let him be anathema). [Gal. 1:8]

4. Since there are no more articles to be revealed to the Church about the substance of our faith, a person must not merely reject new revelations about the faith, but he should out of caution repudiate other kinds of knowledge mingled with them. In order to preserve the purity of his faith, a person should not believe already revealed truths because they are again revealed, but because they were already sufficiently revealed to the Church. Closing his mind to them, he should rest simply on the doctrine of the Church and its faith which, as St. Paul says, enters through hearing. [Rom. 10:17] And if he wants to escape delusion, he should not adapt his credence and intellect to those truths of faith revealed again, no matter how true and conformed to the faith they may seem. To deceive and introduce lies, the devil first lures a person with truths and verisimilitudes that give assurance; and then he proceeds with his beguilement. These truths of his are like the bristle used in sewing leather: It is put through the holes first in order to pull along after it the soft thread; without the bristle the thread would never pass through.

5. Let this be kept in mind: Even if there is actually no danger of deception to the soul, a person should be undesirous of knowing the truths of faith clearly, that he may thereby conserve pure and entire the merit of faith and also pass through this night of intellect to the divine light of union.

Closing the eyes to any new revelation and focusing them upon former prophecies is so important that even though St. Peter in some way saw the glory of the Son of God on Mount Tabor, he declared in his Second Epistle: *Et habemus firmiorem propheticum sermonem, cui benefacitis attendentes,* etc. (Although our vision of Christ on the mount was true, the word of the prophecy revealed to us is more certain and unshaken, and you do well by resting your soul on it). [2 Pt. 1:19]

6. If it is true for the reason already mentioned that one should close one's eyes to these revelations about the propositions of faith, how much greater need is there to repel and disbelieve other revelations impertinent to the faith and in which the devil usually meddles! Because of the apparent truth and convincing quality with which the devil clothes them, I consider it impossible for a person not striving to reject them to go undeceived. For to make one believe, the devil joins together so many apparent and appropriate facts, and implants them so firmly in the imagination and senses, that it seems the events will undoubtedly occur. And he causes the soul to be so convinced and tenacious about them that if it has no humility it will hardly be torn from its opinion and made to believe the contrary.

The pure, cautious, simple, and humble soul should resist and reject revelations and other visions with as much effort and care as it would extremely dangerous temptations, for in order to reach the union of love there is no need of desiring them, but rather of rejecting them. Solomon meant this when he exclaimed: *What need has a man to desire and seek what is above his natural capacity?* [Eccl. 7:1] This means that to be perfect there is no need to desire to receive goods in a way that is supernatural and beyond one's capacity.

7. Any objection that could be made against these instructions has already been answered in Chapters 19 and 20 of this book. Referring to the doctrine given there, I only say that a person should be on his guard against these revelations so that through the night of faith he may journey to union purely and without error.

Chapter 28

The nature and kinds of supernatural locutions received by the spirit.

1. The discreet reader must always keep in mind my intention and goal in this book: to guide the soul in purity of faith through all its natural and supernatural apprehensions, in freedom from every deception and obstacle, to the divine union with God. Thereby he should understand that though I am not giving abundant instruction about these apprehensions of the soul, nor examining the divisions and subject matter as minutely as may be necessary, I am not being brief on this topic either. For I think I have imparted sufficient advice, light, and instruction on the prudent

behavior required for advancement in the midst of these exterior and interior apprehensions.

This is why I discussed prophetic apprehensions so briefly, as I also did the others. There is so much to expound about each of these kinds of prophecy (about their difference and their ways and modes of being received) that I think one would never know it all fully. I am content that, in my opinion, the substantial part of the doctrine has been pointed out, as well as the caution that is necessary in dealing with these apprehensions or anything resembling them.

2. I shall now follow the same method with the third kind of apprehension, the supernatural locutions usually produced in the souls of spiritual persons without the use of the bodily senses as means. Although there are so many classes, I find they can be reduced to three: successive, formal, and substantial locutions.

Successive locutions are the words and reasonings that the spirit usually forms and deduces while recollected.

Formal locutions are certain distinct and formal words that the spirit receives, whether or not recollected, not from itself but from another party.

Substantial locutions comprise other words that are also produced formally in the spirit, regardless of whether or not it is recollected, and that cause in the substance of the soul that power and very substance they signify.

We shall discuss all these in due order.

CHAPTER 29

The first kind of locution the recollected spirit sometimes forms. A discussion of its origin and of the profit or harm it may occasion.

1. Successive words always occur when the spirit is recollected and attentively absorbed in some consideration. A person will reason about his subject, proceeding thought by thought, forming precise words and judgments, deducing and discovering such unknown truths, with so much ease and clarity, that it will seem to him he is doing nothing and that another person is interiorly reasoning, answering, and teaching him.

Indeed, there is every reason for this belief, since he reasons with himself and replies as if carrying on a dialogue. In a way he really is speaking with another for, though he reasons by using his intellect as the instrument, the Holy Spirit frequently helps him to form these true concepts, words, and judgments, and thus he utters them to himself as though to another person. Since his intellect is recollected and united with the truth, which is the subject of his thought, and the Holy Spirit is also united with him in that truth—for He is in every truth—it results that, while his intellect is thus communing with the divine Spirit by means of that truth, it simultaneously forms interiorly and successively the other truths about its subject, while the Holy Spirit, the Teacher, leads the way and gives light. This is one of the Holy Spirit's methods of teaching.

2. The intellect thus enlightened and taught by this Master forms propositions while understanding those truths communicated to it from elsewhere. Accordingly we could say that the voice is of Jacob, but the hands, of Esau. [Gn. 27:22] Anyone having this experience is unable to believe that these propositions originate with himself. Because of his ignorance about the ease with which the intellect can by itself form statements, which seemingly originate from another and which rest on concepts and truths communicated by another, he thinks they do come from some other person.

3. Though in that communication or illumination itself there is actually no deception of the intellect, yet there can be and frequently is deception in the formal words and propositions the intellect deduces from it. That light is often so delicate and spiritual that the intellect does not succeed in being completely informed by it; and it is the intellect that of its own power, as we stated, forms the propositions. Consequently the statements are often false, or only apparent, or defective. Since the intellect afterwards joins its own lowly capacity and awkwardness to the thread of truth it had already begun to grasp, it easily happens that it changes the truth in accordance with this lowly capacity; and all as though another person were speaking to it.

4. I knew someone who in his experience of these successive locutions formed, among some very true and solid ones about the Blessed Sacrament, others that were outright heresies.

And I greatly fear what is happening in these times of ours: If any soul whatever after a bit of meditation has in its recollection one of these locutions, it will immediately baptize all as coming from God and with such a supposition say, "God told me," "God answered me." Yet this is not so, but, as we pointed out, these persons themselves are more often the origin of their locution.

5. Furthermore, their desire for such locutions and their attachment to them cause these persons to answer themselves and think that God is responding and speaking to them. They will commit serious blunders if they do not practice great restraint and if their directors do not oblige them to renounce these discursive methods. For through these methods they usually derive more vanity of speech and impurity of soul than humility and mortification of spirit. They think something extraordinary

has occurred and that God has spoken, whereas in reality little more than nothing will have happened, or nothing at all, or even less than nothing. If an experience fails to engender humility, charity, mortification, holy simplicity, and silence, etc., of what value is it?

I insist, therefore, that this locution can be a serious obstacle to an individual in his journey toward divine union because by paying attention to it the soul is drawn far from the abyss of faith. The intellect should remain in this obscurity and journey by love in darkness of faith and not by much reasoning.

6. If you ask me why the intellect must be deprived of those truths, since the Spirit of God illumines it through them, I answer: the Holy Spirit illumines the intellect that is recollected, and He illumines it according to the mode of its recollection, and the intellect can find no better recollection than in faith, and thus the Holy Spirit will not illumine it in any other recollection more than in faith. The purer and more refined a soul is in faith, the more infused charity it possesses, and the more charity it has the more the Holy Spirit illumines it and communicates His gifts, because charity is the means by which they are communicated.

In that illumination of truths the Holy Spirit indeed communicates some light to the soul, yet the light given in faith—in which there is no clear understanding—is qualitatively as different from the other as is the purest gold from the basest metal, and quantitatively as is the sea from a drop of water. In the first kind of illumination, wisdom concerning one, two, or three truths, etc., is communicated; and in the second, all God's wisdom is communicated in general, that is, the Son of God, Who is imparted to the soul in faith.

7. Should you tell me that everything will be all right since the first kind of illumination is no obstacle to the second, I would reply that it is a serious obstacle if the soul pays attention to it. For this involves attention to distinct truths, which are of little importance and enough to hinder the communication of the abyss of faith. In this faith God supernaturally and secretly teaches the soul, and, in a way unknown to it, raises it up in virtues and gifts.

The profit produced by a successive locution will not be received from focusing one's attention on it. Through such behavior a person instead would be driving away the locution, for Wisdom says to the soul in the Canticle: *Withdraw your eyes from me, for they make me fly away* [Ct. 6:4], that is, they make me fly far from you and ascend higher. The benefit will be received through a simple application of the will to God through love, and in this way the communication will be more abundant than before.

If in the supernatural and passive communication of these truths the natural intellect and the other faculties intervene actively, they will not attain these heights, because of their own mode and obtuseness, and thus they will be forced to modify the truths according to their mode of knowing, and consequently change them. The intellect, then, will necessarily err and form judgments of its own, which will be neither supernatural nor similar to the supernatural, but singularly natural, erroneous, and base.

8. Yet some intellects are so lively and subtle that, while recollected in meditation, they reason naturally and easily about some concepts, and form locutions and propositions very vividly, and consequently think that these locutions are from God. But that notion is false, for an intellect, freed from the operation of the senses, has the capacity to do this and even more with its own natural light and without any other supernatural help. Such an occurrence is frequent. And many are deluded by it in thinking that theirs is the enjoyment of a high degree of prayer and communion with God; consequently they either write the words down themselves or have others do so. It comes about that the experience amounts to nothing, that no substantial virtue is derived from it, and that it serves for little more than inducing vainglory.

9. These people should learn to give importance to nothing other than sincere effort, the establishment of their wills in humble love, and suffering in imitation of the life and mortifications of the Son of God. This is the road to the attainment of every spiritual good, and not that other one of copious interior reasoning.

10. The devil too meddles a great deal in this kind of interior locution, especially in cases where the individuals have a particular attachment to them. When they begin recollecting themselves, the devil usually offers ample matter for digression by supplying through suggestion ideas or words for the intellect. Subtly deceiving them with verisimilitudes, he gradually brings about their ruin. This is one of his ways of communicating with those who have made a tacit or express pact with him, or of informing heretics—or especially heresiarchs—about extremely subtle, false, and erroneous ideas and arguments.

11. Manifestly, then, these successive locutions can originate in the intellect from any of three causes: the divine Spirit, Who moves and illumines the intellect; the natural light of the intellect; and the devil, who can speak to it through suggestion.

It would be a difficult task now to discuss completely all the signs for the discernment of the cause from which these locutions proceed, although we can easily give some general ones. They are the following:

When together with the words and concepts the soul is loving God and simultaneously experiencing this love with humility and reverence, there is indication that the Holy Spirit is at work within it. Whenever He bestows favors, He clothes them with this love.

When the locution originates from the vivacity and light of the intellect, the cause of everything is the intellect, and there is no accompanying activity of the virtues. The will can love naturally in the knowledge and light of those truths, yet after the meditation, it will remain dry. But the soul will have no inclination toward vanity unless the devil again tempts it about its experience. In the locutions arising from the Divine Spirit, this aridity is not felt, because after the locution the will is ordinarily attached to God and inclined toward good. Yet sometimes the will is arid afterwards even if the communication is from the divine Spirit, for God so ordains for the benefit of the soul. At other times the soul will not have much experience of the operations or movements of those virtues, nevertheless the locution will be good. This is the reason for the difficulty I mentioned in discerning the cause of these locutions through their varied effects. The effects already referred to are the common ones, though at times they are more abundant and at other times less.

Even locutions caused by the devil are sometimes difficult to discern and recognize. Ordinarily, indeed, they leave the will in dryness as to the love of God, and the intellect inclined toward vanity and self-esteem or complacency; still, they can bring about a false humility and a fervent tendency of the will rooted in self-love. A person in consequence will have to be very spiritual to recognize this. The devil effects these false virtues in order to be more hidden. That he might fix in souls the attachments he desires them to have, he is expert at inducing the flow of tears from the feelings he introduces. He always endeavors to move the will toward an esteem for these interior communications so that it might devote and occupy itself with things that instead of increasing the virtues occasion the loss of what it already possessed.

12. Let us conclude then with this precaution necessary for the avoidance of any delusion or hindrance from these variously caused locutions: We should pay no heed to them, but be only interested in firmly directing the will through them toward God; we should carry out His law and holy counsels perfectly—for such is the wisdom of the saints—content with knowing the mysteries and truths in the simplicity and verity with which the Church proposes them. An attitude of this kind is sufficient for a vigorous enkindling of the will; hence we do not have to pry into profundities and curiosities in which danger is seldom lacking. St. Paul in regard to this conduct states: *One should not have more knowledge than befits him.* [Rom. 12:3]

This exposition on successive locutions is sufficient.

Chapter 30

Interior words formally and supernaturally produced in the spirit. A warning about their danger and a necessary precaution against delusion.

1. The second kind of interior locution is called formal and is produced supernaturally in the spirit without the use of the senses. Its origin is independent of any spiritual recollection. I give it the name "formal locution" because another person formally utters it to the spirit without intervention of the soul. It is consequently far different from the successive locution. It differs not only by the fact that the spirit itself is not involved in the cause, but also, as I say, it occurs sometimes when there is no recollection and the soul is far from any thought of what is spoken. In successive locutions such is not the case, for they always have to do with the subject of one's meditation.

2. Sometimes these words are very explicit and at other times not. They are like ideas spoken to the spirit, either as a reply to something or in another manner. At times only one word is spoken, and then again more than one; sometimes the locutions are successive, like the others, for they may endure while the soul is being taught, or while something is being discussed. All these words come without any intervention of the spirit, because they are received as though one person were speaking to another. Daniel experienced this when, as he says, the angel spoke to him. The angel reasoned formally and successively in his spirit and also declared that he had come to teach him. [Dn. 9:22]

3. When these words are no more than formal they bear little effect. Ordinarily they are given merely for the purpose of teaching or shedding light upon some truth. Accordingly the efficacy of their effect need be no more than required for the attainment of their purpose. When God is the cause of the locution, this effect is always produced in the soul, for it renders the soul ready to accomplish the command and discerning in understanding it. Yet these locutions do not always remove repugnance and difficulty, rather they sometimes augment it. God does this for the further instruction, humility, and good of the soul. God more frequently allows this repugnance when He orders something pertinent to a prelacy or to some other factor that will bring honor to the soul. And in matters of humility and lowliness He imparts more facility and readiness. We read in Exodus that when God ordered Moses to go to Pharao and obtain liberation for the people, Moses felt such repulsion that God had to command him three times and show him signs; yet none of this was of any avail, until God gave him Aaron to share in the honor. [Ex. 3:10-22; 4:1-18]

4. On the other hand, when the locutions and communications are of diabolic origin, it will happen that facility and readiness will be given in matters involving an increase of honor, whereas only repugnance will be felt for lowly tasks. God surely finds souls inclined toward prelacies a sight so abhorrent that even when He gives such a command and puts a soul in office, He is undesirous of its becoming eager to govern. Formal locutions differ from the successive ones in relation to this readiness God usually bestows. Successive locutions do not move the soul as much as these do, because these are more formal, and the intellect does less on its own. Yet this does not prevent the successive locutions from sometimes producing a greater effect because of a greater communication between the divine Spirit and the human spirit. However, there is considerable difference in the manner in which the effect is produced. The soul has no reason for doubting that these locutions come from another, for it is clearly aware that it does not form them itself, especially by the fact that it is not thinking upon what is said to it. If it does happen to be pondering over this, it experiences very clearly and distinctly that the locution is from another source.

5. A person should pay no more attention to all these formal locutions than he should to the other kind, for besides occupying the spirit with matters irrelevant to faith, the legitimate and proximate means of union with God, they will make him an easy victim for the devil's deceits. It will be difficult sometimes to discern those spoken by a good spirit from those coming from a bad one. Since these locutions do not produce much effect, they can hardly be discerned by their effects. Sometimes those of the devil will even have more efficacy in imperfect souls than the others will have in spiritual ones. A person must not do what these words tell him, nor should he—whether they are from a good or bad spirit—pay any attention to them. Nevertheless, they should be manifested to an experienced confessor or to a discreet and wise person who will give instructions and counsel and decide what is to be done. But the individual's attitude toward them ought to be one of resignation and negation. If such an expert person cannot be found, it is better not to speak of these locutions to anyone, but simply pay no attention to them, for a soul can easily fall into the hands of some persons who will tear it down rather than build it up. Souls should not discuss these locutions with just anyone, since in so serious a matter being right or wrong is of such importance.

6. It should be kept in mind that a person must never follow his own opinion, nor do or admit anything told to him through these locutions, without ample advice and counsel from another. For in this matter of locutions strange and subtle deceits will occur—so much so that I believe a person who is unopposed to them cannot but be deceived in many.

7. Since I intentionally discussed these delusions and dangers, and the necessary precaution concerning them, in Chapters 17 to 20 of this book—to which I refer the reader—I shall not enlarge any more upon them here. I only repeat that my main teaching is to pay no heed whatever to them.

CHAPTER 31

Substantial locutions produced in the spirit. How these differ from formal locutions, the profit they cause, and the resignation and respect that should be had concerning them.

1. The third kind of interior locution, we said, is the substantial locution. Although these locutions are also formal, since they are impressed very formally in the soul, they nevertheless are different in that their effect is vital and substantial, which is not the case with formal locutions. Though, indeed, every substantial word is formal, it does not follow that every formal word is substantial—only the word that impresses its significance substantially upon the soul. For example, if our Lord should say formally to the soul: "Be good," it would immediately be substantially good; or if He should say: "Love Me," it would at once have and experience within itself the substance of the love of God; or if He should say to a soul in great fear: "Do not fear," it would without delay feel ample fortitude and tranquillity. For as the Wise Man declares, God's word and utterance is full of power [Eccl. 8:4], and thus it produces substantially in the soul what is said. David meant this when he stated: *Behold He will give His voice the voice of power.* [Ps. 67:34] God did this to Abraham, for when He said: *Walk in my presence and be perfect* [Gn. 17:1], Abraham immediately became perfect and always proceeded with reverence for God. We remark the power of God's word in the Gospel when with a mere expression He healed the sick, and raised the dead, etc.

In this fashion He bestows substantial locutions upon certain souls. These locutions are important and valuable because of the life, virtue, and incomparable blessings they impart to the soul. A locution of this sort does more good for a person than a whole lifetime of deeds.

2. As for these locutions the soul has nothing to do, desire, refrain from desiring, reject, or fear.

There is nothing to be done, because God never grants them for that purpose, but He bestows them in order to accomplish Himself what they express. For this reason they differ from the formal and successive locutions.

And there is nothing for the soul to desire nor refrain from desiring. A desire for these locutions is not necessary in order that God grant them, nor would not wanting them hinder their effect. The soul should rather be resigned and humble about them.

A person has nothing to reject, because the effect of these locutions remains substantiated in the soul and replete with God's blessings. Since the soul receives this passively, its activity would be entirely superfluous.

It need not fear any deceit, because neither the intellect nor the devil can intervene in this communication. The devil is incapable of passively producing the substantial effect of his locution upon the soul, unless, as it may happen, the soul has surrendered itself to him by a voluntary pact. Thus, the devil dwelling in it as its lord would produce such effects—not good, but evil ones. Since this soul would already be united with him in voluntary wickedness, he could easily impress in it the evil effects of his locutions and words. Through experience we observe that in many matters he has great power through suggestion even with good souls, and injects notable efficacy into these locutions. If these souls were evil, then, he could produce the effect in them completely. But he is unable to produce effects similar to those arising from God's locutions, for there is no comparison between God's words and the devil's. In comparison with God's locutions and their effect, those of the devil and their effect are nothing. God affirms this through Jeremias: *What has the chaff to do with the wheat? Are not my words perhaps like fire and the hammer that breaks rocks?* [Jer. 23:28–29]

Consequently these substantial locutions are a great aid to union with God. And the more interior and substantial they are, the more advantageous they are for the soul. Happy the soul to whom God speaks these substantial words. *Speak, Lord, for your servant is listening.* [1 Kgs. 3:10]

CHAPTER 32

The intellectual apprehensions of the spiritual feelings supernaturally imparted to the soul. The cause of these interior feelings and the attitude necessary for the avoidance of impediments in the journey toward union with God.

1. It is time now for a discussion of the fourth and last kind of intellectual apprehension. This kind, we said, the intellect receives from the spiritual feelings which are often granted supernaturally to spiritual persons. We count these spiritual feelings among the distinct apprehensions of the intellect.

2. These distinct spiritual feelings are of two kinds:
The first comprises feelings in the affection of the will; the second,

feelings in the substance of the soul. These kinds are possible in many ways.

Those in the will are very sublime when from God, but the feelings in the substance of the soul are the loftiest, and are exceptionally advantageous and good. Neither the soul nor its director can know their origin, nor because of what works God bestows them.

These favors are not dependent upon the works or meditations of the soul, though these exercises do dispose it well for the reception of such gifts. For God grants them to whom He wills and for the reason He wills. It can happen that someone will have done many works, and yet God will not bestow these touches; and another will have accomplished far fewer works and nevertheless receive an abundance of the most sublime touches. Accordingly, although it may be a better preparation, it is unnecessary for a person to be actually employed and occupied in spiritual matters in order that God grant the touches from which it experiences these feelings. Most of the time this favor is given when it is farthest from the mind.

Some of these touches are distinct and of short duration, others are not so distinct and last longer.

3. These feelings, as such, are not allied to the intellect but to the will. Thus it is not my purpose to discuss them here. This I shall do in the following book while dealing with the night and purgation of the attachments of the will.

Yet because most of the time the apprehension, knowledge, and understanding of them overflows into the intellect, we ought to mention them here.

It is noteworthy that from these feelings the apprehension of knowledge or understanding frequently redounds, as I say, to the intellect. This is true with both the touches in the will and those in the substance of the soul, whether they be sudden touches or lasting and successive. This apprehension is usually an exceptionally sublime and delightful perception of God in the intellect. It cannot be given a name, as neither can the feeling from which it overflows. This knowledge is now of one kind and then again of another. According to the touches produced by God (which cause the feelings from which the knowledge is derived), and according to the property of these touches, this knowledge is sometimes more sublime and clear than at other times.

4. It is unnecessary to waste many words here in cautioning the intellect and directing it through this knowledge to union with God in faith. Just as the feelings we mentioned are produced passively in an individual without any of his own effective activity, so too the knowledge of them is received passively in the intellect (which the philosophers call "possible") without any active effort. To avoid error on their account,

and any impediment to the profit coming from them, the intellect should do nothing about them other than behave passively and refrain from meddling through the use of its natural capacity. For as in the case of successive locutions, the intellect by its own activity easily disturbs and undoes that delicate knowledge, which is a delightful, supernatural understanding unattainable through one's natural capacity; nor does the intellect find this knowledge comprehensible through its own activity, but only by receiving does it comprehend it.

Thus a person should not strive after this knowledge, nor be desirous of admitting it, lest the intellect begin to form the knowledge on its own, or the devil find an entrance for his other various and false knowledge. The devil can easily effect false knowledge, either by means of these feelings or by others which he himself can bestow on the soul that is attached to this knowledge. A person's attitude toward this knowledge should be one of resignation, humility, and passivity. For since it is received passively from God, it will be received when He is pleased to grant it and when He sees that the soul is humble and unpossessive. In this way one will not hinder the tremendous profit this knowledge affords to the divine union, for all these feelings are touches of union; and the union is produced passively in the soul.

5. The doctrine expounded is sufficient, for in the divisions we gave the soul will find precautions and instructions for any of its intellectual apprehensions. There is no intellectual apprehension unreducible to one of these kinds, even if it may seem different or unincluded. A person can therefore obtain the proper instructions by referring to my discussion of the particular kind of apprehension he has received.

BOOK THREE

The active night or purgation of the memory and will. Doctrine about the attitude required in the apprehensions of these two faculties that a soul may reach union with God in perfect hope and charity.

CHAPTER 1

1. We have already given instructions for the intellect, the first faculty of the soul, so that in all its apprehensions it may be united with God through pure faith, the first theological virtue. The same has to be done for the other two faculties, memory and will. They must undergo a

purification relative to their respective apprehensions in order to reach union with God in perfect hope and charity.

Our exposition in this third book will be brief. For it is unnecessary to enlarge so much in our treatise on these faculties, since in the instructions given for the intellect (the receptacle in its own way of all the other objects) we have covered a great portion of the matter. If the spiritual person directs his intellect in faith according to the doctrine given him, it is impossible for him not to instruct his other two faculties simultaneously in the other two virtues. For these faculties depend on one another in their operations.

2. To continue the method we have been using and for the sake of clarity, we shall discuss each point particularly and list the proper apprehensions of each faculty. We begin with those of the memory and here give a division of them that should suffice for our purpose. We form this division from the three different objects of the memory: natural, imaginative, and spiritual. In accordance with these objects the knowledge of the memory is also of three kinds: natural, supernatural imaginative, and spiritual.

3. With God's help we shall discuss these three here, beginning with natural knowledge which arises from a more exterior object. Afterwards we shall deal with the affections of the will, and thereby this third book of the active spiritual night will be brought to a close.

CHAPTER 2

The natural apprehensions of the memory. The emptiness required for union with God according to this faculty.

1. In each of these books the reader must keep in mind the intention we have in writing. Failure to do so will give rise to many doubts about what he reads. He may already have them concerning the instructions given for the intellect, or he may experience them upon reading what we say about the memory and the will.

Observing how we annihilate the faculties in their operations, it will perhaps seem that we are tearing down rather than building up the way of spiritual exercise. This would be true if our doctrine here were destined merely for beginners, who have to prepare themselves through these discursive apprehensions.

2. But we are imparting instructions here for advancing in contemplation to union with God. All these sensory means and exercises of the faculties must, consequently, be left behind and in silence so that God Himself may effect the divine union in the soul. As a result one has to

follow this method of disencumbering, emptying, and depriving the faculties of their natural rights and operations to make room for the inflow and illumination of the supernatural. If a person does not turn his eyes from his natural capacity, he will not attain to so lofty a communication; rather he will hinder it.

3. Thus, if it is true—as indeed it is—that the soul must journey by knowing God through what He is not, rather than through what He is, it must journey, insofar as possible, by way of the denial and rejection of natural and supernatural apprehensions. This is our task now with the memory. We must draw it away from its natural props and capacities and raise it above itself (above all distinct knowledge and apprehensible possession) to supreme hope in the incomprehensible God.

4. To begin with natural knowledge in the memory, I include under this heading all that can be formed from the objects of the five corporal senses (hearing, sight, smell, taste, and touch), and everything like this sensory knowledge that the memory can evoke and fashion.

The annihilation of the memory in regard to all forms is an absolute requirement for union with God. This union cannot be wrought without a complete separation of the memory from all forms that are not God. For as we mentioned in the night of the intellect, God cannot be contained in any form or distinct knowledge. Since, as Christ affirms, no one can serve two masters [Mt. 6:24], and the memory cannot at the same time be united with God and with forms and distinct knowledge, and since God has no form or image comprehensible to the memory, the memory is without form, figure, or phantasy when united to God; and in great forgetfulness, without the remembrance of anything, it is absorbed in a supreme good. This is noted every day through experience. That divine union empties and sweeps the phantasy of all forms and knowledge, and elevates the memory to the supernatural.

5. It is worthwhile noting what sometimes takes place in this state. When God on occasion produces these touches of union in the memory, a sudden jolt is experienced in the brain (where the memory has its seat), so sensible that it seems the whole head swoons and that consciousness and sensibility are lost. This is sometimes more perceptible, sometimes less, according to the force of the touch. Then, owing to the union, the memory is emptied and purged, as I say, of all knowledge and remains in oblivion, at times in such great oblivion that it must occasionally force itself and struggle in order to remember something.

6. Sometimes this forgetfulness of the memory and suspension of the imagination reaches such a degree—because the memory is united with God—that a long time passes without awareness or knowledge of what has happened. Even though others may inflict pain on a person

in this state, he does not feel it, since the imaginative power is in suspension, and without the imagination there is no feeling. That God may produce these touches of union, the soul must disunite the memory from all apprehensible knowledge. These suspensions, it should be noted, occur at the beginning of union, and are not thus found in souls who have reached perfection, because the union is then perfect.

7. Someone may object that this doctrine seems good, but that it results in the destruction of the natural activity and use of the faculties, and that man then lives in oblivion like an animal and, even worse, without remembrance of natural necessities and operations. The objection will be made that God does not destroy, but perfects nature, and that the destruction of nature is a necessary consequence of this doctrine. For according to these instructions the carrying out of the natural operations and of the moral and rational acts would be forgotten. None of this could be remembered due to the deprivation of concepts and forms, the means of reminiscence.

8. I answer that this is actually so. For the more the memory is united with God, the more the distinct knowledge is perfected, until the memory loses it entirely; that is, when the soul is perfect and has reached the state of union. Thus in the beginning, when this union is in the process of being perfected, a person cannot but experience great forgetfulness of all things, since forms and knowledge are gradually being erased from the memory. Owing to the absorption of his memory in God, a person will show many deficiencies in exterior behavior and customs. He will forget to eat or drink, or fail to remember whether or not he performed some task, or saw a particular object, or said something—all because of the absorption of his memory in God.

Yet once he has the habit of union—which is a supreme good—he no longer experiences these lapses of memory in matters concerning his moral and natural life. Rather he will possess greater perfection in actions which are necessary and fitting. These operations, however, are no longer produced through forms and knowledge in the memory, for by possessing the habitual union, which is now a supernatural state, the memory and other faculties fail entirely in their natural operations and pass from these natural boundaries to those of God, which are supernatural. Thus, when the memory is transformed in God, the knowledge and forms of things cannot be impressed on it.

As a result all the operations of the memory and other faculties in this state are divine. God now possesses the faculties as their complete lord, because of their transformation in Him. And consequently it is He Who divinely moves and commands them according to His spirit and will. As a result the operations are not different from those of God; but those the soul performs are of God and are divine operations. Since he who is united with God is one spirit with Him, as St. Paul says [1 Cor. 6:17], the operations of the soul united with God are of the divine Spirit and are divine.

9. These souls, consequently, perform only fitting and reasonable works, and none that are not so. For God's Spirit makes them know what must be known and ignore what must be ignored, remember what ought to be remembered—with or without forms—and forget what ought to be forgotten, and makes them love what they ought to love, and keeps them from loving what is not in God. Accordingly, all the first movements of these faculties are divine. And it is no wonder that the movements and operations of these faculties are divine, for they are transformed into divine being.

10. Here are some examples of these divine operations. A person will ask a soul in this state for prayers. The soul will not remember to carry out this request through any form or idea of that person remaining in the memory. If it is expedient to pray for him (that is, if God wants to receive prayer for this person), God will move its will and impart a desire to do so; at times God will give it a desire to pray for others whom it has never known nor heard of.

The reason is that God alone moves these souls to do those works that are in harmony with His will and ordinance, and they cannot be moved toward others. Thus the works and prayer of these souls always produce their effect.

Such was the prayer and work of our Lady, the most glorious Virgin. Raised from the very beginning to this high state, she never had the form of any creature impressed in her soul, nor was she moved by any, for she was always moved by the Holy Spirit.

11. Another example. At a particular time a person will have to attend to a necessary business matter. He will not remember through any form, but, without his knowing how, the time and suitable way of attending to it will be impressed on his soul without fail.

12. The Holy Spirit illumines such souls not merely in these matters but in many other present or future matters and about many events, even distant ones. Although He sometimes accomplishes this through intellectual forms, He often does so without them so that these souls are unaware of how they come by this knowledge. But its origin is the divine wisdom. Since these souls are practiced in not knowing or understanding anything with the faculties, they generally attain, as we mentioned in the drawing of the Mount, to the knowledge of everything; as the Wise Man states: *The artificer of all, who is Wisdom, taught me all things.* [Wis. 7:21]

13. You may object, perhaps, by asserting the impossibility of voiding and depriving the memory of all forms and phantasies in order to reach this high state. In your view there will be two difficulties insurmountable by human strength and capacity: the banishment of the natural through one's natural strength, and contact and union with the supernatural (which is far more difficult, and, to be truthful, impossible by one's natural ability alone).

I reply that, indeed, God must place the soul in this supernatural state. Nevertheless, an individual must insofar as possible prepare himself. This he can do naturally with God's help. In the measure that he embarks through his own efforts upon this negation and emptiness of forms, he will receive from God the possession of union. God effects this union in him passively, as we shall explain, *Deo dante*, in *The Passive Night of the Soul*. Thus God will give the habit of the perfect divine union when He is pleased to do so and in accordance with the individual's preparation.

14. We shall not discuss in this active night and purgation the divine effects that the union, when perfect, produces in the intellect, memory, and will, because the divine union is not perfected by this night alone. But we will speak of them in the passive night, for it is by means of this passive night that union with God is wrought.

I shall only treat here of the manner in which the memory through the spiritual person's own efforts must be brought into this night and purgation. In short, the spiritual person should ordinarily take this precaution: do not store up in the memory the objects of hearing, sight, smell, taste, or touch, but leave them immediately and forget them, and endeavor, if necessary, to be as successful in forgetting them as others are in remembering them. This should be practiced in such a way that no form or figure of any of these objects remains in the memory, as though one were not in the world at all. The memory, as though it were nonexistent, should be left free and disencumbered and unattached to any earthly or heavenly consideration. It should be freely forgotten, as though it were a hindrance, since everything natural is an obstacle rather than a help to anyone who would desire to use it in the supernatural.

15. If those doubts and objections we discussed in dealing with the intellect (that nothing is accomplished, that time is lost, and that the soul is deprived of the spiritual goods receivable through the memory) should arise, the answers to them are all in that part. We shall also refer to these objections further on, in the *Passive Night*. Accordingly there is no reason for delay with them here.

It is only proper to give a warning that although at times the spiritual person does not experience the benefit of this suspension of knowledge and forms, he should not grow weary, for God will not fail to come to his aid at a suitable time. And it is expedient to endure and suffer patiently and with hope for so remarkable a blessing.

16. Although it is true that a person will hardly be found whose union with God is so continuous that his faculties, without any form, are always divinely moved, nevertheless there are those who are very habitually moved by God and not by themselves in their operations, as St. Paul says: the children of God (those who are transformed in God and united to Him) are moved by the Spirit of God (that is, moved to divine works in their faculties). [Rm. 8:14] It is no marvel that the operations are divine, since the union of the soul with God is divine.

CHAPTER 3

Three kinds of harm resulting from not darkening the memory of its knowledge and discursive reflection. A discussion of the first kind.

1. The spiritual person who still wishes to make use of natural knowledge and discursive reflection in his journey to God, or for anything else, is subject to three kinds of harm and difficulty. Two are positive and one privative.

The first kind arises from the things of the world; the second from the devil; and the third, the privative, is the impediment and hindrance to the divine union that this knowledge causes.

2. The first, coming from the world, involves the subjection to many evils arising from this knowledge and reflection, such as: falsehoods, imperfections, appetites, judgments, loss of time, and numerous other evils engendering many impurities in the soul.

Manifestly the spiritual person allowing himself this knowledge and reflection will necessarily be the victim of many falsehoods. Often the true will appear false, and the certain doubtful, and vice versa, since we can hardly have complete understanding of a truth. A man frees himself of this if he darkens his memory to all knowledge and reflection.

3. Imperfections meet him at every step, if he turns his memory to the objects of hearing, sight, touch, smell, and taste. By so doing, some emotion will cling to him, whether it be sorrow, fear, hatred, vain hope, vain joy, or vainglory, etc. All these are at least imperfections, and sometimes real venial sins. They subtly contaminate the soul with impurity, even though the knowledge and reflection concerns God.

And it is also clear that appetites will be engendered, since they naturally arise from this knowledge and reflection. And the mere desire for this knowledge and reflection is already an appetite.

Obviously a man will also encounter many occasions to judge others, since by using his memory he cannot help but stumble upon their good or evil deeds. And at times the evil seems good and the good evil. I am of the opinion that no man can free himself entirely from all these evils, if he does not blind and darken his memory as to all things.

4. You may say that a man is easily capable of conquering all these dangers when they come upon him. I reply that it is simply impossible to achieve this completely if one pays attention to this knowledge, for intermingled with it are a thousand imperfections and trifles, some so subtle and slight that without a person's realizing it they stick to him just as pitch does to anyone who touches it. These imperfections are better overcome all at once through complete denial of the memory.

You may also make the objection that the soul will suffer the deprivation of numerous holy thoughts and considerations about God, which are conducive to the reception of favors from God. I answer that purity of soul is more helpful toward this, for purity of soul indicates that no attachment or advertence to creatures or temporal things cling to the soul. I think these creatures will not fail to adhere to it a great deal owing to the imperfections the faculties of themselves have in their operations. It is better to learn to silence and quiet the faculties so that God may speak. For in this state, as we pointed out, the natural operations must fade from sight. This is realized when the soul arrives at solitude in these faculties, and God speaks to its heart, as the prophet asserts. [Os. 2:14]

5. If you still insist, claiming that a person will obtain no benefits if the memory does not consider and reflect about God, and that many distractions and weaknesses will gradually find entrance, I answer that this is impossible. If the memory is recollected as to both heavenly and earthly things, there is no entry for evils, distractions, trifles, or vices—which all enter through the wandering of the memory. Distractions would result if, upon closing the door to considerations and discursive meditation, we opened it to thoughts about earthly matters. But in our case we close the memory to all ideas—from which distractions and evils arise—by rendering it silent and mute, and applying the hearing of the spirit to God in silence, saying with the prophet: *Speak Lord, for your servant is listening.* [1 Kgs. 3:10] The Spouse in the Canticle of Canticles proclaimed that this was to be the attitude of the bride: *My sister is a garden enclosed and a fountain sealed up.* [Ct. 4:12]

6. The soul should remain closed, then, without cares or afflictions, for He who entered the room of His disciples bodily, while the doors were closed (without their knowing how this was possible), and gave them peace, will enter the soul spiritually (without its knowing how or using

any effort of its own), once it has closed the doors of its intellect, memory, and will to all apprehensions. And He will fill them with peace, descending upon them, as the prophet says, like a river of peace. [Is. 66:12] In this peace He will remove all the misgivings, suspicions, disturbances, and darknesses that made the soul fear it had gone astray. The soul should persevere in prayer and should hope in the midst of nakedness and emptiness, for its blessings will not be long in coming.

CHAPTER 4

The second kind of harm, that which comes from the devil through the natural apprehensions of the memory.

1. The second kind of positive harm possible from knowledge in the memory is due to the devil. He has tremendous influence in the soul by this means. For he can add to its knowledge other forms, ideas, and reasonings, and by means of them move it to pride, avarice, anger, envy, etc., and insert unjust hatred, vain love, and many kinds of delusions. Moreover he usually so impresses images on the phantasy that the false ones seem true and the true ones false. And finally all the greatest delusions and evils he produces in the soul enter through the ideas and discursive acts of the memory. If the memory is darkened as to all this knowledge, and annihilated through oblivion, the door is closed entirely to this kind of diabolical harm, and the soul is liberated from these evils; and that is a wonderful blessing.

The devil is unable to do anything in the soul save through the operations of its faculties, and principally by means of its knowledge, because almost all the activity of the other faculties depends upon its knowledge. If the memory is annihilated concerning this knowledge, the devil is powerless. For he finds no means of getting his grip on the soul, and consequently can do nothing.

2. I should like spiritual persons to have full realization of how many evils the devils cause in souls that make use of their memories; of how much sadness, affliction, vain and evil joy from both spiritual and worldly thoughts these devils occasion; and of the number of impurities they leave rooted in the spirit. They also seriously distract these souls from the highest recollection, a recollection which consists in the concentration of all the faculties on the incomprehensible Good and the withdrawal of them from all apprehensible things, for these apprehensible things are not a good that is beyond comprehension.

Although the good derived from this void is not as excellent as that arising from the application of the soul to God, by the mere fact that it liberates us from a lot of sorrow, affliction, and sadness—over and above imperfections and sins—it is an exceptional blessing.

CHAPTER 5

The third kind of harm which follows from the natural, distinct knowledge of the memory.

1. The third kind of evil engendered by the natural apprehensions of the memory is privative. These apprehensions can be an impediment to moral good and deprive one of spiritual good.

An explanation of how these apprehensions are a hindrance to moral good demands a precise idea of moral good. Moral good consists in the control of the passions and the restriction of the inordinate appetites. The result for the soul is tranquillity, peace, repose, and moral virtue, which is the moral good.

The soul is incapable of truly acquiring the control of the passions and the restriction of the inordinate appetites without forgetting and withdrawing from the sources of these emotions. Disturbances never arise in a soul unless through the apprehensions of the memory. When all things are forgotten, nothing disturbs the peace or stirs the appetites. As the saying goes: What the eye doesn't see, the heart doesn't want.

2. We have experience of this all the time. We observe that as often as a person begins to think about some matter, he is moved and aroused about it according to the kind of apprehension. If the apprehension is bothersome and annoying, he feels sadness or hatred, etc.; if agreeable, he will experience a desire and joy, etc.

Accordingly, when the apprehension is changed, agitation necessarily results. Thus he will sometimes be joyful, at other times sad, now he will feel hatred, now love. And he is unable to persevere in equanimity, the effect of moral tranquillity, unless he endeavors to forget all things.

Evidently, then, this knowledge is a serious impediment to the possession of the moral virtues.

3. That an encumbered memory is also a hindrance to the possession of spiritual good is clearly proved from our remarks. For an unsettled soul, which has no foundation of moral good, is incapable as such of receiving spiritual good. For this spiritual good is only impressed upon a restrained and peaceful soul.

Besides, if a person bestows importance and attention upon the apprehensions of the memory, he will find it impossible to remain free for the Incomprehensible Who is God, for he will be unable to advert to more than one thing. As we have always been insisting, the soul must go to

God by not comprehending rather than by comprehending, and it must exchange the mutable and comprehensible for the Immutable and Incomprehensible.

CHAPTER 6

The benefits derived from forgetting the natural thoughts and knowledge of the memory.

1. From the kinds of harm occasioned by the apprehensions of the memory, we can also determine the opposite benefits which come from forgetting them; as the philosophers say: The doctrine for one thing serves also for its contrary.

In contrast to the first kind of harm, the spiritual person enjoys tranquillity and peace of soul due to the absence of disturbance and change which derives from thoughts and ideas in the memory, and consequently he possesses purity of conscience and soul, which is a greater benefit. As a result, he is disposed excellently for human and divine wisdom and virtues.

2. In contrast to the second, he is freed from many suggestions, temptations, and movements which the devil inserts in souls through their thoughts and ideas, thereby occasioning many impurities and sins; as David says: *They thought and spoke wickedness.* [Ps. 72:8] When the thoughts are removed the devil has nothing naturally with which to wage his war on the spirit.

3. Contrary to the third kind of harm, the soul is disposed, by means of this recollection and forgetfulness of all things, to be moved by the Holy Spirit and taught by Him. As the Wise Man declares: *He withdraws from thoughts that are without reason.* [Wis. 1:5]

Even though no other benefit would come to a man through this oblivion and void of the memory than freedom from afflictions and disturbances, it would be an immense advantage and blessing for him. For the afflictions and disturbances engendered in a soul through adversities are no help in remedying these adversities; rather, distress and worry ordinarily makes things worse and even does harm to the soul itself. Thus David proclaimed: *Indeed every man is disturbed in vain.* [Ps. 38:7] Clearly, it is always vain to be disturbed, since being disturbed is never any help.

Thus if the whole world were to crumble and come to an end and all things were to go wrong, it would be useless to get disturbed, for this would do more harm than good. The endurance of all with tranquil and peaceful equanimity not only reaps many blessings, but also helps the soul so that in these very adversities it may succeed in judging them and employing the proper remedy.

4. Solomon, having clear knowledge of this harm and this advantage, exclaimed: *I knew there was nothing better for man than to rejoice and do good in his life.* [Eccl. 3:12] By this he indicates that in all events, however unfavorable, we ought to rejoice rather than be disturbed, and bear them all with equanimity so as not to lose a blessing greater than all prosperity: tranquillity of soul and peace in all things, in adversity as well as in prosperity. A man would never lose this tranquillity if he were to forget ideas and lay aside his thoughts, and also, insofar as possible, withdraw from dealing with others and from hearing and seeing. Our nature is so unstable and fragile that even when well disciplined it will hardly fail to stumble upon thoughts with the memory; and these thoughts become a disturbance to a soul that was residing in peace and tranquillity through the forgetfulness of all. As a result Jeremias proclaimed: *With the memory I shall remember, and my soul will faint in me with sorrow.* [Lam. 3:20]

CHAPTER 7

The second kind of apprehension, which is of supernatural imaginative knowledge.

1. Though in our discussion of the first kind of apprehension, we also gave doctrine for the natural, imaginative visions, we find this division suitable owing to the other forms and ideas the memory preserves. These ideas are from supernatural apprehensions, such as visions, revelations, locutions, and sentiments. When these apprehensions occur, they usually leave an image, form, figure, or idea impressed either in the soul or in the memory or phantasy. At times this impression is most vivid and efficacious.

It is also necessary to give advice about these apprehensions, lest they become an encumbrance to the memory and hinder it from union with God in pure and integral hope.

2. I declare that to obtain this blessing a person should never reflect upon the clear and distinct supernatural apprehensions for the purpose of preserving within himself their forms, figures, and ideas. We must always bear in mind this principle: the more importance given to any clear and distinct apprehension, natural or supernatural, the less capacity and preparedness the soul has for entering the abyss of faith, where all else is absorbed. As we pointed out, none of the supernatural forms and ideas that can be had by the memory is God, and the soul must empty

itself of all that is not God in order to go to God. Consequently the memory must also dismiss all these forms and ideas in order to reach union with God in hope. Every possession is against hope; as St. Paul says, hope is for that which is not possessed. [Heb. 11:1]

In the measure that the memory becomes dispossessed of things, in that measure it will have hope, and the more hope it has the greater will be its union with God; for in relation to God, the more a soul hopes the more it attains. And when, precisely, it is more dispossessed of things, it hopes more; and when it has reached perfect dispossession, it will remain with the perfect possession of God in divine union. But there are many who do not want to go without the sweetness and delight of this knowledge in the memory, and therefore they do not reach supreme possession and complete sweetness. For whoever does not renounce all his possessions cannot be Christ's disciple. [Lk. 14:33]

CHAPTER 8

The harm caused from reflection upon this supernatural knowledge. Tells how many kinds of harm there are.

1. The spiritual person exposes himself to five types of harm if he prizes and reflects upon the ideas and forms impressed within him through supernatural apprehensions.

2. The first is that he will often be deluded in mistaking the natural for the supernatural.

Second, he puts himself in the occasion of falling into presumption and vanity.

Third, the devil finds ample power to deceive him through these apprehensions.

Fourth, so doing would be an impediment to union with God in hope.

Fifth, his judgment of God for the most part will be base.

3. As for the first, if the spiritual person reflects upon these forms and ideas and assigns importance to them, he will frequently be deceived in his judgment. Since no one is capable of knowing perfectly the things that pass naturally through his imagination, or of forming an integral and certain judgment about them, how much less is one able to make judgments about supernatural things which transcend our capacity and occur but rarely.

A person will often have the opinion that the apprehensions are from God, whereas they will be only the product of his imagination; and often he will think that what is from God is from the devil and that what is from the devil is from God. He will frequently receive among other images strong impressions about the goods and evils of himself or others. He will think they are certain and true, however they will not be true, but utterly false. Others will be true, and he will judge them false; though this, I believe, is safer because it is usually the outcome of humility.

4. If he escapes delusion about the truth, he can still suffer a quantitative or qualitative deception. He will think the small, large and the large, small; or as to quality, that which in his imagination he judges to be this particular kind will in reality be another kind. He will be taking, as Isaias says, the darkness for light and the light for darkness, the bitter for the sweet and the sweet for the bitter. [Is. 5:20] If, finally, his surmise in one instance is correct, it will be a wonder if he avoids error in another. Even if he is unwilling to make judgments, it is sufficient that he place some importance on these apprehensions for some sort of harm to cling to him, at least passively. And if it is not this type of harm, it will be one of the other four kinds we shall discuss.

5. To avoid in his judgments this evil of deception, the spiritual person should be unwilling to judge the nature of his experiences, or the kind of visions, knowledge, or feeling he has; he should be undesirous of knowing this or attributing importance to it, except for the sake of informing his spiritual director and of thereby receiving instructions on how to void the memory of these apprehensions. Whatever they are in themselves, they are not as great a help toward the love of God as is the least act of living faith and hope made in the emptiness and renunciation of all things.

CHAPTER 9

The second kind of harm—the danger of falling into self-esteem and vain presumption.

1. These supernatural apprehensions of the memory, if esteemed, are also for spiritual persons a decided occasion for slipping into some presumption or vanity. Since anyone not receiving these is liberated from falling into this vice, because nothing within him warrants this presumption, so, on the other hand, anyone receiving them will be exposed to the idea that he is now worth something on account of these supernatural communications. Though, indeed, a person, in considering himself unworthy, can attribute them to God and be thankful for them, yet there usually remains in the spirit a certain hidden satisfaction and an esteem both for the communication and for oneself. Consequently, without one's realizing it, an abundant spiritual pride will be bred.

2. This is quite evident from the displeasure and aversion these individuals feel toward anyone who does not laud their spirit nor value their communications, and from the affliction they experience upon thinking or being told that others receive the same favors or even better ones. All this is born of hidden self-esteem and pride. And these persons are not fully aware that they are steeped in pride. They think that a certain degree of knowledge of one's own misery is sufficient. Yet at the same time they are full of hidden self-esteem and satisfaction, more pleased with their own spirit and spiritual goods than with those of their neighbor. They resemble the pharisee who thanked God that he was not like other men, and that he had the various virtues, and who from the thought of these virtues derived self-satisfaction and presumption. [Lk. 18:11–12] Though they may not express this as the pharisee did, they habitually feel this way in their spirit. Indeed, some become so proud that they are worse than the devil. Since they observe interiorly some apprehensions and devout and sweet feelings, which they think are of divine origin, they become self-satisfied to the extent of thinking that they are very close to God, and that others who are without them are very far from Him, and, like the pharisee, they look down upon these others.

3. To avoid this pestiferous evil, abhorrent in the eyes of God, they should consider two truths:

First, virtue does not consist in apprehensions and feelings of God, however sublime they may be, nor in any similar experience. But on the contrary, it comprises what they do not experience, that is, deep humility, contempt for themselves and for all things—very explicit and conscious to the soul—delight that others feel contempt for them also, and the desire to be worth nothing in the hearts of others.

4. Second, all the visions, revelations, and feelings from heaven, or whatever else one may desire to think upon, are not worth as much as the least act of humility. Humility has the effects of charity: it neither esteems nor seeks its own, it thinks no evil save of self, it thinks no good of self but of others.

Consequently, souls should not content themselves with these supernatural apprehensions, but strive to forget them for the sake of being free.

CHAPTER 10

The third kind of harm that comes from the devil through the imaginative apprehensions of the memory.

1. It can be deduced and easily understood from all we have said how much evil can come from the devil by way of these supernatural ap-

prehensions. He can present to the memory many false ideas and forms under the guise of truth and falsehood. This he does through suggestion by impressing them on the spirit and the senses in a very efficacious way. He makes these ideas seem so certain that the soul thinks they cannot be false, but that what it feels is in accord with truth. Since the devil transforms himself into an angel of light [2 Cor. 11:14], he seems to be light to the soul. But this is not all. In the true visions from God, he can also tempt it in many ways, by causing inordinate movements of the spiritual and sensory appetites and affections toward these visions. If the soul is pleased with these apprehensions, it is very easy for the devil to occasion an increase of its appetites and affections and a lapse into spiritual gluttony and other evils.

2. To accomplish this more expertly, he usually suggests and places pleasure, savor, and delight in the senses relevant to the things of God so that, sweetened and dazzled in that delight, the soul may become blind and fix its eyes more upon the pleasure than the love—or at least not so intensely on the love—and pay more attention to the apprehension than to the nakedness and emptiness of faith, hope, and love. And in so doing the devil deceives the soul little by little and readily makes it believe his falsehoods.

To a blind soul, falsehood no longer seems falsehood, and evil no longer evil, etc., for the darkness appears to be light, and the light darkness. [Is. 5:20] On this account, the soul will fall into a thousand blunders in matters natural, moral, and spiritual; and what was wine will have turned into vinegar. All this comes about because of failure to deny the pleasure of those supernatural apprehensions from the beginning. Since this satisfaction is slight, or not so evil at first, the soul is not careful and allows it to remain so that, like the mustard seed, the evil grows into a large tree. [Mt. 13:31-32] As the saying goes, a slight error in the beginning is a great one in the end.

3. To flee from this gross error of the devil, therefore, a person should be unwilling to take pleasure in these apprehensions, for most certainly this pleasure will gradually blind him and cause him to fall. By their very own nature, without the devil's help, pleasure, delight, and savor blind the soul. David indicated this when he said: *Darkness will perhaps blind me in my delights and I shall have the night for my life.* [Ps. 138:11]

CHAPTER 11

An impediment to union with God, the fourth kind of harm resulting from the distinct supernatural apprehensions of the memory.

1. Little remains to be said about this fourth kind of harm since we are explaining it all along in this third book. We have given proof that a soul must renounce all possession of the memory in order to reach union with God in hope, for if hope is to be centered entirely on God, nothing that is not God should reside in the memory.

And we have also given proof that no form, figure, image, or idea (whether heavenly or earthly, natural or supernatural) that can be grasped by the memory is God or like to Him. Accordingly, David teaches: *Lord, among the gods no one is like You.* [Ps. 85:8]

2. If the memory, consequently, is desirous of paying attention to this knowledge, it is hindered from union with God: first, because of the encumbrance; second, because the more possessions it has the less hope it has.

The soul, therefore, must live in the nakedness and forgetfulness of distinct forms and knowledge about supernatural apprehensions, so as not to impede union of the memory with God through perfect hope.

CHAPTER 12

Base and improper judgments of God, the fifth kind of harm arising from supernatural imaginative forms and apprehensions.

1. The fifth kind of harm derived from the desire of preserving in the memory and imagination these forms and images of supernatural communications is no less evil than the others, especially if the soul desires to use these images as means toward the divine union. It is extremely easy to judge the being and height of God less worthily and sublimely than is suitable to His incomprehensibility. Though a person may not form an explicit idea that God is similar to these apprehensions, nevertheless the very esteem for them—if, in fact, he esteems them—produces in the soul an esteem and opinion of God less elevated than that given in the teaching of faith: that He is incomparable, incomprehensible, etc.

Besides taking from God all this attention it gives to creatures, the soul will naturally form in its interior, through esteem for these apprehensions, a certain comparison between them and God. This comparison prevents it from having as lofty a judgment and esteem of God as it ought.

Creatures, earthly or heavenly, and all distinct ideas and images, natural and supernatural, that can be the objects of a person's faculties, are incomparable and unproportioned to God's being. God does not fall under the classifications of genus and species, whereas, according to theologians, creatures do. Thus St. John affirms that no one has ever seen God. [Jn. 1:18] Isaias declares that it has not entered the heart of man what God is like. [1 Cor. 2:9] And God told Moses: *You cannot see Me in this life.* [Ex. 33:20]

Therefore, anyone encumbering the memory and the other faculties of the soul with what is comprehensible, cannot have the proper esteem or opinion of God.

2. Here is a poor example. The more a person sets his eyes on the king's servants and the more attention he pays to them, the less heed he pays to the king and the less he esteems him. Though this estimation is not in the intellect formally and explicitly, it is practically; because the more attention he gives to the servants, the more he takes away from his lord. And then his judgment of the king is not very high, since the servants seem to him somewhat important in comparison with the king, his lord. This is what happens in relation to God when a person pays attention to these creatures; although the comparison is very inadequate, because, as we have mentioned, the being of God is different from the being of His creatures. God, by His being, is infinitely distant from all of them. The soul should consequently turn its eyes from these creatures so as to focus them upon God in faith and hope.

3. Those who not only pay heed to these imaginative apprehensions, but think God resembles some of them, and that one can journey to union with God through them, are already in great error and will gradually lose the light of faith in their intellects; and it is by means of faith that the intellect is united with God. Furthermore they will not increase in the loftiness of hope, the means for union with God in the memory. This union is effected by disuniting oneself from everything imaginative.

CHAPTER 13

The benefits obtained through the rejection of the apprehensions of the imagination. Answers certain objections and explains the difference between the natural and the supernatural imaginative apprehensions.

1. Like the observation we made concerning natural forms, the benefits from voiding the imagination of supernatural apprehensions can be

ascertained through the five kinds of harm caused in the soul if it desires to possess these forms interiorly. But besides these, there are other benefits of deep spiritual repose and quietude. In addition to the tranquillity a person naturally enjoys when freed from images and forms, there is a freedom from care about the discernment of the good ones from the evil, and about how one ought to behave with the different kinds. Finally one would be absolved from the drudgery and waste of time with spiritual directors which would result from desiring the director to discern the good apprehensions from the evil ones and to ascertain the kind of apprehension received. A person does not have to know this, since he should not pay attention to any of these apprehensions.

The time and energy that would be wasted in trying to discern them can be employed in another more profitable exercise (the movement of the will toward God), and in solicitude about the search after spiritual and sensory nakedness and poverty (the desire to lack all the consoling support of the apprehensions, both interior and exterior). A person practices this latter by desiring and striving after detachment from these forms, since he thereby receives the great gain of approaching God, Who has neither image, form, nor figure. He will approach God the more closely the more he withdraws from all imaginative forms, images, and figures.

2. Perhaps your question will be: Why do many spiritual persons counsel souls to strive for profit in the communications and feelings God gives, and to desire favors from Him in order to have something to give Him, since if He gives nothing to us, we shall have nothing to give to Him? And you will establish this with a text from St. Paul: *Do not extinguish the spirit* [1 Thes. 5:19]; also with one from the Canticle of Canticles in which the Bridegroom says to the bride: *Put me as a seal upon your heart, as a seal upon your arm* [Ct. 8:6], for this seal is a certain apprehension. And all of this, you will say, according to our doctrine must not only be unsought, but rejected and put aside, even though God bestows it; and that evidently, since God grants this gift, He does so for a good purpose, and it will be effective. You will add that we must not throw away pearls and that it is a kind of pride to refuse God's gifts, as though we are self-sufficient without them.

3. In answer to this objection, our explanation in Chapters 15 and 16 of Book Two [Chapters 16 and 17 in the present state of the text] must necessarily be kept in mind. To a great extent the objection is answered there. We stated that the good resulting in the soul from supernatural apprehensions coming from a good source is produced passively, without any operation of the faculties, at the very moment these apprehensions are represented to the senses.

It is consequently unnecessary for the will to act in order to admit them. As we said, if a man were to desire to act with his faculties, he would through his base natural operation impede the supernatural (which God is producing in the soul by means of these apprehensions) rather than derive profit from his own labor. But since the spirit of these imaginative apprehensions is given passively to the soul, he must maintain a passive attitude without application of his interior or exterior actions to anything.

And this attitude would preserve the spiritual feelings of God, because a person would not then lose them through his own lowly kind of operation. Nor would he extinguish the spirit. A person extinguishes the spirit by wanting to conduct himself in a way different from that in which God is leading him. He acts in this way if he desires, when God gives him the spirit passively—as He does through these apprehensions—to be active, by working with the intellect or by desiring something in these apprehensions.

This is clear, for if the soul would then want to work, its activity would necessarily be no more than natural. On its own it can do no more, since a soul does not move itself to a supernatural work, nor can it, but God moves it and places it in this supernatural activity. If then a person were to desire to make use of his own efforts, he would necessarily impede by his activity the passive communication of God, which is the spirit. He would be engaging in his own work, which is of another and lower kind than that which God is communicating to him. The work of God is passive and supernatural, that of man active and natural. This natural activity of man is what would extinquish the spirit.

4. That this is a more lowly work is also clear, because the faculties of the soul cannot of themselves reflect and operate except upon some form, figure, and image, which would be the rind and accident of the substance and spirit.

This substance and spirit is not united with the faculties of the soul in true understanding and love until the operation of the faculties ceases. For the aim of this activity is the reception of substantial understanding and love through those forms. The difference between the active and passive operation is the same as that between what is being done and what is already done, or what one intends to attain and what is already attained.

Thus we also deduce that if a person were to desire to employ his faculties actively in these supernatural apprehensions by which, as we said, he receives the spirit passively from God, he would be doing nothing less than abandoning what has been accomplished in order to redo it; neither would he be enjoying what was done, nor by his activity doing anything other than impeding God's work. For, as we said, these actions cannot independently attain the spirit God was giving to the soul without them. If the soul pays heed to these imaginative apprehensions, it directly extinguishes the spirit which God infuses by means of them.

Consequently, a person should abandon these apprehensions and behave passively and negatively, because then God moves the soul to what transcends its power and knowledge. The prophet accordingly declared: *I shall stand upon my watch and fix my foot upon my tower, and I shall contemplate what is said to me.* [Hb. 2:1] This is like saying: I shall stand upon the watch of my faculties and take no step forward in my operations; thus I shall be able to contemplate what is told me: I shall understand and taste what is communicated to me supernaturally.

5. The words of the Bridegroom, which were quoted in the objection, should be interpreted as referring to the love he asks of the bride. It is a characteristic of love to assimilate lovers to one another in their spiritual faculties. As a result He tells her to set Him as a mark upon her heart [Ct. 8:6], there where all the arrows of love (the actions and motives of love) that come from the quiver strike. He does this so that all the arrows might strike Him who is there as their target, and thus all are directed to Him. And the soul becomes like Him through its actions and movements of love until transformed in Him. He tells her to set Him also as a mark upon her arm, because the act of love is on the arm, since by the arm the beloved is held and caressed.

6. In these apprehensions coming from above (imaginative or any other kind—it matters not if they be visions, locutions, spiritual feelings, or revelations), a person should only advert to the love of God they interiorly cause. He should pay no attention to the letter and rind (what they signify, represent, or make known). Thus he should pay heed not to the feelings of delight or sweetness, not to the images, but to the feelings of love that are caused.

Only for the sake of moving the spirit to love should the soul at times recall the images and apprehensions which produced love. Though the effect produced by the remembrance of this communication is not as strong as at the time the communication was received, yet, when the communication is recalled, there is a renewal of love and an elevation of the mind to God. This is especially true when the soul remembers some figures, images, or supernatural feelings. These are usually so imprinted on it that they last a long time; some are never erased from the soul. These apprehensions produce, almost as often as remembered, divine effects of love, sweetness, light, etc.—sometimes in a greater degree, sometimes in a lesser—because God impressed them for this reason. This is consequently a great grace, for the person upon whom God bestows it possesses within himself a mine of blessings.

7. The figures producing such effects are vividly impressed upon the soul and are unlike other images and forms preserved in the phantasy. The soul has no need of recourse to this faculty when it desires to remember them, for it is aware that it has them within itself as an image in a mirror. When a soul possesses these figures formally within itself, it can safely recall them for the procuring of the effect of love I mentioned, because they will not be a hindrance to the union of love in faith, providing it is undesirous of being absorbed with the figure. It must profit from the love by immediately leaving aside the figure. By such procedure the remembrance will instead be a help to the soul.

8. It is difficult to discern when these images are impressed on the soul and when on the phantasy. For those of the phantasy are also quite frequent. Some persons who usually have imaginative visions find that these same visions are very frequently represented in their phantasy, either because they themselves possess a very lively faculty, so that with little thought the ordinary figure is immediately represented and sketched upon it, or because the devil causes these representations, or also because God causes them without impressing them formally in the soul.

Nonetheless they can be discerned through their effects. For those that are of natural or diabolical origin produce no good effect or spiritual renovation in the soul, no matter how often they are remembered. The individual beholds them in dryness. When remembered, however, the imaginative apprehensions from God produce some good effect by means of that which they imparted to the soul the first time. Yet the formal apprehensions—those impressed on the soul—yield some effect almost every time they are recalled.

9. Anyone with the experience of these will easily be able to tell the difference between the two, for the diversity between them is very clear. I merely assert that those impressed formally on the soul in such a way as to be long-lasting are of rarer occurrence. But whatever may be their kind, it is good for the soul to have no desire to comprehend anything save God alone in hope through faith.

As for the other point in the objection (that it is apparently pride to reject these apprehensions if they are good), I answer: It is rather prudent humility to benefit by them in the best way, as has been mentioned, and be guided along the safest path.

CHAPTER 14

Spiritual knowledge in the memory.

1. We placed apprehensions of spiritual knowledge in the third class, not because they pertain to the corporeal phantasy—for they do not have

a corporal image and form—as the others do, but because they are like-wise the object of spiritual reminiscence and memory. For after the soul receives knowledge of this sort, it can at will bring it back to memory. It remembers this not through the effigy or image left in the corporal sense faculty—for in being a corporal sense faculty, the phantasy has no capacity for spiritual forms—but it remembers intellectually and spiritually through the form impressed on the soul (which is also a spiritual or formal form, idea, or image), or through the effect produced. As a result I classify these apprehensions among those of the memory, even though they do not belong to those of the phantasy.

2. We have given a sufficient explanation in Chapter 24 of Book Two [Chapter 26], where we discussed intellectual apprehensions, of this kind of knowledge and of the attitude toward it required for advancement to union with God. See that chapter, because there we have explained how these apprehensions are of the two kinds: one referring to the Creator, and the other to creatures.

Concerning what has to do with our intention here (which is to ex-plain the way the memory should conduct itself in order to advance to union), I merely state, as I have just explained in the preceding chapter about formal images, to which class this knowledge of creatures belongs, that this knowledge may be remembered when it produces a good ef-fect, not in order to retain it but to awaken the knowledge and love of God. But if the remembrance of this knowledge of creatures produces no good effect, the soul should never desire the memory of it.

But as for knowledge of the Creator, I declare that a person should strive to remember it as often as possible because it will produce in the soul a notable effect. For, as we affirmed there, the communications of this knowledge are touches and spiritual feelings of union with God, the goal to which we are guiding the soul. The memory does not recall these through any form, image, or figure that may have been impressed on the soul, for those touches and feelings of union with the Creator do not have any; it remembers them through the effect of light, love, delight, and spiritual renewal, etc., produced in it. Something of this effect is renewed as often as the soul recalls them.

CHAPTER 15

A general rule of conduct for spiritual persons in their use of the memory.

1. To conclude this discussion on the memory, then, it will be worth-while to delineate briefly a general method for the use of the spiritual person that he may be united with God according to this faculty. Even if clearly understood from what we said, the reader will grasp it more easily in a summary.

The following must be kept in mind: Our aim is union with God in the memory; the object of hope is something unpossessed; the less other objects are possessed, the more capacity and ability there is to hope for this one object, and consequently the more hope; the greater the possessions, the less capacity and ability for hope, and consequently so much less of hope; accordingly, in the measure that a person dispossesses his memory of forms and objects, which are not God, he will fix it upon God and preserve it empty, in the hope that God will fill it. That which a person must do in order to live in perfect and pure hope in God is this: As often as distinct ideas, forms, and images occur to him, he should immediately, without resting in them, turn to God with loving affection, in emptiness of everything rememberable. He should not think or look upon these things for a longer time than is sufficient for the understanding and fulfillment of his obligations, if they refer to this. And then he should consider these ideas without becoming attached or seeking gratification in them, lest they leave their effects in the soul. Thus a man is not required to cease recalling and thinking about what he must do and know, for, since he is not attached to the possession of these thoughts, he will not be harmed. The verses of the *Mount* in Chapter 13 of the first book are helpful for this practice.

2. Yet it must be noted here that by our doctrine we are not in agreement, nor do we desire to be, with that of those pestiferous men who, persuaded by the pride and envy of Satan, have sought to remove from the eyes of the faithful the holy and necessary use and the renowned cult of the images of God and of His saints. Our doctrine is far different from theirs. We are not asserting, as they do, that there be no images or veneration of them; we are explaining the difference between these images and God, and how souls should use the painted image in such a way that they do not suffer an impediment in their movement toward the living image, and how they should pay no more attention to images than is required for advancing to what is spiritual.

The means is good and necessary for the attainment of the end, as are images for reminding us of God and the saints. But when a person uses and dwells upon the means more than he ought, his excessive use of them becomes as much an impediment as anything else. This is even truer in the case of supernatural visions and images, with which I am especially dealing here and which are the cause of many delusions and dangers.

There is no delusion or danger in the remembrance, veneration, and esteem of images that the Catholic Church proposes to us in a natural manner, since in these images nothing else is esteemed than the person represented. The memory of these images will not fail to be profitable to a person, because this remembrance is accompanied with love for whoever is represented. Images will always help a person toward union with God, provided that he does not pay more attention to them than is necessary, and that he allows himself to soar—when God bestows the favor—from the painted image to the living God, in forgetfulness of all creatures and things pertaining to creatures.

Chapter 16

The beginning of the treatise on the dark night of the will. A division of the emotions of the will.

1. We would achieve nothing by purging the intellect and memory in order to ground them in the virtues of faith and hope if we neglected the purification of the will through charity, the third virtue. Through charity works done in faith are living works and have high value; without it they are worth nothing, as St. James affirms: *Without works of charity, faith is dead.* [Jas. 2:20]

For a treatise on the active night and denudation of this faculty, with the aim of instructing and educating it in this virtue of the love of God, I have found no more appropriate passage than the one in Chapter 6 of Deuteronomy, where Moses commands: *You shall love the Lord, your God, with all your heart, and with all your soul, and with all your strength.* [Dt. 6:5] This passage contains all that a spiritual man must do and all that I must teach him here if he is to reach God by union of the will through charity. In it man receives the command to employ all the faculties, appetites, operations, and emotions of his soul in God so that he may avoid the use of his ability and strength for anything else, in accord with David's declaration: *Fortitudinem meam ad te custodiam.*[1] [Ps. 58:10]

2. The strength of the soul comprises the faculties, passions, and appetites. All this strength is ruled by the will. When the will directs these faculties, passions, and appetites toward God, turning them away from all that is not God, the soul preserves its strength for God, and comes to love Him with all its might.

That a person may effect this, we shall discuss here the purification of the will of all inordinate feelings. These inordinate feelings are the sources of unruly appetites, affections, and operations, and the basis for failure to preserve one's strength for God.

There are four of these feelings or passions: joy, hope, sorrow, and fear. These passions manifestly keep the strength and ability of the soul for God, and direct it toward Him, when they are so ruled that the

---

[1] I will keep my strength for you.

individual rejoices only in what is purely for God's honor and glory, hopes for nothing else, feels sorrow only about matters pertaining to this, and fears only God. The more a person rejoices over something outside God, the less intense will be his joy in God; and the more his hope goes out toward something else, the less there is for God; and so on with the others.

3. To give a complete doctrine on this subject, we shall as is our custom discuss individually these four passions as well as the appetites of the will. The entire matter of reaching union with God consists in purging the will of its appetites and feelings, so that from a human and lowly will it may be changed into the divine will, made identical with the will of God.

4. The less strongly the will is fixed on God, and the more dependent it is upon creatures, the more these four passions combat the soul and reign in it. It then very easily finds joy in what deserves no rejoicing, and hope in what brings it no profit, and sorrow over what should perhaps cause rejoicing, and fear where there is no reason for fear.

5. When these feelings are unbridled, they are the source of all the vices and imperfections, and when they are in order and composed they give rise to all the virtues.

It should be known that, in the measure that one of the passions is regulated according to reason, the others are also. These four passions are so brother-like that where one goes actually the others go virtually; if one is recollected actually, the other three in the same measure are recollected virtually. If the will rejoices over something, it must consequently in the same degree hope for it, with the virtual inclusion of sorrow and fear. And with the removal of satisfaction in this object, fear, sorrow, and hope will also be removed.

We find a reference to the will and the four passions in that figure Ezechial saw: four animals with four faces and but one body, and in which the wings of one were bound to those of the other; each one went forward, and while going ahead they did not turn back. [Ez. 1:6–12] The feathers of each of these emotions are so connected to those of the others that wherever the one actually directs its face (its operation), the others need to go virtually; and when one is lowered, as is affirmed there, all the others must be lowered; and when it is raised, the others are raised too. [Ez. 1:19–25] Where your hope goes, there too will go your joy, fear, and sorrow; and if it turns back, they too will turn back; and so on with each of the other passions.

6. Accordingly, you should keep in mind that wherever one of these passions goes the entire soul (the will and the other faculties) will also

go, and they will live as prisoners of this passion; and the other three passions will dwell in the one to afflict the soul with their chains, and they will prevent it from soaring to the liberty and repose of sweet contemplation and union. As a result Boetius claimed that if you desire a clear understanding of the truth, you must cast from yourself joys, hope, fear, and sorrow. [*De Consolatione Philosophiae*, lib. 2, m. 7–PL 63, 656–58] As long as these passions reign in the soul, they will not allow it to live in the tranquillity and peace necessary for the wisdom it can receive naturally and supernaturally.

CHAPTER 17

The first emotion of the will. The nature of joy and a division of the objects of joy.

1. The first passion of the soul and emotion of the will is joy. Joy—to give a definition suited to our purpose—is nothing else than a satisfaction of the will with esteem for an object it considers fitting. For the will never rejoices unless in something which is valuable and satisfying to it.

We are speaking of active joy, which occurs when a person understands distinctly and clearly the object of its joy, and which means that one has power either to rejoice or not. For there is another joy, which is passive. In this kind of joy the will finds itself rejoicing without any clear and distinct understanding—though at times it has—of the object of its joy. It has no power either to possess this joy or not possess it.

We shall discuss this passive joy afterwards. Our topic now is the joy derived from distinct and clear objects, insofar as it is active and voluntary.

2. Joy can have as its source six kinds of objects or goods: temporal, natural, sensory, moral, supernatural, and spiritual. We must treat of these in their proper order, regulating the will according to reason, lest it fail to concentrate the vigor of its joy upon God because of the hindrance these goods may occasion.

We must in all of this presuppose a fundamental principle which will be like a staff, a continual support for our journey. It must be kept in mind, because it is the light which will be our guide and master in this doctrine. By it we must, amid all these goods, direct joy to God. The principle is: The will should rejoice only in what is for the honor and glory of God, and the greatest honor we can give Him is to serve Him according to evangelical perfection; anything unincluded in such service is without value to man.

CHAPTER 18

Joy in temporal goods. How the soul should direct it to God.

1. We listed the first kind of goods as temporal. By temporal goods we mean: riches, status, positions, and other dignities, and children, relatives, and marriages, etc. All these are possible objects of joy for the will.

But the vanity of rejoicing over riches, titles, status, positions, and other similar goods after which men usually strive is clear. If by being richer, a man were to be a better servant of God, he would need to rejoice in riches. But riches are rather the occasion of his offending God, as the Wise Man teaches: *Son, if you be rich you shall not be free from sin.* [Ecclus. 11:10] Though it is true that temporal goods of themselves are not necessarily the cause of sin, yet, due to the weakness of its tendencies, the heart of man usually becomes attached to them and fails God—which is a sin. Thus the Wise Man says you will not be free from sin.

This is why the Lord in the Gospel calls them thorns—he who handles them with the will shall be wounded with some sin. [Mt. 13:22; Lk. 8:14] His exclamation, *How difficult will it be for those who have riches to enter the kingdom of heaven* (those who have joy in them), demonstrates clearly man's obligation of not rejoicing in riches, since a man is thereby exposed to this danger. [Mt. 19:23; Lk. 18:24] In order to turn us from this danger, David also taught: *If riches abound, do not set your heart on them.* [Ps. 61:11]

2. I do not want to add any more references here on so clear a matter, for I would never finish quoting Scripture or speaking of the evils Solomon attributes to them in Ecclesiastes. Solomon, a man who had abundant riches, and knowledge of what riches are, claimed that everything under the sun was vanity of vanities, affliction of spirit, and vain solicitude of soul [Eccl. 1:14]; and that the lover of riches will not reap fruit from them [Eccl. 5:9]; and that riches are kept to the harm of their owner. [Eccl. 5:12] This last claim is evident too in the Gospel, where the man who rejoiced, because for many years he had stored away a good portion of the harvest, heard these words from heaven: *Fool, this night they will seek your soul that you may give an account, and whose will be all that you stored away?* [Lk. 12:20] Finally, David imparts the same teaching: that we should not be envious when our neighbor becomes rich, since this will profit him nothing for the next life. [Ps. 48:17–18] He indicates thus that we should rather take pity on him.

3. Man should not be joyous over riches, neither when he possesses them nor when his brother possesses them, unless God is served through them. If it is in some way tolerable to rejoice in riches, it is so when they are spent and employed in the service of God. For in no other way will profit be drawn from them.

The same holds true for the other goods, titles, and positions, etc. It is vain for a man to rejoice in these goods if he does not serve God by them and walk more securely on the road of eternal life. And because he cannot know with certitude that he is serving God more, it would be vain of him to rejoice over these goods, for such joy cannot be reasonable. As our Lord asserts, even though one gains the whole world, he can lose his soul. [Mt. 16:26] The only reason for rejoicing then is the greater service of God.

4. Neither, indeed, is there any reason for joy in children because they are many, or rich, or endowed with natural talents and gifts, or because they are wealthy. The motive for rejoicing in them should be the service they render to God. The beauty, riches, and lineage of Absalom, David's son, was of no avail, since he did not serve God. [2 Kgs. 14:25] The joy he found, therefore, in these goods was vain.

It is also vain to desire children, as some do in upsetting and troubling the whole world with their longing for them. For they do not know whether the children will be good and serve God, or whether the expected happiness will instead be sorrow, or the rest and comfort, trial and grief, or the honor, dishonor. And because of the children they might, as many do, offend God more. Christ says of these people, that they circle the earth and the sea in order to enrich their children, and they make them children of perdition twofold more than they themselves are. [Mt. 23:15]

5. Even though all things smile upon a man and succeed prosperously, he should have misgivings rather than joy, since the occasion and danger of forgetting God thereby increases. This is the motive Solomon gave in Ecclesiastes for taking precaution: *I judged laughter an error, and to joy I said: Why are you deceived in vain?* [Eccl. 2:2] This was like saying: When things went well with me, I considered it error and deceit to be glad over them, for doubtless the error and foolishness of a man who is joyous over what apparently brings him prosperity and success is gross, because he does not know whether or not some eternal good will result. *The heart of the fool,* states the Wise Man, *is present where there is joy; but that of the Wise Man is where there is sadness.* [Eccl. 7:5] Joy is blinding to the heart and does not allow it to consider and ponder things, while sadness makes a man open his eyes and see their advantage or harm. Accordingly, the Wise Man also affirms that anger is better than laughter. [Eccl. 7:4] Hence it is better to go to the house

of mourning than to that of feasting, for there we see the end of all men, as the Wise Man also says. [Eccl. 7:3]

6. Indeed, it would also be vanity for a husband and wife to rejoice in their marriage, when they are uncertain whether God is being better served by it. They should rather be perplexed, for as St. Paul declares, matrimony is the cause of not centering the heart entirely on God, since the hearts of the couple are set on one another. [1 Cor. 7:32, 33] He advises consequently: If you are free from a wife do not seek one, but if you already have one, be as free of heart as if you had none. [1 Cor. 7:27, 29] He teaches us this together with what we affirmed about temporal goods: *This, therefore, that I say to you brothers is certain, the time is short; what remains is that those who have wives be as those who have them not; and those who weep as those who do not weep; and those who have joy as those who do not rejoice; and those who are buyers as those who do not possess; and those who are users of this world as those who use it not* [1 Cor. 7:29–31].

The reason he says all this is to explain that nothing but what belongs to the service of God should be the object of our joy. Any other joy would be vain and worthless, for joy that is out of harmony with God is of no value to the soul.

CHAPTER 19

The harm caused from joy in temporal goods.

1. Ink, paper, and time would be exhausted were we to describe the harm which beleaguers the soul because it turns its affection to temporal goods. A small beginning can lead a person into great evils and destroy notable blessings, just as an unextinguished spark can enkindle immense fires capable of burning up the world.

All this harm has its origin and root in one main privative harm embodied in this joy: withdrawal from God. Just as every good is due to an approach toward God through the affection of the will, so withdrawal from Him through creature affection breeds every harm and evil in the soul. The measure of the harm is the intensity of the joy and affection with which the will is joined to the creature, for in that proportion is its withdrawal from God. The harm incurred will be greater or less according to the degree of one's withdrawal from God and, for the most part, both extensive and intensive.

2. This privative harm, from which the other negative and positive kinds arise, has four degrees, one worse than the other. When a person reaches the fourth, he will have encountered all the harm and evil that

can be described in this matter. Moses notes these four degrees very clearly in Deuteronomy with these words: *The beloved was surfeited and hobbled backwards; he was surfeited, grew fat, and spread out. He forsook God his Maker, and departed from God his Saviour.* [Dt. 32:15]

3. To surfeit the soul—which was beloved before this surfeit—is to engulf oneself in the joy of creatures. The first degree of harm springs from this, that is, backsliding: a blunting of the mind in relation to God, darkening of God's goods, just as a cloud darkens the air and prevents the sun's illumination.

By the very fact that a spiritual person rejoices in something and gives reign to the appetite in trifles, his relationship with God is darkened and his intellect clouded. This is what the divine Spirit teaches in the Book of Wisdom: *Contact with vanity and trifles, and the use of them, obscures good things, and the inconstancy of the appetite overturns and perverts the sense and judgment that is without malice.* [Wis. 4:12] The Holy Spirit teaches by this that although the intellect is without the thought of any malice, joy in these trifles and concupiscence for them is alone sufficient to produce the first degree of this harm: dullness of mind and darkness of judgment in understanding truth and judging well of each thing as it is in itself.

4. If a man gives way to concupiscence or joy about temporal goods, his sanctity and keen judgment will be insufficient to prevent this injury. God therefore warned us through Moses: *Do not receive gifts that blind even the prudent.* [Ex. 23:8] This admonition was directed toward those who were to be judges, since their judgment must be clear and alert, which would not be the case if they were to covet and rejoice in gifts.

Similarly God commanded Moses to appoint as judges those who abhorred avarice, that their judgment would not be blunted by gratification of the passions. [Ex. 18:21] He speaks not merely of a lack of desire but of the abhorrence of avarice. To enjoy perfect protection from the emotion of love, a person must maintain this abhorrence, and defend himself from one contrary by means of another. The reason the prophet Samuel was always so upright and enlightened a judge is, as he asserted in the Book of Kings, that he never accepted a gift from anyone. [1 Kgs. 12:3]

5. The second degree of this privative harm issues from the first. It is disclosed in the passage already quoted: *he was surfeited, grew fat, and spread out.* [Dt. 32:15] Accordingly, this second degree is dilation of the will in temporal things—and in a way that involves even greater liberty. This consists in making little of joy and pleasure in creatures, in not being afflicted about it, nor considering it to be so serious a matter. The root of this injury is the reign that was given to joy in the beginning,

for in giving way to it the soul grew fat, as is indicated in Exodus, and that fatness of joy and appetite dilated the will and made it reach out more toward creatures.

Many kinds of serious harm are the consequence. For this second degree causes a withdrawal from spiritual exercises and the things of God, and a lack of satisfaction in these exercises because of the pleasure found in other things, and the surrender to many imperfections, trifles, joys, and vain pleasures.

6. When consummated, this second degree takes away entirely the spiritual practices to which the individual was accustomed and causes him to seek worldly things with his whole mind and all his longing.

Those in the second degree not only possess darkened intellects and judgment in the understanding of truths and justice, as those in the first, but they are now extremely weak, lukewarm, and careless in knowing and practicing true judgment. Isaias affirms this in these words: *They all love gifts and allow themselves to be carried away by retributions, and they do not judge the orphan, and the widow's cause does not come to them and their attention.* [Is. 1:23] This attitude did not exist without their fault, especially when duty was incumbent upon them by their office. Those who have reached this degree are not without malice, as are those in the first degree. Thus they gradually turn from justice and virtue because their will reaches out more and more into affection for creatures.

The trait of those in this second degree is extreme lukewarmness in spiritual matters, and carelessness about them, the observance of them through mere formality, force, or habit, rather than through love.

7. The third degree of this privative harm is the complete abandonment of God. The individual grows careless about the observance of God's law in order to attend to worldly goods, and allows himself to fall into mortal sins through covetousness. This third degree is indicated in the next assertion of this passage from Exodus: *he forsook God his Maker.* [Dt. 32:15]

This degree includes all those who are so engrossed in the things, riches, and affairs of this world that they care nothing about the fulfillment of the obligations of God's law. Forgetful and sluggish about matters pertinent to their salvation, they become much more alive and astute in the things of the world—so much so that Christ in the Gospel calls them children of this world. He says they are more prudent and keen in their affairs than are the children of light in theirs. [Lk. 16:8] Thus, in the affairs of God they are nothing, and in those of the world they are everything.

These, precisely, are the greedy. Their appetite and joy is already so extended and dispersed among creatures—and with such anxiety—that they cannot be satisfied. The more their appetite and thirst increases, the further they regress from God, the fount which alone can satisfy them. God Himself refers to these individuals through Jeremias: *They have abandoned Me, the fount of living water, and dug for themselves leaking cisterns that cannot hold water.* [Jer. 2:13] The reason for this dissatisfaction is that creatures do not slake the thirst, but rather intensify it.

These greedy persons fall into thousands of kinds of sins out of love for temporal goods, and the harm they suffer is indeterminable. David says of them: *Transierunt in affectum cordis.*[2] [Ps. 72:7]

8. The fourth degree of this privative harm is noted in the final statement of the text: *and departed from God his Saviour.* [Dt. 32:15] This is the degree into which the avaricious ones we just mentioned fall. The avaricious man, because of temporal goods, is unconcerned about setting his heart on God's law, and consequently his will, memory, and intellect wander far from God, and he forgets Him, as though He were not his God at all. The reason is that he has made for himself gods out of money and temporal goods. St. Paul indicates this in declaring that avarice is a form of idolatry. [Col. 3:5] Those who are in this fourth degree forget God and deliberately turn their heart—which should be centered on Him —to money, as though they had no other God.

9. We find in this fourth degree those who are unhesitant about ordaining divine and supernatural things to temporal things, as to gods. They should do just the contrary, they should direct the temporal to God, if they take Him for their God as is right. Wicked Balaam belongs in this category, for he sold the grace God had given him. [Nm. 22:32] Also Simon Magus: by contriving to buy God's grace, he thought of putting a monetary value on it. [Acts 18:18–19] He put higher value on money because he thought he could find someone who would esteem money more by selling grace.

Many, today, in various ways belong to the category of this fourth degree. Out there in the world, their reason darkened through covetousness in spiritual matters, they serve money and not God, and they are motivated by money rather than by God, and they give first consideration to the temporal price and not to the divine value and reward. In countless ways they make money their principal god and goal and give it precedence to God, their ultimate end.

10. Likewise included in the category of this last degree are all those miserable souls who value earthly goods as their god and are so enamored of them that they do not hesitate to sacrifice their lives when they observe that this god of theirs undergoes some temporal loss. They

[2] They have passed into the affection of the heart.

despair and commit suicide for wretched reasons, and demonstrate with their own hands the miserable reward that comes from such a god. Since there is nothing to hope for from him, he gives despair and death. And anyone whom he does not pursue right up to death, the ultimate injury, dies from living in the affliction of anxieties and many other miseries. He does not permit gladness to enter their hearts, nor any earthly goods to be profitable to them. Insofar as they are afflicted about money, they are always paying the tribute of their hearts to it. They cling to it unto the final calamity of just perdition, as the Wise Man warns: *Riches are hoarded to the harm of their owner.* [Eccl. 5:12]

11. Belonging to this fourth degree are those of whom St. Paul says: *Tradidit illos in reprobum sensum.*[3] [Rm. 1:28] For joy in possessions ultimately drags man down even to these evils.

But even they to whom less harm comes should be pitied greatly, since, as we affirmed, this joy causes the soul to fall far back in the way of God. As David declares: *Do not fear when a man becomes rich* (do not be envious, thinking that he has an advantage over you) *for when he dies he will take nothing with him, nor will his glory and joy descend with him.* [Ps. 48:17–18]

CHAPTER 20

Benefits derived through the withdrawal of joy from temporal goods.

1. The spiritual man must exercise great care that his heart and joy do not become attached to temporal goods. He must fear lest small attachments through a gradual increase will become great ones. Great things can come from little things, and what is small in the beginning can be immense in the end, just as a spark is enough to set a mountain on fire, and even the whole world. [Jas. 3:5] And he should never assure himself that since his attachment is small, he will break away from it in the future even if he does not do so immediately. If he has not the courage to uproot it when it is small and in its first stages, how does he think and presume he will have the ability to do so when it becomes greater and more deeply rooted? Especially since our Lord affirms in the Gospel that *he who is unfaithful in the little things will also be unfaithful in the great.* [Lk. 16:10] He who avoids small attachments will not fall into greater ones. But there is serious harm in little matters, since through them the enemy has passed beyond the enclosure and wall around the heart; and as the saying goes: once begun, half done. Accordingly, David warns us that *even though riches abound we must not set our heart upon them.* [Ps. 61:11]

[3] He has given them up to a reprobate sense.

2. Even if a man does not free his heart of joy in temporal goods for God and for the sake of his obligation to strive after perfection, he ought to do so on account of the resulting temporal advantages, prescinding from the spiritual ones. By dismissing joy over temporal goods, he is not only delivered from the pestiferous kinds of harm we mentioned in the preceding chapters, but in addition he acquires the virtue of liberality. Liberality is one of God's principal attributes and can in no way coexist with covetousness.

Moreover, he acquires liberty of spirit, clarity of reason, rest, tranquillity, peaceful confidence in God, and, in his will, the true cult and homage of God.

He obtains more joy and recreation in creatures through the dispossession of them. He cannot rejoice in them if he beholds them with possessiveness, for this is a care which, like a bond, fastens the spirit to earth and does not allow it freedom of heart.

In detachment from things he acquires a clearer knowledge of them so that he has a better understanding of both natural and supernatural truths concerning them. His joy, consequently, in these temporal goods is far different from that joy of one who is attached to them, because he receives advantages and ameliorations from it. The satisfaction he finds in these goods harmonizes with their truth, whereas that of the attached man is in accord with what is false in them; he is gratified by the best in them, the attached man by the worst; he rejoices in their substance, the man who is sensibly attached to them rejoices in their accidents. The senses cannot grasp or attain to more than the accident, whereas the spirit purged of the clouds and appearances of accident penetrates the truth and value of things, which is the object of the spirit. Joy clouds the judgment like a mist. For there can be no voluntary joy over creatures without voluntary possessiveness, just as there can be no joy, insofar as it is a passion, unaccompanied by habitual possessiveness of heart. The denial and purgation of such joy leaves the judgment as clear as the air when the vapors vanish.

3. He, then, whose joy is unpossessive of things rejoices in them all as though he possessed them all; another, beholding them with a possessive mind, loses the satisfaction of them all in general.

Inasmuch as one has nothing in his heart, he possesses them, as St. Paul states, with great liberty; another, insofar as he possesses them with attachment, neither has nor possesses anything, rather his heart is held by them and he suffers as a captive. As many as are the joys he longs to uncover in creatures, so many will necessarily be the straits and afflictions of his attached and possessed heart.

Cares are no molestation to the detached man, neither in prayer nor outside of it, and thus, losing no time, he easily stores up an abundance of spiritual good; yet the other spends all his time going to and fro about the snare to which his heart is tied and attached, and even with effort he can hardly free himself for a short while from this snare of thought and joy over the object of his attached heart.

At the first movement of joy toward things, the spiritual person ought to repress it with remembrance of the principle we are here following: There is nothing worthy of a man's joy save the service of God and the procurement of His honor and glory in all things. His use of things should be directed to this and turned away from vanity, and exclude concern for his own satisfaction and consolation.

4. There is another exceptional and principal benefit of detachment from joy in creatures which is a preparatory condition for all the favors God will grant to the soul and without which He does not bestow them; it is freedom of the heart for God. The favors are such that for each joy the soul renounces out of love of God and evangelical perfection, it will receive a hundredfold in this life, as promised in the Gospel. [Mt. 19:29; Mk. 10:30]

But even if such gains were not to be had, the spiritual person would have to quell these joys because they displease God. In the Gospel we mark that merely because the rich man rejoiced for having stored up goods for many years God was so angered that He told him he must give an account of his soul that very night. [Lk. 12:20]

We should believe, therefore, that as often as we rejoice vainly, God is watching and planning some chastisement and bitter drink according to our merits; for at times the sadness redounding from the joy is a hundred times greater than the joy. What St. John says of Babylon in the Apocalypse is true: she would receive torment in the measure in which she rejoiced and lived in delights. [Ap. 18:7] Yet, the text does not mean that the sadness will not be greater than the joy. It shall be greater, since eternal torments are inflicted for brief pleasures. But it indicates that no fault will escape a particular punishment. For He who will punish the idle word shall not pardon vain joy.

CHAPTER 21

The vanity of joy in natural goods, and the method of directing joy through them to God.

1. By natural goods we mean: beauty, grace, elegance, bodily constitution, and all other corporal endowments; also in the soul, good intelligence, discretion, and other talents pertinent to the rational part of man.

A person is vain and deceitful if he rejoices in these gifts only because he or his relatives have them, without giving thanks to God who grants them in order to be better known and loved. As Solomon says: *Grace*

is deceitful and beauty vain; she that fears the Lord will be praised.
[Prv. 31:30] We are taught in this text that a man should rather have
misgivings about these natural gifts, since he can readily be distracted
from the love of God through them and fall into vanity and delusion
because of their allurement. This is why he says that bodily grace is
deceptive, deludes man along the way, and attracts him to inappropriate
things through vain joy and complacency with self or with the possession
of this grace. And he declares that beauty is vain because it causes the
man who esteems and rejoices in it to fall in countless ways; his only
norm of joy should be whether or not he serves God through it. He
ought rather to be diffident and fearful lest his natural gifts and graces
occasion his offending God, in which he would turn his eyes toward them
in vain presumption or inordinate attachment.

Whoever has these endowments should be careful and live cautiously
lest through vain ostentation he be the occasion that someone withdraw
his heart one iota from God. These natural graces and gifts are such a
provocation and occasion both to the possessor and the beholder that
there is scarcely a heart that escapes from this snare or birdlime. We
have known many spiritual persons with these endowments who have
prayed God to disfigure them, in fear lest they be an occasion to themselves or others of some vain joy or attachment.

2. The spiritual man, then, must purge and darken his will of this
vain joy, and bear in mind the following: beauty and all other natural
endowments are but earth, arising from the earth and returning to it;
grace and elegance are but the smoke and air of this earth, and should
be considered and valued as such for the sake of avoiding a lapse into
vanity; in these goods he must direct his heart to God in joy and gladness that God is Himself all these beauties and graces—eminently and
infinitely, above all creatures; and, as David affirms, all these will grow
old and pass away like a garment, while God alone will remain immutable forever. [Ps. 101:27] Accordingly, if a man does not turn his joy
to God in all things, it will always be false and illusory. This is the kind
Solomon referred to when he spoke to joy in creatures: *To joy I said:
Why do you let yourself be deceived in vain?* [Eccl. 2:2], that is, when
the heart is allowed to be allured by creatures.

CHAPTER 22

The harm resulting from joy of will in natural goods.

1. A good deal of the harm as well as the benefit I am describing in
each of these kinds of joy is common to them all. Because this harm or
benefit is the direct result of either joy, or detachment from it, no
matter what class the joy belongs to, I am mentioning this harm and

benefit in each of these categories, since, as I say, the harm or advantage is annexed to all these kinds of joy.

My main intention, however, is to speak of the particular kinds of harm and benefit arising in the soul by rejoicing or not rejoicing in each of these goods. I refer to them as particular because they are the primary and immediate result of a particular kind of joy. They are only caused by other kinds secondarily and mediately.

For example: tepidity of spirit is the outcome of each and every kind of joy, and so this harm is common to all six; yet fornication is a particular evil that follows directly only from joy in natural goods, of which we are now speaking.

2. The spiritual and bodily harm directly and effectively ensuing from joy in natural goods can be reduced to six principal kinds.

The first is vainglory, presumption, pride, and disesteem of neighbor (a person cannot fasten the eyes of esteem upon one object without withdrawing them from others). The result is at least a material disesteem of other things, for when the heart values one thing naturally it turns from others on account of its concentration upon the esteemed object. And through this material contempt it is exceptionally easy in a general or particular way to slip into intentional and voluntary contempt for some of these other things. Such contempt may be internal, or may manifest itself externally through speech: this thing is not like that, or so and so is not like this person.

The second harm is the incitement of the senses to complacency, sensual delight, and lust.

The third kind of harm is that it induces flattery and vain praises, which involves deception and vanity, as Isaias warns: *My people, whoever praises you deceives you.* [Is. 3:12] The reason is that even though the truth is told by lauding natural grace and beauty, this praise rarely fails to contain some harm, either by causing the person praised to fall into vain complacency and joy, or by directing one's own imperfect affections and intentions toward the person endowed with this beauty.

The fourth kind of harm is general, for the reason and judgment of the spirit becomes very dull, as in the case of joy over temporal goods, and in some ways even duller. Since natural goods are more intimate to a man than temporal goods, joy in them produces its imprint more quickly and effectively and ravishes more forcibly. Thus the reason and judgment do not remain free but are clouded by that emotion of very intimate joy.

This gives rise to the fifth harm: distraction of the mind with creatures.

The next outgrowth is spiritual lukewarmness and weakness. This sixth harm is also general and usually reaches such a point that it causes the soul to find extreme tedium and sadness in the things of God, even to the extent of abhorring them.

Pure spirit is infallibly lost in this kind of joy, at least in the beginning. If some spirituality is felt, it will be very sensible, gross, unspiritual, exterior, and unrecollected. It will comprise sensory pleasure more than strength of spirit. The spirit is so lowly and weak that it does not suppress the habit of this joy, for the possession of this imperfect habit is sufficient to impede pure spirit, even though the acts of joy are not consented to. Consequently the soul lives more in the weakness of the senses than in strength of spirit. If it does not it will notice the perfection and strength it has when occasions arise. Though I do not deny that many virtues can coexist with many imperfections, yet due to the reign of the flesh which militates against the spirit [Gal. 5:17], there can be neither a pure nor a savorous interior spirit dwelling together with these unquelled joys. And even if the spirit is unaware of any harm, distraction at least is secretly caused.

3. Let us go back to that second kind of harm which contains in itself innumerable other indescribable kinds. The extent and enormity of the disaster arising from joy in natural graces and beauty is patent, since on account of this joy we hear everyday of many murders, lost reputations, insults, squandered fortunes, rivalries, quarrels, and of so many adulteries, rapes, and fornications, and of fallen saints so numerous that they are compared to the third part of the stars of heaven cast down to earth by the tail of the serpent [Ap. 12:4], to the fine gold which has lost its beauty and luster in the mire, and to the illustrious and noble men of Sion clothed with the best gold, yet esteemed as broken, clay jars. [Lam. 4:1-2]

4. Where does this poisonous harm fail to reach? And who fails to drink little or much from the golden chalice of the Babylonian woman of the Apocalypse? [Ap. 17:4] By the fact that she is seated on that large beast with the seven heads and ten crowns, it is signified that there is hardly anyone of high rank or low, saint or sinner, who does not drink of her wine, subjecting his heart somewhat. For as is pointed out there, all the kings of the earth were inebriated with the wine of her prostitution. [Ap. 17:2] She reaches out to all states, even to the supreme and illustrious state of the sanctuary and divine priesthood, by setting her abominable cup in the holy place, as Daniel asserts [Dn. 9:27], and she hardly leaves a strong man who has not drunk a small or large quantity of wine from her chalice, which is this kind of vain joy. As a result it is said that all the kings of the earth were inebriated by this wine, since so few will be found, no matter how holy, who have not been somewhat

ravished and perplexed by this drink of joy and pleasure in natural beauty and graces.

5. It is worth remarking that the text says they were inebriated. No matter how little is the amount of this wine of joy, it immediately takes a hold on the heart and subdues it, producing obscurity in the reason, as happens with those who get drunk from wine. If some antidote is not taken immediately, the life of the soul will be in danger. For spiritual weakness will augment and bring such evil upon the soul that it will find itself grinding at the mill, a captive of its enemies, like Samson with his eyes plucked out and the hair of his first strength cut. And afterwards it will perhaps die the second death as he did together with his enemies. This is the harm the drink of this joy will cause spiritually, as it did physically to Samson and as it does to many today. The enemies of the soul will come and say to it afterwards what the Philistines said to Samson, to his great confusion: Were you not the one who broke the knotted cords, broke the jaws of the lions, killed the thousand Philistines, pulled out the gates and freed yourself from all your enemies?

6. Let us conclude, then, with necessary instructions for the prevention of this poison. As soon as the heart feels drawn by vain joy in natural goods, it should recall how dangerous and pernicious it is to rejoice in anything other than the service of God. One should consider how harmful it was for the angels to have rejoiced and grown complacent in their natural beauty and goods, since they thereby fell into the ugly abyss; and how many evils come upon man every day because of this very vanity. Therefore one should take courage and use in time the remedy the poet suggests for those beginning to become attached to this joy: *Hurry now in the beginning to apply the remedy, for when evils have had time to increase in the heart, medicine and remedies arrive late.* [Ovid, *Remedia amoris*, 1, 91–92] *Look not at wine*, warns the Wise Man, *when its color is scarlet and it shines in the glass; it enters smoothly, but bites like a snake and spreads poison like the basilisk.* [Prv. 23:31]

CHAPTER 23

The benefits the soul acquires from not rejoicing in natural goods.

1. Many are the benefits derived through withdrawal of the heart from this joy. Besides preparing the soul for the love of God and for other virtues, it directly paves the way for humility toward self and general charity toward one's neighbor. In remaining unattached to everyone in spite of these apparent and deceptive natural goods, a person is unencumbered and free to love all rationally and spiritually, which is the way

God wants him to love. As a result he realizes that nobody merits love except for his virtues. And when he loves with this motive, his love is according to God and exceedingly free. If the love contains some attachment there is greater attachment to God, for as the love of neighbor increases the love of God increases and vice versa. For that which proceeds from God has one and the same reason and cause.

2. Another excellent benefit coming from the denial of this kind of joy is the fulfillment of the counsel our Lord gives in the Gospel of St. Matthew, that whoever would follow Him should deny himself. [Mt. 16:24] In no way could a person do this if he were to rejoice in his natural goods, because whoever pays some attention to self does not deny himself nor follow Christ.

3. Another notable benefit of the denial of this kind of joy is that such denial begets deep tranquillity of soul, a void of distractions, and recollection to the senses, especially to the eyes. Undesirous of this joy, a person does not want to look at or occupy the other senses with these things that he may avoid being attracted or ensnared by them and wasting time or thought. He bears resemblance to the prudent serpent that stops its ears so as not to hear the charmers, lest they make some impression upon it. [Ps. 57:5] By guarding the senses, the gates of the soul, one decidedly safeguards and brings increase to one's peace and purity of soul.

4. There is another benefit of no less importance for those who are already advanced in the mortification of this kind of joy. And it is that obscene objects and ideas do not cause in them the impression and impurity they do in those who still become content with some of this joy. Consequently, from the denial and mortification of this joy, spiritual purity of soul and body (of spirit and sense) arises; and the individual gradually acquires angelic likeness to God, and his soul and body become a worthy temple of the Holy Spirit. This could not be so if his heart rejoiced in natural goods and graces. It is not necessary that there be consent to some obscene thing or a remembrance of it in order to soil the purity of soul, since this kind of joy coupled with knowledge of the natural good is sufficient to cause impurity of spirit and sense. The Wise Man declares that the Holy Spirit will withdraw from thoughts that are without understanding, that is, without the superior reason ordered to God. [Wis. 1:5]

5. Another general benefit coming to the soul, besides freedom from the above-mentioned evils, is freedom from countless vanities and other kinds of spiritual and temporal harm, and especially from being held in disesteem, which is the lot of those who boast about natural endowments and rejoice in them, whether they are their own or another's. Accordingly,

those who pay no attention to such things, but are interested in what is pleasing to God, are considered and esteemed to be discreet and wise—and indeed they are.

6. The last benefit follows upon these, that is, liberty of spirit by which the soul easily conquers temptations, passes through trials, and grows prosperously in virtue. This is an excellent good and very necessary in serving God.

CHAPTER 24

Sensory goods, the third kind that can be the object of the feeling of joy. An exposition of their nature and number and of how the will should be directed to God through the purgation of this joy.

1. Our next subject is joy in sensory goods, the third kind in which the will can rejoice. It should be known that by sensory goods we mean all the goods apprehensible to the senses of sight, hearing, smell, taste, and touch, and to the interior faculty of discursive imagination. They are goods pertinent to the exterior and interior senses.

2. To darken and purge the will of joy in these sensory goods and lead it through them to God, we must presuppose a truth. It is, as we have often said, that the senses of the lower part of man's nature with which we are dealing, neither are nor can be capable of the knowledge or comprehension of God as He is in Himself. The eye cannot see Him or anything like Him, nor the hearing perceive His voice or any sound resembling it, nor can the sense of smell apprehend a fragrance so sweet, nor the sense of taste relish so sublime and delightful a savor, nor can the sense of touch experience a feeling so delicate and ravishing, nor anything similar. Neither is God's form or any figure representing it apprehensible to thought or imagination. Isaias thus affirms: *Eye has not seen Him, nor ear heard Him, nor has it entered into the heart of man.* [Is. 64:4]

3. It is noteworthy that the senses can receive satisfaction and delight either from the spirit, through some communication received interiorly from God, or from exterior things apprehended by them. And, as was said, the sensory part of man can have knowledge of God through neither the senses nor the spirit. Being incapable of such an attainment, it receives the spiritual and sensible in only a sensorial way. As a result it would be at least vanity for the will to pause to rejoice in the gratification caused by any of these apprehensions. And the strength of the will would

be hindered from employing all its joy in God alone. One cannot concentrate one's joy entirely on God save through the purgation and darkening of joy in this kind of good, as well as in the others.

4. I purposely said that it would be vanity for the will to pause to rejoice in any of these apprehensions. For when the will, in becoming aware of the satisfaction afforded by the object of sight, hearing, or touch, does not stop with this joy but immediately elevates itself to God, rejoicing in Him who motivates and gives strength to its joy, it is doing something very good. The will, then, does not have to avoid such experiences when they produce this devotion and prayer, but it can profit by them, and even ought to for the sake of so holy an exercise. For there are souls who are greatly moved toward God by sensible objects.

Yet one should be careful in this matter and take into consideration its effects. Frequently spiritual persons use this refreshment of the senses under the pretext of prayer and devotion to God; and they so perform these exercises that we could call this recreation rather than prayer, and the pleasing of self rather than God. Though the intention of these persons is directed to God, the effect they receive is recreation of the senses, from which they obtain weakness and imperfection more than the quickening of their will and its surrender to God.

5. I should like to offer a norm for discerning when this gratification of the senses is beneficial and when not. Whenever a person, upon hearing music or other things, seeing agreeable objects, smelling sweet fragrance, or feeling the delight of certain tastes and delicate touches, immediately at the first movement directs his thought and the affection of his will to God, receiving more satisfaction in the thought of God than in the sensible object that caused it, and finds no gratification in the senses save for this motive, it is sign that he is profiting by the senses and that the sensory part is a help to the spirit. The senses can then be used because the sensorial objects serve the purpose for which God created them: that He be more known and loved through them.

It should be understood here that he in whom these sensible objects cause this purely spiritual effect does not on that account have an appetite for them, nor does he hardly care for them at all, even though they do provide great satisfaction when presented to him; for, as I mentioned, they cause him pleasure in God. Thus he is not solicitous about these sensible goods; and when, as I say, they are offered to him, his will immediately leaves them aside, passing on to God.

6. The reason this person pays no attention to these sensible motives even though they help him go to God is that his spirit, which has this readiness to go to God in and through all things, is so provided for,

nourished, and satisfied by God's spirit that it is unwanting and unde-sirous of anything else; and if it is desirous of something in order to turn to God, it immediately passes beyond this object, forgetting and paying no attention to it.

Yet anyone who does not feel this freedom of spirit in these sensible objects and gratifications, but finds that his will pauses in and feeds upon them, suffers harm from them and ought to turn from their use. Though according to reason he may want help from them in order to go to God, nonetheless, they assuredly prove more a hindrance than a help, and a harm rather than a benefit, since the appetite finds gratification in them according to the senses; and the effect is always conformed to the pleas-ure. When he sees that the appetite for these recreations reigns within himself, he should mortify it, because the stronger his appetite the weaker and more imperfect he is.

7. The spiritual person, then, in whatever sensory gratification comes his way, intentionally or by chance, ought to benefit from it only for the sake of going to God, by raising his joy of soul to Him that this joy may be useful, profitable, and perfect. He should avert that every joy unac-companied by this negation and annihilation of all other joys—even when they concern something apparently very elevated—is vain and profitless, and a hindrance to union of the will with God.

Chapter 25

The harm incurred by the desire for joy of will in sensory goods.

1. In the first place, all the kinds of harm born of other types of joy spring from this joy in sensory goods if it is not darkened and quelled through direction to God. These kinds of harm are, for example: obscurity of reason, lukewarmness, spiritual tedium, etc. But in particular there are many types—spiritual and corporal or sensory—which can be directly in-curred through this joy.

2. First, through failure to deny for God joy in visible objects, the fol-lowing evils result directly: vanity of spirit, mental distraction, inordinate covetousness, indecency, interior and exterior discomposure, impurity in thought, and envy.

3. Joy in hearing useless things gives direct rise to distraction of the imagination, gossiping, envy, uncertain judgments, and wandering thoughts, followed by many other pernicious kinds of harm.

4. Joy in sweet fragrance foments disgust for the poor, which is con-trary to Christ's doctrine, aversion for servants, unsubmissiveness of heart

in humble things, and spiritual irresponsiveness, at least in the measure of the appetite.

5. Joy in the delights of food directly engenders gluttony and drunkenness, anger, discord, and lack of charity toward one's neighbor and the poor, as in the case of Lazarus and the rich man who ate sumptuously each day. [Lk. 16:19–21] Accordingly, there arise bodily disorders, infirmities, and impure movements due to increasing incentives of lust. A decided spiritual torpor is directly engendered and the desire for spiritual things is so spoiled that one finds no satisfaction in them and is unable to discuss or take part in them. Distraction of the other senses and of the heart and discontent over many things are also born of this joy.

6. Enjoyment in the touch of soft objects foments more numerous and more pernicious kinds of harm, and by it the senses more quickly pervert the spirit and extinguish its strength and vigor. The consequence is the abominable vice of effeminacy or incentives toward it in proportion to this kind of joy. This joy foments lust, it makes the spirit unmanly and timid, and the senses flattering, honey-mouthed, disposed toward sin and the causing of harm. It pours vain gladness and mirth into the heart, engenders license of the tongue and freedom of the eyes, and brings on ravishment and stupefaction of the other senses according to the intensity of the appetite. It confounds the judgment, nurturing it on spiritual insipience and stupidity, and morally engenders cowardice and inconstancy. And by this darkness of soul and weakness of heart, it makes one fear where there is no reason for fear. This joy sometimes begets the spirit of confusion and unresponsiveness of conscience and spirit, since it seriously debilitates reason and reduces it to such a state that one knows not how either to take counsel or to give it, and it leaves the soul incapable of moral and spiritual blessings, as useless as a broken jar.

7. All these evils are caused by this kind of joy according to the intensity of the joy and also according to the disposition, weakness, or inconstancy of the individual. For some temperaments receive more detriment from one small occasion than others do from many.

8. Finally from this kind of rejoicing in touch one can fall into so much evil and harm, as we pointed out, from natural goods, that since it is discussed there I shall not refer to it here. Neither shall I speak of many other kinds of harm caused, such as, the diminution of spiritual exercises and corporal penances, and lukewarmness and lack of devotion in the use of the sacraments of penance and the Eucharist.

CHAPTER 26

The spiritual and temporal benefits resulting from the denial of joy in sensory goods.

1. The benefits acquired from the negation of this joy are admirable; some are spiritual, others temporal.

2. First, by withdrawing his joy from sensible things, a man is restored from the distraction into which he had fallen through excessive use of his senses. He becomes recollected in God and conserves the spirit and virtues he has acquired. These virtues increase and the soul advances.

3. The second spiritual benefit a person procures from not desiring joy in sensible things is excellent; we can truthfully say that from sensual he becomes spiritual, and from animal, rational, and even that from what is of man in him he advances to the angelic, and from earthly and human he becomes heavenly and divine. As the man who looks for gratification and enjoyment in sensible objects deserves no other title than these we mentioned: sensual, animal, earthly, etc., so when he elevates his joy above these sensible goods he deserves all those other titles: spiritual, heavenly, etc.

4. This is obviously true. For since the exercise of the senses and the strength of sensuality are contrary, as the Apostle says, to spiritual exercises and vigor [Gal. 5:17], it follows that upon the enervation of one of these forces the other contrary one, unaugmentable due to this impediment, must grow and increase. Thus in the perfecting of the spirit (the superior portion of the soul which refers to God and communicates with Him), a person merits all these attributes, since he is perfected in the spiritual and heavenly goods and gifts of God.

St. Paul proves both instances. He calls the sensual man, the one who occupies his will with sensory things, the animal man, who is unperceptive of the things of God; and the other who raises his will to God, he calls the spiritual man, and he is the one who penetrates and judges all things, even the deep things of God. [1 Cor. 2:14, 10] Consequently the soul possesses here the admirable benefit of a great preparedness for God's spiritual goods and gifts.

5. But the third benefit is that the satisfaction and joy of the will is temporally and exceedingly increased, since, as the Saviour says, in this life for one joy they will receive a hundredfold. [Mk. 10:30] If you deny one joy, the Lord will give you a hundredfold, spiritually and temporally

in this life, as also from one joy taken in these sensible goods, grief and distress will be yours a hundredfold.

From the eye already purged of enjoyment in seeing things, spiritual joy directed to God at the sight of all divine or profane things follows. Resulting from the purgation of enjoyment in hearing things is a most spiritual joy, a hundred times greater, directed to God in all that is heard, divine or profane; and so on with the other senses already purged. In the state of innocence all that our first parents saw, spoke of, and ate in the garden of paradise served them for more abundant delight in contemplation, since the sensory part of their souls was truly subjected and ordered to reason. He whose sense is purged of sensible objects and ordered to reason from the first movements procures the delight of savorous contemplation and awareness of God.

6. In the pure, therefore, all things, high and low, engender greater good and purity, just as the impure soul usually derives impurity from things, whether high or low. But anyone failing to conquer the joy of appetite will not experience the serenity of habitual joy in God by means of His creatures and works.

The man who does not live according to the senses directs all the operations of his senses and faculties to divine contemplation. Indeed, in good philosophy, the operation of each thing corresponds to its being or life. If the soul through mortification of the animal life lives a spiritual life, it must obviously, without contradiction, go to God in all things, since all its spiritual actions and movements will pertain to the spiritual life. Consequently, this person, now of pure heart, finds in all things a joyful, pleasant, chaste, pure, spiritual, glad, and loving knowledge of God.

7. I deduce the following doctrine from all that was said: Until a man is so habituated to the purgation of sensible joy that at the first movement of this joy he procures the benefit spoken of (that these goods turn him immediately to God), he must necessarily deny his joy and satisfaction in sensible goods in order to draw his soul away from the sensory life. Since he is not spiritual, he should be fearful lest through the use of these goods he may perhaps get more satisfaction and strength for the senses than for the spirit. Because of their predominance in his activity, the sensory forces increase sensuality, and sustain and nourish it. Our Saviour declares: *That which is born of the flesh is flesh; and that which is born of the spirit is spirit.* [Jn. 3:6]

And this we should ponder considerably, for it is really true. No one who has not yet mortified his pleasure in sensory things should dare to look for notable benefit from the vigor and activity of his senses regarding these goods in the belief that they are a help to the spirit. For

the forces of the soul will increase more without these sensible things—
by quelling the appetite for them—than by employing one's joy in them.

8. It is unnecessary to discuss the goods of glory that come in the next
life through the negation of this joy. Besides the fact that the bodily
endowments of glory, such as agility and clarity, will be far more excellent in those who denied themselves than in others who did not, there
will be an increase of essential glory in the soul that responds to the
love of God and denies sensible goods for Him. For every momentary
and perishable joy a person denies, as St. Paul states, there will be worked
in him eternally an immense weight of glory. [2 Cor. 4:17]

Now I do not want to refer here to the additional benefits (moral,
temporal, and spiritual) derived from this night regarding joy, for they
are the same as those mentioned in dealing with the other kinds of joy.
But here they are of a more eminent degree, since the sensible joys
denied are more closely conjoined with one's nature, and therefore a more
intimate purity is acquired through their negation.

CHAPTER 27

*The nature of moral goods, the fourth kind, and the permissible manner
of rejoicing in them.*

1. Moral goods are the fourth kind in which the will can rejoice. By
moral goods we mean: the virtues and their habits insofar as they are
moral; the exercise of any of the virtues; the practice of the works of
mercy; the observance of God's law; urbanity and good manners.

2. When possessed and practiced these moral goods perhaps merit
more joy of will than any of the other three kinds spoken of. For either
of two reasons, or for both together, a man can rejoice in these goods;
that is, because of what they are in themselves, or because of the good
effected through their instrumentality.

We discovered that the possession of the three kinds of good already
mentioned deserves no joy of will. Of themselves, as was said, they have
no good nor produce any in man because they are so perishable and
frail; rather, as was also pointed out, they engender pain, sorrow, and
affliction of spirit. Though they merit some joy for the second reason,
that is, when a man makes use of them to go to God, this benefit is so
uncertain that, as we commonly observe, a person contracts harm from
them more than help.

But even for the first reason (for what they are in themselves), moral
goods merit some rejoicing by their possessor. For they bring along in
their company peace, tranquillity, a right and ordered use of reason, and

actions resulting from mature deliberation. Humanly speaking, a man cannot have any nobler possession in this life.

3. Because virtues in themselves merit love and esteem from a human viewpoint, and because of their nature and the good they humanly and temporally effect, a man can well rejoice in the practice and possession of them. Under this aspect and for this reason the philosophers, wise men, and ancient princes, esteemed, praised, and endeavored to acquire and practice them. Though gentiles, who only cared for these goods in a temporal way, because of the temporal, corporal, and natural benefits they knew would result, they acquired the goods and renown which was their aim. But this was not their only acquisition. God, who loves every good, even in the barbarian and gentile, and does not hinder any good work from being accomplished, as the Wise Man says [Wis. 7:22], bestowed on them honor, dominion, and peace, besides an increase of life. He did this with the Romans because of their just laws. He subjected almost the entire world to them, paying them temporally for their commendable customs, since they were incapable of eternal reward on account of their paganism.

God so loves these moral goods that merely because Solomon asked for wisdom in order to instruct his people, govern them justly, and teach them worthwhile customs, He was exceedingly pleased. And He told him that He had given it to him and that moreover He had granted him what he had not asked for—riches and honor—in such a way that no king in the past or future was like him. [3 Kgs. 3:11–13]

4. Though the Christian ought to rejoice in the moral goods and works he performs temporally, insofar as they are the cause of the temporal goods we spoke of, he ought not do so as the gentiles, who did not penetrate with the eyes of their soul beyond the things of this mortal life. Since the Christian has the light of faith, in which he hopes for eternal life, and without which nothing from above or below will have any value, he ought to rejoice in the possession and exercise of these moral goods only and chiefly in the second manner: that insofar as he performs these works for the love of God, they procure eternal life for him.

Thus, through his good customs and virtues he should fix his eyes only upon the service and honor of God. Without this aspect the virtues are worth nothing in God's sight. This is evident in the Gospel in the case of the ten virgins; they had all preserved their virginity and done good works, yet because five of them had not rejoiced in this second way (by directing their joy in these works to God), but rather in the first, rejoicing vainly in the possession of these works, they were rejected from heaven and left without any gratitude or reward from their spouse. [Mt. 25:1–13] Also many of the ancients possessed numerous virtues and engaged in good works, and many Christians have them today and accomplish wonderful deeds; but such works are of no profit for eternal life, because of failure to seek only the honor and glory of God.

The Christian, then, should not be joyful if he accomplishes good works and abides by good customs, but if he does them out of love for God alone, without any other motive. As those who work only for the service of God will receive a more elevated reward of glory, so those who work for other motives will suffer greater shame when they stand before God.

5. For the sake of directing his joy in moral goods to God, the Christian should keep in mind that the value of his good works, fasts, alms, penances, etc., is not based upon their quantity and quality so much as upon the love of God practiced in them, and that consequently they are deeper in quality the purer and more entire the love of God is by which they are performed, and the less self-interest there is concerning earthly or heavenly joy, pleasure, comfort, and praise. He should not set his heart on the pleasure, comfort, savor, and other interests these good works and practices usually entail, but he must recollect his joy in God and desire to serve Him through these means. And through purgation and darkness as to this joy he should in secret desire that only God be pleased and joyful over them, and he should have no other interest or satisfaction than the honor and glory of God. Thus all the strength of his will in these moral goods will be recollected in God.

CHAPTER 28

Seven kinds of harm which can result from joy of the will in moral goods.

1. I find there are seven kinds of harm that can be incurred through vain joy in one's good works and customs; and because this harm is spiritual it is particularly ruinous.

2. The first is vanity, pride, vainglory, and presumption. For one is unable to rejoice over his works without esteeming them. This gives rise to boasting, etc., as is said of the pharisee in the Gospel: he prayed and sought friendship with God by boasting of his fasting and performance of other good works. [Lk. 18:11-12]

3. The second is usually linked with the first. It is that a person judges others, comparatively speaking, to be evil and imperfect, supposing that their deeds and works are not as good as his own. Interiorly he has less regard for them, and he sometimes manifests this exteriorly in word. The pharisee also had this defect, since he said in his prayer: *I give You thanks that I am not like other men: robbers, unjust, and adulterers.*

[Lk. 18:11] Through one act he incurred the two kinds of harm: self-esteem and contempt for others. Many today also do so when they boast: "I am not like so and so, nor do I do anything similar to what this or that one does." Many are even worse than the pharisee. Though the pharisee not only bore contempt for others in general, but even indicated a particular individual in declaring: *I am not like this publican* [Lk. 18:11], many persons, content with neither of these two attitudes, even become angry and envious in noticing that others receive praise or accomplish more or have greater value than they themselves.

4. The third is that, since they look for satisfaction in their works, they usually do not perform them unless they see that some gratification or praise will result from them. As Christ pointed out, they do everything *ut videantur ab hominibus*[4] [Mt. 23:5]; and they do not undertake their works only out of love for God.

5. The fourth follows from this third; and it is that they will not find their reward in God since they wished to find joy, comfort, honor, or some other thing in this life. Referring to such an attitude, the Saviour says they have received their pay in these goods. [Mt. 6:2] Consequently, they are left alone with the labor of their work and confused without any reward.

There is so much misery in mankind as regards this kind of harm that I believe most of the works publicly achieved are either faulty, worthless, or imperfect in God's sight, because people are not detached from these human respects and interests. How else can one judge the works performed by some and the memorials they have constructed, when they do not desire them unless for some honors or human and vain considerations; or when they perpetuate in the memorials their name, lineage, or nobility; or when they even go to the extent of having their coat of arms or heraldry put in the church, as if they want to put themselves instead of the image there where all bend the knee? It can be said that in these works some adore themselves more than God. And this is true if they undertake such works for these reasons and would not do so without them.

Aside from these individuals, who are the worst, how many are there who in various ways suffer this harm in their works? Some want praise for their works; others, thanks; others talk about them and are pleased if this person or that or even the whole world knows about them; at times they want their alms, or whatever they are doing, to pass through the hands of another that it may be better known; others desire all these aspects together. The Saviour in the Gospel compares this to sounding the trumpet, which is the practice of vain men, and He declares that as

[4] in order to be seen by men

a result they will not receive a reward from God for their works. [Mt. 6:2]

6. To avoid this kind of harm, then, these persons must hide their work so that only God might see it, and they should be undesirous of anyone's paying attention to it. Not only should a man hide it from others, but even from himself: he should desire neither the complacency of esteeming his work as if it had value, nor the procurement of satisfaction. This is the meaning of our Saviour's words: *Let not the left hand know what the right hand does* [Mt. 6:3], which is like saying: Do not esteem with the temporal and carnal eye the spiritual work you do. The strength of the will is thereby recollected in God, and the work bears fruit in His sight. Consequently, a person will not lose the work but reap abundant merit from it.

A passage from Job has this meaning: *I have kissed my hand with my mouth and my heart rejoiced in secret, which is a great iniquity and sin.* [Jb. 31:27–28] The hand in this affirmation refers to the work, and the mouth to the complacency of the will in it. And because it is self-complacency, as we said, he adds: my heart rejoiced in secret, which is a great iniquity and denial against God. And this was equivalent to saying that he was neither complacent nor secretly glad in his heart.

7. The fifth kind of harm is failure to advance in the way of perfection. As a result of attachment to satisfaction and consolation in their works, some usually become discouraged and lose the spirit of perseverance. This ordinarily happens when God leads them on by giving them hard bread, the bread of the perfect, and takes away the infants' milk so as to prove their strength and purge their weak appetite that they may taste the substantial fare of adults. This is the spiritual interpretation of the Wise Man's words: *Dying flies spoil the sweetness of the ointment.* [Eccl. 10:1] For when the occasion of practicing some mortification is presented to these persons, they die to their good works by ceasing to accomplish them, and they lose the spirit of perseverance, which would give them spiritual sweetness and interior consolation.

8. The sixth is that they are usually deluded by the thought that the exercises and works which give satisfaction are better than those which do not. And they have praise and esteem for the one kind, but disesteem for the other. Yet those works which usually require more mortification from a man—especially when he is not advanced in the way of perfection—are more acceptable and precious in God's sight, because of the self-denial exercised in them, than those from which a man can derive consolation, which very easily leads him to self-seeking. Apropos of this, Micheas asserts: *Malum manuum suarum dicunt bonum*

(What is evil in his works they say is good). [Mi. 7:3] This evil is born when they seek to please themselves in their works and not God alone.

An account of how this harmful defect reigns in spiritual persons as well as in ordinary people would involve prolixity, for hardly anyone will be found who is motivated in his work by God alone, without grasping for the support of some consolation or satisfaction or other consideration of self.

9. The seventh is that a man becomes more incapable of taking counsel and receiving reasonable instructions about the works he ought to do, insofar as he does not quell vain joy in his moral deeds. The habitual weakness which he has from working with this vain joy enchains him so that he either believes the counsel of another is not better, or does not wish to follow it even if in his opinion it is, because he is without the courage to do so.

Such people become very slack in charity toward God and neighbor, for the self-love contained in their works makes them grow cold in charity.

CHAPTER 29

Benefits derived through the removal of joy from moral goods.

1. Great are the benefits derived from restraining the desire for vain rejoicing in this kind of good.

As for the first, the soul is freed from falling into many temptations and deceits of the devil, concealed in the joy of these good works. This is understandable from what was said in Job: *He sleeps under the shadow, in the covert of the reed, and in moist places.* [Jb. 40:16] The passage refers to the devil, because in the moisture of joy and the vanity of the reed (of the vain work) he deludes the soul. The devil's hidden deceptiveness in this joy is nothing to marvel at, because, prescinding from his suggestion, the vain joy is itself a deception—especially when there is some boastfulness of heart over one's works—according to Jeremias's affirmation: *Arrogantia tua decepit te.* (Your arrogance has deceived you.) [Jer. 49:16] For what greater deceit is there than boasting? The soul is freed from this deception by purging itself of such joy.

2. The second benefit is a more diligent and precise accomplishment of these works. Such is not the case when one takes pleasure in them with the passion of joy. Through this passion of joy the irascible and concupiscible appetites become so strong that they do not allow leeway for the judgment of reason. As a result a person usually becomes inconstant in his practice of good works and resolutions; he leaves these

aside and takes up others, starting and stopping without ever finishing anything. Since he is motivated by satisfaction, which is changeable—and in some temperaments more so than in others—his work ends when the satisfaction does, and his resolution too, even though it may concern an important endeavor. We can say of those for whom the energy and soul of their work is the joy they find in it that when the joy dies out the good work ceases, and they do not persevere.

Christ spoke of them when He said: *They receive the word with joy, and the devil immediately takes it away from them that they may not persevere.* [Lk. 8:12] And the reason for this lack of perseverance is that they have no other roots or strength than this joy. Withdrawal of the will from such joy, then, is the cause of perseverance and success. This benefit is immense, as is also the contrary harm. A wise man is concerned about the substance and profit of a work, not about the delight and satisfaction it yields. Thus he does not beat the air [1 Cor. 9:26], but procures a stable joy without paying the tribute of displeasure.

3. The third is a divine benefit. It is that through the subdual of vain joy in these works a person becomes poor in spirit, which is one of the beatitudes the Son of God mentions: *Blessed are the poor in spirit, because theirs is the kingdom of heaven.* [Mt. 5:3]

4. The fourth benefit is that anyone denying this joy will be meek, humble, and prudent in his work. For he will act neither impetuously and hastily, compelled by concupiscible and irascible joy; nor presumptuously, affected by his esteem for the work due to the joy it gives; nor uncautiously, blinded by joy.

5. The fifth benefit is to become pleasing to both God and man, and freedom from spiritual avarice, gluttony, sloth, envy, and a thousand other vices.

CHAPTER 30

Supernatural goods, the fifth class in which the will can rejoice. Their nature, the factors distinguishing them from spiritual goods, and how joy in them must be directed to God.

1. Now we ought to discuss supernatural goods, the fifth class in which the will can rejoice. By these we mean all the gifts and graces of God that exceed our natural faculties and powers, called *gratiae gratis datae.* Examples of these are the gifts of wisdom and knowledge God gave to Solomon and the graces St. Paul enumerates: faith, the grace of healing, working of miracles, prophecy, knowledge and discernment of spirits, interpretation of words, and also the gift of tongues. [1 Cor. 12:9–10]

2. Though it is true these goods are also spiritual like the ones we shall speak of later, yet, I must draw a distinction because there is considerable difference between them. For the exercise of these gifts immediately concerns the profit of other men, and God bestows them for that purpose, as St. Paul points out: *the spirit is given to no one save for the benefit of the others* [1 Cor. 12:7]; this assertion is understood in reference to these graces. But the exercise and use of spiritual goods is only between the soul and God, and God and the soul, in a communion of intellect and will, etc., as we shall say afterwards.

There is a difference in their objects, since the object of the spiritual goods is only the Creator and the soul, whereas the object of the supernatural goods is the creature. There is a difference too in substance, consequently in operation, and also necessarily as regards doctrine.

3. Speaking now of supernatural gifts and graces as we here understand them, I assert that for the purgation of vain joy regarding them, it is fitting here to note two benefits included in this kind of goods: temporal and spiritual.

The temporal comprehends cure of the sick, restoration of sight to the blind, raising of the dead, expulsion of devils, prophecy of the future so that men may be careful, and other similar things.

The spiritual and eternal benefit is the knowledge and love of God caused by these works in him who performs them or in those in whom, or before whom, they are accomplished.

4. As for the first, the temporal benefit, supernatural works, and miracles merit little or no joy of soul. When the second benefit is excluded they are of little or no importance to man, since they are not in themselves means for uniting the soul with God, as is charity. And the exercise of these supernatural works and graces does not require grace and charity; either God truly bestows them as He did to the wicked prophet Balaam and to Solomon, or they are effected falsely by means of the devil, as in the case of Simon Magus, or by means of other secret, natural powers. If any of these marvels are to be beneficial to their agent, they will be the true ones that are given by God.

St. Paul teaches what they are worth without the second benefit: *If I speak with the tongues of men and of angels and have not charity, I am become as the sounding metal or bell. And if I should have prophecy and know all mysteries and all knowledge, and if I should have all faith so as to move mountains, and have not charity, I am nothing, etc.* [1 Cor. 13:1–2] When those who so esteem their works seek glory from Christ saying: *Lord, did we not prophesy in your name and work many miracles?* He will answer: *Depart from Me, workers of iniquity.* [Mt. 7: 22–23]

5. A man should rejoice, then, not in the possession and exercise of these graces, but in the procurement of the second spiritual benefit: serving God by them with true charity, for in charity lies the fruit of eternal life. Accordingly, our Saviour reproved the disciples who were glorying in their success at casting out devils: *In this do not desire to rejoice, that the devils are subject to you, but that your names are written in the book of life.* [Lk. 10:20] In sound theology this is like saying: Rejoice if your names are written in the book of life. Hence it should be understood that a man ought only rejoice in treading the path that leads to life, in doing works with charity. What profit is there in anything that is not the love of God, and what value has it in His sight? Love is not perfect if it is not strong and discreet in purifying joy of all things, centering it only upon the fulfillment of God's will. Thus the will is united with God through these supernatural goods.

CHAPTER 31

Harm incurred from rejoicing in this class of goods.

1. It seems to me that three chief kinds of harm follow from rejoicing in supernatural goods: active and passive deception; detriment to the soul's faith; and vainglory or some vanity.

2. As for the first it is very easy to deceive oneself and others by rejoicing in these accomplishments. The reason is that discernment of the true ones from the false and knowledge of how and at what time they may be exercised demands much counsel and light from God, both of which are exceedingly hindered by esteeming and rejoicing in these works.

There are two reasons for this: first, because joy blunts and darkens the judgment; second, due to his joy in the work, a man is not merely desirous of believing in it more quickly, but even impelled toward performing the work outside the proper time.

Granted that the wonders and works be genuine, one can be sufficiently deluded by these two defects, either by not understanding them as they ought to be understood or by not benefitting by and making suitable use of them as to time and manner. Though it is true that when God bestows these gifts and graces He gives light for them and an impulse as to the time and manner of their exercise, yet, souls can err seriously because of possible attachment and imperfection concerning them, and by not using them with the perfection desired by God, at the time and in the way He desires. We read that Balaam was thus at fault when, against God's will, he determined to go and curse the Israelites; consequently, God being angered, desired to kill him. [Nm. 22:22-23]

St. James and St. John wanted to make fire descend from heaven upon the Samaritans who refused lodging to our Saviour, but the Lord reproved them for this. [Lk. 9:54–55]

3. Obviously in these cases they were moved to perform their works at an inopportune time by some imperfect passion that was clothed in joy and esteem for these works. When this imperfection is not present, a person decides to perform these works when and in the manner that God moves him; until then he should not work them. For this reason God complained through Jeremias: *I did not send the prophets and they ran; I did not speak and they prophesied.* [Jer. 23:21] Further on He says: *They deceived my people with their lying and prodigies, for I had not commanded it nor sent them.* [23:32] He also says of them there that they beheld the visions of their own heart and published them about. [23:26] This would never have happened had they overcome their abominable attachment to these works.

4. Through these passages we learn that the harm engendered by this joy comes not only from the wicked and perverse use of God's graces —as in the case of Balaam and those who deceived the people with their miracles—but even from performing them without God's grace, as in those who prophesied their fancies and spoke of visions manufactured by either themselves or the devil. When the devil observes their attachment to these wonders, he opens a wide field and provides ample material for their endeavors and meddles extensively. And these individuals with such means spread wide their sails, become shamelessly audacious, and abound in prodigious works.

5. And this is not all! The joy and covetousness they have in these works reaches such a point that if previously their pact with the devil was secret—for often the works are performed through a secret pact— now through their boldness they make an express and open one with him and by an agreement subject themselves to him as his disciples and friends. Hence we have wizards, enchanters, magicians, soothsayers, and witches.

Joy in these works goes so far that some, as Simon Magus, not merely want to buy the gifts and graces with money [Acts 18:18] for the service of the devil, but they even try to get hold of sacred and divine objects—which cannot be mentioned without trembling—as has already been witnessed in the theft of the most sacred body of our Lord Jesus Christ for evil practices and abominations. May God extend and show forth His infinite mercy in this matter!

6. Everyone can readily understand how pernicious these individuals are and how detrimental to Christianity. It should be noted that all those

magicians and soothsayers who lived among the children of Israel and were expelled from the land by Saul had fallen into so many abominations and delusions because of their desire to imitate the genuine prophets.

7. Anyone, then, who has this supernatural gift should not desire or rejoice in its use, nor should he care about exercising it. God, who grants the grace supernaturally for the utility of the Church or its members, will also move him supernaturally as to the manner and time in which he should use it. Since the Lord commanded His disciples not to be anxious about what or how to speak, because it was a supernatural matter of faith, and since these works are also a supernatural matter, He will want a man to wait until He becomes the worker, by moving the heart toward the practice of the work. [Mt. 10:19; Mk. 13:11] For it is by the power of God that every other power should be exercised. In the Acts of the Apostles the disciples beseeched Him in prayer to extend His hand for the work of signs and cures that the faith of our Lord Jesus Christ would be introduced into hearts. [Acts 4:29–30]

8. The second harm proceeds from the first. It is a twofold detriment to the faith.

First, in regard to others: When a person tries to increase these prodigies or powers outside the proper time and without necessity, it can happen that besides tempting God—which is a serious sin—he will be unsuccessful and thereby engender in hearts a distrust and contempt of the faith. Sometimes one is successful because God wishes it for other reasons and motives, as with Saul's sorceress—if Samuel really appeared there. [1 Kgs. 28:7–15] Yet this will not always be so; but when a person does succeed, he errs and is culpable for using these graces inopportunely.

Second, there is detriment to the individual himself in the merit of faith. By giving importance to these miracles one loses the support of the substantial habit of faith, which is an obscure habit. Where signs and testimonies abound, there is less merit in believing. St. Gregory declares that faith is without merit when it has proof from human reason. [*Hom. 26 in Evang.:* PL 76, 1197]

God never works these marvels except when they are a necessity for believing. Lest His disciples should go without merit by having sensible proof of His resurrection, He did many things to further their belief before they saw Him. Mary Magdalen was first shown the empty sepulcher, and afterwards the angels told her about the resurrection so that she would believe before seeing. As St. Paul says: *Faith comes through hearing.* [Rom. 10:17] And though she beheld Him, He seemed only an ordinary man, that by the warmth of His presence He could finish instructing her in the belief she was lacking. [Mt. 28:1–6; Lk. 24:4–6; Jn. 20:15] And first the women were sent to tell the disciples; then these disciples set out to see the sepulcher. [Mt. 28:7] And journeying incognito to Emmaus with two of His followers, He inflamed their hearts in faith before allowing them to see. [Lk. 24:15–32] Finally He reproved all his disciples for refusing to believe those who had told them of His resurrection. [Mk. 16:14] And announcing to St. Thomas that they are blessed who believe without seeing, He reprimanded him for desiring to see and touch His wounds. [Jn. 20:25, 29]

9. It is not God's desire that miracles be performed; when He works them He does so out of necessity. He consequently reprimanded the pharisees because they were unwilling to believe without signs: *If you do not see signs and wonders, you do not believe.* [Jn. 4:48]

Those, then, who love to rejoice in these supernatural works suffer a great loss in faith.

10. Third, through joy in these works one ordinarily falls into vainglory or some kind of vanity. Even the very joy in these marvels that is not wholly in and for God is vanity. Our Lord's reproval of the disciples for having rejoiced that the devils were subject to them is a demonstration of this truth; if this joy were not vain He would not have made the reprimand. [Lk. 10:20]

CHAPTER 32

The two benefits acquired through the negation of joy in supernatural goods.

1. Besides the advantage of being freed from these kinds of harm, the soul acquires two excellent benefits.

The first refers to the praise and the extolling of God; the second to the exaltation of the soul itself.

God is exalted in the soul in two ways. First, the heart and the joy of will is withdrawn from all that is not God and concentrated upon Him alone. David intended this in the verse we quoted at the beginning of the night of this faculty: *The heart of man will reach high, and God will be exalted.* [Ps. 63:7–8] By lifting the heart above all things, the soul is exalted above them all.

2. And because the soul in this way concentrates only upon God, God receives praise and extollment in manifesting to it His excellence and grandeur. In this elevation of joy in Him, God gives testimony of Who He is. This is only done when the will is empty of joy and comfort

in all things, as He also declares through David: *Leave all and see that I am God.* [Ps. 45:11] And again David says: *In a desert way, dry and pathless, I appeared before You to see Your power and glory.* [Ps. 62:3] God is truly extolled when joy is withdrawn from all things and centered upon Him, but He receives much more glory when it is removed from these more marvelous goods and applied to Him alone, since by being supernatural they are of higher entity. To leave them behind for the sake of joy in God alone is to attribute greater glory and excellence to God than to them. Commensurate with the quality and the number of things despised for the sake of another person is the esteem and praise given to that person.

3. Moreover, through the withdrawal of the will from these works, God is exalted in the second manner. The more faith and service rendered to God without testimonies and signs, the more extollment He receives from the soul, since it believes more of Him than what the signs and miracles can teach.

4. The second benefit, the exaltation of the soul, owes its origin to the withdrawal of the will from all apparent testimonies and signs. Because of this the soul is exalted in purest faith, which God then infuses and augments much more abundantly. And together with this the other two theological virtues—charity and hope—receive increase. As a result the soul enjoys divine and lofty knowledge by means of the dark and naked habit of faith; and the admirable delight of love through charity, by which it rejoices in no one other than the living God; and satisfaction in the memory by means of hope. All of this is a splendid benefit, essentially and directly required for the perfect union of the soul with God.

CHAPTER 33

The nature and division of the sixth kind of good which is a possible object of joy for the will.

1. Our intention in this work is to guide the soul through spiritual goods to the divine union with God. Now that we are about to discuss this sixth kind (those very goods that are the most helpful in this matter), both the reader and I myself will have to pay particular attention. Because of their lack of knowledge, it is a common and certain occurrence with some to let spiritual things serve only for the senses and to leave the spirit empty. Hardly will anyone be found in whom sensory satisfaction does not in some way spoil a good part of what was destined for the spirit, for senses drink up the waters before they reach the spirit, and thus leave the spirit dry and empty.

2. To come, then, to our subject, I refer by spiritual goods to all those that are an aid and motivating force in turning the soul to divine things and to converse with God, as well as a help in God's communications to the soul.

3. According to their main headings we can divide spiritual goods into two classes: the delightful, and the painful.

Each of these can again be divided into two kinds: the delightful comprise goods that are clearly and distinctly understood, and others that do not afford clear or distinct understanding; the painful likewise include those that are clear and distinct, and others that are vague and obscure.

4. We can also divide these goods according to the faculties of the soul. Those dealing with knowledge are pertinent to the intellect, those referring to affections belong to the will, and others insofar as they are imaginary pertain to the memory.

5. We will discuss the painful goods afterwards, because they belong to the passive night. The discussion of the vague and indistinct delightful goods will be left for the end, since they are pertinent to the general, vague, loving knowledge in which union with God is effected. In the second book we also deferred this to the end when we listed the divisions of intellectual apprehensions. Here we shall treat of delightful goods that are clear and distinct.

CHAPTER 34

The proper conduct of the will as to joy in the distinct spiritual goods communicable to the intellect and memory.

1. We would have had to cover a great deal of matter here to instruct the will about the proper conduct concerning joy in the multitudinous apprehensions of the intellect and memory if we had not amply discussed these apprehensions in the second and third book. Since we indicated there the conduct suitable for these two faculties in this kind of apprehension, there is no necessity for repetition here. The conduct of the will should be the same in their regard. It is sufficient to remark that wherever instructions are given about emptying these faculties of certain apprehensions, the will too, it is understood, should be voided of joy in them.

And the conduct required of the memory and intellect concerning these apprehensions is also necessary for the will. Since the intellect and other faculties cannot admit or deny anything without the intervention of the will, the same doctrine that serves for the one faculty will evidently apply to the others also.

2. The reader will find in those sections what is required here. For the soul will fall into all those kinds of harm if it is ignorant of how to direct to God its joy in these apprehensions.

CHAPTER 35

Delightful spiritual goods. A division.

1. All goods giving distinct joy to the will can be reduced to four kinds: motivating, provocative, directive, and perfective. We shall discuss them in due order, beginning with motivating goods: statues, paintings of saints, oratories, and ceremonies.

2. There can be considerable vain joy in relation to statues and paintings. Although they are vital to the divine cult and necessary to move the will to devotion, as the approbation and use of our Holy Mother the Church demonstrates (we should always take advantage of them in order to be awakened from our lukewarmness), many rejoice more in the painting and ornamentation than in the object represented.

3. The Church established the use of statues for two principal reasons: the reverence given to the saints through them; and the motivation of the will and the awakening of devotion to the saints by their means. Insofar as they serve this purpose their use is profitable and necessary. We should consequently choose those statues that are more lifelike and move the will more to devotion. Our concentration should be centered upon this devotion more than upon the elaborateness of the workmanship and its ornamentation.

There are, as I say, some people who pay more attention to the decorations and the value of the statue than to the object represented. And the interior devotion which they should direct spiritually toward the invisible saint in immediate forgetfulness of the statue—since the purpose of the statue is to give motivation—is so taken up with the exterior elaboration and ornamentation that the senses receive the satisfaction and delight, and then both the love and joy of the will dwell upon that satisfaction. This is a total obstacle to authentic spirituality which demands the annihilation of the affections in all particular things.

4. Such an attitude is obvious in the abominable custom some have in these times of ours. Without any repugnance for vain worldly fashions, they adorn statues with the jewelry conceited people in the course of time invent to satisfy themselves in their pastimes and vanities, and they clothe the statues in garments that would be reprehensible if worn

by themselves—a practice that was and still is abhorrent to the saints represented by the statues. In company with the devil they strive to canonize their vanities, not without serious offense to the saints. By this usage the authentic and sincere devotion of the soul, which in itself uproots and rejects every vanity and trace of it, is reduced to little more than doll-dressing. Some use the statues for nothing more than idols upon which they center their joy.

You will see some who never tire of adding statue upon statue to their collection, of insisting that they be of this particular kind and workmanship and placed in a certain niche and in a special way—all so that these statues will give delight to the senses. As for devotion of heart, there is very little. They are as attached as were Michas and Laban to their idols. For Michas left his house shouting because they were stolen; and Laban, after a long journey and being enraged, turned over all of Jacob's household furnishings in search for them. [Jgs. 18:23-24; Gn. 31:23-27]

5. The truly devout person directs his devotion mainly to the invisible object represented, has little need for many statues, and uses those that are conformed more to the divine traits than to human ones. He brings these images—and himself through them—into conformity with the fashion and condition of the other world, not with this one. He does this so that worldly images will not be stirring his appetite and so that he will not even be reminded of the world, as he would in having before his eyes any object apparently a part of this world. His heart is not attached to these goods, and if they are taken away, his grief is slight. He seeks the living image of Christ crucified within himself, and thereby he is pleased rather to have everything taken from him and to be left with nothing.

Even when the motives and means that bring his soul closer to God are taken from him, he remains calm. A person is more perfect when he remains tranquil and joyous in the privation of these motives than when he possesses them with desire and attachment. It is good to be pleased with images that help the soul toward deeper devotion; a person should always choose that image which is most devotional for him. Yet there is no perfection in being so attached to those that are possessed as to become sad if they are taken away.

6. A person should be certain that the more he is attached with a possessive spirit to the image or motive, the less will his prayer and devotion ascend to God. Indeed, since some statues are truer likenesses than others and excite more devotion, it is fit to be attached more to some than to others. However, not with that attachment and possessiveness, I mentioned, for the engulfment of the senses in the joy of the means would expend the good which the spirit should gain by soaring from the image to God in immediate forgetfulness of this thing or that.

These means which should be an aid in one's flight to God now become through this imperfection a hindrance, and no less so than in the case of attachment to or possessiveness relative to any other object.

7. Although on this subject of statues you may have some objection due to lack of a clear understanding of the nakedness and spiritual poverty demanded for perfection, at least you will not be able to defend through your objections the imperfection commonly found in the use of rosaries. You will hardly meet anyone who does not have some weakness in this matter. They want the rosary to be made in one style rather than another, or that it be of this color or that metal rather than the other, or of this or that particular design. One rosary is no more influential with God than is another; His answer to the rosary prayer is not dependent upon the kind of rosary used. The prayer He hears is that of the simple·and pure heart, which is concerned only about pleasing God and does not bother about the kind of rosary used, unless in regard to indulgences.

8. Our vain covetousness is such that it clings to everything. It is like the wood borer which gnaws at both good and bad objects. What else is your motive in carrying around an overdecorated rosary with the desire that it be this kind rather than another and in wanting to choose this statue instead of that other if not the joy you find in the instrument? And in your concern about their value and ornamentation, you neglect to consider their faculty for awakening the divine love in you. Should you employ your appetite and joy only in the love of God, you would be indifferent to these various religious articles. It is pitiful to see how attached some persons are to the style and craftsmanship of these instruments and motives as well as to their elaborateness and to the vain satisfaction that is to be gotten from them. You will never see them satisfied. They are always setting aside one thing for another and forgetting spiritual devotion because of these visible means; their attachment and possessive spirit is no different with these religious articles than it is with temporal furnishings. The harm done through such an attitude is by no means slight.

CHAPTER 36

A continued discussion of statues; the ignorance of some in their use of them.

1. Much could be said about the ignorance of many in their use of statues. Their foolishness reaches such a point that they trust more in one statue than in another and think that God will answer them more

readily through it, even when both statues represent the same person, such as those of our Lord or our Blessed Lady. At the bottom of this idea is their greater attachment to the one work than to the other, which entails gross ignorance about communion with God and the cult and honor due Him Who looks only upon the faith and purity of the prayerful heart.

If God sometimes bestows more favors through one statue than through another, He does not do so because of its greater ability to produce this effect—even though there may be notable difference in the workmanship —but because the devotion of individuals is awakened more by means of the one statue than the other. Should the persons have equal devotion in the presence of both—and even this same devotion without the aid of either statue—God would grant them the same favors.

2. God does not work miracles and grant favors by means of some statues in order that these statues may be held in higher esteem than others, but that through His wonderful works He may awaken the dormant devotion and affection of the faithful. Since, consequently, through the instrumentality of this statue, devotion is enkindled and prayer prolonged—both means by which God hears and grants one's petitions—God continues to bestow favors and work miracles through that statue. God certainly does not work miracles because of the image, which in itself is no more than a painting, but He does so because of the faith and devotion that is had toward the saint represented. Thus, if you had equal devotion to and faith in our Lady before two different images of her—and even without them, as we said—you would receive the same favors.

Experience even teaches that if God grants some favors and works miracles, He does so through some statues that are not very well carved or carefully painted, or that are poor representations, so that the faithful will not attribute any of these wonders to the statue or painting.

3. Our Lord frequently bestows these favors by means of images situated in remote and solitary places. The reason for this is that the effort required in journeying to these places makes the affection increase and the act of prayer more intense. Another motive is that a person may withdraw from people and noise in order to pray, as our Lord did. [Mt. 14:23]

Whoever makes a pilgrimage, therefore, does well to make it alone, even if he must do so at an unusual time. I would never advise going along with a large crowd, because one ordinarily returns more distracted than before. Many who go on pilgrimages do so more for the sake of recreation than devotion.

Where there is devotion and faith, any image will be sufficient; but if this is lacking, none will suffice. Our Lord was indeed a living image during His sojourn in this world; nevertheless, those who were faithless received no spiritual gain, even though they frequently went about with Him and beheld His wondrous works. This is why He did not perform many mighty works in His own country, as the Evangelist declared. [Mt. 13:58; Mk. 6:5–6]

4. I would also like to mention here some supernatural effects that certain images occasionally cause in particular individuals. God gives to some images a special spiritual influence upon souls so that their figure and the devotion they cause remain fixed in the mind as though they were present; when a person suddenly recalls the image, he will discover that it exercises the same spiritual influence it did when seen, sometimes less and occasionally even more. And he will not find that spiritual influence in another image, even if it is one of more perfect craftsmanship.

5. Many also experience more devotion through statues of one kind of workmanship than another. In some people this devotion will be caused by no more than a natural liking and attachment, just as some will like the face of one person more than that of another, become more attached to it naturally, and preserve it more readily in their imagination because they are naturally inclined to that type of form and figure, even though the face itself may not be as beautiful as those of others. Thus some people will think the attachment they have to a certain image is devotion when in reality it will perhaps be no more than a natural attachment and preference.

Occasionally when looking at an image they see it move and make signs and gestures, or they hear words and instructions. Although these signs and the supernatural effects produced by the images are authentic and good, destined by God to either increase devotion or give the soul some support against distractions because of its weakness, the devil frequently produces them in order to cause deception and harm.

We will thus expound the doctrine regarding all this in the following chapter.

CHAPTER 37

The direction of joy of the will to God in order to avoid errors and obstacles arising from images.

1. Just as images are notably beneficial for the remembrance of God and His saints, and for moving the will to devotion through their proper use, so too they will be the cause of serious error if the soul is ignorant of the conduct proper for its journey to God when supernatural phe-

nomena occur relative to these images. One of the means with which the devil readily catches uncautious souls, and impedes them in the way of spiritual truthfulness, is the supernatural and extraordinary phenomena he manifests through images, either through the material and corporal ones the Church uses, or through those he fixes in the phantasy in the guise of a particular saint. He transforms himself into an angel of light for the sake of deception. [2 Cor. 11:14] Crafty as he is, he will disguise himself, in order to catch us off guard, in the very means we use to procure help for ourselves. The good soul should consequently be more cautious in the use of good things, for evil in itself gives testimony to itself.

2. That the soul may escape the harm which in these circumstances can affect it (such as: a hindrance in its flight to God, the use of images with ignorance and an inferior attitude, or suffering delusion by them, either naturally or supernaturally, which are subjects we dwelt on above), purify its will of the joy it finds in images and direct itself through them to God, which is the intention of the Church in their use, I wish to set down only one maxim here, which will be sufficient for all cases: Since images serve as a motivating means toward invisible things, we should strive that the motivation, affection, and joy of will derived from them be directed toward the living object they represent.

The faithful man should therefore take this precaution: Upon seeing the image he should not allow his senses to become absorbed in it (whether it be corporal or imaginary, of beautiful workmanship or richly adorned, the cause of sensible or spiritual devotion, or whether it may make gestures through supernatural power); he should pay no attention to these accidents, dwell not upon the image but immediately raise his mind to what is represented. He should prayerfully and devotedly center the satisfaction and joy of his will in God or the saint being invoked, so that the painting and senses will not absorb what belongs to the spirit and the living person represented. He will accordingly be safe from delusion, since he will pay no attention to what the image supernaturally says to him, nor so employ his senses as to hinder his free elevation to God, nor put more trust in one image than in another. And that image which does excite his devotion will do this more copiously, since his affection will be immediately raised to God. Whenever God bestows these and other favors, He does so by inclining the passion of joy toward the invisible, and He wishes us to do likewise by annihilating the strength and satisfaction of the faculties in regard to sensory and visible objects.

CHAPTER 38

A continued discussion of motivating goods. Oratories and dedicated places of prayer.

1. I think I have explained clearly how in relation to these images or accidents a spiritual person can have as much imperfection—and perhaps more if he sets his liking and joy on them—as in the use of other corporal and temporal objects. And I add that perhaps these images are more dangerous, for in saying, "they are holy objects," a person becomes more assured and does not fear natural possessiveness and attachment. Spiritual persons are thus at times seriously deluded by thinking they are filled with devotion because of their satisfaction in the use of these holy objects, yet, perhaps, this devotion will be no more than a natural inclination and appetite which is centered on these holy things as upon any other object.

2. Hence, to begin our discussion on the subject of oratories, some individuals never grow tired of adding images of one kind or another to their oratories, of taking delight in the order and adornment with which they are arranged, so that their place of prayer will appear well decorated and attractive. But they do not love God more when it is arranged in this way instead of that, rather they love Him less, since the delight they find in these ornate paintings withholds their attention from the living person represented, as we pointed out. It is true, indeed, that every decoration, adornment, and reverence that can be given to images is very small. Those, therefore, who show little respect or reverence for their statues deserve sharp reproof, as well as those who carve so inexpertly that the finished statue subtracts from devotion rather than adding to it. Some artisans so unskilled and unpolished in the art of carving should be forbidden to continue their craft. Still, what pertinence has this to the possessiveness, attachment, and appetite you have in these exterior decorations and adornments which so engross the senses that your heart is impeded from turning to God, loving Him, and forgetting all things out of love for Him? If you fail in this love because of these other objects, He will not merely fail to reward you, but will punish you for not having sought His pleasure in all things instead of your own.

We get a clear understanding of this in the festivity that was celebrated in honor of His Majesty when He entered Jerusalem; while they were expressing thanks to Him with songs and palm branches, He was weeping because He knew that in spite of those exterior signs and decorations their hearts were far from Him. [Lk. 19:35-44] Evidently they were celebrating their own selves more than God, which often happens today when there is a solemn festival in some locality. Many are usually happier because of the recreation derived from the celebration—by seeing or being seen, or by eating, or through some other means than because of God's pleasure. In these inclinations and intentions they do not please God. This is especially so with those who in organizing the religious festivals invent ridiculous and undevout things to incite laughter among the people, which only adds to the distraction. Others design displays meant to please the people more than arouse their devotion.

3. What shall I say about the desires for personal profit of some of those who organize the festivals? If they have more concern and covetousness for this than for the service of God they are well aware of the fact, but so is God Who sees them. Yet, if the right intention is lacking, whatever kind of celebration they may have, they are having a festival for themselves rather than for God.

God does not record for their merit what they do for their own pleasure or for that of others; on the contrary, many taking part in the festivals in honor of God will be only diverting themselves, and God will be angry with them. He was angry in this way with the children of Israel when He killed many thousands of them while they were celebrating a festival, singing and dancing to their idol, thinking their festivity was in honor of God. [Ex. 32:7–28] God also killed the priests Nadab and Abiud, children of Aaron, while they still held the censers in their hands, because they offered strange fire. [Lv. 10:1–2] And the one who came to the wedding feast badly dressed and without the wedding garment was commanded by the king to be bound hand and foot and cast into exterior darkness. [Mt. 22:12–13] We learn from these instances how intolerable to God these irreverences are in the gatherings organized for His service.

How many festivals, my God, do the children of men celebrate in Your honor in which the devil has a greater role than You! And the devil, like a merchant, is pleased with these gatherings because he does more business on those days. How many times will You say of them: *This people honors Me with their lips alone, but their heart is far from Me, because they serve Me without cause.* [Mt. 15:8–9]

God must be served because He is Who is; and other motives must not be intermingled with this one. If a person does not serve God because of Who He is, God would not be the final cause of this person's service.

4. Returning, then, to the subject of oratories, I say that some persons decorate them more for their own pleasure than for that of God. Some pay so little attention to the devotional aspect of their oratories that they have no more regard for them than they do for their profane dressing rooms; some do not even have this much interest in them, since they find more gratification in profane things than in divine.

5. Let us turn our discussion rather to the more spiritual persons, those who are considered devout. Many of them in their desire and gratification grow so attached to their oratory and its decoration that all their energy, which should be employed in prayer and interior recollection, is expended on these things. They do not realize that, by not arranging their oratory in a way that would further interior recollection and peace of soul, they receive as much distraction as they would from other things; and at every step they become disquieted about this pleasure, and even more so if anyone wants to take it away from them.

CHAPTER 39

How a person should use oratories and churches and direct his spirit to God through them.

1. To direct the spirit to God in this kind of good, we should keep in mind that for beginners it is permissible and even fitting to find some sensible gratification and satisfaction in the use of images, oratories, and other visible objects of devotion so that with this pleasure they may renounce worldly things from whose taste they are not yet weaned or detached. This is what we do with a child when we desire to take something away from him; we give him another thing to play with so that he will not begin to cry when left empty-handed.

But in order to advance, the spiritual person should likewise divest himself of all these satisfactions and appetites, for the pure spirit is bound to none of these objects, but turns only to interior recollection and mental communion with God. Although he derives profit from images and oratories, this is very transitory, for his spirit is immediately elevated to God in forgetfulness of all sensory objects.

2. Even though it is better to pray in the place that is more respectable, one should in spite of this choose that place which least hinders the elevation of sense and spirit to God. This is the interpretation we should give to Christ's reply to the query of the Samaritan woman about the place best suited for prayer—the temple or the mountain. His answer was that true prayer is annexed neither to the temple nor to the mountain, but that the adorers who please the Father are those who adore Him in spirit and truth. [Jn. 4:20–24]

Churches and quiet places are dedicated and suitable for prayer, for the church should be used for no other purpose. Nevertheless, in a matter of communion with God as interior as this, that place should be chosen which least occupies and attracts the senses. A spiritual person should not look for a spot pleasant and delightful to the senses, as some usually do, lest he become absorbed with the recreation, gratification, and delight of the senses rather than with God in spiritual recollection. A solitary and austere location is beneficial for the sure and direct ascent of the spirit to God without the impediment or detainment caused by visible things. Sometimes visible objects do aid in the elevation of the spirit, but this elevation is the result of immediately forgetting them in order to remain recollected in God. Our Saviour, to give us an example, chose for His prayer solitary places, those that were undistracting to the senses and raised the soul to God (such as the mountains that are elevated above the earth and usually barren of the objects that would provide sensitive recreation). [Mt. 14:23]

3. The truly spiritual person never considers nor becomes attached to the particular comfort of a place of prayer, for this would result from attachment to the senses. His interest is interior recollection in the forgetfulness of other things. He chooses the site that is freest of sensible objects and satisfactions and turns his attention from all these considerations so that unimpeded by any creature he may rejoice more in solitude with God. Some spiritual persons noticeably spend all their time in adorning oratories and making places agreeable to their own temperament or inclination and they pay little heed to interior recollection, which is the important factor. They are not very recollected, for if they were they would be unable to find any satisfaction in these ways, but would grow tired of them.

CHAPTER 40

The continuation of this topic on the direction of the spirit toward interior recollection.

1. The reason some spiritual persons never entirely enter into the true joys of spirit is a failure to renounce their desire for joy in these exterior and visible things. These persons should keep in mind that although the place dedicated and suited to prayer is the visible oratory or church and the motivating good is the image, these means should not be so used that the satisfaction and delight of the soul stems entirely from them, thereby causing one to forget to pray in the living temple which is interior recollection of soul.

To remind us of this the Apostle said: *Behold, your bodies are living temples of the Holy Ghost, who dwells within you.* [1 Cor. 3:16] This thought brings to mind that affirmation of Christ which we quoted: *The true adorers should adore in spirit and truth.* [Jn. 4:24] God pays little attention to your oratories and places arranged for prayer if in your desire and liking for them you become attached and, in consequence, have less interior nakedness, that is, spiritual poverty in the renunciation of things possessable.

2. To purge the will of its desires and vain joy in these objects, and direct it to God, you should strive in your prayer for a pure conscience, a will that is wholly with God, and a mind truly set upon Him. And, as I mentioned, you ought to choose the most withdrawn and solitary place possible, convert all your joy of will into the invocation and glorification of God, and pay no attention to these other little exterior satisfactions which you should rather seek to deny. Should a soul become bound to the delight of sensory devotion, it will never succeed in passing on to the strength of spiritual delight, which is discovered through interior recollection in spiritual nakedness.

CHAPTER 41

Some harm resulting from the surrender to sensible gratification in the use of devotional objects and places.

1. Spiritual persons incur many kinds of interior and exterior harm by their desire to get sensible delight from the use of devotional objects. As for interior harm, one will never reach inward recollection of spirit, which consists in passing beyond all these sensory delights, making the soul forget them, entering into the living temple of spiritual recollection, and acquiring solid virtue. With regard to the exterior harm, a person will be rendered incapable of praying everywhere, but will be able to pray only in those places suited to his taste, and thus be frequently wanting in prayer. As the saying runs, he knows no other book than that of his own village.

2. Moreover, the appetites of these individuals will be the occasion of considerable inconstancy. Some never persevere in one place—nor even at times in one state—but now you see them in one spot, and now in another; now choosing one hermitage, now another; at one moment they will be decorating one oratory, and at the next, another.

Some also pass their time here below changing states and modes of life. The fervor and joy they find in their spiritual practices is merely sensible, and they have never made any effort to reach spiritual recollection through denial of their wills and submission to the suffering of discomforts. Consequently, as often as they see a seemingly devotional place, or way, or state of life adapted to their disposition and inclination, they immediately leave what they have and follow after it. And since they are motivated by sensible gratification, they soon begin to look for something else; for sensible satisfaction is inconstant and very quick to fail.

CHAPTER 42

The proper conduct of the will in the use of three different kinds of devotional places.

1. There are three different kinds of places, I find, by which God usually moves the will.

The first includes those sites which have pleasant variations in the arrangement of the land and the trees, and provide solitary quietude, all of which naturally awakens devotion. It is advantageous to use these places if one immediately directs the will to God in the forgetfulness of the place itself, since one should not be detained by the means and motive more than necessary for the attainment of the end. If a person strives for recreation of his appetites and for sensory satisfaction, he will rather encounter spiritual dryness and distraction, because spiritual satisfaction and contentment is found only in interior recollection.

2. When a person, therefore, prays in a beautiful site, he should endeavor to be interiorly with God and forget the place, as though he were not there at all. For when people wander about looking for delight and gratification from a particular site, they are in search, as we said, for sensory recreation and spiritual instability more than spiritual tranquillity.

The anchorites and other holy hermits, while in the loveliest and vastest wildernesses, chose for themselves as small an area as possible, built narrow cells and caves, and enclosed themselves within. St. Benedict lived in one of these for three years, and St. Simon tied himself with a cord so as not to use up more space or go farther than the cord allowed him. There are many other examples of this kind of mortification of which we would never finish speaking. For those saints clearly understood that without extinguishing their appetite and covetousness for spiritual gratification and delight they would never become truly spiritual.

3. The second kind of place in which God moves the will to devotion is more particular. It includes those localities, whether wildernesses or not, in which God usually grants some very delightful spiritual favors to particular individuals. He so grants His favor that the recipient will have a natural inclination toward that place, and will sometimes experience immense desires and longings to return there. But when he returns he discovers that the place is not to him what it was before, because these favors do not lie within his power. God bestows these

graces when, and how, and where He wills without being bound to place, or time, or to the free will of the recipient.

Yet it is good sometimes to return there for prayer, provided one's soul is divested of the desire for spiritual possessions. There are three reasons: first, it seems that although God is not bound to any place, He desires in granting the favor to receive praise there from that soul; second, the soul when there will be more mindful of thanking God for His favors; third, while remembering the graces received there, a more fervent devotion will be awakened.

4. These are the reasons for returning to that place. And one, consequently, should not think that God is bound to grant favors there as if He were unable to do so wherever He wishes, for the soul is a more becoming and suitable place for God than any material site.

We read in Sacred Scripture that Abraham built an altar in the very place God appeared and there called upon His holy name. Afterwards, on his return from Egypt, he went to the same place where God had appeared and invoked Him again at that very altar he had built there. [Gn. 12:7-8; 13:3-4] By setting up a stone anointed with oil, Jacob also marked the place where God, leaning upon a ladder, had appeared to him. [Gn. 28:13-18] Agar, with highest esteem for that place where the angel appeared to her, gave it a name, saying: *Certainly, here have I seen the shoulders of Him who sees me.* [Gn. 16:13-14]

5. The third kind of place comprises those in which God chooses to be invoked and worshiped. For example: Mount Sinai, where He presented the law to Moses [Ex. 24:12]; and the place He marked for the sacrifice of Abraham's son [Gn. 22:2]; and also Mount Horeb, to which He sent our Father Elias for the sake of appearing to him there [3 Kgs. 19:8]; and Mount Garganus, the place St. Michael dedicated to God's cult by appearing to the Bishop of Siponto and telling him how he guarded that place so that a chapel might be dedicated to God there in memory of the angels; and the site which the Blessed Virgin through the miracle of snow pointed out for a church which she desired Patritius to build in her name.

6. Why God chooses one place in which to receive praise more than another, He alone knows. What we should know is that He does all for our own benefit and so that He may hear our prayers in these places— or anywhere in which we beseech Him with integral faith. Yet there is much greater occasion to be heard in those places consecrated to His cult, since the Church has so marked and dedicated them.

CHAPTER 43

The large variety of ceremonies as another motivating means which
many people use for prayer.

1. The useless joy and imperfect possessiveness of many apropos of
the goods we have mentioned is perhaps somewhat tolerable because of
their innocence in the matter. Yet the strong attachment of some to
many kinds of ceremonies which were introduced by people uninstructed
and wanting in the simplicity of faith is unsufferable.

We shall prescind from those ceremonies which make use of extrava-
gant names or terms without meaning and other unsacred things that
ignorant, rude, and questionable persons usually intermingle with their
prayers, since these ceremonies are obviously evil and sinful. And in many
of them there is a secret pact with the devil by which God is provoked to
anger and not mercy.

2. I want to speak only of those ceremonies used by many today with
indiscreet devotion, since these are not included in those other suspect
kinds. These people attribute so much efficacy to methods of carrying out
their devotions and prayers and so trust in them that they believe that if
one point is missing or certain limits have been exceeded their prayer will
be profitless and go unanswered. As a result they put more trust in
these methods than they do in the living prayer, not without great
disrespect and offense toward God. For example, they demand that the
Mass be said with a certain number of candles, no more nor less; or
that it be celebrated at a particular hour, no sooner nor later; or that it
be said after a certain day, not before; or that the prayers and stations
be a particular number and kind and that they be recited at certain times
and with certain ceremonies, and neither before nor after, nor in any
other way; and that the person performing the ceremonies have certain
endowments and characteristics. And they are of the opinion that nothing
will be accomplished if one of these points is lacking.

3. What is worse—and intolerable—is that some desire to experience
an effect in themselves: either the granting of their petition or the knowledge that it will be granted at the end of those superstitious ceremonies.
Such a desire would amount to nothing more than tempting God and
would thereby seriously provoke His wrath. Sometimes God gives the
devil permission to deceive them through an experience and knowledge
of things far from profitable to their souls. They deserve this because of
the possessiveness they bring into their prayer, by not willing what God

wills but what they themselves will. Hence, because they do not put all their trust in God, nothing turns out well for them.

<h2 style="text-align:center">CHAPTER 44</h2>

The manner of directing the joy and strength of the will to God in these devotions.

1. These individuals should know, then, that the more trust they put in these ceremonies the less confidence they have in God, and that they will not obtain from Him the object of their desire.

Some pray more for their own intention than for the honor of God. Although they pray with the supposition that if God is to be served their petition will be granted, and if otherwise, it will not, they nevertheless overmultiply their prayers for that intention because of their attachment to the object of their request and their vain joy in it. It would be better to convert these prayers into practices of greater importance, such as the purification of their consciences, and serious concentration upon matters pertinent to their salvation; and thus they ought to have far less regard for all these other petitions irrelevant to this. Through the attainment of more important goals, they will also obtain all that in this other intention is good for them, even though they do not ask for it. And they receive this answer to their prayer sooner and in a better way than if they had directed all their strength toward making the request.

2. The Lord has promised in the Gospel: *Seek first and chiefly the kingdom of God and His justice, and all these other things will be added unto you.* [Mt. 6:33] This is the aim and petition that is most pleasing to God. To obtain an answer to the requests we bear in our hearts, there is no better means than to concentrate the strength of our prayer upon what is more pleasing to God. For then He will give us not only the salvation we beg for, but whatever else He sees is fit and good for us, even though we do not ask for it. David shows this clearly in a psalm: *The Lord is near to those who call upon Him in truth* [Ps. 114:18], to those who ask for things that are most true, such as things pertinent to salvation. Of these individuals he says afterwards: *He will fulfill the will of those who fear Him, and He will hear their prayers and save them. For God is the guardian of those who love Him.* [Ps. 144:19–20] God's being near is nothing more than His satisfying them and granting what it did not even enter their minds to ask for. We read that because Solomon had asked for something pleasing to God (that is, wisdom) so as to be certain of ruling the people justly, God answered him: *Because wisdom pleased you more than any other thing, and you did not seek victory through the death of your enemies, nor riches, nor a long life, I will give*

you not only the wisdom you seek to rule my people justly, but I will even give you what you have not asked for, that is, riches, and substance, and glory so that neither before nor afterwards will a king have equaled you. [2 Par. 1:11–12] And God in fact did this and pacified Solomon's enemies too so that all who were around him paid him tribute and did not perturb him. [3 Kgs. 4:21, 24] Similarly, we read in Genesis that God, according to Abraham's request, promised to multiply the offspring of his legitimate son like the stars of heaven: *I shall also multiply the offspring of the son of the bondwoman because he is your son.* [Gn. 15:2, 5; 21:13]

3. In one's petitions, then, the energies of the will and its joy should be directed to God in the manner described. One should be distrustful of ceremonies unapproved by the Catholic Church; and the manner of saying Mass should be left to the priest, who represents the Church at the altar, for he has received directions from her as to how Mass should be said. And persons should not desire new methods as if they knew more than the Holy Spirit and His Church. If in such simplicity God does not hear them, let them be convinced that God will not answer them even if they invent more ceremonies. For God is such that if a person lives in harmony with Him and does His will, He will give him whatever he wants; but if the person seeks his own interests, it will be useless for him to speak to God.

4. And regarding other ceremonies in vocal prayers and other devotions, one should not become attached to any ceremonies or modes of prayer other than those Christ taught us. When His disciples asked Him to teach them to pray, Christ obviously, as one Who knew so well His Father's will, would have told them all that was necessary in order to obtain an answer from the Eternal Father; and, in fact, He only taught them those seven petitions of the *Pater Noster,* which include all our spiritual and temporal necessities, and He did not teach numerous other kinds of prayers and ceremonies. [Lk. 11:1–4] At another time, rather, He told them that in praying they should not desire much speaking because our heavenly Father clearly knows our needs. [Mt. 6:7–8] He only charged us with great insistence to persevere in prayer—that is, in the *Pater Noster*—teaching in another place that one should pray and never cease. [Lk. 18:1] He did not teach us a quantity of petitions but that these seven be repeated often, and with fervor and care. For in these, as I say, are embodied everything that is God's will and all that is fitting for us. Accordingly, when His Majesty had recourse three times to the Eternal Father, all three times He prayed with the same petition of the *Pater Noster,* as the Evangelists recount: *Father, if it cannot be but that I drink this chalice, may Your will be done.* [Mt. 26:39, 42; Mk. 14:36; Lk. 22:42]

And He taught us only two ceremonies for use in our prayers. Our prayer should be made either in the concealment of our secret chamber (where without noise and without telling anyone we can pray with a more perfect and pure heart), as He said: *When you pray enter into your secret chamber, and having closed the door, pray* [Mt. 6:6]; or if not in one's chamber, in the solitary wilderness, and at the best and most quiet time of night, as He did. [Lk. 6:12] No reason exists, hence, for designating fixed times or set days, or for choosing some days more than others for our devotions; neither is there reason for using other kinds of prayer, or phrases having a play on words, but only those prayers that the Church uses, and as she uses them, for all are reducible to the *Pater Noster.*

5. By this I do not condemn—but rather approve—the custom of setting aside certain days for devotions, such as novenas, fastings, and other similar practices. I condemn the fixed methods and ceremonies with which the devotions are carried out, just as Judith reproved the Bethulians for having established a certain time to await God's mercy: *You have fixed a time for God's mercies. This does not serve for moving God to clemency, but for stirring up His wrath.* [Jdt. 8:13, 12]

CHAPTER 45

The second kind of distinct goods in which the will can vainly rejoice.

1. The second kind of distinct delightful goods in which the will can vainly rejoice comprises those which arouse or persuade one to serve God. We call these provocative goods. Preachers belong to this class, and we can speak of them in two ways: through whatever applies to the preacher himself, and through whatever pertains to his hearers. It is needful to counsel both preacher and hearer as to how joy of will should be directed to God in this practice.

2. As for the preacher, he should, in order to benefit the people and avoid the impediment of vain joy and presumption, keep in mind that preaching is more a spiritual practice than a vocal one. For although it is practiced through exterior words, it has no force or efficacy save from the interior spirit. No matter how lofty the doctrine preached, or polished the rhetoric, or sublime the style in which the preaching is clothed, the profit does not ordinarily increase because of these means in themselves; it comes from the spirit of the preacher. God's word is indeed efficacious of itself according to David, who says that God will give to His voice the voice of power [Ps. 67:34]; yet fire also has power to burn, but will not burn if the material is unprepared.

3. A twofold preparation is required if the doctrine is to communicate its force: that of the preacher, and that of his hearer. As for the one who teaches, the profit is usually commensurate with his interior preparedness. It is commonly said that as the master, so usually is the disciple.

When, in the Acts of the Apostles, those seven sons of the chief priest of the Jews were casting out devils with the same formula St. Paul used, the devil was enraged against them, crying: *"Jesus I know, and Paul I know; but you, who are you?"* And he attacked and stripped and wounded them. [Acts 19:14–16] This unfortunate outcome was due to their lack of proper attitudes, and not because Christ was unwilling that they perform these works in His name. Once the Apostles forbade a man, who was not a disciple, to continue casting out devils in the name of Christ, and the Lord in turn reproved them: *Do not forbid him, for no one, if in My name he does mighty works, will be able forthwith to speak badly of Me.* [Mk. 9:38] But He is opposed to those who preach the law of God, yet do not keep it, and who preach to others the good spirit, yet do not possess it themselves. He admonishes consequently through St. Paul: *You teach others, but you do not teach yourselves. You who preach that others must not steal, steal.* [Rom. 2:21] And the Holy Ghost says through David: *God said to the sinner: Why do you preach my statutes and take My law in your mouth, though you have abhorred discipline and cast My words behind you?* [Ps. 49: 16–17] From this we deduce that He will not give them the spirit from which they may bear fruit.

4. We frequently see, insofar as it is possible to judge here below, that the better the life of the preacher the more abundant the fruit, no matter how lowly his style, poor his rhetoric, and plain the doctrine. For the living spirit enkindles fire. But when this spirit is wanting, the gain is small, however sublime the style and doctrine. Although it is true that good style, gestures, sublime doctrine, and well-chosen words are more moving and productive of effect when accompanied by this good spirit, yet, without it, even though delightful and pleasing to the senses and the intellect, the sermon imparts little or no devotion to the will. For the will in this case will ordinarily be left as weak and remiss as before, even though wonderful things were admirably spoken; and the sermon merely delights the sense of hearing, like a musical concert or sounding bells. But the spirit, as I said, will not leave its natural ties any more than previously, since the voice does not possess the power to raise a dead man from his sepulcher.

5. It is of little significance that one kind of music is more pleasing to me than another if it fails to move me to the practice of works more than the other. Although the preacher may speak remarkable truths,

these will soon be forgotten since they do not enkindle the will. Besides the fact of their unproductivity, the sensory adherence to the gratification the truths afford hinders their effect upon the spirit, and the individual is left only with esteem for the mode and accidents of the sermon. He praises the preacher and listens to him for these reasons more than for the motivation he receives to amend his life.

St. Paul gives an exceptionally clear explanation of this doctrine to the Corinthians: *I, brothers, when I came to you, did not come preaching with sublimity of doctrine and wisdom, and my words and my preaching were not in the rhetoric of human wisdom, but in the manifestation of the spirit and of truth.* [1 Cor. 2:1, 4]

6. Indeed, neither is it the Apostle's intention nor mine to condemn good style, and rhetoric, and effective delivery; these rather are most important to the preacher, as they are in all matters. Elegant style and delivery lifts up and restores even those things that have fallen into ruin, just as poor presentation spoils what is good and destroys[5]

[5] Here *The Ascent of Mount Carmel* ends abruptly.

The Dark Night

THE DARK NIGHT

An explanation of the stanzas describing a soul's conduct along the spiritual road which leads to the perfect union with God through love, insofar as it is attainable in this life. A description also of the characteristics of one who has reached this perfection.

Prologue for the Reader

In this book we will first cite the entire poem, then each stanza will be repeated separately and explained, and finally we will do the same thing with the individual verses.

The first two stanzas proclaim the effects of the two kinds of spiritual purgation: one, a purification of the sensory part; the other, a purification of the spiritual part. The remaining six stanzas proclaim some of the marvelous results which are obtained from the spiritual illumination and from the union with God through love.

Stanzas of the Soul

1. One dark night,
   Fired with love's urgent longings
   —Ah, the sheer grace!—
   I went out unseen,
   My house being now all stilled;

2. In darkness, and secure,
   By the secret ladder, disguised,
   —Ah, the sheer grace!—
   In darkness and concealment,
   My house being now all stilled;

3. On that glad night,
   In secret, for no one saw me,
   Nor did I look at anything,
   With no other light or guide
   Than the one that burned in my heart;

4. This guided me
   More surely than the light of noon
   To where He waited for me
   —Him I knew so well—
   In a place where no one else appeared.

5. O guiding night!
   O night more lovely than the dawn!
   O night that has united
   The Lover with His beloved,
   Transforming the beloved in her Lover.

6. Upon my flowering breast
   Which I kept wholly for Him alone,
   There He lay sleeping,
   And I caressing Him
   There in a breeze from the fanning cedars.

7. When the breeze blew from the turret
   Parting His hair,
   He wounded my neck
   With His gentle hand,
   Suspending all my senses.

8. I abandoned and forgot myself,
   Laying my face on my Beloved;
   All things ceased; I went out from myself,
   Leaving my cares
   Forgotten among the lilies.

(Beginning of the explanation of the stanzas which deal with the way a soul must conduct itself along the road leading to union with God through love.)

Before embarking upon an explanation of these stanzas, we should remember that the soul recites them when it has already reached the state of perfection—that is, union with God through love—and has now passed through severe trials and conflicts by means of the spiritual exercise which leads one along the narrow way to eternal life, of which our Saviour speaks in the Gospel. [Mt. 7:13] The soul must ordinarily walk this path to reach that sublime and joyous union with God. Recognizing the narrowness of the path and the fact that so very few tread it—as the Saviour Himself says [Mt. 7:14]—the soul's song in this first stanza is one of happiness in having marched along it to this perfection of love. Appropriately, this narrow road is called a dark night, as we shall explain in later verses of this stanza.

The soul, therefore, happy at having trod this narrow road from which it derived so much good, speaks in this manner:

BOOK ONE

(A treatise on the passive night of the senses)

> One dark night,
> Fired with love's urgent longings
> —Ah, the sheer gracel—
> I went out unseen,
> My house being now all stilled;

EXPLANATION

1. In this first stanza, the soul is speaking of the way it followed in its departure from love of self and of all things through a method of true mortification, which causes it to die to itself and to all these things and to begin the sweet and delightful life of love with God. And it declares that this departure was a "dark night." As we shall explain later, this dark night signifies here purgative contemplation, which passively causes in the soul this negation of self and of all things.

2. The soul states that it was able to make this escape because of the vigor and warmth gained from loving its Spouse in this obscure contemplation. It emphasizes the intense happiness it possessed in journeying to God through this dark night; so great was the soul's success that none of the three enemies (the world, the flesh, and the devil, which are always in opposition to the journey along this road) could impede it, for that night of purifying contemplation lulled to sleep and deadened all the inordinate movements of the passions and appetites in the house of sense.

The verse then states:

> One dark night,

CHAPTER 1

Quotes the first verse and begins to discuss the imperfections of beginners.

1. Souls begin to enter this dark night when God, gradually drawing them out of the state of beginners (those who practice meditation on

the spiritual road), begins to place them in the state of proficients (those who are already contemplatives) so that by passing through this state they might reach that of the perfect, which is the divine union of the soul with God.

We should first mention here some characteristics of beginners for the sake of a better explanation and understanding of the nature of this night and of God's motive for placing the soul in it. Although our treatment of these things will be as brief as possible, beginners will be helped by it to understand the feebleness of their state and take courage and desire that God place them in this night where the soul is strengthened in virtue and fortified for the inestimable delights of the love of God. And, although we shall be delayed for a moment, it will be no longer than our discussion of this dark night requires.

2. It should be known, then, that God nurtures and caresses the soul, after it has been resolutely converted to His service, like a loving mother who warms her child with the heat of her bosom, nurses it with good milk and tender food, and carries and caresses it in her arms. But as the child grows older, the mother withholds her caresses and hides her tender love; she rubs bitter aloes on her sweet breast and sets the child down from her arms, letting it walk on its own feet so that it may put aside the habits of childhood and grow accustomed to greater and more important things. The grace of God acts just as a loving mother by re-engendering in the soul new enthusiasm and fervor in the service of God. With no effort on the soul's part, this grace causes it to taste sweet and delectable milk and to experience intense satisfaction in the performance of spiritual exercises, because God is handing the breast of His tender love to the soul, just as if it were a delicate child.

3. The soul finds its joy, therefore, in spending lengthy periods at prayer, perhaps even entire nights; its penances are pleasures; its fasts, happiness; and the sacraments and spiritual conversations are its consolations. Although spiritual persons do practice these exercises with great profit and persistence and are very careful about them, spiritually speaking, they conduct themselves in a very weak and imperfect manner. Since their motivation in their spiritual works and exercises is the consolation and satisfaction they experience in them, and since they have not been conditioned by the arduous struggle of practicing virtue, they possess many faults and imperfections in the discharge of their spiritual activities. For, assuredly, everyone's actions are in direct conformity to the habit of perfection he has acquired, and since these persons have not had time to acquire those firm habits, their work must of necessity be feeble, like that of weak children.

For a clearer understanding of this and of how truly imperfect beginners are, insofar as they practice virtue readily because of the satisfaction attached to it, we shall describe, using the seven capital vices as our basis, some of the numerous imperfections beginners commit. Thus we shall see how very similar are their deeds to those of children. Then the benefits of the dark night will become evident, since it cleanses and purifies the soul of all these imperfections.

CHAPTER 2

Some of the imperfections of pride possessed by beginners.

1. These beginners feel so fervent and diligent in their spiritual exercises and undertakings that a certain kind of secret pride is generated in them which begets a complacency with themselves and their accomplishments, despite the fact that holy works do of their very nature cause humility. Then they develop a desire somewhat vain—at times very vain—to speak of spiritual things in others' presence, and sometimes even to instruct rather than be instructed; in their hearts they condemn others who do not seem to have the kind of devotion they would like them to have, and sometimes they give expression to this criticism like the pharisee who despised the publican while he boasted and praised God for the good deeds he himself accomplished. [Lk. 18: 11–12]

2. The devil, desiring the growth of pride and presumption in these beginners, often increases their fervor and readiness to perform such works, and other ones, too. For he is quite aware of the fact that all these works and virtues are not only worthless for them, but even become vices. Some of these persons become so evil-minded that they do not want anyone except themselves to appear holy; and so by both word and deed, they condemn and detract others whenever the occasion arises, seeing the little mote in their brother's eye, and failing to consider the beam in their own eye [Mt. 7:3]; they strain at the other's gnat and swallow their own camel. [Mt. 23:24]

3. And when at times their spiritual directors, their confessors or superiors, disapprove their spirit and method of procedure, they feel that these directors do not understand, or perhaps that this failure to approve derives from a lack of holiness, since they want these directors to regard their conduct with esteem and praise. So they quickly search for some other spiritual adviser more to their liking, someone who will congratulate them and be impressed by their deeds, and they flee, as they would death, those who attempt to place them on the safe road by forbidding these things—and sometimes they even become hostile toward such spiritual directors. Frequently, in their presumption, they make many res-

olutions but accomplish very little. Sometimes they want others to recognize their spirit and devotion, and as a result occasionally contrive to make some manifestations of it, such as movements, sighs, and other little ceremonies; sometimes, with the assistance of the devil, they experience raptures, more often in public than in private, and they are quite pleased, and often eager, for others to take notice of these.

4. Many want to be the favorites of their confessors, and thus they are consumed by a thousand envies and disquietudes. Embarrassment forbids them from relating their sins clearly, lest their reputation diminish in their confessor's eyes. They confess their sins in the most favorable light so as to appear better than they actually are, and thus they approach the confessional to excuse themselves rather than accuse themselves. Sometimes they confess the evil things they do to a different confessor so that their own confessor might think they commit no sins at all. Therefore, in their desire to appear holy, they enjoy relating their good behavior to their confessor, and in such careful terms that these good deeds appear greater than they actually are. It would be more humble of them, as we shall point out later on, to make light of the good they do and to wish that no one, neither their confessor nor anybody else, should consider it of any importance at all.

5. Sometimes they minimize their faults, and at other times they become discouraged by them, since they felt they were already saints, and they become impatient and angry with themselves, which is yet another fault.

They are often extremely anxious that God remove their faults and imperfections, but their motive is personal peace rather than God. They fail to realize that were God to remove their faults they might very well become more proud and presumptuous.

They dislike praising anyone else, but they love to receive praise, and sometimes they even seek it. In this they resemble the foolish virgins who had to seek oil from others when their own lamps were extinguished. [Mt. 25:8]

6. The number of these imperfections in some people is serious and causes them a good deal of harm. Some have fewer, some have more, and yet others have little more than the first movements toward them. But there are scarcely any beginners who do not fall victim to some of these imperfections at the time of their initial fervor.

Souls, however, who are advancing in perfection act in an entirely different manner and with a different quality of spirit during this period. They receive great benefit from their humility by which they not only place little importance on their deeds, but also take very little self-satisfaction from them. They think everyone else is far better than themselves, and usually possess a holy envy of them and would like to emulate their service of God. Since they are truly humble, their growing fervor and the increased number of their good deeds and the gratification they receive from them only cause them to become more aware of their debt to God and the inadequacy of their service to Him, and thus the more they do, the less satisfaction they derive from it. Their charity and love makes them want to do so much for God that what they actually do accomplish seems as nothing. This loving solicitude goads them, preoccupies them, and absorbs them to such an extent that they never notice what others do or do not accomplish, but if they should, they then think, as I say, that everyone is better than they. They think they themselves are insignificant, and want others to think this too and to belittle and slight their deeds. Moreover, even though others do praise and value their works, they are unable to believe them; such praises seem strange to them.

7. These souls humbly and tranquilly long to be taught by anyone who might be a help to them. This desire is the exact opposite of that other desire we mentioned above, of those who want to be themselves the teachers in everything. When these others notice that someone is trying to give them some instruction, they themselves take the words from their very mouths as though they already know everything.

Yet these humble souls, far from desiring to be anyone's teacher, are ready to take a road different from the one they are following, if told to do so. For they do not believe they could ever be right themselves. They rejoice when others receive praise, and their only sorrow is that they do not serve God as these others do.

Because they consider their deeds insignificant, they do not want to make them known. They are even ashamed to speak of them to their spiritual directors because they think these deeds are not worth mentioning.

They are more eager to speak of their faults and sins, and reveal these to others, than their virtues. They have an inclination to seek direction from one who will have less esteem for their spirit and deeds. Such is the characteristic of a pure and simple and true spirit, one that is very pleasing to God. Since the wise Spirit of God dwells within these humble souls, He moves them to keep these treasures hidden, and to manifest only their faults. God gives this grace to the humble, together with the other virtues, just as He denies it to the proud.

8. These souls would give their life's blood to anyone who serves God, and they will do whatever they can to help others serve Him. When they see themselves fall into imperfections, they suffer this with humility, with docility of spirit, and with loving fear of God and hope in Him.

Yet I believe very few souls are so perfect in the beginning. We would be happy enough if they managed not to fall into these imperfections of pride. As we shall point out later, then, God places these souls in the dark night so as to purify them of these imperfections and make them advance.

CHAPTER 3

Some imperfections of spiritual avarice commonly found in beginners.

1. Sometimes many beginners also possess great spiritual avarice. They will hardly ever seem content with the spirit God gives them. They become unhappy and peevish owing to a lack of the consolation they desire to have in spiritual things.

Many never have enough of hearing counsels, or of learning spiritual maxims, or of keeping them and reading books about them. They spend more time doing this than striving after mortification and the perfection of the interior poverty to which they are obliged. Furthermore, they weigh themselves down with overly decorated images and rosaries; they will now put these down, now take up others; at one moment they are exchanging, and at the next re-exchanging; now they want this kind, now they want another; and they will prefer one cross to another because of its elaborateness. Others you will see decked out in *agnusdeis* and relics and lists of saints' names, like children in trinkets.

What I condemn in this is possessiveness of heart and attachment to the number, workmanship, and overdecoration of these objects. For this attachment is contrary to poverty of spirit which is intent only upon the substance of the devotion, benefits by no more than what procures this sufficiently, and tires of all this other multiplicity and elaborate ornamentation. Since true devotion comes from the heart and looks only to the truth and substance represented by spiritual objects, and since everything else is imperfect attachment and possessiveness, any appetite for these things must be uprooted if some degree of perfection is to be reached.

2. I knew a person who for more than ten years profited by a cross roughly made out of a blessed palm and held together by a pin twisted around it. He carried it about and never would part with it until I took it from him—and he was not a person of poor judgment or little intelligence. I saw someone else who prayed with beads made out of bones from the spine of a fish. Certainly, his devotion was not for this reason less precious in the sight of God. In neither of these two instances, obviously, did these persons base their devotion on the workmanship and value of any spiritual object.

They, therefore, who are well guided from the outset do not become attached to visible instruments, nor burden themselves with them. They do not care to know any more than what is necessary to accomplish good works, because their eyes are fixed only upon God, upon being His friend and pleasing Him; this is what they long for. They very generously give all they have. Their pleasure is to know how to live for love of God or neighbor without these spiritual or temporal things. As I said, their eyes are fastened on the substance of interior perfection, on pleasing God and not themselves.

3. Yet until a soul is placed by God in the passive purgation of that dark night, which we shall soon explain, it cannot purify itself completely from these imperfections nor from the others. But a person should insofar as possible strive to do his part in purifying and perfecting himself and thereby merit God's divine cure; in this cure God will heal him of what through his own efforts he was unable to remedy. No matter how much an individual does through his own efforts, he cannot actively purify himself enough to be disposed in the least degree for the divine union of the perfection of love. God must take over and purge him in that fire that is dark for him, as we shall explain.

CHAPTER 4

The imperfections of lust, the third capital vice, usually found in beginners.

1. A number of these beginners have many more imperfections in each vice than those I am mentioning. But to avoid prolixity, I am omitting them and touching on some of the principal ones which are as it were the origin of the others.

As for the vice of lust—aside from what it means for spiritual persons to fall into this vice, since my intent is to treat of the imperfections that have to be purged by means of the dark night—spiritual persons have numerous imperfections, many of which can be called spiritual lust, not because the lust is spiritual, but because it proceeds from spiritual things. It happens frequently that in one's very spiritual exercises, without one's being able to avoid it, impure movements will be experienced in the sensory part of the soul, and even sometimes when the spirit is deep in prayer or when receiving the sacrament of penance or of the Eucharist. These impure feelings arise from any of three causes outside one's power.

2. First, they often proceed from the pleasure human nature finds in spiritual exercises. Since both the spiritual and sensory part of the soul receive gratification from that refreshment, each part experiences de-

light according to its own nature and properties. The spirit, the superior part of the soul, experiences renewal and satisfaction in God; and the sense, the lower part, feels sensory gratification and delight because it is ignorant of how to get anything else and hence takes whatever is nearest, which is the impure sensory satisfaction. It will happen that while a soul is with God in deep spiritual prayer, it will on the other hand passively experience sensual rebellions, movements, and acts in the senses, not without its own great displeasure. This frequently happens at the time of communion. Since the soul receives joy and gladness in this act of love—for the Lord grants the grace and gives Himself for this reason—the sensory part also takes its share, as we said, according to its mode. Since, after all, these two parts form one *suppositum*, each one usually shares according to its mode in what the other receives. As the Philosopher says: Whatever is received is received according to the mode of the receiver. Because in the initial stages of the spiritual life, and even in more advanced ones, the sensory part of the soul is imperfect, it frequently receives God's spirit with this very imperfection. Once the sensory part is reformed through the purgation of the dark night, it no longer has these infirmities. For then the spiritual part of the soul rather than the sensory part receives God's spirit, and the soul thus receives everything according to the mode of the spirit.

3. The second origin of these rebellions is the devil. To bring disquietude and disturbance upon a soul when it is praying, or trying to pray, he endeavors to excite impure feelings in the sensory part. And if a person pays any attention to them, the devil does him great harm. Some souls, through fear, grow slack in their prayer—which is what the devil wants—in order to struggle against these movements, and others give it up entirely, for they think these feelings come while they are engaged in prayer rather than at any other time. And this is true, because the devil excites these feelings while souls are at prayer, instead of when they are engaged in other works, so that they might abandon prayer. And that is not all, for to make them cowardly and afraid he brings vividly to their minds foul and impure thoughts. And sometimes the thoughts will concern spiritual things and persons who have been a help to them. Those who attribute any importance to such thoughts, therefore, do not even dare look at anything or think about anything, lest they thereupon stumble into them.

These impure thoughts so affect people who are afflicted with melancholia that one should have great pity for them; indeed, they suffer a sad life. In some who are troubled with this bad humor the trial reaches such a point that the devil, they think, definitely has access to them without their having the freedom to prevent it; yet some of these melancholiacs are able through intense effort and struggle to forestall this power of the devil.

If these impure thoughts and feelings arise from melancholia, a person is not ordinarily freed from them until he is cured of that humor, unless the dark night flows in upon the soul and deprives it successively of all things.

4. The third origin from which these impure feelings usually proceed and wage war on the soul is fear of them. The fear that springs up in people at the sudden remembrance of these thoughts, caused by what they see, are dealing with, or thinking of, produces impure feelings without their being at fault.

5. Some people are so delicate that when gratification is received from the spirit or from prayer, they immediately experience a lust which so inebriates them and caresses their senses that they become as it were engulfed in the delight and satisfaction of that vice; and this experience will endure passively with the other. Sometimes these individuals become aware that certain impure and rebellious acts have taken place.

The reason for such occurrences is that since these natures are, as I say, delicate and tender, their humors and blood are stirred up by any change. For these persons will also experience these feelings when they are inflamed with anger or agitated by some other disturbance or affliction.

6. Sometimes too, in their spiritual conversations or works, they manifest a certain sprightliness and gallantry upon considering who is present, and they carry on with a kind of vain satisfaction. Such behavior is also a by-product of spiritual lust (in the way we here understand it), which generally accompanies complacency of the will.

7. Some will spiritually acquire a liking for other individuals which often arises from lust rather than from the spirit. This lustful origin will be recognized if, upon recalling that affection, there is not an increase in the remembrance and love of God, but remorse of conscience.

The affection is purely spiritual if the love of God grows when it grows, or if the love of God is remembered as often as the affection is remembered, or if the affection gives the soul a desire for God—if by growing in one the soul grows also in the other. For this is a trait of God's spirit: the good increases with the good, since there is likeness and conformity between them.

But when the love is born of this sensual vice it has the contrary effects. As the one love grows greater, the other lessens, and the remembrance of it lessens too. If the inordinate love increases, then, as will be seen, the soul will grow cold in the love of God, and, owing to the recollection of that other love, forget Him—not without the feeling of some remorse of conscience. On the other hand, as the love of God increases, the soul will grow cold in the inordinate affection, and come to forget it. For not only do these loves fail to benefit one another, but, since they are contrary loves, the predominating one, while becoming stronger itself, will stifle and extinguish the other, as the philosophers say. Hence our Saviour proclaimed in the Gospel: *That which is born of the flesh is flesh, and that which is born of the spirit is spirit* [Jn. 3:16], that is: Love derived from sense terminates in sense, and the love which is of the spirit terminates in the spirit of God, and brings it increase. And this, then, is the difference between these two loves which enables us to discern the one from the other.

8. The dark night, when it enters the soul, puts all these loves in reasonable order. It strengthens and purifies the love of God, and takes away and destroys the other. But in the beginning it will cause the soul to lose sight of both of them, as will be explained.

CHAPTER 5

The imperfections of the capital vice of anger into which beginners fall.

1. Because of the strong desire of many beginners for spiritual gratification, they usually have many imperfections of anger. For when the delight and satisfaction procured in their spiritual exercises passes, these beginners are naturally left without any spiritual savor. And because of this distastefulness, they become peevish in the works they do and easily angered by the least thing, and occasionally they are so unbearable that nobody can put up with them. This frequently occurs after they have experienced in prayer some recollection pleasant to the senses. After the delight and satisfaction is gone, the sensory part of the soul is naturally left vapid and zestless, just as a child when withdrawn from the sweet breast. These souls are not at fault if they do not allow this dejection to influence them, for it is an imperfection which must be purged through the dryness and distress of the dark night.

2. Among these spiritual persons there are also those who fall into another kind of spiritual anger. Through a certain indiscreet zeal they become angry over the sins of others, they reprove these others, and sometimes even feel the impulse to do so angrily, which in fact they occasionally do, setting themselves up as lords of virtue. All such conduct is contrary to spiritual meekness.

3. Others, in becoming aware of their own imperfections, grow angry with themselves in an unhumble impatience. So impatient are they about these imperfections that they would want to become saints in a day.

Many of these beginners will make numerous plans and great resolutions, but since they are not humble and have no distrust of themselves, the more resolves they make the more they break, and the greater becomes their anger. They do not have the patience to wait until God gives them what they need when He so desires. Their attitude is contrary to spiritual meekness and can only be remedied by the purgation of the dark night. Some, however, are so patient about their desire for advancement that God would prefer to see them a little less so.

CHAPTER 6

The imperfections of spiritual gluttony.

1. A great deal can be said on spiritual gluttony, the fourth vice. There is hardly anyone among these beginners, no matter how excellent his conduct, who will not fall into some of the many imperfections of this vice. These imperfections arise because of the delight beginners find in their spiritual exercises.

Many, lured by the delight and satisfaction procured in their religious practices, strive more for spiritual savor than for spiritual purity and discretion; yet it is this purity and discretion which God looks for and finds acceptable throughout a soul's entire spiritual journey. Besides the imperfection of seeking after these delights, the sweetness these persons experience makes them go to extremes and pass beyond the mean in which virtue resides and is acquired.

Some, attracted by the delight they feel in their spiritual exercises, will kill themselves with penances, and others will weaken themselves by fasts and, without the counsel or command of another, overtax their weakness; indeed they try to hide these penances from the one to whom they owe obedience in such matters. Some will even dare perform these penances contrary to obedience.

2. Such individuals are unreasonable and most imperfect. They subordinate submissiveness and obedience (which is a penance of reason and discretion, and consequently a sacrifice more pleasing and acceptable to God) to corporal penance. But corporal penance without obedience is no more than a penance of beasts. And like beasts, they are motivated in these penances by an appetite for the pleasure they find in it. Since all extremes are vicious and since by such behavior these persons are doing their own will, they grow in vice rather than in virtue. For, through this conduct they at least become spiritually gluttonous and proud, since they do not tread the path of obedience.

The devil, increasing the delights and appetites of these beginners and thereby stirring up this gluttony in them, so impels many of them that when they are unable to avoid obedience they either add to, change, or modify what was commanded them. Any obedience in this matter is distasteful to them. Some will reach such a point that the mere obligation of obedience to perform their spiritual exercises makes them lose all desire and devotion. Their only yearning and satisfaction is to do what they feel inclined to do, whereas it would be better in all likelihood for them not to do this at all.

3. Some are very insistent that their spiritual director allow them to do what they themselves want to do, and finally almost force the permission from him. And if they do not get what they want, they become sad and go about like testy children. They are under the impression that they do not serve God when they are not allowed to do what they want. Since they take gratification and their own will as their support and their god, they become sad, weak, and discouraged when their director takes these from them and desires that they do God's will. They think that gratifying and satisfying themselves is serving and satisfying God.

4. Others, too, because of this sweetness have so little knowledge of their own lowliness and misery and such lack of the loving fear and respect they owe to God's grandeur that they do not hesitate to insist boldly that their confessors allow them the frequent reception of Communion. And worse than this, they often dare communicate without the permission and advice of the minister and dispenser of Christ. They are guided here solely by their own opinion, and they endeavor to hide the truth from him. As a result, with their hearts set on frequent Communion, they make their confessions carelessly, more eager just to receive Communion than to receive it with a pure and perfect heart. It would be sounder and holier of them to have the contrary inclination and to ask their confessor not to let them receive Communion so frequently. Although humble resignation is better than either of these two attitudes. But the boldnesses referred to first will bring great evil and chastisement upon the others.

5. In communicating they spend all their time trying to get some feeling and satisfaction rather than humbly praising and reverencing God dwelling within them. And they go about this in such a way that, if they do not procure any sensible feeling and satisfaction, they think they have accomplished nothing. As a result they judge very poorly of God and fail to understand that the sensory benefits are the least among those that this Most Blessed Sacrament bestows, for the invisible grace it gives is a greater blessing. God often withdraws sensory delight and pleasure so that souls might set the eyes of faith upon this invisible grace. Not only in receiving communion, but in other spiritual exercises as well, beginners

desire to feel God and taste of Him as if He were comprehensible and accessible. This desire is a serious imperfection and, because it involves impurity of faith, opposed to God's way.

6. They have the same defect in their prayer, for they think the whole matter of prayer consists in looking for sensory satisfaction and devotion. They strive to procure this by their own efforts and tire and weary their heads and their faculties. When they do not get this sensible comfort, they become very disconsolate and think they have done nothing. Because of their aim they lose true devotion and spirit, which lies in distrust of self and in humble and patient perseverance so as to please God. Once they do not find delight in this, or any other spiritual exercise, they feel extreme reluctance and repugnance in returning to it, and sometimes even give it up. For after all, as we mentioned, they are like children who are prompted to act not by reason but by pleasure.

All their time is spent looking for satisfaction and spiritual consolation; they can never read enough spiritual books, and one minute they are meditating upon one subject and the next upon another, always in search for some gratification in the things of God. God very rightly and discreetly and lovingly denies this satisfaction to these beginners, for if He did not, they would fall into innumerable evils because of their spiritual gluttony and craving for sweetness. Wherefore it is important for these beginners to enter the dark night and be purged of this childishness.

7. Those who are inclined toward these delights have also another serious imperfection, that is, they are weak and remiss in treading the rough way of the cross. A soul given up to pleasure naturally feels aversion toward the bitterness of self-denial.

8. These people incur many other imperfections because of this spiritual gluttony, of which the Lord in time will cure them through temptations, aridities, and other trials, which are all a part of the dark night. So as not to be too lengthy, I do not want to discuss these imperfections any more, but only point out that spiritual sobriety and temperance beget another very different quality, one of mortification, fear, and submissiveness in all things; an individual thereby becomes aware that the perfection and value of his works does not depend upon their number, nor the satisfaction found in them, but upon knowing how to practice self-denial in them. These beginners ought to do their part in striving after this self-denial, until God in fact brings them into the dark night and purifies them. In order to get to our discussion of this dark night, I am passing over these imperfections hurriedly.

CHAPTER 7

The imperfections of spiritual envy and sloth.

1. As for the other two vices, spiritual envy and sloth, these beginners also have many imperfections.

In regard to envy, many of them will feel sad about the spiritual good of others and experience sensible grief in noting that their neighbor is ahead of them on the road to perfection, and they will not want to hear others praised. To learn of the virtues of others makes them sad; they cannot bear to hear others praised without contradicting and undoing these compliments as much as possible. Their annoyance grows because they themselves do not receive these plaudits and because they long for preference in everything.

All of this is contrary to charity, which, as St. Paul says, rejoices in goodness. [1 Cor. 13:6] If any envy accompanies charity, it is a holy envy, saddened at not having the virtues of others, rejoicing that others have them, happy that all others are ahead of it in the service of God, since it is so wanting in His service.

2. Also regarding spiritual sloth, these beginners usually become weary in the more spiritual exercises and flee from them, since these exercises are contrary to sensory satisfaction. Since they are so used to finding delight in spiritual practices, they become bored when they do not find it. If they do not receive in prayer the satisfaction they crave—for after all it is fit that God withdraw this so as to try them—they do not want to return to it or at times they either give up prayer or go to it begrudgingly. Because of their sloth, they subordinate the way of perfection (which requires the denial of one's will and satisfaction for God's sake) to the pleasure and delight of their own will. As a result they strive to satisfy their own will rather than God's.

3. Many of these beginners want God to desire what they want, and become sad if they have to desire God's will. They feel an aversion toward adapting their will to God's. Hence they frequently believe that what is not their will, or that which brings them no satisfaction, is not God's will, and, on the other hand, that if they are satisfied, God is too. They measure God by themselves and not themselves by God, which is in opposition to His teaching in the Gospel: that he who loses his life for His sake will gain it, and that he who desires to gain it will lose it. [Mt. 16:25]

4. Beginners also become bored when told to do something unpleasant. Because they look for spiritual gratifications and delights, they

are extremely lax in the fortitude and labor perfection demands. Like those who are reared in luxury, they run sadly from everything rough, and they are scandalized by the cross, in which spiritual delights are found. And in the more spiritual exercises their boredom is greater. Since they expect to go about in spiritual matters according to the whims and satisfactions of their own will, to enter by the narrow way of life, about which Christ speaks, is saddening and repugnant to them. [Mt. 7:14]

5. It is enough to have referred to the many imperfections of those who live in this beginner's state to see the need there is that God put them in the state of proficients. He does this by introducing them into the dark night, of which we shall now speak. There, through pure dryness and interior darkness, He weans them from the breasts of these gratifications and delights, takes away all these trivialities and childish ways, and makes them acquire the virtues by very different means. No matter how earnestly the beginner in all his actions and passions practices the mortification of self, he will never be able to do so entirely—far from it—until God accomplishes it in him passively by means of the purgation of this night.

May God be pleased to give me His divine light that I may say something worthwhile about this subject, for in a night so dark and a matter so difficult to treat and expound His enlightenment is very necessary.

The verse, then, is:

One dark night,

CHAPTER 8

The beginning of the exposition of this dark night. An explanation of verse 1 of the first stanza.

1. This night, which as we say is contemplation, causes two kinds of darkness or purgation in spiritual persons according to the two parts of the soul, the sensory and the spiritual.

Hence the one night or purgation will be sensory, by which the senses are purged and accommodated to the spirit; and the other night or purgation will be spiritual, by which the spirit is purged and denuded as well as accommodated and prepared for union with God through love.

The sensory night is common and happens to many; these are the beginners of whom we shall treat first. The spiritual night is the lot of very few, of those who have been tried and are proficient, and of whom we shall speak afterwards.

2. The first purgation or night is bitter and terrible to the senses. But

nothing can be compared to the second, for it is horrible and frightful to the spirit.

Because the sensory night is first in order, we shall speak briefly of it now—since it is a more common occurrence one finds more written on it—and then pass on to discuss more at length the spiritual night, for hardly anything has been said of it, in sermons or in writing, and even the experience of it is rare.

3. Since the conduct of these beginners in the way of God is lowly and not too distant from love of pleasure and of self, as was explained, God desires to withdraw them from this base manner of loving and lead them on to a higher degree of divine love. And He desires to liberate them from the lowly exercise of the senses and of discursive meditation, by which they go in search of Him so inadequately and with so many difficulties, and lead them into the exercise of spirit, in which they become capable of a communion with God that is more abundant and freer of imperfections. God does this after beginners have exercised themselves for a time in the way of virtue and have persevered in meditation and prayer. For it is through the delight and satisfaction they experience in prayer that they have become detached from worldly things and have gained some spiritual strength in God. This strength has helped them somewhat to restrain their appetites for creatures, and through it they will be able to suffer a little oppression and dryness without turning back. Consequently, it is at the time they are going about their spiritual exercises with delight and satisfaction, when in their opinion the sun of divine favor is shining most brightly on them, that God darkens all this light and closes the door and spring of the sweet spiritual water they were tasting as often and as long as they desired. For since they were weak and tender, no door was closed to them, as St. John says in the Apocalypse. [Ap. 3:8] God now leaves them in such darkness that they do not know which way to turn in their discursive imaginings; they cannot advance a step in meditation, as they used to, now that the interior sensory faculties are engulfed in this night. He leaves them in such dryness that they not only fail to receive satisfaction and pleasure from their spiritual exercises and works, as they formerly did, but also find these exercises distasteful and bitter. As I said, when God sees that they have grown a little, He weans them from the sweet breast so that they might be strengthened, lays aside their swaddling bands, and puts them down from His arms that they may grow accustomed to walking by themselves. This change is a surprise to them because everything seems to be functioning in reverse.

4. This usually happens to recollected beginners sooner than to others, since they are freer from occasions of backsliding and they more quickly reform their appetites for worldly things. A reform of the appetites is

the requirement for entering the happy night of the senses. Not much time ordinarily passes after the initial stages of their spiritual life before beginners start to enter this night of sense. And the majority of them do enter it, because it is common to see them suffer these aridities.

5. We could adduce numerous passages from Sacred Scripture, for since this sensory purgation is so customary, we find throughout, especially in the Psalms and Prophets, a great many references to it. But I do not want to waste time citing them, because the prevalence of the experience of this night should be enough for those who are unable to find the scriptural references to it.

CHAPTER 9

Signs for discerning whether a spiritual person is treading the path of this sensory night and purgation.

1. Because the origin of these aridities may not be the sensory night and purgation, but sin and imperfection, or weakness and lukewarmness, or some bad humor or bodily indisposition, I will give some signs here for discerning whether the dryness is the result of this purgation or of one of these other defects. I find there are three principal signs for knowing this.

2. The first is that as these souls do not get satisfaction or consolation from the things of God, they do not get any out of creatures either. Since God puts a soul in this dark night in order to dry up and purge its sensory appetite, He does not allow it to find sweetness or delight in anything.

Through this sign it can in all likelihood be inferred that this dryness and distaste is not the outcome of newly committed sins and imperfections. If this were so, some inclination or propensity to look for satisfaction in something other than the things of God would be felt in the sensory part. For when the appetite is allowed indulgence in some imperfection, the soul immediately feels an inclination toward it, little or great in proportion to the degree of its satisfaction and attachment.

Yet, because the want of satisfaction in earthly or heavenly things could be the product of some indisposition or melancholic humor, which frequently prevents one from being satisfied with anything, the second sign or condition is necessary.

3. The second sign for the discernment of this purgation is that the memory ordinarily turns to God solicitously and with painful care, and the soul thinks it is not serving God but turning back, because it is aware of this distaste for the things of God. Hence it is obvious that this aversion and dryness is not the fruit of laxity and tepidity, for a lukewarm

person does not care much for the things of God nor is he inwardly solicitous about them.

There is, consequently, a notable difference between dryness and lukewarmness. A lukewarm person is very lax and remiss in his will and spirit, and has no solicitude about serving God; a person suffering the purgative dryness is ordinarily solicitous, concerned, and pained about not serving God. Even though the dryness may be furthered by melancholia or some other humor—as it often is—it does not thereby fail to produce its purgative effect in the appetite, for the soul will be deprived of every satisfaction and concerned only about God. If this humor is the entire cause, everything ends in disgust and does harm to one's nature, and there are none of these desires to serve God which accompany the purgative dryness. Even though, in this purgative dryness, the sensory part of the soul is very cast down, slack, and feeble in its actions, because of the little satisfaction it finds, the spirit is ready and strong.

4. The reason for this dryness is that God transfers His goods and strength from sense to spirit. Since the sensory part of the soul is incapable of the goods of spirit, it remains deprived, dry, and empty, and thus, while the spirit is tasting, the flesh tastes nothing at all and becomes weak in its work. But the spirit through this nourishment grows stronger and more alert, and becomes more solicitous than before about not failing God. If in the beginning the soul does not experience this spiritual savor and delight, but dryness and distaste, it is because of the novelty involved in this exchange. Since its palate is accustomed to these other sensory tastes, the soul still sets its eyes on them. And since, also, its spiritual palate is neither purged nor accommodated for so subtle a taste, it is unable to experience the spiritual savor and good until gradually prepared by means of this dark and obscure night; the soul rather experiences dryness and distaste because of a lack of the gratification it formerly enjoyed so readily.

5. Those whom God begins to lead into these desert solitudes are like the children of Israel; when God began giving them the heavenly food which contained in itself all savors and, as is there mentioned, changed to whatever taste each one hungered after [Wis. 16:20, 21], they nonetheless felt a craving for the tastes of the fleshmeats and onions they had eaten in Egypt, for their palate was accustomed and attracted to them more than to the delicate sweetness of the angelic manna. And in the midst of that heavenly food, they wept and sighed for fleshmeat. [Nm. 11:4–6] The baseness of our appetite is such that it makes us long for our own miserable goods and feel aversion for the incommunicable heavenly good.

6. Yet, as I say, when these aridities are the outcome of the purgative way of the sensory appetite, the spirit feels the strength and energy to

work, which is obtained from the substance of that interior food, even though in the beginning, for the reason just mentioned, it may not experience the savor. This food is the beginning of a contemplation that is dark and dry to the senses. Ordinarily this contemplation, which is secret and hidden from the very one who receives it, imparts to the soul, together with the dryness and emptiness it produces in the senses, an inclination to remain alone and in quietude. And the soul will be unable to dwell upon any particular thought, nor will it have the desire to do so.

If those in whom this occurs know how to remain quiet, without care or solicitude about any interior or exterior work, they will soon in that unconcern and idleness delicately experience the interior nourishment. This refection is so delicate that usually if the soul desires or tries to experience it, it cannot. For, as I say, this contemplation is active while the soul is in idleness and unconcern. It is like air that escapes when one tries to grasp it in one's hand.

7. In this sense we can interpret what the Spouse said to the bride in the Canticle: *Turn your eyes from me, because they make me fly away.* [Ct. 6:4] God conducts the soul along so different a path, and so puts it in this state, that a desire to work with the faculties would hinder rather than help His work; whereas in the beginning of the spiritual life everything is quite the contrary.

The reason is that now in this state of contemplation, when the soul has left discursive meditation and entered the state of proficients, it is God who works in it. He therefore binds the interior faculties and leaves no support in the intellect, nor satisfaction in the will, nor remembrance in the memory. At this time a person's own efforts are of no avail, but an obstacle to the interior peace and work God is producing in the spirit through that dryness of sense. Since this peace is something spiritual and delicate, its fruit is quiet, delicate, solitary, satisfying, and peaceful, and far removed from all these other gratifications of beginners, which are very palpable and sensory. For this is the peace that David says God speaks in the soul in order to make it spiritual. [Ps. 84:9] The third sign follows from this one.

8. The third sign for the discernment of this purgation of the senses is the powerlessness, in spite of one's efforts, to meditate and make use of the imagination, the interior sense, as was one's previous custom. At this time God does not communicate Himself through the senses as He did before, by means of the discursive analysis and synthesis of ideas, but begins to communicate Himself through pure spirit by an act of simple contemplation, in which there is no discursive succession of thought. The exterior and interior senses of the lower part of the soul cannot attain

to this contemplation. As a result the imaginative power and phantasy can no longer rest in any consideration nor find support in it.

9. From the third sign it can be deduced that this dissatisfaction of the faculties is not the fruit of any bad humor. For if it were, a person would be able with a little care to return to his former exercises and find support for his faculties when that humor passed away, for it is by its nature changeable. In the purgation of the appetite this return is not possible, because upon entering it the powerlessness to meditate always continues. It is true, though, that at times in the beginning the purgation of some souls is not continuous in such a way that they are always deprived of sensory satisfaction and the ability to meditate. Perhaps, because of their weakness, they cannot be weaned all at once. Nevertheless, if they are to advance, they will ever enter further into the purgation and leave further behind their work of the senses. Those who do not walk the road of contemplation act very differently. This night of the aridity of the senses is not so continuous in them, for sometimes they experience the aridities and at other times not, and sometimes they can meditate and at other times they cannot. God places them in this night solely to exercise and humble them, and reform their appetite lest in their spiritual life they foster a harmful attraction toward sweetness. But He does not do so in order to lead them to the life of the spirit, which is contemplation. For God does not bring to contemplation all those who purposely exercise themselves in the way of the spirit, nor even half. Why? He best knows. As a result He never completely weans their senses from the breasts of considerations and discursive meditations, except for some short periods and at certain seasons, as we said.

CHAPTER 10

The conduct required of souls in this dark night.

1. At the time of the aridities of this sensory night, God makes the exchange we mentioned by withdrawing the soul from the life of the senses and placing it in that of spirit—that is, He brings it from meditation to contemplation—where the soul no longer has the power to work or meditate with its faculties on the things of God. Spiritual persons suffer considerable affliction in this night, owing not so much to the aridities they undergo as to their fear of having gone astray. Since they do not find any support or satisfaction in good things, they believe there will be no more spiritual blessings for them and that God has abandoned them. They then grow weary and strive, as was their custom, to concentrate their faculties with some satisfaction upon a subject of medita-

tion, and they think that if they do not do this and are unaware of their activity, they are doing nothing. This effort of theirs is accompanied by an interior reluctance and repugnance on the part of the soul, for it would be pleased to dwell in that quietude and idleness without working with the faculties.

They consequently impair God's work and do not profit by their own. In searching for spirit, they lose the spirit which was the source of their tranquillity and peace. They are like someone who turns from what has already been done in order to do it again, or one who leaves a city only to re-enter it, or they are like the hunter who abandons his prey to go hunting again. It is useless then for the soul to try to meditate, because it will no longer profit by this exercise.

2. If there is no one to understand these persons, they either turn back and abandon the road or lose courage, or at least they hinder their own progress because of their excessive diligence in treading the path of discursive meditation. They fatigue and overwork themselves, thinking that they are failing because of their negligences or sins. Meditation is now useless for them, because God is conducting them along another road, which is contemplation and which is very different from the first. For the one road belongs to discursive meditation and the other is beyond the range of the imagination and discursive reflection.

3. Those who are in this situation should feel comforted; they ought to persevere patiently and not be afflicted. Let them trust in God Who does not fail those who seek Him with a simple and righteous heart; nor does He fail to impart what is needful for the way until getting them to the clear and pure light of love. God will give them this light by means of that other night, the night of spirit, if they merit that He place them in it.

4. The attitude necessary in the night of sense is to pay no attention to discursive meditation, since this is not the time for it. They should allow the soul to remain in rest and quietude, even though it may seem very obvious to them that they are doing nothing and wasting time, and even though they think this disinclination to think about anything is due to their laxity. Through patience and perseverance in prayer, they will be doing a great deal without activity on their part. All that is required of them here is freedom of soul, that they liberate themselves from the impediment and fatigue of ideas and thoughts and care not about thinking and meditating. They must be content simply with a loving and peaceful attentiveness to God, and live without the concern, without the effort, and without the desire to taste or feel Him. All these desires disquiet the soul and distract it from the peaceful quiet and sweet idleness of the contemplation which is being communicated to it.

5. And even though more scruples come to the fore concerning the loss of time and the advantages of doing something else, since it cannot do anything nor think of anything in prayer, the soul should endure them peacefully, as though going to prayer means remaining in ease and freedom of spirit. If a person should desire to do something himself with his interior faculties, he would hinder and lose the goods which God engraves upon his soul through that peace and idleness. If a model for the painting or retouching of a portrait should move because of a desire to do something, the artist would be unable to finish, and his work would be disturbed. Similarly, any operation, affection, or advertency a soul might desire when it wants to abide in interior peace and idleness, would cause distraction and disquietude, and make it feel sensory dryness and emptiness. The more a person seeks some support in knowledge and affection the more will the soul feel its lack, for this cannot be supplied through these sensory means.

6. Accordingly, a person should not mind if the operations of his faculties are being lost to him; he ought to desire rather that this be done quickly so that he may be no obstacle to the operation of the infused contemplation which God is bestowing, that he may receive it with more peaceful plenitude and make room in his spirit for the enkindling and burning of the love that this dark and secret contemplation bears and communicates to his soul. For contemplation is nothing else than a secret and peaceful and loving inflow of God, which, if not hampered, fires the soul in the spirit of love, as is brought out in the following verse:

Fired with love's urgent longings

CHAPTER 11

Explains three verses of the stanza.

1. The fire of love is not commonly felt at the outset, either because it does not have a chance to take hold, owing to the impurity of the sensory part, or because the soul for want of understanding has not made within itself a peaceful place for it; although at times with or without these conditions a person will begin to feel a certain longing for God. In the measure that the fire increases, the soul becomes aware of being attracted by the love of God and enkindled in it, without knowing how nor where this attraction and love originates. At times this flame and enkindling increases to such an extent that the soul desires God with urgent longings of love, as David, while in this night, said of himself: *Because my heart was inflamed* (in contemplative love), *my reins were likewise changed.* [Ps. 72:21] That is, my appetites of sensible affection were

changed from the sensory life to the spiritual life, which implies dryness and cessation of all those appetites we are speaking of. *And, he says, I was brought to nothing and annihilated, and I knew not.* [Ps. 72:22] For, as we pointed out, the soul, with no knowledge of its destination, sees itself annihilated in all heavenly and earthly things in which it formerly found satisfaction; and it only sees that it is enamored, but knows not how.

Because the enkindling of love in the spirit sometimes increases exceedingly, the longings for God become so intense that it will seem to a person that his bones are drying up in this thirst, his nature withering away, and his ardor and strength diminishing through the liveliness of the thirst of love. A person will feel that this is a living thirst. David also had such experience when he proclaimed: *My soul thirsts for the living God* [Ps. 41:3], as though to say, this thirst my soul experiences is a living thirst. Since this thirst is alive, we can assert that it is a thirst which kills. Yet it should be noted that its vehemence is not continual, but only experienced from time to time; although usually some thirst is felt.

2. Yet it must be kept in mind that, as I explained before, a person generally does not perceive this love in the beginning, but he experiences rather the dryness and void we are speaking of. Then, instead of this love which is afterwards enkindled, he will, in the midst of the dryness and emptiness of his faculties, harbor a habitual care and solicitude for God accompanied by grief or fear about not serving Him. It is a sacrifice most pleasing to God—that of a spirit in distress and solicitude for His love.

Secret contemplation produces this solicitude and concern in the soul until, after having somewhat purged the sensory part of its natural propensities by means of this aridity, it begins to enkindle in the spirit this divine love. Meanwhile, however, as in one who is undergoing a cure, all is suffering in this dark and dry purgation of the appetite, and the soul being relieved of numerous imperfections acquires many virtues, thereby becoming capable of this love, as will be shown in the explanation of the following verse.

—Ah, the sheer grace!—

3. Since God introduces a person into this night to purge his senses, and accommodate, subject, and unite the lower part of his soul to the spiritual part by darkening it and causing a cessation of discursive meditation (just as afterwards in order to purify the spirit and unite it to Himself, He brings it into the spiritual night), this person gains so many benefits—though at the time this may not be apparent to him—that he

considers his departure from the fetters and straits of the senses a sheer grace. The verse therefore proclaims: "—Ah, the sheer grace!—"

We ought to point out the benefits procured in this night, for it is because of them that the soul says it was a sheer grace to have passed through it. All these benefits are included in the next verse:

I went out unseen,

4. This going out bears reference to the subjection the soul had to its senses, in seeking God through operations so feeble, limited, and exposed to error as are those of this lower part, for at every step it stumbled into numerous imperfections and much ignorance as was noted above in relation to the seven capital vices. This night frees the soul from all these vices by quenching all its earthly and heavenly satisfactions, darkening its discursive meditations, and producing in it other innumerable goods through the acquisition of the virtues, as we shall now explain. For it will please and comfort one who treads this path to know that a way seemingly so rough and adverse and contrary to spiritual gratification engenders so many blessings.

These blessings are attained when the soul departs from all created things, in its affection and operation, by means of this night and marches on toward eternal things. This is a great happiness and grace: first, because of the signal benefit of quenching one's appetite and affection for all things; second, because there are very few who will endure the night and persevere in entering through this small gate and in treading this narrow road that leads to life, as our Saviour says. [Mt. 7:14]

This small gate is the dark night of sense, in which the soul is despoiled and denuded—in order to pass through it—and grounded in faith, which is foreign to all sense, that it may be capable of walking along the narrow road which is the night of spirit. The soul enters this second night that it may journey to God in pure faith, for pure faith is the means whereby it is united with God. Few there are who walk along this road, because it is so narrow, dark, and terrible that, in obscurities and trials, the night of sense cannot be compared to it, as shall be explained. Yet the benefits of this night are incomparably greater than those of the night of sense.

We shall say something now about the benefits of the night of sense as briefly as possible in order to pass on to our exposition of the other night.

CHAPTER 12

The benefits this night causes in the soul.

1. This glad night and purgation causes many benefits, even though seemingly to the soul it deprives it of them. So numerous are these bene-

fits that, just as Abraham made a great feast on the day of his son Isaac's weaning [Gn. 21:8], there is rejoicing in heaven: that God now has taken from this soul its swaddling clothes; that He has put it down from His arms and is making it walk alone; that He is weaning it from the delicate and sweet food of infants and making it eat bread with crust; and that the soul is beginning to taste the food of the strong (the infused contemplation of which we have spoken), which in these sensory aridities and darknesses is given to the spirit that is dry and empty of the satisfactions of sense.

2. The first and chief benefit that this dry and dark night of contemplation causes is the knowledge of self and of one's own misery. Besides the fact that all the favors God imparts to the soul are ordinarily enwrapped in this knowledge, the aridities and voids of the faculties in relation to the abundance previously experienced, and the difficulty encountered in the practice of virtue make the soul recognize its own lowliness and misery, which was not apparent in the time of its prosperity.

There is a good figure of this in Exodus where God, desiring to humble the children of Israel and make them know themselves, ordered them to remove their festive garments and adornments which they were ordinarily wearing in the desert: *From now on leave aside your festive ornaments and put on common working garments that you may be aware of the treatment you deserve.* [Ex. 33:5] This was like saying: Since the clothing you wear, being of festivity and mirth, is an occasion for your not feeling as lowly as you in fact are, put it aside, so that seeing the foulness of your dress you may know yourself and your deserts.

As a result the soul recognizes the truth about its misery, of which it was formerly ignorant. When it was walking in festivity, gratification, consolation, and support in God, it was more content, believing that it was serving God in some way. Though this idea of serving God may not be explicitly formed in a person's mind, at least some notion of it is deeply embedded within him owing to the satisfaction he derives from his spiritual exercises. Now that the soul is clothed in these other garments of labor, dryness, and desolation, and that its former lights have been darkened, it possesses more authentic lights in this most excellent and necessary virtue of self-knowledge. It considers itself to be nothing and finds no satisfaction in self because it is aware that of itself it neither does nor can do anything.

God esteems this lack of self-satisfaction and the dejection a person has about not serving Him more than all former deeds and gratifications, however notable they may have been, since they were the occasion of many imperfections and a great deal of ignorance. Not only the benefits we mentioned result from this garment of dryness but also those of which we shall now speak, and many more, for they flow from self-knowledge as from their fount.

3. First, a person communes with God more respectfully and courteously, the way one should always converse with the Most High. In the prosperity of satisfaction and consolation the beginner did not act thus, for that satisfying delight made him somewhat more daring with God than was proper, and more discourteous and inconsiderate. This is what happened to Moses: when he heard God speaking to him, he was blinded by that gratification and desire and without any further thought would have dared to approach God, if he had not been ordered to stop and take off his shoes. [Ex. 3:4-5] This instance denotes the respect and discretion, the nakedness of appetite, with which one ought to commune with God. Consequently when Moses was obedient to this command, he was so discreet and cautious that Scripture says he not only dared not approach but did not even dare look. [Ex. 3:6; Acts 7:32] Having left aside the shoes of his appetites and gratifications, he was fully aware of his misery in the sight of God; for this was the manner in which it was fitting for him to hear God's word.

Similarly, Job was not prepared for converse with God by means of those delights and glories of which he tells he was accustomed to experience in his God. But the preparation for this converse embodied: nakedness on a dunghill; abandonment and even persecution by his friends; the fullness of anguish and bitterness; and the sight of the earth round about him covered with worms. [Jb. 2:8; 30:17-18] Yet then the most high God, He who raises the poor from the dunghill [Ps. 112:7], was pleased to descend and speak face to face with him and reveal the deep mysteries of His wisdom, which He never did before in the time of Job's prosperity. [Jb. 38:1 et seq.]

4. Since this is the proper moment, we ought to point out another benefit resulting from this night and dryness of the sensory appetite. So that the prophecy—*Your light will illumine the darkness* [Is. 58:10]—may be verified, God will give illumination by bestowing upon the soul not only knowledge of its own misery and lowliness but also knowledge of His grandeur and majesty. When the sensory appetites, gratifications, and supports are quenched, the intellect is left limpid and free to understand the truth, for even though these concern spiritual things they blind and impede the spirit. Similarly the anguish and dryness of the senses illumines and quickens the intellect, as Isaias affirms: *vexation makes one understand.* [Is. 28:19] But God also, by means of this dark and dry night of contemplation, supernaturally instructs in His divine wisdom the soul that is empty and unhindered (which is the requirement for His divine inflow), which He did not do through the former satisfactions and pleasures.

5. Isaias explains this clearly: *Whom shall God teach His knowledge? And to whom shall He explain His message? To them that are weaned,*

he says, *from the milk, and to them who are drawn away from the breasts.* [Is. 28:9] This passage indicates that the preparation for this divine influx is not the former milk of spiritual sweetness, nor aid from the breast of the discursive meditations of the sensory faculties which the soul enjoyed, but the privation of the one and a withdrawal from the other.

In order to hear God, a person should stand firm and be detached in his sense life and affections, as the prophet himself declares: *I will stand upon my watch* (with detached appetite) *and will fix my foot* (I will not meditate with the sensory faculties) *in order to contemplate* (understand) *what God says to me.* [Hb. 2:1]

We conclude that self-knowledge flows first from this dry night, and that from this knowledge as from its source proceeds the other knowledge of God. Hence St. Augustine said to God: *Let me know myself Lord, and I will know You.* [*Soliloq.*, lib. 2, c. 1–PL 32, 885] For as the philosophers say, one extreme is clearly known by the other.

6. For a more complete proof of the efficacy of this sensory night in occasioning through its dryness and destitution the light here received from God, we shall quote that passage from David in which the great power of this night in relation to the lofty knowledge of God is clearly shown. He proclaims: *In a desert land, without water, dry, and without a way, I appeared before You to be able to see Your power and Your glory.* [Ps. 62:3] David's teaching here is admirable: that the means to the knowledge of the glory of God were not the many spiritual delights and gratifications he had received, but the sensory aridities and detachments referred to by the dry and desert land. And it is also wonderful that, as he says, the way to the experience and vision of the power of God did not consist in ideas and meditations about God, of which he had made extensive use, but that it embodied his inability to grasp God with ideas and to walk by means of discursive, imaginative meditation, which is here indicated by the land without a way.

Hence the dark night with its aridities and voids is the means to the knowledge of God and self, although the knowledge given in this night is not as plenteous and abundant as that of the other night of spirit, for the knowledge of this night is as it were the foundation of the other.

7. In the dryness and emptiness of this night of the appetite, a person also procures spiritual humility, that virtue opposed to the first capital vice, spiritual pride. Through this humility acquired by means of self-knowledge, a person is purged of all those imperfections of the vice of pride into which he fell in the time of his prosperity. Aware of his own dryness and wretchedness, the thought of his being more advanced than others does not even occur in its first movements, as it did before; on the contrary, he realizes that others are better.

8. From this humility stems love of neighbor, for he will esteem them and not judge them as he did before, when he was aware that he enjoyed an intense fervor while others did not.

This person will know only his own misery and keep it so much in sight that he will have no opportunity to watch anyone else's conduct. David while in this night gives an admirable manifestation of such a state of soul: *I became dumb, and was humbled, and I kept silent in good things, and my sorrow was renewed.* [Ps. 38:3] He says this because it seemed to him that his blessings had so come to an end that he not only was unable to find words for them, but he also became silent concerning his neighbor, in the sorrow he experienced from the knowledge of his own misery.

9. These individuals also become submissive and obedient in their spiritual journey. Since they are so aware of their own wretchedness, they not only listen to the teaching of others but even desire to be directed and told what to do by anyone at all. The affective presumption they sometimes had in their prosperity leaves them.

And, finally, as they proceed on their journey, all the other imperfections of this first vice, spiritual pride, are swept away.

CHAPTER 13

Other benefits of this night of senses.

1. In this arid and obscure night the soul undergoes a thorough reform in its imperfections of avarice, in which it coveted various spiritual objects and was never content with any of its spiritual exercises because of the gratification derived from them and the covetousness of its appetite. Since it does not obtain the delight it formerly did in its spiritual practices, but rather finds them distasteful and laborious, it uses them so moderately that now perhaps it might fail through defect rather than excess. Nevertheless, God usually imparts to those whom He brings into this night the humility and the readiness, even though they feel displeasure, to do what is commanded of them for His sake alone, and they become detached from many things because of this lack of gratification.

2. It is also evident regarding spiritual lust that through the sensory dryness and distaste experienced in its spiritual exercises, the soul is freed of those impurities we noted. For we said that they ordinarily proceed from the delight of the spirit redounding in the senses.

3. The imperfections of the fourth vice, spiritual gluttony, from which a person is freed in this dark night are listed above, although not all of them since they are innumerable. Thus I will not refer to them here,

since I am anxious to conclude this dark night in order to pass on to the important doctrine we have concerning the other night.

To understand the countless benefits gained in this night in regard to the vice of spiritual gluttony, let it suffice to say that the soul is liberated from all the imperfections we mentioned and from many other greater evils and foul abominations, not listed, into which many have fallen, as we know from experience, because they did not reform their desire for this spiritual sweetness.

God so curbs concupiscence and bridles the appetite through this arid and dark night that the soul cannot feast on any sensory delight from earthly or heavenly things, and He continues this purgation in such a way that the concupiscence and the appetites are brought into subjection, reformed, and mortified. The passions, as a result, lose their strength and become sterile from not receiving any satisfaction, just as the courses of the udder dry up when milk is not drawn through them daily.

Once the soul's appetites have withered, and it lives in spiritual sobriety, admirable benefits besides those mentioned result. For when the appetites and concupiscences are quenched, the soul dwells in spiritual peace and tranquillity. Where neither the appetites nor concupiscence reign, there is no disturbance but only God's peace and consolation.

4. A second benefit following upon this one is that the soul bears a habitual remembrance of God, accompanied by a fear and dread of turning back on the spiritual road. This is a notable benefit and by no means one of the least in this dryness and purgation of the appetite, because the soul is purified of the imperfections which of themselves make it dull and dark, and cling to it by means of appetites and affections.

5. Another very great benefit for the soul in this night is that it exercises all the virtues together. In the patience and forbearance practiced in these voids and aridities, and through perseverance in its spiritual exercises without consolation or satisfaction, the soul practices the love of God, since it is no longer motivated by the attractive and savory gratification it finds in its work, but only by God. It also practices the virtue of fortitude, because it draws strength from weakness in the difficulties and aversions experienced in its work, and thus becomes strong. Finally, in these aridities the soul practices corporally and spiritually all the virtues, theological as well as cardinal and moral.

6. David affirms that a person obtains in this night these four benefits: the delight of peace; a habitual remembrance of God, and solicitude concerning Him; cleanness and purity of soul; and the practice of virtue. For David himself had this experience upon enduring the night: *My soul refused consolations, I remembered God and found consolation, and exercised myself, and my soul swooned away* [Ps. 76:3-4]; and then he

adds: *I meditated at night in my heart, and I exercised myself, and swept and purified my spirit* (of all its imperfections). [Ps. 76:7]

7. In relation to the imperfections of the other three vices (anger, envy, and sloth), the soul is also purged in this dryness of appetite, and it acquires the virtues to which these vices are opposed. Softened and humbled by aridities and hardships and by other temptations and trials in which God exercises the soul in the course of this night, a person becomes meek toward God and himself, and also toward his neighbor. As a result he will no longer become impatiently angry with himself and his faults, nor with his neighbor's, neither is he displeased or disrespectfully querulous with God for not making him perfect quickly.

8. As for envy, the individual will also be charitable toward others. For if he does have envy, it will not be vicious as before, when he was distressed that others were preferred to him and more advanced. Now, aware of how miserable he is, he is willing to concede this about others. The envy he has—if he does have any—is a holy envy that desires to imitate them, which indicates solid virtue.

9. The sloth and tedium he feels in spiritual things is not vicious as before. Previously this sloth was the outcome of the spiritual gratification he either enjoyed or tried to obtain when not experienced. Yet this wearisomeness does not flow from any weakness relative to sensory gratification, for in this purgation of the appetite God takes from the soul all its satisfaction.

10. Besides these benefits, innumerable others flow from this dry contemplation. In the midst of these aridities and straits, God frequently communicates to the soul, when it least expects, spiritual sweetness, a very pure love, and a spiritual knowledge which is sometimes most delicate. Each of these communications is more valuable than all that the soul previously sought. Yet in the beginning one will not think so because the spiritual inflow is very delicate and the senses do not perceive it.

11. Finally, insofar as a person is purged of his sensory affections and appetites, he obtains liberty of spirit in which he acquires the twelve fruits of the Holy Ghost.

He is also wondrously liberated from the hands of his enemies, the world, the flesh, and the devil. For when the sensory delight and gratification of things is quenched, neither the devil, nor the world, nor sensuality has arms or power against the spirit.

12. These aridities, then, make a person walk with purity in the love of God, for he is no longer moved to act by the delight and satisfaction he finds in a work, as he was perhaps when he derived this from his deeds, but by the desire of pleasing God. He is neither presumptuous

nor self-satisfied, as was his custom in the time of his prosperity, but fearful and disquieted about himself and lacking in any self-satisfaction. This is the holy fear which preserves and gives increase to the virtues.

This dryness also quenches the natural concupiscences and vigor, as we also said. Were it not for the satisfaction God Himself sometimes infuses, it would be a wonder if the soul through its own diligence could get any sensible gratification or consolation out of its spiritual works and exercises.

13. In this arid night solicitude for God and yearnings about serving Him increase. Since the sensory breasts (through which the appetites pursued by these souls were sustained and nurtured) gradually dry up, only the anxiety about serving God remains, in dryness and nakedness. These yearnings are very pleasing to God, since as David proclaims: *the afflicted spirit is a sacrifice to God.* [Ps. 50:19]

14. Since the soul knows that, from this dry purgation through which it passed, it procured so many and such precious benefits, as are those referred to here, the verse of this stanza is no exaggeration: "—Ah, the sheer grace!—I went out unseen." That is, I went forth from subjection to my sensory appetites and affections, unseen, so that the three enemies were unable to stop me. These enemies entrap the soul—as with snares—in its appetites and gratifications and keep it from going forth to the freedom of the love of God. But without these satisfactions and appetites the enemies cannot fight against the soul.

15. Having calmed the four passions (joy, sorrow, hope, and fear) through constant mortification, and lulled to sleep the natural sensory appetites, and having achieved harmony in the interior senses by discontinuing discursive operations (all of which pertains to the household or dwelling of the lower part of the soul, here referred to as its house), the soul says:

My house being now all stilled;

CHAPTER 14

An explanation of the last verse of the first stanza.

1. When this house of the senses was stilled (that is, mortified), its passions quenched, and its appetites calmed and put to sleep through this happy night of the purgation of the senses, the soul went out in order to begin its journey along the road of the spirit, which is that of proficients and which by another terminology is referred to as the illuminative way or the way of infused contemplation, in which God Himself pastures and

refreshes the soul without any of its own discursive meditation or active help.

Such is the sensory night and purgation of the soul. For those who must afterwards enter into the other more oppressive night of the spirit in order to reach the divine union of love—because not everyone but only a few usually reach this union—this night is ordinarily accompanied by burdensome trials and sensory temptations which last a long time, and in some longer than in others.

An angel of Satan [2 Cor. 12:7], which is the spirit of fornication, is given to some to buffet their senses with strong and abominable temptations, and afflict their spirit with foul thoughts and very vivid images, which sometimes is a pain worse than death for them.

2. At other times the blasphemous spirit is added; it commingles intolerable blasphemies with all their thoughts and ideas. Sometimes these blasphemies are so strongly suggested to the imagination that the soul is almost made to pronounce them, which is a grave torment to it.

3. Sometimes another loathsome spirit, which Isaias calls *spiritus vertiginis* [Is. 19:14], is sent to these souls, not for their downfall but to try them. This spirit so darkens the senses that it fills them with a thousand scruples and perplexities, and these seem so intricate to them that they can never be content with anything, nor can their judgment receive the support of any counsel or idea. This is one of the most burdensome goads and horrors of this night—very similar to what occurs in the spiritual night.

4. God generally sends these storms and trials in this sensory night and purgation to those whom He will afterwards put in the other night—although not all pass on to it—so that thus chastised and buffeted, the senses and faculties may be gradually exercised, prepared, and inured for the union with wisdom which will be granted there. For if a soul is not tempted, tried, and proved through temptations and trials, its senses will not be strengthened in preparation for wisdom. It is said, therefore, in Ecclesiasticus: *He who is not tempted, what does he know? And he who is not tried, what are the things he knows?* [Ecclus. 34:9, 11] Jeremias gives good testimony of this truth: *You have chastised me Lord, and I was instructed.* [Jer. 31:18]

And the most fitting kind of chastisement for entering into wisdom consists of the interior trials we mentioned, since they most efficaciously purge the senses of all the satisfaction and consolation the soul was attached to through natural weakness. By these trials it is truly humbled in preparation for its coming exaltation.

5. Yet, we cannot say certainly how long the soul will be kept in this fast and penance of the senses. Not everyone undergoes this in the same

way, neither are the temptations identical. All is meted out according to God's will and the greater or lesser amount of imperfection that must be purged from each one. In the measure of the degree of love to which God wishes to raise a soul, He humbles it with greater or less intensity, or for a longer or shorter period of time.

Those who have more considerable capacity and strength for suffering, God purges more intensely and quickly.

But those who are very weak He keeps in this night for a long time. Their purgation is less intense and their temptations abated, and He frequently refreshes their senses to keep them from backsliding. They arrive at the purity of perfection late in life. And some of them never reach it entirely, for they are never wholly in the night nor wholly out of it. Although they do not advance, God exercises them for short periods and on certain days in those temptations and aridities to preserve them in humility and self-knowledge; and at other times and seasons He comes to their aid with consolation, lest through loss of courage they return to their search after worldly consolation.

God acts with other weaker souls as though He were showing Himself and then hiding; He does this to exercise them in His love, for without these withdrawals they would not learn to reach Him.

6. Yet, as is evident through experience, souls who will pass on to so happy and lofty a state as is the union of love must usually remain in these aridities and temptations for a long while no matter how quickly God leads them.

It is time to begin our treatise on the second night.

BOOK TWO

The Dark Night of the Spirit

CHAPTER 1

The beginning of the treatise on the dark night of the spirit. Explains when this night commences.

1. If God intends to lead the soul on, He does not put it in this dark night of spirit immediately after its going out from the aridities and trials of the first purgation and night of sense. Instead, after having emerged from the state of beginners, it usually spends many years exercising itself in the state of proficients. In this new state, as one liberated from a cramped prison cell, the soul goes about the things of God with much more freedom and satisfaction of spirit and with more abundant

interior delight than it did in the beginning before entering the night
of sense. Its imagination and faculties are no longer bound to discursive
meditation and spiritual solicitude, as was their custom. The soul readily
finds in its spirit, without the work of meditation, a very serene, loving
contemplation and spiritual delight. Nonetheless, since the purgation of
the soul is not complete (the purgation of the principal part, that of the
spirit, is lacking, and without it the sensory purgation, however strong it
may have been, is incomplete because of a communication existing between the two parts of the soul which form only one *suppositum*), certain needs, aridities, darknesses, and conflicts are felt. These are sometimes far more intense than those of the past and are like omens or
messengers of the coming night of the spirit.

But they are not lasting, as they will be in the night that is to come.
For after enduring the short period or periods of time, or even days, in
this night and tempest, the soul immediately returns to its customary
serenity. Thus God purges some individuals who are not destined to
ascend to so lofty a degree of love as are others. He brings them into
this night of contemplation and spiritual purgation at intervals, frequently
causing the night to come and then the dawn so that David's affirmation
might be fulfilled: *He sends His crystal* (contemplation) *like morsels.*
[Ps. 147:17] These morsels of dark contemplation, though, are never
as intense as is that frightful night of contemplation we are about to
describe, in which God places the soul purposely in order to bring it to
the divine union.

2. The delight and interior gratification which these proficients enjoy
abundantly and readily is communicated more copiously to them than
previously and consequently overflows into the senses more than was
usual before the sensory purgation. Since the sensory part of the soul is
now purer, it can, after its own mode, experience the delights of the
spirit more easily.

But since, after all, the sensory part of the soul is weak and incapable of vigorous spiritual communications, these proficients, because
of such communications experienced in the sensitive part, suffer many
infirmities, injuries, and weaknesses of stomach, and as a result fatigue
of spirit. As the Wise Man says: *The corruptible body is a load upon the
soul.* [Wis. 9:15] Consequently the communications imparted to proficients cannot be very strong, nor very intense, nor very spiritual—which
is a requirement of the divine union—because of the weakness and
corruption of the senses which have their share in them.

Thus we have raptures and transports and the dislocation of bones,
which always occur when the communications are not purely spiritual
(communicated to the spirit alone) as are those of the perfect, who are
already purified by the night of spirit. For in the perfect, these raptures

and bodily torments cease, and they enjoy freedom of spirit without a detriment to or transport of their senses.

3. To point out why these proficients must enter this night of spirit, we shall note some of their imperfections and some of the dangers they confront.

CHAPTER 2

Other imperfections of these proficients.

1. The imperfections in these proficients are of two kinds: habitual and actual.

The habitual are the imperfect affections and habits still remaining like roots in the spirit, for the sensory purgation could not reach the spirit. The difference between the two purgations is like the difference between pulling up roots and cutting off a branch, or rubbing out a fresh stain and an old, deeply embedded one. As we said, the purgation of the senses is only the gate to and beginning of the contemplation which leads to the purgation of spirit. This sensitive purgation, as we also explained, serves more for the accommodation of the senses to the spirit than for the union of the spirit with God. The stains of the old man still linger in the spirit, although this may not be apparent or perceptible. If these are not wiped away by the use of the soap and strong lye of this purgative night, the spirit will be unable to reach the purity of divine union.

2. These proficients also have the so-called *hebetudo mentis*, the natural dullness everyone contracts through sin, and a distracted and inattentive spirit. The spirit must be illumined, clarified, and recollected by means of the hardships and conflicts of this night.

All those who have not passed beyond the state of proficients possess these habitual imperfections which cannot, as we said, coexist with the perfect state of the union of love.

3. Not all of these proficients fall into actual imperfections in the same way. Some encounter greater difficulties and dangers than those we mentioned, for their experience of these goods in the senses is so exterior and easily come by. Since they receive such abundance of spiritual communications and apprehensions in the sensory and spiritual parts of their souls and frequently behold imaginative and spiritual visions (for all of this plus other delightful feelings are the lot of those who are in this state, and a soul is often tricked through them by its own phantasy as well as by the devil), and since the devil is so pleased to suggest to souls and impress upon them apprehensions and feelings,

these proficients are easily charmed and beguiled, if they are not careful to renounce such apprehensions and feelings and energetically defend themselves through faith.

This is the stage in which the devil induces many into believing vain visions and false prophecies. He strives to make them presume that God and the saints speak with them; and frequently they believe their phantasy. It is here that the devil customarily fills them with presumption and pride. Drawn by vanity and arrogance, they will allow themselves to be seen in exterior acts of apparent holiness, such as raptures and other exhibitions. They become audacious with God and lose holy fear which is the key to and guardian of all the virtues. Illusions and deceptions so multiply in some, and they become so inveterate in them, that it is very doubtful whether they will return to the pure road of virtue and authentic spirituality. They fall into these miseries by being too secure in their surrender to these apprehensions and spiritual feelings; and this, just when they were beginning to make progress along the way.

4. So much could be said about the imperfections of these proficients and of how irremediable they are—since proficients think their blessings are more spiritual than formerly—that I desire to pass over the matter. I only assert, in order to establish the necessity of the spiritual night (the purgation) for anyone who is to advance, that no proficient, however strenuous his efforts, will avoid many of these natural affections and imperfect habits; and these must be purified before he passes on to the divine union.

5. Furthermore, to repeat what was said above, these spiritual communications cannot be so intense, so pure, and so vigorous as is requisite for this union, because the lower part of the soul still shares in them. Thus, to reach union, the soul must enter the second night of the spirit. In this night both the sensory and spiritual parts are despoiled of all these apprehensions and delights, and the soul is made to walk in dark and pure faith, which is the proper and adequate means to divine union, as God says through Osee: *I will espouse you* (unite you) *to me through faith.* [Os. 2:20]

CHAPTER 3

An explanation for what is to follow.

1. These souls, then, are now proficients. Their senses have been fed with sweet communications so that, allured by the gratification flowing from the spirit, they could be accommodated and united to the spirit.

Each part of the soul can now in its own way receive nourishment from the same spiritual food and from the same dish of only one *suppositum* and subject. These two parts thus united and conformed are jointly prepared to suffer the rough and arduous purgation of the spirit which awaits them. In this purgation, these two portions of the soul will undergo complete purification, for one part is never adequately purged without the other. The real purgation of the senses begins with the spirit. Hence the night of the senses we explained should be called a certain reformation and bridling of the appetite rather than a purgation. The reason is that all the imperfections and disorders of the sensory part are rooted in the spirit and from it receive their strength. All good and evil habits reside in the spirit and until these habits are purged, the senses cannot be completely purified of their rebellions and vices.

2. In this night that follows both parts are jointly purified. This was the purpose of the reformation of the first night and the calm that resulted from it: that the sensory part, united in a certain way with the spirit, might undergo the purgation and suffering with greater fortitude. Such is the fortitude necessary for so strong and arduous a purgation that if the lower part in its weakness is not reformed first and afterwards strengthened in God through the experience of sweet and delightful communion with Him, it has neither the fortitude nor the preparedness to endure it.

3. These proficients are still very lowly and natural in their communion with God and in their activity directed toward Him because the gold of the spirit is not purified and illumined. They still think of God and speak of Him as little children, and their knowledge and experience of Him is like that of little children, as St. Paul asserts. [1 Cor. 13:11] The reason is that they have not reached perfection, which is union of the soul with God. Through this union, as full-grown men, they do mighty works in their spirit, since their faculties and works are more divine than human, as we shall point out. Wishing to strip them in fact of this old man and clothe them with the new which is created according to God in the newness of sense, as the Apostle says [Col. 3:9–10; Eph. 4:22–24; Rom. 12:2], God divests the faculties, affections, and senses, both spiritual and sensory, interior and exterior. He leaves the intellect in darkness, the will in aridity, the memory in emptiness, and the affections in supreme affliction, bitterness, and anguish, by depriving the soul of the feeling and satisfaction it previously obtained from spiritual blessings. For this privation is one of the conditions required that the spiritual form, which is the union of love, may be introduced in the spirit and united with it. The Lord works all of this in the soul by means of a pure and dark contemplation, as is indicated in the first stanza. Although we explained this stanza in reference to the first night of the senses, the

soul understands it mainly in relation to this second night of the spirit, since this night is the principal purification of the soul. With this in mind, we shall quote it and explain it again.

CHAPTER 4

First Stanza

One dark night,
Fired with love's urgent longings
—Ah, the sheer grace!—
I went out unseen,
My house being now all stilled;

EXPLANATION

1. Understanding this stanza now to refer to contemplative purgation or nakedness and poverty of spirit (which are all about the same), we can thus explain it, as though the soul says:

Poor, abandoned, and unsupported by any of the apprehensions of my soul (in the darkness of my intellect, the distress of my will, and in the affliction and anguish of my memory), left to darkness in pure faith, which is a dark night for these natural faculties, and with only my will touched by the sorrows, afflictions, and longings of love of God, I went out from myself. That is, I departed from my low manner of understanding, and my feeble way of loving, and my poor and limited method of finding satisfaction in God. I did this unhindered by either the flesh or the devil.

2. This was great happiness and a sheer grace for me, because through the annihilation and calming of my faculties, passions, appetites, and affections, by which my experience and satisfaction in God was base, I went out from my human operation and way of acting to God's operation and way of acting. That is:

My intellect departed from itself, changing from human and natural to divine. For, united with God through this purgation, it no longer understands by means of its natural vigor and light, but by means of the divine wisdom to which it was united.

And my will departed from itself and became divine. United with the divine love, it no longer loves in a lowly manner, with its natural strength, but with the strength and purity of the Holy Spirit; and thus the will does not operate humanly in relation to God.

And the memory, too, was changed into presentiments of eternal glory.

And finally, all the strength and affections of the soul, by means of this night and purgation of the old man, are renewed with divine qualities and delights.

An explanation of the first verse follows:

One dark night,

CHAPTER 5

Begins to explain how this dark contemplation is not only night for the soul but also affliction and torment.

1. This dark night is an inflow of God into the soul, which purges it of its habitual ignorances and imperfections, natural and spiritual, and which the contemplatives call infused contemplation or mystical theology. Through this contemplation, God teaches the soul secretly and instructs it in the perfection of love without its doing anything nor understanding how this happens.

Insofar as infused contemplation is loving wisdom of God, it produces two principal effects in the soul: it prepares the soul for the union with God through love by both purging and illumining it. Hence the same loving wisdom that purges and illumines the blessed spirits, purges and illumines the soul here on earth.

2. Yet a doubt arises: Why, if it is a divine light (for it illumines and purges a person of his ignorances), does the soul call it a dark night?

In answer to this, there are two reasons why this divine wisdom is not only night and darkness for the soul, but also affliction and torment. First, because of the height of the divine wisdom which exceeds the capacity of the soul. Second, because of the soul's baseness and impurity; and on this account it is painful, afflictive, and also dark for the soul.

3. To prove the first reason, we must presuppose a certain principle of the Philosopher: that the clearer and more obvious divine things are in themselves, the darker and more hidden they are to the soul naturally. [Aristotle, *Metaphys.*, lib. brevior, c. 1, ed. Didot, 486] The brighter the light, the more the owl is blinded; and the more one looks at the brilliant sun, the more the sun darkens the faculty of sight, deprives it and overwhelms it in its weakness.

Hence when the divine light of contemplation strikes a soul not yet entirely illumined, it causes spiritual darkness, for it not only surpasses the act of natural understanding but it also deprives the soul of this act and darkens it. This is why St. Dionysius and other mystical theologians call this infused contemplation a "ray of darkness"—that is, for the soul not yet illumined and purged. [Pseudo-Dionysius Areopagita, *De Mystica Theologia*, c. 1: PG 3, 999] For this great supernatural light overwhelms the intellect and deprives it of its natural vigor.

David also said that clouds and darkness are near God and surround Him [Ps. 17:12], not because this is true in itself, but because it appears thus to our weak intellects, which in being unable to attain so bright a light are blinded and darkened. Hence he immediately added: *clouds passed before the great splendor of His presence* [Ps. 17:13], that is, between God and our intellect. As a result, when God communicates this bright ray of His secret wisdom to the soul not yet transformed, He causes thick darkness in its intellect.

4. It is also evident that this dark contemplation is painful to the soul in these beginnings. Since this divine infused contemplation has many extremely good properties, and the still unpurged soul that receives it has many extreme miseries, and because two contraries cannot coexist in one subject, the soul must necessarily undergo affliction and suffering. Because of the purgation of its imperfections caused by this contemplation, the soul becomes a battlefield in which these two contraries combat one another. We shall prove this by induction in the following way.

5. In regard to the first cause of one's affliction: because the light and wisdom of this contemplation is very bright and pure, and the soul in which it shines is dark and impure, a person will be deeply afflicted in receiving it within himself. When eyes are sickly, impure, and weak, they suffer pain if a bright light shines on them.

The soul, because of its impurity, suffers immensely at the time this divine light truly assails it. When this pure light strikes in order to expel all impurity, a person feels so unclean and wretched that it seems God is against him and that he is against God.

Because it seems that God has rejected it, the soul suffers such pain and grief that when God tried Job in this way it proved one of the worst of Job's trials, as he says: *Why have You set me against You, and I am heavy and burdensome to myself?* [Jb. 7:20] Clearly beholding its impurity by means of this pure light, although in darkness, the soul understands distinctly that it is worthy neither of God nor of any creature. And what most grieves it is that it thinks it will never be worthy, and that there are no more blessings for it. This divine and dark light causes deep immersion of the mind in the knowledge and feeling of one's own miseries and evils; it brings all these miseries into relief so that the soul sees clearly that of itself it will never possess anything else. We can interpret that passage from David in this sense: *You have corrected*

*man because of his iniquity and have undone and consumed his soul, as
a spider is eviscerated in its work.* [Ps. 38:12]

6. A person suffers affliction in the second manner because of his
natural, moral, and spiritual weakness. Since this divine contemplation
assails him somewhat forcibly in order to subdue and strengthen his soul,
he suffers so much in his weakness that he almost dies, particularly at
times when the light is more powerful. Both the sense and the spirit, as
though under an immense and dark load, undergo such agony and pain
that the soul would consider death a relief. The prophet Job, having
experienced this, declared: *I do not desire that He commune with me
with much strength that He might not overwhelm me with the weight
of His greatness.* [Jb. 23:6]

7. Under the stress of this oppression and weight, a man feels so much
a stranger to being favored that he thinks, and so it is, that even that
which previously upheld him has ended along with everything else, and
that there is no one who will take pity on him. It is in this sense that
Job also cried out: *Have pity on me, at least you my friends, for the
hand of the Lord has touched me.* [Jb. 19:21]

How amazing and pitiful it is that the soul be so utterly weak and
impure that the hand of God, though light and gentle, should feel so
heavy and contrary. For the hand of God does not press down or weigh
upon the soul, but only touches it; and this mercifully, for God's aim is to
grant it favors and not chastise it.

CHAPTER 6

Other kinds of affliction suffered in this night.

1. The two extremes, divine and human, which are joined here, produce the third kind of pain and affliction the soul suffers here. The
divine extreme is the purgative contemplation and the human extreme is
the soul, the receiver of this contemplation. Since the divine extreme
strikes in order to renew the soul and divinize it (by stripping it of the
habitual affections and properties of the old man to which it is strongly
united, attached, and conformed), it so disentangles and dissolves the
spiritual substance—absorbing it in a profound darkness—that the soul
at the sight of its miseries feels that it is melting away and being undone
by a cruel spiritual death; it feels as if it were swallowed by a beast and
being digested in the dark belly, and it suffers an anguish comparable
to Jonas's when in the belly of the whale. [Jon. 2:1–3] It is fitting that the
soul be in this sepulcher of dark death in order that it attain the
spiritual resurrection for which it hopes.

2. David describes this suffering and affliction—although it is truly beyond all description—when he says: *The sighs of death encircled me, the sorrows of hell surrounded me, in my tribulation I cried out.* [Ps. 17: 5-7]

But what the sorrowing soul feels most is the conviction that God has rejected it, and with an abhorrence of it cast it into darkness. The thought that God has abandoned it is a piteous and heavy affliction for the soul. When David also felt this affliction he cried: *In the manner of the wounded, dead in the sepulchers, abandoned now by Your hand so that You remember them no longer, so·have You placed me in the deepest and lowest lake, in the darkness and shadow of death, and Your wrath weighs upon me, and all Your waves You have let loose upon me.* [Ps. 87:6-8]

When this purgative contemplation oppresses a man, he feels very vividly indeed the shadow of death, the sighs of death, and the sorrows of hell, all of which reflect the feeling of God's absence, of being chastised and rejected by Him, and of being unworthy of Him, as well as the object of His anger. The soul experiences all this and even more, for now it seems that this affliction will last forever.

3. A person also feels forsaken and despised by creatures, particularly by his friends. David immediately adds: *You have withdrawn my friends and acquaintances far from me; they have considered me an abomination.* [Ps. 87:9] Jonas, as one who also underwent this experience, both physically and spiritually in the belly of the whale, testifies: *You have cast me out into the deep, into the heart of the sea, and the current surrounded me; all its whirlpools and waves passed over me and I said: I am cast from the sight of Your eyes; yet I shall see Your holy temple again* (he says this because God purifies the soul that it might see His temple); *the waters encircled me even to the soul, the abyss went round about me, the open sea covered my head, I descended to the lowest parts of the mountains, the locks of the earth closed me up forever.* [Jon. 2:4-7] The "locks" refer to the soul's imperfections which hinder it from enjoying the delights of this contemplation.

4. Another excellence of dark contemplation, its majesty and grandeur, causes a fourth kind of affliction to the soul. This property makes the soul feel within itself the other extreme—its own intimate poverty and misery. Such awareness is one of the chief afflictions it suffers in the purgation.

The soul experience an emptiness and poverty in regard to three classes of goods (temporal, natural, and spiritual) which are directed toward pleasing it, and is conscious of being in the midst of the contrary evils (the miseries of imperfections, aridities and voids in the apprehensions of the faculties, and an abandonment of the spirit in darkness).

Since God purges both the sensory and spiritual substance of the soul, and its interior and exterior faculties, it is fitting that it be brought into emptiness and poverty and abandonment in these parts, and left in dryness and darkness. For the sensory part is purified by aridity, the faculties by the void of their apprehensions, and the spirit by thick darkness.

5. God does all this by means of dark contemplation. And the soul not only suffers the void and suspension of these natural supports and apprehensions, which is a terrible anguish (like hanging in midair, unable to breathe), but it is also purged by this contemplation. As fire consumes the tarnish and rust of metal, this contemplation annihilates, empties, and consumes all the affections and imperfect habits the soul contracted throughout its life. Since these imperfections are deeply rooted in the substance of the soul, it usually suffers besides this poverty and this natural and spiritual emptiness an oppressive undoing and an inner torment. Thus the passage of Ezechiel may be verified: *Heap together the bones, and I shall burn them in the fire, the flesh shall be consumed, and the whole composition burned, and the bones destroyed.* [Ez. 24:10] He refers here to the affliction suffered in the emptiness and poverty of both the sensory and the spiritual substance of the soul. And he then adds: *Place it also thus empty on the embers that its metal may become hot and melt and its uncleanness be taken away from it and its rust consumed.* [Ez. 24:11] This passage points out the heavy affliction the soul suffers from the purgation caused by the fire of this contemplation. For the prophet asserts that in order to burn away the rust of the affections the soul must, as it were, be annihilated and undone in the measure that these passions and imperfections are connatural to it.

6. Because the soul is purified in this forge like gold in the crucible, as the Wise Man says [Wis. 3:6], it feels terrible annihilation in its very substance and extreme poverty as though it were approaching its end. This experience is expressed in David's cry: *Save me, Lord, for the waters have come in even unto my soul; I am stuck in the mire of the deep, and there is nowhere to stand; I have come unto the depth of the sea, and the tempest has overwhelmed me. I have labored in crying out, my throat has become hoarse, my eyes have failed while I hope in my God.* [Ps. 68:2–4]

God humbles the soul greatly in order to exalt it greatly afterwards. And if He did not ordain that these feelings, when quickened in the soul, be soon put to sleep again, a person would die in a few days. Only at intervals is one aware of these feelings in all their intensity. Sometimes this experience is so vivid that it seems to the soul that it sees hell and perdition open before it. These are the ones who go down into hell alive [Ps. 54:16], since their purgation on earth is similar to that of purgatory. For this purgation is that which would have to be undergone there. The soul that endures it here on earth either does not enter purgatory, or is detained there for only a short while. It gains more in one hour here on earth by this purgation than it would in many there.

CHAPTER 7

A continuation of the same subject; other afflictions and straits of the will.

1. The afflictions and straits of the will are also immense. Sometimes these afflictions pierce the soul when it suddenly remembers the evils in which it sees itself immersed, and it becomes uncertain of any remedy. To this pain is added the remembrance of past prosperity, because usually persons who enter this night have previously had many consolations in God and rendered Him many services. They are now sorrowful in knowing that they are far from such good and can no longer enjoy it. Job tells also of his affliction: *I who was wont to be wealthy and rich am suddenly undone and broken; he has taken me by the neck, He has broken me and set me up as His mark so as to wound me. He has surrounded me with His lances, He wounded all my loins, He has not pardoned, He has scattered my bowels on the ground, He has torn me with wound upon wound, He has attacked me like a strong giant. I sewed sackcloth upon my skin and covered my flesh with ashes. My face is swollen with weeping, and my eyes blinded.* [Jb. 16:13–17]

2. So numerous and burdensome are the pains of this night, and so many are the scriptural passages we could cite that we would have neither the time nor the energy to put it all in writing; and, doubtless, all that we can possibly say would fall short of expressing what this night really is. Through the texts already quoted we have some idea of it.

To conclude my commentary on this verse and further explain what this night causes in the soul, I shall refer to what Jeremias felt in it. Because his tribulations were so terrible, he speaks of them and weeps over them profusely: *I am the man who sees my poverty in the rod of His indignation. He has led me and brought me into darkness and not into light. He has turned and turned again His hand against me all the day. He has made my skin and my flesh old; He has broken my bones. He has built a fence round about me; and He has surrounded me with gall and labor. He has set me in darkness, as those who are dead forever. He has made a fence around me and against me that I might not go out; He has made my fetters heavy. And also when I might have cried out and entreated, He has shut out my prayer. He has closed up my exits and ways with square stones; He has destroyed my paths. He is become to me like a bear lying in wait, as a lion in hiding. He has turned aside my paths, and broken me in pieces; He has made me desolate. He has bent His bow and set me as a mark for His arrow. He has shot into my reins the daughters of His quiver. I have become a derision to all the people and laughter and scorn for them all the day. He has filled me with bitterness, He has inebriated me with absinthe. One by one He has broken my teeth; He has fed me with ashes. My soul is far removed from peace. I have forgotten good things. And I said: My end, my aim and my hope from the Lord is frustrated and finished. Remember my poverty and my distress, the absinthe and the gall. I shall be mindful and remember, and my soul will languish within me in afflictions.* [Lam. 3:1–20]

3. Jeremias gives vent to all these lamentations about his afflictions and trials and depicts very vividly the sufferings of a soul in this purgation and spiritual night.

One ought to have deep compassion for the soul God puts in this tempestuous and frightful night. It may be true that the soul is fortunate because of what is being accomplished within it, for the great blessings will proceed from this night. Job affirms that out of darkness God will raise up in the soul profound blessings and change the shadow of death into light. [Jb. 12:22] He will do this in such a way that, as David says, the light will become what the darkness was. [Ps. 138:12] Nevertheless the soul is deserving of great pity because of the immense tribulation it suffers and its extreme uncertainty about a remedy. It believes, as Jeremias says [Lam. 3:18], that its evil will never end. And it feels as David that God has placed it in darkness like the dead of old, and that its spirit as a result is in anguish within it and its heart troubled. [Ps. 142:3–4]

Added to this, because of the solitude and desolation this night causes, is the fact that a person in this state finds neither consolation nor support in any doctrine or spiritual director. Although his spiritual director may point out many reasons for being comforted on account of the blessings contained in these afflications, he cannot believe this. Because he is engulfed and immersed in that sentiment of evils by which he so clearly sees his own miseries, he believes his directors say these things because they do not understand him and do not see what he sees and feels. Instead of consolation he experiences greater sorrow thinking that the director's doctrine is no remedy for his evil. Indeed, it is not a remedy, for until the Lord finishes purging him in the way He desires, no remedy is a help to him in his sorrow. His helplessness is even greater because of the little he can do in this situation. He resembles one who is imprisoned in a dark dungeon, bound hands and feet, and able neither to move, nor see, nor feel any favor from heaven or earth. He remains in this condition until his spirit is humbled, softened, and purified, until it becomes so delicate, simple, and refined that it can be one with the Spirit of God, according to the degree of union of love that God, in His mercy, desires to grant. In conformity with this degree, the purgation is of greater or lesser force and endures for a longer or shorter time.

4. But if it is to be truly efficacious, it will last for some years, no matter how intense it may be; although there are intervals in which this dark contemplation ceases to assail the soul in a purgative mode and shines upon it illuminatively and lovingly. Then the soul, like one who has been unshackled and released from a dungeon and who can enjoy the benefit of spaciousness and freedom, experiences great sweetness of peace and loving friendship with God in a ready abundance of spiritual communication.

This illumination is for the soul a sign of the health the purgation is producing within it and a foretaste of the abundance for which it hopes. Sometimes the experience is so intense that it seems to the soul that its trials are over. For when the graces imparted are more purely spiritual they have this trait: When they are trials, it seems to a soul that it will never be liberated from them and that no more blessings await it, as was mentioned in the passages previously cited; when they are spiritual goods, the soul believes its evils have passed and that it will no longer lack blessings, as David confessed on being aware of these goods: *I said in my abundance: I shall never move.* [Ps. 29:7]

5. The soul experiences this because in the spirit the possession of one contrary removes of itself the actual possession and sentiment of the other contrary. This does not occur in the sensory part because of the weakness of its apprehensive power. But since the spirit is not yet completely purged and cleansed of affections contracted from the lower part, it can, insofar as it is affected by them, be changed and suffer affliction; although insofar as it is a spirit it does not change. We note that David changed [Ps. 29:8] and that he experienced many afflictions and evils, although in the time of his abundance he had thought and said that he would never be moved. Since the soul beholds itself actuated with that abundance of spiritual goods, and is unable to see the imperfection and impurity still rooted within it, it thinks its trials have ended.

6. But this thought is rare, for until the spiritual purification is completed, the tranquil communication is seldom so abundant as to conceal the roots which still remain. The soul does not cease to feel that something is lacking or remaining to be done and this feeling keeps it from fully enjoying the alleviation. It feels as though an enemy is within it who, although pacified and put to sleep, will awaken and cause trouble.

And this is true, for when a person feels safest, and least expects it, the purgation returns to engulf him in another degree more severe, dark, and piteous than the former and which lasts for another period of time, perhaps longer than the first. He thereby believes that his blessings are gone forever. That enjoyment of blessing that was his after the first trial, in which he thought he no longer had anything more to suffer, is not sufficient to prevent him from thinking in this second degree of anguish that now all is over and that the blessings formerly experienced will never more return. As I say, this strong conviction is caused by the actual apprehension of the spirit which annihilates within itself everything contrary to this conviction.

7. This is the reason the souls in purgatory suffer great doubts about whether they will ever leave and whether their afflictions will end. Although they habitually possess the three theological virtues (faith, hope, and charity), the actual feeling of the privation of God and of the afflictions does not permit them to enjoy the actual blessing and comfort of these virtues. Although they are aware that they love God, this gives them no consolation, because they think that God does not love them and that they are unworthy of His love. Because they see themselves deprived of Him and established in their own miseries, they feel that they truly bear within themselves every reason for being rejected and abhorred by God.

Thus, although a person suffering this purgation knows that he loves God and that he would give a thousand lives for Him (he would indeed, for souls undergoing these trials love God very earnestly), he finds no relief. This knowledge rather causes him deeper affliction. For in loving God so intensely that nothing else gives him concern, and aware of his own misery, he is unable to believe that God loves him. He believes that he neither has nor ever will have within himself anything deserving of God's love, but rather every reason for being abhorred not only by God but by every creature forever. He grieves to see within himself reasons for meriting rejection by Him Whom he so loves and longs for.

CHAPTER 8

Other afflictions that trouble the soul in this state.

1. Yet something else grieves and troubles a man in this state, and it is that, since this dark night impedes his faculties and affections, he cannot beseech God nor raise his mind and affection to Him. It seems as it did to Jeremias that God has placed a cloud in front of the soul so that its prayer might not pass through. [Lam. 3:44] That passage we already cited refers to this difficulty also: *He closed and locked my ways with square stones.* [Lam. 3:9] And if sometimes the soul does beseech God,

it does this with so little strength and fervor that it thinks God does not hear or pay any attention to it, as the prophet Jeremias also lamented: *when I cried out and entreated, He excluded my prayer.* [Lam. 3:8]

Indeed, this is not the time to speak with God, but the time to put one's mouth in the dust, as Jeremias says, that perhaps there might come some actual hope [Lam. 3:29], and the time to suffer this purgation patiently. God it is who is working now in the soul, and for this reason the soul can do nothing. Consequently, a person can neither pray vocally nor be attentive to spiritual matters, nor still less attend to temporal affairs and business. Furthermore, he frequently experiences such absorption and profound forgetfulness in the memory that long periods pass without his knowing what he did or thought about, and he knows not what he is doing or about to do, nor can he concentrate on the task at hand, even though he desires to.

2. Since this night not only purges the intellect of its light and the will of its affections, but also the memory of its discursive knowledge, it is fitting that the memory be annihilated in all things to fulfill what David said of this purgation: *I was annihilated and knew not.* [Ps. 72:22] David's unknowing refers to forgetfulness and a lack of knowledge in the memory. This abstraction and oblivion is caused by the interior recollection in which this contemplation absorbs the soul.

That the soul with its faculties be divinely tempered and prepared for the divine union of love, it must first be engulfed in this divine and dark spiritual light of contemplation, and thereby be withdrawn from all creature affections and apprehensions. The duration of this absorption is proportionate to the intensity of the contemplation. The more simply and purely the divine light strikes the soul, the more it darkens and empties and annihilates it in its particular apprehensions and affections concerning both earthly and heavenly things; and, also, the less simply and purely it shines, the less it deprives and darkens the soul.

It seems incredible that the brighter and purer the supernatural, divine light is, the darker it is for the soul; and that the less bright it is, the less dark it is to the soul. We can understand this truth clearly if we consider what we proved above from the teaching of the Philosopher: that the clearer and more evident supernatural things are in themselves, the darker they are to our intellects.

3. A comparison with natural light will illustrate this. We observe that the more a ray of sunlight shining through a window is void of dust particles, the less clearly it is seen, and that it is perceived more clearly when there are more dust particles in the air. The reason is that the light in itself is invisible and is rather the means by which the objects it strikes are seen; but it is also seen when it reflects on them. Were the light not to strike these objects, it would not be seen and neither would

they. As a result, if a ray of sunlight should enter through one window, traverse the room, and go out through another window without coming in contact with any object or dust particles on which it could reflect, the room would have no more light than previously, neither would the ray be visible. Instead, upon close observation one notes that there is more darkness where the ray is present, because it takes away and darkens some of the other light; and this ray is invisible as we said because there are no objects on which it can reflect.

4. This, precisely then, is what the divine ray of contemplation does. In striking the soul with its divine light, it surpasses the natural light and thereby darkens and deprives a man of all the natural affections and apprehensions he perceives by means of his natural light. It leaves an individual's spiritual and natural faculties not only in darkness, but in emptiness too. Leaving the soul thus empty and dark, the ray purges and illumines it with divine spiritual light, while the soul thinks it has no light and that it is in darkness, as illustrated in the case of the ray of sunlight which is invisible even in the middle of a room if the room is pure and void of any object on which the light may reflect. Yet when this spiritual light finds an object on which to shine, that is, when something is to be understood spiritually concerning perfection or imperfection, no matter how slight, or about a judgment on the truth or falsity of some matter, a man will understand more clearly than he did before he was in this darkness. And easily recognizing the imperfection which presents itself, a man grows conscious of the spiritual light he possesses; for the ray of light is dark and invisible until a hand or some other thing passes through it, and then both the object and the ray are recognized.

5. Since this light is so simple, so pure, and so general and is unaffected and unrestricted by any particular intelligible object, natural or divine, and since the faculties are empty and annihilated of all these apprehensions, the soul with universality and great facility perceives and penetrates anything earthly or heavenly presented to it. Hence the Apostle says that the spiritual man penetrates all things, even the deep things of God. [1 Cor. 2:10] What the Holy Spirit says through the Wise Man applies to this general and simple wisdom, that is, that it touches everywhere because of its purity [Wis. 7:24], because it is not particularized by any distinct object or affection.

And this is characteristic of the spirit purged and annihilated of all particular knowledge and affection: not finding satisfaction in anything, nor understanding anything in particular, and remaining in its emptiness and darkness, it embraces all things with great preparedness. And St. Paul's words are verified: *Nihil habentes, et omnia possidentes.*[1] [2 Cor. 6:10] Such poverty of spirit deserves this blessedness.

[1] Having nothing, yet possessing all things.

CHAPTER 9

Although this night darkens the spirit, it does so to give light.

1. It remains to be said, then, that even though this happy night darkens the spirit, it does so only to impart light concerning all things; and even though it humbles a person and reveals his miseries, it does so only to exalt him; and even though it impoverishes and empties him of all possessions and natural affection, it does so only that he may reach out divinely to the enjoyment of all earthly and heavenly things, with a general freedom of spirit in them all.

That elements be commingled with all natural compounds, they must be unaffected by any particular color, odor, or taste, and thus they can concur with all tastes, odors, and colors. Similarly, the spirit must be simple, pure, and naked as to all natural affections, actual and habitual, in order to be able to freely communicate in fullness of spirit with the divine wisdom, in which, on account of the soul's purity, the delights of all things are tasted in a certain eminent degree. Without this purgation the soul would be wholly unable to experience the satisfaction of all this abundance of spiritual delight. Only one attachment or one particular object to which the spirit is actually or habitually bound is enough to hinder the experience or reception of the delicate and intimate delight of the spirit of love which contains eminently in itself all delights.

2. Because of their one attachment to the food and fleshmeat they had tasted in Egypt [Ex. 16:3], the children of Israel were unable to get any taste out of the delicate bread of angels—the manna of the desert, which, as Scripture says, contained all savors and was changed to the taste each one desired. [Wis. 16:20–21] Similarly the spirit, still affected by some actual or habitual attachment or some particular knowledge or any other apprehension, is unable to taste the delights of the spirit of freedom.

The reason is that the affections, sentiments, and apprehensions of the perfect spirit, because they are divine, are of another sort and are so eminent and so different from the natural that their actual and habitual possession demands the annihilation and expulsion of the natural affections and apprehensions; for two contraries cannot coexist in one subject.

Hence, that the soul pass on to these grandeurs, this dark night of contemplation must necessarily annihilate it first and undo it in its lowly ways by putting it in darkness, dryness, conflict, and emptiness. For the light imparted to the soul is a most lofty divine light which transcends all natural light and which does not belong naturally to the intellect.

3. That the intellect reach union with the divine light and become

divine in the state of perfection, this dark contemplation must first purge and annihilate it of its natural light and bring it actually into obscurity. It is fitting that this darkness last as long as is necessary for the expulsion and annihilation of the intellect's habitual way of understanding which was a long time in use, and that the divine light and illumination take its place. Since that strength of understanding was natural to the intellect, the darkness it here suffers is profound, frightful, and extremely painful. This darkness seems to be substantial darkness, since it is felt in the deep substance of the spirit.

The affection of love which is bestowed in the divine union of love is also divine, and, consequently, very spiritual, subtle, delicate, and interior, exceeding every affection and feeling of the will and every appetite. The will, as a result, must be first purged and annihilated of all its affections and feelings in order to experience and taste through union of love this divine affection and delight, which is so sublime and which does not naturally belong to the will. The soul is left in a dryness and distress proportionate with its habitual natural affections (whether for divine or human things), so that every kind of demon may be debilitated, dried up, and tried in the fire of this divine contemplation, as when Tobias placed the fish heart in the fire [Tb. 6:8], and the soul may become pure and simple, with a palate purged and healthy and ready to experience the sublime and marvelous touches of divine love. After the expulsion of all actual and habitual obstacles, it will behold itself transformed in these divine touches.

4. Furthermore, in this union for which the dark night is a preparation, the soul in its communion with God must be endowed and filled with a certain glorious splendor embodying innumerable delights. These delights surpass all the abundance the soul can possess naturally, for nature, so weak and impure, cannot receive these delights, as Isaias says: *Eye has not seen, nor ear heard, nor has it entered the heart of man what He has prepared,* etc. [Is. 64:4] As a result the soul must first be set in emptiness and poverty of spirit and purged of every natural support, consolation, and apprehension, earthly and heavenly. Thus empty, it is truly poor in spirit and stripped of the old man, and thereby able to live that new and blessed life which is the state of union with God, attained by means of this night.

5. Extraneous to its common experience and natural knowledge, the soul will have a very abundant and delightful divine sentiment and knowledge of all divine and human things. It must then be refined and inured, as far as its common and natural experience goes (for the eyes by which it now views these things will be as different from those of the past as is spirit from sense and divine from human), and placed in terrible

anguish and distress by means of this purgative contemplation. And the memory must be abstracted from all agreeable and peaceful knowledge and feel interiorly alien to all things, in which it will seem that all things are different than before.

This night withdraws the spirit from its customary manner of experience to bring it to the divine experience which is foreign to every human way. It seems to the soul in this night that it is being carried out of itself by afflictions. At other times a man wonders if he is not being charmed, and he goes about with wonderment over what he sees and hears. Everything seems so very strange even though he is the same as always. The reason is that he is being made a stranger to his usual knowledge and experience of things so that annihilated in this respect he may be informed with the divine, which belongs more to the next life than to this.

6. A man suffers all these afflictive purgations of spirit that he may be reborn in the life of the spirit by means of this divine inflow, and through these sufferings the spirit of salvation is brought forth in fulfillment of the words of Isaias: *In your presence, O Lord, we have conceived and been in the pains of labor and have brought forth the spirit of salvation.* [Is. 26:17–18]

Moreover, the soul should leave aside all its former peace, because it is prepared by means of this contemplative night to attain inner peace, which is of such a quality and so delightful that, as the Church says, it surpasses all understanding. [3rd Sun. of Advent, Epis. Phil. 4:7] That peace was not truly peace, because it was clothed with many imperfections; although to the soul walking in delight it seemed to be peace. It seemed to be a twofold peace, sensory and spiritual, since the soul beheld within itself a spiritual abundance. This sensory and spiritual peace, since it is still imperfect, must first be purged; the soul's peace must be disturbed and taken away. In the passage we quoted to demonstrate the distress of this night, Jeremias felt disturbed and wept over his loss of peace: *My soul is withdrawn and removed from peace.* [Lam. 3:17]

7. This night is a painful disturbance involving many fears, imaginings, and struggles within a man. Due to the apprehension and feeling of his miseries, he suspects that he is lost and that his blessings are gone forever. The sorrow and moaning of his spirit is so deep that it turns into vehement spiritual roars and clamoring, and sometimes he pronounces them vocally and dissolves in tears (if he has the strength and power to do so); although such relief is less frequent.

David, one who also had experience of this trial, refers to it very clearly in one of the psalms: *I was very afflicted and humbled; I roared with the groaning of my heart.* [Ps. 37:9] This roaring embodies great suffering. Sometimes due to the sudden and piercing remembrance of his wretchedness, a man's roaring becomes so loud and his affections so surrounded by suffering and pain that I know not how to describe it save by the simile holy Job used while undergoing this very trial: *as the overflowing waters so is my roaring.* [Jb. 3:24] As the waters sometimes overflow in such a way that they inundate everything, this roaring and feeling so increases that in seeping through and flooding everything, it fills all one's deep affections and energies with indescribable spiritual anguish and suffering.

8. These are the effects produced in the soul by this night which enshrouds the hopes one has for the light of day. The prophet Job also proclaims: *In the night my mouth is pierced with sufferings, and they that feed upon me do not sleep.* [Jb. 30:17] The mouth refers to the will pierced through by these sufferings which neither sleep nor cease to tear the soul to shreds. For these doubts and fears that penetrate the soul are never at rest.

9. This war or combat is profound because the peace awaiting the soul must be exceedingly profound; and the spiritual suffering is intimate and penetrating because the love to be possessed by the soul will also be intimate and refined. The more intimate and highly finished the work must be, so the more intimate, careful, and pure must the labor be; and commensurate with the solidity of the edifice is the energy involved in the work. As Job says, the soul is withering within itself and its inmost parts boiling without any hope. [Jb. 30:16, 27]

Because in the state of perfection toward which it journeys by means of this purgative night, the soul must reach the possession and enjoyment of innumerable blessings of gifts and virtues in both its substance and its faculties, it must first in a general way feel a withdrawal, deprivation, emptiness, and poverty regarding these blessings. And a person must be brought to think that he is far removed from them, and become so convinced that no one can persuade him otherwise or make him believe anything but that his blessings have come to an end. Jeremias points this out when he says in the passage already cited: *I have forgotten good things.* [Lam. 3:17]

10. Let us examine now why this light of contemplation, which is so gentle and agreeable and which is the same light to which the soul must be united and in which it will find all its blessings in the desired state of perfection, produces such painful and disagreeable effects when in these initial stages it shines upon the soul.

11. We can answer this question easily by repeating what we already explained in part; that is, there is nothing in contemplation or the divine inflow which of itself can give pain, contemplation rather bestows sweet-

ness and delight. The cause for not experiencing these agreeable effects is the soul's weakness and imperfection at the time, its inadequate preparation, and the qualities it possesses which are contrary to this light. Because of these the soul has to suffer when the divine light shines upon it.

CHAPTER 10

Explains this purgation thoroughly by means of a comparison.

1. For the sake of further clarity in this matter, we ought to note that this purgative and loving knowledge or divine light we are speaking of, has the same effect on a soul that fire has on a log of wood. The soul is purged and prepared for union with the divine light just as the wood is prepared for transformation into the fire. Fire, when applied to wood, first dehumidifies it, dispelling all moisture and making it give off any water it contains. Then it gradually turns the wood black, makes it dark and ugly, and even causes it to emit a bad odor. By drying out the wood, the fire brings to light and expels all those ugly and dark accidents which are contrary to fire. Finally, by heating and enkindling it from without, the fire transforms the wood into itself and makes it as beautiful as it is itself. Once transformed, the wood no longer has any activity or passivity of its own, except for its weight and its quantity which is denser than the fire. For it possesses the properties and performs the actions of fire: it is dry and it dries; it is hot and it gives off heat; it is brilliant and it illumines; and it is also light, much lighter than before. It is the fire that produces all these properties in the wood.

2. Similarly, we should philosophize about this divine, loving fire of contemplation. Before transforming the soul, it purges it of all contrary qualities. It produces blackness and darkness and brings to the fore the soul's ugliness; thus the soul seems worse than before and unsightly and abominable. This divine purge stirs up all the foul and vicious humors of which the soul was never before aware; never did it realize there was so much evil in itself, since these humors were so deeply rooted. And now that they may be expelled and annihilated they are brought to light and seen clearly through the illumination of this dark light of divine contemplation. Although the soul is no worse than before, neither in itself nor in its relationship with God, it feels undoubtedly so bad as to be not only unworthy that God should see it but deserving of His abhorrence; in fact, it feels that God now does abhor it.

This comparison illustrates many of the things we have been saying and shall say.

3. First, we can understand that the very loving light and wisdom into which the soul will be transformed is that which in the beginning purges and prepares it, just as the fire which transforms the wood by incorporating it into itself is that which was first preparing it for this transformation.

4. Second, we discern that the experience of these sufferings does not derive from this wisdom—for as the Wise Man says: *All good things come to the soul together with her* [Wis. 7:11]—but from the soul's own weakness and imperfection. Without this purgation it cannot receive the divine light, sweetness, and delight of wisdom, just as the log of wood until prepared cannot be transformed by the fire that is applied to it. And this is why the soul suffers so intensely. Ecclesiasticus confirms our assertion by telling what he suffered in order to be united with wisdom and enjoy it: *My soul wrestled for her, and my entrails were disturbed in acquiring her; therefore shall I possess a good possession.* [Ecclus. 51:25, 29]

5. Third, we can infer the manner in which souls suffer in purgatory. The fire, when applied, would be powerless over them, if they did not have imperfections from which to suffer. These imperfections are the fuel which catches on fire, and once they are gone there is nothing left to burn. So it is here on earth; when the imperfections are gone, the soul's suffering terminates, and joy remains.

6. Fourth, we deduce that as the soul is purged and purified by this fire of love, it is further enkindled in love, just as the wood becomes hotter as the fire prepares it. A person, however, does not always feel this enkindling of love. But sometimes the contemplation shines less forcibly that he may have the opportunity to observe and even rejoice over the work being achieved, for then these good effects are revealed. It is as though one were to stop work and take the iron out of the forge to observe what is being accomplished. Thus the soul is able to perceive the good of which it was unaware while the work was proceeding. So too, when the flame stops acting upon the wood, there is a chance to see how much it has enkindled it.

7. Fifth, we can also gather from this comparison why, as we previously mentioned, the soul after this alleviation suffers again, more intensely and inwardly than before. After that manifestation and after a more exterior purification of imperfections, the fire of love returns to act more interiorly on the consumable matter of which the soul must be purified. The suffering of the soul becomes more intimate, subtle, and spiritual in proportion to the inwardness, subtlety, spirituality, and deep-rootedness of the imperfections which are removed. This more interior purgation resembles the action of fire upon wood: As the fire penetrates more

deeply into the wood its action becomes stronger and more vehement, preparing the innermost part in order to gain possession of it.

8. Sixth, we discover the reason it seems to the soul that all blessings are past and that it is full of evil. For at this time it is conscious of nothing but its own bitterness; just as in the example of the wood, for neither the air nor anything else gives it more than a consuming fire. Yet, when other manifestations like the previous are made, the soul's joy will be more interior because of the more intimate purification.

9. Seventh, we deduce that when the purification is soon to return, even though the soul's joy is ample during these intervals (so much so that it sometimes seems, as we pointed out, that the bitterness will never recur), there is a feeling, if it adverts (and sometimes it cannot help adverting), that some root remains. And this advertence does not allow complete joy, for it seems that the purification is threatening to assail it again. And when the soul does have this feeling, the purification soon returns. Finally, that more inward part still to be purged and illumined cannot be completely concealed by the portion already purified, just as there is a very perceptible difference between that inmost part of the wood still to be illumined and that which is already purged. When this purification returns to attack more interiorly, it is no wonder that once again the soul thinks all its good has come to an end and that its blessings are over. Placed in these more interior sufferings, it is blinded as to all exterior good.

10. With this example in mind as well as the explanation of verse 1 of the first stanza concerning this dark night and its terrible properties, it will be a good thing to leave these sad experiences and begin now to discuss the fruit of the soul's tears and the happy traits about which it begins to sing in this second verse:

Fired with love's urgent longings

CHAPTER 11

The beginning of an explanation of verse 2 of the first stanza. Tells how the fruit of these dark straits is a vehement passion of divine love.

1. In this second verse the soul refers to the fire of love which, like material fire acting on wood, penetrates it in this night of painful contemplation. Although this enkindling of love we are now discussing is in some way similar to that which occurs in the sensory part of the soul, it is as different from it in another way as is the soul from the body or the spiritual part from the sensory part. For this enkindling of love occurs in

the spirit and through it the soul in the midst of these dark conflicts feels vividly and keenly that it is being wounded by a strong divine love, and it has a certain feeling and foretaste of God. Yet it understands nothing in particular, for as we said the intellect is in darkness.

2. The spirit herein experiences an impassioned and intense love, because this spiritual inflaming engenders the passion of love. Since this love is infused, it is more passive than active and thus generates in the soul a strong passion of love. This love is now beginning to possess something of union with God and thereby shares to a certain extent in its properties. These properties are actions of God more than of the soul and they reside in it passively, although the soul does give its consent. But only the love of God which is being united to the soul imparts the heat, strength, temper, and passion of love, or fire, as the soul terms it here. This love finds that the soul is equipped to receive the wound and union in the measure that all its appetites are brought into subjection, alienated, incapacitated, and unable to be satisfied by any heavenly or earthly thing.

3. This happens very particularly in this dark purgation, as was said, since God so weans and recollects the appetites that they cannot find satisfaction in any of their objects. God proceeds thus so that by withdrawing the appetites from other objects and recollecting them in Himself, He strengthens the soul and gives it the capacity for this strong union of love, which He begins to accord by means of this purgation. In this union the soul will love God intensely with all its strength and all its sensory and spiritual appetites. Such love is impossible if these appetites are scattered by their satisfaction in other things. In order to receive the strength of this union of love, David proclaimed to God: *I will keep my strength for You* [Ps. 58:10], that is, all the ability, appetites, and strength of my faculties, by not desiring to make use of them or find satisfaction in anything outside of You.

4. One might, then, in a certain way ponder how remarkable and how strong this enkindling of love in the spirit can be. God gathers together all the strength, faculties, and appetites of the soul, spiritual and sensory alike, that the energy and power of this whole harmonious composite may be employed in this love. The soul consequently arrives at the true fulfillment of the first commandment which, neither disdaining anything human nor excluding it from this love, states: *You shall love your God with your whole heart and with your whole mind and with your whole soul and with all your strength.* [Dt. 6:5]

5. When the soul is wounded, touched, and impassioned, all its strength and its appetites are recollected in this burning of love. How will we be able to understand the movements and impulses of all this strength and these appetites? They are aroused when the soul becomes

aware of the fire and wound of this forceful love and still neither possesses it nor gets satisfaction from it, but remains in darkness and doubt. Doubtless, suffering hunger like dogs, as David says, these souls wander about the city and howl and sigh because they are not filled with this love. [Ps. 58:7, 15–16]

The touch of this divine love and fire so dries up the spirit and so enkindles the soul's longings to slake its thirst for this love that a person will go over these longings in his mind a thousand times and pine for God in a thousand ways. David expresses this state very well in a psalm: *My soul thirsts for You; in how many ways does my flesh long for You* [Ps. 62:2], that is, in its desires. And another translation puts it this way: *My soul thirsts for You, my soul loses itself or dies for You.*

6. As a result the soul proclaims in this verse: fired "with love's urgent longings," and not, "with an urgent longing of love." In all its thoughts and in all its business and in all events, it loves in many ways and desires and also suffers in its desire in many ways, and at all times and in many places. It finds rest in nothing, for it feels this anxiety in the burning wound, as the prophet Job explains: *As the hart desires the shade and as the hireling desires the end of his work, so have I had empty months and numbered to myself long and wearisome nights. If I lie down to sleep I shall say: When will I arise? And then I will await the evening and will be filled with sorrows until the darkness of the night.* [Jb. 7:2–4]

Everything becomes narrow for this soul: there is no room for it within itself, neither is there any room for it in heaven or on earth; and it is filled with sorrows unto darkness, as Job says speaking spiritually and from our point of view. This affliction the soul undergoes here is a suffering unaccompanied by the comfort of certain hope for some spiritual light and good.

7. A man's anxiety and affliction in this burning of love is more intense because it is doubly increased: first, through the spiritual darknesses in which he is engulfed and which afflict him with doubts and fears; second, through the love of God which inflames and stimulates and wondrously stirs him with a loving wound. Isaias clearly explains these two ways of suffering in this state when he says: *My soul desired You in the night* [Is. 26:9], that is, in the midst of misery. This is the one way of suffering in this dark night. *Yet within my spirit,* he says, *until the morning I will watch to You.* [Is. 26:9] And this is the second way of suffering: with desire and anxiety of love in the innermost parts of the spirit. Nonetheless, in the midst of these dark and loving afflictions, the soul feels the presence of someone and an interior strength which so fortifies and accompanies it that when this weight of anxious darkness passes, it often feels alone, empty, and weak. The reason is that since the strength

and efficacy of the dark fire of love which assails it is communicated and impressed upon it passively, the darkness, strength, and warmth of love ceases when the assault terminates.

CHAPTER 12

The resemblance of this frightful night to purgatory. How the divine wisdom illumines men who suffer this night on earth by the same illumination with which He illumines and purges the angels in heaven.

1. We can therefore understand that just as this dark night of loving fire purges in darkness it also inflames the soul in darkness. We can also note that as the spirits in the other life are purged with a dark material fire, so in this life souls are purged and cleansed with a dark, loving spiritual fire. For such is the difference: Souls are cleansed in the other life by fire, but here on earth they are cleansed and illumined by love. David asked for this love when he said: *Cor mundum crea in me Deus*, etc.[2] [Ps. 50:12] Purity of heart is nothing less than the love and grace of God. The clean of heart are called blessed by our Saviour [Mt. 5:8], and to call them blessed is equivalent to saying they are taken with love, for blessedness is derived from nothing else but love.

2. Jeremias shows clearly that the soul is purged by the illumination of this fire of loving wisdom (for God never bestows mystical wisdom without love, since love itself infuses it) where he says: *He sent fire into my bones and instructed me.* [Lam. 1:13] And David says that *God's wisdom is silver tried in the fire* [Ps. 11:7], that is, in the purgative fire of love. This contemplation infuses both love and wisdom in each soul according to its capacity and necessity. It illumines the soul and purges it of its ignorances, as the Wise Man declares it did to him.

3. Another deduction is that this very wisdom of God, which purges and illumines these souls, purges the angels of their ignorances and gives them understanding by illumining them on matters they are ignorant of. This wisdom descends from God through the first hierarchies unto the last, and from these last unto men. It is rightly and truly said in Scripture that all the works of the angels and the inspirations they impart are also accomplished or granted by God. For ordinarily these works and inspirations are derived from God by means of the angels, and the angels also in turn give them one to another without delay. This communication is like that of a ray of sunlight shining through many windows placed one after the other. Although it is true that of itself the

2 A clean heart create for me, O God.

ray of light passes through them all, nevertheless each window communicates this light to the other with a certain modification according to its own quality. The communication is more or less intense insofar as the window is closer to or farther from the sun.

4. Consequently, the nearer the higher spirits (and those that follow) are to God, the more purged and clarified they are by a more general purification; the last spirits will receive a fainter and more remote illumination. Man, the last one to whom this loving contemplation of God is communicated, when God so desires, must receive it according to his own mode, which is limited and painful.

God's light, which illumines the angels by clarifying and giving them the savor of love—for they are pure spirits prepared for this inflow—illumines man, as we said, by darkening him and giving him pain and anguish, since naturally he is impure and feeble. This communication affects him as sunlight affects the sick and bleared eye. This very fire of love enamors a man impassionedly and afflictively until it spiritualizes and refines him through purification, and he becomes capable of the tranquil reception of this loving inflow, as are the angels and those already purified. With the Lord's help we will explain this state later. In the meanwhile, however, the soul receives this contemplation and loving knowledge in distress and longing of love.

5. The soul does not always feel this inflaming and urgent longing of love. In the beginning of the spiritual purgation, the divine fire spends itself in drying out and preparing the wood—that is, the soul —rather than in heating it. Yet as time passes and the fire begins to give off heat, the soul usually experiences the burning and warmth of love. As the intellect becomes more purged by means of this darkness, it happens sometimes that this mystical and loving theology besides inflaming the will also wounds the intellect, by illumining it with some knowledge and light, so delightfully and delicately that the will is thereby marvelously enkindled in fervor. This divine fire burns in the will— while the will remains passive—like a living flame and in such a way that this love now seems to be a live fire because of the living knowledge communicated. David says in the psalm: *My heart grew hot within me and a certain fire was enkindled while I was knowing.* [Ps. 38:4]

6. This enkindling of love and the union of these two faculties, the intellect and the will, is something immensely rich and delightful for the soul, because it is a certain touch of the divinity and already the beginning of the perfection of the union of love for which the soul hopes. Thus one does not receive this touch of so sublime an experience and love of God without having suffered many trials and a great part of the

purgation. But so extensive a purgation is not required for other inferior and more common touches.

7. You may deduce from our explanation that when God infuses these spiritual goods the will can very easily love without the intellect understanding, just as the intellect can know without the will loving. Since this dark night of contemplation consists of divine light and love—just as fire gives off both light and heat—it is not incongruous that this loving light, when communicated, sometimes acts more upon the will through the fire of love and leaves the intellect in darkness by not wounding it with light, or that at other times it illumines the intellect with understanding and leaves the will in dryness. All of this is similar to feeling the warmth of fire without seeing its light or seeing the light without feeling the fire's heat. The Lord works in this way because He infuses contemplation as He wills.

Chapter 13

Other delightful effects of this dark night of contemplation in the soul.

1. Through this inflaming of love we can understand some of the delightful effects this dark night of contemplation now gradually produces in the soul. Sometimes, as we said, it illumines in the midst of these darknesses, and the light shines in the darkness [Jn. 1:5], serenely communicating this mystical knowledge to the intellect and leaving the will in dryness, that is, without the actual union of love. The serenity is so delicate and delightful to the feeling of the soul that it is ineffable. This experience of God is felt now in one way and now in another.

2. Sometimes, as we said, this contemplation acts upon the intellect and will together and sublimely, tenderly, and forcibly enkindles love. We already pointed out that once the intellect is more purged these two faculties are sometimes united; and in the measure that they are both purged, this union becomes so much more perfect and deeper in quality. Yet before reaching this degree, it is more common to experience the touch of burning in the will than the touch of understanding in the intellect.

3. A question arises here: Why does one in the beginning more commonly experience in the purgative contemplation an inflaming of love in the will rather than understanding in the intellect, since these two faculties are equally being purged?

We may answer that this passive love does not act upon the will directly because the will is free, and that this burning of love is more the passion of love than a free act of the will. The warmth of love

wounds the substance of the soul and thus moves the affections passively. As a result the enkindling of love is called the passion of love
rather than a free act of the will. An act of the will is such only insofar
as it is free. Yet, since these passions and affections bear a relation to the
will, it is said that if the soul is impassioned with some affection, the
will is. This is true, because the will thus becomes captive and loses its
freedom, carried away by the impetus and force of the passion. As
a result we say that this enkindling of love takes place in the will, that
is, the appetites of the will are enkindled. This enkindling is called the
passion of love rather than the free exercise of the will. Since only the
receptive capacity of the intellect can take in the naked and passive
knowledge and since the intellect, unless purged, cannot receive this
knowledge, the soul, prior to the purgation of the intellect, experiences
the touch of knowledge less frequently than the passion of love. For to
feel the passion of love, it is unnecessary that the will be so purged in
relation to the passions; the passions even help it experience impassioned
love.

4. Since this fire and thirst of love is spiritual, it is far different from
the other enkindling of love we discussed in the night of the senses.
Although the senses share in this love, because they do not fail to
participate in the work of the spirit, the root and keenness of the thirst
is felt in the higher part of the soul. The spirit so feels and understands
what it experiences and the lack which this desire causes in it that all
the suffering of sense—even though incomparably greater than that of
the night of senses—is nothing in comparison to this spiritual suffering.
For the soul is conscious deeply within itself of the lack of an immense
and incomparable good.

5. We ought to point out that the burning of love is not felt at
the beginning of this spiritual night because the fire of love has not
begun to catch. Nevertheless, God gives from the outset an esteeming
love of Himself, so intense that, as we said, the soul's greatest suffering
in the trials of this night is the anguish of thinking it has lost God and
been abandoned by Him. We can always assert, then, that from the
commencement of this night the soul is touched with urgent longings of
love; of esteeming love, sometimes, at other times also of burning love.
Seemingly the greatest suffering the soul experiences in these trials
is this fear. If a man could be assured that all is not over and lost but
that what he suffers is for the better—as indeed it is—and that God is
not angry with him, he would be unconcerned about all these sufferings,
rather he would rejoice in the knowledge that God is pleased with them.
His love of esteem for God is so intense, even though obscure and
imperceptible, that he would be happy not only to suffer these things
but even die many times in order to please Him. When the fire now

inflames the soul together with the esteem of God already possessed, an individual usually acquires such strength, courage, and longing relative to God, through the warmth of the love which is being communicated, that with singular boldness he would do strange things, in whatever way necessary, in order to encounter Him Whom he loves. Because of the strength and inebriation of his love and desire, he would perform these actions without any considerations or concerns.

6. Mary Magdalen, in spite of her past, paid no heed to the crowds of men, prominent as well as unknown, at the banquet. She did not consider the opportuneness of weeping and shedding tears in the presence of our Lord's guests. Her only concern was to reach Him, for Whom her soul was already wounded and on fire, without any delay and without waiting for another more appropriate time. [Lk. 7:37–38] And such is the inebriation and courage of love: knowing that her Beloved was shut up in the tomb by a huge sealed rock and surrounded by guards so that the disciples could not steal His body, she did not permit this to keep her from going out with ointments before daybreak to anoint Him. [Mt. 27:64–66; Mk. 16:1–2]

7. Finally, this inebriation and urgent longing of love prompted her to ask the man she thought was gardener if he had stolen Him and, that if he had, to tell her where he put Him so that she could take Him away. [Jn. 20:15] She did not stop to realize that her question in the light of sound judgment was foolish, for obviously if he had stolen the Lord he would not have told her, and still less would he have allowed her to take Him away.

The strength and vehemence of love has this trait: Everything seems possible to it and it believes everyone is occupied as it is; it does not believe anyone could be employed in any other way or seek anyone other than Him Whom it seeks and loves; it believes there is nothing else to desire or to occupy it and that everyone is engaged in seeking and loving Him. When the bride went searching for her Beloved in the plazas and suburbs, she thought that others were doing the same and told them that if they found Him they should inform Him that she was suffering for love of Him. [Ct. 3:2; 5:8] Mary's love was so ardent that she thought she would go and take Him away, however great the impediments, if the gardener would tell where He was hidden.

8. Such are the traits of these longings of love which the soul experiences when it is advanced in this spiritual purgation. The wounded soul rises up at night, in this purgative darkness, according to the affections of the will; as the lioness or she-bear that goes in search of her cubs when they are taken away and cannot be found, it anxiously and forcibly goes out in search of its God. Since it is immersed in

darkness, it feels His absence and that it is dying with love of Him. Such is impatient love, which one cannot long endure without either receiving its object or dying. Rachel bore this love for children when she said: *Give me children, otherwise I will die.* [Gn. 30:1]

9. It should be explained here why, even though the soul feels as miserable and unworthy of God as it does in these purgative darknesses, it possesses an energy bold enough to go out to be joined with God.

The reason is that since love now imparts a force by which the soul loves authentically, and since it is the nature of love to seek to be united, joined, equaled, and assimilated to the loved object in order to be perfected in the good of love, the soul hungers and thirsts for this union or perfection of love still unattained. And the strength love has now bestowed, and by which the will has become impassioned, makes this inflamed will daring. Since the intellect is not illumined but in darkness, the soul feels unworthy and knows that it is miserable.

10. I do not want to fail to explain why this divine light, even though it is always light for the soul, does not illumine immediately upon striking as it will afterwards, but instead causes trials and darknesses.

We already said something on this matter. Yet, we may reply particularly that the darknesses and evils the soul experiences when this light strikes are not darknesses and evils of the light but of the soul itself. And it is this light which illumines it so it may see these evils. From the beginning the divine light illumines the soul; yet at the outset it can only see through this light what is nearest—or rather within—itself, namely, its own darknesses and miseries. It sees these by the mercy of God, and it did not see them before because this supernatural light did not shine in it. Accordingly, it only feels darknesses and evils at the outset. After being purged through the knowledge and feeling of these darknesses and evils, it will have eyes capable of the vision of the goods of the divine light. Once all these darknesses and imperfections are expelled, it seems that the immense benefits and goods the soul is acquiring in this happy night of contemplation begin to appear.

11. It is clear, consequently, how God grants the soul a favor by cleansing and curing it. He cleanses it with a strong lye and a bitter purge in its sensory and spiritual parts of all imperfect affections and habits relative to temporal, natural, sensory, and spiritual things, by darkening the interior faculties and emptying them of all these objects, and by restraining and drying up the sensory and spiritual affections and weakening and refining the natural forces of the soul with respect to these things. A man would never have been able to accomplish this work himself, as we shall soon explain. Accordingly, God makes the soul die to all that He is not, so that when it is stripped and flayed of its

old skin, He may clothe it anew. Its youth is renewed like the eagle's [Ps. 102:5], clothed in the new man which is created, as the Apostle says, according to God. [Eph. 4:24] This renovation is: an illumination of the human intellect with supernatural light so that it becomes divine, united with the divine; an informing of the will with love of God so that it is no longer less than divine and loves in no other way than divinely, united and made one with the divine will and love; and also a divine conversion and change of the memory, the affections, and the appetites according to God. And thus this soul will be a soul of heaven, heavenly and more divine than human.

As we have gradually seen, God accomplishes all this work in the soul by illumining it and firing it divinely with love's urgent longing for God alone. Rightly and reasonably does the soul add the third verse of the canticle:

—Ah, the sheer grace!—

CHAPTER 14

An explanation of the three last verses of the first stanza.

1. This sheer grace resulted from what is expressed in the following verses:

> I went out unseen,
> My house being now all stilled;

We have the metaphor of one who in order to execute his plan better, and without hindrance, goes out at night, in darkness, when everybody in the house is sleeping.

The soul had to go out to accomplish so heroic and rare a feat— to be united with its divine Beloved outside—because the Beloved is not found except alone, outside, and in solitude. The bride accordingly desired to find Him alone, saying: *Who will give you to me, my brother, that I may find you alone outside and communicate to you my love.* [Ct. 8:1] The enamored soul must leave its house, then, in order to reach its desired goal. It must go out at night when all the members of its house are asleep, that is: when the lower operations, passions, and appetites of its soul are put to sleep or quelled by means of this night. These are the people of its household who when awake are a continual hindrance to the reception of any good and hostile to the soul's departure in freedom from them. Our Saviour declares that a man's enemies are those of his own household. [Mt. 10:36] The operations and movements of these members had to be put to sleep in order not to keep the soul from receiving the supernatural goods of the union of love of God, for this union cannot be wrought while they are awake and active. All the soul's natural activity hinders rather than helps it to receive the spiritual goods of the union of love. All natural ability is insufficient to produce the supernatural goods which God alone infuses in the soul passively, secretly, and in silence. All the faculties must receive this infusion, and in order to do so, they must be passive and not interfere through their own lowly activity and vile inclinations.

2. It was a sheer grace for this soul that God in this night put to sleep all the members of its household, that is: all the faculties, passions, affections, and appetites which live in its sensory and spiritual parts. God put them to sleep to enable the soul to go out to the spiritual union of the perfect love of God without being seen, that is, without the hindrance of these affections, etc. For these members of the household are put to sleep and mortified in this night, which leaves them in darkness, that they may not be able to observe or experience anything in their lowly, natural way which would impede the soul's departure from itself and the house of the senses.

3. Oh what a sheer grace it is for the soul to be freed from the house of its senses! This fortune, in my opinion, can only be understood by the man who has savored it. For then a person will become clearly aware of the wretched servitude and the many miseries he suffered when he was subject to the activity of his faculties and appetites. He will understand how the life of the spirit is true freedom and wealth and embodies inestimable goods. In the following stanzas we will specify some of these goods and see more clearly how right the soul is in singing about the journey through this horrendous night as being a great grace.

CHAPTER 15

Second Stanza

In darkness, and secure,
By the secret ladder, disguised,
—Ah, the sheer grace!—
In darkness and concealment,
My house being now all stilled;

EXPLANATION

1. The soul in its song continues to recount some of the properties of the darkness of this night and mentions again the happiness resulting from them. It speaks of these traits in response to a certain tacit

objection. It says that we should not think a person runs a more serious risk of being lost because of the torments of anguish, the doubts, the fears, and the horrors of this night and darkness, for rather a man is saved in the darkness of this night. In this night the soul subtly escapes from its enemies, who were always opposed to its departure. In its journey in the darkness of this night its garb is changed and thus it is disguised by three differently colored garments, which we shall discuss later; and it departs by a very secret ladder of which no one in the house knows. This ladder, as we will also explain, is the living faith by which it departs in so concealed a way in order to carry out its plan successfully, and by which it cannot but escape very securely. The soul is particularly secure in this purgative night because its appetites, affections, and passions, etc. were put to sleep, mortified, and deadened. These are the members of the household that when awake and alive would not consent to this departure.

The following verse then states:

In darkness, and secure,

Chapter 16

An explanation of how the soul is secure when it walks in darkness.

1. We already said that the darkness the soul mentions here relates to the sensory, the interior, and the spiritual appetites and faculties, because this night darkens their natural light so that through the purgation of this light they may be illumined supernaturally. It puts the sensory and spiritual appetites to sleep, deadens them, and deprives them of the ability to find pleasure in anything. It binds the imagination and impedes it from doing any good discursive work. It makes the memory cease, the intellect become dark and unable to understand anything, and hence it causes the will also to become arid and constrained, and all the faculties empty and useless. And over all this hangs a dense and burdensome cloud which afflicts the soul and keeps it withdrawn from God. As a result it asserts that in darkness it walked securely.

2. The reason for this security has been clearly explained. Usually a soul never strays except through its appetites, or its gratifications, or its discursive meditation, or through its knowledge or affections. By these, a man usually fails through excess or defect, or he changes because of them or goes astray, or experiences inordinate inclinations. Once all these operations and movements are impeded, he is obviously freed of error in them, because he is not only liberated from himself but also from his other enemies, the world and the devil. The world and

the devil have no other means of warring against the soul when its affections and operations are deadened.

3. In the measure that the soul walks in darkness and emptiness in its natural operations, it walks securely. As the prophet says, the soul's perdition comes only from itself (from its senses and interior and sensory appetites); and its good, says God, comes only from Me. [Os. 13:9] Since the soul's evils are thus impeded, only the goods of union with God are imparted to the appetites and faculties; these appetites and faculties become divine and heavenly in this union. If a person at the time of these darknesses observes closely, he will see clearly how little the appetites and faculties are distracted with useless and harmful things and how secure he is from vainglory, from pride and presumption, from an empty and false joy, and from many other evils. By walking in darkness the soul not only avoids going astray but advances rapidly, because it thus gains the virtues.

4. A question immediately arises here: Since the things of God in themselves produce good, profit, and assurance in the soul, why does God in this night darken the appetites and faculties so that they derive no satisfaction in these good things and find it difficult to be occupied with them—in some ways even more difficult than to be occupied with other things?

The answer is that at this time there should not be any activity or satisfaction relative to spiritual objects, because the soul's faculties and appetites are impure, lowly, and very natural. And even if God were to give these faculties the activity and delight of supernatural, divine things, they would be unable to receive it except in their own way, very basely and naturally. As the philosopher says, whatever is received is received according to the mode of the receiver.

Since these natural faculties do not have the purity, strength, or capacity to receive and taste supernatural things in a supernatural or divine mode, but only according to their own mode which is human and lowly, as we said, these faculties must also be darkened regarding the divine so that weaned, purged, and annihilated in their natural way they might lose that lowly and human mode of receiving and working. Thus all these faculties and appetites of the soul are tempered and prepared for the sublime reception, experience, and savor of the divine and supernatural, which is unreceivable until the old man dies.

5. Consequently, if all spiritual communication does not come from on high, from the Father of lights, from above the free will and human appetite [Jas. 1:17], man will not taste it divinely and spiritually but rather humanly and naturally, no matter how much his faculties are employed in God and no matter how much satisfaction he derives

from this. For goods do not go from man to God, but they come from God to man.

Here we could explain, if this were the place, how many persons have numerous inclinations toward God and spiritual things, employ their faculties in them, derive great satisfaction by so doing, and think their actions and appetites are supernatural and spiritual, when perhaps they are no more than natural and human. Because of a certain natural facility they have for moving the appetites and faculties toward any object at all, their activity with spiritual things and the satisfaction they derive are the same as with other things.

6. If by chance the opportunity arises we will give some signs for recognizing when the movements and interior actions of the soul in its communion with God are only natural and when only spiritual, and when they are both natural and spiritual. Here it is sufficient to know that if the soul in its interior acts is to be moved by God divinely, it must first be obscured, put to sleep, and pacified in regard to its natural ability and operations so that these operations might weaken.

7. Oh, then, spiritual soul, when you see your appetites darkened, your inclinations dry and constrained, your faculties incapacitated for any interior exercise, do not be afflicted; think of this as a grace, since God is freeing you from yourself and taking from you your own activity. However well your actions may have succeeded you did not work so completely, perfectly, and securely—owing to their impurity and awkwardness—as you do now that God takes you by the hand and guides you in darkness, as though you were blind, along a way and to a place you know not. You would never have succeeded in reaching this place no matter how good your eyes and your feet.

8. Another reason the soul not only advances securely when it walks in darkness but even gains and profits is that when in a new way it receives some betterment, it usually does so in a manner it least understands, and thus ordinarily thinks it is getting lost. Since it has never possessed this new experience which makes it go out, blinds it, and leads it astray with respect to its first method of procedure, it thinks it is getting lost rather than marching on successfully and profitably; indeed, it is getting lost to what it knew and tasted, and going by a way in which it neither tastes nor knows.

To reach a new and unknown land and travel unknown roads, a man cannot be guided by his own knowledge, rather he has doubts about his own knowledge and seeks the guidance of others. Obviously he cannot reach new territory nor attain this added knowledge if he does not take these new and unknown roads and abandon those familiar ones. Similarly, when a person is learning new details about his art or trade, he must work in darkness and not with what he already knows. If he refuses to lay aside his former knowledge, he will never make any further progress. The soul, too, when it advances, walks in darkness and unknowing.

Since God, as we said, is the master and guide of the soul, this blind man, it can truly rejoice, now that it has come to understand as it has here, and say: in darkness, and secure.

9. There is another reason why the soul walks securely in these darknesses: it advances by suffering. Suffering is a surer and even more advantageous road than that of joy and action. First, in suffering God gives strength to the soul, whereas in its deeds and its joys it exercises its own weakness and imperfections. Second, in suffering, virtues are practiced and acquired and the soul is purified, made wiser and more cautious.

10. Another more basic reason why the soul walks securely in darkness is that this light or obscure wisdom so absorbs and engulfs it in the dark night of contemplation and brings it so near God that it protects and frees it from all that is not God. Since the soul as it were is undergoing a cure to regain its health, which is God Himself, His Majesty restricts it to a diet, to abstinence from all things, and causes it to lose its appetite for them all. This effect resembles the cure of a sick man esteemed by the members of his household: they keep him inside so that neither air nor light may harm him, and they try not to disturb him by the noise of footsteps or even their whisperings, and they give him a very delicate and limited food, a substantial rather than a tasty food.

11. Because dark contemplation brings the soul closer to God, it has all these characteristics; it safeguards and cares for the soul. Because of his weakness, a person feels thick darkness and more profound obscurity the closer he comes to God, just as he would feel greater darkness and pain, because of the weakness and impurity of his eyes, the closer he approached the immense brilliance of the sun. The spiritual light is so bright and so transcendent that it blinds and darkens the natural intellect as it approaches.

Accordingly, David says in Psalm 17 [Ps. 17:12] that God made *darkness his hiding place and covert, and dark waters in the clouds of the air His tabernacle round about him.* The dark water in the clouds of the air signifies dark contemplation and divine wisdom in these souls. When God is joining them closer to Himself they feel that this darkness is near Him as though it were a tabernacle in which He dwells. That which is light in God and of the loftiest clarity is dense darkness for the soul, as St. Paul affirms [1 Cor. 2:14] and as David points out immediately in the same psalm: *Because of the splendor encircling His presence, the clouds and cataracts came out* [Ps. 17:13], that is, they came out over the natural intellect, whose light, as Isaias says in Chapter 5, *obtenebrata est in caligine eius.*[3] [Is. 5:30]

12. Oh, what a miserable lot this life is! We live in the midst of so much danger and find it so hard to arrive at truth. The clearest and truest things are the darkest and most dubious to us and consequently we flee from what most suits us. We embrace what fills our eyes with the most light and satisfaction and run after what is the very worst thing for us, and we fall at every step. In how much danger and fear does man live, since the very light of his natural eyes which ought to be his guide is the first to deceive him in his journey to God and since he must keep his eyes shut and tread the path in darkness if he wants to be sure of where he is going and be safeguarded against the enemies of his house, his senses and faculties.

13. The soul, then, is well hidden and protected in this dark water—close to God. Since the dark water serves God Himself as a tabernacle and dwelling place, it will also serve the soul in this way, as a perfect safeguard and security, even though it causes darkness to it. In this darkness the soul is hidden and protected from itself and the harm of creatures.

David's assertion in another psalm is also applicable to these souls: *You will hide them in the secret of Your face from the disturbance of men. You will protect them in Your tabernacle from the contradiction of tongues.* [Ps. 30:21] This passage applies to every kind of protection. To be hidden in the face of God from the disturbance of men refers to the fortification this dark contemplation provides against all the occasions that may arise because of men. To receive protection in His tabernacle from the contradiction of tongues indicates the absorption of the soul in this dark water. This dark water is the tabernacle we said David mentions, in which the soul, with weaned appetites and affections and darkened faculties, is freed of all imperfections contradictory to the spirit, whether they originate with its own flesh or with other creatures. The soul can therefore truly say that its journey is in darkness, and secure.

14. There is another no less efficacious reason to help us understand clearly that this soul's journey is in darkness, and secure, that is, the fortitude this obscure, painful, and dark water of God bestows on the soul from the beginning. After all, even though it is dark, it is water, and thereby refreshes and fortifies the soul in what most suits it—although in darkness, and painfully.

From the outset a person is conscious of a true determination and power to do nothing it recognizes as an offense against God and to omit nothing which seems to be for His service. That dark love enkindles in

---

[3] is darkened with the mist thereof

the soul a remarkably vigilant care and interior solicitude about what to do or omit in order to please God. A man will ponder whether or not he may have angered God and go over this in his mind a thousand times. He does this with much greater care and solicitude than the previous concern we mentioned in discussing the yearnings of love. In this dark contemplation the soul's appetites, strength, and faculties are withdrawn from all other things, and its effort and strength is expended only in paying homage to God. This is the way it goes out from itself and from all created things to the sweet and delightful union with God through love: In darkness, and secure,

By the secret ladder, disguised,

CHAPTER 17

An explanation of the secrecy of this dark contemplation.

1. We ought to explain three properties of this night indicated in the three terms of this verse. Two of them, "secret" and "ladder" pertain to the dark night of contemplation now under discussion; the third, "disguised," refers to the soul and the way it conducts itself in this night.

Relative to the first two, it should be known that in this verse the soul calls dark contemplation, by which it goes out to the union of love, a "secret ladder" because of two properties that are found in it: it is secret, and it is a ladder. We will discuss them separately.

2. First, it calls this dark contemplation "secret" since, as we mentioned, contemplation is the mystical theology which theologians call secret wisdom and which St. Thomas says is communicated and infused into the soul through love. This communication is secret and dark to the work of the intellect and the other faculties. Insofar as these faculties do not acquire it but the Holy Spirit infuses it and puts it in order in the soul, as the bride says in the Canticle of Canticles [Ct. 2:4], the soul neither knows nor understands how this comes to pass and thus calls it secret. Indeed, not only does the soul fail to understand, but no one understands, not even the devil, since the Master who teaches the soul dwells within it substantially where neither the devil, the natural senses, nor the intellect can reach.

3. Not only because of this inability to understand contemplation is it called "secret" but also because of the effects it produces in the soul. The wisdom of love is not secret merely in the darknesses and straits of the soul's purgation (for the soul does not know how to describe it) but also afterwards in the illumination, when it is communicated more clearly. Even then it is so secret that it is ineffable. Not only does a man feel

unwilling to give expression to this wisdom, but he finds no adequate means or similitude to signify so sublime an understanding and delicate a spiritual feeling. Even if the soul should desire to convey this experience in words and think up many similitudes, the wisdom would always remain secret and still to be expressed.

Since this interior wisdom is so simple, general, and spiritual that in entering the intellect it is not clothed in any sensory species or image, the imaginative faculty cannot form an idea or picture of it in order to speak of it; this wisdom did not enter through these faculties nor did they behold any of its apparel or color. Yet the soul is clearly aware that it understands and tastes that delightful and wondrous wisdom. If a man were to behold an object never before seen in itself or in its likeness, he would be unable to describe it or give it a name no matter how much he tried, even though he does understand and find satisfaction in it. And if he should encounter such difficulty in describing what he perceives through the senses, how much greater difficulty he will have in expressing what does not enter through the senses. The language of God has this trait: Since it is very spiritual and intimate to the soul, transcending everything sensory, it immediately silences the entire ability and harmonious composite of the exterior and interior senses.

4. We have examples of this ineffability of the divine language in Sacred Scripture. Jeremias manifested his incapacity to describe it when, after God had spoken to him, he knew of nothing more to say than *ah, ah, ah.* [Jer. 1:6] Moses also declared before God, present in the burning bush, his interior inability (the inability of both his imagination and his exterior senses). [Ex. 4:10] He asserted that he was not only unable to speak of this converse but that he did not even dare consider it in his imagination, as is said in the Acts of the Apostles. [Acts 7:32] He believed that his imagination was not only as it were dumb in the matter of forming some image of what he understood in God, but also incapable of receiving this knowledge.

Since the wisdom of this contemplation is the language of God to the soul, of Pure Spirit to the spirit alone, all that is less than spirit such as the sensory, fails to perceive it. Consequently this wisdom is secret to the senses; they have neither the knowledge nor ability to speak of it, nor do they even desire to do so because it is beyond words.

5. We understand, then, why some persons who tread this road and desire to give an account of this experience to their director—for they are good and God-fearing—are unable to describe it. They feel great repugnance in speaking about it, especially when the contemplation is so simple that they are hardly aware of it. All they can manage to say is that they are satisfied, quiet, and content, and aware of God, and that

in their opinion all goes well. But the experience is ineffable, and one will hear from the soul no more than these general terms. It is a different matter when the communications the soul receives are particular, such as visions, feelings, etc. These communications are ordinarily received through some species in which the sense participates and which are describable through that species or a similar one. Yet pure contemplation is indescribable, as we said, and on this account called "secret."

6. Not for this reason alone do we call mystical wisdom "secret"— and it is actually so—but also because it has the characteristic of hiding the soul within itself. Besides its usual effect, this mystical wisdom will occasionally so engulf a person in its secret abyss that he will have the keen awareness of being brought into a place far removed from every creature. He will accordingly feel that he has been led into a remarkably deep and vast wilderness, unattainable by any human creature, into an immense, unbounded desert, the more delightful, savorous, and loving, the deeper, vaster, and more solitary it is. He is conscious of being so much the more hidden the more he is elevated above every temporal creature.

A man is so elevated and exalted by this abyss of wisdom, which leads it into the veins of the science of love, that he realizes that all the conditions of creatures in relation to this supreme knowing and divine experience are very base, and he perceives the lowliness, deficiency, and inadequacy of all the terms and words used in this life to deal with divine things. He will also note the impossibility, without the illumination of this mystical theology, of a knowledge or experience of these divine things as they are in themselves through any natural means, no matter how wisely or loftily one speaks of them. Beholding this truth—that it can neither grasp nor explain this wisdom—the soul rightly calls it secret.

7. This divine contemplation has the property of being secret and above one's natural capacity, not merely because it is supernatural, but also because it is the way which guides the soul to the perfections of union with God, toward which one must advance humanly by not knowing and divinely by ignorance, since they are not humanly knowable.

8. Speaking mystically, as we are here, the divine things and perfections are not known as they are in themselves while they are being sought and acquired, but when they are already found and acquired. Accordingly, the prophet Baruch speaks of this divine wisdom: *There is no one able to know her ways or think of her paths.* [Bar. 3:31] The royal prophet of this road also speaks of this kind of wisdom in his converse with God: *And your illuminations enlightened and illumined the entire world; the earth shook and trembled. Your way is in the sea and your paths are in many waters, and your footsteps shall not be known.*

[Ps. 76:19–20] Spiritually speaking, this passage refers to our subject. The lightning of God illumining the whole earth signifies the illumination this divine contemplation produces in the faculties of the soul; the shaking and trembling of the earth applies to the painful purgation it causes in the soul; and to assert that the way and road of God, by which the soul travels toward Him, is in the sea, and His footsteps in many waters, and thereby unknowable, is similar to stating that the way to God is as hidden and secret to the sensory part of the soul as are the footsteps of one walking on water imperceptible to the bodily senses. The traces and footsteps God leaves in those whom He desires to bring to Himself, by making them great in the union with His wisdom, are unrecognizable. In the Book of Job this fact is stressed in these words: *Do you perchance know the paths of the great clouds or the perfect sciences?* [Jb. 37:16] This passage refers to the ways and roads by which God exalts souls (here referred to by the clouds) and perfects them in His wisdom.

Consequently, this contemplation which is guiding the soul to God is secret wisdom.

CHAPTER 18

An explanation of how this secret wisdom is also a ladder.

1. The second characteristic has yet to be discussed, that is, of how this secret wisdom is also a ladder. It should be known that there are many reasons for calling this secret contemplation a ladder.

First, as one climbs a ladder to pillage the fortresses containing goods and treasures, so too, by this secret contemplation, the soul ascends in order to plunder, know, and possess the goods and treasures of heaven. The Royal Prophet points this out clearly in saying: *Blessed is the man who receives Your favor and help. In his heart he has prepared his ascent, in the vale of tears, in the place which he set. For in this way the Lord of the law will give a blessing, and they will go from virtue to virtue* (as from step to step) *and the God of gods will be seen on Sion.* [Ps. 83:6–8] (He is the treasure of the fortress of Sion, and this treasure is beatitude.)

2. We can also call this secret wisdom a "ladder" because as the same steps of a ladder are used for both ascent and descent, so also the same communications this secret contemplation produces in the soul extol it in God and humiliate it within itself. Communications which are truly from God have this trait: they simultaneously exalt and humble the soul. For on this road, to descend is to ascend and to ascend is to descend, since he who humbles himself is exalted and he who exalts himself is humbled.

[Lk. 14:11] Besides this (that the virtue of humility exalts), God usually makes the soul ascend by this ladder so that it might descend, and He makes it descend that it might ascend. Accordingly, the Wise Man's words are fulfilled: *Before the soul is exalted, it is humbled, and before it is humbled, it is exalted.* [Prv. 18:12]

3. Naturally speaking, and disregarding the spiritual which it does not understand, the soul, if it desires to pay close attention, will clearly recognize how on this road it suffers many ups and downs, and how immediately after prosperity some tempest and trial follows, so much so that seemingly that calm was given to forewarn and strengthen it against the future penury; it sees too how abundance and tranquillity succeed misery and torment, and in suchwise that it thinks it was made to fast before celebrating that feast.

This is the ordinary procedure in the state of contemplation until one arrives at quietude; the soul never remains in one state, but everything is ascent and descent.

4. The reason is that since the state of perfection, which consists in perfect love of God and contempt of self, cannot exist without knowledge of God and of self, the soul necessarily must first be exercised in both. It is now given the one, in which it finds satisfaction and exaltation, and now it is made to experience the other and is humbled until the ascent and descent cease through the acquisition of perfect habits, for the soul will then have reached God and united itself with Him. For He is at the end of the ladder and it is in Him that the ladder rests.

This ladder of contemplation, derived as we have said from God, is prefigured in that ladder Jacob saw in his sleep and by which the angels were ascending and descending from God to man and from man to God, while God leaned on the top. [Gn. 28:12–13] The divine Scriptures say that all this happened at night, while Jacob was sleeping, to disclose how secret is the way and ascent to God and how it differs from human knowledge. The secrecy of this ascent is evident since ordinarily the losing and annihilation of self, which brings the most profit to a man, will be considered the worst for him, whereas consolation and satisfaction (which are of less value and ordinarily involving loss rather than gain if attachment is involved) will be considered the best.

5. Speaking now somewhat more particularly of this ladder of secret contemplation, we declare that the principal property involved in calling contemplation a "ladder" is its being a science of love, which as we said is an infused loving knowledge, that both illumines and enamors the soul, elevating it step by step unto God, its Creator.

For greater clarity we shall note the steps of this divine ladder and briefly point out the signs and effects of each one so that a person may surmise which of these steps he is on. We shall distinguish them by their effects as do St. Bernard and St. Thomas. [He refers to the work *De Decem Gradibus Amoris Secundum Bernardum,* attributed for a long time to St. Thomas and published among his work (cf. Ed. Vivès, Vol. 28, Paris 1889, pp. 351–67). The true author is Helwich Teutonicus, O.P. (13th–14th century).] Knowing these steps in themselves naturally is impossible, since this ladder of love is, as we said, so secret that God alone is He Who measures and weighs it.

CHAPTER 19

An explanation of the first five of the ten steps on the mystical ladder of divine love.

1. We mentioned that there are ten successive steps on this ladder of love by which the soul ascends to God.

The first step of love makes the soul sick in an advantageous way. The bride speaks of this step of love when she says: *I conjure you, daughters of Jerusalem, if you encounter my Beloved, to tell Him that I am lovesick.* [Ct. 5:8]

Yet this sickness is not unto death but for the glory of God [Jn. 11:4], because in this sickness the soul's languor pertains to sin and things that are not God. It languishes for the sake of God Himself, as David testifies: *My soul has languished* (in regard to all things) *for Your salvation.* [Ps. 118:81] As a sick person changes color and loses his appetite for all foods, so on this step of love the soul changes the color of its past life and loses its appetite for all things. The soul does not get this sickness unless an excess of heat is sent to it from above, as is brought out in this verse of David: *Pluviam voluntariam segregabis, Deus, haereditati tuae, et infirmata est,* etc. (You shall set aside for Your inheritance a free rain, O God, and it was weakened.). [Ps. 67:10]

We clearly explained this sickness and languor in respect to all things when we mentioned the annihilation of which the soul becomes aware when it begins to climb this ladder of contemplation. It becomes unable then to find satisfaction, support, consolation, or a resting place in anything.

The soul therefore begins immediately to ascend from this step to the next.

2. The second step causes a person to search for God unceasingly. When the bride said that seeking Him by night in her bed (when in accord with the first step of love she was languishing), she did not find Him, she added: *I shall rise up and seek Him whom my soul loves* [Ct. 3:1–2], which as we said the soul does unceasingly, as David

counsels: *Seek the face of God always.* [Ps. 104:4] Searching for Him in all things, it pays heed to nothing until it finds Him. It resembles the bride who, after asking the guards for Him immediately passed by and left them behind. [Ct. 3:3–4] Mary Magdalen did not even pay attention to the angels in the sepulcher. [Jn. 20:14]

The soul goes about so solicitously on this step that it looks for its Beloved in all things. In all its thoughts it turns immediately to the Beloved; in all converse and business it at once speaks about the Beloved; when eating, sleeping, keeping vigil, or doing anything else, it centers all its care on the Beloved, as we pointed out in speaking of the yearnings of love.

Since the soul is here convalescing and gaining strength in the love found on this second step, it immediately begins to ascend to the third through a certain degree of new purgation in the night, as we shall point out, which produces the following effects.

3. The third step of this loving ladder prompts the soul to the performance of works and gives it fervor that it might not fail. The royal prophet exclaims: *Blessed is the man who fears the Lord, because in His commandments he longs to work.* [Ps. 111:1] If fear, a child of love, produces this eagerness in the soul, what will love itself do? On this step the soul thinks the great works it does for the Beloved are small; its many works, few; the long time spent in His service, short. It believes all of this because of the fire of love in which it is now burning. Thus Jacob, obliged to serve seven more years in addition to the seven years he had already served, did not think these were many because of the intensity of his love. [Gn. 29:20, 30] If Jacob's love for a creature could do so much, what will love of the Creator do when it takes hold of the soul on this third step?

Because of his intense love of God, a person at this stage feels deep sorrow and pain about the little he does for God, and if it were licit he would destroy himself a thousand times for God and be greatly consoled. He consequently considers himself useless in all his works and thinks his life is worthless.

Another admirable effect produced here is that a person thinks inwardly that he is really worse than all others. One reason for this effect is that love is teaching him what God deserves; another is that because the works he performs for God are many and he knows them to be wanting and imperfect, he is confused and pained by them all, conscious that his work is so lowly for so high a Lord. On this third step the soul is far removed from vainglory, presumption, and the condemnation of others.

This third step causes these effects of solicitude and many other similar ones in the soul. And thus one acquires the courage and strength to ascend to the fourth step.

4. On the fourth step of this ladder of love a habitual yet unwearisome suffering is engendered on account of the Beloved. As St. Augustine says, love makes all burdensome and heavy things nearly nothing. [Serm. 9, *De verbis Domini in Mt.*; PL 38, 444] The bride spoke of this step when in desiring to reach the last one she said to her Spouse: *Put me as a seal upon Your heart, as a seal upon Your arm, for love* (the act and work of love) *is as strong as death, and emulation and importunity endure as long as hell.* [Ct. 8:6]

The spirit possesses so much energy on this step that it brings the flesh under control and takes as little account of it as would a tree of one of its leaves. The soul in no way seeks consolation or satisfaction either in God or in anything else; neither does it desire or ask favors of God, for it is clearly aware that it has already received many from Him. All its care is directed toward how it might give some pleasure to God and render Him some service because of what He deserves and the favors He has bestowed, even though the cost might be high. This person will proclaim in his heart and spirit: Ah, my Lord and my God! How many go to You looking for their own consolation and gratification and desiring that You grant them favors and gifts, but those wanting to give You pleasure and something at a cost to themselves, setting aside their own interests, are few. What is lacking is not that You, O my God, desire to grant us favors again, but that we make use of them for Your service alone and thus oblige You to grant them to us continually.

This degree of love is a very elevated step. For as the soul at this stage through so genuine a love pursues God in the spirit of suffering for His sake, His Majesty frequently gives it joy by paying it visits of spiritual delight. For the immense love of Christ, the Word, cannot long endure the sufferings of its beloved without response to them. God affirms this through Jeremias: *I have remembered you, pitying your youth and tenderness when you followed me in the desert.* [Jer. 2:2] Spiritually speaking, the desert is an interior detachment from every creature in which the soul neither pauses nor rests in anything.

This fourth step so inflames a person and enkindles him with desire for God that it enables him to ascend to the fifth step.

5. The fifth step of this ladder of love imparts an impatient desire and longing for God. On this step the desire of the lover to apprehend and be united with the Beloved is so ardent that any delay, no matter how slight, is long, annoying, and tiresome. The soul is ever believing that it is finding its Beloved; and when it sees its desire frustrated, which is at almost every step, it faints in its longing, as the Psalmist declares: *My soul longs and faints for the dwelling places of the Lord.* [Ps. 83:2] On

this step the lover must either see its love or die. With such love Rachel in her immense longing for children declared to Jacob her spouse: *Give me children or I will die.* [Gn. 30:1] On this step, *they suffer hunger like dogs and encircle the city of God.* [Ps. 58:7]

On this step of hunger, the soul so feeds on love—for in accord with its hunger is its satisfaction—that it can ascend to the sixth step which produces the following effects.

CHAPTER 20

The remaining five steps of love.

1. The sixth step makes the soul run swiftly toward God and experience many touches in Him. And it runs without fainting by reason of its hope. The love that has invigorated it makes it fly swiftly. The prophet Isaias also speaks of this step: *The saints who hope in God shall renew their strength. They shall take wings like the eagle and shall fly and not faint* [Is. 40:31], as is characteristic of the fifth step. The following verse of the psalm also pertains to this step: *As the hart desires the waters, so does my soul desire Thee, my God* [Ps. 41:2], for the hart when thirsty races toward the waters.

The reason for the swiftness of love on this step is that the soul's charity is now highly increased and almost completely purified, as is also stated in the psalm: *Sine iniquitate cucurri*[4] [Ps. 58:5]; and in another psalm: *I have run the way of Your commandments, when You enlarged my heart.* [Ps. 118:32] The soul is soon brought from the sixth to the seventh step.

2. The seventh step of the ladder gives it an ardent boldness. At this stage love neither profits by the judgment to wait nor makes use of the counsel to retreat, neither can it be curbed through shame. For the favor God now gives it imparts an ardent daring. Hence the Apostle says: *Charity believes all things, hopes all things, and endures all things.* [1 Cor. 13:7] Moses spoke from this step when he besought God to forgive the people or else strike his name out of the book of life. [Ex. 32:31-32] These souls obtain from God what they ask of Him with pleasure. David accordingly declares: *Delight in God, and He will grant you the petitions of your heart.* [Ps. 36:4] On this step the bride became bold and exclaimed: *Osculetur me osculo oris sui.*[5] [Ct. 1:1] It is illicit for the soul to become daring on this step if it does not perceive the divine favor of the king's scepter held out toward it [Est. 5:2; 8:4], for it might

4 Without iniquity have I run.
5 Let Him kiss me with the kiss of His mouth.

then fall down the steps it has already climbed. On these steps it must always conserve humility.

From the free hand and boldness God gives on this seventh step, that one may be daring in His presence with an ardent love, follows the eighth step. Here the soul captures the Beloved and is united with Him as follows.

3. The eighth step of love impels the soul to lay hold of the Beloved without letting Him go, as the bride proclaims: *I found Him Whom my heart and soul loves, I held Him and did not let Him go.* [Ct. 3:4] Although the soul satisfies its desire on this step of union, it does not do so continually. Some manage to get to it, but soon turn back and leave it. If one were to remain on this step, a certain glory would be possessed in this life; and so the soul rests on it for only short periods of time. Because the prophet Daniel was a man of desires, God ordered him to stay on this step: *Daniel, remain on your step, because you are a man of desires.* [Dn. 10:11]

After this step comes the ninth, which is that of the perfect.

4. The ninth step of love causes the soul to burn gently. It is the step of the perfect who burn gently in God. The Holy Spirit produces this gentle and delightful ardor by reason of the perfect soul's union with God. St. Gregory accordingly says of the Apostles that when the Holy Spirit came upon them visibly, they burned interiorly and gently with love [*Homil. in Evang.*: PL 76, 1220]

We cannot speak of the goods and riches of God a man enjoys on this step, because even were we to write many books about them, the greater part would remain unsaid. For this reason and also because we shall say something about them later, I will mention no more here than that this step of the ladder of love is succeeded by the tenth and final step, which is no longer of this life.

5. The tenth and last step of this secret ladder of love assimilates the soul to God completely because of the clear vision of God which a person possesses as soon as he reaches it. After reaching the ninth step in this life, the soul departs from the body. Since these souls— few that they are—are already extremely purged through love, they do not enter purgatory. St. Matthew says: *Beati mundo corde, quoniam ipsi Deum videbunt.*[6] [Mt. 5:8] As we mentioned, this vision is the cause of the soul's complete likeness to God. St. John says: *We know that we shall be like Him* [1 Jn. 3:2], not because the soul will have as much capacity as God—this is impossible—but because all that it is will become like God. Thus it will be called, and shall be, God through participation.

[6] Blessed are the clean of heart, for they shall see God.

6. Such is the secret ladder of which the soul here speaks, although on these higher steps it is not very secret to the soul, for love through the remarkable effects it produces reveals a great deal. But on this last step of clear vision at the top of the ladder, where God rests as we said, nothing is any longer hid from the soul because of its total assimilation. Accordingly our Saviour exclaimed: *On that day you will not ask Me anything*, etc. [Jn. 16:23] Nevertheless, until that day, however high it may ascend, something will still be hidden in proportion to its lack of total assimilation to the divine essence.

Thus, by means of this mystical theology and secret love, the soul departs from itself and all things and ascends to God. For love is like a fire which always rises upwards as though longing to be engulfed in its center.

CHAPTER 21

An explanation of the term "disguised" and a description of the colors of the disguise the soul wears in this night.

1. Now then, after having explained why the soul calls this contemplation a secret ladder, we have still to comment on the third word of this verse, "disguised," and tell why it also says that it departed by this "secret ladder, disguised."

2. It should be known for the sake of understanding this verse that a person disguises himself by simply dissembling his identity under a garb and appearance different from his own. And he does this either to show exteriorly by means of that garment his will and aspiration toward gaining the favor and good pleasure of his beloved, or also to hide from rivals and better execute his plan. He then chooses the garments and livery which most represent and signify his heart's affections and with which he can better dissemble himself from his enemies.

3. The soul, then, touched with love for Christ, its Spouse, and aspiring to win His favor and friendship, departs in the disguise that more vividly represents the affections of its spirit. Its advance in this disguise makes it more secure against its adversaries: the world, the flesh, and the devil. The livery it thus wears is of three principal colors: white, green, and red. These three colors stand for the three theological virtues: faith, hope, and charity, by which the soul not only gains the favor and good will of its Beloved but also advances very safely, fortified against its three enemies.

4. Faith is an inner tunic of such pure whiteness that it blinds the sight of every intellect. When the soul is clothed in faith the devil

is ignorant of how to hinder it, neither is he successful in his efforts, for faith gives the soul strong protection—more than do all the other virtues—against the devil, who is the mightiest and most astute enemy.

As a result St. Peter found no greater safeguard than faith in freeing himself from the devil, when he advised: *Cui resistite fortes in fide.*[7] [1 Pt. 5:9] To obtain the favor of the Beloved and union with Him, the soul can have no better inner tunic than this white garment of faith, the foundation and beginning of the other garments or virtues. Without faith, as the Apostle says, it is impossible to please God [Heb. 11:6]; and with faith it is impossible not to please Him, since He Himself declares through the prophet Osee: *Desponsabo te mihi in fide* [Os. 2: 20], which is similar to saying: If you desire, soul, union and espousal with Me, you must come interiorly clothed in faith.

5. The soul wore this white tunic of faith when it departed on this dark night and walked, as we said, in the midst of interior darknesses and straits, without the comfort of any intellectual light—neither from above, because heaven seemed closed and God hidden, nor from below, because it derived no satisfaction from its spiritual masters—and suffered with constancy and perseverance, passing through these trials without growing discouraged or failing the Beloved. The Beloved so proves the faith of His bride in tribulations that she can afterwards truthfully declare what David says: *Because of the words of Your lips I have kept hard ways.* [Ps. 16:4]

6. The soul over this white tunic of faith puts on a second colored garment, a green coat of mail. Green, as we said, signifies the virtue of hope, by which one in the first place is defended and freed, as before, from the second enemy, the world. This greenness of living hope in God imparts such courage and valor and so elevates the soul to the things of eternal life that in comparison with these heavenly hopes all earthly things seem, as they truly are, dry, withered, dead, and worthless. A person is thus divested of all worldly garments and does not set his heart on anything of what there is, or will be, in the world; he lives clothed only in the hope of eternal. life. Having his heart so lifted up above the things of the world, he is not only unable to touch or take hold of worldly things, but he cannot even see them.

7. By this green livery and disguise, the soul is therefore protected against its second enemy, the world. St. Paul calls hope the "helmet of salvation." [1 Thes. 5:8] A helmet is a piece of armor which protects the entire head and so covers it that there is no opening except for a visor through which to see. Hope has this characteristic: it covers all

---

[7] Resist him, steadfast in the faith.

the senses of a person's head so that they do not become absorbed in any worldly thing, nor is there any way in which some arrow from the world might wound them. Hope allows the soul only a visor that it may look toward heavenly things, and no more. This is the ordinary task of hope in the soul: it raises the eyes to look only at God, as David asserts it did with him: *Oculi mei semper ad Dominum.*[8] [Ps. 24: 15] David hoped for nothing from anyone else as he says in another psalm: *Just as the eyes of the handmaid are fixed on the hands of their mistress, so are our eyes on the Lord our God until He has mercy on us who hope in Him.* [Ps. 122:2]

8. As a result, this green livery, by which one always gazes upon God, looks at nothing else, and is not content save with Him alone, so pleases the Beloved that it is true to say the soul obtains from God all that it hopes to receive from Him. The Spouse of the Canticle consequently says of His bride that she wounded His heart by merely the look of her eye. [Ct. 4:9] Without this green livery of hope in God alone, it would not behoove a person to go out toward this goal of love; he would obtain nothing, since what moves and conquers is unrelenting hope.

9. The soul advances through this dark and secret night in the disguise of the green livery of hope, since it walks along so empty of all possession and support that neither its eyes nor its care are taken up with anything but God. It places its mouth in the dust that there might be hope [Lam. 3:29], as we previously quoted from Jeremias.

10. Over the white and green, as the finishing touch and perfection of this disguise, the soul puts on a third color, which is a precious red toga. This color denotes charity, the third virtue, which not only adds elegance to the other two colors but so elevates the soul as to place it near God. Charity makes it so beautiful and pleasing to God that it dares to say: *Although I am black O daughters of Jerusalem, I am beautiful, and for this reason the king has loved me and brought me into his chamber.* [Office of the Blessed Virgin Mary, third antiphon of Vespers]

With this livery of charity, a livery of love which increases love for the Beloved, the soul receives protection and concealment from the flesh, its third enemy. For where there is true love of God, love of self and of one's own things finds no entry. Not only does charity protect it, but it even makes the other virtues genuine, strengthens and invigorates them in order to fortify the soul, and bestows on them loveliness and charm so as to please the Beloved thereby. For without charity no

[8] My eyes are ever toward the Lord.

virtue is pleasing to God. This is the seat draped in purple on which God rests, as is said in the Canticle of Canticles. [Ct. 3:10]

The soul is clothed in this red livery when, as explained in the first stanza, it departs in the dark night from itself and from all creatures, fired with love's urgent longings, and advances by the secret ladder of contemplation to perfect union with God who is its beloved salvation.

11. This, then, is the disguise the soul says it wore on this secret ladder in the night of faith, and these are its colors. These colors are a most suitable preparation for union of the three faculties (intellect, memory, and will) with God.

Faith darkens and empties the intellect of all its natural understanding and thereby prepares it for union with the divine wisdom.

Hope empties and withdraws the memory from all creature possessions, for as St. Paul says, hope is for that which is not possessed. [Rom. 8:24] It withdraws the memory from what can be possessed and fixes it on that for which it hopes. Hence, only hope in God prepares the memory perfectly for union with Him.

Charity also empties and annihilates the affections and appetites of the will of whatever is not God and centers them on Him alone. Thus charity prepares the will and unites it with God through love.

Because these virtues have the function of withdrawing the soul from all that is less than God, they consequently have the mission of joining it with God.

12. Without walking sincerely in the garb of these three virtues, it is impossible to reach perfect union with God through love. This garb and disguise worn by the soul was very necessary that it reach its goal, which was this loving and delightful union with its Beloved. It was a great grace that the soul put on this vesture and persevered in it until attaining its end or goal. Consequently it proclaims in the next verse:

—Ah, the sheer grace!—

CHAPTER 22

An explanation of verse 3 of the second stanza.

1. It was manifestly a great grace for the soul to have successfully undertaken this departure, in which it liberated itself from the devil, the world, and its own sensuality. In having reached the happy freedom of spirit desired by all, the soul went from the lowly to the sublime; being earthly, it became heavenly; and being human, it became divine, and arrived at having its conversation in heaven [Phil. 3:20], as is proper

to this state of perfection which we shall now discuss, although somewhat more briefly.

2. What was more important and the reason I undertook this task was to explain this night to many souls who in passing through it do not understand it, as is pointed out in the prologue. Now the nature of this night has been explained to some extent. We have also discussed the many blessings this night brings to the soul—though in a way that makes them seem less than what they in fact are—and how great a grace it is for one who passes through it. We have written of these blessings so that when souls become frightened by the horror of so many trials they might take courage in the sure hope of the many advantageous blessings obtained from God through these trials.

This night was, besides, a sheer grace for the soul on account of what it says in the next verse:

In darkness and concealment,

CHAPTER 23

An explanation of the fourth verse. Tells of the soul's wondrous hiding place during this night and how, though the devil enters other very high ones, he is unable to gain entry to this one.

1. "In concealment" amounts to saying in hiding or under cover. As a result, departing in darkness and concealment more fully indicates the security the soul speaks of in the first verse of this stanza. It received this security along the way toward union with God through love by means of this dark contemplation. "In darkness and concealment" is like saying that since the soul walked in darkness in the way we mentioned, it was concealed and hidden from the devil and his deceits and wiles.

2. The reason the darkness of this contemplation frees and hides the soul from the wiles of the devil is that the contemplation experienced here is infused passively and secretly without the use of the exterior and interior faculties of the sensory part of the soul. The soul's journey, consequently, is not only hidden and freed from the obstacle these faculties in their natural weakness can occasion, but also from the devil, who without these faculties of the sensory part cannot reach the soul nor know what is happening within it. Accordingly, the more spiritual and interior the communication and the more remote it is from the senses, the less the devil understands it.

3. It is very important to the soul's security that in its inner communion with God its senses remain in darkness, without this communication, and that they do not attain to it: first, so that, without any hindrance to freedom of spirit from the weakness of the sensory part, there may be room for a more abundant spiritual communication; second, that, as we say, the soul might journey more securely, since the devil cannot enter so far within it. Hence, we can understand spiritually those words of our Saviour: *Let not your left hand know what your right hand is doing.* [Mt. 6:3] This is like saying: Do not allow the left side, the lower portion of your soul, to know or attain to what happens on the right side, the superior and spiritual part of the soul; let this be a secret between the spirit and God alone.

4. It is quite true that even though the devil is ignorant of the nature of these very interior and secret spiritual communications, he frequently perceives that one is receiving them because of the great quietude and silence some of them cause in the sensory part. And since he is aware that he cannot impede them in the depths of the soul, he does everything possible to excite and disturb the sensory part, which he can affect with sufferings, horrors, and fears. He intends by this agitation to disquiet the superior and spiritual part of the soul in its reception and enjoyment of that good.

Yet when the communication of such contemplation shines in the spirit alone and produces strength in it, the devil's assiduity in disturbing the soul is often of no avail. It receives instead new benefits and a deeper, more secure peace. For what a wonderful thing it is! In experiencing the troublesome presence of the enemy, the soul enters more deeply into its inner depths without knowing how and without any efforts of its own, and it is sharply aware of being placed in a certain refuge where it is more hidden and withdrawn from the enemy. There the peace and joy which the devil planned to undo increases. All that fear remains outside; and the soul exults in a very clear consciousness of secure joy, in that quiet peace and delight of the hidden Spouse which neither the world nor the devil can either give or take away. A man experiences the truth of the bride's exclamation in the Canticle: *Behold sixty men surround the bed of Solomon,* etc., *because of the fears of the night.* [Ct. 3:7–8] He is aware of this strength and peace even though he frequently feels that outside his flesh and bones are being tormented.

5. At other times, when the spiritual communication is not bestowed exclusively on the spirit, but on the senses too, the devil more easily disturbs and agitates the spirit with these horrors by means of the senses. The torment and pain he then causes it is immense, and sometimes it is ineffable. For since it proceeds nakedly from spirit to spirit, the horror the evil spirit causes within the good spirit (in that of the

soul), if he reaches the spiritual part, is unbearable. The bride of the Canticle also speaks of this disturbance in telling of her desire to descend to interior recollection and enjoy these goods: *I went down into the garden of nuts to see the apples of the valleys and if the vineyard was in flower; I knew not; my soul was troubled by the chariots* (by the carts and roaring) *of Aminadab* (the devil). [Ct. 6: 10–11]

6. At other times, when the communications are accorded by means of the good angels, the devil detects some of the favors God desires to grant the soul. God ordinarily permits the adversary to recognize favors granted through the good angel so that he may do what he can, in accord with the measure of justice, to hinder them. Thus the devil cannot protest his rights, claiming that he is not given the opportunity to conquer the soul, as was his complaint in the story of Job. [Jb. 1:9–11; 2:4–5] He could do this if God did not allow for a certain parity between the two warriors (the good angel and the bad) in their struggle for the soul. Hence the victory of either one will be more estimable, and the soul, victorious and faithful in temptation, will receive a more abundant reward.

7. We must note that this is why God permits the devil to deal with the soul in the same measure and mode in which He conducts and deals with it Himself. True visions ordinarily come from the good angel, even if Christ is represented, for He hardly ever appears in His own Person. If a person receives true visions from the good angel, God permits the bad angel to represent false ones of the same kind. Thus a man, if he be uncautious, can be deceived, as many have been. There is a figure of this in Exodus where it says that all the true signs Moses worked were seemingly worked by Pharoa's magicians: if he produced frogs, they also did; if he turned water into blood, they also did so. [Ex. 8:6–7; 7:19–22]

8. Not only does the devil imitate this kind of corporal vision, but he also simulates and interferes with spiritual communications coming from a good angel, since he can discern them, as we said, and as Job said: *Omne sublime videt.*[9] [Jb. 41:25] Yet, he cannot imitate and form these spiritual communications as he can those granted under some appearance or figure, for these are without form and figure and it is of the nature of the spirit to be formless and figureless. He represents his frightful spirit to the soul in order to attack it in the same way in which it receives the spiritual communication, and to assail and destroy the spiritual with the spiritual.

[9] He sees every high thing.

In this case, when the good angel communicates spiritual contempla-tion, the soul cannot enter the hiding place and concealment of this contemplation quickly enough to go unnoticed by the devil. He then presents himself to it with some spiritual horror and disturbance, at times very painful. Sometimes the soul can withdraw speedily without giving this horror of the evil spirit an opportunity to make an impression upon it, and it recollects itself by the efficacious grace the good angel then gives it.

9. At other times the devil prevails, and disturbance and horror seize upon it. This consternation is a greater suffering than any other torment in this life. Since this horrendous communication proceeds from spirit to spirit manifestly and somewhat incorporeally, it in a way transcends all sensory pain. This spiritual suffering does not last long, for if it did the soul would depart from the body due to this violent communication. Afterwards, the soul keeps a remembrance of this diabolic communica-tion, which is enough to cause great suffering.

10. All we have mentioned here takes place passively without one's doing or undoing anything. Yet it should be understood that when the good angel allows the devil the advantage of reaching the soul with this spiritual horror, he does so that it may be purified and prepared through this spiritual vigil for some great feast and spiritual favor which God, Who never mortifies but to give life nor humbles but to exalt [1 Kgs. 2:6–7], desires to give. This favor will be granted a short time after-wards, and the soul in accord with the dark and horrible purgation it suffered will enjoy a wondrous and delightful spiritual communication, at times ineffably sublime. The preceding horror of the evil spirit refined the soul so that it could receive this good. These spiritual visions belong more to the next life than to this, and each is a preparation for the one following.

11. We have been speaking of God's visits by means of the good angel, in which the soul does not walk in such complete darkness and con-cealment that the enemy cannot somehow reach it. Yet, when God visits the soul directly, this verse is fully verified. In receiving the spiritual favors from God, the soul is in total darkness and concealment as far as the enemy is concerned.

The reason for this concealment is that since His Majesty dwells sub-stantially in that part of the soul to which neither the angel nor the devil can gain access and thereby see what is happening, the enemy cannot learn of the intimate and secret communications there between the soul and God. Since the Lord grants these communications directly, they are wholly divine and sovereign. They are all substantial touches of divine union between God and the soul. In one of these touches, since this is the highest degree of prayer, the soul receives greater good than in all else.

12. These are the touches the soul began to ask for in the Canticle upon saying: *Osculetur me osculo oris sui,*[10] etc. [Ct. 1:1] Since a substantial touch is wrought in such close intimacy with God, which the soul longs for with so many yearnings, a person will esteem and covet a touch of the divinity more than all God's other favors. After the bride in the Canticle had received many favors which she related there, she was unsatisfied and asked for these divine touches: *Who will give You to me, my brother, that I might find You alone, outside nursing at the breasts of my mother so that* (with the mouth of my soul) *I might kiss You and no one might despise me* (nor attack me)? [Ct. 8:1] This passage refers to the communication God gives to the soul by Himself alone, outside and exclusive of all creatures, for this is the meaning of the terms, "alone," "outside," and "nursing at the breasts." The breasts of the appetites and affections of the sensory part are dried up when in freedom of spirit the soul enjoys these blessings with intimate delight and peace, unhindered by the sensory part or the devil (who opposes them through the senses). The devil, then, would not assail the soul because he would be unable to reach these blessings or arrive at the understanding of these divine touches of the loving substance of God in the substance of the soul.

13. No one attains to this blessing except through an intimate nakedness, purgation, and spiritual hiding from all that is of creature. Accordingly, one reaches this good in darkness (as we have explained at length and now repeat in reference to this verse), and in concealment (in which the hidden soul, as we said, is strengthened in its union with God through love). The soul in its song consequently exclaims: "In darkness and concealment."

14. When these favors are bestowed in concealment (only in the spirit, as we said), a person is usually aware without knowing how that the superior and spiritual part of his soul is withdrawn and alienated from the lower and sensory part. This withdrawal makes him conscious of two parts so distinct that the one seemingly has no relation to the other and is far removed from it. And indeed, this is in a way true, for in the then entirely spiritual activity there is no communication with the sensory part.

A person in this way becomes wholly spiritual, and in these hiding places of unitive contemplation, and by their means, the passions and

10 Let Him kiss me with the kiss of His mouth.

spiritual appetites are to a great degree eliminated. Referring thus to the superior part, the soul says in this last verse:

My house being now all stilled;

CHAPTER 24

The concluding explanation of this second stanza.

1. This is like saying: Since the superior portion of my soul is now, like the lower, at rest in its appetites and faculties, I went out to the divine union with God through love.

2. Insofar as the soul is buffeted and purged through the war of the dark night in a twofold way (in the sensory and spiritual parts with their senses, faculties, and passions), it also attains a twofold peace and rest, in the faculties and appetites of both the sensory and spiritual parts. Consequently, the soul repeats this verse of the first stanza. The sensory and spiritual parts of the soul, in order to go out to the divine union of love, must first be reformed, put in order, and pacified, as was their condition in Adam's state of innocence. This verse, which in the first stanza refers to the quiet of the lower and sensory part, refers particularly in this second stanza to the superior and spiritual part, and consequently the soul has repeated it.

3. The soul obtains habitually and perfectly (insofar as the condition of this life allows) the rest and quietude of the spiritual house by means of the acts of substantial touches of divine union which, in concealment and hiding from the disturbance of the devil and of the senses and passions, are received from the divinity. With these touches the soul is purified, quieted, strengthened, and made stable that it may be able to receive permanently this divine union, which is the divine espousal between the soul and the Son of God.

As soon as these two parts of the soul are wholly at rest and strengthened, together with all the members of the household, the faculties and appetites (also put to sleep and in silence regarding earthly and heavenly things), Divine Wisdom unites Himself with the soul in a new bond of the possession of love. This union is wrought, as is asserted in the Book of Wisdom, *Dum quietum silentium contineret omnia, et nox in suo cursu medium iter haberet, omnipotens sermo tuus, Domine a regalibus sedibus prosilivit.*[11] [Wis. 18:14-15] The bride in the Canticle explains the same thing when she states that after she passed by

[11] When peaceful stillness compassed everything and the night in its course was half spent, Your all-powerful word, O Lord, leapt down from Your royal throne.

those who took away her veil and wounded her, she found Him Whom her soul loved. [Ct. 5:7; 3:4]

4. One cannot reach this union without remarkable purity, and this purity is unattainable without vigorous mortification and nakedness regarding all creatures. Taking off the bride's veil and wounding her at night in her search and desire for her Spouse, signifies this denudation and mortification, for she could not put on the new bridal veil without the removal first of her other one. Whoever refuses to go out at night in search for the Beloved and to divest and mortify his will, but rather seeks the Beloved in his own bed and comfort, as did the bride [Ct. 3:1], will not succeed in finding Him; as this soul declares, it found Him when it departed in darkness and with longings of love.

CHAPTER 25

A brief explanation of the third stanza.

Third Stanza

On that glad night,
In secret, for no one saw me,
Nor did I look at anything,
With no other light or guide
Than the one that burned in my heart;

EXPLANATION

1. Still using the metaphor and similitude of temporal night to describe this spiritual night, the soul enumerates and extols its good properties. It found and made use of these properties by means of this night and thereby obtained securely and in a short while its desired goal. We shall list three of them here.

2. The first is that in this glad contemplative night, God conducts the soul by so solitary and secret a contemplation, one so remote and alien to all sense, that nothing pertinent to the senses, nor any touch of creature, can reach or detain it on the route leading to the union of love.

3. The second property of this night, mentioned in this stanza, has as its cause the spiritual darkness of this night in which all the faculties of the higher part of the soul are in obscurity. In neither looking nor being able to look at anything, the soul is not detained in its journey to God by anything outside of Him, for in its advance it is free of hindrance

from the forms and figures of the natural apprehensions, which are those that usually prevent it from union with the eternal being of God.

4. The third property is that, although the soul in its progress has not the support of any particular, interior light of the intellect or of any exterior guide that may give it satisfaction on this lofty path—since these dense darknesses have deprived it of all satisfaction—love alone, which at this period burns by soliciting the heart for the Beloved, is what guides and moves it and makes it soar to God in an unknown way along the road of solitude.

The next verse is:

On that glad night,[12]

[12] Here *The Dark Night* ends.

The Spiritual Canticle

INTRODUCTION TO *THE SPIRITUAL CANTICLE*

THE THEME AND THE ORIGIN OF THE POEM

In *The Spiritual Canticle* St. John of the, Cross tells in lyric verse of the loving exchange which takes place between a soul and Christ, its Bridegroom. Since the soul in this case is undoubtedly the soul of Fray John of the Cross, it can be concluded that the stanzas lay before us a colloquy of love between the Mystical Doctor and Christ, his Beloved.

The first question that confronts us in a study of *The Spiritual Canticle* is: Why did the Saint give expression to this loving exchange in poetic form? He supplies the clue for an answer to this question in his prologue, by pointing out that the stanzas are utterances of love arising from mystical understanding. Again, in his commentary on stanza 25 we find a further enlightening indication of how these verses originated. Explaining the effect of one of God's intense communications to the soul, he writes: ". . . it should be known that this touch of a spark is a very subtle touch which the Beloved sometimes produces in the soul, even when least expected, and which inflames her in the fire of love, as if a hot spark were to leap from the fire and set her ablaze. Then, with remarkable speed, as when one suddenly remembers, the will is enkindled in loving, desiring, praising, and thanking God, and reverencing, esteeming, and praying to Him in savor of love. She calls these acts flowings from the balsam of God . . . The spark touches and then passes, although its effect lasts for a while, and sometimes for a long while." (C25, 5–8) We might conclude, then, that these stanzas of St. John of the Cross represent the flowings or outpourings from the balsam of God; they were born out of the abundant mystical understanding which was communicated to his soul in the touch of the spark produced by his Beloved.

St. Teresa in her *Life* speaks even more explicitly of how a soul sometimes feels the impulse to convey a plentiful spiritual experience in poetic forms, even though talent as a poet may be lacking. "O God, what must that soul be like when it is in this state! It would desire to be all tongue in order to praise the Lord. It utters a thousand holy absurdities, striving ever to please Him who thus possesses it. I know a person who, though no poet, composed some verses in a very short time, which full of feeling described her pain very well. They did not come from her intellect, but, in order to enjoy better the bliss which came to her from such delectable pain, she complained of it to her God." (*Life,* Ch. 16)

THE NATURE OF MYSTICAL UNDERSTANDING

To understand the process by which this poem evolved and to analyze the structure of both the poem and its commentary, it is necessary, first of all, since the verses "were composed in a love flowing from abundant mystical understanding," to examine more carefully what St. John of the Cross means by mystical understanding. In the prologue of the *Canticle* he does not speak of this kind of knowledge only as mystical understanding, but likewise as mystical wisdom and mystical theology. This mystical understanding, wisdom, or theology is also what spiritual persons call contemplation. As a result we have in stanza 27 the following clarification: "The sweet and living knowledge she says He taught her is mystical theology, that secret knowledge of God which spiritual persons call contemplation." (C27, 5) Or again, he explains: "On this account contemplation is also termed mystical theology, meaning the secret or hidden knowledge of God. In contemplation God teaches the soul very quietly and secretly, without its knowing how, without the sound of words, and without the help of any bodily or spiritual faculty, in silence and quietude, in darkness to all sensory and natural things. Some spiritual persons call this contemplation knowing by unknowing." (C39, 12) These texts make it clear above all that the knowledge is called mystical because it is secret or hidden knowledge.

The Mystical Doctor then proceeds to explain why this understanding is secret or hidden: "For this knowledge is not produced by the intellect which the philosophers call the agent intellect, which works upon forms, phantasies, and apprehensions of the corporal faculties; rather, it is produced in the possible or passive intellect. This possible intellect, without the reception of these forms, etc., receives passively only substantial knowledge, which is divested of images and given without any work or active function of the intellect." (C39, 12; 14–15, 14, 16; A2, 8, 5–6) Mystical understanding is hidden or secret, therefore, because it excludes discursive reflection and meditation, and because it has no sensory image from which a distinct idea may be formed. Since it is not clothed in any sensory species or image, a man will encounter great difficulty in his attempt to describe it; he will find that it is not even similar to anything that comes through the senses. "Since the wisdom of this contemplation is the language of God to the soul, of Pure Spirit to the spirit alone, all that is less than spirit, such as the sensory, fails to perceive it. Consequently this wisdom is secret to the senses. . . ." (N2, 17, 4)

But even though this knowledge is liberated of sensory images, we cannot thereby draw the conclusion that it gives a clear vision of God or of the divine truths; and this is another reason for its being secret. "It must not be thought that, because what the soul understands is the naked substance, there is perfect and clear fruition as in heaven. Although the knowledge is stripped of accidents, it is not for this reason clear, but dark; for it is contemplation, which in this life, as St. Dionysius says, is a ray of darkness." (C14-15, 16) Regardless of how heightened the contemplative experience may be, there is never a clear vision of God as in glory, for the knowledge always remains hidden or secret. "Neither must it be thought that, because the soul has so sublime an experience of God, we are asserting that she has essential and clear vision of Him." (C14-15, 5, 20) Just as contemplation, then, is called mystical understanding, it is also termed a ray of darkness, for it bestows knowledge or light, but this knowledge is hidden, it is not understood clearly, it is darkness to the intellect. The light of contemplation is a dark night to the soul (depriving it of distinct understanding), a hidden or secret or mystical knowledge of God. (A2, 13-14; N2, 17, 3, 6; F3, 32-34)

If we assert that the soul does not fashion this knowledge actively by means of the agent intellect working upon the sensory image present in the phantasy, and likewise that no clear vision of God is had, we nevertheless do not deny thereby that knowledge is received in the passive intellect. Accordingly, in contemplation, there is a vital activity of the soul, a knowing "stripped of accidents," of particular images and phantasms, a knowing communicated by God supernaturally, "according to the mode of faith." Being received according to the mode of faith, this mystical understanding is supernatural by reason of its eliciting principle and also its object. But it is likewise supernatural because of the manner in which it is wrought—not through discursive reflection, but through contemplation. (F3, 34-37)

So far as this mystical understanding implies knowledge and wisdom, it belongs to the cognitive order, but in addition, St. John of the Cross affirms repeatedly that it is a loving knowledge, that it involves both knowledge and love. "Since God communicates this knowledge and understanding in the love with which He communicates Himself to the soul, it is very delightful to the intellect, since it is a knowledge belonging to the intellect, and it is delightful to the will since it is communicated in love, which pertains to the will." (C27, 5) Thus he states most clearly in the *Living Flame of Love*:

"Since the soul cannot function naturally except by means of the senses, it is God who in this state is the agent, and the soul is the receiver. The soul conducts itself only as the receiver and as one in whom something is being done. God is the giver and the one who works in it, by according spiritual goods in contemplation (which is knowledge and love together, that is, loving knowledge), without the soul's natural acts and discursive reflections, for it can no longer engage in these acts as before." (F3, 32)

Speaking descriptively, St. John sometimes refers to the love as an effect of the knowledge, and at other times to the knowledge as an effect of the love. But when he does pose the precise question on the causal relation between the knowledge and love, he admits as normal the principle by which love is looked upon as an effect of knowledge. (C26, 8) Thus it is only insofar as the loving knowledge proceeds from God as a gift to the soul that love is said to be the cause of the knowledge:

". . . the Bridegroom calls this love of the soul a "breeze," because it proceeds from the contemplation and knowledge that she has of God at this time.
"It is noteworthy that the Bridegroom does not say He comes at the flight, but at the breeze of the flight, because, properly speaking, God does not communicate Himself to the soul through its flight (the knowledge it has of Him), but through the love it has from this knowledge." (C13, 11)

We find in effect throughout *The Spiritual Canticle* a mutual causality between knowledge and love. The knowledge communicated in contemplation gives rise to love, and love in turn is the reason the Lord communicates more abundant and profound knowledge.

It is true that this loving knowledge is not understood clearly and distinctly and that in this sense it is dark to the soul; but, on the other hand, it is a knowledge which is experienced—in mystical theology "one not only knows but at the same time experiences." On account of this experience it is certain, even though it cannot be explained adequately through concepts and images. "I do not think anyone who has not had such experience will understand this well. But, since the soul experiencing this is aware that what she has so sublimely experienced remains beyond her understanding, she calls it 'I-don't-know-what.' Since it is not understandable, it is indescribable, although, as I say, one may know what the experience of it is." (C7, 10) Stanzas 14 and 15, for instance, describe in exuberant terms what the soul tastes or experiences in God in one of the very intense and lofty communications bestowed on her by her Beloved (for mystical understanding, it must also be remembered, has varied degrees of intensity and spirituality).

EXPRESSION OF THE INEFFABLE

But despite the fact that these verses were written in a love flowing from abundant mystical understanding, they cannot give full expression to or explain clearly what is understood or experienced. For "who can describe the understanding He gives to loving souls in whom He dwells? And who can express the experience He imparts to them? Who, finally, can explain the desires He gives them? Certainly, no one can! Not even they who receive these communications." (C. Prol. 1) No matter how one may seek to describe this knowledge and experience, it will always seem that ". . . there is a certain 'I-don't-know-what' which one feels is yet to be said, something unknown still to be spoken, and a sublime trace of God, as yet uninvestigated, revealed to the soul; a lofty understanding of God which cannot be put into words." (C7, 9) The effort to convey this in words becomes sheer stammering, for when a person stammers he does not succeed in voicing his thoughts. (C7, 10)

Accordingly, it is due to the inexpressibleness of this experience as well as to the loving impulse to convey it outwardly that these persons "from the abundance of their spirit pour out secrets and mysteries rather than rational explanations." But from the viewpoint of the reader: "if these similitudes are not read with the simplicity of the spirit of knowledge and love they contain, they will seem to be absurdities rather than reasonable utterances." (C. Prol. 1) Given, then, the high mystical experience of St. John of the Cross and the ineffableness of that experience, the lyric verses of the *Canticle* were the best means he could find to set in words what in itself remained beyond words. Indeed, the apparent absurdities of the poetic figures and similes are less inadequate than the rational explanations. Such in fact is the manner of the Holy Spirit, who ". . . unable to express the plentitude of His meaning in ordinary words, utters mysteries in strange figures and likenesses," as in "the divine Canticles of Solomon and other books of Sacred Scripture."

If the figures and similitudes of poetry tell more adequately of the inexpressible exchange of love between Christ and Fray John of the Cross than do common and ordinary words, we need not conclude that every mystic must be a poet. The work of art as such is the creation of the poet, not the mystic. Yet the mystical understanding and experience will doubtless affect the creative activity of the poet. The lines of poetry may flow forth either under the direct impulse of the mystical understanding or they may be composed in the burning love that endures for some days after the spark of the divine touch has passed. For "the spiced wine—which is, as I say, sweet love in the soul—usually lasts, together with its effect, a long while, and sometimes a day or two, or many days, though not always in the same degree of intensity." (C25, 8)

Admitting that St. John of the Cross invests his living mystical experiences in poetic figures and symbols, one might query whether these figures are wholly original. It can hardly be denied that in the *Canticle* as well as in his other poems there abound elements representative of Castilian poetic tradition. But more than any other work, the inspired text of the Canticle of Canticles served as a source. It provided the theme and the pastoral surroundings. St. John's years of reflection upon these "strange figures and likenesses" of Solomon's song enabled him to make them his own and put them to use according to his need, weaving them in a personal way into new patterns.

THE LOVING EXCHANGE

Since *The Spiritual Canticle,* created in the lyric form of an eclogue, presents a loving colloquy between Fray John of the Cross and Christ, the exercise of love constitutes the core of the poem. This love, being essentially dynamic, is conceived and delineated in the *Canticle* as an uninterrupted progression in sanctity. In recounting the history of his love of Christ, its forward movement, St. John marks for us the degrees and stages of his spiritual life, which develops along lines parallel with and dependent upon love. In the *Canticle,* it is the progress of love which sustains the poem and supplies the direction and the structure for the sequence of the stanzas. This advance in love, obviously, is expressed through verses that retain a decidedly personal coloring; yet, we need not expect the poem to propose for us explicitly each and every moment of loving communion with Christ. This account of Fray John's loving exchange with Christ does not afford us a view of his spiritual life that has precise temporal perspective; we cannot discern in the sequence of the stanzas a progressive chronological order developing verse by verse and stanza by stanza. The development is present rather in blocks of stanzas pointing to key situations and moments in the life of divine love.

We can separate these blocks in the following simple manner: The bride goes in search of her Beloved to the mountains and the watersides, learning many things of Him, but never satisfied; all this knowledge serves only to increase her longing for Him, only wounds her with deeper love. (st. 1–12) Now, after so much longing, she sees Him, in sight on the hill. Her condition changes; He is for her: the mountains, lonely wooded valleys, strange islands, silent music, the tranquil night, and so on. Yet the bride and her Beloved are not wholly free from disturbances; there are the foxes, the deadening north wind, the girls of Judea, the swift-winged birds, lions, stags, fears of night, etc., all seeking to unsettle the exchange of love between the bride and Bridegroom. (st. 13–21) Ultimately, the bride enters the sweet garden of her desire, laying her neck on the gentle arms of her Beloved, and in the inner wine cellar of perfect love drinks of her Beloved. There He gives her His breast and there teaches her a sweet and living knowledge. She is no longer seen or found on the common. (st. 22–35) But in the end she desires to go forth with her Beloved to the mountain and to the hill, further, deep into the thicket, and then on to the high caverns in the rock—there where He will show her and there where He will give her the vision of His beauty in glory. (st. 36–40)

Such is the general plan of the poem; it dwells upon four main aspects of the life of love: 1) the anxious loving search for the Beloved; 2) the first encounter with Him, the spiritual espousal, and the life of union with Him which is not yet perfect; 3) perfect union with the Bridegroom, or, the spiritual marriage, and the life of love in this state of perfection; 4) the desire for the perfect union with and transformation in the Beloved in glory.

Since this evolution of love is delineated poetically, the flow of verses renders an allegorical description of the different stages of the spiritual life. The poetical symbols, as we learn in the commentary, represent the gracious gifts which the soul receives from her Beloved. These gifts are the communications of knowledge and love: the favors, visits, wounds, and touches of love. The increasingly more intimate communion with God is wrought by means of an increasingly more elevated knowledge and love of the divine Bridegroom. First, this knowledge and love is born out of the consideration of creatures; second, it flows from a consideration of God's works manifested in the mysteries of faith, particularly the Incarnation; third, it originates with a touch of supreme knowledge of the divinity. (C7, 2–4)

As the loving knowledge of God grows more intense, the soul withdraws from every affection contrary to the will of the divine Bridegroom. But if it is true that in ascending to God by a progression in love, the soul both purifies itself and increases in perfection, the stanzas, it is worth repeating, do not mark this progression through a precise arrangement of the steps of love, one following upon the other, but limit themselves to singing of only certain vital instances in the exchange of love.

THE DATES OF COMPOSITION

The entire poem was not composed at once, but it springs from different periods of inspiration. Fray John began fashioning the verses in his mind in the prison of Toledo, and later, with the writing materials supplied by his sympathizing jailer, jotted down thirty-one stanzas. Madre

Magdalena del Espíritu Santo testifies that she saw the little notebook he had made from the paper given him while in prison and the poems he had recorded in it. He probably wrote the eight additional stanzas at two distinct periods while Prior of Granada (1582–84). In regard to the last five of these, the event is related that, passing through Beas one Lent, while Prior of Granada, he asked Madre Francisca de la Madre de Dios her manner of prayer, and she answered that it consisted in looking upon God's beauty and rejoicing that He possessed it. So exultant was the Saint with her answer that for several days he spoke very sublime and wonderful things concerning the beauty of God. And carried away by love, he wrote five stanzas on this beauty, beginning with: "Let us rejoice, Beloved,/And let us go forth to behold ourselves in Your Beauty."

THE COMMENTARY

Undoubtedly the symbolic imagery of the *Canticle* was permeated with meaning for the Saint, and the rich lines of poetry were the best means he could find to express or to stammer something of the overflowing love and fervor he experienced in the touch of mystical understanding of God. But to anyone else, especially to one having no experience of mystical understanding, the stanzas might seem "absurdities" —certainly, unintelligible. The Carmelite nuns at Beas, the first to read the *Canticle,* were astonished by the beauty of its lines and, recognizing vaguely the staggering depth of meaning hidden within them, began to ask for further enlightenment. How could the nuns, left to themselves, come to any understanding of the profound doctrine hidden beneath those rich symbols? Thus Fray John began his commentary. First, in spiritual conferences, later in writing, he unraveled the meanings of his verses, until, finally, at the request of Madre Ana de Jesús, he compiled the complete and systematic commentary.

The commentary is an effort to shed some general light on the meaning of the poem by explaining the symbolic terminology. In translating the imagery verse by verse, St. John of the Cross unveils the basic order contained in the poem, which, he assures us, corresponds to the personal experience of the poet and, in its general plan, to the common path which leads to spiritual perfection. In addition to his proposal in the prologue to give a commentary on the poem, he promises to dwell more at length on some matters concerning prayer and its effects, making use of scholastic theology.

Forming a unified whole of the commentary and the poem, however, did not come easily to the master of spiritual theology, for the lyric, artistic creation of the poet did not lend itself perfectly to all the logical demands of the theologian. What finally occurred is that, ever seeking to present an orderly analysis of the evolution of the spiritual life, the Saint rearranged the stanzas so that he could establish the chronological order more exactly. This he did in a revision of the first commentary he had written with the result that two redactions of *The Spiritual Canticle* have come down to us. The change of order in the sequence of the stanzas, however, did harm, in the judgment of critics, to the poetic spontaneity and inspiration of the poem, but we must admit that even though damage was done to the poetry in the second redaction, the doctrinal value was thereby enhanced. Nevertheless, in spite of the improvement, a want of precise time sequence is still noticeable even in the second redaction.

Hence, wishing to explain the order contained in the verses, he tells us that the soul begins by the practice of mortification and meditation which, he continues, is referred to in the first four stanzas and that then it passes along the paths and straits of love until stanza 13. But the first two stanzas do not speak of the practice of mortification and meditation; they refer very clearly to the pains, longings, and straits of love. The state of the soul in the first two stanzas is equivalent rather to that expressed in the group of stanzas in which she suffers from "impatient love." Only stanzas 3 and 4 describe the soul's search for the Beloved through mortification and meditation.

In stanza 7 he speaks of a touch of supreme knowledge of the divinity. This touch, he points out, is granted to proficients, souls already advanced:

"Sometimes God favors advanced souls, through what they hear, see, or understand—and sometimes independently of this—with a sublime knowledge by which they receive an understanding or experience of the height and grandeur of God . . . One of the outstanding favors God grants briefly in this life is an understanding and experience of Himself so lucid and lofty as to make one know clearly that He cannot be completely understood or experienced." (C7, 9)

This touch, then, is a favor belonging more properly to the stanzas which in the general plan deal with a higher period of the spiritual life (a favor sometimes bestowed on advanced souls) than does stanza 7.

In stanza 22 the soul reaches the state of spiritual marriage, a state "incomparably greater" than the spiritual espousal, for the spiritual marriage is "a total transformation in the Beloved." And he goes on to say that one does not attain this full transformation of spiritual marriage without first passing through the spiritual espousal, the loyal and mutual love of betrothed persons. Still, in stanzas 27, 28, and 30, he speaks again, not too precisely, of the spiritual espousal.

The stanzas themselves need not always be confined to the determined period of the spiritual life attributed to them in the commentary. Those expressing impatient love need not apply merely to the first period of search for the Beloved; they may very well be uttered again in those absences of the Beloved which the soul suffers in the state of spiritual espousal. For some of those absences are of such kind that there is no suffering comparable to them. "The reason for such affliction is that, since she has a singular and intense love for God in this state, His absence is a singular and intense torment for her." (C17, 1) Stanzas 14 and 15, referring to an abundant communication received in the state of spiritual espousal, could apply as well to a communication received in the state of spiritual marriage.

This difficulty involved in the attempt to adjust the poetical work of art to the logical framework of the commentary ought to be kept in mind in any endeavor to determine the period of the spiritual life to which the stanzas refer, even though these periods, from the "initial steps in the service of God" to "the ultimate state of perfection," are declared in the *Theme* at the beginning and also in stanza 22.

The Elements of the Commentary

The chief elements constituting the commentary are as follows:

1) After the particular quotation of each stanza there usually follows a *general summary* of its meaning. This summary brings into relief the content of the stanza and its relation to the previous one or to the following.

2) In addition there is a *detailed explanation* of each verse which gives a literal interpretation of the words in relation to the narrative as a whole. These explanations make reference to the various moments of the spiritual life to which the poem alludes, and they may be separate from or united with the doctrinal explanations.

3.) The *doctrinal explanations* on the one hand seek to justify theologically the teaching contained in the explanation of the verses, or, on the other hand, to accommodate the teaching as well as possible to the real development of the spiritual life. These explanations are constructed through texts from Sacred Scripture and theoretical reasoning, all of which enlarges considerably the doctrinal scope of the simple commentary. It is important to note these doctrinal explanations, for they do not always correspond to the spiritual moment laid before us in the lines of the stanza. Sometimes these explanations are plainly digressions and form something apart from the commentary on the verses. In these instances they are the lengthier explanations, promised in the prologue, "of some matters concerning prayer and its effects." (*cf.*, e.g., C12, 7–8; 14–15, 17–20; 17, 8; 25, 9–11; 26, 14–17) More frequently they appear as clarifications of the direct commentary and in immediate relation to the literary and doctrinal content of the stanza. In these cases the additional elucidation fits well with the spiritual moment described in the poem, but at the same time establishes general principles which do not belong to this state alone. (C1, 4–11, etc.)

4) Finally we have the *introductions* placed before most of the stanzas molding them into a systematic whole. These introductions are proper to the second redaction of the commentary (for here again, as with the poem, we have two commentaries or redactions); only one is found in the first redaction, that placed before the commentary on stanzas 13 and 14. The second redaction also includes at the beginning, after a quotation of the entire poem, a section under the title *Theme,* which indicates generally how the stanzas refer to the different stages of the spiritual life. But considering all the elements constituting the commentary, it is understandable how we must not look for doctrine on some particular period of the spiritual life solely in those stanzas which are designated as referring to that stage.

THE COMPOSITIONS AND THE REDACTIONS OF THE COMMENTARY

The two different redactions of *The Spiritual Canticle* are commonly distinguished as *Canticle A* and *Canticle B.* These two redactions differ from one another in regard to both the sequence and the number of stanzas; also, the commentary of the second redaction is more detailed. *Canticle A* comprises thirty-nine stanzas; *Canticle B,* forty, the additional one being stanza 11, which begins, *Reveal Your presence.* The first fourteen stanzas follow the same order in both redactions, except that *Canticle B* has the added stanza appearing in the eleventh place and causing the other four to be one number higher than in *Canticle A.* The last seven stanzas, from *The small white dove* (stanza 33 in *Canticle A,* and stanza 34 in *Canticle B*) to *No one looked at her* (stanza 39 in *Canticle A,* and stanza 40 in *Canticle B*), also follow in the same order. The reorganizing of the stanzas occurs in the middle section of the poem, from stanza 15 in *Canticle A* (stanza 16 in *Canticle B*) to stanza 32 (stanza 33 in *Canticle B*).

The sanjuanist authorship of the first redaction has never been seriously questioned. But the authenticity of the second redaction has been denied, and this by means of some quite inadequate arguments. However, this unwarranted denial has given rise, happily, to such excellent critical studies in favor of the sanjuanist authorship of the second redaction that it cannot be seriously doubted. It was not unthinkable or even uncommon for St. John of the Cross to review his writings and make additions and revisions for the sake of greater clarity. We have indeed an excellent example of this in the *Codex of Sanlucar,* in which, in St. John's handwriting, there are many marginal and interlinear corrections, changes, and additions, paving the way for his *Canticle B.*

All the codices which are preserved of both redactions state explicitly that the commentary "was written at the request of Madre Ana de Jesús, Prioress of the Discalced Carmelite nuns of St. Joseph's in Granada, 1584." This statement at first hand seems to solve the questions concerning destination, date, and place of composition. But in regard to the first redaction, we know from the testimony of Madre Magdalena that the Saint began to comment upon the *Canticle* in Beas, answering the questions put to him by the religious of that community, and that later he continued in Granada. These stanzas, then, in all likelihood frequently provided inspirational themes for his spiritual conferences to the nuns. Thus, when Padre Juan Evangelista testifies that the saint began and finished his commentary on the *Canticle* while at Granada, he is in all probability referring to the actual drafting of the first redaction of the commentary, which was done at the request of Madre Ana de Jesús, as stated in the prologue.

As for the second redaction, it is difficult to determine the date and place of composition. Certainly it was written after the first redaction of *The Living Flame of Love*, since in *Canticle B* (st. 31, 7) the Saint makes reference to the *Living Flame*, which was written between 1585–86.

Since the commentary of the second redaction is clearer, better arranged, and more valuable from a doctrinal viewpoint (we might call it the final draft of the *Canticle*), we are using this redaction. We have followed the *Codex of Jaen*, which is the most trustworthy copy of the second redaction. Later, in the poetry section, we will present the first redaction of the poem.

It is noteworthy, finally, that St. John of the Cross wishes "to explain the utterances of love in their broadest sense so that each one may derive profit from them according to the mode and capacity of his spirit, rather than narrow them down to a meaning unadaptable to every palate." (C. Prol. 2) So, in passing over the more common effects of prayer, "I will briefly deal with the more extraordinary ones, which take place in those who with God's help have passed beyond the state of beginners." (C. Prol. 3) And in the very first stanza St. John of the Cross reminds all who read of these lofty experiences of God:

"You do very well, O soul, to seek Him ever as one hidden, for you exalt God immensely and approach very near Him when you consider Him higher and deeper than anything you can reach. Hence, pay no attention, neither partially nor entirely, to anything which your faculties can grasp. I mean that you should never desire satisfaction in what you understand about God, but in what you do not understand of Him. Never stop with loving and delighting in your understanding and experience of God, but love and delight in what is neither understandable nor perceptible of Him. Such is the way, as we said, of seeking Him in faith. However surely it may seem that you find, experience, and understand God, you must, because He is inaccessible and concealed, always regard Him as hidden, and serve Him Who is hidden in a secret way. Do not be like the many foolish ones who, in their lowly understanding of God, think that when they do not understand, taste, or experience Him, He is far away and utterly concealed." (C1, 12)

GENERAL PLAN OF THE SPIRITUAL CANTICLE

The search for her Beloved.

The initial burst into song announcing the theme: the bride laments the absence of her Bridegroom.

The first steps of the spiritual journey.

The longings and the weariness of impatient love.

1. She records her longings of love and complains to Him of His absence.

2. She seeks to take advantage of her desires, affections, and moanings as messengers that know how to reveal to the Beloved her need of Him and her suffering in His absence.

3. She decides to go herself in search of her Beloved through the practice of virtue and mortification and by avoiding the snares of her three enemies.

4. She begins to walk along the path of the knowledge of God by considering His greatness and excellence manifested in creatures.

5. Creatures reveal to her some traces of the beauty and grandeur of God.

6. These traces of His beauty and excellence increase her love for Him and her sorrow at His absence.

7. She is also wounded with love by the knowledge she receives of her Beloved through rational creatures.

8. She continues her complaint of love.

9. She shows the longings of impatient love in every way.

10. She begs her Beloved to put an end to her longings and let her eyes behold Him.

11. She asks for the vision of His beauty, displaying before Him the sickness and longing of her heart.

12. Aware that she finds no remedy in any creature, she turns to faith as to that which most vividly sheds light on her Beloved.

Preparations for the
perfect union.
The first encounter.
The spiritual espousal.

13. Since she desires the divine eyes with such yearnings, the Beloved reveals to her some rays of His grandeur and divinity, which cause her to go out of herself in rapture and ecstasy.

14, 15. This flight in which the soul is placed after much spiritual activity is called spiritual espousal. God communicates great things about Himself, beautifies her and adorns her with gifts and virtues. Her vehement longings and complaints of love cease, and a state of peace, delight, and gentleness of love commences. Although the bride enjoys so much good in these visits in the state of espousal, still she suffers from her Beloved's withdrawals and from disturbances and afflictions coming either from the senses or from the devil.

16. She invokes the angels, telling them to catch all the disturbances caused by the sensory appetites, by the wanderings of the imagination, and by the devil.

17. The absences of the Beloved which the soul suffers are very afflictive. Her love for her Bridegroom is now so intense that His absence is a great torment to her. She invokes the Holy Spirit to awaken love.

18. She begs the sensory part of the soul not to disturb the goods being communicated to the spiritual part.

19. Since the sensory part is unable to endure abundant spiritual communications, she asks the Beloved to communicate them to the spirit alone.

20, 21. The Bridegroom gives the bride peace and tranquillity by conforming the lower part to the higher, cleansing it of all its imperfections, quieting the appetites, and bringing the natural faculties under the control of reason.

22. Being duly prepared, the bride is now brought into the state of spiritual marriage, the highest state attainable in this life.

23. The Bridegroom reveals His admirable plan in redeeming and espousing the soul to Himself.

24. The bride tells about the happy and high state in which she has been placed. She possesses the virtues with fortitude; they are perfect and heroic; she has perfect love and perfect peace of soul.

25. The bride praises the Beloved for the favors devout souls receive from Him.

26. Even though the soul is always in this sublime state of spiritual marriage once God has placed her in it, the faculties are not always in actual union, although the substance is. God recollects the soul in one of these actual unions in the intimacy of His love.

27. Tells of the mutual surrender made between God and the soul.

28. Gives the method of accomplishing this surrender.

The perfect union with and transformation in the Beloved.
The spiritual marriage.
The desires for the vision of glory.

29. The bride proclaims to the world how she has acted and she rejoices and glories in having lost the world and herself for her Beloved.

30. The interior exchange of the virtues and gifts which the bride and Bridegroom enjoy mutually.

31-33. She observes her state and reviews how she has attained it. If the Beloved looked at her before clothing her in His beauty, how much more reason is there for Him to look at her now.

34, 35. The Bridegroom describes the soul's purity in this state and praises her for having desired to live in solitude, withdrawn from every satisfaction, comfort, and support of creature, for her Beloved alone.

36-40. Knowing that she is detached from all things and attached to God in intimate love, that the sensory part is brought into subjection, the devil conquered, that she is united to her Beloved with an abundance of heavenly riches and gifts, the bride longs in these stanzas to be brought to the glorious marriage of the beatific vision in the Church Triumphant, where she will know and enjoy His secrets and mysteries.

THE SPIRITUAL CANTICLE

This commentary on the stanzas which deal with the exchange of love between the soul and Christ, its Bridegroom, explains certain matters about prayer and its effects. It was written at the request of Mother Ann of Jesús, prioress of the Discalced Carmelite nuns of St. Joseph's in Granada, 1584.

PROLOGUE

1. These stanzas, Reverend Mother, were obviously composed with a certain burning love of God. The wisdom and charity of God is so vast, as the Book of Wisdom states, that it reaches from end to end [Wis. 8:1], and a person informed and moved by it bears in some way this very abundance and impulsiveness in his words. As a result I do not plan to expound these stanzas in all the breadth and fullness that the fruitful spirit of love conveys to them. It would be foolish to think that expressions of love arising from mystical understanding, like these stanzas, are fully explainable. The Spirit of the Lord, who abides in us and aids our weakness, as St. Paul says [Rom. 8:26], pleads for us with unspeakable groanings in order to manifest what we can neither fully understand nor comprehend.

Who can describe the understanding He gives to loving souls in whom He dwells? And who can express the experience He imparts to them? Who, finally, can explain the desires He gives them? Certainly, no one can! Not even they who receive these communications. As a result these persons let something of their experiences overflow in figures and similes, and from the abundance of their spirit pour out secrets and mysteries rather than rational explanations.

If these similitudes are not read with the simplicity of the spirit of knowledge and love they contain, they will seem to be absurdities rather than reasonable utterances, as will those comparisons of the divine Canticle of Solomon and other books of Sacred Scripture where the Holy Spirit, unable to express the fullness of His meaning in ordinary words, utters mysteries in strange figures and likenesses. The saintly doctors, no matter how much they have said or will say, can never furnish an exhaustive explanation of these figures and comparisons, since the abundant meanings of the Holy Spirit cannot be caught in words. Thus the explanation of these expressions usually contains less than what they in themselves embody.

2. Since these stanzas, then, were composed in a love flowing from abundant mystical understanding, I cannot explain them adequately, nor is it my intention to do so. I only wish to shed some general light on them, since Your Reverence has desired this of me. I believe such an explanation will be more suitable. It is better to explain the utterances of love in their broadest sense so that each one may derive profit from them according to the mode and capacity of his spirit, rather than narrow them down to a meaning unadaptable to every palate. As a result, though we give some explanation of these stanzas, there is no reason to be bound to this explanation. For mystical wisdom, which comes through love and is the subject of these stanzas, need not be understood distinctly in order to cause love and affection in the soul, for it is given according to the mode of faith, through which we love God without understanding Him.

3. I shall then be very brief, although I do intend to give a lengthier explanation when necessary and where the occasion arises for a discussion of some matters concerning prayer and its effects. Since these stanzas refer to many of the effects of prayer, I ought to treat of at least some of these effects.

Yet, passing over the more common effects, I will briefly deal with the more extraordinary ones, which take place in those who with God's help have passed beyond the state of beginners. I do this for two reasons: first, because there are many writings for beginners; second, because I am addressing Your Reverence, at your request. And our Lord has favored you and led you beyond the state of beginners into the depths of His divine love.

I hope that, although some scholastic theology is used here in reference to the soul's interior converse with God, it will not prove vain to speak in such a manner to the pure of spirit. Even though Your Reverence lacks training in scholastic theology by which the divine truths are understood, you are not wanting in mystical theology which is known through love and by which one not only knows but at the same time experiences.

4. And that my explanations—which I desire to submit to anyone with better judgment than mine and entirely to Holy Mother the Church—may be worthy of belief, I do not intend to affirm anything of myself nor trust in any of my own experiences nor in those of other spiritual persons

whom I have known or heard of. Although I plan to make use of these experiences, I want to explain and confirm at least the more difficult matters through passages from Sacred Scripture. In using these passages, I will quote the words in Latin, and then interpret them in regard to the matter being discussed.

I shall now record the stanzas in full and then in due order quote each one separately before its explanation; similarly, I will quote each verse before commenting on it.

END OF THE PROLOGUE

STANZAS BETWEEN THE SOUL AND THE BRIDEGROOM

Bride

1. Where have You hidden,
Beloved, and left me moaning?
You fled like the stag
After wounding me;
I went out calling You, and You were gone.

2. Shepherds, you that go
Up through the sheepfolds to the hill,
If by chance you see
Him I love most,
Tell Him that I sicken, suffer, and die.

3. Seeking my Love
I will head for the mountains and for watersides,
I will not gather flowers,
Nor fear wild beasts;
I will go beyond strong men and frontiers.

4. O woods and thickets
Planted by the hand of my Beloved!
O green meadow,
Coated, bright, with flowers,
Tell me, has He passed by you?

5. Pouring out a thousand graces,
He passed these groves in haste;
And having looked at them,
With His image alone,
Clothed them in beauty.

6. Ah, who has the power to heal me?
Now wholly surrender Yourself!
Do not send me
Any more messengers,
They cannot tell me what I must hear.

7. All who are free
Tell me a thousand graceful things of You;
All wound me more
And leave me dying
Of, ah, I-don't-know-what behind their stammering.

8. How do you endure
O life, not living where you live?
And being brought near death
By the arrows you receive
From that which you conceive of your Beloved.

9. Why, since You wounded
This heart, don't You heal it?
And why, since You stole it from me,
Do You leave it so,
And fail to carry off what You have stolen?

10. Extinguish these miseries,
Since no one else can stamp them out;
And may my eyes behold You,
Because You are their light,
And I would open them to You alone.

11. Reveal Your presence,
And may the vision of Your beauty be my death;
For the sickness of love
Is not cured
Except by Your very presence and image.

12. O spring like crystal!
If only, on your silvered-over face,
You would suddenly form
The eyes I have desired,
Which I bear sketched deep within my heart.

13. Withdraw them, Beloved,
I am taking flight!

Bridegroom   Return, dove,
The wounded stag
Is in sight on the hill,
Cooled by the breeze of your flight.

Bride

14. My Beloved is the mountains,
And lonely wooded valleys,
Strange islands,
And resounding rivers,
The whistling of love-stirring breezes,

15. The tranquil night
At the time of the rising dawn,
Silent music,
Sounding solitude,
The supper that refreshes, and deepens love.

16. Catch us the foxes,
For our vineyard is now in flower,
While we fashion a cone of roses
Intricate as the pine's;
And let no one appear on the hill.

17. Be still, deadening north wind;
South wind come, you that waken love,
Breathe through my garden,
Let its fragrance flow,
And the Beloved will feed amid the flowers.

18. You girls of Judea,
While among flowers and roses
The amber spreads its perfume,
Stay away, there on the outskirts:
Do not so much as seek to touch our thresholds.

19. Hide Yourself, my Love;
Turn Your face toward the mountains,
And do not speak;
But look at those companions
Going with her through strange islands.

Bridegroom

20. Swift-winged birds,
Lions, stags, and leaping roes,
Mountains, lowlands, and river banks,
Waters, winds, and ardors,
Watching fears of night:

21. By the pleasant lyres
And the siren's song, I conjure you
To cease your anger
And not touch the wall,
That the bride may sleep in deeper peace.

22. The bride has entered
The sweet garden of her desire,
And she rests in delight,
Laying her neck
On the gentle arms of her Beloved.

23. Beneath the apple tree:
There I took you for My own,
There I offered you My hand,
And restored you,
Where your mother was corrupted.

Bride

24. Our bed is in flower,
Bound round with linking dens of lions,
Hung with purple,
Built up in peace,
And crowned with a thousand shields of gold.

25. Following Your footprints
Maidens run along the way;
The touch of a spark,
The spiced wine,
Cause flowings in them from the balsam of God.

26. In the inner wine cellar
I drank of my Beloved, and, when I went abroad
Through all this valley
I no longer knew anything,
And lost the herd which I was following.

27. There He gave me His breast;
There He taught me a sweet and living knowledge;
And I gave myself to Him,
Keeping nothing back;
There I promised to be His bride.

28. Now I occupy my soul
And all my energy in His service;
I no longer tend the herd,
Nor have I any other work
Now that my every act is love.

29. If, then, I am no longer
Seen or found on the common,
You will say that I am lost;
That, stricken by love,
I lost myself, and was found.

30. With flowers and emeralds
Chosen on cool mornings
We shall weave garlands
Flowering in Your love,
And bound with one hair of mine.

31. You considered
That one hair fluttering at my neck;
You gazed at it upon my neck
And it captivated You;
And one of my eyes wounded You.

32. When You looked at me
Your eyes imprinted Your grace in me;
For this You loved me ardently;
And thus my eyes deserved
To adore what they beheld in You.

33. Do not despise me;
For if, before, You found me dark,
Now truly You can look at me
Since You have looked
And left in me grace and beauty.

Bridegroom 34. The small white dove
Has returned to the ark with an olive branch;
And now the turtledove
Has found its longed-for mate
By the green river banks.

35. She lived in solitude,
And now in solitude has built her nest;
And in solitude He guides her,
He alone, Who also bears
In solitude the wound of love.

Bride   36. Let us rejoice, Beloved,
And let us go forth to behold ourselves in Your beauty,
To the mountain and to the hill,
To where the pure water flows,
And further, deep into the thicket.

37. And then we will go on
To the high caverns in the rock
Which are so well concealed;
There we shall enter
And taste the fresh juice of the pomegranates.

38. There You will show me
What my soul has been seeking,
And then You will give me,
You, my Life, will give me there
What You gave me on that other day:

39. The breathing of the air,
The song of the sweet nightingale,
The grove and its living beauty
In the serene night,
With a flame that is consuming and painless.

40. No one looked at her,
Nor did Aminadab appear;
The siege was still;
And the cavalry,
At the sight of the waters, descended.

THE THEME

1. These stanzas begin with a person's initial steps in the service of God and continue until he reaches spiritual marriage, the ultimate state of perfection. They refer, consequently, to the three states or ways of spiritual exercise (purgative, illuminative, and unitive) through which a person passes in his advance to this state, and they describe some of the characteristics and effects of these ways.

2. The initial stanzas treat of the state of beginners, that of the purgative way.

The subsequent ones deal with the state of proficients in which the spiritual espousal is effected, that is, of the illuminative way.

The stanzas following these refer to the unitive way, that of the perfect, where the spiritual marriage takes place. This unitive way of the perfect follows the illuminative way of the proficients.

The final stanzas speak of the beatific state, that sole aspiration of a person who has reached perfection.

The beginning of a commentary on the love songs between the bride and Christ, the Bridegroom.

STANZA 1

Introduction

1. The soul at the beginning of this song has grown aware of her obligations and observed that life is short [Jb. 14:5], the path leading to eternal life narrow [Mt. 7:14], the just man scarcely saved [1 Pt. 4:18], the things of the world vain and deceitful [Eccl. 1:2], that all comes to an end and fails like falling water [2 Kgs. 14:14], and that the time is uncertain, the accounting strict, perdition very easy, and salvation very difficult. She knows on the other hand of her immense indebtedness to God for having created her solely for Himself, and that for this she owes Him the service of her whole life; and that because He redeemed her solely for Himself she owes Him every response of love. She knows too of the thousand other benefits by which she has been obligated to God from before the time of her birth, and that a good part of her life has vanished, that she must render an account of everything—of the beginning of her life as well as the later part—unto the last penny [Mt. 5:26], when God will search Jerusalem with lighted candles [So. 1:12], and that it is already late—and the day far spent [Lk. 24:29]—to remedy so much evil and harm. She feels on the other hand that God is far off and hidden because she desired to forget Him so in the midst of creatures. Touched with dread and interior sorrow of heart over so much loss and danger, renouncing all things, leaving aside all business, and not delaying a day or an hour, with desires and sighs pouring from her heart, wounded now with love for God, she begins to call her Beloved and say:

> Where have You hidden,
> Beloved, and left me moaning?
> You fled like the stag
> After wounding me;
> I went out calling You, and You were gone.

Commentary

2. In this first stanza the soul, enamored of the Word, her Bridegroom, the Son of God, longs for union with Him through clear and essential vision. She records her longings of love and complains to Him of His absence, especially since His love wounds her. Through this love she departed from all creatures and from herself, and yet she must suffer her Beloved's absence, for she is not freed from mortal flesh as the enjoyment of Him in the glory of eternity requires. Accordingly she says:

3.   Where have You hidden . . . ?

This is like saying: O Word, my Spouse, show me where You are hidden.

In her petition she seeks the manifestation of His divine essence, because the hiding place of the Word of God is, as St. John asserts [Jn. 1:18], the bosom of the Father, that is the divine essence, which is alien to every mortal eye and hidden from every human intellect. Isaias proclaimed in speaking to God: *Indeed, You are a hidden God.* [Is. 45:15]

It is noteworthy that, however elevated God's communications and the experiences of His presence are, and however sublime a person's knowledge of Him may be, these are not God essentially, nor are they comparable to Him because, indeed, He is still hidden to the soul. Hence, regardless of all these lofty experiences, a person should think of Him as hidden and seek Him as one who is hidden, saying: "Where have You hidden?"

Neither is the sublime communication nor the sensible awareness of His nearness a sure testimony of His gracious presence, nor is dryness and the lack of these a reflection of His absence. As a result, the prophet Job exclaims: *If He comes to me I shall not see Him, and if He goes away I shall not understand.* [Jb. 9:11]

4. It must be understood that if a person experiences some grand spiritual communication or feeling or knowledge, he should not think that his experiences are similar to the clear and essential vision or possession of God, or that the communication, no matter how remarkable it is, signifies a more notable possession of God or union with Him. It should be known too that if all these sensible and spiritual communications are wanting and a person lives in dryness, darkness, and dereliction, he must not thereby think that God is any more absent than in the former case. A person, actually, cannot have certain knowledge from the one state that he is in God's grace, nor from the other that he is not. As the Wise Man says, *No one knows if he is worthy of love or abhorrence before God.* [Eccl. 9:1]

The soul's chief aim in this verse is not to ask for sensible devotion in which there is neither certain nor clear possession of the Bridegroom in this life, but for the manifest presence and vision of His divine essence, in which she desires to be secure and satisfied in the next life.

5. The bride of the divine Canticle had this very idea when, longing for union with the divinity of the Word, her Bridegroom, she asked the Father: *Show me where you pasture and where you rest at midday.* [Ct. 1:6] In requesting Him to disclose His place of pasture, she wanted Him to reveal the essence of the divine Word, His Son. For the Father does not pasture in any other than His only Son, since the Son is the

glory of the Father. And in begging that He show her His place of rest, she was asking to see that same Son. The Son is the only delight of the Father, Who rests nowhere else, nor is present in any other than in His beloved Son. He rests wholly in His Son, communicating to Him His essence at midday, which is eternity, where He ever begets Him and has begotten Him.

When the soul, the bride, cries: "Where have You hidden . . . ?" she seeks this pasture, the Word, her Bridegroom, where the Father feeds in infinite glory, and she seeks the flowering bed, where He rests with infinite delight of love, deeply hidden from every mortal eye and every creature.

6. That this thirsting soul might speak with her Bridegroom and be united with Him in this life through union of love insofar as possible, that she might slake her thirst with the drop of Him that is receivable in this life, it would be well for us to answer for her Spouse, since she asks Him, and point out the place where He is most surely hidden. She may then surely find Him there with the perfection and delight possible in this life, and thus not wander in vain after the footprints of her companions. [Ct. 1:6]

It should be known that the Word, the Son of God, together with the Father and the Holy Ghost, is hidden by His essence and His presence in the innermost being of the soul. A person who wants to find Him should leave all things through affection and will, enter within himself in deepest recollection, and regard things as though they were nonexistent. St. Augustine, addressing God in the *Soliloquies*, said: I did not find You without, Lord, because I wrongly sought You without, Who were within. [*cf.* Pseudo-Augustine: *Soliloquiorum animae ad Deum liber unus*, c. 30: PL 40, 888]

God, then, is hidden in the soul, and there the good contemplative must seek Him with love, exclaiming: "Where have You hidden . . . ?"

7. Oh, then, soul, most beautiful among all the creatures, so anxious to know the dwelling place of your Beloved that you may go in quest of Him and be united with Him, now we are telling you that you yourself are His dwelling and His secret chamber and hiding place. This is something of immense gladness for you, to see that all your good and hope is so close to you as to be within you, or better, that you cannot be without Him. *Behold*, exclaims the Bridegroom, *the kingdom of God is within you.* [Lk. 17:21] And His servant, the apostle St. Paul, declares: *You are the temple of God.* [2 Cor. 6:16]

8. It brings special happiness to a person to understand that God is never absent, not even from a soul in mortal sin (and how much less from one in the state of grace).

What more do you want, O soul! And what else do you search for outside, when within yourself you possess your riches, delights, satisfactions, fullness, and kingdom—your Beloved whom you desire and seek? Be joyful and gladdened in your interior recollection with Him, for you have Him so close to you. Desire Him there, adore Him there. Do not go in pursuit of Him outside yourself. You will only become distracted and wearied thereby, and you shall not find Him, nor enjoy Him more securely, nor sooner, nor more intimately than by seeking Him within you. There is but one difficulty: Even though He does abide within you, He is hidden. Nevertheless, it is vital for you to know the place of His hiding that you may search for Him there with assuredness. And this, soul, is also what you ask, when with the affection of love you question: "Where have You hidden . . . ?"

9. Yet you inquire: Since He Whom my soul loves is within me, why don't I find Him or experience Him?

The reason is that He remains concealed and you do not also conceal yourself in order to encounter and experience Him. Anyone who is to find a hidden treasure must enter the hiding place secretly, and once he has discovered it, he will also be hidden just as the treasure is hidden. Since, then, your beloved Bridegroom is the treasure hidden in a field, for which the wise merchant sold all his possessions [Mt. 13:44], and that field is your soul, in order to find Him you should forget all your possessions and all creatures and hide in the interior, secret chamber of your spirit. And there, closing the door behind you (your will to all things), you should pray to your Father in secret. [Mt. 6:6] Remaining hidden with Him, you will experience Him in hiding, and love and enjoy Him in hiding, and you will delight with Him in hiding, that is, in a way transcending all language and feeling.

10. Come, then, O beautiful soul! Since you know now that your desired Beloved lives hidden within your heart, strive to be really hidden with Him, and you will embrace Him within you and experience Him with loving affection. Note that through Isaias He calls you to this secret chamber: *Come enter into your secret chambers, shut the door behind you* (your faculties to all creatures), *hide yourself a little, even for a moment* [Is. 26:20], for this moment of life on earth. If, O soul, in this short space of time you keep diligent watch over your heart, as the Wise Man advises [Prv. 4:23], God will undoubtedly give you what He also promises further on through Isaias: *I shall give you hidden treasures and reveal to you the substance and mysteries of secrets.* [Is. 45:3] The substance of the secrets is God Himself, for God is the substance and concept of faith, and faith is the secret and the mystery. And when that which faith covers and hides from us is revealed—that perfect vision of God spoken of by St. Paul [1 Cor. 13:10]—then the substance and mysteries of the secrets will be uncovered to the soul.

However much the soul hides herself, she will never in this mortal life attain to so perfect a knowledge of these mysteries as she will possess in the next. Nevertheless, if like Moses she hides herself in the cleft of the rock (in real imitation of the perfect life of the Son of God, her Bridegroom), she will merit that, while God protects her with His right hand, He will show her His shoulders [Ex. 33:22-23], that is, He will bring her to the high perfection of union with the Son of God, her Spouse, and transformation in Him through love. In this union she experiences such closeness to Him and is so instructed and wise in His mysteries that, as for knowing Him in this life, she has no need to say, "Where have You hidden . . . ?"

11. You have been told, O soul, of the conduct you should observe if you want to find the Bridegroom in your hiding place. Still, if you want to hear this again, listen to a word abounding in substance and inaccessible truth: seek Him in faith and love, without desire for the satisfaction, taste, or understanding of any other thing than what you ought to know. Faith and love are like the blind man's guides. They will lead you along a path unknown to you, to the place where God is hidden. Faith, the secret we mentioned, is comparable to the feet by which one journeys to God, and love is like one's guide. In dealing with these mysteries and secrets of faith, the soul will merit through love the discovery of the content of faith, that is, the Bridegroom Whom she desires to possess in this life through the special grace of divine union with God, as we said, and in the next through the essential glory, by which she will rejoice in Him not in a hidden way, but face to face. [1 Cor. 13:12]

In the meantime, even though the soul reaches union in this life (the highest state attainable here below), she always exclaims: "Where have You hidden . . . ?" For even in the state of union He is still hidden from her in the bosom of the Father, which is how she wants to enjoy Him in the next life.

12. You do very well, O soul, to seek Him ever as one hidden, for you exalt God immensely and approach very near Him when you consider Him higher and deeper than anything you can reach. Hence, pay no attention, neither partially nor entirely, to anything which your faculties can grasp. I mean that you should never desire satisfaction in what you understand about God, but in what you do not understand about Him. Never stop with loving and delighting in your understanding and experience of God, but love and delight in what is neither understandable nor perceptible of Him. Such is the way, as we said, of seeking Him in faith. However surely it may seem that you find, experience, and understand God, you must, because He is inaccessible and concealed, always regard Him as hidden, and serve Him Who is hidden in a secret way. Do not be like the many foolish ones who, in their lowly under-

standing of God, think that when they do not understand, taste, or experience Him, He is far away and utterly concealed. The contrary belief would be truer. The less distinct is their understanding of Him, the closer they approach Him, since in the words of the prophet David, *He made darkness His hiding place.* [Ps. 17:12] Thus in drawing near Him, you will experience darkness because of the weakness of your eye.

You do well, then, at all times, in both adversity and prosperity, whether spiritual or temporal, to consider God as hidden, and call after Him thus:

13.   Where have You hidden,
                     Beloved, and left me moaning?

She calls Him "Beloved" to move Him more to answer her prayer. When God is loved He very readily answers the requests of His lover. This He teaches through St. John: *If you abide in Me, ask whatever you desire and it shall be done unto you.* [Jn. 15:7] A person can truthfully call God Beloved when he is wholly with Him, does not allow his heart attachment to anything outside of Him, and thereby ordinarily centers his mind on Him. This is why Dalila asked Samson how he could say he loved her, since his spirit was not with her [Jgs. 16:15], and this spirit includes the mind and the affection.

Some call the Bridegroom beloved, whereas He is not really their beloved because their heart is not wholly set on Him. As a result their petition is not of much value in His sight. They do not obtain their request until through perseverance in prayer they keep their spirit more continually with God, and their heart with its affectionate love more entirely set on Him. Nothing is obtained from God except by love.

14. It is noteworthy of her next remark, "and left me moaning," that the absence of the Beloved causes continual moaning in the lover. Since she loves nothing outside of Him, she finds no rest or relief in anything. This is how we recognize the person who truly loves God: if he is content with nothing less than God. But what am I saying, if he is content? Even if he possesses everything, he will not be content; in fact the more he has, the less satisfied he will be. Satisfaction of heart is not found in the possession of things, but in being stripped of them all and in poverty of spirit. Since perfection consists in this poverty of spirit, in which God is possessed by a very intimate and special grace, the soul, having attained it, lives in this life with some satisfaction, although not complete. For David, in spite of all his perfection, hoped to have this fullness in heaven, saying: *When your glory appears, I shall be filled.* [Ps. 16:15]

As a result, the peace, tranquillity, and satisfaction of heart attainable in this life is insufficient to prevent the soul from moaning within itself—although this moan may be tranquil and painless—hoping for what it lacks. Moaning is connected with hope, and the Apostle affirmed that he and others moaned even though they were perfect: *We ourselves who have the first fruits of the spirit moan within ourselves, hoping for the adoption of the sons of God.* [Rom. 8:23]

The soul, then, bears this moan within herself, in her enamored heart. For there where love wounds is the moan rising from the wound, and it ever cries out in the feeling of His absence; especially when the soul, after the taste of some sweet and delightful communication of the Bridegroom, suffers His absence and is left alone and dry. She thus says:

15.   You fled like the stag

It is noteworthy that in the Canticle the bride compares the Bridegroom to the stag and the mountain goat: *My beloved is like a gazelle or a young stag.* [Ct. 2:9] She makes this comparison not only because He is withdrawn and solitary and flees from companions like the stag, but also because of the swiftness with which he shows and then hides Himself. He usually visits devout souls in order to gladden and liven them, and then leaves in order to try, humble, and teach them. Because of His visits His withdrawals are felt with keener sorrow, as is evident in the following verse:

16.   After wounding me;

This is like saying: The pain and sorrow I ordinarily suffer in Your absence was not enough for me, but having inflicted upon me a deeper wound of love with Your arrow, and increasing my desire to see You, You flee as swiftly as the stag and do not let Yourself be captured even for a moment.

17. In further explanation of this verse, it should be known that besides the many other different kinds of visits God grants to the soul, in which He wounds and raises it up in love, He usually bestows some secret touches of love, which like fiery arrows pierce and wound it, leaving it wholly cauterized by the fire of love. And these wounds, mentioned here, are properly called wounds of love. They so inflame the will in its affection that it burns up in this flame and fire of love. So intense is this burning that the soul is seemingly consumed in that flame, and the fire makes it go out of itself, wholly renews it, and changes its manner of being, as in the case of the phoenix which burns itself in the fire and rises anew from the ashes. David said in this regard: *My heart was inflamed and my reins have been changed, and I was brought to nothing, and I knew not.* [Ps. 72:21–22]

18. The appetites and affections which the prophet refers to as reins are all changed to divine ones in that inflammation of the heart, and the soul, through love, is brought to nothing, and knows nothing save love. The changing of these reins at this time is accompanied by a kind of

immense torment and yearning to see God. So extreme is this torment that Love seems to be unbearably rigorous with the soul, not because He has wounded her—she rather considers these wounds to be favorable to her health—but because He left her thus, suffering with love, and did not slay her for the sake of her seeing and being united with Him in the life of perfect love.

19. In stressing or declaring her sorrow, she says: "After wounding me," that is, leaving me thus wounded, thus dying with wounds of love for You, You have hidden as swiftly as the stag.

This feeling is so strong because in that love-wound which God produces in the soul, the affection of the will rises with sudden rapidity toward the possession of the Beloved, Whose touch was felt. Just as quickly, she feels His absence and the impossibility of possessing Him here as she wants. And together with this feeling, she then experiences "moaning" over His absence. These visits are not like others in which God refreshes and satisfies the soul. He bestows these to wound more than heal, and afflict more than satisfy, since they serve to stimulate knowledge and increase the appetite (consequently the sorrow and longing) to see God.

These are termed spiritual wounds of love, and are very delightful and desirable. The soul would desire to be ever dying a thousand deaths from these thrusts of the lance, for they make her go out of herself and enter into God. She explains this in the following verse:

20.   I went out calling You, and You were gone.

No medicine can be gotten for these wounds of love except from the One Who causes them. Thus the wounded soul, strengthened from the fire caused by the wound, went out after her Beloved Who wounded her, calling for Him, that He might heal her.

This spiritual departure, it should be pointed out, refers to the two ways of going after God: one consists of a departure from all things, effected through a contempt for them; the other, in going out from oneself through self-forgetfulness, which is achieved by the love of God. When the love of God really touches the soul, as we are saying, it so raises her up that it not only impels her to go out from self in this forgetfulness, but even draws her away from her natural supports, manners, and inclinations, thus inducing her to call after God.

Accordingly, this verse is like saying: My Spouse, in that touch and wound of Your love, You have not only drawn my soul away from all things, but have also made it go out from self—indeed, it even seems that You draw it out of the body—and You have raised it up to Yourself, while it was calling after You, now totally detached so as to be attached to You.

21. "And You were gone" is like saying: At the time I desired to hold fast to Your presence, I did not find You, and the detachment from one without attachment to the other left me suspended in air and suffering, without any support from You or from myself.

What the soul refers to as going out in search of the Beloved, the bride of the Canticle calls "rising": *I will rise and seek Him whom my soul loves, by going about the city, through the squares and the suburbs . . . but,* she adds, *I did not find Him, and they wounded me.* [Ct. 3:2; 5:7] The rising of the soul, the bride, is spiritually understood of rising from the lowly to the sublime. The same is understood of the soul's words here, "I went out," that is, from her lowly manner and love to the sublime love of God.

Yet the bride states that she was wounded because she did not find Him. And the soul also declares that she was wounded with love and that He left her thus. The loving soul lives in constant suffering at the absence of her Beloved, for she is already surrendered to Him and hopes for the reward of that surrender: the surrender of the Beloved to her. Yet He does not do so. Now lost to herself and to all things for the sake of her loved One, she has gained nothing from her loss, since she does not possess Him.

22. The suffering and the pain arising from God's absence is usually so intense in those who are nearing the state of perfection, at the time of these divine wounds, that if the Lord did not provide, they would die. Since the palate of their will is healthy and their spirit is cleansed and well prepared for God, and they have been given some of the sweetness of divine love, which they desire beyond all measure, they suffer immeasurably. For an immense good is shown them, as through the fissure of a rock, but not granted them. Thus their pain and torment is unspeakable.

STANZA 2

Shepherds, you that go
Up through the sheepfolds to the hill,
If by chance you see
Him I love most,
Tell Him that I sicken, suffer, and die.

Commentary

1. The soul in this stanza desires the advantage of intercessors and intermediaries with her Beloved, by begging them to bring Him word

of her grief and pain. This is the trait of a lover: When she herself cannot converse with her loved one, she does so through the best means possible. The soul wants to take advantage of her desires, affections, and moanings as messengers that know so well how to manifest to the Beloved the secret of the lover's heart.

She entreats them to go, crying:

2. **Shepherds, you that go**
She calls her desires, affections, and moanings, "shepherds," because they pasture the soul with spiritual goods (a shepherd or pastor is one who feeds or pastures), and by means of these yearnings God communicates Himself to her and gives her the divine pasture. Without them His communications are slight.

"You that go," is like saying, you that go out through pure love. Not all the affections and desires go to Him, but only those that go out of true love.

3. **Up through the sheepfolds to the hill,**
She calls the hierarchies and choirs of angels "sheepfolds." Through them, from choir to choir, our moanings and prayers go to God. She refers to God as "the hill," because He is the supreme height and because in Him, as on a hill, one has a view of all things, and both the higher and the lower sheepfolds. Our prayers rise up to Him through the angels, who offer them to Him, as we said. The angel told Tobias: *When you were praying with tears and burying the dead, I was offering your prayer to God.* [Tb. 12:12]

These shepherds can also be the angels, who not only carry our messages to God, but also God's messages to us. They feed our souls, like good shepherds, with sweet communications and inspirations from God —they are the means by which God grants them—and they protect us from the wolves, which are the devils.

Whether, then, these shepherds refer to the affections or to the angels, the soul longs that they all be helps and intermediaries with her Beloved. She pleads with them all:

4. **If by chance you see**
This means: if by my good luck you so reach His presence that He sees and hears you.

It is noteworthy that even though God has knowledge and understanding of all, and even sees the very thoughts of the soul, as Moses asserts [Dt. 31:21], it is said, when He remedies our necessities, that He sees them and, when He answers our prayers, that He hears them. Not all needs and petitions reach the point at which God, in hearing, grants them. They must wait until in His eyes they arrive at the suitable time, season, and number, and then it is said that He sees and hears them.

This is evident in Exodus. After the four hundred years in which the children of Israel had been afflicted by the Egyptian slavery, God declared to Moses: *I have seen the affliction of my people and have come down to free them* [Ex. 3:7–8], even though He had always seen it.

And St. Gabriel, too, told Zacharias not to fear, because God had heard his prayer and given him the son for which he had prayed those many years, even though God had always heard that prayer. [Lk. 1:13]

Every soul should know that even though God does not answer its prayer immediately, He will not on that account fail to answer it at the opportune time if it does not become discouraged and give up its prayer. He is, as David remarks, *a helper in opportune times and tribulations.* [Ps. 9:10]

The soul means in saying "If by chance you see" that if by chance the time is at hand for my petitions to be heard by

5.   Him I love most,

That is, by Him I love more than all things. She loves Him more than all things when nothing intimidates her in doing and suffering for love of Him whatever is for His service. And when she can also say truthfully what she proclaims in the following verse, it is a sign that she loves Him above all things. The verse is:

6.   Tell Him that I sicken, suffer, and die.

In this line the soul discloses three needs: sickness, suffering, and death. The soul that truly loves God with some perfection usually suffers from His absence in three ways (in the intellect, the will, and the memory).

She says she sickens through the intellect because she does not see God, the health of the intellect. God says through David: *I am your health.* [Ps. 34:3]

She declares she suffers through the will because she does not possess Him, the will's refreshment and delight. David also says: *You shall fill them with the torrent of Your delight.* [Ps. 35:9]

She says she dies through the memory because, in remembering that she lacks all the goods of the intellect (the vision of God) and the delights of the will (the possession of God), and that it is highly possible, among the dangers and sinful occasions of this life, to be without Him forever, she suffers a distress that resembles death. For she sees her want of the sure and perfect possession of God, Who, as Moses affirms, is the soul's life: *He is certainly your life.* [Dt. 30:20]

7. Jeremias also indicated these three kinds of needs in Lamentations, saying: *Remember my poverty, the wormwood, and the gall.* [Lam. 3:19]

The poverty relates to the intellect, because to the intellect belong the riches of the wisdom of the Son of God, in Whom, as St. Paul says, are hidden all the treasures of God. [Col. 2:3]

The wormwood, a most bitter herb, refers to the will, because to this faculty belongs the sweetness of the possession of God. When this possession is lacking, the will is left in bitterness. And that bitterness pertains to the will is understood spiritually in the Apocalypse where the angel told St. John that eating the book would bring bitterness to the belly [Ap. 10:9], meaning to the will.

The gall refers not only to the memory but to all a person's faculties and strength. Gall signifies the death of the soul, as Moses indicates speaking of the condemned in Deuteronomy: *Their wine will be the gall of dragons and the incurable poison of asps.* [Dt. 32:33] Gall refers to their lack of God, which is death to the soul.

These three needs and sufferings are based on the three theological virtues (faith, charity, and hope), which reside in the three faculties of the soul in the order given here, intellect, will, and memory.

8. It should be pointed out that in this verse the soul does no more than disclose her need and suffering to the Beloved. The discreet lover does not care to ask for what she lacks and desires, but only indicates this need that the Beloved may do what He pleases. When the Blessed Virgin spoke to her beloved Son at the wedding feast in Cana in Galilee, she did not ask directly for the wine, but merely remarked: *They have no wine.* [Jn. 2:3] And the sisters of Lazarus did not send to ask our Lord to cure their brother, but to tell Him that Lazarus whom He loved was sick. [Jn. 11:3] There are three reasons for this: first, the Lord knows what is suitable for us better than we do; second, the Beloved has more compassion when He beholds the need and resignation of a soul that loves Him; third, the soul is better safeguarded against self-love and possessiveness by indicating its lack, rather than asking for what in its opinion is wanting. The soul, now, does likewise by just indicating her three needs. Her words are similar to saying: Tell my Beloved, since I sicken and He alone is my health, to give me health; and, since I suffer and He alone is my joy, to give me joy; and, since I die and He alone is my life, to give me life.

STANZA 3

Seeking my Love
I will head for the mountains and for watersides,
I will not gather flowers,
Nor fear wild beasts;
I will go beyond strong men and frontiers.

Commentary

1. The soul is aware that neither her sighs and prayers nor the help of good intermediaries, about which she spoke in stanzas 1 and 2, are sufficient for her to find her Beloved. Since the desire in which she seeks Him is authentic and her love intense, she does not want to leave any possible means untried. The soul that truly loves God is not slothful in doing all she can to find the Son of God, her Beloved. Even after she has done everything, she is dissatisfied and thinks she has done nothing.

And accordingly she seeks Him in this third stanza. She desires to look for Him herself through works, and she describes the method to be employed in order to find Him: she must practice the virtues and engage in the spiritual exercises of both the active and the contemplative life. As a result she must tolerate no delights or comforts, and the powers and snares of her three enemies (the world, the flesh, and the devil) must neither detain nor impede her. She says,

2.   Seeking my Love

That is, seeking my Beloved. She points out here that for the attainment of God it is not enough to pray with the heart and the tongue and receive favors from others, but that together with this a soul must through its own efforts do everything possible. God usually esteems a work done by the individual himself more than many others done for him. And mindful of the words of the Beloved, *Seek and you shall find* [Lk. 11:9], the soul decides to go out searching for Him in the way we mentioned, to seek Him through works that she may not be left without finding Him. Many desire that God cost them no more than words, and even these they say badly. They scarcely desire to do anything for Him that might cost them something. Some would not even rise from a place of their liking, if they were not to receive thereby some delight from God in their mouth and heart. They will not even take one step to mortify themselves and lose some of their satisfactions, comforts, and useless desires.

Yet, unless they go in search for God, they will not find Him, no matter how much they cry for Him. The bride of the Canticle cried after Him, but did not find Him until she went out looking for Him. She affirms: *In my bed by night I sought Him whom my soul loves; I sought Him and did not find Him. I will rise up and go about the city; in the suburbs and the squares I will look for Him whom my soul loves.* [Ct. 3:1–2] And she says that she found Him after undergoing some trials. [Ct. 3:4]

3. He who seeks God and yet wants his own satisfaction and rest, seeks Him at night and thus will not find Him. He who looks for Him through the practice and works of the virtues and gets up from the bed of his own satisfaction and delight, seeks Him by day and thus will find Him. What is not found at night appears during the day. The Bridegroom Himself points this out in the Book of Wisdom: *Wisdom is bright and never fades and is easily seen by them that love her, and found by them that seek her. She goes out before them that covet her that she might first show herself to them. He who awakes early in the morning to seek her shall not labor, because he will find her seated at the door of his house.* [Wis. 6:13-15] This passage indicates that when the soul has departed from the house of her own will and the bed of her own satisfaction, she will find outside divine Wisdom, the Son of God, her Spouse. As a result, she says here: "Seeking my Love"

4.   I will head for the mountains and for watersides,
The mountains, which are high, refer to the virtues: first, because of their height; second, because of the difficulty and labor one undergoes in climbing them. She says she will exercise the contemplative life by means of these virtues.

The watersides, which are low, apply to the mortifications, penances, and spiritual exercises by which she says she will practice the active and contemplative life together. To seek God in the right way and acquire the virtues, both are necessary.

These words, then, are like saying: Seeking my Beloved, I will practice the high virtues and humble myself by lowly mortifications and humble exercises.

She recites this line because the way to look for God is to do good works for Him and mortify evil within oneself in the following manner:

5.   I will not gather flowers,
Since seeking God demands a heart naked, strong, and free from all evils and goods which are not purely God, the soul speaks in this and the following verses of the freedom and fortitude one should possess in looking for Him.

She declares she will not gather the flowers she sees along the way. The flowers are all the gratifications, satisfactions, and delights which may be offered to her in this life, and which will hinder her should she desire to gather and accept them.

They are of three kinds: temporal, sensory, and spiritual. All three occupy the heart and hinder the spiritual nakedness required for the narrow way of Christ, if the soul pays attention to them or becomes attached. Consequently she says that in order to seek Him she will not gather these things. This line is equivalent to saying: I will not set my heart on the riches and goods the world offers, neither will I tolerate the pleasures and delights of my flesh, nor will I pay heed to the satisfactions and consolations of my spirit in a way that may detain me from seeking my Love in the mountains of virtues and trials.

She makes this declaration in order to take the advice the prophet David gives those who journey along this path: *Divitiae si affluant, nolite cor apponere* (If riches abound, do not set your heart on them). [Ps. 61:11] These riches refer to both sensory and temporal goods and to spiritual consolations.

It should be known that not only temporal goods and bodily delights are contradictory to the path leading to God, but also spiritual consolations, if possessed or sought with attachment, are an obstacle to the way of the cross of Christ, the Bridegroom. He who is to advance must not gather these flowers. More than this, he must also have the courage and fortitude to say:

6.   Nor fear wild beasts;
         I will go beyond strong men and frontiers.

In these verses she records the soul's three enemies: the world, the devil, and the flesh. They are causes of war and hardship along the road. The wild beasts refer to the world, the strong men to the devil, and the frontiers to the flesh.

7. She calls the world "wild beasts" because, in the imagination of the soul that begins to tread the path leading to God, the world is pictured as wild animals threatening and scaring her. The world frightens her in three ways:

First, it makes her think she must live without its favor, and lose her friends, reputation, importance, and even wealth.

Second, through another beast, no less ferocious, it makes her wonder how she will ever endure the permanent lack of the contentments and delights of the world and all its comforts.

The third is still worse. It makes her think that tongues will rise up against her and mock her, that there will be many remarks and jeers, and that she will be considered almost worthless.

These fears are brought before some souls in such a way that not only does perseverance against these wild beasts become most difficult, but it even becomes difficult to determine to embark on this road.

8. Yet some generous souls will be faced with other wild beasts, more interior and spiritual: hardships and temptations and many kinds of trials through which they must pass. God sends these to those He wants to raise to high perfection by trying them like gold in the fire. According to David, *Multae tribulationes justorum* (Many are the tribulations of the just), *but out of these the Lord will deliver them.* [Ps. 33:20]

Yet the truly loving soul, esteeming her Beloved above all things, trusting in His love and friendship, does not find it hard to say: "Nor fear wild beasts," and "I will go beyond strong men and frontiers."

9. She calls devils, the second enemy, "strong men," because they strive mightily to entrap her on this road and because, too, their temptations are stronger and their wiles more baffling than those of the world and the flesh, and, finally, because the devils reinforce themselves with these other two enemies, the world and the flesh, in order to wage a rugged war.

David, in alluding to them, calls them strong men: *Fortes quaesierunt animam meam* (The strong men sought after my soul). [Ps. 53:5] The prophet Job also remarked concerning this strength that there is no power on earth comparable to that of the devil, who was made to fear no one [Jb. 41:24], that is, no human strength is comparable to his. Only the divine power is sufficient to conquer him and only the divine light can understand his wiles.

A man who must overcome the devil's strength will be unable to do so without prayer, nor will he be able to understand his deceits without mortification and humility. St. Paul counsels the faithful: *Induite vos armaturam Dei, ut possitis stare adversus insidias diaboli, quoniam non est nobis colluctatio adversus carnem et sanguinem* (Put on the armor of God that you may be able to resist the wiles of the devil, for this struggle is not against flesh and blood). [Eph. 6:11–12] By blood he means the world, and by the armor of God, prayer and the cross of Christ, in which is found the humility and mortification we mentioned.

10. The soul affirms also that she will pass by frontiers, which refer to the natural rebellions of the flesh against the spirit. As St. Paul says: *Caro enim concupiscit adversus spiritum* [Gal. 5:17], which is like saying: The flesh covets against the spirit, and sets itself up as though on the frontier to oppose the spiritual journey. A person must pass these frontiers by breaking through these difficulties and throwing down with willful strength and determination all sensory appetites and natural affections. In the measure that these are present in the soul, the spirit is impeded by them and cannot go on to true life and spiritual delight. St. Paul indicated this clearly: *Si spiritu facta carnis mortificaveritis, vivetis* (If by the spirit you mortify the inclinations and appetites of the flesh, you shall live). [Rom. 8:13]

Such is the method the soul, in this stanza, claims she must follow in order to seek her Beloved on this road. The method, in sum, consists of steadfastness and courage in not stooping to gather flowers; of bravery in not fearing the wild beasts; of strength in passing by strong men and frontiers; and of the sole intention to head for the mountains and the watersides of virtues, as we explained.

STANZA 4

O woods and thickets
Planted by the hand of my Beloved!
O green meadow,
Coated, bright, with flowers,
Tell me, has He passed by you?

Commentary

1. The soul has made known the manner of preparing oneself to begin this journey: to pursue no longer delights and satisfactions, and to overcome temptations and difficulties through fortitude. This is the practice of self-knowledge, the first requirement for advancing to the knowledge of God. Now, in this stanza, she begins to walk along the way of the knowledge and consideration of creatures which leads to the knowledge of her Beloved, the Creator.

On this spiritual road the consideration of creatures is first in order after the exercise of self-knowledge. The soul thereby advances in the knowledge of God by considering His greatness and excellence manifested in creatures, as is brought out in that passage of St. Paul: *Invisibilia enim ipsius a creatura mundi, per ea quae facta sunt intellecta conspiciuntur* (The invisible things of God are known by the soul through creatures, both visible and invisible). [Rom. 1:20]

She addresses creatures, then, in this stanza, asking them about her Beloved. And it is noteworthy, as St. Augustine says, that the soul's interrogation of creatures is the very consideration of the Creator it has through them. [*cf.* Pseudo-Augustine: *Soliloquiorum animae ad Deum liber unus*, c. 31: PL 40, 888]

This stanza embodies a meditation upon the elements and other inferior creatures, and on the heavens together with the other material things in them which God created, and also upon the heavenly spirits.

2.   O woods and thickets

She calls the elements (earth, water, air, and fire) "woods," because like pleasant woods they are thickly populated with creatures. She labels these creatures "thickets" because of their vast number and the notable difference among them in each of the elements. On the earth there is a countless variety of animals and plants; in the water, numberless kinds of fish; and in the air, a remarkable diversity of birds; and the element fire concurs with the others for the animation and preservation of these creatures. Each kind of animal lives in its element, and is placed and planted in it as in the woods and region where it is born and nurtured. Indeed, God commanded this when He created the elements. He ordered the earth to produce the plants and the animals; and the sea and water, the fish; and He made the air a habitation for birds. [Gn. 1:11, 12, 20, 21, 24, 28]

Seeing that as He commanded it was done, the soul says in the following verse:

3.   Planted by the hand of my Beloved!

This verse contains the following reflection: Only the hand of God, her Beloved, was able to create this diversity and grandeur.

It is noteworthy that she deliberately says "by the hand of my Beloved." Although God often acts through the hand of another—as through those of angels and men—He never created, nor does He carry on this work of creation by any other hand than His own. This reflection on creatures, this observing that they are things made by the very hand of God, her Beloved, strongly awakens the soul to love Him.

She then continues:

4.   O green meadow,

This verse refers to her reflection upon the heavens. She calls them a "green meadow" because the created things in them are as verdure that neither dies nor fades with time, and in them, as in cool, verdant meadows, the just find their recreation and delight. The diversity of the beautiful stars and other heavenly planets is also included in this meditation.

5. The Church likewise uses the word "green" to express heavenly things. In praying to God for the souls of the faithful departed, she says, speaking to them: *Constituat vos Dominus inter amoena virentia,* which means: May God set you among delightful, green places. [Rit. Rom., tit. 6, c. 7]

And she says that this green meadow is also

6.   Coated, bright, with flowers,

By these flowers she understands the angels and saintly souls which adorn and beautify that place like a costly enamel on a vase of fine gold.

7.   Tell me, has He passed by you?

This question is the reflection mentioned above; it is similar to saying: Tell me of the excellent qualities He has created in you.

STANZA 5

Pouring out a thousand graces,
He passed these groves in haste;
And having looked at them,
With His image alone,
Clothed them in beauty.

Commentary

1. In this stanza the creatures answer the soul. Their answer, as St. Augustine declares in that same place, is the testimony that they in themselves give the soul of God's grandeur and excellence. [Pseudo-Augustine: *Soliloquiorum animae ad Deum liber unus,* c. 31: ML 40, 888] It is for this testimony that she asked in her meditation. The substance of this stanza is: God created all things with remarkable ease and brevity, and in them He left some trace of Who He is, not only in giving all things being from nothing, but even by endowing them with innumerable graces and qualities, making them beautiful in a wonderful order and unfailing dependence on one another. All of this He did through His own Wisdom, the Word, His only begotten Son by Whom He created them.

She then says:

2.   Pouring out a thousand graces,

These thousand graces she says He was pouring out refer to the numberless multitude of creatures. She records the high number, a thousand, to indicate their multitude. She calls them graces because of the many graces He has endowed creatures with. Pouring these out, that is, stocking the whole world with them,

3.   He passed these groves in haste;

To pass the groves is to create the elements, which are here termed "groves." She declares that He passed by them pouring out a thousand graces, because He adorned them with all the creatures that are favored with graces. And in addition, He poured out on them the thousand graces by giving them the power to concur in generation and conservation.

And she says He passed by because creatures are like a trace of God's passing. Through them one can track down His grandeur, might, wisdom, and other divine attributes.

She declares that this passing was in haste. Creatures are the lesser works of God, because He made them as though in passing. The greater works, in which He manifested Himself more and to which He gave greater attention, were those of the Incarnation of the Word and the mysteries of the Christian faith. Compared to these, all the others were done as though in passing and with haste.

4.   And having looked at them,
                          With His image alone,
                          Clothed them in beauty.

St. Paul says: *the Son of God is the splendor of His glory and the image of His substance.* [Heb. 1:3] It should be known that only with this figure, His Son, did God look at all things, that is, He communicated to them their natural being and many natural graces and gifts, and made them complete and perfect, as is said in Genesis: *God looked at all things that He made, and they were very good.* [Gn. 1:31] To look and behold that they were very good was to make them very good in the Word, His Son.

Not only by looking at them did He communicate natural being and graces, as we said, but also with this image of His Son alone, He clothed them in beauty by imparting to them supernatural being. This He did when He became man and elevated human nature in the beauty of God and consequently all creatures, since in human nature He was united with them all. Accordingly, the Son of God proclaimed: *If I be lifted up from the earth, I will elevate all things to Me.* [Jn. 12:32] And in this elevation of all things through the Incarnation of His Son and through the glory of His resurrection according to the flesh, the Father did not merely beautify creatures partially, but rather we can say, clothed them wholly in beauty and dignity.

STANZA 6

Introduction

1. In addition to all this, from the viewpoint of contemplative experience, it should be known that in the living contemplation and knowledge of creatures the soul sees such fullness of graces, powers, and beauty with which God has endowed them that seemingly all are arrayed in wonderful beauty and natural virtue. This beauty and virtue is derived from above and imparted by that infinite supernatural beauty of the Image of God; His look clothes the world and all the heavens with beauty and gladness, just as He also, upon opening His hand, fills every animal with blessing, as David says. [Ps. 144:16]

The soul, wounded with love through a trace of the beauty of her

Beloved, which she has known through creatures, and anxious to see
that invisible beauty which caused this visible beauty, declares in the
following verses:

> Ah, who has the power to heal me?
> Now wholly surrender Yourself!
> Do not send me
> Any more messengers,
> They cannot tell me what I must hear.

Commentary

2. Since creatures gave the soul signs of her Beloved and showed
within themselves traces of His beauty and excellence, love increased in
her and, consequently, sorrow at His absence. Since she is conscious that
nothing can cure her grief other than her Beloved's presence and the
sight of Him, she asks Him in this stanza, distrusting any other remedy,
to surrender His presence that she may possess Him. She asks Him
that from henceforth He no longer detain her with any other knowledge,
communications, and traces of His excellence, for these increase her
desire and suffering rather than bring her satisfaction. The will is content
with nothing less than His presence and the sight of Him. She asks,
therefore, if it be His will, that He truly surrender Himself to her in
complete and perfect love. She says:

3.   Ah, who has the power to heal me?
This is like saying: Among all worldly delights and sensible satisfactions and spiritual gratification and sweetness, there is certainly nothing
with the power to heal me, nothing to satisfy me. And then she adds:

4.   Now wholly surrender Yourself!
It is noteworthy that any soul with authentic love cannot be satisfied
until it really possesses God. Everything else not only fails to satisfy it
but, as we said, increases the hunger and appetite to see Him as He is.
Every glimpse of the Beloved received through knowledge, or feeling,
or any other communication (which is like a messenger bringing to the
soul news of Who He is) further increases and awakens her appetite,
like the crumbs given to a famished man. Finding it difficult to be delayed
by so little, she pleads: "Now wholly surrender Yourself!"

5. All the knowledge of God possible in this life, however extensive it
may be, is inadequate, for it is only partial knowledge and very remote.
Essential knowledge of Him is the real knowledge for which the soul
asks here, unsatisfied by these other communications. She says next:

6.   Do not send me
                            Any more messengers,

This is like saying: Do not let my knowledge of You, communicated through these messengers of news and sentiments about You, any longer be so measured, so remote and alien to what my soul desires. How well You know, my Spouse, that messengers redouble the sorrow of one who grieves over Your absence: first, through knowledge they enlarge the wound; second, they seem to postpone Your coming. From now on do not send me this remote knowledge. If up to this time I could be content with it, because I did not have much knowledge or love of You, now the intensity of my love cannot be satisfied with these messages; therefore: "Now wholly surrender Yourself!"

More clearly, this is like saying: My Lord, my Spouse, You have given Yourself to me partially; now may You give me Yourself more completely. You have revealed Yourself to me as through fissures in a rock; now may You give me that revelation more clearly. You have communicated by means of others, as if joking with me; now may You truly grant me a communication of Yourself by Yourself. In Your visits, at times, it seems You are about to give me the jewel of possessing You; but when I become aware of this possession, I discover that I do not have it, for You hide this jewel as if You had given it jokingly. Now wholly surrender Yourself by giving Yourself entirely to all of me, that my entire soul may have complete possession of You.

7.   Do not send me
                            Any more messengers,
                            They cannot tell me what I must hear.

This verse is equivalent to saying: I desire complete knowledge of You, and they have neither knowledge nor ability to tell of You entirely. Nothing in heaven or on earth can give the soul the knowledge she desires of You. Thus, "they cannot tell me what I must hear." Instead of these other messengers, may You, then, be both the messenger and message.

Stanza 7

All who are free
Tell me a thousand graceful things of You;
All wound me more
And leave me dying
Of, ah, I-don't-know-what behind their stammering.

Commentary

1. In the previous stanza the soul has shown her sickness or wound of love for her Bridegroom, caused by the knowledge irrational creatures gave of Him. In this stanza she asserts that she is wounded with love because of another higher knowledge she receives of the Beloved through rational creatures (angels and men), creatures more noble than the others. She asserts, too, that she is not merely wounded, but also dying of love. This dying of love is due to an admirable immensity these creatures disclose to her; yet not completely. Because this immensity is indescribable she calls it an "I-don't-know-what." And because of it the soul is dying of love.

2. We can deduce that in this matter of love there exist three ways of suffering for the Beloved corresponding to the three kinds of knowledge of Him.

The first is called a wound. It is the mildest and heals the most quickly, as does a wound. This wound arises from the knowledge the soul receives from creatures, the lowest of God's works. The bride of the Canticle refers to this wound, which we also call sickness, saying: *Adjuro vos, filiae Jerusalem, si inveneritis dilectum meum ut nuntietis ei quia amore langueo* (I adjure you, daughters of Jerusalem, if you find my Beloved that you tell Him that I am sick with love). [Ct. 5:8] By the daughters of Jerusalem she refers to creatures.

3. The second is called a sore wound and cuts more deeply into the soul than the simple wound. As a result it is longer-lasting because it is like a wound that has now become sore, from which she feels she is indeed sorely wounded by love. This sore wound is produced in the soul by knowledge of the Incarnation of the Word and of the mysteries of faith. Since these are more remarkable works of God, embodying in themselves a greater love than that shown forth in creatures, they produce in the soul a more intense love. Thus, if the first is like a wound, this second is like a sore wound, which lasts longer. Speaking of this to the soul in the Canticle of Canticles, the Bridegroom says: *You have wounded my heart, my sister, with one of your eyes and with one hair of your neck.* [Ct. 4:9] The eye refers to faith in the Incarnation of the Bridegroom, and the hair signifies love for this very Incarnation.

4. The third kind of suffering of love is like dying. It is equivalent to having a festered wound, since the soul is now wholly festered. She lives by dying until love, in killing her, makes her live the life of love, transforming her in love. This death of love is caused in the soul by means of a touch of supreme knowledge of the divinity, the "I-don't-

know-what," which she says lies behind their stammering. This touch is
not continual or prolonged, for if it were the soul would be loosed from
the body. It passes quickly, and she is left dying of love. And she dies
the more in growing aware that she does not wholly die of love.

This love is called impatient love. Genesis points to it in telling that the
longing Rachel had to conceive was so intense that she pleaded with
her spouse Jacob: *Da mihi liberos, alioquin moriar* (Give me children,
otherwise I will die). [Gn. 30:1] And the prophet Job exclaimed: *Quis
mihi det ut qui coepit, ipse me conterat* (Who will grant that He Who
gave me a beginning might destroy me?). [Jb. 6:9]

5. The soul says in this stanza that these rational creatures cause two
kinds of suffering of love in her, the sore wound and death; the sore
wound because, as she asserts, they relate a thousand graces of the
Beloved in both the mysteries of faith and the wisdom of God which
they teach her; death, in that which, as she says, lies "behind their
stammering": the feeling and knowledge of the divinity sometimes unveiled in what she hears about God. She says then:

6.   All who are free
She refers here to rational creatures (angels and men) as those who
are free. For they alone among all creatures are free to engage in
knowing God. This is the significance of the term "are free," which
rendered in Latin is *vacant*. This verse, as a result, is like saying: All
of them are free for God. Some, the angels, are free for God in con-
templating and enjoying Him in heaven; others, men, by loving and
desiring Him on earth.

Through these rational creatures the soul acquires a more vivid knowledge of God; sometimes through the consideration of His excellence
which transcends all created things, at other times through what the
rational creatures teach about God. The angels teach us interiorly through
secret inspirations; others teach exteriorly, through the truths of Scripture. As a result she says:

7.   Tell me a thousand graceful things of You;
This line means: They teach me choice things about Your grace and
mercy manifested in both the works of Your Incarnation and the truths
of faith. And they forever tell more, because the more they desire to
tell, the more of Your graces they are able to reveal.

8.   All wound me more
Insofar as angels inspire me and men teach me about You, they
inspire me to love You more. Thus all wound me more with love.

9.   And leave me dying
       Of, ah, I-don't-know-what behind their stammering.

These lines amount to saying: Beside the fact that these creatures wound me with the thousand graceful things they explain about You, there is a certain "I-don't-know-what" which one feels is yet to be said, something unknown still to be spoken, and a sublime trace of God, as yet uninvestigated, revealed to the soul, a lofty understanding of God which cannot be put into words. Hence she calls this something "I-don't know-what." If what I understand wounds me with love, this which I do not understand completely, yet have sublime experience of, is death to me.

Sometimes God favors advanced souls, through what they hear, see, or understand—and sometimes independently of this—with a sublime knowledge by which they receive an understanding or experience of the height and grandeur of God. Their experience of God in this favor is so lofty that they understand clearly that everything remains to be understood. This understanding and experience that the divinity is so immense as to surpass complete understanding is indeed a sublime knowledge.

One of the outstanding favors God grants briefly in this life is an understanding and experience of Himself so lucid and lofty as to make one know clearly that He cannot be completely understood or experienced. This understanding is somewhat like that of the Blessed in heaven: Those who understand God more, understand more distinctly the infinitude which remains to be understood; whereas those who see less of Him do not realize so clearly what remains to be seen.

10. I do not think anyone who has not had such experience will understand this well. But, since the soul experiencing this is aware that what she has so sublimely experienced remains beyond her understanding, she calls it "I-don't-know-what." Since it is not understandable, it is indescribable, although, as I say, one may know what the experience of it is. As a result, she says the creatures are stammering, for they do not make it completely known. Stammering, a trait we notice in children's speech, means that one is unsuccessful in saying and explaining what one has to say.

Stanza 8

Introduction

1. When God favors the soul by disclosing to it a spiritual knowledge and experience of other creatures, he gives it some illuminations concerning these creatures, in the way we mentioned, although these illuminations are not always so sublime as the others. It seems these creatures impart to the soul an understanding of the grandeurs of God

which are not entirely understandable; and it is as if they were making these grandeurs understood while yet they remain to be understood. Hence it is an "I-don't-know-what behind their stammering."

The soul continues with her complaint, and in the following stanza speaks to her life, saying:

> How do you endure
> O life, not living where you live?
> And being brought near death
> By the arrows you receive
> From that which you conceive of your Beloved.

Commentary

2. Since the soul is aware that she is dying of love, as she has just declared, but that she does not die entirely and thus enjoy love freely, she complains about the duration of life in the body, on account of which the spiritual life is delayed.

In this stanza she addresses her own life, stressing the grief it causes her. The meaning of the stanza is as follows: Life of my soul, how can you endure in this bodily life, for it is death to you and a privation of that true spiritual life of God, in which through essence, love, and desire you live more truly than in the body? And now that this understanding of God's grandeur has not caused you to go out and be freed from the body of this death [Rom. 7:24] so as to live and enjoy the life of your God, how can you still live in a body so fragile? Moreover, the wounds of love which you receive from the grandeurs of the Beloved communicated to you are, in themselves alone, enough to end your life. For all of them leave you wounded with vehement love. And the things you experience and understand of Him are as numerous as the touches and wounds you receive of a love that slays.

The verse follows:

3.   How do you endure
        O life, not living where you live?

To understand these lines it should be known that the soul lives where she loves more than in the body she animates; for she does not live in the body, but rather gives life to the body, and lives through love in the object of her love.

Yet, beside this life of love through which the soul that loves God lives in Him, her life is radically and naturally centered in God, like that of all created things, centered in God, as St. Paul says: *In Him we live and move and are.* [Acts 17:28] This was like saying: In God we have our life and our movement and our being. And St. John says that all that was made was life in God. [Jn. 1:3–4] Since the soul knows she has her natural life in God by the being she has in Him, and her spiritual life through the love by which she loves Him, she complains and laments that so fragile a life in the mortal body can achieve so much as to hinder her from the enjoyment of a life so strong, true, and delightful as the one she lives in God through nature and love.

The soul lays great stress on this complaint, for she announces here that she suffers from two contraries: natural life in the body, and spiritual life in God. They are contraries insofar as the one wars against the other. [Rom. 7:23] And living both in the body and in God, she necessarily feels great torment, since the one painful life thwarts the other delightful one, so much so that the natural life is like death to her, because through it she is deprived of the spiritual life in which she has all her being and life by nature and all her operations and affections through love.

To indicate further the hardship of this fragile life, she says next:

> 4.   And being brought near death
>   By the arrows you receive

This is like saying: Moreover, how can you endure in the body, since the touches of love (indicated by the arrows) which the Beloved causes in your heart are enough to take away your life. These touches so impregnate the soul and heart with the knowledge and love of God that she can truthfully say she conceives, as she does in the following verse:

> 5.   From that which you conceive of your Beloved.

That is, from the grandeur, beauty, wisdom, grace, and virtues you understand of Him.

STANZA 9

Introduction

1. A stag, wounded by a poison arrow, neither rests nor remains calm, but searches everywhere for remedies, plunging now into these waters, now into those, and the effect of the poison arrow ever increases in all circumstances and with all remedies taken, until finally it seizes upon the heart, and the stag dies. Similarly, the soul touched by the poison arrow of love, as is this soul we are discussing, never stops seeking remedies for her sorrow. Yet she not only fails to find them, but everything she thinks, says, and does brings her greater sorrow. Conscious of this, and knowing that she has no other remedy than to put herself in the hands of the one who wounded her, so that in relieving her He may

slay her now entirely with the force of love, she turns to her Bridegroom, Who is the cause of all this, and speaks to Him in the following stanza:

> Why, since You wounded
> This heart, don't You heal it?
> And why, since You stole it from me,
> Do you leave it so,
> And fail to carry off what You have stolen?

Commentary

2. The soul, then, in this stanza, still complaining of her grief, turns once more to speak with the Beloved. For the impatient love here manifested will endure no idleness and allow no rest to the soul in its affliction, but shows its longings in every way until it discovers a remedy. Aware that she is sorely wounded and alone, without any other remedy or medicine than her Beloved, the one who wounded her, she questions Him: Why didn't He heal her with the vision of His presence, since He wounded her heart with love coming from knowledge of Himself? She also asks, since He stole her through the love by which He captivated her and carried her away from her own power, why He leaves her thus drawn out of her own power (for the lover does not possess her heart but has given it to the beloved) and does not truly place her heart in His own, taking it for Himself in complete transformation of love in glory.

She asks then:

3.   Why, since You wounded
                  This heart, don't You heal it?

Her complaint is not that He wounded her—for the more a loving soul is wounded the more its love is repaid—but that in sorely wounding her heart, He did not heal her by slaying her completely. The wounds of love are so sweet and delightful that if they do not cause death they cannot satisfy. Yet they are so delightful that she would want them to wound her sorely until they slay her completely. Consequently, she says: "Why, since You wounded this heart, don't You heal it?"

This is equivalent to saying: Why, since You wounded this heart until it has become sorely wounded, do You not heal it by wholly slaying it with love? Since You cause the sore wound in the sickness of love, may You cause health in the death of love. As a result, the heart, wounded with the sorrow of Your absence, will be healed with the delight and glory of Your sweet presence. And she adds:

4.   And why, since You stole it from me,
                      Do You leave it so,

To steal is to dispossess an owner of what belongs to him and take possession of it oneself. This is the complaint the soul here sets before the Beloved in asking, since He has robbed her heart through love and taken it out of her power and possession, why He left it so, without really taking possession of it, as the thief does with the stolen goods he in fact carries off.

5. He who is in love is said to have his heart stolen or seized by the object of his love, for his heart will go out of self and become fixed on the loved object. Thus his heart or love is not for himself, but for what he loves.

Accordingly, the soul can know clearly whether or not she loves God purely. If she loves Him, her heart or love will not be set on herself or her own satisfaction and gain, but upon pleasing God and giving Him honor and glory. In the measure she loves herself that much less she loves God.

6. Whether the heart has been truly stolen by God will be evident in either of the two following signs: if it has longings for God; or if it finds no satisfaction in anything but Him, as the soul demonstrates here. The reason is that the heart cannot have peace and rest while not possessing, and when it is truly in love it no longer has possession of self or of any other thing. And if it does not possess completely what it loves, it cannot help being weary, in proportion to its loss, until it possesses the loved object and is satisfied. Until this possession, the soul is like an empty vessel waiting to be filled, or like a hungry man craving for food, or like a sick person moaning for health, or like one suspended in the air with nothing to lean on. Such is the truly loving heart.

The soul experiencing this love exclaims: "Why do You leave it so," that is: empty, hungry, alone, sorely wounded and sick with love, and suspended in the air,

7.   And fail to carry off what You have stolen?

That is: Why do You fail to carry off the heart You have stolen through love; and why do You fail to fill, satisfy, accompany, and heal it, giving it complete stability and repose in You?

The loving soul, however great her conformity to the Beloved, cannot cease longing for the wages of her love, for which she serves the Beloved. Otherwise there would not be true love, because the payment for love is nothing else—neither can the soul desire anything else—than more love, until the perfection of love is reached.

Love is paid only with love itself, as the prophet Job brought out when he exclaimed with the same yearning and desire the soul has:

Just as the servant desires the shade, and the day laborer waits for the end of his work, so I had empty months and I counted the nights wearisome for myself. If I lie down to sleep, I shall say: When will the day come that I might arise? Then again I turn to awaiting the evening, and I shall be full of sorrows till the darkness of night. [Jb. 7:2–4] The soul, then, enkindled with love of God yearns for the fulfillment and perfection of love in order to have therein complete refreshment. As the servant, wearied by the summer heat, longs for the refreshing shade, and as the hireling awaits the end of his work, the soul awaits the end of hers.

It is noteworthy that the prophet Job did not say that the hireling was awaiting the end of his labor, but the end of his work, in order to indicate what we are explaining, that is, that the soul that loves does not await the end of her labor but the end of her work. Her work is to love, and of this work, love, she awaits the end, which is the perfection and completeness of it. Until this work is accomplished the soul is always in the condition of the picture Job paints in this passage; she considers her days and months empty and counts her nights as long and wearisome.

We have explained how the soul that loves God must not desire or hope for any other reward for her services than the perfect love of God.

STANZA 10

Introduction

1. The soul, then, in this condition of love is like a sick man who is extremely tired and, having lost his taste and appetite, finds all food nauseating and everything a disturbance and annoyance. In everything he thinks or sees he has only one desire, the desire for health, and all that does not lead to this is a bother and burden to him.

Since the soul has reached this sickness of love of God, she has three traits: in all things that are offered to her or with which she deals, she has ever before her that longing for her health, which is her Beloved (even though she cannot help being occupied with them, she always has her heart fixed on Him); the second trait, arising from this first, is the loss of taste for all things; the third then results, which is that all these things molest her and all dealings with others are burdensome and annoying.

2. The reason for these traits, deduced from what has been said, is that, since the palate of the soul's will has tasted this food of love of God, her will is inclined immediately to seek and enjoy her Beloved in everything that happens and in all her occupations, without looking for any

satisfaction or concern of her own. Mary Magdalen acted similarly when with ardent love she was searching for Him in the garden: thinking that He was the gardener, without any further reasoning or consideration, she pleaded with Him: *If you have taken Him from me, tell me, and I will take Him away.* [Jn. 20:15] Having a similar yearning to find Him in all things, and not immediately finding Him as she desires—but rather quite the contrary—not only does the soul fail to find satisfaction in these things, but they also become a torment to her, and sometimes a very great one. Such souls suffer much in dealing with people and with business matters, for these contacts hinder rather than help them to their goal.

3. The bride clearly indicates in the Canticle these three traits she had when searching for her Bridegroom: *I looked for Him and did not find Him. But they who go about the city found me and wounded me, and the guards of the walls took my mantle from me.* [Ct. 5:6–7] Those who go about the city refer to the affairs of the world. When they find the soul who is searching for God, they inflict upon her many wounds of sorrow, pain, and displeasure, for not only does she fail to find her desire in them, but she is also impeded by them. Those who guard the wall of contemplation, to prevent the soul from entering, are the devils and the negotiations of the world, and they take away the mantle of the peace and quietude of loving contemplation.

The soul that loves God derives a thousand displeasures and annoyances from all of these. Conscious that as long as she is in this life without the vision of God, she cannot free herself from them to either a small or great degree, she continues her prayers to the Beloved and recites the following stanza:

> Extinguish these miseries,
> Since no one else can stamp them out;
> And may my eyes behold You,
> Because You are their light,
> And I would open them to You alone.

Commentary

4. She continues in this stanza to ask the Beloved to put an end to her longings and pains, since He alone can do this, and no one else; and to accomplish this so that the eyes of her soul may be able to see Him, since He alone is the light they behold, and she wants to employ them in Him alone:

5.   Extinguish these miseries,

A characteristic of the desires of love is that all deeds and words unconformed with what the will loves, weary, tire, annoy, and displease the soul as she beholds that her desire goes unfulfilled. She refers to this weariness she suffers in order to see God as "these miseries." And nothing but possession of the Beloved can extinguish them. She says He extinguishes them by His presence and refreshes her as cool water soothes a man exhausted from the heat. She uses the word "extinguish" to indicate that she is suffering from the fire of love.

6.   Since no one else can stamp them out;

To further urge and persuade her Beloved to grant her petition, she declares that, since He alone suffices to satisfy her need, He must be the one to extinguish these miseries. It is noteworthy that God is very ready to comfort and satisfy the soul in her needs and afflictions when she neither has nor desires consolation and satisfaction outside of Him. The soul possessing nothing that might withhold her from God cannot remain long without a visit from the Beloved.

7.   And may my eyes behold You,

That is: May I see You face to face with the eyes of my soul,

8.   Because You are their light,

Regardless of the fact that God is the supernatural light of the soul's eyes, and that without this light she is enveloped in darkness, she affectionately calls Him here the light of her eyes, just as a man might call the one he loves the light of his eyes in order to show his affection.

These two verses are like saying: Since my eyes have no other light (neither through nature nor through love) than You, may my eyes behold You because You are their light in every way. David noted the absence of this light when he lamented: *the light of my eyes itself is not with me.* [Ps. 37:11] Tobias did the same: *What joy can be mine, since I am seated in darkness and do not see the light of heaven?* [Tb. 5:12] Through these words he gave expression to his desire for the clear vision of God, because the light of heaven is the Son of God, as St. John says: *The heavenly city has no need of the sun nor of the moon to shine in it, because the brightness of God illumines it, and the Lamb is the lamp thereof.* [Ap. 21:23]

9.   And I would open them to You alone.

With this line the soul desires to oblige the Bridegroom to reveal this light of her eyes, not only because she lives in darkness in that her eyes have no other light, but also because she wants to keep her eyes for Him alone. As the soul longing to focus the eyes of her will upon the light of something outside of God is justly deprived of the divine light—insofar as the spiritual powers she has for receiving God's light are occupied with this other light—so also does the soul that closes its eyes to all things in order to open them to God alone merit congruously the illumination of the divine light.

Stanza 11

Introduction

1. It should be known that the loving Bridegroom of souls cannot long watch them suffering alone—as this soul is suffering—because as He says through Zacharias, their afflictions touch Him in the apple of His eye [Za. 2:8]; especially when these afflictions are the outcome of love for Him, as are those of this soul. He also declares through Isaias: *Before they call, I will hear; while they are yet with the word in their mouth, I will hear them.* [Is. 65:24] The Wise Man says of Him, that if the soul seeks Him as money, she will find Him. [Prv. 2:4–5]

Apparently God granted a certain spiritual feeling of His presence to this loving soul whose prayers are so enkindled and who seeks Him more covetously than one would seek money, since she has left herself and all things for Him. In this spiritual sense of His presence, He revealed some deep glimpses of His divinity and beauty by which He greatly increased her fervor and desire to see Him. As a man throws water into the forge to stir up and intensify the fire, so the Lord usually grants to some souls that walk in these fiery longings of love certain signs of His excellence to make them more fervent and further prepare them for the favors He wishes to grant them later.

Since the soul saw and experienced through that obscure presence the Supreme Good and Beauty hidden there, she recites the following stanza, dying with the desire to see Him:

> Reveal Your presence,
> And may the vision of Your beauty be my death;
> For the sickness of love
> Is not cured
> Except by Your very presence and image.

Commentary

2. The soul, desiring to be possessed by this immense God, for love of Whom she feels that her heart is robbed and wounded, unable to endure her sickness any longer, deliberately asks Him in this stanza to show her His beauty, His divine essence, and to kill her with this revelation, and thereby free her from the flesh since she cannot see and enjoy Him as she wants. She makes this request by displaying before Him the sickness and yearning of her heart, in which she perseveres suffering for love of

Him, unable to find a cure in anything less than this glorious vision of His divine essence. The verse follows:

3.   Reveal Your presence,

In explanation of this verse it should be known that God's presence can be of three kinds:

The first is His presence by essence. In this way He is present not only in the holiest souls, but also in sinners and in all other creatures. For with this presence He gives them life and being. Should this essential presence be lacking to them, they would all be annihilated. Thus this presence is never wanting to the soul.

The second is His presence by grace, in which He abides in the soul, pleased and satisfied with it. Not all have this presence of God; those who fall into mortal sin lose it. The soul cannot know naturally if it has this presence.

The third is His presence by spiritual affection, for God usually grants His spiritual presence to devout souls in many ways, by which He refreshes, delights, and gladdens them.

Yet, these many kinds of spiritual presence, just as the others, are all hidden, for in them God does not reveal Himself as He is, since the conditions of this life will not allow such a manifestation. Thus the above verse, "reveal Your presence," could be understood of any of these three ways in which God is present.

4. Since it is certain that at least in the first way God is ever present in the soul, she does not ask Him to be present in her, but that He so reveal His hidden presence, whether natural, spiritual, or affective, that she may be able to see Him in His divine being and beauty. As he gives the soul natural being through His essential presence, and perfects her through His presence by grace, she begs Him to glorify her also with His manifest glory.

Yet insofar as this soul is full of fervor and tender love of God, we should understand that this presence she asks the Beloved to reveal refers chiefly to a certain affective presence which the Beloved accords her. This presence is so sublime that the soul feels an immense hidden being is there from which God communicates to her some semi-clear glimpses of His divine beauty. And these bear such an effect on the soul that she ardently longs and faints with desire for what she feels hidden there in that presence, which is similar to what David felt when he exclaimed: *My soul longs and faints for the courts of the Lord.* [Ps. 83:3]

At this time the soul faints with longing to be engulfed in that supreme good she feels present and hidden, for although it is hidden she has a notable experience of the good and delight present there. Accordingly she is drawn and carried toward this good more forcibly than any material object is pulled toward its center by gravity. With this longing and heartfelt desire, unable to contain herself any longer, the soul begs: Reveal Your presence,

5. Moses had this very experience on Mount Sinai. While standing in God's presence, he was able to get such sublime and profound glimpses of the height and beauty of the hidden divinity that, unable to endure it, he asked God twice to reveal His glory: *You say that You know me by name and that I have found favor before You. If therefore I have found favor in Your presence, show me Your face that I may know You and find before Your eyes the grace which I desire fulfilled* [Ex. 33:12–13], that is, to reach the perfect love of the glory of God. Yet the Lord answered: *You shall not be able to see My face, for no man shall see Me and live.* [Ex. 33:20] This is like saying: You ask a difficult thing of Me, Moses, for such is the beauty of My face and the delight derived from the sight of My being that your soul will be unable to withstand it in a life as weak as this.

The soul knows that she cannot see Him in His beauty in this kind of life. She knows this either through God's answer to Moses or through her experience of what is hidden here in the presence of God. For even though He appears but vaguely, she faints. Hence she anticipates the reply that can be made to her as it was to Moses and says:

6.   And may the vision of Your beauty be my death;
This is like saying: Since the delight arising from the sight of Your being and beauty is unendurable, and since I must die in seeing You, may the vision of Your beauty be my death.

7. It is known that there are two visions which will kill a man because of the inability of human nature to suffer their force and vigor: one is that of the basilisk, from which it is said one dies immediately; the other is the vision of God. Yet the causes are very different, for the sight of one kills with a terrible poison, and that of God by an immense health and glorious good.

The soul does nothing very outstanding by wanting to die at the sight of the beauty of God in order to enjoy Him forever. Were she to have but a foreglimpse of the height and beauty of God, she would not only desire death in order to see Him now forever, as she here desires, but she would very gladly undergo a thousand singularly bitter deaths to see Him only for a moment; and having seen Him, she would ask to suffer just as many more that she might see Him for another moment.

8. To shed further light on this verse, it should be known that when the soul asks that the vision of His beauty be her death she speaks conditionally, under the supposition that she cannot see Him without dying. Were she able to see Him without dying, she would not ask Him to slay her, for to desire death is a natural imperfection. Yet with the supposition

that this corruptible life of man is incompatible with the other incorruptible life of God, she says, "may the vision of Your beauty be my death."

9. St. Paul teaches this doctrine to the Corinthians, saying: *we do not wish to be unclothed, but we desire to be clothed over, that that which is mortal may be absorbed in life.* [2 Cor. 5:4] This is like saying: we do not desire to be despoiled of the flesh but to be clothed over with glory. Yet observing that one cannot live simultaneously in glory and in the mortal flesh, he says to the Philippians that he desires to be loosed and to be with Christ. [Phil. 1:23]

Yet one may question: Why did the children of Israel formerly flee God and fear to see Him lest they die, as Manue and his wife [Jgs. 13:22], whereas this soul desires to die at the sight of God? We reply that there are two reasons for this:

First, even though the children of Israel at that time died in the grace of God, they were not to see Him until the coming of Christ. It was much better for them to live in the flesh, increasing their merits and enjoying their natural life, than to be in limbo, without ability to merit, and suffering the darkness and spiritual absence of God. As a result they considered it a wonderful gift and favor from God to live for many years.

10. The second reason is based on love. Since the Israelites were not so fortified in love, nor so close to God through love, they feared to die upon seeing Him. But because now in the law of grace the soul when separated from the body can see God, the desire to live but a short while and die in order to see Him is more perfect. And even if this were false, the soul, loving God as intensely as this one does, would not fear to die from seeing Him. True love receives all things that come from the Beloved—prosperity, adversity, even chastisement—with the same evenness of soul, since they are His will. And they afford her joy and delight, because, as St. John says: *Perfect charity casts out all fear.* [1 Jn. 4:18]

Death cannot be bitter to the soul that loves, for in it she finds all the sweetness and delight of love. The thought of death cannot sadden her, for she finds that gladness accompanies this thought. Neither can the thought of death be burdensome and painful to her, for death will put an end to all her sorrows and afflictions and be the beginning of all her bliss. She thinks of death as her friend and bridegroom, and at the thought of it she rejoices as she would over the thought of her betrothal and marriage, and she longs for that day and that hour of her death more than earthly kings yearn for kingdoms and principalities.

The Wise Man proclaims of this kind of death: *O death! Your sentence is welcome to the man who feels need.* [Ecclus. 41:3] If it is welcome to the man who feels need for earthly things, even though it does not provide for these needs but rather despoils him of the possessions he has, how much better will its sentence be for the soul in need of love, as is this one who is crying out for more love. For death will not despoil her of the love she possesses, but rather be the cause of love's completeness, which she desires, and the satisfaction of all her needs.

The soul is right in daring to say, may the vision of Your beauty be my death, since she knows that at the instant she sees this beauty she will be carried away by it, and absorbed in this very beauty, and transformed in this same beauty, and made beautiful like this beauty itself, and enriched and provided for like this very beauty.

David declares, consequently, that the death of the saints is precious in the sight of the Lord. [Ps. 115:15] This would not be true if they did not participate in His very grandeurs, for in the sight of God nothing is precious but what He in Himself is.

Accordingly, the soul does not fear death when she loves, rather she desires it. Yet the sinner is always fearful of death. He foresees that death will take everything away and bring him all evils. As David says, *the death of sinners is very evil.* [Ps. 33:22] And hence, as the Wise Man says, the remembrance of it is bitter. [Ecclus. 41:1] Since sinners love the life of this world intensely and have little love for that of the other, they have an immense fear of death.

The soul that loves God lives more in the next life than in this, for the soul lives where it loves more than where it gives life, and thus has but little esteem for this temporal life. She says then, "may the vision of Your beauty be my death."

11.   For the sickness of love
       Is not cured
       Except by Your very presence and image.

The reason love-sickness has no other remedy than the presence and the image of the Beloved is that, since this sickness differs from others, its medicine also differs. In other sicknesses, following sound philosophy, contraries are cured by contraries, but love is incurable except by what is in accord with love.

The reason for this is that love of God is the soul's health, and the soul does not have full health until love is complete. Sickness is nothing but a want of health, and when the soul has not even a single degree of love, she is dead. But when she possesses some degrees of love of God, no matter how few, she is then alive, yet very weak and infirm because of her little love. In the measure that love increases she will be healthier, and when love is perfect she will have full health.

12. It should be known that love never reaches perfection until the lovers are so alike that one is transfigured in the other. And then the love

is in full health. The soul experiences within herself a certain sketch of love, which is the sickness she mentions, and she desires the completion of the sketch of this image, the image of her Bridegroom, the Word, the Son of God, who as St. Paul says, *is the splendor of His glory and the image of His substance* [Heb. 1:3], for this is the image referred to in this verse and into which the soul desires to be transfigured through love. As a result she says: For the sickness of love is not cured except by Your very presence and image.

13. She does well to call imperfect love "sickness." For just as a sick man is too weak for work, so is the soul, feeble in love, too weak to practice heroic virtue.

14. It is also noteworthy that he who feels in himself the sickness of love, a lack of love, shows that he has some love, because he is aware of what he lacks through what he has. Whoever does not feel this sickness shows that he either has no love or is perfect in love.

Stanza 12

Introduction

1. At this period the soul feels that she is rushing toward God as impetuously as a falling stone when nearing its center. She also feels that she is like wax in which an impress is being made, but not yet completed. She knows too that she is like a sketch or the first draft of a drawing and calls out to the one who did this sketch to finish the painting and image. And her faith is so enlightened that it gives her a glimpse of some clear divine reflections of the height of her God. As a result she does not know what to do other than turn to this very faith, which contains and hides the image and the beauty of her Beloved, and from which she also receives these sketches and tokens of love, and speak to it in the following stanza:

> O spring like crystal!
> If only, on your silvered-over face,
> You would suddenly form
> The eyes I have desired,
> Which I bear sketched deep within my heart.

Commentary

2. Since the soul longs so ardently for union with the Bridegroom, and is aware that she finds no remedy in any creature, she turns to speak to

faith, as to that which most vividly sheds light concerning her Beloved, and takes it as a means toward this union. Indeed, there is no other means by which one reaches true union and spiritual espousal with God, as Osee indicates: *I will espouse you to me in faith.* [Os. 2:20] With this burning desire she exclaims the following, which is the meaning of the stanza: O faith of Christ, my Spouse, would that you might show me clearly now the truths of my Beloved, which you have infused in my soul and which are covered with obscurity and darkness (for faith, as the theologians say, is an obscure habit), in such a way that, what you communicate to me in inexplicit and obscure knowledge, you would show suddenly, clearly, and perfectly, changing it into a manifestation of glory! Would that you might do this by drawing back from these truths (for faith is the veil of the truths of God)! The verse then runs:

3.   O spring like crystal!

She says faith is like crystal for two reasons: first, because it concerns Christ, her Spouse; second, because it has the characteristics of crystal. It is pure in its truths, and strong and clear, cleansed of errors and natural forms.

And she calls it a "spring" because from it the waters of all spiritual goods flow into the soul. Christ, our Lord, speaking with the Samaritan woman, called faith a "spring," declaring that in those who believed in Him He would make a fountain whose waters would leap up unto life everlasting. [Jn. 4:14] This water was the Spirit which believers were to receive through faith. [Jn. 7:39]

4.   If only, on your silvered-over face,

She calls the propositions and articles of faith a "silvered-over face." To understand this verse as well as the others, it should be known that faith is compared to silver in the propositions it teaches us, and that the truths and substance it contains are compared to gold. For in the next life we shall see and enjoy openly this very substance which, clothed and covered with the silver of faith, we now believe.

David says of faith: *If you sleep between the two choirs, the feathers of the dove will be silvery and the hinder parts will be of the color of gold.* [Ps. 67:14] This means that if we close the eyes of the intellect to earthly and heavenly things, which he terms "sleeping between," we will remain in faith. He calls faith "the dove"; and its feathers (the truths it tells us) are silvery, because in this life faith proposes these truths to us covered and in darkness. As a result she calls these truths a silvered-over face. Yet when faith comes to an end, when it terminates through the clear vision of God, the substance of faith, in having been stripped of the veil of silver, will have the color of gold.

Faith, consequently, gives us God, but covered with the silver of faith. Yet it does not for this reason fail to give Him to us truly. Were someone to give us a gold vase plated with silver, he would not fail to give a gold vase merely because it is silver-plated. When the bride of the Canticle wanted this possession of God, He promised to make her, insofar as possible in this life, gold earrings, plated with silver. [Ct. 1:10] He thereby promised to give Himself to her, but hidden in faith.

The soul, then, exclaims to faith: Oh, if only on your silvered-over face (the articles we mentioned) by which you cover the gold of the divine rays (the eyes I have desired), and she adds:

5.   You would suddenly form
                   The eyes I have desired,

The eyes refer to the divine truths and rays. Faith, as we mentioned, proposes these truths to us in its covered and inexplicit articles. The soul, in other words, says: Oh, if only the truths hidden in your articles, which you teach me in an inexplicit and dark manner, you would give me now completely, clearly, and explicitly, freed of their covering, as my desire begs!

She calls these truths "eyes" because of the remarkable presence of the Beloved she experiences. It seems that He is now always looking at her. Thus she says:

6.   Which I bear sketched deep within my heart.

She says these truths are sketched deep within her, that is, in her soul, in her intellect and will.

For these truths are infused by faith into her intellect. And since the knowledge of them is imperfect, she says they are sketched. Just as a sketch is not a perfect painting, so the knowledge of faith is not perfect knowledge. Hence, the truths infused in the soul through faith are as though sketched, and when they will be clearly visible they will be like a perfect and finished painting in the soul. As the Apostle says: *Cum autem venerit quod perfectum est evacuabitur quod ex parte est* [1 Cor. 13:10]; this means that when what is perfect, the clear vision, comes, that which is in part, the knowledge of faith, will end.

7. Over this sketch of faith is drawn in the will of the lover the sketch of love. When there is union of love, the image of the Beloved is so sketched in the will and drawn so intimately and vividly, that it is true to say that the Beloved lives in the lover and the lover in the Beloved. Love produces such likeness in this transformation of lovers that one can say each is the other and both are one. The reason is, that in the union and transformation of love each gives possession of self to the other, and each leaves and exchanges self for the other. Thus each one lives in the other and is the other, and both are one in the transformation of love.

8. This is the meaning of St. Paul's affirmation: *Vivo autem, iam non ego; vivit vero in me Christus* (I live, now not I, but Christ lives in

me). [Gal. 2:20] In saying, I live, now not I, he meant that, even though he had life it was not his, because he was transformed in Christ, and it was divine more than human. He consequently asserts that he does not live, but that Christ lives in him. In accord with this likeness and transformation, we can say that his life and Christ's were one life through union of love. This transformation into divine life will be effected perfectly in heaven, in all those who merit the vision of God. Transformed in God, these blessed souls will live the life of God and not their own life—although, indeed, it will be their own life, because God's life will be theirs. Then they will truly proclaim: We live, now not we, but God lives in us.

Although transformation in this life can be what it was in St. Paul, it still cannot be perfect and complete, even though the soul reaches such transformation of love as is found in the spiritual marriage, the highest state attainable in this life. Everything can be called a sketch of love in comparison with that perfect image, the transformation in glory. Yet the attainment of such a sketch of transformation in this life is a great blessing, for with this transformation the Beloved is very pleased. Desiring the bride to put Him as a sketch in her soul, He said in the Canticle: *Put Me as a seal upon your heart, as a seal upon your arm.* [Ct. 8:6] The heart signifies the soul in which God dwells in this life as a seal, which is the sketch of faith, mentioned above; the arm signifies the strong will in which He is present as the seal, which is the sketch of love we just discussed.

9. The soul's state at this time is such that I do not want to neglect saying something about it, even though briefly, regardless of the fact that it is indescribable. It seems to the soul that its bodily and spiritual substance is drying up with thirst for this living spring of God. Its thirst is like David's when he said: *As the hart longs for the fount of waters, so does my soul long for You, my God. My soul has thirsted for God the living fount; when shall I see and appear before the face of God?* [Ps. 41:2–3] This thirst so exhausts the soul that she would think nothing of breaking through the midst of the camp of the Philistines, as did David's strong men to fill their containers with water from the cistern of Bethlehem, which was Christ. [1 Par. 11:18] She would consider all the difficulties of the world, and the fury of demons, and infernal afflictions nothing if by passing through them she could plunge into the unfathomable spring of love. In this respect it is said in the Canticle: *Love is as strong as death and its jealousy as hard as hell.* [Ct. 8:6]

It is incredible how ardent the longing and pain is that the soul experiences when she sees that she is near the enjoyment of that good, and that yet it is not given to her. The more the object of her desire comes into sight and the closer it draws, while yet being denied her, so much more pain and torment does it cause. In this spiritual sense Job says: *Before I eat, I sigh; and the roaring and bellowing of my soul is like overflowing waters* [Jb. 3:24], with craving for food (by the food is meant God), because the yearning for food, or the knowledge of Him, is commensurate with the suffering for Him.

Stanza 13

Introduction

1. This is the reason the soul's suffering for God at this time is so intense: she is drawing nearer to Him, and so she has greater experience within herself of the void of God, of very heavy darkness, and of spiritual fire which dries up and purges her, so that thus purified she may be united with Him. Inasmuch as God does not communicate some supernatural ray of light from Himself, He is intolerable darkness to her when He is spiritually near her, for the supernatural light darkens with its excess the natural light. David indicated all this when he said: *Clouds and darkness are round about Him; fire goes before Him.* [Ps. 96:2-3] And in another psalm he asserts: *He made darkness His covert and hiding place, and His tent round about Him is dark water in the clouds of the air; because of His great splendor there are in His presence clouds, hail, and coals of fire* [Ps. 17:12-13], that is, for the soul drawing near Him. As the soul comes closer to Him, and until God introduces her into His divine splendors through transformation of love, she experiences within herself all that David described. In the meanwhile, like Job, she exclaims over and over: *Who will grant me to know Him and find Him and come unto His throne?* [Jb. 23:3]

Just as God through His immense mercy grants the soul favors and consolations in the measure of her darknesses and voids (for *sicut tenebrae ejus, ita et lumen ejus*[1] [Ps. 138:12], and because in exalting and glorifying her He humbles and wearies her), so in a like way He sends the soul suffering these fatigues some of His divine rays with such strong love and glory that He stirs her completely and causes her to go out of her senses. Thus in great fear and trembling, she spoke to her Beloved the first part of the following stanza, and her Beloved then spoke the remaining verses.

> Withdraw them, Beloved,
> I am taking flight!

[1] as is its darkness, so is its light

The Bridegroom

> Return, dove,
> The wounded stag
> Is in sight on the hill,
> Cooled by the breeze of your flight.

Commentary

2. The Beloved usually visits His bride chastely, delicately, and with strong love amid the intense loving desires and ardors she has shown in the previous stanzas. God's favors and visits are generally in accord with the intensity of the yearnings and ardors of love which precede them.

Since, as the soul just finished saying in the previous stanza, she desired these divine eyes with such yearnings, the Beloved revealed to her some rays of His grandeur and divinity. He communicated these so sublimely and forcibly that He carried her out of herself in rapture and ecstasy. At the beginning this is accompanied by great pain and fear in the sensory part. Unable in her weakness to endure such excess, she proclaims in this stanza: "withdraw them, Beloved," that is, these Your divine eyes, "for they cause me to take flight and go out of myself to supreme contemplation, which is beyond what the sensory part can endure." She makes this plea because seemingly the soul is flying away from the body. This flight from the body is what she desired; this is why she begged Him to withdraw His eyes, to cease communicating them to her in the body, in which she is unable to suffer and enjoy them as she would, and communicate them to her in her flight outside the body.

The Bridegroom then impedes this desire and flight, saying: "Return, dove, for the communication you receive from Me is not yet of the state of glory to which you now aspire. Return to Me, for I am He Whom you, wounded with love, seek. For I too, like the stag, wounded by your love begin to reveal Myself to you in your high contemplation, and I am refreshed and renewed in the love which arises from your contemplation."

The soul, then, says to the Bridegroom:

3.   Withdraw them, Beloved . . . !

As we mentioned, the soul in accordance with her intense desire for these divine eyes, for the divinity, received interiorly from the Beloved such divine communication and knowledge that she had to say, "withdraw them, Beloved."

The misery of human nature is such that when the communication and knowledge of the Beloved, which gives more life to the soul and for which she longs so ardently, is about to be imparted, she cannot receive

it save almost at the cost of her life. When she receives the eyes she has
been searching for so anxiously and in so many ways, she cries: "Withdraw them, Beloved . . . !"

4. The torment experienced in these rapturous visits is such that there
is no other which so disjoins the bones and endangers the sensory part.
Were God not to provide, she would die. And indeed, it seems so to the
soul in which this happens, that she is being loosed from the flesh and
is abandoning the body.

The reason for this is that such favors cannot be received wholly in
the body, for the spirit is elevated to commune with the divine Spirit
Who comes to the soul. Thus the soul must in some fashion abandon the
body. As a result the body must suffer and, consequently, the soul in
the body, because of their unity in one *suppositum*. The torment she
experiences at the time of this visit and the terror arising from her awareness of being treated in this supernatural way make her cry: "Withdraw
them, Beloved . . . !"

5. Yet, it should not be thought that because she says withdraw them,
she desires Him to do so. Those words spring from natural fear, as we
said. No matter what the cost, she would not want to lose these visits
and favors of the Beloved. Although the sensory part suffers, the spirit
takes flight to supernatural recollection and enjoyment of the Beloved's
Spirit, which is what she desired and sought. Yet she would not want to
receive the Spirit in the body, for there she cannot receive Him fully,
but only in a small degree and with considerable suffering. But she would
want to receive Him in the flight of the spirit, outside the body, where
she can freely rejoice with Him. Accordingly, she says, withdraw them,
Beloved, that is, cease communicating them to me in the body,

6.   I am taking flight!

This is like saying: I am taking flight from the body in order that you
may communicate them to me outside of it, since they cause me to fly
out of the body.

For a better understanding of the nature of this flight, it should be
noted that, as we said, in this visit of the divine Spirit, the spirit of the
soul is carried away violently to communicate with Him, and it abandons
the body and ceases to have its feelings and actions in it, for they are
in God. Thus St. Paul said that in his rapture he did not know if his
soul was receiving the communication in the body or out of the body. [2
Cor. 12:2]

However, it should not be thought because of this that the soul for-
sakes the body, which is its sensory life, but rather that the soul's actions
are not in the body. This is why in these raptures and flights the body
has no feeling, and even though severely painful things are done to it,

it does not feel them. This rapture is not like other natural transports and swoons in which one returns to self when pain is inflicted.

These feelings are experienced in such visits by those who have not yet reached the state of perfection, but are advancing along in the state of proficients. Those who have reached perfection receive all communications in peace and gentle love. These raptures then cease, for they are communications preparatory to the reception of the total communication.

7. This would be an apt place to treat of the different kinds of raptures, ecstasies, and other elevations and flights of the soul which are customarily experienced by spiritual persons. But since, as I promised in the prologue, my intention is only to give a brief explanation of these stanzas, such a discussion will have to be left for someone who knows how to treat the matter better than I. Then too, the blessed Teresa of Jesus, our Mother, left writings about these spiritual matters, which are admirably done and which I hope will soon be printed and brought to light.

What the soul then says about flight here should be understood in reference to rapture and ecstasy of the spirit in God.

And the Beloved then says:

8.   Return, dove,

The soul went out of the body very willingly in that spiritual flight and thought that now her life was at an end and that she would be able to see her Bridegroom openly and enjoy Him forever. But the Bridegroom intercepted her flight saying, "return, dove." This is like saying: in your sublime and swift contemplation and in your burning love and in the simplicity of your advance—for the dove has these three properties—return from this lofty flight in which you aim after true possession of Me; the time has not yet come for such high knowledge, adapt yourself to this lower knowledge which I am communicating to you in this rapture of yours. And it is as follows:

9.   The wounded stag

The Bridegroom in this verse compares Himself to a stag. It is characteristic of the stag to climb to high places and when wounded to race in search of refreshment and cool waters. If he hears the cry of his mate and senses that she is wounded, he immediately runs to her to comfort and coddle her.

The Bridegroom now acts similarly. Beholding that the bride is wounded with love for Him, He also, because of her moan, is wounded with love for her. Among lovers, the wound of one is a wound for both, and the two have but one feeling. Thus, in other words, He says: Return to Me, My bride, because if you go about like the stag wounded with love for Me, I too, like the stag, will come to you wounded by your wound.

10. Also by appearing in a high place I am like the stag. Hence He says, the stag

Is in sight on the hill,

That is, in the height of your contemplation in this flight. For contemplation is a high place where God in this life begins to communicate and show Himself to the soul, but not completely. Hence He does not say that He is fully in sight, but that He is in sight. However sublime may be the knowledge God gives the soul in this life, it is but like a glimpse of Him from a great distance.

The third characteristic of the stag, contained in the next verse, follows:

11.   Cooled by the breeze of your flight.

By the "flight," He means the contemplation received in that ecstasy, and by the breeze, that spirit of love which this flight of contemplation causes in the soul. He very appropriately terms this love which is caused by the flight a "breeze," because the Holy Spirit, who is Love, is also compared to a breeze in Scripture, for the Holy Spirit is the breath of the Father and the Son. And just as the Holy Spirit is like a breeze from the flight (that is, He proceeds through spiration from the contemplation and wisdom of the Father and the Son), so the Bridegroom calls this love of the soul a "breeze" because it proceeds from the contemplation and knowledge that she has of God at this time.

It is noteworthy that the Bridegroom does not say He comes at the flight, but at the breeze of the flight, because, properly speaking, God does not communicate Himself to the soul through its flight (the knowledge it has of Him), but through the love it has from this knowledge. For just as love is the union of the Father and the Son, so is it the union of the soul with God. Hence it is that even though a soul may have the highest knowledge and contemplation of God and know all mysteries, yet if it does not love, this knowledge will be of no avail to her union with God, as St. Paul teaches. [1 Cor. 13:2] St. Paul also says: *Charitatem habete quod est vinculum perfectionis* (Have this charity which is the bond of perfection). [Col. 3:14]

This charity, then, causes the Bridegroom to run to the spring of His bride's love, as the wounded and thirsty stag races for refreshment to the cool waters. Consequently He uses the word "cooled."

12. As a breeze cools and refreshes a man worn out by the heat, so this breeze of love refreshes and renews the soul burning with the fire of love. The fire of love bears this property: The breeze by which it is

cooled and refreshed makes it increase. For in the lover, love is a flame that burns with a desire to burn more, like the flame of natural fire. He refers to the fulfillment of this desire to burn more in His ardent love for His bride as, being cooled. In other words He says: In the ardor of your flight you burn more, because one love enkindles another.

It is worthy of note that God does not place His grace and love in the soul except according to its desire and love. Anyone truly loving God must strive not to fail in this love, for he will thereby induce God, if we may so express it, to further love him and find delight in his soul.

And for the acquisition of this charity, the soul must practice what St. Paul taught: *Charity is patient, is kind, is not envious, does no evil, does not become proud, is not ambitious, seeks not its own, does not become disturbed, thinks no evil, rejoices not in iniquity, but rejoices in the truth, suffers all things* (that are to be suffered), *believes all things* (that must be believed), *hopes all things, and endures all things* (that are in accord with charity). [1 Cor. 13:4–7]

STANZAS 14 AND 15

Introduction

1. Since this little dove was flying in the breeze of love above the flood waters of her loving fatigues and yearnings, which she has shown until now, and could find nowhere to alight, the compassionate father Noah, stretching out his merciful hand, caught her on her last flight and placed her in the ark of his charity. [Gn. 8:9] This occurred when in the stanza we just explained the Bridegroom said, "return, dove."

Finding in this recollection all that she desired and more than is expressible, the soul begins to sing the praises of her Beloved in the following stanzas. They apply to His grandeurs, which she experiences and enjoys in this union.

> My Beloved is the mountains,
> And lonely wooded valleys,
> Strange islands,
> And resounding rivers,
> The whistling of love-stirring breezes,
>
> The tranquil night
> At the time of the rising dawn,
> Silent music,
> Sounding solitude,
> The supper that refreshes, and deepens love.

2. Before commenting on these stanzas, we should call to mind for the sake of a clearer understanding of them, and those that follow, that this spiritual flight denotes a high state and union of love, in which, after much spiritual exercise, the soul is placed by God. This state is called spiritual expousal with the Word, the Son of God. And at the beginning, when this flight is experienced the first time, God communicates to the soul great things about Himself, beautifies her with grandeur and majesty, adorns her with gifts and virtues, and clothes her with the knowledge and honor of God, as the betrothed is clothed on the day of her betrothal.

Not only do her vehement yearnings and complaints of love cease, but, in being graced with the blessings mentioned, a state of peace and delight and gentleness of love begins in her. This state is indicated in these stanzas, in which she does no more than tell in song her Beloved's grandeurs, which she knows and enjoys in Him through this union of espousal. In the remaining stanzas she no longer speaks of sufferings and longings as she did before, but of the communion and exchange of sweet and peaceful love with her Beloved, because now in this state all those sufferings have ceased.

It should be noted that these two stanzas describe the most that God communicates to the soul at this time. Yet it must not be thought that He communicates to all those who reach this state everything declared in these two stanzas, or that He does so in the same manner and measure of knowledge and feeling. To some souls He gives more and to others less, to some in one way and to others in another, although all alike may be in this same state of spiritual-espousal. But the greatest possible communication is recorded here because it includes everything else. The commentary follows.

Commentary on the two stanzas

3. In Noah's ark, as the divine Scripture says, there were many rooms for different kinds of animals, and all the food that could be eaten. [Gn. 6:14, 19–21] It should be noted that, similarly, the soul in her flight to the divine ark, the bosom of God, not only sees there the many mansions that His Majesty through St. John declared were in His Father's house [Jn. 14:2], but sees and knows there all the foods (all the grandeurs the soul can enjoy) included in these two stanzas and signified by these common terms. These grandeurs in substance are as follows:

4. The soul sees and tastes abundance and inestimable riches in this divine union. She finds all the rest and recreation she desires, and understands secrets and strange knowledge of God, which is another one of the foods that taste best to her. She experiences in God an awesome

power and strength which sweeps away every other power and strength. She tastes there a splendid spiritual sweetness and gratification, discovers true quiet and divine light, and tastes sublimely the wisdom of God reflected in the harmony of His creatures and works. She has the feeling of being filled with blessings and of being empty of evils and far removed from them. And above all she understands and enjoys inestimable refreshment of love which confirms her in love. These in substance are the affirmations of the two stanzas.

5. The bride says in these stanzas that the Beloved is all these things in Himself, and that He is so also for her, because in such superabundant communications from God, the soul experiences and knows the truth of St. Francis' prayer: *My God and my all.* Since God is all things to the soul and the good that is in all things, the communication of this superabundance is explained through its likeness to the goodness of the things mentioned in these stanzas, which we shall explain in our commentary on each of the verses. It should be known that what is explained here is present in God eminently and infinitely, or better, each of these sublime attributes is God, and all of them together are God.

Inasmuch as the soul in this case is united with God, she feels that all things are God, as St. John experienced when he said: *Quod factum est, in ipso vita erat* (That which was made, had life in Him). [Jn. 1:4] It should not be thought that what the soul is said to feel here is comparable to seeing things by means of the light, or creatures by means of God; rather in this possession the soul feels that God is all things for her. Neither must it be thought that, because the soul has so sublime an experience of God, we are asserting that she has essential and clear vision of Him. This experience is nothing but a strong and overflowing communication and glimpse of what God is in Himself, in which the soul feels the goodness of the things mentioned in these verses, which we shall now comment upon.

6.   My Beloved is the mountains,
Mountains have heights and they are affluent, vast, beautiful, graceful, bright, and fragrant. These mountains are what my Beloved is to me.

7.   And lonely wooded valleys,
Lonely valleys are quiet, pleasant, cool, shady, and flowing with fresh waters; in the variety of their groves and in the sweet song of the birds, they afford abundant recreation and delight to the senses, and in their solitude and silence they refresh and give rest. These valleys are what my Beloved is to me.

8.   Strange islands,
Strange islands are surrounded by water and situated across the sea,

far withdrawn and cut off from communication with other men. Many things very different from what we have here are born and nurtured in these islands; they are of many strange kinds and powers never before seen by men, and they cause surprise and wonder in anyone who sees them. Thus, because of the wonderful new things and the strange knowledge (far removed from common knowledge) which the soul sees in God, she calls Him "strange islands."

A man is called strange for either of two reasons: He is withdrawn from people; or, compared with other men, he is singular and superior in his deeds and works. The soul calls God "strange" for these two reasons. Not only is He all the strangeness of islands never seen before, but also His ways, counsels, and works are very strange and new and wonderful to man.

It is no wonder that God is strange to men who have not seen Him, since He is also strange to the holy angels and to the blessed. For the angels and the blessed are incapable of seeing Him fully, nor will they ever be capable of doing so. Until the day of the Last Judgment they will see so many new things in Him concerning His deep judgments and His works of mercy and justice that they will forever be receiving new surprises and marveling the more. Hence not only men but also the angels can call Him strange islands. Only to Himself is He neither strange nor new.

9.   And resounding rivers,

Rivers have three properties: first, they besiege and inundate everything they encounter; second, they fill up all the low and empty spots found along their path; third, they are so loud that they muffle and suppress every other sound. Since in this communication the soul has in God a delightful experience of these three properties, she says that her Beloved is resounding rivers.

As for the first property, it should be known that the soul is conscious at this time that the torrent of God's spirit is besieging and taking possession of her so forcibly that all the rivers of the world seem to have flooded in upon her and to be assailing her. She feels that all the actions and passions in which she was formerly occupied are drowned therein. This is not a torment to her, although it is a thing of tremendous force, because these rivers are rivers of peace, as God declared of this onslaught through Isaias: *Ecce ego declinabo super eam quasi fluvium pacis, et quasi torrentem inundantem gloriam* (See that I will descend and besiege her—the soul—like a river of peace and like a torrent overflowing with glory). [Is. 66:12] Hence this divine onslaught God causes in the soul is like a resounding river which fills everything with peace and glory.

The second property the soul experiences at this time is that of the divine water filling the low places of her humility and the voids of her appetites, as St. Luke says: *Exaltavit humiles. Esurientes implevit bonis* (He exalted the humble and filled the hungry with good things). [Lk. 1: 52–53]

The third property she experiences in these resounding rivers of her Beloved is a spiritual clamor and outcry, louder than any other sound or call. This cry prevails against all other cries and its sound exceeds all the sounds of the world.

To explain how this comes about we will have to delay a short while.

10. This clamor or resounding of these rivers which the soul refers to here is such an abundant plenitude that she is filled with goods, and it is so powerful a force that she is possessed by it, for it seems to be not merely the sound of rivers but the sound of roaring thunder. Nevertheless this cry is a spiritual cry which does not contain these other material sounds, nor their pain and disturbance, but rather grandeur, strength, power, delight, and glory. It is like an immense interior clamor and sound which clothes the soul in power and strength.

This spiritual cry and noise was made in the souls of the Apostles when the Holy Spirit descended upon them like a mighty wind, as is related in the Acts of the Apostles. [Acts 2:2] To manifest the spiritual voice bestowed on them interiorly, that sound was heard exteriorly as of a fierce wind by all who were in Jerusalem. [Acts 2:5–6] This sound denoted what the Apostles received interiorly, a fullness of power and fortitude.

St. John says that while the Lord Jesus was praying to His Father in the conflict and anguish occasioned by His enemies, an interior voice came to Him from heaven, comforting Him in His humanity. The sound of this voice which the Jews heard as though coming from outside was so deep and loud that some said it had thundered and others that an angel from heaven had spoken. [Jn. 12:27–29] The reason is that that voice, which was heard as though coming from without, denoted and manifested the fortitude and strength which was interiorly bestowed on Christ in His humanity.

It must not be thought on this account that the soul fails to receive in its spirit the sound of the spiritual voice. It should be noted that the spiritual voice is the effect produced in the spirit, just as the sound in the ear and the knowledge in the spirit is an effect of the material voice. David meant this when he said: *Ecce dabit voci suae vocem virtutis* (Behold that God will give to His voice the voice of power). [Ps. 67:34] This power is the interior voice, because when David said He will give to His voice the voice of power he meant that to the exterior voice, heard from without, He will give the voice of power that is heard from within.

Hence it should be known that God is an infinite voice, and by communicating Himself to the soul in this way He produces the effect of an immense voice.

11. St. John heard this voice and says in the Apocalypse that the voice he heard from heaven *erat tamquam vocem aquarum et tamquam vocem tonitrui magni* (was like the voice of many waters and like the voice of a great thunder). [Ap. 14:2] That it might not be thought that because this voice was so great it was harsh and painful, he immediately adds that it was so gentle it sounded *sicut citharoedorum citharizantium in citharis suis* (like many harpers laying on their harps). [Ap. 14:2] And Ezechiel says that this sound as of many waters was *quasi sonum sublimis Dei* (like the sound of the most high God), that is, this infinite voice was communicated in a most lofty and gentle way. For as we said, it is God Himself who communicates Himself by producing this voice in the soul. But He limits Himself in each soul, measuring out the voice of power according to the soul's capacity, and this voice produces great delight and grandeur. As a result He said to the bride in the Canticle: *Sonet vox tua in auribus meis, vox enim tua dulcis* (Let your voice sound in my ears, for your voice is sweet). [Ct. 2: 14]

12.   The whistling of love-stirring breezes,
The soul refers to two things in this verse: the breezes and the whistling.

By "love-stirring breezes" is understood the attributes and graces of the Beloved which by means of this union assail the soul and lovingly touch it in its substance.

This most sublime and delightful knowledge of God and His attributes which overflows into the intellect from the touch these attributes of God produce in the substance of the soul, she calls the whistling of these breezes. This is the most exalted delight of all the soul here enjoys.

13. To understand this better it should be noted that just as two things are felt in the breeze (the touch and the whistling or sound), so in this communication of the Bridegroom two things are experienced: knowledge and a feeling of delight. As the feeling of the breeze delights the sense of touch, and its whistling the sense of hearing, so the sentiment of the Beloved's attributes are felt and enjoyed by the soul's power of touch, which is in its substance, and the knowledge of these attributes is experienced in its hearing, which is the intellect.

It should also be known that the love-stirring breeze is said to come when it wounds in a pleasant way by satisfying the appetite of the one desiring such refreshment, because the sense of touch is then filled with enjoyment and refreshment; and the hearing, through this delectable touch, experiences great pleasure and gratification in the sound and whistling of the breeze. The delight of hearing is much greater than that of feeling, because the sound in the sense of hearing is more spiritual; or, better, it more closely approaches the spiritual than does feeling. Consequently, the delight of hearing is more spiritual than that of feeling.

14. Since this touch of God gives intense satisfaction and enjoyment to the substance of the soul, and gently fulfills her desire for this union, she calls this union or these touches, love-stirring breezes. As we have said, the Beloved's attributes are lovingly and sweetly communicated in this breeze, and from it the intellect receives the knowledge or whistling.

She calls the knowledge a "whistling," because just as the whistling of the breeze pierces deeply into the hearing organ, so this most subtle and delicate knowledge penetrates with wonderful savoriness into the innermost part of the substance of the soul, and the delight is greater than all others.

The reason for the delight is that the already understood substance, stripped of accidents and phantasms, is bestowed. For this knowledge is given to that intellect which philosophers call the passive or possible intellect, and the intellect receives it passively without any efforts of its own. This knowing is the soul's main delight because it is pertinent to the intellect, and as theologians say fruition, the vision of God, is proper to the intellect.

Since this whistling refers to the substantial knowledge mentioned, some theologians think our Father Elias saw God in that whistling of the gentle breeze heard on the mount at the mouth of his cave. [3 Kgs. 19: 11–13] Scripture calls it "the whistling of the gentle breeze," because knowledge was begotten in his intellect from the delicate spiritual communication. The soul calls this knowledge "the whistling of love-stirring breezes" because it flows over into the intellect from the loving communication of the Beloved's attributes. As a result she calls the knowledge "the whistling of the love-stirring breezes."

15. This divine whistling which enters through the soul's hearing is not only, as I have said, the understood substance, but also an unveiling of truths about the divinity and a revelation of His secrets. When Scripture refers to a communication of God which enters by hearing, this communication ordinarily amounts to a manifestation of these naked truths to the intellect, or a revelation of the secrets of God. These are pure spiritual revelations or visions, which are given only to the spirit without the service and help of the senses. Thus what is called the communication of God through hearing is very certain and lofty.

Accordingly, St. Paul in order to declare the height of his revelation did not say: *vidit arcana verba,* and still less: *gustavit arcana verba,* but: *audivit arcana verba quae non licet homini loqui* (he heard secret words which men are not permitted to utter). [2 Cor. 12:4] It is thought that he saw God there as our Father Elias also did in the whistling.

Since faith, as St. Paul also says [Rom. 10:17], comes through hearing, so too that which faith tells us, the understood substance, comes through spiritual hearing. The prophet Job indicates this clearly in speaking with God Who revealed Himself: *Auditu auris audivi te, nunc autem oculus meus videt te* (With the hearing of the ear I heard You and now my eye sees You). [Jb. 42:5] This passage points out clearly that to hear Him with the hearing of the soul is to see Him with the eye of the passive intellect. Consequently, he does not say I heard You with the hearing of my ears, but of my ear, nor, I saw You with my eyes, but with my eye, which is the intellect. This hearing of the soul, therefore, is the vision of the intellect.

16. It must not be thought that, because what the soul understands is the naked substance, there is perfect and clear fruition as in heaven. Although the knowledge is stripped of accidents, it is not for this reason clear, but dark, for it is contemplation, which in this life, as St. Dionysius says, is a ray of darkness. [Pseudo-Dionysius Areopagita, *De Mystica Theologia*, c. 1: PG 3, 999] We can say that it is a ray and image of fruition, since it is in the intellect that fruition takes place.

This understood substance that the soul calls "whistling" is equivalent to "the eyes I have desired," of which the soul said, when they were being revealed to her, "Withdraw them, Beloved," because her senses could not endure them.

17. Because it seems to me that a passage from Job which confirms a great deal of what I said about this rapture and espousal is very appropriate, I will refer to it here, even though we may be detained some more, and I will explain its pertinent parts. First, I will cite the entire passage in Latin, and then render it in the vernacular, afterwards I will offer a brief explanation of what interests us. After this I shall go on with the commentary on the verses of the other stanza.

In the Book of Job, then, Eliphaz the Temanite speaks in the following way: *Porro ad me dictum est verbum absconditum et quasi furtive suscepit auris mea venas susurri ejus. In horrore visionis nocturnae, quando solet sopor occupare homines, pavor tenuit me et tremor, et omnia ossa mea perterrita sunt; et cum spiritus, me praesente, transiret, inhorruerunt pili carnis meae. Stetit quidam, cujus non agnoscebam vultum, imago coram oculis meis, et vocem quasi aurae lenis audivi* (Truly a hidden word was spoken to me, and my ear as though by stealth received the veins of his whisper. In the horror of the nocturnal vision, when sleep usually occupies men, fear and trembling took hold of me and all my bones were disturbed; and as the spirit passed before me the hair of my flesh shriveled. There stood one before me whose countenance I knew not, an image before my eyes, and I heard the voice of a gentle wind). [Jb. 4:12–16] The passage contains almost everything we have said about this rapture, from stanza 13 (beginning, "Withdraw them, Beloved") up to this point.

18. What Eliphaz, the Temanite, refers to (in saying that a hidden word was spoken to him) was given to the soul when, unable to endure it, she said, "Withdraw them, Beloved."

By saying that his ear, as though by stealth, received the veins of his whisper, he refers to the naked substance the intellect receives. The veins here denote the interior substance, and the whisper signifies that communication and touch of attributes by which the understood substance is imparted to the intellect. He calls the communication a "whisper" because it is very gentle, just as the soul calls it "love-stirring breezes" because it is lovingly bestowed. He says he received it as though by stealth because, as a stolen article is not one's own, so that secret from a natural viewpoint is foreign to man, for Eliphaz received what did not belong to him naturally. Thus it was unlawful for him to receive it just as it was unlawful for St. Paul to disclose the secret words he heard. [2 Cor. 12:4] Hence the other prophet twice declared: *My secret for myself.* [Is. 24:16]

In saying that in the horror of the nocturnal vision when sleep usually occupies men, fear and trembling took hold of him, he refers to the fear and trembling naturally caused in the soul by that rapturous communication, unendurable to nature, in the imparting of God's spirit. The prophet here indicates that just as men are oppressed and frightened by the vision they call a nightmare which occurs when they are about to sleep (at that moment between sleeping and waking, the point at which sleep begins), so at the time of this spiritual transport, between the sleep of natural ignorance and the wakefulness of supernatural knowledge, which is the beginning of the rapture or ecstasy, the communication of a spiritual vision gives rise to this fear and trembling.

19. And he adds that all his bones were terrified or disturbed, which amounts to saying that they were shaken and dislocated. He refers here to the great disjuncture of the bones which we said they suffer at this time. Daniel clearly indicates this when he says upon his vision of the angel: *Domine in visione tua dissolutae sunt compages meae* (Lord, upon seeing you the joints of my bones are loosed). [Dn. 10:16]

And in what he says next, that is, "and as the spirit passed before me" (by making my spirit pass beyond its natural limits and ways through the rapture we have mentioned), "the hair of my flesh shriveled," he attests to our teaching concerning the body: that in this transport, as in death, it remains frozen, and the flesh stiff.

20. And continuing: "there stood before me one whose countenance I knew not, an image before my eyes." He who stood before him was God, who communicated Himself in the manner mentioned. And he says that he did not know His countenance, to signify that in such a communication and vision, even though most sublime, the countenance and essence of God is neither known nor seen. Yet he says that it was an image before his eyes, because that knowledge of the hidden word was most high, like an image and trace of God, but he does not refer to the essential vision of God.

21. Then he concludes, saying: "and I heard the voice of a gentle wind." This voice of the gentle wind refers to the whistling of love-stirring breezes, which the soul says is her Beloved.

It must not be thought that these visits are always accompanied by natural tremblings and torments; for, as we said, these are found only in those who are beginning to enter the state of illumination and perfection and this kind of communication; in others they are very gentle.

The commentary continues:

22.   The tranquil night

In this spiritual sleep in the bosom of the Beloved, the soul possesses and relishes all the tranquillity, rest, and quietude of the peaceful night; and she receives in God, together with this peace, a fathomless and obscure divine knowledge. As a result she says that her Beloved is a tranquil night to her.

23.   At the time of the rising dawn,

Yet she does not say that the tranquil night is equivalent to a dark night, but, rather, that it is like the night that has reached the time of the rising dawn. This quietude and tranquillity in God is not entirely obscure to the soul as is a dark night; but it is a tranquillity and quietude in divine light, in the new knowledge of God, in which the spirit elevated to the divine light is in quiet.

She very appropriately calls this divine light "the rising dawn," which means the morning. Just as the rise of morning dispels the darkness of night and unveils the light of day, so this spirit, quieted and put to rest in God, is elevated from the darkness of natural knowledge to the morning light of the supernatural knowledge of God. This morning light is not clear, as was said, but dark as night at the time of the rising dawn. Just as the night at the rise of dawn is not entirely night or entirely day, but is, as they say, at the break of day, so this divine solitude and tranquillity, informed by the divine light, has some share in that light, but not its complete clarity.

24. In this tranquillity the intellect is aware of being elevated, with strange newness, above all natural understanding to the divine light,

just as a person who after a long sleep opens his eyes to the unexpected light.

I think David was referring to this knowledge when he said: *Vigilavi et factus sum sicut passer solitarius in tecto* (I have kept watch and am become like a solitary sparrow on the housetop). [Ps. 101:8] This was like saying: I opened the eyes of my intellect and found myself above all natural knowledge, without this knowledge and alone on the housetop, which is above all low things.

He says he became like the solitary sparrow, because in this contemplation the spirit has the traits of a solitary sparrow. There are five of these traits:

First, the sparrow ordinarily perches on the highest thing. And so the spirit at this stage is placed in the highest contemplation.

Second, it always turns its beak toward the wind. Thus the spirit ever turns the beak of its affection toward the Spirit of Love, Who is God.

Third, it is usually alone and allows no other bird close to it, for when another perches nearby it flies away. Thus the spirit in this contemplation is alone in regard to all things, stripped of them all, nor does it allow within itself anything other than solitude in God.

The fourth trait is that it sings very sweetly. And so does the spirit sing sweetly to God at this time, for the praises it renders Him are of the most delightful love, pleasant to the soul and precious in God's eyes.

The fifth is that it possesses no definite color. So neither does the perfect spirit, in this excess, have any color of sensible affection or self-love; it does not even have any particular consideration in either its lower or higher part, nor will it be able to describe the mode or manner of this excess, for what it possesses is an abyss of the knowledge of God.

25.   Silent music,

In that nocturnal tranquillity and silence and in that knowledge of the divine light the soul becomes aware of Wisdom's wonderful harmony and sequence in the variety of His creatures and works. Each of them is endowed with a certain likeness of God and in its own way gives voice to what God is in it. So creatures will be for the soul a harmonious symphony of sublime music surpassing all concerts and melodies of the world.

She calls this music "silent" because it is tranquil and quiet knowledge, without the sound of voices. And thus there is in it the sweetness of music and the quietude of silence. Accordingly, she says that her Beloved is silent music because in Him she knows and enjoys this symphony of spiritual music. Not only is He silent music, but He is also

26.   Sounding solitude,

This is almost identical with silent music, for even though that music is silent to the natural senses and faculties, it is sounding solitude for the spiritual faculties. When these spiritual faculties are alone and empty of all natural forms and apprehensions, they can receive in a most sonorous way the spiritual sound of the excellence of God, in Himself and in His creatures. We said above that St. John speaks of this spiritual vision in the Apocalypse, that is: *the voice of many harpers playing on their harps*. [Jn. 14:2] This vision was spiritual and had nothing to do with material harps. It involved a knowledge of the praises that each of the blessed in his own degree of glory gives continually to God. This praise is like music, for as each one possesses God's gifts differently, each one sings His praises differently, and all of them together form a symphony of love, as of music.

27. In this same way the soul perceives in that tranquil wisdom that all creatures, higher and lower ones alike, according to what each in itself has received from God, raise their voice in testimony to what God is. She beholds that each in its own way, bearing God within itself according to its capacity, magnifies God. And thus all these voices form one voice of music praising the grandeur, wisdom, and wonderful knowledge of God.

This is the meaning of the Holy Spirit in the Book of Wisdom when He said: *Spiritus Domini replevit orbem terrarum, et hoc quod continet omnia, scientiam habet vocis* (The spirit of the Lord filled the whole earth, and this world which contains all things has knowledge of the voice). [Wis. 1:7] This voice is the sonorous solitude the soul knows here, that is, the testimony to God which, in themselves, all things give.

Since the soul does not receive this sonorous music without solitude and estrangement from all exterior things, she calls it "silent music" and "sounding solitude," which she says is her Beloved. And what is more:

28. The supper that refreshes, and deepens love.

Supper affords lovers refreshment, satisfaction, and love. Since in this gentle communication the Beloved produces these three benefits in the soul, she calls it "the supper that refreshes, and deepens love."

It should be known that in the divine Scripture this term "supper" refers to the divine vision. Just as supper comes at the end of a day's work and at the beginning of the evening rest, this tranquil knowledge causes the soul to experience a certain end of her evils and the possession of good things in which her love of God is deepened more than before. As a result, He is the supper that refreshes by being the end of evils for her, and that deepens love by being to her the possession of all goods.

29. Yet for a better understanding of what this supper is to the soul— it is as we said her Beloved—we should note in this appropriate place

what the beloved Bridegroom says in the Apocalypse: *I stand at the door and knock; if anyone opens, I shall enter and sup with him, and he with Me.* [Ap. 3:20] In this text He indicates that He carries His supper with Him, and it is nothing but His own very delights and savors that He himself enjoys. In uniting Himself with the soul He imparts them, and she likewise enjoys them. For such is the meaning of the words, *I shall sup with him, and he with Me.* Hence these words declare the effect of the divine union of the soul with God, in which God's very own goods are graciously and bounteously shared in common with His bride, the soul. He Himself is for her the supper that refreshes and enamors, for in being bounteous He refreshes her, and in being gracious He enamors her.

30. Before continuing with the commentary on the remaining stanzas, we ought to point out here that even though we have said that in this state of espousal the soul enjoys complete tranquillity and receives the most abundant communication possible in this life, it should be understood that this tranquillity refers only to the superior part (until the state of spiritual marriage the sensory part never completely loses the dross left from bad habits, or brings all its energies into subjection, as will be said later) and that this communication is the most abundant possible to the state of espousal. In the spiritual marriage there are striking advantages over this state of espousal, for although the bride, the soul, enjoys so much good in these visits of the state of espousal, still she suffers from her Beloved's withdrawals and from disturbances and afflictions in her sensory part and from the devil; all of these cease in the state of marriage.

Stanza 16

Introduction

1. Since the virtues of the bride are perfect and she enjoys habitual peace in the visits of her Beloved, she sometimes has a sublime enjoyment of their sweetness and fragrance when her Beloved touches these virtues, just as a man enjoys the sweetness and beauty of flowers and lilies when they have blossomed, and he must handle them. In many of these visits the soul sees within herself all her virtues by means of the light the Bridegroom causes. And then in a wonderful delight of love she gathers them together and offers them to Him as a bouquet of beautiful flowers. And He, in accepting them—for indeed He accepts them—receives great service.

This all occurs interiorly. The soul feels that the Beloved is within her as in His own bed. She offers herself together with her virtues, which is the greatest service she can render Him. Thus one of the most remarkable delights she receives in her interior communion with God comes from this gift of herself to her Beloved.

2. The devil, who in his great malice is envious of all the good he sees in the soul, knowing of her prosperity, now employs all his ability and engages all his crafts to disturb even a slight part of this good. It is worth more to him to hinder a small fraction of this soul's rich and glorious delight than to make many others fall into numerous serious sins, for these others have little or nothing to lose and this soul has very much to lose because of all her precious gain. The loss of a little pure gold is much worse than the loss of many other base metals.

The devil at this point takes advantage of the sensory appetites, although most of the time he can do very little or nothing, since these appetites in persons having reached this state are already deadened. When he is unable to stir these appetites, he produces a great variety of images in the imagination. He is sometimes the cause of many movements of the sensory part of the soul and of many other disturbances, spiritual as well as sensory. It is not in a person's power to be free of these until the Lord sends His angel, as is said in the Psalm, round about them that fear Him and delivers them [Ps. 33:8], and until He brings peace and tranquillity, both in the sensory and spiritual part of the soul.

Referring to the devil's disturbances and distrustful of the wiles he uses to cause her harm at this time, the soul, seeking this favor from God, speaks to the angels whose duty it is to assist her now by putting the devil to flight. She recites the following stanza:

> Catch us the foxes,
> For our vineyard is now in flower,
> While we fashion a cone of roses
> Intricate as the pine's;
> And let no one appear on the hill.

Commentary

3. Desirous that neither the envious and malicious devils, nor the wild sensory appetites, nor the various wanderings of the imagination, nor any other knowledge or awareness hamper the continuance of this interior delight of love, which is the flower of her vineyard, the bride invokes the angels, telling them to catch all these disturbances and keep them from interfering with the interior exercise of love, in the delight of which the virtues and graces are communicated and enjoyed by the soul and the Son of God.

And thus she says:

4.   Catch us the foxes,
                    For our vineyard is now in flower,

The vineyard spoken of is the nursery of all the virtues in this holy soul; these virtues supply her with a sweet-tasting wine. This vineyard is in flower when the soul is united with her Bridegroom according to the will and gladdened in Him according to all these virtues together.

Frequently, as we said, many various kinds of images are brought to the memory and phantasy and many appetites and inclinations are stirred up in the sensory part. These are of so many kinds that when David was drinking this delicious spiritual wine with intense thirst for God, he proclaimed upon experiencing the hindrance they caused: *My soul has thirsted for You; Oh how many ways my flesh for You!* [Ps. 62:2]

5. The soul calls all this harmonious composite of appetites and sensory movements "foxes" because of the great resemblance. As foxes pretend to be asleep when they are out to catch their prey, so all these appetites and sensory powers are tranquil and asleep until these flowers of virtues rise and blossom in the soul in an exercise of love. At that moment, then, it seems that the sensual flowers of the appetites and sense powers awaken and arise in the sensory part of the soul in an effort to contradict the spirit and reign. Covetousness will reach such a point, as St. Paul says, that the flesh covets against the spirit. [Gal. 5:17] Since the flesh has a strong inclination to sensory things, that which pleases the spirit is distasteful and unpleasant to all flesh. As a result these appetites are a notable disturbance to the sweet spirit. Thus she says: "Catch us the foxes."

6. The malicious demons on their part disturb the soul in two ways: They vehemently incite and stimulate these appetites and by means of them and other imaginations, etc., wage war on this peaceful and flowering kingdom of the soul.

In the second way, which is worse, they assail her with bodily torments and noises in order to distract her, when it is impossible for them to do so in the first way. And what is still worse they struggle against her with spiritual terrors and horrors that sometimes become a frightful torment. If permission is given them they can do this very easily, for since the soul at this time enters into great nakedness of spirit for the sake of this spiritual exercise, the devil can easily show himself to her, because he is also spirit.

At other times he attacks her with different horrors, before she begins to enjoy these sweet flowers, when God is beginning to withdraw her from the house of the senses that she may enter, through this interior exercise, the garden of her Bridegroom. The devil knows that once the soul has entered into that recollection, she is so fortified that however much he may try he cannot do her harm. Frequently when he goes out to block the soul she recollects herself very quickly in her deep interior hiding place, where she finds intense delight and protection. Then the terrors she suffers seem so exterior and far away that the devils not only fail to frighten her, but they cause happiness and joy.

7. The bride of the Canticle spoke of these terrors, saying: *My soul troubles me because of the chariots of Aminadab.* [Ct. 6:11] By Aminadab she refers to the devil, and she calls his attacks and assaults chariots because of the terrible violence and clamor he produces with them.

The soul afterwards says here: "Catch us the foxes"; this very request was made by the bride of the Canticles: *Catch us the little foxes that damage the vines, for our vineyard is in flower.* [Ct. 2:15] She does not say "catch me" but "catch us" because she is speaking of both herself and the Beloved. They are united and enjoying the flower of the vine.

The reason she says the vine is in flower rather than with fruit is that, even though the virtues in this life are enjoyed with all this perfection we have been discussing, she merely enjoys them as though in flower. Only in the next life will they be enjoyed as the fruit.

And she adds:

8.   While we fashion a cone of roses
                     Intricate as the pine's;

While the soul at this stage is enjoying the flower of this vineyard and delighting in the bosom of her Beloved, it will happen that all her virtues are suddenly and clearly revealed in their perfection and that they give her immense sweetness and delight. The soul feels that these virtues are both in her and in God so that they seem to form a very flowering and pleasant vineyard belonging to the Bridegroom as well as to herself and in which they both feed and delight. She then gathers all these virtues and makes very delightful acts of love in each of them and in all together. She offers this bouquet to the Beloved with remarkable tenderness and sweetness of love. The Beloved Himself helps her, for without His favor and help she would not be able to gather these virtues and offer them to Him. Hence she says: "While we fashion a cone of roses."

9. She fashions this bouquet in the shape of a pine cone, for as a pine cone is something sturdy, with many pieces, or pine kernels, firmly fastened together, so this cone or bouquet of virtues which the soul arranges for her Beloved forms one perfect whole embodying in itself many perfect and strong virtues and very rich gifts. All perfections and virtues are incorporated in orderly fashion in the one solid perfection of the soul. This perfection, while being formed through the practice of the virtues—as well as when already formed—is offered by the soul to the Beloved in that spirit of love we are discussing. These foxes should, then, be caught so that they do not hinder the interior communion of the two.

The bride not only asks for the ability to make a good bouquet, but also for what follows in the next verse:

10.   And let no one appear on the hill.

To attain this divine interior exercise there is also need for solitude and withdrawal from all things presentable to the soul, whether from the lower, sensory portion, or from the higher, rational part. These two parts comprise the entire compound of man's faculties and senses, and she calls this compound a "hill." All the natural knowledge and the appetites dwelling on the hill in this harmonious composite are like prey to the devil, who hunts and catches them in order to harm the soul.

She says: "And let no one appear on the hill," that is, let no image of any object belonging to any of these faculties or senses we have mentioned appear before the soul and the Bridegroom. This is like saying: let there be no particular knowledge or affection or other consideration in any of the spiritual faculties (memory, intellect, and will); and let there be no other digressions, forms, images, or figures of objects or other natural operations in any of the bodily senses and faculties, either interior or exterior (the imaginative power and phantasy, etc., sight and hearing, etc.).

11. The reason the soul says this is that for the perfect enjoyment of this communion with God all the senses and faculties, interior and exterior, should be unoccupied, idle, and empty of their own operations and objects. The more active they are in themselves at such a time, the more they hinder the communication. When the soul reaches a certain degree of interior union of love, the spiritual faculties are no longer active, and much less the corporal ones, since the union of love is already wrought and the soul is actuated in love. Thus the faculties cease their work, since upon attaining the end the activity of the means ceases. Then the soul attends to God with love, which is to love in the continuance of unitive love.

"And let no one appear on the hill," then. Let only the will appear, attending to the Beloved in a surrender of self and of all the virtues in the way described.

Stanza 17

Introduction

1. For a greater understanding of the following stanza it should be pointed out that the absences of the Beloved, which the soul suffers in this state of spiritual espousal, are very painful; some are of such a kind that there is no suffering comparable to them. The reason for such af-

fliction is that since she has a singular and intense love for God in this state, His absence is a singular and intense torment for her. Added to this torment is the disturbance which at this time she receives from any kind of converse or communication with creatures. Since she lives with that driving force of a fathomless desire for union with God, any delay whatever is very burdensome and disturbing, just as anything in the path of a stone which is racing on toward its center would cause in that void a violent jolt. Since the soul has already received the delight of these sweet visits, they are more desirable than gold and all beauty. Fearing as a result the great lack—even if momentary—of so precious a presence, she speaks in this stanza both to dryness and to the Spirit of her Bridegroom:

> Be still, deadening north wind;
> South wind come, you that waken love,
> Breathe through my garden,
> Let its fragrance flow,
> And the Beloved will feed amid the flowers.

Commentary

2. Besides what was said in the previous stanza, spiritual dryness also hampers the interior satisfaction and sweetness of which she spoke. Dreading this, she does two things here:

First, she impedes dryness by closing the door to it through continual prayer and devotion.

Second, she invokes the Holy Spirit; He it is Who will dispel this dryness and sustain and increase her love for the Bridegroom. He also moves the soul to the interior exercise of the virtues, so that the Son of God, her Bridegroom, may rejoice and delight more in His bride. She invokes the Holy Spirit because her entire aim is to please her Bridegroom.

3.   Be still, deadening north wind;

The north wind is very cold, it dries up and withers the flowers and plants, or at least when striking them makes them shrink and close. Because the spiritual dryness and affective absence of the Beloved produces this same effect in the soul by extinguishing the satisfaction, delight, and fragrance of the virtues she was enjoying, she calls it a "deadening north wind." It deadens the virtues and affective exercise, and as a result the soul pleads, "Be still, deadening north wind."

It should be understood that this plea of the soul flows from prayer and the spiritual exercises and is directed toward a detainment of the dryness. Yet since God's communications to the soul are so interior that she cannot actively move her own faculties to the enjoyment of these communications, unless the Spirit of the Bridegroom causes this movement of love, she invokes Him, saying:

4.   South wind come, you that waken love,

The south wind is a delightful breeze: it causes rain, makes the herbs and plants germinate, opens the flowers, and scatters their fragrance. Its effects are the opposite of those of the north wind. The soul, by this breeze, refers to the Holy Spirit, who awakens love. When this divine breeze strikes her, it wholly enkindles and refreshes her, and quickens and awakens the will, and elevates the previously fallen appetites that were asleep to the love of God; it does so in such a way that she can easily add, you that waken love, both His love and hers.

What she asks of the Holy Spirit is expressed in the following verse:

5.   Breathe through my garden,

This garden is the soul. As the soul above calls herself a "vineyard . . . in flower," because the flower of the virtues within her supply sweet-tasting wine, here she calls herself a garden, because the flowers of perfections and virtues planted within her come to life and begin to grow.

It should be noted that the bride does not say "breathe in my garden," but "breathe through my garden," for there is a considerable difference between God's breathing in the soul and His breathing through the soul. To breathe in the soul is to infuse graces, gifts, and virtues. To breathe through the soul is to touch and put in motion the virtues and perfections already given, renewing and moving them in such a way that they of themselves afford the soul a wonderful fragrance and sweetness, as when you shake aromatic spices and they spread their abundant fragrance, which prior to this was neither so strong nor so highly perceptible. The soul is not always experiencing and enjoying the acquired or infused virtues actually, because, as we shall say later, they remain within her in this life like flowers enclosed in the bud or like aromatic spices whose scent is not perceived until shaken and uncovered.

6. God sometimes grants these favors to the soul, His bride. He breathes through her flowering garden, opens all these buds of virtues, and uncovers these aromatic spices of gifts, perfections, and riches, and, disclosing this interior treasure and wealth, He reveals all her beauty. And then it is something wonderful to behold and pleasant to feel: the richness from her gifts unveiled to the soul and the beauty of these flowers of virtues now in full bloom. And the fragrant scent each one with its own characteristics gives to her is inestimable.

She calls this the flowing of the garden's fragrance when she says in the following verse:

7.   Let its fragrance flow,

Sometimes the fragrance is so abundant that it seems to the soul she is clothed with delight and bathed in inestimable glory, to such an extent that the experience is not only within her but overflows and becomes manifest outside of her, and those capable of recognizing it are aware of her experience. It seems to them that she is in a pleasant garden filled with the delights and riches of God. And not only when these flowers are open can you see this in these holy souls, but they ordinarily bear in themselves an "I-don't-know-what" of greatness and dignity. This causes awe and respect in others because of the supernatural effect diffused in such persons from their close and familiar conversation with God. It is said of Moses in Exodus, that others were unable to look upon his countenance because of the honor and glory that remained with him after he conversed face to face with God. [Ex. 34:29–30; 2 Cor. 3:7]

8. In this breathing through the soul, which is the Holy Spirit's visit of love, the Bridegroom, the Son of God, is Himself sublimely communicated. He sends His Spirit, as He sent His Apostles [Lk. 22:8], to act as His quartermaster, to prepare His dwelling, the bride-soul, by raising her up in delight and adorning this garden, opening its flowers, uncovering the gifts, and decorating her with the tapestry of graces and riches.

And thus the bride has immense longing that the north wind be stilled, and that the south wind come and breathe through her garden.

For then the soul gains many things together: she gains the agreeable exercise of the perfect virtues; she gains enjoyment of the Beloved in them, since by their means He communicates Himself to her with more intimate love and grants her a more particular favor than before; she obtains that her Beloved delight more in her through this exercise of the virtues, and this is what she most enjoys (pleasing the Beloved); and she also gains the continuation of this delight and sweetness of the virtues. This endures as long as the Bridegroom thus sustains His bride and gives her sweetness in her virtues, as she says in the Canticle: *While the king was at his repose* (in the soul) *my flowering spikenard gave forth its fragrance.* [Ct. 1:11] This fragrant spikenard refers to the soul herself, who from the flowers of the virtues within her gives forth the scent of sweetness to her Beloved dwelling in her in this union.

9. Hence this divine breeze of the Holy Spirit should be greatly desired. Let each soul petition that He breathe through her garden that the divine fragrance might flow.

Since this is so necessary and brings such glory and good to the soul, the bride in the Canticle desired and asked for it in the same terms as here, saying: *Arise north wind, come south wind and blow through my garden, and its fragrance and precious spices will flow.* [Ct. 4:16]

The soul desires this, not for her own pleasure and glory, but because she knows her Bridegroom delights in this, and that it is a preparation and foretelling of the coming of the Son of God to take His delight in her. She says next:

10.   And the Beloved will feed amid the flowers.

The soul applies the word "feed" to the delight the Son of God takes in her at this time. This term provides an appropriate description, since food is something which not only gives pleasure but also sustains. The Son of God finds delight in the soul in these her delights, and is sustained in her, that is, He dwells in her as in a place that pleases Him, for the soul is indeed pleasing to Him. This, I believe, is what He meant through what Solomon said in Proverbs: *My delights are with the sons of men* [Prv. 8:31], that is, when their delight is to be with Me, Who am the Son of God.

It should be noted that the soul does not say the Beloved will feed on the flowers, but amid the flowers. Since the Bridegroom communicates Himself to the soul by means of the adornment of these virtues, He feeds on the soul, transforming her into Himself, now that she is prepared and seasoned with the flowers of virtues, gifts, and perfections, the seasonings with which, and among which, He feeds on her. By means of the Holy Spirit, who prepares the dwelling, these virtues delight the Son of God so that through them He may feed more on the love of the soul. This is characteristic of the Bridegroom: to unite Himself with the soul amid the fragrance of these flowers.

The bride of the Canticle, as one who knows so well, notes this characteristic in these words: *My Beloved is gone down into the garden, to the small threshing floor and the air scented with the aromatic spices, to pasture in the gardens and gather lilies.* [Ct. 6:1] And again she says: *I for my Beloved and my Beloved for me, who feeds among the lilies* [Ct. 6:2], that is, who feeds and delights in my soul, which is His garden, amid the lilies of my virtues, perfections, and graces.

STANZA 18

Introduction

1. Since in this state of spiritual espousal the soul is able to see her excellent qualities and ample riches and also that she does not possess and enjoy them as she would like because she still dwells in the body, her suffering is often intense, especially so when her awareness of this lack is heightened. Her presence in the body makes her feel like a noble lord held in prison. Such a prisoner is subject to a thousand miseries while his dominions are confiscated and he is prevented from making use of his lordship and wealth; all he gets from his riches is a little food, and that very sparingly. The extent of his suffering is obvious, for even the members of his own household are not submissive to him, and his servants and slaves without any respect turn against him every chance they have,

even to the point of taking from his plate the morsel of food meant for him. For at the moment God favors the soul with the taste of a morsel of the goods and riches He has prepared for her, a bad servant or appetite, sometimes an inordinate movement, sometimes other sensory rebellions, rise up in the lower part to impede this good.

2. As a result the soul feels as though she were in the land of enemies and tyrannized among strangers and like one dead among the dead. She has a definite experience of what the prophet Baruch discloses in stressing the misery of Jacob's captivity: *How is it Israel that you are in enemy land? You have grown old in a foreign land, you are defiled with the dead, you are counted with those who go down into hell.* [Bar. 3:10–11] And Jeremias, feeling this miserable treatment the soul suffers because of its captivity in the body, speaks in a spiritual sense to Israel: *Is Israel perhaps a servant or a slave? Why is he thus imprisoned? The lions have roared upon him,* etc. [Jer. 2:14–15] By the lions he refers here to the appetites and rebellions of this tyrant king, sensuality.

To manifest the trouble she receives and her desire that this kingdom of sensuality with all its armies and disturbances come to an end or be entirely subjected to her, she raises her eyes to the Bridegroom as to one who will accomplish all of this and speaks against these movements and rebellions:

> You girls of Judea,
> While among flowers and roses
> The amber spreads its perfume,
> Stay away, there on the outskirts:
> Do not so much as seek to touch our thresholds.

Commentary

3. It is the bride who speaks in this stanza; aware in her spiritual part of rich and beneficial gifts and delights from her Beloved, she desires to preserve the security and possession found in them. She referred to these gifts and delights, of which the Bridegroom makes her conscious, in the two preceding stanzas. Realizing that because of the lower, sensory part this good can be disturbed, and in fact is, she begs the operations and movements of the lower faculties and senses to be still and not to transcend the limits of this sensory region to molest and disquiet the higher and spiritual part. She asks this so that the good and delight enjoyed will not be impeded by even the slightest motion in this lower part. When the spirit is rejoicing, the movements of the senses and its faculties, in the measure that they are active and lively, molest and disquiet it. She says then:

4.   You girls of Judea,

The lower, sensory part of the soul is Judea because it is weak and carnal and, of itself, blind like the Judean people.

She names the imaginations, phantasies, movements, and affections of the lower part "girls." She calls them all "girls" because as girls attract lovers to themselves by their affection and grace, so these pleasant sensory operations and movements strive persistently to attract the will of the rational part to themselves. They try to draw it out of its interior to a desire for the exterior things which they crave. They also endeavor to move and attract the intellect that it may be wed to them in their base way of feeling, and they strive to bring the rational part into conformity and union with the sensory.

You, then, O sensory operations and movements, she says,

5.   While among flowers and roses

The flowers, as we said, are the soul's virtues. The rose bushes are the faculties (memory, intellect, and will), which bear and nurture in themselves the flowers of divine concepts, acts of love, and these same virtues.

While, then, among these virtues and faculties of my soul

6.   The amber spreads its perfume,

By "the amber" she refers to the Bridegroom's divine Spirit abiding within her. The divine amber spreading its perfume among the flowers and rose bushes is a reference to the overflow and communication of the Spirit in the faculties and virtues of the soul by which He imparts through them the perfume of divine sweetness.

While the divine Spirit is giving my soul this sweetness,

7.   Stay away, there on the outskirts:

The outskirts of Judea (and Judea, we said, refers to the lower or sensory part of the soul) are the interior senses (sensible memory, phantasy, and imagination) in which the forms, images, and phantasms of the objects gather and reside. By means of these images the sensory appetites are moved. These forms are what she refers to as girls. When they are quiet and tranquil, the appetites are also asleep. These images enter the outskirts, the interior senses, through the gates of the exterior senses, hearing, sight, smell, etc. They do so in such a way that we can call both the interior and exterior sense faculties "outskirts," for they are the districts outside the walls of the city. That part of the soul called the city is the innermost part, the rational portion, which is capable of communion with God; its operations are contrary to those of the sensory part.

Yet because there is a natural communication between the people, or girls, dwelling in these outskirts of the sensory part with the superior part or city, this communication is of such a kind that what occurs in this lower part is usually felt in the interior part, and consequently distracts and deprives it of the peace it has from its spiritual activity and attentiveness to God. As a result she tells those dwelling in the outskirts, in the interior and exterior senses, to remain quiet.

8.   Do not so much as seek to touch our thresholds.

This means that they should not even touch the superior part through the first movements. The first movements are the entrances and thresholds of the soul. When these girls pass beyond first movements to the rational part of the soul, they cross the thresholds. But in the case of first movements, it is said they merely set foot on the thresholds or knock at the door. This happens when the sensory part attacks the rational for the sake of some inordinate act. The soul not only tells these girls not to enter, but also not to distract the quietude and good she enjoys.

STANZA 19

Introduction

1. The soul in this state becomes such an enemy of the lower part and its operations that she does not want God to communicate to it any of the spiritual good He gives to the higher part. For on account of its weak condition, the sensory part is unable to endure an abundant spiritual communication without fainting. Consequently the spirit suffers and is afflicted and cannot enjoy this communication peacefully. As the Wise Man says: *The body on account of its corruption is a burden to the soul.* [Wis. 9:15] Since the soul desires the highest and most excellent communications from God, and is unable to receive them in the company of the sensory part, she desires God to bestow them apart from it.

St. Paul states of his sublime vision of the third heaven, in which he saw God, that he does not know whether he received it in the body or out of it. [2 Cor. 12:2] Nevertheless, no matter how it did take place, it occurred outside the body. For if the body had participated, St. Paul would have known of this and the vision would not have been as sublime as he implied by stating that he heard such secret words that it is unlawful for man to speak of them. [2 Cor. 12:4] Knowing full well that such favors are unreceivable in so fragile a vessel [2 Cor. 4:7] and desiring that the Bridegroom grant them outside of her, or at least without her, the soul asks Him in this stanza:

> Hide Yourself, my Love;
> Turn Your face toward the mountains,
> And do not speak;
> But look at those companions
> Going with her through strange islands.

Commentary

2. The bride-soul asks the Bridegroom four things in this stanza:

First, that He be pleased to communicate Himself to her very inwardly, in the hiding place of the soul.

Second, that He inform and shine upon her faculties with the glory and excellence of His divinity.

Third, that this communication be so sublime and profound that she may neither desire nor know how to give a description of it, and that the sensory and exterior part be incapable of receiving it.

Fourth, that He be enamored of the many virtues and graces He has placed in her. These accompany her in her ascent to God through a very lofty and elevated knowledge of the divinity and through excesses of love, which are very strange and extraordinary in comparison with those she ordinarily has. Thus she says:

3.   Hide Yourself, my Love,

This is like saying: My dear Spouse, withdraw to the innermost part of my soul and communicate Yourself in secret, manifest Your hidden wonders, alien to every mortal eye.

4.   Turn Your face toward the mountains,

The face of God is the divinity, and the mountains are the soul's faculties (memory, intellect, and will). This verse is like saying: Let Your divinity shine on my intellect by giving it divine knowledge, and on my will by imparting to it the divine love, and on my memory with the divine possession of glory.

The soul asks in this line for everything she possibly can ask of Him. She is no longer satisfied with the knowledge and communication of the "back" of God—which was His communication to Moses [Ex. 33:23]—and which is knowledge of Him in His effects and works; she can only be satisfied with God's face, which is an essential communication of the divinity to the soul. This communication is not brought about through any means, but through a certain contact of the soul with the divinity. This contact is something foreign to everything sensory and accidental, since it is a touch of naked substances—of the soul and the divinity. Consequently she adds:

5.   And do not speak;

This means: Do not speak as before when the communications You granted me were such that You spoke them to the exterior senses; that is, You spoke things apprehensible to the senses, since these things were not so high and deep that the sensory part could not attain to them. But now let these communications be so lofty and substantial and interior that You do not speak of them to the senses, that is, such that the senses may be unable to attain to the knowledge of them. Spiritual substance cannot be communicated to the senses, and anything imparted to sense, especially in this life, cannot be pure spirit, since sense is incapable of it.

The soul, then, desiring this communication of God, which is so substantial and essential that it is imperceptible to sense, asks the Bridegroom to refrain from speaking, which is like saying: Let the depth of this hiding place, which is spiritual union, be of such a kind that the senses will be unable to feel or speak of it, as with the secrets heard by St. Paul about which it was unlawful for man to speak. [2 Cor. 12:4]

6.   But look at those companions

When God looks, He loves and grants favors. And the companions whom the soul tells God to look at are the many virtues, gifts, perfections, and other spiritual riches He has placed in her as the pledges, tokens, and jewels of espousal. Thus this verse is like saying: But Beloved, first turn to the interior of my soul, and be enamored of the company—the riches—You have placed there, so that loving the soul through them You may dwell and hide in her. For, indeed, even though they are Yours, since You gave them to her, they also belong to her,

7.   Going with her through strange islands.

That is, they belong to the soul that goes to You by means of strange knowledge of You and by modes and ways that are foreign to all the senses and to common natural knowledge. And thus it is as though, desiring to oblige Him, she were to say: Since I go to You through a spiritual knowledge strange and foreign to the senses, let Your communication be so interior and sublime as to be foreign to all of them.

STANZAS 20 and 21

Introduction

1. The attainment of so high a state of perfection as that which the soul here aims after, which is spiritual marriage, requires the purification of all the imperfections, rebellions, and imperfect habits of the lower part, which, by putting off the old man, is surrendered and made subject to the higher part; but there is also needed a singular fortitude and a

very sublime love for so strong and intimate an embrace from God. The soul obtains not only a very lofty purity and beauty, but also an amazing strength because of the powerful and intimate bond effected between God and her by means of this union.

2. In order that she reach Him, it is necessary for her to attain an adequate degree of purity, fortitude, and love. The Holy Spirit, He Who intervenes to effect this spiritual union, desiring that the soul attain the possession of these qualities in order to merit this union, speaks to the Father and the Son in the Canticle: *What shall we do for our sister on the day of her courtship, for she is little and has no breasts? If she is a wall, let us build upon it silver bulwarks and defenses; and if she is a door, let us reinforce it with cedar wood.* [Ct. 8:8–9] The silver bulwarks and defenses refer to the strong and heroic virtues clothed with faith, which is signified by the silver. These heroic virtues are those of spiritual marriage and their foundation is in the strong soul, referred to by the wall. The peaceful Bridegroom rests in the strength of these virtues without any weakness disturbing Him. The cedar wood applies to the affections and properties of lofty love. This lofty love is signified by cedar and it is the love proper to spiritual marriage. The bride must first be a door in order to receive the reinforcement of cedar wood, that is, she must hold the door of her will open to the Bridegroom that he may enter through the complete and true "yes" of love. This is the yes of espousal which is given before the spiritual marriage. The breasts of the bride also refer to this perfect love which she should possess in order to appear before the Bridegroom, Christ, for the consummation of this state.

3. The text, however, mentions that the bride answered immediately by stating her desire to be courted: *I am a wall and my breasts are as a tower.* [Ct. 8:10] This means: My soul is strong and my love lofty, and so I should not be held back. Desiring this perfect union and transformation, the bride also manifested this strength in the preceding stanzas, especially in the one just explained, in which to oblige her Spouse further she sets before Him the virtues and preparative riches received from Him. As a result the Bridegroom, desiring to conclude this matter, speaks the two following stanzas in which He finishes purifying the soul, strengthening and disposing her in both sensory and spiritual parts for this state. He speaks these lines against all the oppositions and rebellions from the sensory part and the devil.

> Swift-winged birds,
> Lions, stags, and leaping roes,
> Mountains, lowlands, and river banks,
> Waters, winds, and ardors,
> Watching fears of night:

By the pleasant lyres
And the siren's song, I conjure you
To cease your anger
And not touch the wall,
That the bride may sleep in deeper peace.

Commentary

4. In these two stanzas the Bridegroom, the Son of God, gives the bride-soul possession of peace and tranquillity by conforming the lower part to the higher, cleansing it of all its imperfections, bringing under rational control the natural faculties and motives, and quieting all the other appetites mentioned in these two stanzas. The meaning of these stanzas is as follows:

First the Bridegroom conjures and commands the useless wanderings of the phantasy and imaginative power to cease once and for all.

He also puts under the control of reason the two natural powers, the irascible and the concupiscible, which were previously somewhat of an affliction to the soul.

And, insofar as is possible in this life, He perfects the three faculties (memory, intellect, and will) in regard to their objects.

What is more, He conjures and commands the four passions (joy, hope, fear, and sorrow) that from now on they be mitigated and controlled by reason.

Such is the meaning of the terms used in the first of these stanzas. The Bridegroom makes these disturbing activities and movements cease by means of the immense delight and sweetness and strength received in the spiritual communication and surrender He makes of Himself at this time. Because God vitally transforms the soul into Himself, all these faculties, appetites, and movements lose their natural imperfection and are changed to divine.

And thus He says:

5.   Swift-winged birds,

He calls the wanderings of the imagination "swift-winged birds," for these digressions are quick and restless in flying from one place to another. When the will is enjoying in quietude the delightful communication of the Beloved, these wanderings usually displease her by their restless flights and put an end to her satisfaction. The Bridegroom says that He conjures them by the pleasant lyres, etc. (by sweetness and delight so abundant and frequent that they cannot be the impediment they were before she reached so high a state) to cease their restless flights, impulses, and excesses.

This should be understood similarly regarding the other verses we will comment on here, such as:

6.   Lions, stags, and leaping roes,

By the "lions," He refers to the acrimony and impetuosity of the irascible power, for in its acts this power is bold and daring like the lion.

By the "stags" and the "leaping roes," He refers to that other power, the concupiscible, which is an appetitive power. This faculty causes two classes of effects: the one of cowardice and the other of daring. It produces the effects of cowardice when things are found difficult, for it then retires, withdraws within itself, and becomes cowardly. Because of these effects this faculty is comparable to stags, for since the stag has a more intense concupiscible power than many other animals, it is very cowardly and withdrawn. This faculty produces the effects of daring when things are found easy, for then it does not withdraw and become cowardly but makes bold to admit these things by its appetites and affections. And because of these effects this faculty is compared to the roes, which have such concupiscence that they do not merely run after their desires but even leap after them. And thus He calls them leaping roes.

7. In conjuring the lions, He bridles the impulses and excesses of anger. And in conjuring the stags, He strengthens the concupiscible power against the cowardice and pusillanimity which previously made it withdrawn. And in conjuring the leaping roes, He satisfies the appetites, previously restless and leaping like roes from one thing to another, trying to satisfy concupiscence. This concupiscence is now satisfied by the pleasant lyres, whose sweetness it enjoys, and by the siren's song, the delight of which it feeds on.

It should be observed that the Bridegroom does not conjure anger and concupiscence to cease, for these powers are never wanting to the soul. But He conjures their disturbances and inordinate actions, signified by the lions, stags, and leaping roes. It is necessary that in this state these inordinate movements be lacking.

8.   Mountains, lowlands, and river banks,

These expressions denote the vicious and inordinate acts of the three faculties, memory, intellect, and will. These acts are inordinate and vicious when they reach either a high level or a low level, or even when they are inclined toward one of them without actually reaching it.

Thus the "mountains," which are high, refer to acts that are extreme through an inordinate excess.

The "lowlands," being low, refer to the acts that are extreme through defect.

The "river banks," which are neither high nor low, but still not level, participate somewhat in both extremes and refer to the acts that exceed or lack something of the mean or right measure. Although these are not extremely inordinate as would be the case with mortal sin, they are nonetheless partly so, either through venial sin or through imperfection, however slight, in the intellect, memory, and will.

He also conjures by means of the pleasant lyres and the siren's song all these acts in excess of the just measure to cease. These lyres perfect the three faculties of the soul by bringing them to an operation which lies in the just measure, without extremes or even any part in extremes.

The remaining verses follow:

9.   Waters, winds, and ardors,
                       Watching fears of night:

These four references indicate the four passions: sorrow, hope, joy, and fear.

The waters denote the emotions of sorrow which afflict the soul, for they enter like water. David, referring to them, says to God: *Salvum me fac, Deus, quoniam intraverunt aquae usque ad animam meam* (Save me my God, for the waters have come in even unto my soul). [Ps. 68:2]

The winds allude to the emotions of hope, for like the wind they fly toward the absent object. David also says: *Os meum aperui et attraxi spiritum, quia mandata tua desiderabam* (I opened the mouth of my hope and drew in the breath of my desire because I longed and hoped for your commandments). [Ps. 118:131]

The ardors refer to the emotions of the passion of joy which inflame the heart like fire. David says: *Concaluit cor meum intra me, et in meditatione mea exardescet ignis* (My heart grew hot within me, and in my meditation a fire shall be enkindled). [Ps. 38:4] This is like saying: In my meditation joy shall be enkindled.

By the watching fears of night are understood the emotions of fear, the other passion. These fears are usually very great in spiritual persons who have not reached this state of spiritual marriage of which we are speaking. Sometimes when God wishes to grant them some favors, He causes fear and trembling in the spirit and also shriveling of the flesh and the senses, because the sensory part is not fortified, perfected, and habituated to such favors. Sometimes, too, the devil, being envious and sad over the soul's peace and good when God grants it recollection and sweetness in Himself, strives to put horror and fear in the spirit in order to hinder that good. And sometimes he does this as though he were threatening her there in the spirit. When he becomes aware of his inability to reach the inmost part of the soul because of her deep recollection and union with God, he tries to cause distraction, wanderings, conflicts, sorrows, and dread, at least in the sensory part, in order to disturb the bride in her bridal chamber.

He calls these emotions "fears of night," because they are produced by the devil, who endeavors by their means to diffuse obscurity in the soul and darken the divine light she enjoys.

He calls them "watching fears," because of themselves they awaken her from her peaceful interior sleep, and also because the devils are always awake and watching for their chance to cause these fears. These fears, as I said, are passively introduced by God or the devil into the souls of those who are already spiritual. I am not speaking here of other temporal or natural fears, for such fears are not characteristic of spiritual people; but these spiritual fears are.

10. The Beloved also conjures these four passions of the soul and makes them cease and be calm insofar as He gives the bride in this state riches, strength, and satisfaction through the pleasant lyres of His sweetness and the siren's song of His delight. He does this so that they may cease not only to reign in her but also to cause her any displeasure.

If previously the waters of sorrow over something reached the soul —especially concerning her own sins or those of others, since sin is what usually causes the most sorrow in spiritual persons—her grandeur and stability is now so great that even though she knows what these sins are they do not produce sorrow or grief. And she does not have compassion, that is, the feeling of compassion, even though she possesses its work and perfection. In this state the soul lacks what involved weakness in her practice of the virtues, whereas the strength, constancy, and perfection of them remains. For the soul in this transformation of love resembles the angels who judge perfectly the things that give sorrow, without the feeling of sorrow, and exercise the works of mercy without the feeling of compassion. Sometimes, however, and at certain periods, God allows her to feel things and suffer from them that she might gain more merit and grow in the fervor of love, or for other reasons, as He did with the Virgin Mother, St. Paul, and others. Yet in itself the state does not comprise this feeling of sorrow.

11. Neither is she afflicted with the desires of hope, for being now satisfied in this union with God insofar as is possible in this life, she has nothing to hope for from the world, nor anything to desire spiritually, for she has the awareness and experience of the fullness of God's riches. In life and in death she is conformed to the will of God, saying in both the sensory and spiritual part, without the impulse of any other longing or appetite: *Fiat voluntas tua.* [Mt. 6:10] Thus her desire for the vision of God is painless.

Neither do the emotions of joy, which usually caused her a feeling of possessing more or less, make her aware of less or added abundance, for what she ordinarily enjoys is so great that, like the sea, she neither decreases by the outflowing waters nor increases by the inflowing waters.

For this is the soul in which is established the fount of whose waters, as Christ says through St. John, leap up unto life everlasting. [Jn. 4:14]

12. Because I asserted that this soul does not receive anything new in this state of transformation, in which it seems that accidental joys are taken from her (which are not lacking even in the glorified), it should be pointed out that even though these joys and accidental sweetnesses are not lacking—ordinarily they are numberless—they do not on this account add anything to the substantial spiritual communication. She already possesses everything that could come to her anew. Thus what she possesses within herself is more than what comes to her anew.

Hence, every time joyous and happy things are offered to this soul, whether they are exterior or interior and spiritual, she immediately turns to the enjoyment of the riches she already has within herself, and experiences much greater gladness and delight in them than in those new joys. Thus she in some way resembles God who, even though He has delight in all things, does not delight in them as much as He does in Himself, for He possesses within Himself a good eminently above all others. Thus all new joys and satisfactions serve more to awaken the soul to a delight in what she already possesses and experiences within herself than to new delights, for, as I say, what she already possesses is greater than these.

13. It is natural for a person when something gives him joy and contentment to turn his thoughts to an object he likes and esteems even more, and to rejoice and take pleasure in that object. Thus what is accidental in these new spiritual joys is so little in comparison with the substantial good the bride already has within herself that we can call it a nothing. The soul that has attained this fulfillment, which is transformation, in which she has reached full stature, does not grow through these new spiritual things as do others who have not arrived. Yet it is a wonderful thing to behold how, although the soul receives no new delights, it always seems to her that she receives them anew and also that she has had them before. The reason is that she ever takes pleasure in them anew, since they are her good that is ever new. Thus it seems to her that she is always receiving new things without need.

14. Yet were we to desire to speak of the glorious illumination He sometimes gives to the soul in this habitual embrace, which is a certain spiritual turning toward her in which He bestows the vision and enjoyment of this whole abyss of riches and delight He has placed within her, our words would fail to explain anything about it. As the sun shining brightly upon the sea lights up great depths and caverns and reveals pearls and rich veins of gold and other minerals, etc., so the Bridegroom, the divine sun, in turning to the bride so reveals her riches

that even the angels marvel and utter those words of the Canticle: *Who is she that comes forth like the morning rising, beautiful as the moon, resplendent as the sun, terrible as the armies set in array?* [Ct. 6:9] In spite of the excellence of this illumination, it gives no increase to the soul; it only brings to light what was previously possessed that she may have enjoyment of it.

15. Finally, the watching fears of night do not reach her, for she is now so clearly illumined and strong and rests so firmly in her God that the devils can neither cause her obscurity through their darknesses, nor frighten her with their terrors, nor awaken her by their attacks. Nothing can reach or molest her now that she has withdrawn from all things and entered into her God where she enjoys all peace, tastes all sweetness, and delights in all delight insofar as this earthly state allows. The Wise Man's words refer to this soul: *The peaceful and tranquil soul is like a continual banquet.* [Prv. 15:15] As one at a banquet enjoys the taste of a variety of foods and the sweetness of many melodies, the soul in this banquet, now received through her repose on the bosom of her Beloved, enjoys every delight and tastes every sweetness.

So little of this is describable that we would never succeed in fully explaining what takes place in the soul that has reached this happy state. If she attains the peace of God which, as the Church says, surpasses all understanding [*cf.* 3rd Sun. of Advent, Epis., Phil. 4:7], all understanding will be inadequate and mute when it comes to explaining this peace.

Verses from the second stanza follow:

16.   By the pleasant lyres
                        And the siren's song, I conjure you

We have already explained that by "the pleasant lyres" the Bridegroom refers here to the sweetness bestowed on the soul in this state. By it He causes the cessation of all the disturbances we mentioned. As the music of the lyres fills the soul with sweetness and refreshment and so absorbs and suspends her as to keep her away from bitterness and sorrow, so this sweetness takes such an inward hold on her that nothing painful can reach her. These words are like saying: May all bitter things cease for the soul by means of the sweetness I place in her.

We also said that the "siren's song" signifies the soul's habitual delight. He calls this delight the "siren's song" because, as they say, its song is so charming it enraptures and enamors its hearer and makes him forget all things as though he were in a transport. Similarly the delight of this union absorbs the soul within herself and gives her such refreshment that it makes her insensible to the disturbances and troubles mentioned. These disturbances are referred to in this verse:

17.   To cease your anger

He calls these troubles and disturbances of the inordinate passions and operations "anger." Just as anger is a certain impulse which troubles peace by going beyond its limits, so all the passions, etc., which we mentioned, exceed by their movements the limits of peace and tranquillity, and when they touch the soul they cause disquietude. As a result He says:

18.   And not touch the wall,

By "the wall" He refers to the enclosure of peace and the fence of virtues and perfections by which the soul is shut in and protected, for she is the garden mentioned above, which is enclosed and protected solely for the Beloved, and among whose flowers He browses. In the Canticle He calls her an enclosed garden: *My sister is an enclosed garden.* [Ct. 4:12] Thus He tells them here not to touch even the wall of His garden

19.   That the bride may sleep in deeper peace.

That she may delight more freely in the quietude and sweetness she enjoys in her Beloved. It should be known that there is now no door closed to the soul, but that it is in her power to enjoy this gentle sleep of love at will, as the Bridegroom indicates in the Canticle: *I conjure you daughters of Jerusalem by the roes and harts of the fields, that you do not stir up or wake the beloved until she wishes.* [Ct. 3:5]

STANZA 22

Introduction

1. Great was the desire of the Bridegroom to free and ransom His bride completely from the hands of sensuality and the devil. Like the good shepherd rejoicing and holding on his shoulders the lost sheep for which he had searched along many winding paths [Lk. 15:4–5], and like the woman who, having lit the candle and hunted through her whole house for the lost drachma, holding it up in her hands with gladness and calling to her friends and neighbors to come and celebrate, saying, rejoice with me, etc. [Lk. 15:8–9], now, too, that the soul is liberated, this loving Shepherd and Bridegroom rejoices. And it is wonderful to see His pleasure in carrying the rescued, perfected soul on His shoulders, held there by His hands in this desired union.

Not only does He Himself rejoice, but He also makes the angels and saintly souls share in His gladness, saying in the words of the Canticle: *Go forth daughters of Sion and behold king Solomon in the crown with which his mother crowned him on the day of his espousal and on the*

day of the joy of his heart. [Ct. 3:11] By these words He calls the soul
His crown, His bride, and the joy of His heart, and He takes her now in
His arms and goes forth with her as the bridegroom from his bridal
chamber. [Ps. 18:6] He refers to all this in the following stanza.

> The bride has entered
> The sweet garden of her desire,
> And she rests in delight,
> Laying her neck
> On the gentle arms of her Beloved.

Commentary

2. Now that the bride has diligently sought to catch the foxes, still
the north wind, and calm the girls of Judea, all of which are obstacles
to the full delight of the state of spiritual marriage; and now that she
has also invoked and obtained the breeze of the Holy Spirit, as in the
preceding stanzas, which entails the proper preparation and instrument
for the perfection of this state, we must treat of this state by explaining
the stanza. Here the Bridegroom speaks and, in calling the soul "bride,"
declares two things:

First He tells how, now victorious, she has reached this pleasant state
of spiritual marriage, which was His as well as her ardent longing.

And second, He enumerates the properties of this state which the soul
now enjoys, such as: resting in delight and laying her neck on the gentle
arms of her Beloved, as we shall explain.

3.   The bride has entered

To offer a more lucid explanation of the order of these stanzas and of
what the soul usually passes through before reaching this state of spiritual marriage, which is the highest (that which, with the divine help,
we will now speak of), it should be noted that before the soul reaches
this state she first exercises herself both in the trials and the bitterness
of mortification and in meditation on spiritual things. This is referred to
from the first stanza until that which says: "Pouring out a thousand
graces." Afterwards she embarks upon the contemplative way. Here she
passes along the paths and straits of love about which she sings in the
sequence of the verses until that stanza which begins, "Withdraw them,
Beloved," where the spiritual espousal is wrought. Afterwards, she advances along the unitive way, in which she receives many remarkable
communications, visits, gifts, and jewels from her Bridegroom, and, as
one betrothed, learns of her Beloved and becomes perfect in loving Him;
this she relates starting at the stanza in which the espousal was made
("Withdraw them, Beloved") until this one beginning with, "The bride

has entered," where the spiritual marriage between this soul and the Son of God is effected.

This spiritual marriage is incomparably greater than the spiritual espousal, for it is a total transformation in the Beloved in which each surrenders the entire possession of self to the other with a certain consummation of the union of love. The soul thereby becomes divine, becomes God through participation, insofar as is possible in this life. And thus I think that this state never occurs without the soul's being confirmed in grace, for the faith of both is confirmed when God's faith in the soul is here confirmed. It is accordingly the highest state attainable in this life.

Just as in the consummation of carnal marriage there are two in one flesh, as Sacred Scripture points out [Gn. 2:24], so also when the spiritual marriage between God and the soul is consummated, there are two natures in one spirit and love, as St. Paul says in making this same comparison: *He who is joined to the Lord is one spirit with Him.* [1 Cor. 6:17] This union resembles the union of the light of a star or candle with the light of the sun, for what then sheds light is not the star or the candle, but the sun, which has absorbed the other lights into its own.

The Bridegroom speaks of the state in this verse saying: The bride has entered, that is, she has entered, leaving behind everything temporal and natural and all spiritual affections, modes, and manners, and has set aside and forgotten all temptations, disturbances, pains, solicitude, and cares, and is transformed in this high embrace.

The next line follows:

4.   The sweet garden of her desire,

This is like saying: She has been transformed into her God, here referred to as "the sweet garden," because of the sweet and pleasant dwelling she finds in Him. One does not reach this garden of full transformation, which is the joy, delight, and glory of spiritual marriage, without first passing through the spiritual espousal and the loyal and mutual love of betrothed persons. For after the soul has been for some time the betrothed of the Son of God in gentle and complete love, God calls her and places her in His flowering garden to consummate this most joyful state of marriage with Him. The union wrought between the two natures and the communication of the divine to the human in this state is such that even though neither change their being, both appear to be God. Yet in this life the union cannot be perfect, although it is beyond words and thought.

5. The Bridegroom points this out clearly in the Canticle where He invites the soul, now His betrothed, to this state: *Veni in hortum meum, soror mea sponsa, messui myrrham meam cum aromatibus meis* (Come

and enter my garden, my sister, my bride, for now I have gathered my myrrh with my fragrant spices). [Ct. 5:1] He calls her sister and bride because she was a sister and bride in the love and surrender she had made of herself to Him before He called her to this state of spiritual marriage, where, as He says, He has now gathered His fragrant myrrh and aromatic spices, which are the fruits of the flowers now ripe and ready for the soul. These are the delights and grandeurs which of Himself and in Himself He communicates to her in this state.

Consequently He is for her an enchanting, desirable garden. For her entire aim in all her works is the consummation and perfection of this state. She never rests until reaching it. She finds in this state a much greater abundance and fullness of God, a more secure and stable peace, and an incomparably more perfect delight than in the spiritual espousal; here it is as though she were placed in the arms of her Bridegroom. As a result she usually experiences an intimate spiritual embrace, which is a veritable embrace, by means of which she lives the life of God. The words of St. Paul are verified in this soul: *I live, now not I, but Christ lives in me.* [Gal. 2:20]

Wherefore, since the soul lives in this state a life as happy and glorious as is God's, let each one consider here, if he can, how pleasant her life is; just as God is incapable of feeling any distaste neither does she feel any, for the delight of God's glory is experienced and enjoyed in the substance of the soul now transformed in Him.

As a result the next verse continues:

6.   And she rests in delight,
                       Laying her neck

The "neck" refers here to the soul's strength by means of which, as we said, is effected this union with her Bridegroom; because she would be unable to endure so intimate an embrace if she were not now very strong. And because the soul labored by means of this strength, practiced the virtues, and conquered, it is right that with the strength by which she struggled and conquered she repose, laying her neck

7.   On the gentle arms of her Beloved.

To recline her neck on the arms of God is to have her strength, or, better, her weakness, now united to the strength of God, for the "arms" signify God's strength. Accordingly this state of spiritual marriage is very aptly designated by the laying of her neck on the gentle arms of the Beloved, for now God is the soul's strength and sweetness, in which she is sheltered and protected against all evils, and habituated to the delight of all goods.

Desirous of this state, the bride spoke to the Bridegroom in the Canticle: *Who will give you to me for my brother, nursed at the breasts of my mother, that I may find you alone outside and kiss you, and no one despise me?* [Ct. 8:1] In calling Him "brother," she indicates the equality of love between the two in the espousal before this state is reached. And in saying, "nursed at the breasts of my mother," she means: You dried up and subdued in me the appetites and passions which in our flesh are the breasts and milk of mother Eve, and an impediment to this state. And when this is accomplished "that I may find you alone outside," that is, outside of all things and of myself, in solitude and nakedness of spirit, which is attained when the appetites are dried up. And alone there, "kiss you" alone, that is, that my nature now alone and denuded of all temporal, natural, and spiritual impurity may be united with You alone, with Your nature alone, through no intermediary. This union is found only in the spiritual marriage, in which the soul kisses God without contempt or disturbance from anyone. For in this state neither the flesh, the world, the devil, nor the appetites molest her. Here we find also the fulfillment of what is said in the Canticle: *Winter is now past, the rain is gone, and the flowers have appeared in our land.* [Ct. 2:11]

STANZA 23

Introduction

1. In this high state of spiritual marriage the Bridegroom reveals His wonderful secrets to the soul, as to His faithful consort, with remarkable ease and frequency, for true and perfect love knows not how to keep anything hidden from the beloved. He communicates to her, mainly, sweet mysteries of His Incarnation and of the ways of the Redemption of mankind, which is one of the loftiest of His works, and thus more delightful to the soul. Even though He communicates many other mysteries to her, the Bridegroom in the following stanza mentions only the Incarnation, as the most important. In speaking to the soul He says:

> Beneath the apple tree:
> There I took you for My own,
> There I offered you My hand,
> And restored you,
> Where your mother was corrupted

Commentary

2. The Bridegroom explains to the soul in this stanza His admirable plan in redeeming and espousing her to Himself through the very means by which human nature was corrupted and ruined, telling her that as human nature through Adam was ruined and corrupted by means of the

forbidden tree in the Garden of Paradise, so on the tree of the cross it was redeemed and restored when He gave it there, through His Passion and Death the hand of His favor and mercy, and broke down the barriers between God and man which were built up through original sin.

Thus He says:

3.　　　　　　　　　Beneath the apple tree:

That is: beneath the favor of the tree of the cross (referred to by the apple tree), where the Son of God redeemed human nature and consequently espoused it to Himself and then espoused each soul by giving it through the cross grace and pledges for this espousal.

And thus He says:

4.　　　　　　　　　There I took you for My own,
　　　　　　　　　　There I offered you My hand,

That is: there I offered you My kind regard and help by raising you from your low state to be My companion and spouse.

5.　　　　　　　　　And restored you,
　　　　　　　　　　Where your mother was corrupted.

For human nature, your mother, was corrupted in your first parents, under the tree, and you too under the tree of the cross were restored. If your mother, therefore, brought you death under the tree, I, under the tree of the cross, brought you life. In such a way God manifests the decrees of His wisdom; He knows how to draw good from evil so wisely and beautifully, and to ordain to a greater good what was a cause of evil.

The Bridegroom Himself literally speaks this stanza to the bride in the Canticle: *Sub arbore malo suscitavi te; ibi corrupta est mater tua, ibi violata est genitrix tua* (Under the apple tree I raised you up; there your mother was corrupted, there she who bore you was violated). [Ct. 8:5]

6. The espousal made on the cross is not the one we now speak of. For that espousal is accomplished immediately when God gives the first grace, which is bestowed on each one at baptism. The espousal of which we speak bears reference to perfection and is not achieved save gradually and by stages. For though it is all one espousal, there is difference in that one is attained at the soul's pace, and thus little by little, and the other at God's pace, and thus immediately.

This espousal we are dealing with is that which God makes known through Ezechiel by saying to the soul: *You were cast out upon the earth in contempt of your soul on the day you were born. And passing by you I saw you trodden under foot in your blood. And I said to you as you were in your blood: live and be as multiplied as the grass of the field. Increase and grow great and enter and reach the stature of woman-*

hood. And your breasts grew and your hair increased, and you were naked and full of confusion. And I passed by you and looked at you and saw that your time was the time of lovers, and I held my mantle over you and covered your ignominy. And I swore to you and entered into a pact with you and made you mine. And I washed you with water and cleansed the blood from you and anointed you with oil; and I clothed you in color and shod you with violet shoes, girded you with fine linen and clothed you with fine woven garments. And I adorned you with ornaments, put bracelets on your hands and a chain on your neck. And above your mouth I placed a ring, and I put earrings in your ears and a beautiful crown upon your head. And you were adorned with gold and silver and clothed with fine linen and embroidered silk and many colors. You ate very choice bread and honey and oil, and you became exceedingly beautiful and advanced to rule and be a queen. And your name was spread among the people because of your beauty. [Ez. 16:5-14] These are the words of Ezechiel. And so it happens with the soul of which we are speaking.

STANZA 24

Introduction

1. But that which immediately follows this delightful surrender of the bride and the Beloved is their bed, in which the bride tastes much more steadily the delights of her Bridegroom. In the following stanza she speaks of their bed, which is divine, pure, and chaste and in which the soul is divine, pure, and chaste. For the bed is none but her very Bridegroom, the Word, the Son of God, as will soon be said, upon whom she reclines through the union of love. She calls her bed a flourishing one because her Bridegroom is not only flourishing, but the very flower of the fields and the lily of the valleys, as He Himself says in the Canticle. [Ct. 2:1] Thus the soul reclines not merely upon the bed in flower but upon the flower itself, the Son of God, who bears within Himself divine fragrance, grace, and beauty, as He likewise declares through David: *The beauty of the field is with me.* [Ps. 49:11] The soul thus relates in song the properties and graces of her bed:

> Our bed is in flower,
> Bound round with linking dens of lions,
> Hung with purple,
> Built up in peace,
> And crowned with a thousand shields of gold.

Commentary

2. In the two preceding stanzas the bride-soul's song told of the graces and grandeurs of her Beloved, the Son of God.

In this stanza the theme continues, but also includes the happy and high state in which she has been placed, and its security. Thirdly, she tells of the rich gifts and virtues with which she sees herself endowed and adorned in the nuptial chamber of her Bridegroom, for she says she is now in union with God and possesses the virtues with fortitude. Fourth, she relates that she now has perfect love. Fifth, that she has perfect spiritual peace, and that all is enriched and made beautiful with gifts and virtues in the measure that they are possessable and enjoyable in this life, as will be said in commenting on the verses.

First, then, she tells about her delight in the union with her Beloved, saying:

3.   Our bed is in flower,

We have already mentioned that this bed of the soul is the Bridegroom, the Son of God, who is in flower for the soul. For now that she is united with and reclines upon Him and has become His bride, her Beloved's breast and love is communicated to her. This means that He communicates to her His wisdom, secrets, graces, virtues, and gifts, and that through them He makes her so beautiful and rich and so imbues her with delights that it seems to her she rests upon a bed, made of a variety of sweet divine flowers, that delights with its touch and refreshes with its fragrance. Very appropriately does she call this union with God through love a "bed in flower," for this is what the bride speaking to the Bridegroom in the Canticle calls it: *Lectulus noster floridus* (our bed in flower). [Ct. 1:15]

She calls it "our," because both have the same virtues and the same love (which are the Beloved's) and both have the same delight, as the Holy Spirit says in Proverbs: *My delights are with the children of men.* [Prv. 8:31] She also says that it is in flower because the virtues of the soul in this state are now perfect and heroic. This, though, could not have come about until the bed was in flower in the perfect union with God.

Next she declares the second property of this union:

4.   Bound round with linking dens of lions,

By the "dens of lions," she understands the virtues she possesses in this state of union with God, for dens of lions are very safe and protected against all other animals. Fearful of the strength and boldness of the lion within, these animals not only dare not enter, but they dare not even stay nearby. Thus when the soul possesses the perfect virtues, each of them is like a den of lions in which Christ, the Bridegroom, united with the soul in that virtue and in each of the others, dwells and assists like a strong lion. And the soul herself, united with Him in these same virtues, is also like a strong lion, because she thereby receives the properties of God.

In this state the soul is so protected and strong in each of the virtues and in all of them together—while at rest upon this bed in flower of union—that the devils not only fear to attack her, but they do not even venture to appear before her. For they become greatly frightened upon seeing her so exalted, courageous, and bold, with the perfect virtues in the bed of her Beloved. When she is united with Him in transformation, they fear her as much as they do Him, and they have not even the courage to look at her. The devil has an extraordinary fear of the perfect soul.

5. She also says that the bed is bound round with linking dens of lions, because in this state the virtues are bound together, united, and fortified by each other, and fitted to the full perfection of the soul, sustaining one another in such fashion that no part remains open or weak. They are so fastened that not only does the devil fail to find entry, but nothing in the world, high or low, is able to disquiet, molest, or even move the soul. Liberated now from all the disturbance of the natural passions, and estranged from and stripped of the torment and variety of temporal cares, she enjoys in security and quietude the participation of God.

This is what the bride wanted to say in the Canticle: *Who will give you to me for my brother, nursed at the breasts of my mother, that I may find you alone outside and kiss you, and no one despise me?* [Ct. 8:1] This kiss is the union of which we speak, in which the soul is made equal with God through love. Owing to this desire she asks who will give her the Beloved as her brother (which would both signify equality and produce it), nursed at the breasts of her mother (which is a destroying of all her natural imperfections and appetites received from her mother Eve), that she may find Him alone outside (be united with Him alone, outside of all things, stripped of all things according to the appetite and will). Thus no one will despise her, that is, neither the world, the flesh, nor the devil will dare attack her. For none of these can disturb the soul that is liberated and purged of all things and united with God. She enjoys now in this state a habitual sweetness and tranquillity which is never lost or lacking to her.

6. Yet besides this habitual satisfaction and peace, the flowers of the virtues of this garden are so wont to open within her and spread their fragrance that it seems—and so it is—that she is filled with the delights of God.

And I said that the flowers of the virtues within her are wont to open, because even though she is filled with perfect virtues she is not always enjoying them actually; although, as I said, she ordinarily does enjoy the peace and tranquillity they cause. We can say that in this life they are present in the soul as flower buds in a garden. It is sometimes a wonderful thing to see them all open through the Holy Spirit and diffuse a marvelous variety of fragrance.

It will happen that the soul will behold in herself the mountain of flowers mentioned above, which are the abundance, grandeur, and beauty of God; and intertwined among them, the lilies of the wooded valleys, which stand for rest, refreshment, and protection; and next, interspersed there, the fragrant roses of the strange islands, which we said was the strange knowledge of God. Then too she will be struck by the scent of the lilies beside the resounding rivers, which we said represented the greatness of God filling every soul. And she will perceive from the jasmine interwoven there a fragrance diffused by the whistling of love-stirring breezes, which we also said the soul enjoys in this state. Likewise she is aware of all the other virtues and gifts we mentioned: the tranquil knowledge, silent music, sounding solitude, and the delightful and loving supper.

And sometimes her experience and enjoyment of these flowers united together is such that she can very truthfully say: Our bed is in flower, bound round with linking dens of lions. Happy is the soul who in this life merits at some time the enjoyment of the fragrance of these divine flowers!

And she says that this bed is also

7.   Hung with purple,

In Scripture, purple denotes charity, and kings use and clothe themselves in purple. The soul says this bed in flower is hung with purple because it is only by the charity and love of the King of heaven that all the virtues, riches, and goods flourish, receive sustenance, and give enjoyment. Without such love, the soul could not enjoy this bed and its flowers. Thus all these virtues are present in her as though hung with love of God, as in a subject in which they are well preserved. And they are as though bathed in love because each one of them is ever making her love God, and in all things and in all works they lovingly move her to more intense love of God.

Such is the meaning of "hung with purple." A clear reference to this is found in the divine Canticle. For there it is said that the couch or bed Solomon made for himself was of wood from Lebanon, and that the columns were of silver, the seat of gold, and the hangings purple, and it is said that he put order in all by means of charity. [Ct. 3:9–10] The virtues and endowments, signified by the wood from Lebanon and the silver columns, and which God places in the soul, have their couch and reclining place made of gold. For as we have said, the seat of the virtues is love, and by love they are conserved. And all of them are put in order and exercised by means of the charity of both God and the soul.

And she also says of this bed

8.   Built up in peace,

Here she lists the fourth excellence of this bed, which is dependent upon the third. The third was perfect love, and from perfect love, whose property as St. John says is to cast out all fear [1 Jn. 4:18], stems perfect peace of soul, the fourth characteristic of this bed.

For a greater understanding of this it should be known that each of the virtues is of itself peaceful, meek, and strong, and consequently produces in the soul these three effects: peace, meekness, and fortitude. And because this bed is in flower, made from the flowers of virtues, and all these virtues are peaceful, meek, and strong, the bed itself is built up in peace, and the soul peaceful, meek, and strong. These are three properties against which no war can be waged, neither by the world, nor by the devil, nor by the flesh. And the virtues keep the soul so tranquil and safe that to her it seems she is built up in peace.

And besides what has already been said, she adds the fifth property of this bed in flower:

9.   And crowned with a thousand shields of gold.

These shields are the virtues and gifts. Even though these virtues and gifts, as we said, are the flowers, etc., of this bed, they also serve as the soul's crown and her reward for having struggled to acquire them. Not only this, but they also have a defensive value, like strong shields, against the vices which were conquered through the practice of virtue. As a result the bride's bed in flower is crowned with them as her reward, and protected by them as by a shield.

She states that they are gold in order to designate the high value of the virtues. The bride made this same assertion in other terms in the Canticle: *Behold that sixty strong men of the strongest in Israel surround the bed of Solomon, each with a sword at his thigh in defense against the fears of night.* [Ct. 3:7–8]

And she asserts that there are a thousand to denote the multitude of virtues, graces, and gifts with which God endows the soul in this state. To signify the vast number of the bride's virtues, the same term was used in the Canticle: *Thy neck is like the tower of David which is built with defenses; a thousand shields hang from it, and all the armor of the strong men.* [Ct. 4:4]

STANZA 25

Introduction

1. The soul that has reached this state of perfection is not content with extolling and praising the excellences of her Beloved, the Son of God, nor of telling in song and rendering thanks for the favors she receives from Him and the delights she enjoys in Him; for she makes reference also to those He bestows on other souls. In this blessed union of love she is aware of both. In praising and thanking Him for the favors He grants to other souls, she recites this stanza:

> Following Your footprints
> Maidens run along the way;
> The touch of a spark,
> The spiced wine,
> Cause flowings in them from the balsam of God.

Commentary

2. In this stanza the bride praises the Beloved for the three favors devout souls receive from Him, which animate them further and raise them to the love of God. Because she herself has experience of them in this state, she mentions them here.

The first, she says, is the sweetness that He gives them, which is so efficacious that it makes them run along the road to perfection.

The second is a visit of love by which He suddenly inflames them in love.

The third is abundance of charity which He infuses in them and by which He so inebriates them that He causes the spirit—as in the visit of love—to be elevated and to burst forth in praise and delightful affections of love before God.

Thus she says:

3.   Following Your footprints

A man's footprints are the traces by which we can track him. God's sweetness and knowledge, given to the soul seeking Him, is a trace by which she goes on knowing and searching for Him. Yet the soul says to the Word, her Bridegroom: Following Your footprints (after the trace of your sweetness which You infuse and leave impressed on them) and the fragrance which flows from You,

4.   Maidens run along the way;

This means that devout souls run along by the youthful strength received from the sweetness of your footprints, that is, run from place to place and in many ways. This is the meaning of "run along": Each runs along, according to the way and kind of spirit and state God gives, with many differences of spiritual practices and works. They run along the way of eternal life, the way of evangelical perfection, by which they encounter the Beloved in union of love, after their spirit has been stripped of all things.

This sweetness and trace of Himself which God leaves in the soul greatly lightens her and makes her run after Him. For then the soul does very little or nothing of her own in order to advance on this road, rather she is moved and attracted by the divine footprint, not only to go out, but even to run along this road in many ways, as we have said. The bride in the Canticle sought this divine attraction from the Bridegroom, saying: *Trahe me; post te curremus in odorem unguentorum tuorum* (Draw me, and we shall run after You in the odor of Your ointments). [Ct. 1:3] And after He gave her this divine odor she says: *In odorem unguentorum tuorum currimus: adolescentulae dilexerunt te nimis* (We run in the odor of Your ointments; the maidens have loved You exceedingly). [*cf*. Office of Assump. B.V.M.; 3rd ant. 1st vesp.] And David says: *I have run the way of Your commandments when You enlarged my heart.* [Ps. 118:32]

5.   The touch of a spark,
                 The spiced wine,
                 Cause flowings in me from the balsam of God.

Commenting on the first two verses, we have explained that souls, following His footprints, run along the way by external practices and works. And now in these three verses the soul speaks of their interior exercise of will when they are moved by two other inward favors and visits bestowed on them by the Beloved. She calls these favors "the touch of a spark" and "the spiced wine." And she calls the interior exercise of the will arising from these two visits "flowings in me from the balsam of God."

As for the first, it should be known that this touch of a spark is a very subtle touch which the Beloved sometimes produces in the soul, even when least expected, and which inflames her in the fire of love, as if a hot spark were to leap from the fire and set her ablaze. Then with remarkable speed, as when one suddenly remembers, the will is enkindled in loving, desiring, praising, and thanking God, and reverencing, esteeming, and praying to Him in the savor of love. She calls these acts, flowings from the balsam of God. These flowings result from the touch of the sparks shot forth by the divine love which enkindles the fire. This divine love is the balsam of God that with its fragrance and substance comforts and cures the soul.

6. In the Canticle the bride speaks of this divine touch: *Dilectus meus misit manum suam per foramen, et venter meus intremuit ad tactum eius* (My lover put His hand through the opening, and my heart trembled at his touch). [Ct. 5:4]

The Beloved's touch is the touch of love which we said He produces in the soul. The hand is the favor He grants her by this touch. The opening through which this hand entered is the manner, mode, and degree of the soul's perfection, for the touch is usually greater or less and of one kind of spiritual quality or another in accordance with the manner of perfection. Her heart, which she says trembled, is the will in which this touch is produced. And the trembling is the elevation of her appetites and affections toward God through the desire, love, and praise of Him, and all the other acts we mentioned, which are the flowings from the balsam of God redounding from this touch.

7. "The spiced wine." This spiced wine is another much greater favor which God sometimes grants to advanced souls, in which He inebriates them in the Holy Spirit with a wine of sweet, delightful, and fortified love. Accordingly, she calls this love, "spiced wine." As this wine is seasoned and strengthened with many diverse, fragrant, and fortified spices, so this love, which God accords to those who are already perfect, is fermented and established in them and spiced with the virtues they have gained. Prepared with these precious spices, this wine gives such strength and abundance of sweet inebriation in these visits granted by God to the soul that they cause her to direct toward Him, efficaciously and forcefully, flowings or outpourings of praise, love, and reverence, etc., which we have mentioned. And she does this with admirable desires to work and suffer for Him.

8. It should be known that this favor of sweet inebriation, because it has more permanence, does not pass away as quickly as the spark. The spark touches and then passes, although its effect lasts for a while, and sometimes for a long while; but the spiced wine—which is, as I say, sweet love in the soul—usually lasts, together with its effect, a long while, and sometimes a day or two, or many days, though not always in the same degree of intensity, because its lessening and increasing are beyond the soul's power. Sometimes without doing anything on his own, a person feels in his intimate substance that his spirit is being sweetly inebriated and inflamed by this divine wine. As David says: *My heart grew hot within me, and in my meditation a fire shall be enkindled.* [Ps. 38:4]

The flowings from this inebriation of love sometimes last as long as the inebriation itself. At other times, even though this love is present, these flowings are absent; but when they are present, their intensity is greater or less in accordance with the intensity of the inebriation. But the flowings, or effects of the spark, ordinarily last longer than the spark itself, in fact the spark leaves these flowings in the soul, and they are more ardent than those derived from the inebriation, for this divine spark sometimes sets souls on fire and leaves them burning up with love.

9. And since we have mentioned fermented wine it will be worthwhile to note briefly the difference between fermented wine, which is called old wine, and new wine. The difference will be the same as that between old and new lovers. This will help us in giving some instructions to spiritual persons.

With the new wine, the lees are not yet completely fermented and settled. Thus the wine is still in the process of fermentation and one cannot know its good quality and value until the effervescence stops and the lees are entirely fermented. Until then the wine is in danger of going bad, has a rough, sharp savor, and is harmful to the one who drinks much of it. A great deal of its strength lies in the sediment.

In the old wine, the lees are settled and the process of fermentation finished, and thus there is no effervescence as in the new wine. The good quality of the wine is now evident and there is no danger of its going bad, since the fermentation which could have spoiled it has now ceased. The wine that is well fermented is hardly ever spoiled or lost; it has a smooth savor; and its strength lies in the substance and no longer in the taste. Drinking it fortifies one, and gives a good disposition.

10. New lovers are comparable to new wine. They are the beginners in the service of God. The fervors of the wine of love are very exterior, in the sensory part of the soul. The lees of the weak and imperfect sensory part have not yet finished their work of fermentation. These new lovers find their strength in the savor of love, and this sensible savor is what really motivates and strengthens them for the performance of their works. One should not trust this love until these fervors and coarse sensory tastes have passed. Just as this fervor and the warmth of sense can incline one to good and perfect love, and serve as a beneficial means for such love by a thorough fermentation of the lees of imperfection, so too it is very easy in these beginnings and in this novelty of tastes that the new wine of love fail and lose its fervor and delight.

These new lovers always carry about the anxieties and fatigues of sensible love. In this regard they ought to be moderate in their drinking, for, if prompted by the agitation of the wine, they do a great deal of work, their nature will be ruined by these anxieties and fatigues of love, that is, of the new wine. As we said, this new wine is sharp, coarse, and unsmooth until completely fermented, that is, when these anxieties of love have passed, as we shall soon say.

The Wise Man in the Book of Ecclesiasticus makes this same comparison, saying: *A new friend is like new wine; it will grow old and become a smooth drink.* [Ecclus. 9:15]

11. Now, then, the old lovers, those who are exercised and tried in the service of the Bridegroom, are like old wine. The lees of this wine are already fermented, and it does not have the sensitive effervescence or fermentation, nor the ardent external fires. What is more, they taste the sweetness of the wine of love, the substance of which is now well fermented, so that the love is based not on the sensible delights, as is the love of new lovers, but settled within the soul, in spiritual substance and savor, and truly good works. And these individuals do not want to be attached to this sensory taste and fervor, nor do they desire to take pleasure in it, lest weariness and distaste become their lot. For he who gives reign to his appetite for some sensory taste will necessarily suffer affliction and displeasure in both sense and spirit.

Since these old lovers now lack the spiritual sweetness that has its roots in the sensory part, they do not have the anxieties or afflictions of love in the sense and spirit. These old lovers hardly ever fail God, for they now stand above all that would make them fail Him, that is, above sensuality. And their wine of love is not only fermented and purged of the lees, but even spiced, as is said in the verse, with the perfect virtues, which do not let it go bad as does the new wine.

In God's sight, as a result, the old friend is highly esteemed, and thus the Book of Ecclesiasticus says of him: *Do not forsake an old friend, for a new one will not be like him.* [Ecclus. 9:14]

With this wine of love, then, now tried in the soul and spiced, the Beloved causes the divine inebriation we mentioned. By its strength, the soul directs toward God sweet and delightful outpourings.

Thus the meaning of these three verses is: The touch of the spark by which You awaken the soul, and the spiced wine, by which You lovingly inebriate her, cause her to direct to You the flowings of the movements and acts of love which You cause in her.

STANZA 26

Introduction

1. What, then, is the state of this happy soul in her bed of flowers, where these things and so many others take place, in which she has for her couch the Bridegroom, the Son of God, and love of this very Bridegroom for a covering and hanging? She can certainly repeat the words of the bride: *His left hand is under my head.* [Ct. 2:6] We can therefore assert truly that this soul is here clothed with God and bathed in divinity, not as though on the surface, but in the interior of her spirit, superabounding in divine delights. In the fullness of the spiritual waters of life, she experiences what David says of those who have

reached God: *They shall be inebriated with the plenty of Your house; and You will give them to drink of the torrent of Your delight, because with You is the fountain of life.* [Ps. 35:9–10] What fulfillment will the soul have in her being, since the drink given her is no less than a torrent of delight! This torrent is the Holy Spirit, because, as St. John says, He is a resplendent river of living water which flows from the throne of God and of the Lamb. [Ap. 22:1] These waters, since they are the intimate love of God, flow intimately into the soul and give her to drink of this torrent of love, which, as we said, is the Spirit of her Bridegroom infused in this union. As a result she sings this stanza with abundant love:

> In the inner wine cellar
> I drank of my Beloved, and, when I went abroad
> Through all this valley
> I no longer knew anything,
> And lost the herd which I was following.

Commentary

2. In this stanza the soul relates the sovereign favor God granted by recollecting her in the intimacy of His love, which is the union with, or transformation in, Him through love. And she notes two effects of this union: forgetfulness or withdrawal from all worldly things, and mortification of all her appetites and gratifications.

3.   In the inner wine cellar

To explain something about this wine cellar, and what the soul wishes to make known here, it will be necessary for the Holy Spirit to take my hand and guide my pen.

This wine cellar is the last and most intimate degree of love in which the soul can be placed in this life. Accordingly she calls this degree of love, the inner wine cellar, that is, the most interior. As a result, there are other steps of love, not so interior, by which one ascends to this last.

And we can assert that there are seven of these degrees or wine cellars of love. They are all possessed when the seven gifts of the Holy Spirit are possessed perfectly according to the soul's capacity for receiving them. Thus when the soul attains to the perfect possession of the spirit of fear, she has the spirit of love insofar as that fear, which is the last of the seven gifts, is filial. And perfect filial fear arises from perfect paternal love. So when Scripture wishes to point out that a person is perfect in charity, it says he is God-fearing. Isaias, in prophesying the perfection of Christ, said: *Replebit eum spiritus timoris Domini* (The spirit of the fear of God will fill Him). [Is. 11:3] St. Luke likewise called Simeon a God-fearing man: *Erat vir justus et timoratus.* [Lk. 2:25] And so with many others.

4. It should be known that many people reach and enter the first wine cellars, each according to the perfection of his love, but few in this life reach this last and most interior, for in it is wrought the perfect union with God, called spiritual marriage, of which the soul is now speaking. What God communicates to the soul in this intimate union is totally beyond words. One can say nothing about it just as one can say nothing about God Himself that resembles Him. For in the transformation of the soul in God, it is God who communicates Himself with admirable glory. In this transformation the two become one, as we would say of the window united with the ray of sunlight, or of the coal with the fire, or of the starlight with the light of the sun. But this union is not as essential and perfect as in the next life.

Thus to explain what she receives from God in the interior cellar of union, the soul says nothing else—neither do I think she can say anything more adequate—than the following verse.

5.   I drank of my Beloved,
As the drink is diffused through all the members and veins of the body, so this communication is diffused substantially in the whole soul, or better, the soul is transformed in God. In this transformation she drinks of God in her substance and in her spiritual faculties. With the intellect she drinks wisdom and knowledge; with the will, sweetest love; and with the memory she drinks refreshment and delight in the remembrance and the feeling of glory.

As for the first, that the soul receives and drinks delight substantially, the bride speaks of it in the Canticle: *Anima mea liquefacta est, ut sponsus locutus est* (My soul delighted as soon as the bridegroom spoke). [Ct. 5:6] This speaking of the bridegroom is equivalent to God's communication of Himself to the soul.

6. In the same book the bride says that the intellect drinks wisdom, when in desiring to attain this kiss of union and seeking it from the bridegroom she said: *There You will teach me* (wisdom and knowledge and love), *and I shall give You a drink of spiced wine* (my love spiced with Yours, transformed in Yours). [Ct. 8:2]

7. Regarding the third, the will drinks love as the bride says in the Canticle: *He put me in the secret wine cellar and set in order charity in me.* [Ct. 2:4] The meaning is that when I was put in His love, He gave me love to drink; or, more clearly and properly speaking: He put His charity in order in me, accommodating and appropriating His own charity to me. Hence the soul drinks of the Beloved's very own love, which He infuses in her.

8. It should be known that the teaching of some about the will's inability to love what the intellect does not first know ought to be under-

stood naturally. Naturally, it is impossible to love without first under-standing what is loved, but supernaturally, God can easily infuse and increase love without the infusion or increase of particular knowledge.

This is the experience of many spiritual persons; they frequently feel they are burning in love of God, with no more particular knowledge than before. They understand little but love a great deal, or understand a great deal but love little. As a matter of fact those spiritual persons whose understanding of God is not very advanced usually make progress according to their wills, while infused faith suffices for their knowledge. By means of this faith God infuses charity in them, and augments this charity and its act, which means greater love, although, as we said, their knowledge is not increased. Thus the will can drink love without the intellect again drinking knowledge, although in our case, in which the soul says she drank of her Beloved, all the three faculties drink together, insofar as there is union in the inner wine cellar.

9. As to the fourth, in which the memory drinks of the Beloved, it is clear that the memory is illumined by the intellectual light in remem-brance of the goods the soul possesses and enjoys in the union with her Beloved.

10. This divine drink so deifies, elevates, and immerses her in God that she says:

11.   . . . and, when I went abroad
That is, when this favor had passed. For even though the soul is always in this sublime state of spiritual marriage once God has placed her in it, the faculties are not always in actual union, although the substance is. Yet in this substantial union of the soul, the faculties are frequently united too and they drink in this inner wine cellar, the intellect understanding, the will loving, etc. But in saying, "when I went abroad," she does not refer to the essential or substantial union, which is this state she already has, but to the union of the faculties, which is not, nor can be, continuous in this life. "And when I went abroad," then

12.   Through all this valley
That is, through this vast world.

13.   I no longer knew anything,
The reason is that the drink of highest wisdom makes her forget all worldly things. And it seems that her previous knowledge, and even all the knowledge of the world, in comparison with this knowledge is pure ignorance.

For a better understanding of this, it should be known that the most formal cause of the soul's knowing nothing of the world when in this state is that she is being informed with supernatural knowledge, in the presence of which all natural and political knowledge of the world is ignorance rather than knowledge. When the soul is brought into this lofty knowing, she understands by means of it that all other knowledge which has not the taste of this knowledge is not knowledge but ignorance, and that there is nothing to know in it. She declares the truth of the Apostle's words, that what is greater wisdom in the sight of men is foolishness before God. [1 Cor. 3:19] Hence she asserts that she no longer knew anything after drinking of that divine wisdom.

And this truth (that the wisdom of men and of the whole world is pure ignorance and unworthy of being known) cannot be understood except by this favor of God's presence in the soul, by which He communicates His wisdom and comforts her with the drink of love that she may behold this truth clearly, as Solomon explains: *This is the vision that the man who is with God saw and spoke. And being comforted by God's dwelling within him, he said: I am the most foolish of men, and the wisdom of men is not with me.* [Prv. 30:1–2]

The reason is that in the excess of the lofty wisdom of God the lowly wisdom of men is ignorance. The natural sciences themselves and the very works of God, when set beside what it is to know God, are like ignorance. For where God is unknown nothing is known. The high things of God are foolishness and madness to man, as St. Paul also says. [1 Cor. 2:14] Hence the wise men of God and the wise men of the world are foolish in the eyes of each other, for the one group finds the wisdom and knowledge of God imperceptible, and the other finds the same of the knowledge of the world. Wherefore the knowledge of the world is ignorance to the knowledge of God, and the knowledge of God is ignorance to the knowledge of the world.

14. On the other hand, that elevation and immersion of the mind in God, in which the soul is as though carried away and absorbed in love, entirely transformed in God, does not allow attention to any worldly thing. She is not only annihilated before and estranged from all things, but even from herself, as if she had vanished and been dissolved in love; all of which consists in passing out of self to the Beloved. Thus the bride in the Canticle, after having treated of the transformation of her love into the Beloved, refers to this unknowing in which she was left by the word, *nescivi* (I did not know). [Ct. 6:11]

In a way, the soul in this state resembles Adam in the state of innocence, who did not know evil. For she is so innocent that she does not understand evil, nor does she judge anything in a bad light. And she will hear very evil things and see them with her own eyes and be unable to understand that they are so, since she does not have within herself the habit of evil by which to judge them; for God, by means of the perfect habit of true wisdom, has destroyed her habitual imperfections and ignorances which include the evil of sin.

15. And so too in regard to her words, "I no longer knew anything," she takes little part in the affairs of others, for she is not even mindful of her own. This is a characteristic of God's spirit in the soul: He gives her an immediate inclination toward ignoring and not desiring knowledge of the affairs of others, especially that which brings her no benefit. God's spirit is turned toward the soul to draw her away from external affairs rather than involve her in them. Thus she remains in an unknowing, in the manner she was accustomed to.

16. It should not be thought that because she remains in this unknowing that she loses there her acquired knowledge of the sciences; rather these habits are perfected by the more perfect habit of supernatural knowledge infused in her. Yet these habits do not reign in such a way that she must use them in order to know; though at times she may still use them, as this supernatural knowledge does not impede their use. For in this union with divine wisdom these habits are joined to the superior wisdom of God. When a faint light is mingled with a bright one, the bright light prevails and is that which illumines. Yet the faint light is not lost, but rather perfected, even though it is not the light which illumines principally.

Such, I believe, will be the case in heaven. The habits of the acquired knowledge of the just will not be supplanted, but they will not be of great benefit either, since the just will have more knowledge through the divine wisdom than through these habits.

17. Yet particular knowledge, forms of things, imaginative acts, and any other apprehensions involving form and figure are all lost and ignored in that absorption of love. There are two reasons for this:

First, since the soul is absorbed and imbibed in that drink of love, she cannot advert actually to any other thing.

Second, and principally, that transformation in God makes her so consonant with the simplicity and purity of God, in which there is no form or imaginative figure, that it leaves her clean, pure, and empty of all forms and figures, purged, and radiant in simple contemplation. The effect of this contemplation is like that of the sun on a window. In shining upon the window, the sun makes it look bright, and all the stains and smudges previously apparent are lost sight of; yet when the sunlight passes, the stains and smudges reappear.

Since the effect of that act of love endures a while, the unknowing also continues, so that the soul cannot advert to anything in particular until the effect of that act of love passes. Since that act of love inflamed and transformed her into love, it annihilated her and did away with all that was not love, as is understood in what we mentioned above concerning David: *Because my heart was inflamed, my reins were also changed, and I was brought to nothing and knew not.* [Ps. 72:21–22] The change of the reins because of this inflammation of the heart is a change of the soul, according to her operations and appetites, into God, into a new kind of life in which she is undone and annihilated before all the old things she formerly made use of. The prophet thus says that he was brought to nothing and did not know, for these are the two effects we mentioned of this drink from the wine cellar of God. Not only is all her old knowing annihilated, seeming to her to be nothing, but her old life and imperfections are annihilated, and she is restored in the new man, which is the second effect contained in this verse.

18.   And lost the herd which I was following.

It should be known that however spiritual a soul may be there always remains, until she reaches this state of perfection, some little herd of appetites, satisfactions, and other imperfections, natural or spiritual, after which she follows, in an effort to pasture and satisfy it.

In the intellect there usually resides some imperfect appetites for knowing things.

The will is usually allowed to be captivated by some small appetites and gratifications of its own. These may involve temporal things, such as some little possession, or the attachment to one object more than to another, or some presumptions, judgments, and punctilios, and other small things having a worldly savor or tinge. These latter may concern natural things, such as eating, drinking, finding more gratification in this than in that, choosing and desiring the best. Or they may concern spiritual things, such as the desire for spiritual satisfactions, or other trifles we would never finish listing, characteristic of spiritual persons who are not yet perfect.

In the memory there are usually many wanderings, cares, and useless imaginings after which she follows.

Regarding too the four passions of the soul, there are many useless hopes, joys, sorrows, and fears which she follows.

19. Some have more and others less of this herd, and they follow until, having entered the interior wine cellar to drink, all transformed in love, they lose it entirely. In this wine cellar these herds of imperfections are more easily consumed than the rust and tarnish of metal is consumed by fire. Thus the soul now feels free of all the childish likes and trifles which she pursued, and can say: "And lost the herd which I was following."

STANZA 27

Introduction

1. In this interior union God communicates Himself to the soul with such genuine love that no mother's affection, in which she tenderly caresses her child, nor brother's love, nor friendship is comparable to it. The tenderness and truth of love by which the immense Father favors and exalts this humble and loving soul reaches such a degree—O wonderful thing, worthy of all our awe and admiration!—that the Father Himself becomes subject to her for her exaltation, as though He were her servant and she His lord. And He is as solicitous in favoring her as He would be if He were her slave and she His god. So profound is the humility and sweetness of God!

In this communication of love, He exercises in some way that very service that He says in the Gospel He will render to His elect in heaven, that is: girding Himself and passing from one to another, He will minister to them. [Lk. 12:37] He is occupied here in favoring and caressing the soul like a mother who ministers to her child and nurses it at her own breasts. The soul thereby comes to know the truth of Isaias' words: *You shall be carried at the breast of God and upon His knees you will be caressed.* [Is. 66:12]

2. What then will be the soul's experience among such sovereign graces! How she will be dissolved in love! How thankful she will be to see the breasts of God given to her with such supreme and generous love! Aware that she has been set among so many delights, she makes a complete surrender of herself and gives Him the breast of her will and love. She experiences this surrender of her soul in the way the bride did in the Canticle when speaking to her Bridegroom: *I turn to my Beloved, and His turning is toward me. Come my Beloved, let us go into the field, let us abide together on the grange; let us rise very early and go to the vineyards to see if the vine is in flower and if the flowers bear fruit, if the pomegranates flourish; there will I give You my breasts* (that is, I shall employ the delights and strength of my will in Your love). [Ct. 7:10–12]

Because this mutual surrender of God and the soul is made in this union, she refers to it in the following stanza:

> There He gave me His breast;
> There He taught me a sweet and living knowledge;
> And I gave myself to Him,
> Keeping nothing back;
> There I promised to be His bride.

Commentary

3. In this stanza the bride tells of the mutual surrender made in this spiritual espousal between the soul and God, saying that in that interior wine cellar of love they were joined by the communication He made of Himself to her, by freely offering her the breast of His love, in which He taught her wisdom and secrets, and by the complete surrender she made of herself to Him, keeping nothing back for herself or for any other, promising to be His forever. The verse follows:

4.   There He gave me His breast;

Giving one's breast to another signifies the giving of love and friendship to another and the revealing of secrets to him as to a friend. When the soul says that there He gave her His breast, she means that He communicated His love and secrets to her there. God grants this communication to the soul in this state, and also that of which she speaks in the following verse:

5.   There He taught me a sweet and living knowledge;

The sweet and living knowledge she says He taught her is mystical theology, that secret knowledge of God which spiritual persons call contemplation. This knowledge is very delightful because it is a knowledge through love. Love is the master of this knowledge and that which makes it wholly agreeable. Since God communicates this knowledge and understanding in the love with which He communicates Himself to the soul, it is very delightful to the intellect, since it is a knowledge belonging to the intellect, and it is delightful to the will since it is communicated in love, which pertains to the will. Then she says:

6.   And I gave myself to Him,
                       Keeping nothing back;

In that sweet drink of God, in which the soul is imbibed in Him, she most willingly and with intense delight surrenders herself wholly to Him, in the desire to be totally His and never to possess in herself anything other than Him. God causes in this union the purity and perfection necessary for such a surrender. And since He transforms her in Himself, He makes her entirely His own and empties her of all she possesses other than Him.

Hence, not only in her will but also in her works she is really and totally given to God, without keeping anything back, just as God has freely given Himself entirely to her. This union is so effected that the two wills are mutually payed, surrendered, and satisfied (so that neither fails the other in anything) with the fidelity and stability of an espousal.

She therefore adds:

7.   There I promised to be His bride.

Just as one who is espoused does not love, care, or work for any other than her bridegroom, so the soul in this state has no affections of the will, nor knowledge in the intellect, nor care, nor work, nor appetite that is not entirely inclined toward God. She is as it were divine and deified, in such a way that in regard to all she can understand she does not even suffer first movements contrary to God's will.

As an imperfect soul is ordinarily inclined toward evil, as least in the first movements of its will, intellect, memory, and appetites, and as it has imperfections, so on the other hand the soul in this state ordinarily inclines and moves toward God in the first movements of its intellect, memory, will, and appetites, because of the great help and stability it has in God and its perfect conversion toward good.

David clarified all this when he said, speaking of the soul in this state: *Shall not my soul be subject to God? Yes; for from Him do I receive salvation, and because He is my God and my Saviour and my Receiver, I shall no longer move.* [Ps. 61:2–3] By using the expression, my Receiver, he indicates that since his soul is received by God and united to Him, it will no longer suffer any movement contrary to God.

8. Obviously, then, the soul that has reached this state of spiritual espousal knows how to do nothing else than love and walk always with its Spouse in the delights of love. Since in this state she has reached perfection, the form and nature of which, as St. Paul says, is love [Col. 3: 14], and since the more a soul loves the more completely it loves, this soul that is now perfect is all love, if one may express it so, and all her actions love; she employs all her faculties and possessions in loving, giving up everything, like the wise merchant [Mt. 13:44], for this treasure of love she has found hidden in God. She is conscious that love is so valuable in her Beloved's sight that He neither esteems nor makes use of anything else but love, and so she employs all her strength in the pure love of God, desiring to serve Him perfectly.

She does this not merely because He desires it, but also because the love by which she is united to Him moves her to the love of God in and through all things. Like the bee that sucks honey from all the wild-flowers and will not use them for anything else, the soul easily extracts the sweetness of love from all the things that happen to her, that is, she loves God in them. Thus everything leads her to love. And being informed and fortified as she is with love, she neither feels, nor tastes, nor knows the things that happen to her, whether delightful or bitter, since as we said the soul knows nothing else but love. And her pleasure in all things and in all transactions is always the delight of loving God. And to illustrate this she speaks the following stanza.

STANZA 28

Introduction

1. Because we said that God makes use of nothing other than love, it may prove beneficial to explain the reason for this, prior to commenting on the stanza. The reason is that all our works and all our trials, even though they are the greatest possible, are nothing in the sight of God. For through them we cannot give Him anything nor fulfill His only desire, which is the exaltation of the soul. Of these other things He desires nothing for Himself, since He has no need of them. If anything pleases Him, it is the exaltation of the soul. Since there is no way by which He can exalt her more than by making her equal to Himself, He is pleased only with her love. For the property of love is to make the lover equal to the object loved. Since the soul in this state possesses perfect love, she is called the bride of the Son of God, which signifies equality with Him. In this equality of friendship the possessions of both are held in common, as the Bridegroom Himself said to His disciples: *I have now called you my friends, because all that I have heard from my Father I have manifested to you.* [Jn. 15:15]

She then recites the stanza:

> Now I occupy my soul
> And all my energy in His service;
> I no longer tend the herd,
> Nor have I any other work
> Now that my every act is love.

Commentary

2. Since in the last stanza the soul—or better the bride—said she surrendered herself entirely to the Bridegroom without keeping anything back, she now tells her mode and method of accomplishing this, saying that now she occupies her soul and body, her faculties and all her ability, in nothing other than the service of her Bridegroom. And she says that on this account she no longer goes about in search of her own gain or

pleasures, nor occupies herself with things and matters foreign to God; and that even with God Himself she has no other style or manner of dealing than the exercise of love, since she has now traded and changed all her first manner of dealing for love, as is now said:

3. Now I occupy my soul
By saying that she occupies her soul, she refers to her surrender to the Beloved in that union of love where now the soul and all the faculties (intellect, memory, and will) are dedicated and devoted to His service. She employs the intellect in understanding and carrying out the things that are more for His service, and the will in loving all that is pleasing to Him and attaching it to Him in all things, and her memory and care in what most pleases and serves Him.
And she adds:

4. And all my energy in His service;
By all her "energy" she refers to all that pertains to the sensory part of the soul. The sensory part includes the body with all its senses and faculties, interior and exterior, and all the natural ability (the four passions, the natural appetites, and other energies).
All of this, she says, she occupies, as she does the rational and spiritual part referred to in the preceding verse, in the service of her Beloved. By directing the activity of the interior and exterior senses toward God, her use of the body is now conformed to His will. She also binds the four passions of the soul to Him, for she does not rejoice except in God, nor hope in anything other than God; she fears only God and has no sorrow unless in relation to Him. And likewise all her appetites and cares go out only to God.

5. All this energy is occupied in God, and so directed to Him that even without advertence all its parts, which we have mentioned, are inclined from their first movements to work in and for God. The intellect, will, and memory go out immediately toward God, and the affections, senses, desires, appetites, hope, joy, and all the energy from the first instant incline toward God, although, as I say, the soul may not advert to the fact that she is working for Him.
As a result she frequently works for God, and is occupied in Him and in His affairs, without thinking or being aware that she is doing so. For her custom and habit of acting in this way causes her to lack advertence and care and even the fervent acts she used to make in beginning some work.
Because this energy is now all employed in God, the soul necessarily achieves the condition described in the following verse:

6. I no longer tend the herd,
This is like saying: I no longer follow after my pleasures and appetites.

For having placed them in God and given them to Him, she no longer
feeds them nor keeps them for herself.

She does not merely say she no longer tends this herd, but even more:

7.   Nor have I any other work

Before reaching this gift and surrender of herself and her energy to
the Beloved, the soul usually has many unprofitable occupations, by
which she endeavors to serve her own appetite and that of others.
For we can say she had as much work as she had many habitual imperfections. These habitual imperfections can be, for example, the trait or
"work" of speaking about useless things, thinking about them, and also
carrying them out, or of not making use of these actions in accord with
the demands of perfection. She usually has desires to serve the appetites
of others, which she does through ostentatiousness, compliments, flattery,
human respect, the effort to impress and please people by her actions,
and many other useless things; in this fashion she strives to satisfy people,
employing for them all her care, desires, work, and finally energy.

She says she no longer has all this work, because all her words,
thoughts, and works are of God and directed toward Him without any
of the former imperfections. Thus the verse means: I no longer tend to
giving satisfaction to my appetite nor that of others, neither am I occupied or detained with other useless pastimes or things of the world.

8.   Now that my every act is love.

This is like saying that now all this work is directed to the practice
of love of God, that is: All the ability of my soul and body (memory,
intellect, and will, interior and exterior senses, appetites of the sensory
and spiritual part) move in love and because of love. Everything I
do, I do with love, and everything I suffer, I suffer with the delight
of love. David meant this when he said: *I shall keep my strength for
You.* [Ps. 58:10]

9. It should be known that when the soul reaches this state, all the
activity of the spiritual and sensory part (in what it does, or in what
it suffers, and in whatever manner) always causes more love and delight
in God, as we have said. Even the very exercise of prayer and communion with God, in which she was accustomed to considerations and
methods, is now wholly the exercise of love. Hence whether her work is
temporal or spiritual, this soul can always say, "Now that my every act
is love."

10. Happy is the life and state, and happy the person who attains it,
where everything is now the substance of love and the pleasure and delight of espousal. The bride in this state can indeed say to the divine
Bridegroom those words she spoke to Him out of pure love in the Canticle: *All the new and old apples I have kept for You* [Ct. 7:13], which is

equivalent to saying: My Beloved, all that is rough and toilsome I desire for Your sake, and all that is sweet and pleasant I desire for Your sake. Yet the accommodated sense of this verse is that the soul in this state of spiritual espousal ordinarily walks in the union of love of God, which is a habitual and loving attentiveness of the will to God.

STANZA 29

Introduction

1. This soul indeed, lost to all things and won over to love, no longer occupies her spirit in anything else. She even withdraws in matters pertinent to the active life and exterior occupations for the sake of fulfilling the one thing the Bridegroom said was necessary [Lk. 10:42], and that is: attentiveness to God and continual love of Him. This the Lord values and esteems so highly that He reproved Martha when she tried to call Mary away from her place at His feet in order to busy her with other active things in His service; and Martha thought that she herself was doing all the work and that Mary, because she was enjoying the Lord's presence, was doing nothing. [Lk. 10:39-41] Yet, since there is no greater nor more necessary work than love, the contrary is true. He also defends the bride in the Canticle, conjuring all creatures of the world, referred to by the daughters of Jerusalem, not to hinder the bride's spiritual sleep of love, nor cause her to awaken or open her eyes to anything else until she desires. [Ct. 3:5]

2. It should be noted that until the soul reaches this state of union of love, she should practice love in both the active and contemplative life. Yet once she arrives, she should not become involved in other works and exterior exercises that might be of the slightest hindrance to the attentiveness of love toward God, even though the work be of great service to God. For a little of this pure love is more precious to God and the soul and more beneficial to the Church, even though it seems one is doing nothing, than all these other works put together.

Because of her determined desire to please her Spouse and benefit the Church, Mary Magdalen, even though she was accomplishing great good by her preaching and would have continued doing so, hid in the desert for thirty years in order to surrender herself truly to this love. It seemed to her, after all, that by such retirement she would obtain much more because of the notable benefit and gain a little of this love brings to the Church.

3. Great wrong would be done to a person who possesses some degree of this solitary love, as well as to the Church, if we should urge him to

become occupied in exterior or active things, even if the works are very important and demand only a short time. Since God has solemnly entreated that no one awaken a soul from this love [Ct. 3:5], who will dare do so and remain without reproof? After all, this love is the end for which we were created.

Let those, then, who are singularly active, who think they can win the world with their preaching and exterior works, observe here that they would profit the Church and please God much more, not to mention the good example they would give, were they to spend at least half of this time with God in prayer, even though they may not have reached a prayer as sublime as this. They would then certainly accomplish more, and with less labor, by one work than they otherwise would by a thousand. For through their prayer they would merit this result, and themselves be spiritually strengthened. Without prayer, they would do a great deal of hammering but accomplish little, and sometimes nothing, and even at times cause harm.

God forbid that the salt should begin to lose its savor [Mt. 5:13], for however much they may appear to achieve externally, they will in substance be accomplishing nothing; it is beyond doubt that good works can be performed only by the power of God.

4. Oh, how much could be written here on this subject! But this is not the place. I have mentioned it only in explanation of the next stanza. In this stanza the soul replies to all those who impugn her holy idleness, and who desire every work to be the kind that shines outwardly and satisfies the eye, and do not know the secret source from which the water flows and all fruit is produced.

And thus she recites the stanza

> If, then, I am no longer
> Seen or found on the common,
> You will say that I am lost;
> That, stricken by love,
> I lost myself, and was found.

Commentary

5. In this stanza the soul answers a tacit reproof of those in the world who usually criticize persons who are entirely given to God and think these persons excessive in their conduct, estrangement, and withdrawal, and assert that they are useless in important matters and lost to what the world esteems. The soul skillfully answers this reprimand, boldly facing it and all the other possible reproofs of the world; for in having reached the intimate love of God, she considers everything else of little consequence.

But this is not all. She even proclaims how she has acted, and rejoices and glories in having lost the world and herself for her Beloved. This is what she means in the stanza when she addresses the worldly: that, if they no longer see her engaged in her former worldly conversations and pastimes, they should believe and declare that she has lost these things and withdrawn; and that she has counted this loss such a good that she herself, searching for her Beloved and intensely enamored of Him, desired it. That they might see the gain of her loss and not think it an absurdity or a delusion, she declares that her loss was her gain, and that as a result she became lost purposely.

6.   If, then, I am no longer
         Seen or found on the common,

The place where people often gather for diversion and recreation, and where shepherds also feed their flocks, is usually called "the common." Thus, by the common the soul refers to the world, where worldlings engage in their pastimes and conversations and feed the flock of their appetites. In this verse she tells those who are of the world that if they neither see nor find her as they did before her complete surrender to God, they should consider her, by this fact, lost, and they should therefore say (because she rejoices in their saying this and desires them to do so):

7.   You will say that I am lost;

He who loves is not abashed before the world because of the works he performs for God, nor even if everybody condemns them does he hide them in shame. Whoever is ashamed to confess the Son of God before men, by failing to perform His works, will discover that the Son of God, as is recorded in Luke, will be ashamed to confess him before the Father. [Lk. 9:26] The soul possessing the spirit of love glories rather in beholding that she has achieved this work in praise of her Beloved and lost all things of the world. Hence she says: "You will say that I am lost."

8. Few spiritual persons reach such daring and determination in their works. Though some do act this way, and are considered far advanced, they never lose themselves entirely in some matters, whether worldly or natural, and never execute works for Christ with perfection and nakedness of spirit and without thought of what others will say or how their work will appear. Since these persons are not lost to themselves in their work, they cannot declare: "You will say that I am lost." They are still ashamed to confess Christ before men by their works. Because of their human respect they do not live entirely in Christ.

9.   That, stricken by love,

This means that, through the practice of virtue, stricken with love,

10.   I lost myself, and was found.

Aware of the Bridegroom's words in the Gospel, that no one can serve two masters, but must necessarily fail one [Mt. 6:24], the soul claims here that in order not to fail God, she failed all that is not God, that is, herself and all other creatures, losing all these for love of Him. He who truly walks in love lets himself lose all things immediately in order to be found more attached to what he loves. On this account the soul affirms here that she lost herself. She achieved this in two ways: she became lost to herself by paying no attention to herself in anything, by concentrating on her Beloved and surrendering herself to Him freely 'and disinterestedly, with no desire to gain anything for herself; secondly, she became lost to all creatures, paying no heed to all her own affairs, but only to those of her Beloved. And this is to lose herself purposely, which is to desire to be found.

11. He who walks in the love of God seeks neither his own gain nor his reward, but only to lose all things and himself for God; and this loss he judges to be his gain. And thus it is as St. Paul asserts: *Mori lucrum* [Phil. 1:21], that is, my death for Christ is the spiritual gain of all things and of myself. And consequently the soul declares: I was found. He who does not know how to lose himself, does not find himself, but rather loses himself, as Our Lord teaches in the Gospel: *He who desires to gain his soul shall lose it, and he who loses it for My sake shall gain it.* [Mt. 16:25]

Should we desire to interpret this verse more spiritually and in closer accord with what we are discussing here, it ought to be known that when a soul treading the spiritual road has reached such a point that she has lost all roads and natural methods in her communion with God, and no longer seeks Him by reflections, or forms, or sentiments, nor by any other way of creatures and the senses, but has advanced beyond them all and beyond all modes and manners, and enjoys communion with God in faith and love, then it is said that God is her gain, because she has certainly lost all that is not God.

Stanza 30

Introduction

1. Everything is a gain for the soul whose gain is God, because all the strength of her faculties is converted into a spiritual communion with Him of exceedingly agreeable interior love. These interior exchanges between God and the soul bear such delicate and sublime delight that no mortal tongue can describe it nor human intellect understand it. For the

betrothed on the day of her espousal understands nothing else than what belongs to the festivity and delight of love and to the revealing of all her jewels and graces for the sake of pleasing and gladdening the Bridegroom. And similarly her Beloved manifests to her all His wealth and excellent qualities in order to bring her consolation and happiness. In this spiritual espousal then, in which the soul truly experiences what the bride says in the Canticle—*I for my Beloved and my Beloved for me* [Ct. 6:2]—the virtues and graces of the bride as well as the grandeurs and graces of the Bridegroom, the Son of God, are brought to light. They both display these riches in order to celebrate the feast of this espousal, and they mutually communicate their goods and delights with a wine of savory love in the Holy Spirit.

The soul declares this by addressing the Bridegroom in this stanza:

> With flowers and emeralds
> Chosen on cool mornings
> We shall weave garlands
> Flowering in Your love,
> And bound with one hair of mine.

Commentary

2. In this stanza the bride returns to address the Bridegroom in the communion and refreshment of love. She describes the solace and fruition the bride-soul and the Son of God possess in the wealth of the virtues and gifts of each other, and in the interchange of these treasures which they enjoy mutually in the communion of love. In speaking to Him, therefore, she asserts that they will weave rich garlands of gifts and virtues, acquired and gained at a pleasant and suitable time, made beautiful and attractive in the love He bears for her, and sustained and preserved through her love for Him. She calls this enjoyment of the virtues, a weaving of garlands from them, for both the bride and the Bridegroom enjoy them together in their love for each other, as though these virtues were flowers twisted into garlands.

3.   With flowers and emeralds
The flowers are the soul's virtues, and the emeralds are the gifts she has received from God. These flowers and emeralds are

4.   Chosen on cool mornings
This means they are acquired at the time of youth, which is life's cool morning. She points out that they are chosen, because she obtained them during her youth when the vices put up more strenuous opposition and nature is more inclined and ready to lose them; also by beginning to

gather the virtues at this early season, she acquired more perfect and choice ones.

She terms this time of youth, "cool mornings." For just as the fresh spring mornings are more pleasant than the other times of day, so too the virtue of youth pleases God more. And these cool mornings can even refer to the acts of love by which the virtues are acquired. These acts of love give more pleasure to God than do cool mornings to the sons of men.

5. The cool mornings also bear reference to works done in difficulty and dryness of spirit. God highly esteems these works denoted by the chill of the winter mornings and done for Him in aridity and hardship, for by such means the virtues and gifts are acquired in a high degree. Those acquired through this labor are for the most part more select, refined, and stable than if they were obtained with spiritual relish and enjoyment, for virtue takes root in dryness, difficulty, and labor, as God says to St. Paul: *Virtue is made perfect in weakness.* [2 Cor. 12:9] To stress, then, the excellence of the virtues from which garlands for the Beloved are woven, the words, "chosen on cool mornings," are very apt, because the Beloved rejoices only in these flowers and emeralds of select and perfect virtues and gifts, and not in imperfect ones.

As a result the bride declares here that with them

6.   We shall weave garlands

To understand this verse it should be known that all the virtues and gifts the soul (and God within her) acquires are like a garland of various flowers within her, with which she is wonderfully adorned, as though in a robe of rich variety. For a better understanding it should be noted that while gathering material flowers one at the same time weaves them into the garland that is being made, and so too while one acquires the spiritual flowers of virtues and gifts, they are at the same time fixed firmly in the soul. And when these spiritual flowers are wholly obtained, the garland of perfection in the soul is complete. Both the soul and the Bridegroom rejoice in the beauty and adornment of this garland, as is proper to the state of perfection.

These are the garlands she declares they must weave, that is, she must be girded, surrounded with an assortment of flowers and emeralds, which are perfect virtues and gifts, that, wearing this beautiful and costly adornment, she may appear worthily before the King and deserve that He make her His equal and place her at His side like a queen; for this she merits through the beauty of such variety. Hence David speaks to Christ on this subject: *Astitit regina a dextris tuis in vestitu deaurato, circumdata varietate* (The queen stood at your right hand, clothed in a garment of gold, surrounded with variety). [Ps. 44:10] This would be similar to saying: She stood at your right, clothed in perfect love and surrounded with a variety of perfect gifts and virtues.

And she does not say I alone shall weave the garlands, or You alone will, but we shall weave them together. The soul cannot practice or acquire the virtues without the help of God, nor does God effect them alone in the soul without her help. Although it is true that *every good gift and every perfect gift is from above, having come down from the Father of lights,* as St. James says [Jas. 1:17], yet this gift is not received without the ability and help of the soul receiving it. So the bride in the Canticle said to the Bridegroom: *Draw me; we shall run after you.* [Ct. 1:3] The movement toward good, therefore, comes only from God, as is declared here. But she does not state that He alone nor she alone runs, but that we shall both run, which means that God and the soul work together.

7. This verse most appropriately refers to Christ and the Church, for in it, the Church, the Bride of Christ, addresses Him saying: let us weave garlands (understanding by garlands, all the holy souls engendered by Christ in the Church). Each holy soul is like a garland adorned with the flowers of virtues and gifts, and all of them together form a garland for the head of Christ, the Bridegroom.

The lovely garlands can refer as well to what we call aureoles; these are also woven by Christ and the Church and are of three kinds:

The first kind is made from the beautiful white flowers of all the virgins. Each virgin possesses her own aureole of virginity, and all these aureoles together will be joined into one and placed on the head of Christ, the Bridegroom.

The seond aureole contains the resplendent flowers of the holy doctors. All these aureoles will be entwined into one and set upon the head of Christ over that of the virgins.

The third is fashioned from the crimson carnations of the martyrs. Each martyr has his aureole of martyrdom, and all these red aureoles woven together will add the final touch to the aureole of Christ, the Bridegroom.

So beautiful and fair will Christ the Bridegroom be with these three garlands that the bride's words in the Canticle will be repeated in heaven: *Go forth daughters of Sion and behold king Solomon in the crown with which his mother crowned him on the day of his espousal and on the day of the joy of his heart.* [Ct. 3:11]

She continues then:

8.   We shall weave these garlands
                      Flowering in Your love,

The flower of these works and virtues is the grace and power they possess from the love of God. Without love these works will not only fail to flower, but they will all wither and become valueless in God's sight, even though they may be perfect from a human standpoint. Yet, because God bestows His grace and love, they are works that have blossomed in His love.

9.   *And bound with one hair of mine.*

This hair is her will and the love she has for the Beloved. This love assumes the task of the thread in a garland. As the thread binds the flowers together, so love fastens and sustains the virtues in the soul. As St. Paul remarks: *charity is the bond of perfection.* [Col. 3:14] The supernatural virtues and gifts are so necessarily tied together in this soul's love that if the love should break, by an offense against God, the virtues would immediately become loose and disappear, just as the flowers would fall away if the thread of the garland were broken. Consequently it is insufficient that God love us and thereby give us virtues, for we must also love Him in order to receive and preserve them.

She says they were held with only one hair, and not with many, in order to point out that now her will is alone, detached from all other strands of hair, that is, from all extraneous loves. She clearly stresses here the value of these garlands of virtues, for when love is fixed solely and firmly in God, as she says, the virtues are also perfect, complete, and full-flowering in the love of God. Then God's love for the soul is inestimable, as she also experiences.

10. Even if I wanted to, I could not find words to express the beauty arising from the interwreathing of these flowers of virtues and these emeralds, nor could I describe the strength and majesty their order and arrangement gives to the soul, or the loveliness and charm in which this garment of variety clothes her.

In the Book of Job, God declares that the devil's body is like shields of molten metal protected with scales closely knit and so joined that air cannot pass through. [Jb. 41:6] If the devil, since he is clothed with evils (the scales) that are bound and ordained one to the other, is so strong that his body is comparable to a shield of molten metal, and since all evils in themselves are weakness, how tremendous will be the might of this soul that is all clothed with strong virtues and has them so fastened and interwoven that no ugliness or imperfection can get between them! By its strength every virtue adds strength to the soul, by its beauty it adds beauty, by its value it enriches her, and by its majesty it imparts power and grandeur to her. How marvelous, then, to the spiritual eye will this bride-soul appear, at the right hand of the King, her Bridegroom, in the charm of these gifts. *How beautiful are your steps in sandals, O prince's daughter,* exclaims the Bridegroom in the Canticle. [Ct. 7:1] He calls her "prince's daughter" to denote her royal inheritance.

And if he calls her beautiful because of her sandals, what will be the beauty afforded her by her garment!

11. Not only does her beauty in this robe of flowers stir one's admiration, but the strength she possesses from the orderly arrangement of these flowers and the interspersion of both emeralds and innumerable divine gifts fills one with terror. On this account the groom declares of her in the Canticle: *You are terrible, like an army in array.* [Ct. 6:3] As these virtues and gifts of God give refreshment by their spiritual fragrance, so too, when they are joined together in the soul, they impart strength by their substance. As a result the bride in the Canticle, when she was weak and love-sick over not having attained the union and interweaving of these flowers and emeralds by means of the hair of love, desired to be strengthened by this union and asked for it in these words: *Strengthen me with flowers, surround me with apples, because I languish with love.* [Ct. 2:5] By "flowers" she means the virtues, and by "apples," the remaining gifts.

STANZA 31

Introduction

1. I believe it is clear that by means of these garlands, interwoven and placed in the soul, the bride wishes to describe the divine union of love between herself and God. The flowers represent the Bridegroom, since He is *the flower of the fields and the lily of the valleys,* as He affirms. [Ct. 2:1] The hair of the soul's love is what unites and fastens her to this flower of flowers, for as the Apostle teaches: *love is the bond of perfection* (which is union with God). [Col. 3:14] The soul is like the peg on which the garlands are hung, since she is the subject of this glory and no longer appears to be what she was before. But by the perfection and beauty of all the flowers, she resembles the perfect flower Himself. This thread of love joins and binds God and the soul so strongly that it unites and transforms them. So great is this union that even though they differ in substance, in glory and appearance the soul seems to be God and God seems to be the soul.

2. This union is more wonderful than all that can be said of it. Scripture mentions something about it in the First Book of Kings in reference to Jonathan and David. The love Jonathan bore David was so intimate that it knitted his soul to David's. [1 Kgs. 18:1] If the love of one man for another was that strong, what will be the tie caused by the soul's love for God, the Bridegroom; especially since God here is the principal lover, who, in the omnipotence of His fathomless love, absorbs the soul in Him-

self more efficaciously and forcibly than a torrent of fire would devour the drop of morning dew, which usually rises and dissolves in the air! Undoubtedly the hair that joins them must be thin and very strong, since it penetrates with such forcefulness the parts it binds. Accordingly, the soul describes in the following stanza this beautiful hair.

> You considered
> That one hair fluttering at my neck;
> You gazed at it upon my neck
> And it captivated You;
> And one of my eyes wounded You.

Commentary

3. The soul wishes to express three things in this stanza:

First, she wishes to explain that that love which binds the virtues is no other love than solitary and strong love, for it must be this if it is to preserve them.

Second, she wishes to state that God was greatly captivated by this single hair of love when He beheld it alone and strong.

Third, she wishes to declare that God was intimately taken with love for her when He marked the purity and integrity of her faith.

And thus she proclaims:

4.   You considered
>   That one hair fluttering at my neck;

The neck, where the hair of love was fluttering, signifies fortitude. This hair of love weaves the virtues together, that is to say: loves with fortitude. In order to preserve the virtues it is not enough that love be alone; it must also be strong so that no contrary vice on any side of the garland of virtue may be able to break it. This hair of love binds the virtues in such a way that if it breaks where one of these virtues lies, it will immediately, as we said, fail in regard to them all. Just as all the virtues are present there where one is, so they all fail where one fails.

And she says that it was fluttering and flying about at her neck, because in fortitude of soul, this love flies to God mightily and speedily, without anything detaining it. And as the breeze causes the hair to flutter and fly about the neck, so too the breeze of the Holy Spirit moves and arouses the strong love to make its flight to God. Without this divine breeze to stir the faculties to the exercise of divine love, the virtues do not produce their effects, even though they are present in the soul.

In saying that the Beloved considered this hair fluttering at the neck, she points out how much God cherishes a strong love, for to consider an object is to look upon it with very particular attention and esteem; and the strong love urges God to turn His eyes to look at it.

And thus the following:

5.   You gazed at it upon my neck

The soul makes this affirmation to show that God not only values this love of hers because He sees that it is alone, but that He also cherishes it because He sees that it is strong. With God, to gaze at is to love, just as to consider an object is to value it. She repeats the word "neck" in this verse, in speaking of the hair—"You gazed at it upon my neck"—because, as we mentioned, this is why He loved her so much; He saw that her love was strong. Thus it is like saying: You loved it upon seeing that it was strong, without cowardice or fear; and alone, without other loves; and fluttering about quickly and fervently.

6. Until now this hair had not captivated God, because He had not gazed at it, nor had He seen it alone and detached from other strands of other loves, appetites, affections, and pleasures, nor did it flutter about alone at the neck of fortitude. But after love, through mortifications, trials, and penance, becomes so detached and strong that no force or occasion can break it, then God looks at it and takes the flowers of these garlands and binds them with it, since it is strong enough to keep them fastened in the soul.

7. In the explanation of the four stanzas that begin "O Living Flame of Love," we mentioned something about the nature of these temptations and trials, and about how deeply they reach into the soul that she might come to this fortitude of love in which God unites Himself to her. Having passed through these tribulations, the soul has reached such a degree of love that she merits the divine union.

Hence she says:

8.   And it captivated You;

Oh, how worthy of utter admiration and joy! God is taken captive by a hair! The reason this captivity is so estimable is that God wished to stop and gaze at the fluttering of the hair, as the preceding verse asserts. And as we pointed out, for God, to gaze at is to love. If in His infinite mercy He had not gazed at us and loved us first—as St. John declares [1 Jn. 4:10, 19]—and descended, the hair of our lowly love would not have taken Him prisoner, for this love was not so lofty in its flight as to be able to capture this divine bird of heights. But because He came down to gaze at us and arouse the flight of our love by strengthening and giving it the courage for this [Dt. 32:11], He Himself as a result was captivated by the flight of the hair, that is, He was satisfied and pleased. Such is the meaning of the verses: "You gazed at it upon my neck and it captivated You." It is indeed credible that a bird of lowly flight can capture the royal eagle of the heights, if this eagle descends with the desire of being captured.

Continuing:

9.   And one of my eyes wounded You.

The eye refers to faith. She says she wounded Him with only one eye, because if the soul's faith and fidelity toward God were not single, but mixed with some other human respect, it would not attain such an effect as to wound God with love. Thus it is only one eye that wounds Him, just as it is only one hair that captivates the Beloved. And so intimate is the love with which the Bridegroom is captivated by the bride in this single-hearted fidelity He beholds in her that, if the hair of her love captivates Him, the eye of her faith so tightens the bonds of His captivity as to cause a wound of love. This wound of love is the result of the great tenderness of affection with which He loves her, which means He introduces her further into His love.

10. The Bridegroom in addressing the bride in the Canticle makes this same statement about the hair and the eye: *You have wounded my heart, my sister; you have wounded my heart with one of your eyes and with one hair of your neck.* [Ct. 4:9] In this passage He declares twice that His heart was wounded—by the eye and by the hair. The soul accordingly mentions in this stanza the eye and the hair, for through them she denotes her union with God in the intellect and the will. Faith or fidelity, signified by the eye, resides in the intellect, and love, signified by the hair, resides in the will. She is, then, united with God in the intellect through faith, and in the will through love. She glories here in this union and thanks her Spouse for this favor received from His hands, and she values it highly that He should be satisfied and captivated by her love. Consider the joy, happiness, and delight the soul finds in such a prisoner, she who had been for so long His prisoner.

STANZA 32

Introduction

1. The power and the tenacity of love is great, for love captures and binds God Himself. Happy is the loving soul, since she possesses God for her prisoner, and He is surrendered to all her desires. God is such that those who act with love and friendship toward Him will make Him do all they desire, but if they act otherwise there is no speaking to Him nor power with Him, even though they go to extremes. Yet by love they bind Him with one hair.

Knowing this, and knowing how far beyond her merits it was that He should have favored her with such sublime love and the rich tokens of virtues and gifts, she attributes all to Him in the following stanza:

> When You looked at me
> Your eyes imprinted Your grace in me;
> For this You loved me ardently;
> And thus my eyes deserved
> To adore what they beheld in You.

Commentary

2. It is a property of perfect love to be unwilling to take anything for self, nor does it attribute anything to self, but all to the Beloved. If we find this characteristic in base loves, how much more in love of God, where reason so strongly obliges us to this. Because, therefore, it seems in the two previous stanzas that the bride attributed something to herself (saying that she would make garlands with the Bridegroom, and weave them together with one of her hairs—a work of no small importance—and afterwards announcing and glorying in the fact that her hair captivated the Beloved and her eye wounded Him, in which she also takes some credit), she desires in this stanza to explain her intention and remove the false impression which may have been received. For she is anxious and fearful lest she give herself some credit and attribute less to God than is His due and her desire. So she accredits all to Him, and thanks Him, stating that the reason the hair of her love captivated Him and the eye of her faith wounded Him was that He favored her by looking at her with love. By this look of love He made her gracious and pleasing to Himself. And she adds that from this grace and value she received from Him, she merited His love and a value within herself enabling her to adore her Beloved in a fashion pleasing to Him and to perform works worthy of His grace and love.

The verse follows:

3.   When You looked at me

That is, with the affection of love, because we have already pointed out that for God to look is for Him to love.

4.   Your eyes imprinted Your grace in me;

By the eyes of the Bridegroom she refers to God's mercy: He descends upon the soul in mercy, impressing and infusing His love and grace in her, making her beautiful and lifting her so high as to make her a partaker of the very divinity. [2 Pt. 1:4]

Seeing the height and dignity in which He has placed her, the soul proclaims:

5.   For this You loved me ardently;

To love ardently is to love very much. It is more than loving simply;
it is like loving doubly, for two reasons. In this verse the soul points to
the two motives or causes of the Bridegroom's love for her. He not only
loved her in being captivated by her hair, but He loved her ardently
in being wounded by her eye.

And she states in this verse that the cause of His loving her so ardently
and intimately was His desire, in looking at her, to give her grace by
which He could find His pleasure in her. Thus He gave her love, which
is her hair, and He gave her faith, which is her eye, formed with
His charity. She says therefore: "For this You loved me ardently."

By infusing His grace in the soul, God makes it worthy and capable
of His love. This verse, then, is like saying: Because You have infused
Your grace into me, which was a worthy token of Your love, You loved
me ardently, that is, You gave me more grace on this account. St. John
makes the same affirmation: *He gives grace for the grace He has given*
[Jn. 1:16], which is to give more. Without His grace one cannot merit
His grace.

6. It should be noted for an understanding of this that, just as God
loves nothing outside Himself, He bears no lower love for anything
than the love He bears for Himself. He does not love things because of
what they are in themselves, but because of what He is in Himself. Thus
love is the purpose for which He loves. With God, to love the soul is
to put her somehow in Himself and make her His equal. Thus He loves
the soul within Himself, with Himself, that is, with the very love by
which He loves Himself. This is why the soul merits the love of God in
all her works, insofar as she does them in God. Placed in this height,
this grace, she merits God Himself in every work.

Consequently, she continues:

7.   And thus my eyes deserved

That is, by the favor and grace the eyes of Your mercy granted me,
when You looked at me and made me pleasing to Your eyes and worthy
of Your sight, my eyes deserved

8.   To adore what they beheld in You.

This is like saying: My faculties, the eyes through which I can see
You, my Spouse, have merited this elevation which enables them to look
at You. These faculties were previously fallen and lowly in the misery
of their inferior operation and natural ability, for the power to look at
God is, for the soul, the power to do works in the grace of God. The faculties of the adoring soul, because they adored in the grace of their
God, by which every work becomes meritorious, merited this. Illumined
and elevated by His grace and favor, they adored what they beheld in

Him, which they did not previously see on account of their blindness and lowliness.

What was it, then, they beheld? They beheld grandness of virtue, abundance of sweetness, immense goodness, love, and mercy, all these in God, and the numberless benefits received from Him, either before or since these close ties with Him were wrought. The soul's eyes now deserved to adore all this meritoriously, for they were now gracious and pleasing to the Bridegroom. Previously they did not merit to adore or behold this; they did not even deserve to reflect upon some of these things about God. Great is the rudeness and the blindness of the soul without God's grace!

9. There is much to note here and much to grieve over in observing how far from the fulfillment of its obligations is the soul unillumined by the love of God. Having the obligation to know these and the countless other favors, both temporal and spiritual, she has received and continues to receive from God at every step, and to adore and serve God ceaselessly with all her faculties, she fails to do so. Not only this, she does not even merit to look at and know Him, nor even to have cognizance of such a possibility; such is the misery of those who live, or better are dead, in sin.

STANZA 33

Introduction

1. For a better understanding both of what we have said and of the following, it should be known that God's gaze produces four goods in the soul: it cleanses, endows with grace, enriches, and illumines, like the sun that dries and provides warmth and beauty and splendor when it pours down its rays.

After God places these three last kinds of good in the soul, He no longer remembers her former ugliness and sin, as He declares through Ezechiel [Ez. 18:22], for on account of these goods she is very agreeable to Him. And once He has blotted out this sin and ugliness, He no longer reproaches her for it, nor fails to impart more favors, since He never judges a thing twice.

Yet even though God forgets evil and sin once it is pardoned, the soul should not become oblivious of her former sins. As the Wise Man says: *Be not without fear for sin forgiven.* [Ecclus. 5:5] There are three reasons why she should not forget her sins: first, so as always to have a motive against presumption; second, to have cause for rendering thanks; third, to incite herself to greater confidence, for if while in sin the soul received so much good from God, how many more remarkable favors will she be able to hope for now that God has placed her in His love, outside of sin?

2. Remembering here all these mercies and aware that she has been placed with so much dignity close to the Bridegroom, she rejoices immeasurably in the gladness of thanksgiving and love. The memory of that former state, so unsightly and abject, notably promotes this gratitude and love. She was not only unprepared for and unworthy of God's gaze, but she did not even deserve that He pronounce her name, as He says through David. [Ps. 15:4] Conscious that in herself there is no reason, nor possibility of a reason, why God should look at and exalt her, but that this reason is only in God, in His mere will and beautiful grace, she ascribes her misery to herself and all her good possessions to the Beloved. Aware that through them she now merits what previously she did not, she takes courage and becomes bold to request the continuation of the divine spiritual union in which He will go on multiplying His favors in her. She declares all this in the following stanza:

> Do not despise me;
> For if, before, You found me dark,
> Now truly You can look at me
> Since You have looked
> And left in me grace and beauty.

Commentary

3. Taking courage and appraising herself by the tokens and value she has from her Beloved and observing that since they belong to Him she deserves esteem on their account—although in herself she is of small value and merits no esteem—the bride dares to tell her Beloved not to consider her any longer of little account and not to despise her. If she previously merited this treatment because of the ugliness of her fault and the inferiority of her nature, now, after He has looked at her the first time, by which He arrayed her in His grace and clothed her in His beauty, He can easily look at her the second time and many more times, making this grace and beauty grow. Now there is reason enough for Him to look at her, if we consider that He looked at her when she did not have these qualities, or merit that He do so.

4.   Do not despise me;

The soul does not declare this out of a desire for esteem (on the contrary, anyone with a genuine love of God highly esteems and rejoices in being hated and reviled because he is aware that of himself he deserves nothing else), but because of the gifts and graces of God which she possesses, as she points out in saying:

5.   For if, before, You found me dark,
That is, if before You graciously looked upon me, You found in me the
unsightliness of sins and imperfections and the lowness of the natural
condition

6.   Now truly You can look at me
                     Since You have looked
Since You have looked (rubbed out this dark and wretched color of sin
which made me unsightly), in which You bestowed grace on me the
first time, now truly You can look at me. That is, now I can indeed
be seen, and I merit being seen by receiving more grace from Your
eyes. The first time You not only rubbed out the dark color with those
eyes, but You made me worthy to be seen, since You looked with love
and grace,

7.   And left in me grace and beauty.
The soul's affirmations in the two preceding verses explain what St.
John states in the Gospel, that God gives grace for grace [Jn. 1:16] because when God beholds the soul made attractive through grace, He is
impelled to grant her more grace; for He dwells within her well pleased
with her. Knowing this, Moses begged God for more grace, desiring to
oblige Him by the grace he had already received from Him: *You say
that You know me by name and that I have found grace before You; if,
therefore, I have found grace in Your sight, show me Your face that I
might know You and find grace in Your sight.* [Ex. 33:12–13]
Because this grace exalts, honors, and beautifies her in His sight,
God loves her ineffably. If before she had grace, He loved her only on
account of Himself, now that she is in grace He loves her not only on
account of Himself but also on account of herself. And thus enamored
by means of the effects and works of grace, or without them, He ever
continues to communicate more love and more graces. And as He continues to honor and exalt her, He becomes continually more captivated
by and enamored of her.
God manifests this in speaking to His friend Jacob through Isaias:
*Since You have become honorable and glorious in My sight, I have loved
you.* [Is. 43:4] In other words, after I had turned My eyes upon you,
thus giving you grace and making you glorious and worthy of honor
and My presence, you merited the grace of more of My favors.
The bride in the Canticle explains the same thing, saying: *I am black
but beautiful, daughters of Jerusalem; wherefore the King has loved
me and brought me to His inner chamber.* [Ct. 1:4; 3rd ant. of Vesp.
BVM.] This is like saying: Souls, you who do not know of nor recognize
these favors, do not marvel that the heavenly King has granted such
admirable ones, as even to bring me to His inner love. For though of
myself I am dark, He so frequently fixed His eyes on me, after having

looked at me the first time, that He was not satisfied until He had espoused me to Himself and brought me to the inner chamber of His love.

8. Who can express how much God exalts the soul that pleases Him? It is impossible to do so, nor can this even be imagined, for after all, He does this as God, to show who He is. One can only explain something of it through that custom God has of giving more to whomsoever has more. And His gifts are multiplied in proportion to what the soul possesses, as the Gospel makes clear: *To him that has will be given more until he abounds; and from him that has not, even what he has shall be taken from him.* [Mt. 13:12; Lk. 19:26] Thus the money of the servant who did not stand in the lord's good graces was taken from him and given to the servant who had the most money of all those who pleased the lord. [Lk. 19:24]

God gathers together in him who is His closest friend the best and principal goods of His house, of both the Church Militant and Triumphant. This friend receives these goods for his own higher honor and glory, so that he is like a brilliant light absorbing in itself countless fainter lights. God also declared this, according to the spiritual sense, in the passage of Isaias, quoted above, when He spoke to Jacob: *I am your Lord God, the Holy One of Israel, your Savior; I have given Egypt for your propitiation, Ethiopia and Saba for you . . . and I will give men for you and people for your soul.* [Is. 43:3–4]

9. Now, my God, You can easily look upon and bear high esteem for the soul You behold, for by Your look You present her with valuables and jewels and then esteem her and are captivated. After You looked at her, she no longer merits that You look at her only once, but that You look at her often. The Holy Spirit observes in the Book of Esther: *He is worthy of such honor whom the king honors.* [Est. 6:11]

STANZA 34

Introduction

1. The gifts of friendship the Bridegroom bestows on the soul in this state are inestimable, and the praises and endearing expressions of love which frequently pass between the two are indescribable. She praises and thanks Him, and He extols, praises, and thanks her, as is apparent in the Canticle where He tells her: *Behold you are beautiful, my love, behold you are beautiful and your eyes are those of doves.* And she replies: *Behold You are beautiful, my Beloved, and fair.* [Ct. 1:14–15] There are many other expressions of gratitude and praise they repeat to each other throughout the Canticle. In the preceding stanza she belit-

tled herself, calling herself dark and ugly, and lauded Him for His beauty and grace, since with His regard He gave her beauty and grace. And since He customarily exalts him who humbles himself [Lk. 14:11; Mt. 23:12], He fixes His eyes upon her as she requested, and in the next stanza He extols her and does not call her dark, as she called herself, but a white dove, praising her good characteristics which are like those of the dove and the turtledove. Thus He says:

> The small white dove
> Has returned to the ark with an olive branch;
> And now the turtledove
> Has found its longed-for mate
> By the green river banks.

Commentary

2. It is the Bridegroom who takes up the song here and describes the soul's purity in this state and her riches and reward for laboring and preparing herself to come to Him. He also tells of her good fortune in having found her Bridegroom in this union, and of the fulfillment of her desires and of the delight and refreshment she possesses in Him, now that the trials of this life and time are over.

And thus He says:

3.   The small white dove

He calls the soul a "white dove" because of the whiteness and purity imparted by the grace she has found in God. And He calls her "dove," because this is the name He gives her in the Canticle [Ct. 2:10] to denote both the simplicity and meekness of her character and her loving contemplation. For the dove is not only simple and meek, without gall, but also has bright and loving eyes. As a result the Bridegroom also remarked there that she had dove's eyes to denote this property of loving contemplation by which she looks at God. [Ct. 4:1]

He declares that this dove

4.   Has returned to the ark with an olive branch;

Here the Bridegroom compares the soul to the dove of Noah's ark, taking that flight back and forth from the ark as a figure of what has happened to the soul in this case. For the dove flew back and forth from the ark because it found no place among the waters of the flood where it could alight, until it returned with an olive branch in its beak as a sign of God's mercy in the cessation of the deluge. [Gn. 8:8–11] Similarly this soul that left the ark of God's omnipotence when He created her, passed through the waters of sin and imperfection, and finding no place for her appetite to rest, flew back and forth from the Creator's breast. And He did not take her in until He made the waters of all the imperfections upon the land of the soul to cease, and she returned with the olive branch (the symbol of her victory over all things through the clemency and mercy of God) to this happy and perfect recollection on the breast of her Beloved. She returns not only victorious over her enemies, but with the reward of her merits, for both are denoted by the olive branch. Thus the small dove, the soul, not only returns to the ark of her God as clean and white as when He created her prior to her departure, but also carries in addition the olive branch which signifies the reward and peace obtained in her victory over self.

5.
> And now the turtledove
> Has found its longed-for mate
> By the green river banks.

The Bridegroom calls the soul a "turtledove" because, in looking for her Beloved, she acted as the turtledove when it does not find the mate it longs for. To make this clear we ought to recall what they say about the turtledove: when it does not find its mate, it will not perch on the green branch, nor drink the cool, clear water, nor does it rest in the shade or join the company of others; but when it finds its mate, then it will enjoy all these other goods.

The soul possesses all these traits, and it is necessary for her to possess them, in order to reach this union with her Bridegroom, the Son of God. For she must advance with such love and solicitude as not to set the foot of her appetite on the green branch of any delight, or drink the clear water of any worldly honor and glory, nor should she desire the taste of the cool water of any temporal refreshment or comfort, or to settle in the shade of any creature's favor and protection, nor should she desire in any way to rest in anything, or have the company of other affections, but she should always sigh for solitude in all things until she reaches her Bridegroom in complete satisfaction.

6. Because the soul, before reaching this high state, went about with deep love in search of her Beloved and was satisfied with nothing else than Him, the Bridegroom Himself describes in song the end of her fatigues and the fulfillment of her desires, saying that now the turtledove has found its longed-for mate by the green river banks. This is similar to saying: Now the bride alights on the green branch, delighting in her Beloved; now she drinks the clear water of sublime contemplation and wisdom of God, and the cool water of her refreshment and comfort in God; and she also rests in the shade of His protection and favor—which she so longed for—where she is divinely and delightfully consoled, fed, and refreshed, as she happily declares in the Canticle: *I sat down in the shade of Him Whom I desired, and His fruit was sweet to my palate.* [Ct. 2:3]

STANZA 35

Introduction

1. The Bridegroom continues the explanation of His happiness over the blessing the bride has obtained through the solitude in which formerly she desired to live. This blessing is a stable peace and unchanging good. When the soul has become established in the quietude of solitary love of her Spouse, as has this one of whom we are speaking, she is fixed with so much delight in God, and God in her, that she has no need of other masters or means to direct her to Him, for now God is her guide and her light. He accomplishes in her what He promised through Osee: *I shall lead her into solitude and there speak to her heart.* [Os. 2:14] In this promise He reveals that He communicates and unites Himself to the soul in solitude. To speak to the heart is to satisfy the heart, which is dissatisfied with anything less than God. Thus the Bridegroom continues:

> She lived in solitude,
> And now in solitude has built her nest;
> And in solitude He guides her,
> He alone, Who also bears
> In solitude the wound of love.

Commentary

2. The Bridegroom does two things in this stanza:

First, He praises the solitude in which the soul formerly desired to live, telling how it was a means for her to find and rejoice in her Beloved alone, withdrawn from all her former afflictions and fatigues. Since she wished to live in solitude, apart from every satisfaction, comfort, and support of creatures, in order to reach companionship and union with her Beloved, she deserved to discover the possession of peaceful solitude in her Beloved, in Whom she rests, alone and isolated from all these disturbances.

Second, He states that, insofar as she desired to live apart from all created things, in solitude for her Beloved's sake, He Himself was enamored of her because of this solitude and took care of her by accepting her in His arms, feeding her in Himself with every blessing, and guiding her to the high things of God. He asserts not only that He guides her, but that He does so alone without other means (angels, men, forms, or figures), for she now possesses, through this solitude, true liberty of spirit which is not bound to any of these means.

The verse states:

3. She lived in solitude,

The soul, represented by the turtledove, lived in solitude before encountering the Beloved in this state of union. There is no companionship which affords comfort to the soul that longs for God; indeed, until she finds Him everything causes greater solitude.

4. And now in solitude has built her nest;

The solitude in which she lived consisted of the desire to go without the things of the world for her Bridegroom's sake—as we said of the turtledove—by striving for perfection, acquiring perfect solitude in which she reaches union with the Word. She consequently attains to complete refreshment and rest, signified here by the nest which refers to repose. It is similar to saying: She formerly practiced this solitude, in which she lived, in trial and anguish because she was imperfect, but now she has built her nest in it and has found refreshment and repose in having acquired it perfectly in God. David, speaking spiritually, says: *Truly the sparrow has found a house and the turtledove a nest where she can nurture her young* [Ps. 83:4], that is: The soul has found a place in God where she can satisfy her appetites and faculties.

5. And in solitude He guides her,

In this solitude, away from all things the soul is alone with God and He guides, moves, and raises her to divine things. That is: He elevates her intellect to divine understanding, because it is alone and divested of other contrary and alien knowledge; He moves her will freely to the love of God, because it is alone and freed from other affections; and He fills her memory with divine knowledge, because it is now alone and empty of other images and phantasies. Once the soul disencumbers these faculties and empties them of everything inferior and of attachment to even superior things, leaving them alone without these things, God engages them in the invisible and divine. It is God who guides her in this solitude, as St. Paul declares of the perfect: *Qui spiritu Dei aguntur*, etc. (*they are moved by the Spirit of God*). [Rm. 8:14] This is like saying: In solitude He guided her,

6. He alone, Who also bears

The meaning of this is that He not only guided her in her solitude, but that it is He alone who works in her, without any means. This is a characteristic of the union of the soul with God in spiritual marriage: God works in and communicates Himself to her through Himself alone, without the intermediary of angels or natural ability, for the exterior and interior senses, and all creatures, and even the very soul do very little toward the reception of the remarkable supernatural favors which God grants in this state. They do not fall within the province of the soul's natural ability, or work, or diligence, but God alone grants them to her. And the reason He does so is that He finds her alone and does not want to give her any other company, nor does He want her to trust in or profit by any other than Himself alone.

Since the soul has left all and passed beyond all means, ascending above them all to God, it is fitting that God Himself be the guide and means of reaching Himself. And having ascended above all things, in solitude from all things, the soul profits by no other than the Word, the Bridegroom, Who helps her to ascend further. He is taken with love for her and wants to be the only one to grant her these favors. And He goes on:

7.   He alone, Who also bears
                      In solitude the wound of love.

That is, He is wounded with love for the bride. The Bridegroom bears a great love for the solitude of the soul; but He is wounded much more by her love, since being wounded with love for Him, she desired to live alone in respect to all things. And He does not wish to leave her alone, but wounded by the solitude she embraces for His sake, and observing that she is dissatisfied with any other thing, He alone guides her, drawing her to and absorbing her in Himself. Had He not found her in spiritual solitude, He would not have wrought this in her.

STANZA 36

Introduction

1. Strange it is, this property of lovers, that they like to enjoy one another's companionship alone, apart from every creature and all company. If some stranger is present, they do not enjoy each other freely, even though they are together and may speak to one another just as much when he is present as when he is absent, and even though the stranger does not talk to them. The reason they desire to commune with each other alone is that love is a union between two alone.

Once the soul is placed at the peak of perfection and freedom of spirit in God, and all the repugnances and contradictions of sensuality have ceased, she no longer has any other activity to engage her than surrender to the delights and joys of intimate love of her Bridegroom. So it is written of the holy Tobias, that after he had undergone the trials of his poverty and temptations he was enlightened by God and spent all the rest of his days in joy [Tb. 14:4], as does the soul of whom we are now speaking, since the goods she beholds in herself are of such joy and delight.

2. Isaias declares this of the one who has practiced the works of perfection and arrived at the summit which we are discussing. Addressing the soul he says of this perfection: *Then your light will rise up in darkness, and your darkness will be as the noonday. And your Lord God will give you rest always and will fill your soul with brightness, and deliver your bones; and you will be like a watered garden and an unfailing fount of water. And the solitudes of ages will be built in you. You will raise up the beginnings and foundations of generation and generation, and you will be called the builder of the fences, withdrawing your paths and ways to quietude. If you separate your labor from the day of rest and from doing your will on my holy day, and call yourself the delicate, holy, and glorious Lord's day of rest, and if you glorify Him by not doing your own ways and not fulfilling your own will, then you will delight in the Lord, and I will extol you above the heights of the earth and feed you with the inheritance of Jacob.* [Is. 58:10–14] These are the words of Isaias; Jacob's inheritance here is God Himself. Accordingly, as we said, this soul is no longer engaged in anything else than joy in the delights of this pasture. One thing only is left for her to desire: perfect enjoyment of God in eternal life.

In the remaining stanzas she asks her Beloved for this beatific pasture of the manifest vision of God.

Thus she exclaims:

> Let us rejoice, Beloved,
> And let us go forth to behold ourselves in Your beauty,
> To the mountain and to the hill,
> To where the pure water flows,
> And further, deep into the thicket.

Commentary

3. Now that the perfect union of love between God and the soul is wrought, she desires to employ herself in those things proper to love. She it is who addresses the Bridegroom in this stanza, asking for three things proper to love.

First, she desires to receive the joy and savor of love, which is what she asks for in saying, "Let us rejoice, Beloved."

Second, she desires to become like the Beloved, and she asks for this in stating, "And let us go forth to behold ourselves in Your beauty."

Third, she desires to look closely at and know the things and secrets of the Beloved Himself, which is what she requests in saying, "And further, deep into the thicket."

The verse follows:

4.   Let us rejoice, Beloved,

That is: Let us rejoice in the communication of the sweetness of love, not only in that sweetness we already possess in our habitual union, but in that which overflows into the effective and actual practice of love, either interiorly with the will in the affective act, or exteriorly in works directed to the service of the Beloved. As we mentioned, when love takes root it has this characteristic: It makes one always desire to taste its joys and sweetnesses, which are the inward and outward exercise of love. All this the lover does in order to resemble the Beloved more.

And thus she continues:

5.   And let us go forth to behold ourselves in Your beauty,

This means: Let us so act that by means of this loving activity we may attain to the vision of ourselves in Your beauty in eternal life. That is: That I be so transformed in Your beauty that we may be alike in beauty, and both behold ourselves in Your beauty, possessing now Your very beauty; this, in such a way that each looking at the other may see in the other his own beauty, since both are Your beauty alone, I being absorbed in Your beauty; hence, I shall see You in Your beauty, and You shall see me in Your beauty, and I shall see myself in You in Your beauty, and You will see Yourself in me in Your beauty; that I may resemble You in Your beauty, and You resemble me in Your beauty, and my beauty be Your beauty and Your beauty my beauty; wherefore I shall be You in Your beauty, and You will be me in Your beauty, because Your very beauty will be my beauty; and therefore we shall behold each other in Your beauty.

This is the adoption of the sons of God, who will indeed declare to God what the very Son said to the Eternal Father through St. John: *All my things are yours, and yours mine.* [Jn. 17:10] He says this by essence, since He is the natural Son of God, and we say it by participation, since we are adopted sons. He declared this not only for Himself, the Head, but for His whole mystical body, the Church, which on the day of her triumph, when she sees God face to face, will participate in the very beauty of the Bridegroom. Hence the soul makes the petition that she and her Bridegroom go forth to behold each other in His beauty

6.   To the mountain and to the hill,

That is: to the morning and essential knowledge of God, which is knowledge in the divine Word, who, in His height, is signified here by the mountain. Isaias speaks similarly in calling upon men to know the Son of God: *Come let us ascend to the mountain of the Lord* [Is. 2:3]; in another passage: *The mountain of the house of the Lord shall be prepared.* [Is. 2:2]

And to the hill, that is, to the evening knowledge of God, which is God's wisdom in His creatures, works, and wondrous decrees. The hill suggests this wisdom because it is not as high as the morning wisdom. Yet the soul asks for both the evening and the morning wisdom when she says: "To the mountain and the hill."

7. The soul in urging the Bridegroom, "let us go forth to the mountain to behold ourselves in Your beauty," means: Transform me into the beauty of divine Wisdom and make me resemble it, which is the Word, the Son of God. And in adding, the hill, she asks that He inform her with the beauty of this other lesser wisdom, contained in His creatures and other mysterious works. This wisdom is also the beauty of the Son of God by which the soul desires to be illumined.

8. The soul cannot see herself in the beauty of God unless she is transformed in the wisdom of God, in which she sees herself in possession of earthly and heavenly things. The bride wanted to come to this mountain and this hill when she asserted: *I shall go to the mountain of myrrh and to the hill of incense.* [Ct. 4:6] The mountain of myrrh refers to the clear vision of God, and the hill of incense to the knowledge of creatures, for the myrrh on the mountain is more choice than the incense on the hill.

9.   To where the pure water flows,

That is, to where God bestows on the intellect knowledge and wisdom, called water here because it cleanses and removes accidents and phantasies and clears away the clouds of ignorance. The soul always possesses this desire to have clear and pure understanding of the divine truths, and the greater her love, the more she longs to enter further into these truths. Because of this desire she asks for the third property of love, saying:

10.   And further, deep into the thicket.

Into the thicket of your splendid works and profound judgments, whose multitude and variety are such that we can use the term "thicket." In these works and judgments there is abundant wisdom, so full of mysteries, that not only is the term "thicket" apt, but even "curdled thicket," which David uses: *Mons Dei, mons pinguis, mons coagulatus* (The mountain of God is a fat mountain and a curdled mountain). [Ps. 67:16] This thicket of God's wisdom and knowledge is so deep and immense that no matter how much the soul knows she can always enter it further; it is vast and its riches incomprehensible, as St. Paul exclaims: *O height of the riches of the wisdom and knowledge of God, how incomprehensible are His judgments and unsearchable His ways.* [Rom. 11:33]

11. Yet the soul wants to enter this thicket and incomprehensibility of judgments and ways because she is dying with the desire to penetrate them deeply. Knowledge of them is an inestimable delight surpassing all understanding. David, therefore, in speaking of the savoriness of these judgments, says: *The judgments of the Lord are true and in themselves justified. They are more to be desired and coveted than gold and precious stone of great price; and they are sweeter than honey and the honeycomb, so much so that Your servant loved and kept them.* [Ps. 18:10–12] Hence

the soul ardently wishes to be engulfed in these judgments and know them from further within. And, in exchange, it will be a singular comfort and happiness for her to enter all the afflictions and trials of the world, and everything that might be a means to this, however difficult and painful, even the anguish and agony of death, all in order to see herself further within her God.

12. This thicket into which the soul thus wants to enter also signifies very appropriately the thicket and multitude of trials and tribulations, for suffering is very delightful and beneficial to her. Suffering is the means of her penetrating further, deep into the thicket of the delectable wisdom of God. The purest suffering brings with it the purest and most intimate knowing, and consequently the purest and highest joy, because it is a knowing from further within. Not being content with just any kind of suffering, she insists: "And further, deep into the thicket," that is, even to the agony of death in order to see God. The prophet Job, desirous of this suffering in order to see God, exclaimed: *Who will grant that my request be fulfilled and that God will give me what I hope for and that He Who began me may destroy me, and let loose His hand and put an end to me. And that I may have this comfort, that in afflicting me with sorrow He might not spare me?* [Jb. 6:8–10].

13. Oh! If we could but now fully understand how a soul cannot reach the thicket and wisdom of the riches of God, which are of many kinds, without entering the thicket of many kinds of suffering, finding in this her delight and consolation; and how a soul with an authentic desire for divine wisdom, wants suffering first in order to enter this wisdom by the thicket of the cross! Accordingly, St. Paul admonished the Ephesians not to grow weak in their tribulations and to be strong and rooted in charity in order to comprehend with all the saints what is the breadth and height and depth, and to know also the supereminent charity of the knowledge of Christ, in order to be filled with all the fullness of God. [Eph. 3:13, 17–19] The gate entering into these riches of His wisdom is the cross, which is narrow, and few desire to enter by it, but many desire the delights obtained from entering there.

Stanza 37

Introduction

1. One of the main reasons for the desire to be dissolved and to be with Christ [Phil. 1:23] is to see Him face to face and thoroughly understand the profound and eternal mysteries of His Incarnation, which is by no means the lesser part of beatitude. As Christ Himself says to the

Father in St. John's Gospel: *This is eternal life that they might know You, the one true God, and Your Son Jesus Christ Whom You have sent.* [Jn. 17:3] The first thing a person desires to do after having come a long distance is to see and converse with the one he deeply loves; similarly, the first thing the soul desires upon coming to the vision of God is to know and enjoy the deep secrets and mysteries of the Incarnation and the ancient ways of God dependent upon it. Hence after expressing her desire to see herself in the beauty of God, the soul declares in the following stanza:

> And then we will go on
> To the high caverns in the rock
> Which are so well concealed;
> There we shall enter
> And taste the fresh juice of the pomegranates.

Commentary

2. One of the reasons urging the soul most to enter this thicket of God's wisdom and know its beauty from further within is her wish to unite her intellect with God in the knowledge of the mysteries of the Incarnation, in which is contained the highest and most savory wisdom of all His works. The bride states in this stanza that once she has entered further into the divine wisdom (further into the spiritual marriage she now possesses, which will be the face-to-face vision of God in glory as well as union with this divine wisdom, Who is the Son of God), she will know the sublime mysteries of God and man. These mysteries are exalted in wisdom, and the soul enters the knowledge of them, engulfing and immersing herself in them. And both the bride and the Bridegroom will taste the savoriness and the delight caused by the knowledge of these mysteries together with the powers and attributes of God uncovered in them such as: justice, mercy, wisdom, power, charity, etc.

3.   And then we will go on
                    To the high caverns in the rock

The rock mentioned here, as St. Paul says, is Christ. [1 Cor. 10:4] The high caverns of this rock are the sublime, exalted, and deep mysteries of God's wisdom in Christ, in the hypostatic union of the human nature with the divine Word, and in the corresponding union of men with God, and the mystery of the harmony between God's justice and mercy with respect to the manifestations of His judgments in the salvation of the human race. These mysteries are so profound that she very appropriately calls them high caverns; high, because of the height of the sublime mysteries, and caverns, because of the depth of God's wisdom in them. As caverns are deep and have many recesses, so each of the mysteries in

Christ is singularly deep in wisdom and contains many recesses of His secret judgments of predestination and foreknowledge concerning the sons of men.

She then adds:

4.   Which are so well concealed;

They are so well concealed that however numerous are the mysteries and marvels which holy doctors have discovered and saintly souls understood in this earthly life, all the more is yet to be said and understood. There is much to fathom in Christ, for He is like an abundant mine with many recesses of treasures, so that however deep men go they never reach the end or bottom, but rather in every recess find new veins with new riches everywhere. On this account St. Paul said of Christ: *In Christ dwell hidden all treasures and wisdom.* [Col. 2:3] The soul cannot enter these caverns or reach these treasures if, as we said, she does not first pass over to the divine wisdom through the straits of exterior and interior suffering. For one cannot reach in this life what is attainable of these mysteries of Christ without having suffered much, and without having received numerous intellectual and sensible favors from God, and without having undergone much spiritual activity; for all these favors are inferior to the wisdom of the mysteries of Christ in that they serve as preparations for coming to this wisdom. When Moses asked God to reveal His glory, God told Moses that he would be unable to receive such a revelation in this life, but that he would be shown all good, that is all the good revealable in this life. So God put Moses in the cavern of the rock, which is Christ, as we said, and showed His back to him, which was to impart knowledge of the mysteries of the humanity of Christ.

5. The soul, then, earnestly longs to enter these caverns of Christ in order to be absorbed, transformed, and wholly inebriated in the love of the wisdom of these mysteries, and hide herself in the bosom of the Beloved. In the Canticle He invites her to these clefts, saying: *Arise, make haste, my love, my beautiful one, and come into the clefts of the rock and into the cavern of the wall.* [Ct. 2:13-14] These clefts are the caverns we are discussing here of which the soul says next:

6.   There we shall enter

That is, there, into that knowledge and those mysteries, we shall enter. And she does not declare, I alone shall enter—which would seem more suitable since the Bridegroom does not enter again—but we (the Beloved and I) shall enter, and thereby she shows that she does not do this work alone but that the Bridegroom does it with her. Furthermore, since the soul and God are now united in this state of spiritual marriage, which we are discussing, the soul performs no work without God. To say, there we shall enter, is to say there we shall be transformed, that is, I shall be transformed in You through love of these divine and delightful judgments. In her knowledge about the predestination of the just and the fore-knowledge of the damned, in which the Father predisposed the just with the blessings of sweetness [Ps. 20:4], in His Son Jesus Christ, the soul is most sublimely and intimately transformed in the love of God. And with unspeakable delight she thanks and loves the Father again through His Son Jesus. She does this united with Christ, together with Christ. And the savor of this praise is so delicate as to be totally beyond words. Yet the soul states in the following verse:

7.   And taste the fresh juice of the pomegranates.

The pomegranates stand for the mysteries of Christ, the judgments of the wisdom of God and the virtues and attributes uncovered in the knowledge of these innumerable mysteries and judgments. Just as pome-granates have many little seeds, formed and sustained within the circular shell, so each of the attributes, mysteries, judgments, and virtues of God, like a round shell of power and mystery, holds and sustains a multitude of marvelous decrees and wondrous effects.

Let us remark here the circular or spherical figure of the pomegranate, for each pomegranate symbolizes some divine attribute and power, and each divine attribute and power is God Himself, Who is represented by the circular or spherical figure because He has no beginning or end.

Since in God's wisdom there are such countless judgments and mys-teries, the bride told the Bridegroom in the Canticle: *Your belly is of ivory set with sapphires.* [Ct. 5:14] The sapphires represent these mys-teries and judgments of the divine wisdom, signified by the belly; for the sapphire is a precious stone, the color of a clear and serene sky.

8. The juice from these pomegranates which the bride and the Bride-groom will taste is the fruition and delight of the love of God overflowing from the knowledge of His attributes. In eating a pomegranate, one juice alone is tasted from its many seeds; similarly, from all these infused wonders and grandeurs of God there redounds to the soul one fruition and delight of love, which is the drink of the Holy Spirit. With glowing tenderness of love she at once offers this drink to her God, the Word, her Spouse. She had promised Him this divine drink in the Canticle, if He would lead her into this lofty knowledge: *There You will teach me; and I shall give You the drink of spiced wine and of juice from my pomegranates.* [Ct. 8:2] She calls the pomegranates (the divine knowl-edge) her own because, even though they are His, God has given them to her. She offers as a drink to God her joy in and fruition of this knowl-edge in the wine of love. Such is the meaning of the words, "And taste the fresh juice of the pomegranates." Tasting it Himself, He gives it to

her to taste; and she in tasting it turns and offers it to Him—and they both taste it together.

STANZA 38

Introduction

1. In the two preceding stanzas the bride's song focused on the good the Bridegroom will offer her in that eternal bliss. That is, the Spouse will really transform her into the beauty of both His created and uncreated wisdom, and also into the beauty of the union of the Word with His humanity, in which she will know Him face to face as well as from the back.

In the next stanza she discusses two things: first, the manner in which she will taste that divine juice of the sapphires, or rather the pomegranates; second, the glory she will give to her Bridegroom through her predestination.

It should be noted that even though she refers to these goods as successive parts, they are all contained in one essential glory.

She says:

> There You will show me
> What my soul has been seeking,
> And then You will give me,
> You, my Life, will give me there
> What You gave me on that other day:

Commentary

2. The reason why the soul desired to enter these caverns was to reach the consummation of the love of God, which she had always been seeking, that is, to love God as purely and perfectly as He loves her, in order to repay Him by such love. She declares to the Bridegroom in this stanza that there He will show her what was her desire in all her acts, how to love the Spouse as perfectly as He loves her. The second gift she will receive there is the essential glory to which He predestined her from the day of His eternity.

Thus she declares:

3.   There You will show me
        What my soul has been seeking,

The soul's aim is a love equal to God's. She always desired this equality, naturally and supernaturally, for a lover cannot be satisfied if he fails to feel that he loves as much as he is loved. Since the soul sees that through her transformation in God in this life she cannot, even though her love is immense, equal the perfection of God's love for her, she desires the clear transformation of glory in which she will reach this equality. Even though there is a true union of will in this high state she now enjoys, she cannot attain the excellence and power of love which she will possess in the strong union of glory. Just as the soul, according to St. Paul, will know then as she is known by God [1 Cor. 13:12], so she will also love God as she is loved by Him. As her intellect will be the intellect of God, her will then will be God's will, and thus her love will be God's love. The soul's will is not destroyed there, but it is so firmly united with the strength of God's will, with which He loves her, that her love for Him is as strong and perfect as His love for her, for the two wills are so united that there is only one will and love, which is God's. This strength lies in the Holy Spirit, in Whom the soul is there transformed, for by this transformation of glory He supplies what is lacking in her, since He is given to the soul for the sake of the strength of this love. Even in the perfect transformation of this state of spiritual marriage, which the soul reaches in this life, she superabounds with grace and, as above, loves in some way through the Holy Spirit who is given [Rom. 5:5] in this transformation of love.

4. It should be noted that the soul does not say that there He will give her His love—although He really does—because she would thereby manifest only that God loves her. She states rather that there He will show her how to love Him as perfectly as she desires. Although it is precisely by giving her His love there, that He shows her how to love as He loves her. Besides teaching her to love purely, freely, and disinterestedly, as He loves her, God makes her love Him with the very strength with which He loves her. Transforming her into His love, as we said, He gives her His own strength by which she can love Him. As if He were to put an instrument in her hands and show her how it works by operating it jointly with her, He shows her how to love and gives her the ability to do so.

Until attaining this equality of love the soul is dissatisfied, nor would she be satisfied in heaven if, as St. Thomas affirms in the opuscule *De Beatitudine* [ed. Vivès of the works of St. Thomas, v. 28, Paris, 1875, pp. 404-25; this treatise is not an authentic work of the Angelic Doctor], she did not feel that she loved God as much as He loves her. And even though in this state of spiritual marriage which we are discussing there is not that perfection of glorious love, there is nonetheless a living and totally ineffable semblance of that perfection.

5.   And then You will give me,
         You, my Life, will give me there
         What You gave me on that other day:

That which the soul says He will then give her is essential glory, consisting in the vision of God's being. But before proceeding we ought to resolve a doubt: Why, since essential glory lies in seeing God and not in loving, does the soul declare at the beginning of the stanza that she was seeking this love and not the essential glory, and afterwards request, as something of less importance, essential glory?

There are two reasons: First, just as the ultimate reason for everything is love (which is seated in the will), whose property is to give and not to receive, whereas the property of the intellect (which is the subject of essential glory) lies in receiving and not giving, the soul in the inebriation of love does not put first the glory she will receive from God, but rather puts first the surrender of herself to Him through true love, without concern for her own profit. Second, the desire to see is included in the desire to love and already presupposed in the preceding stanzas, for it is impossible to attain to the perfect love of God without the perfect vision of God. Thus the force of this doubt is resolved by the first answer. With love the soul pays God what she owes Him; with the intellect, on the contrary, she receives from Him.

6. But returning to the commentary, let us see what day "that other day" is, which she here mentions, as well as the meaning of the "what" which God gave her on that other day and which she asks to have afterwards in glory. By "that other day," she means the day of God's eternity, which is different from this temporal day. In that day of eternity, God predestined the soul to glory, decreed the glory He would bestow on her, and gave it to her freely from all eternity before He created her. And this "what" is so proper to the soul that no event or adversity, whether great or insignificant, will suffice to take it from her. But she will attain the endless possession of the "what" to which God predestined her from eternity. And this is the "what" which she says He gave her on that other day, and which she now desires to possess openly in glory.

As for understanding the nature of the "what" He there gave her: *Neither eye has seen, nor ear heard, nor has it entered into the heart of man,* as the Apostle says. [1 Cor. 2:9] And again Isaias says: *Eye has not seen, outside of You, Lord, what You have prepared,* etc. [Is. 64:4] Since it has no name, the soul calls it "what." The "what" is in point of fact the vision of God, but that which the vision of God is to the soul has no other name than "what."

7. Yet in order to say something about it, let us repeat what Christ said of it to St. John seven times in the Apocalypse with many expressions and words and comparisons, for this "what" cannot be understood by one word, nor at one time, for even with all these terms it still remains to be expressed. Christ then says: *To him that overcomes I will give to eat of the tree of life which is in the paradise of my God.* [Ap. 2:7]

But since this expression does not explain the "what" suitably, He immediately adds another: *Be faithful unto death and I will give you the crown of life.* [Ap. 2:10]

Because this expression is inadequate also, He uses another which is more obscure, yet explains it better: *To him that overcomes I will give the hidden manna and a white stone, and on the stone a new name will be written which no one knows save he who receives it.* [Ap. 2:17]

And because this is also an insufficient expression of the "what," the Son of God uses another indicating great happiness and power: *He who overcomes and keeps my commandments to the end, to him will I give power over the nations. And he will rule them with a rod of iron, and as a vessel of clay they shall be smashed, as I also received of my Father. And I will give him the morning star.* [Ap. 2:26–28]

And discontent with these expressions for explaining this "what," He then states: *He that overcomes will thus be clothed in white garments, and I will not cross his name from the book of life. And I will confess his name before my Father* [Ap. 3:5]

8. But since everything He said falls short of the mark, He then employs many terms to explain the "what," and they include in themselves unspeakable majesty and grandeur: *And I will make him who overcomes a pillar in the temple of my God, and he shall go out no more. And I will write upon him the name of my God and the name of the city of my God, the new Jerusalem, which comes down out of heaven from my God, and also my new name.* [Ap. 3:12]

And then He makes use of the seventh expression to explain the "what": *To him that overcomes I will give to sit with me on my throne, as I also have conquered and sat with my Father on His throne. He who has ears to hear, let him hear,* etc. [Ap. 3:21–22]

These are the words of the Son of God, explaining the "what." They cast the "what" in very perfect terms, but they still do not explain it. This is a peculiarity of a thing that is immense: All the expressions of excellence, grandeur, and goodness are fitting, but do not explain it, not even when taken together.

9. Let us see if David makes any affirmations about this "what." In a psalm he exclaims: *How great is the multitude of Your sweetness which You have hidden for them that fear You.* [Ps. 30:20] And so in another place he calls the "what" a torrent of delight: *You will give them to drink from the torrent of Your delight.* [Ps. 35:9] And because David finds this term inadequate as well, he calls it the prevenient blessings of God's sweetness. [Ps. 20:4]

Consequently, a suitable expression for the "what" of which the soul here speaks (the happiness toward which God predestined her) is undiscoverable.

Let us set aside this term "what" which the soul uses and explain the verse in this way: What You gave me (that weight of glory to which You predestined me, O my Spouse, on the day of Your eternity when You considered it good to decree my creation), You will give me then on the day of my espousals and nuptials and on my day of gladness of heart [Ct. 3:11], when loosed from the flesh and within the high caverns of Your chamber, gloriously transformed in You, I shall drink with You the juice of the sweet pomegranates.

Stanza 39

Introduction

1. Yet since the soul in this state of spiritual marriage knows something of this "what," she desires to say something about it, for by her transformation in God something of this "what" occurs within her. She now feels within herself the signs and traces of the "what," for as it is said in the book of Job: *Who can keep back the word he has conceived without saying it?* [Jb. 4:2] In the following stanza she says something about the fruition she will enjoy in the beatific vision, by explaining insofar as possible the nature and mode of the "what" which she will there possess.

> The breathing of the air,
> The song of the sweet nightingale,
> The grove and its living beauty
> In the serene night,
> With a flame that is consuming and painless.

Commentary

2. In this stanza the soul declares with five expressions the "what" which she says the Bridegroom will bestow on her in that beatific transformation.

First, she says it is the breath or spiration of the Holy Spirit from God to her and from her to God.

Second, that it is rejoicing in the fruition of God.

Third, that it is the knowledge of creatures and of their orderly arrangement.

Fourth, that it is pure and clear contemplation of the divine essence.

Fifth, that it is a total transformation in the immense love of God.

The verse then is:

3.   The breathing of the air,

This breathing of the air is an ability which the soul states God will give her there in the communication of the Holy Spirit. By His divine breath-like spiration, the Holy Spirit elevates the soul sublimely and informs her and makes her capable of breathing in God the same spiration of love that the Father breathes in the Son and the Son in the Father, which is the Holy Spirit Himself, Who in the Father and the Son breathes out to her in this transformation, in order to unite her to Himself. There would not be a true and total transformation if the soul were not transformed in the three Persons of the Most Holy Trinity in an open and manifest degree.

And this kind of spiration of the Holy Spirit in the soul, by which God transforms her into Himself, is so sublime, delicate, and deep a delight that a mortal tongue finds it indescribable, nor can the human intellect, as such, in any way grasp it. Even that which comes to pass in the communication given in this temporal transformation is unspeakable, for the soul united and transformed in God breathes out in God to God the very divine spiration which God—she being transformed in Him—breathes out in Himself to her.

4. In the transformation which the soul possesses in this life, the same spiration passes from God to the soul and from the soul to God with notable frequency and blissful love, although not in the open and manifest degree proper to the next life. Such I believe was St. Paul's meaning when he said: *Since you are sons of God, God sent the Spirit of His Son into your hearts, calling to the Father.* [Gal. 4:6] This is true of the Blessed in the next life and of the perfect in this life according to the ways described.

One should not think it impossible that the soul be capable of so sublime an activity as this breathing in God, through participation as God breathes in her. For, granted that God favors her by union with the Most Blessed Trinity, in which she becomes deiform and God through participation, how could it be incredible that she also understand, know, and love—or better that this be done in her—in the Trinity, together with it, as does the Trinity itself! Yet God accomplishes this in the soul through communication and participation. This is transformation in the three Persons in power and wisdom and love, and thus the soul is like God through this transformation. He created her in His image and likeness that she might attain such resemblance.

5. No knowledge or power can describe how this happens, unless by explaining how the Son of God attained and merited such a high state for us, the power to be sons of God, as St. John says. [Jn. 1:12] Thus the Son asked of the Father in St. John's Gospel: *Father, I desire that where*

*I am those You have given Me may also be with Me, that they may see
the clarity You have given Me* [Jn. 17:24], that is, that they may perform
in us by participation the same work that I do by nature, that is, breathe
the Holy Spirit. And He adds: *I do not ask, Father, only for these present,
but for those also who will believe in Me through their doctrine; that all
of them may be one as You, Father, in Me and I in You, that thus they
be one as We are one, I in them and You in Me; that they may be perfect
in one; that the world may know that You have sent Me and loved them
as You have loved Me.* [Jn. 17:20–23] The Father loves them by communicating to them the same love He communicates to the Son, though
not naturally as to the Son, but, as we said, through union and transformation of love. It should not be thought that the Son desires here to ask
the Father that the saints be one with Him essentially and naturally as
the Son is with the Father, but that they may be so through the union
of love, just as the Father and the Son are one in essential unity of love.

6. Accordingly, souls possess the same goods by participation that
the Son possesses by nature. As a result they are truly gods by participation, equals and companions of God. Wherefore St. Peter said: *May grace
and peace be accomplished and perfect in you in the knowledge of God
and of Our Lord Jesus Christ, as all things of His divine power which
pertain to life and piety are given us through the knowledge of Him
who called us with His own glory and power, by Whom He has given us
very great and precious promises that by these we may be made par-
takers of the divine nature.* [2 Pt. 1:2–5] These are words of St. Peter in
which he clearly indicates that the soul will participate in God Himself
by performing in Him, in company with Him, the work of the Most
Blessed Trinity, as we mentioned, because of the substantial union between the soul and God. Although this participation will be perfectly
accomplished in the next life, still in this life when the soul has reached
the state of perfection, as has the soul we are here discussing, she obtains
a foretaste and noticeable trace of it in the way we are describing, although as we said it is indescribable.

7. O souls, created for these grandeurs and called to them! What are
you doing? How are you spending your time? Your aims are base and
your possessions miseries! O wretched blindness of your eyes! You are
blind to so brilliant a light and deaf to such loud voices, because you fail
to discern that insofar as you seek eminence and glory you remain miserable, base, ignorant, and unworthy of so many blessings!

The next expression the soul uses to explain the "what," is:

8.   The song of the sweet nightingale,

The result of the soul's breathing the air is that she hears the sweet
voice of her Beloved calling to her. And she in this voice expresses to

Him her delightful jubilation and calls both voices the song of the nightingale. Just as the nightingale begins its song in the spring, once the wintery cold, rain, and changes have passed, and provides melody for the ear and refreshment for the spirit, so in this actual communication and transformation of love which the bride has now attained in this life, in which she is freed from and protected against all temporal disturbances and changes, and divested and purged of imperfections, penalties, and clouds in the senses and the spirit, she feels a new spring, in spiritual freedom and breadth, and gladness. She hears the sweet voice of her Bridegroom Who is her sweet nightingale. Renewing and refreshing the substance of the soul with the sweetness and mellowness of His voice, He calls her as He would call one now disposed to make the journey to eternal life, and she hears this pleasant voice urge: *Arise, make haste, my love, my dove, my beautiful one, and come; for now the winter has passed, the rains have gone far off, the flowers have appeared in our land, the time of pruning has come, and the voice of the turtledove is heard in our land.* [Ct. 2:10–12]

9. The bride feels that this voice of the Bridegroom speaking within her is the end of evil and the beginning of good. In the refreshment, protection, and delightful sentiment afforded by this voice, she too, like the sweet nightingale, sings a new and jubilant song together with God, Who moves her to do this. He gives His voice to her, that so united with Him, she may give it to Him. This is the Bridegroom's aim and desire, that the soul may intone to God with a spiritual voice of jubilance, as He requests in the Canticle: *Arise, make haste my love, and come my dove; in the clefts of the rock; in the hollow of the wall show Me your face, let your voice sound in My ears.* [Ct. 2:13–14] The ears of God signify His desires to have the soul sing to Him with this voice of perfect jubilation. That this voice be perfect, the Bridegroom asks that she sing and let it resound in the caverns of the rock, that is, in the transformation in the mysteries of Christ. Since the soul rejoices in and praises God with God Himself in this union (as we said she loves God with God Himself), it is a praise highly perfect and pleasing to God, for a soul in this state of perfection performs very perfect works. This voice of jubilance, thus, is sweet both to God and to the soul. As a result the Bridegroom declared: *Your voice is sweet* [Ct. 2:14], that is, not only to you but to Me as well, since through union with Me you sing to me—and with Me—like the sweet nightingale.

10. Such is the song of the soul in the transformation that is hers in this life, the delight of which is beyond all exaggeration. Yet since this song is not as perfect as the new song of the glorious life, the soul in this bliss becomes mindful of the new song of glory, hearing faintly in the song of this life the excellence of the possession of glory, which is in-

comparably more precious. And she states that the "what" which He will give her is the song of the sweet nightingale.

She continues:

11. The grove and its living beauty

This is the third gift the Bridegroom will bestow on the soul. Since many plants and animals are nurtured in it, the "grove" refers to God, for He nurtures and gives being to all creatures rooted and living in Him. Through this gift God shows Himself to her and reveals Himself as Creator.

By the "living beauty" of this grove, for which she asks the Bridegroom here, she intends to beg for the grace, wisdom, and beauty which every earthly and heavenly creature not only has from God but also manifests in its wise, well-ordered, gracious, and harmonious relationship to other creatures. Thus we find this accord among the lower creatures and among the higher, and we find it as well in the relationships between the higher and the lower. The knowledge of this harmony fascinates and delights the soul.

The fourth gift follows:

12. In the serene night,

This night is the contemplation in which the soul desires to behold these things. Because of its obscurity, she calls contemplation night. On this account contemplation is also termed mystical theology, meaning the secret or hidden knowledge of God. In contemplation God teaches the soul very quietly and secretly, without its knowing how, without the sound of words, and without the help of any bodily or spiritual faculty, in silence and quietude, in darkness to all sensory and natural things. Some spiritual persons call this contemplation knowing by unknowing. For this knowledge is not produced by the intellect which the philosophers call the agent intellect, which works upon the forms, phantasies, and apprehensions of the corporal faculties; rather it is produced in the possible or passive intellect. This possible intellect, without the reception of these forms, etc., receives passively only substantial knowledge, which is divested of images and given without any work or active function of the intellect.

13. This contemplation, in which the soul, by means of her transformation, has sublime knowledge in this life of the divine grove and its living beauty, is consequently called "night." Yet however sublime this knowledge may be, it is still a dark night when compared with the beatific knowledge she asks for here. In seeking clear contemplation, she asks that this enjoyment of the grove and its fascination, as well as the other goods mentioned, take place now in the serene night, that is, in beatific and clear contemplation, the night of the dark contemplation

of this earth changing into the contemplation of the clear and serene vision of God in heaven. Therefore, by saying, "in the serene night," she means in the clear and serene contemplation of the vision of God. David declares of this night of contemplation: *The night will be my illumination in my delights* [Ps. 138:11], which is like saying: When I shall delight in the essential vision of God, then the night of contemplation will have changed into day and light for my intellect.

The fifth good follows:

14.   With a flame that is consuming and painless.

By the flame she here indicates the love of the Holy Spirit. To consummate means to bring to completion or perfection. The soul then, in affirming that the Beloved will give her all the things she mentioned in this stanza, and that she will possess them with consummate and perfect love, and that these goods will all be absorbed—and she with them—in perfect love that is painless, affirms all this in order to reveal the complete perfection of this love. For love to be perfect it must have these two properties: It must consummate and transform the soul in God; and the inflammation and transformation engendered by this flame must give no pain to the soul, which cannot be true except in the beatific state where this flame is delightful love. For by the transformation of the soul in this flame, there is a beatific conformity and satisfaction of both lover and Beloved, and thus the flame gives no pain from the variety of greater or less intensity, as it did before the soul reached the capacity of this perfect love. Having reached perfection, the soul possesses a love so comforting and conformed to God that, even though God is a consuming fire, as Moses says [Dt. 4:24], He is now a consummator and restorer. This transformation is not like the one the soul possesses in this life, for although the flame in this life is very perfect and consummating in love, it is still also somewhat consuming and destructive, acting as fire does on coal; although the coal is conformed with and transformed into the fire, and does not fume as it did before the transformation, still the flame which consummated the coal in fire consumed and reduced it to ashes.

This is what happens to the soul that in this life is transformed through the perfection of love; although it is conformed, it still suffers a kind of pain and detriment: first, because of the lack of the beatific transformation, whose absence is always felt in the spirit; second, because of the detriment the weak and corruptible sense suffers from the strength and height of so much love, for any excellent thing is a pain and detriment to natural weakness, as it is written: *Corpus quod corrumpitur, aggravat animam.* [Wis. 9:15] Yet in that beatific life she will feel no detriment or pain, although her understanding will be very deep and her love immense.

For God will equip her for the one and strengthen her for the other, consummating her intellect with His wisdom and her will with His love.

15. Since in the preceding stanzas as well as in this one, the bride sought from God immense communications and knowledge for which she needs the strongest and highest love, a love commensurate with the greatness and height of this knowledge, she asks that this knowledge be communicated in consummated, perfect, and strong love.

STANZA 40

No one looked at her,
Nor did Aminadab appear;
The siege was still;
And the cavalry,
At the sight of the waters, descended.

Introduction and Commentary

1. The bride knows that now her will's desire is detached from all things and attached to her God in most intimate love; that the sensory part of her soul, with all its strength, faculties, and appetites is in harmony with the spirit, and its rebelliousness brought into subjection; that the devil is now conquered and far withdrawn as a result of her varied and prolonged spiritual activity and combat; that her soul is united and transformed with an abundance of heavenly riches and gifts; and that consequently she is now well prepared, disposed, and strong, leaning on her Beloved, coming up from the desert of death, flowing with delights, to the glorious thrones of her Bridegroom. [Ct. 8:5] Desiring the Spouse to conclude this matter now, she sets all these facts before Him in this last stanza in order to urge Him the more to do so. In this stanza she mentions five blessings:

First, her soul is detached and withdrawn from all things.
Second, the devil is conquered and put to flight.
Third, the passions are subjected and the natural appetites mortified.
Fourth and fifth, the sensory and lower part is reformed, purified, and brought into conformity with the spiritual part. The sensory part not only offers no obstacle to the reception of these spiritual blessings, but is even accommodated to them, since it participates according to its capacity in the goods the soul now possesses.
She therefore says:

2.   No one looked at her,
This is like saying: My soul is now divested, detached, alone, and

withdrawn from all created things, both from those above and from those below; and it has entered so deeply into interior recollection with You that none of them can discern the intimate delight I now possess in You; that is, these creatures cannot move my soul to relish their sweetness or become displeased and disturbed by their misery and lowness. Since my soul stays so far from them and abides in such profound delight with You, none of them can get a view of me.

Not this alone, but:

3.   Nor did Aminadab appear;

In Sacred Scripture [Ct. 6:11], Aminadab, speaking spiritually, symbolizes the devil, the soul's adversary. He endlessly combated and disturbed her with the countless ammunition of his artillery to prevent her entry into this fort and hiding place of interior recollection with the Bridegroom. But in this place where she now dwells, she is so favored, strong, and victorious with the virtues, and with God's embrace, that the devil dares not come, but with immense fear flees and does not venture to appear. Also because of the practice of virtue and the state of perfection, the soul has so conquered and routed him that he no longer appears before her. And thus, Aminadab did not appear with any right to hinder this blessing I aim after.

4.   The siege was still;

By "the siege" the soul means the passions and appetites. When these passions and appetites are not conquered and calmed, they surround her and fight against her on all sides, and for this reason she calls them a siege. She says "the siege is now still," that is, that the passions are put in order according to reason and the appetites mortified. Since this is true and the siege is no longer capable of impeding these favors, she asks God not to fail to communicate them to her. She says this because she is incapable of the vision of God until her four passions are directed to Him and her appetites mortified and purged.

And the stanza continues:

5.   And the cavalry,
                    At the sight of the waters, descended.

"The waters" refer here to the spiritual goods and delights which the soul enjoys inwardly with God in this state. "The cavalry" signifies the bodily senses, interior as well as exterior, because they bear the phantasms and figures of their objects. The bride declares that in this state the cavalry descended at the sight of the spiritual waters, because in this state of spiritual marriage the sensory and lower part of the soul is so purified and spiritualized that it recollects the sensory faculties and natural strength so that they may thereby share in and enjoy in their own fashion the spiritual grandeurs which God is communicating in the inwardness of the spirit. David described this when he said: *My heart and my flesh have rejoiced in the living God.* [Ps. 83:3]

6. It should be noted that the bride does not state that the cavalry descended to taste the waters, but that it descended at the sight of the waters. For this sensory part with its faculties has no capacity in this life, nor even in the next, for the essential and proper taste of spiritual goods. It can, though, through a certain spiritual overflow, receive sensible refreshment and delight from them. This delight attracts the corporal senses and faculties to the inner recollection where the soul drinks the waters of spiritual goods, and so they descend at the sight of the waters rather than drink and taste them as they are.

The soul declares that they descended (she does not say, they went, or use some other word) in order to point out that in this share which the sensory part has in the spiritual communication, when the soul tastes this drink of spiritual goods, the senses discontinue their natural operations and go down from them to spiritual recollection.

7. The bride sets all this perfection and preparedness before her Beloved, the Son of God, with the desire that He transfer her from the spiritual marriage, to which He desired to bring her in this Church Militant, to the glorious marriage of the Triumphant. May the most sweet Jesus, Bridegroom of faithful souls, be pleased to bring all who invoke His name to this glorious marriage. To Him be honor and glory, together with the Father and the Holy Spirit, *in saecula saeculorum.* Amen.

The Living Flame of Love

INTRODUCTION TO *THE LIVING FLAME OF LOVE*

THE POEM

"Although in the stanzas we have already commented on, we speak of the highest degree of perfection one can reach in this life (transformation in God), these stanzas treat of a love within this very state of transformation that has a deeper quality and is more perfect." With these words of his prologue to the *Living Flame of Love*, St. John of the Cross announces clearly the exalted subject with which this poem deals: a highly perfected love within the state of transformation. A more precise understanding of the nature of the state of transformation in God will be most helpful, then, for a profitable reading of this poem and its commentary.

Since St. John asserts that this state of transformation is the highest state attainable on earth, we know that it is equivalent to what he frequently calls the spiritual marriage. In the *Canticle* he points out concerning the spiritual marriage: "This spiritual marriage . . . is a total transformation in the Beloved . . . It is accordingly the highest state attainable in this life." (C22, 3) And being a total transformation in God, it is also doubtless the goal toward which the soul is directed in the *Ascent-Night* and of which we have already spoken in our introduction to that work; it is the union of likeness. (A2, 5) Thus, whether the saint refers to this highest degree of perfection as the divine union, the spiritual marriage, or the state of transformation, the reality is the same: a union with God through the likeness of love, a state beyond which a person cannot pass in this life.

With the information *The Spiritual Canticle* and *The Living Flame of Love* add to the knowledge we have from the *Ascent-Night*, we can set forth the following essential elements of this state:

1. It is a perfect union of the soul with God, which embodies a total transformation in Him in the operative order. As a result all the cognitive-affective activity of the soul becomes divine through its likeness to or participation in God's activity or life. Just as he explains in the *Ascent* that the soul in this state remains distinct from God in its being or nature, he repeats in *The Spiritual Canticle* that "the union wrought between the two natures, and the communication of the divine to the

human in this state is such that even though neither change their being, both appear to be God." (C22, 4) Pertaining to the operative order, then, the union is dynamic and entails a manner of living:

"Spiritually speaking, there are two kinds of life:
One is beatific, consisting in the vision of God, which must be attained by natural death . . .
The other is the perfect spiritual life, the possession of God through union of love. This is acquired through complete mortification of all the vices and appetites of one's own nature." (F2, 32)

After noting that the old life (which is death to the new life in God) is the engagement of the faculties in the things of the world and the indulgence of the appetites in the pleasures of creatures, he explains that in the transformation of the new perfect life in God:

"The intellect . . . is now moved by another higher principle of supernatural divine light . . .
"And the will . . . loves in a lofty way . . . moved by the strength of the Holy Spirit . . .
"And the natural appetite . . . is moved and satisfied by another principle: the delight of God . . .
"Finally all the movements, operations, and inclinations the soul had previously from the principle and strength of its natural life are now in this union dead to what they formerly were, changed into divine movements, and alive to God." (F2, 34; N2, 4, 2; C38, 3)

2. The affirmation that the activity of the soul is divine does not signify that the acts of the soul cease to be vital acts; rather, it means that God works wholly with the soul, giving the initial impulse to act, accompanying it in the performing of the act, and being the final object to which the act is directed. In this divinization God does not substitute His activity for the soul's activity, but elevates and informs it completely by means of the theological virtues now perfect. Even though he calls the operations of the soul in this state divine operations, he continues also to call them operations of the soul:

"God now possesses the faculties as their complete lord, because of their transformation in Him. And consequently it is He Who divinely moves and commands them according to His spirit and will. As a result the operations are not different from those of God, but those the soul performs are of God and are divine operations. Since he who is united with God is one spirit with Him, as St. Paul says [1 Cor. 6:7], the operations of the soul united with God are of the divine Spirit and are divine." (A3, 2, 8; F1, 9)

3. God in His divine activity tends always toward Himself, and thus the soul in this state is not moved to act by passions, appetites, or purely natural motives, but its activity is determined by the divine

activity. One cannot reach such a degree of transformation, then, without freedom from everything opposed to this divine activity.

"As an imperfect soul is ordinarily inclined toward evil, at least in the first movements of its will, intellect, memory, and appetite, and as it has imperfections; so on the other hand the soul in this state ordinarily inclines and moves toward God in the first movements of its intellect, memory, will, and appetites, because of the great help and stability it has in God and its perfect conversion toward good." (C27, 7)

Being inclined in its first movements to work in and for God, the soul:

". . . employs the intellect in understanding and carrying out the things that are more for His service, and the will in loving all that is pleasing to Him and attaching it to Him in all things, and her memory and care in what most pleases and serves Him . . . The intellect, will, and memory go out immediately toward God and the affections, senses, desires, appetites, hope, joy, and all the energy from the first instant incline toward God, although, as I say, the soul may not advert to the fact that she is working for Him." (C28, 3–5)

4. In this state, there is nothing within the soul impeding the life of glory other than union with the body. Once it is loosed from the body through the death of love, the soul will go directly to enjoy the vision of God.

Both *The Spiritual Canticle* and the *Living Flame* discuss the desire the completely purified soul has for the vision of God in glory. This longing for the beatific vision, however, does not cause affliction as do the urgent longings of the passive purifications, "but with a gentle and delightful desire it seeks this in conformity . . . to God's will." (F1, 27–28) The soul reaches the vision of God by a tearing of three veils. And since in this state the soul has already been purified, that is, two veils have been torn away through the renunciation of all the things of the world, the mortification of natural appetites and affections, and the divinization of natural operations, there remains only the thin veil of this natural life separating it from the clear vision of God. (F1, 29–34)

5. The soul experiences this union habitually in its "substance"; whereas the actual unions are transient. In his commentary, St. John of the Cross figuratively describes the difference between the habitual and actual union:

"Thus in this soul in which neither any appetite nor other images or forms, nor any affections for created things, dwell, the Beloved dwells secretly with an embrace so much the closer, more intimate, and interior, the purer and more alone the soul is to everything other than God . . . Yet it is not secret to the soul itself that has attained this perfection, for within itself it has the experience of this intimate embrace. It does not, however, always experience these awakenings, for when the Beloved produces them, it seems to the soul that He is awakening in its heart, where before He remained as though asleep . . . He is usually there, in this embrace with His bride, as though asleep in the substance of the soul. And it is very well aware of Him and ordinarily enjoys Him. Were He always awake within it, communicating knowledge and love, it would already be in glory. For if, when He does waken, scarcely opening His eyes, He has such an effect on the soul, what would it be like were He ordinarily in it fully awake?" (F4, 14-15)

In heaven the union will be a most intense, continuous, and permanent act. Here on earth the acts of intense, living union cannot be permanent; they come and go, and are more or less prolonged, deep in quality and frequent according to God's will for the soul. The habitual union of love is the permanent union formed by the acts and consists of nothing else than the less intense form of union which the soul lives in its ordinary state after the actual union is passed. The Mystical Doctor speaks of it as the obscure habit of union, no doubt because it lacks the intensity and liveliness of the light and the flame proper to the actual transient unions, which are called "illuminations," "lights," "living flames," "splendors of the lamps of fire," etc. In this respect the saints states clearly:

"The same difference that lies between a habit and an act lies between the transformation in love and the flame of love; it is like the difference between the wood that is on fire and the flame that leaps up from it, for the flame is the effect of the fire that is present there.

"Hence we can compare the soul in its ordinary condition in this state of transformation of love to the log of wood that is ever immersed in fire, and the acts of this soul to the flame that blazes up from the fire of love." (F1, 3-4; C26, 11)

Since this union consists of a transformation in the operative order, it is important to understand rightly the sense in which he speaks of union in the substance of the soul. He uses the word "substance" in various ways, which demands that in seeking to determine the correct meaning in each instance, we note carefully the context. In this case, of a union in the substance of the soul, the substance is that capacity or faculty in one's psychological makeup for experiencing fruition, delight, and joy; or, sadness, anguish, and desolation, etc. And since these experiences are possible in the sensory as well as in the spiritual part of the soul, he speaks sometimes of the sensitive substance, and sometimes of the spiritual substance. Just as the union in the intellect is faith (knowledge) and the union in the will is charity (love), so the union in the substance of the soul is the fruition, peace, and so on; it is intense in the actual transient unions, and subdued, although sometimes profound, in the habitual unions. (F1, 1, 17, 19–20, 26; 2, 9–10, 22; C12, 9; 22, 6; 26, 5, 11)

The poetry of the *Living Flame* is the utterance of a soul advanced within this very state of transformation, ". . . the soul is so inwardly transformed in the fire of love, and has received such quality from it that it is not merely united to this fire but produces within it a living flame . . . as the fire grows hotter and continues to burn, the wood becomes more incandescent and inflamed, even to the point of flaring up and shooting out flames from itself." This flaring of the flame amounts to an actual union, very intense and deep in quality; the habitual state of the soul in this transformation resembles that of "glowing embers," and when the union becomes actual, the embers not merely glow but shoot forth a living flame.

It is through this union of love that the Father, the Son, and the Holy Ghost come to dwell in man, for, as St. John of the Cross makes clear, they take up their abode in man by making him live the life of God, and thus we must not marvel at the sublime and strange gifts He grants to souls, since He promised that the Persons of the Trinity would come and dwell in anyone who loves Him. (F. Prol. 2)

The infused, pure loving knowledge of the intense actual unions to which the stanzas of the *Living Flame* especially refer are the work of the Blessed Trinity, who "inhabits the soul by divinely illumining its intellect with the wisdom of the Son, delighting its will in the Holy Spirit, and absorbing it powerfully and mightily in the delightful embrace of the Father's sweetness." (F1, 15; 2, 1–22) But the intenseness of the loving inflow depends upon the soul's preparation and that which God wills to give. ". . . He burns each soul according to its preparation: He will burn one more, another less, and this He does insofar as He desires, and how and when He desires." (F2, 2)

In stanza 1, then, it seems to the soul that it is singularly close to beatitude, so vigorously is it transformed in God and sublimely possessed by Him. Every time the delicate flame of love assails it, the soul thinks that the veil of mortal life will be torn through; thus it beseeches the Holy Spirit to tear through the veil and give the perfect glory He is seemingly about to bestow each time He encounters it.

In stanza 2, it extolls the Father, the Son, and the Holy Ghost, laying stress on the three favors and blessings they produce in it; these blessings repay it a hundredfold in this life for every suffering it has endured.

In stanza 3, the soul exalts and thanks its Spouse for a lofty and abundant loving knowledge of the divine attributes; these attributes are like lamps of fire transmitting light and heat. Thus the soul, once obscure and blind, receives illumination and the warmth of love; and since it can give this to the Beloved, it has deep satisfaction and joy, for it sees clearly that in offering Him this very divine light and divine warmth it gives Him more than in itself it is worth, "something of its own which is suited to Him according to His infinite being."

In stanza 4, the soul with deep love esteems and thanks the Bridegroom for two admirable effects sometimes produced by Him: an awakening within it in gentleness and love; and a sweet breathing within it filled with good and glory and delicate love of God.

The poem itself comprises only four stanzas in contrast to the forty stanzas of *The Spiritual Canticle* and the eight stanzas of *The Dark Night;* it numbers six lines, however, in each stanza rather than five. Another characteristic of this poem is that, according to the saint's own affirmation in the prologue, it was written for a particular person, for Doña Ana del Mercado y Peñalosa, a widow living in Granada. St. John of the Cross knew Doña Ana at least from January 20, 1582, when he arrived in Granada with Madre Ana de Jesús and the other Carmelite nuns to establish a convent of the Reform in that city. It was Doña Ana who charitably received them into her home when the owner of the house that was promised to them for their convent refused at the last minute to allow them to have it. Very probably, however, the poem, as indicated in some of the manuscripts, was not written until 1584.

The Commentary

As in *The Spiritual Canticle*, the commentary of the *Living Flame* presents a general summary of the meaning of each stanza and then a detailed explanation of every verse. It also includes doctrinal explanations, which again either bear immediate relationship to the content of the stanza or amount to digressions forming something apart from the interpretation of the verses. Hence the commentary includes significant sanjuanist teaching on many matters concerning the spiritual life which lie outside the immediate theme of the poem.

For instance, he discusses: the soul's purgation which is wrought by the flame (F1, 19–25); the cause and mode of the death of those who have reached this state of transformation (F1, 30); the transverberation of the soul and the impression of the stigmata (F2, 9–14); the necessity of suffering in order to reach this state of transformation in God (F2, 25–30); how the soul in order to live this new life in God must die to its old life (F2, 33–35); the thirst, hunger, and longing of the spiritual faculties experienced toward the end of a man's purification and illumination (F3, 18–26); how the spiritual director, the devil, and the soul itself can be obstacles to the contemplation God infuses. (F3, 29–67)

Similarly as with *The Spiritual Canticle*, two redactions have come down to us, and are referred to as *Flame A* and *Flame B*. The differences are not as notable as those between the two redactions of the *Canticle;* no change is made in the sequence of the stanzas, nor are any parts added. The commentary of the second redaction is merely some-what enlarged.

As we read in the prologue, the commentary was also written for Doña Ana de Peñalosa. Its first redaction was composed certainly in Granada between 1585–87, while the Saint was Vicar Provincial in Anda-lusia, a period which was the busiest of his life. Padre Juan Evangelista offers the following testimony: "He wrote *The Living Flame of Love* in this house (Granada), at the request of Doña Ana de Peñalosa, when Vicar Provincial, and he wrote it in fifteen days while here busily occu-pied with many other things besides." From his reference to *The Spirit-ual Canticle* in the prologue, we can conclude that this commentary was written after *Canticle A*, which was finished in Granada at least by 1584.

It is more difficult to fix the time in which the second redaction was written. We have some testimony indicating that he might have worked on it in Segovia (1588–91), and other testimony which speaks of the writing he did while at La Peñuela (August–September 1591). One witness who lived with the saint at La Peñuela asserted that he used to go into the garden for prayer in the morning and remain there until the heat of the sun forced him to return to his cell in the monastery, where he remained "writing some books he had left concerning certain stanzas of poetry."

We have translated the second redaction, or *Flame B*, and have fol-lowed the *Codex of Sevilla*, consulting as well the *Codex of Baeza* and the *Codex of Toledo*, which is a copy of the first redaction.

St. John of the Cross often urges his readers not to think that his de-scriptions of God's graces are incredible or sheer exaggerations, for, he insists, God diffuses Himself abundantly wherever there is room, and He gladly shows Himself "along the highways and byways," and does not hesitate to share His delights with the children of men. (F1, 15) He has only one desire for a soul; and that is to exalt it. (C28, 1) The Saint's descriptions in fact fall far short of the reality. "Who can express how much God exalts the soul that pleases Him? It is impossible to do so, nor can this even be imagined, for, after all, He does this as God, to show Who He is." (C33, 8) Why is it, then, that so few reach this high state of perfect union with God? St. John of the Cross answers that it is not because God wishes that there be few—He would rather want all to be perfect—but because there are few willing to make room for Him and to bear the trials necessary to reach this state. (F2, 27) But neither should one think these trials in themselves are worth anything in God's eyes; ". . . all our works and all our trials, even though they are the greatest possible, are nothing in the sight of God . . . through them we cannot give Him anything, nor fulfill His only will, which is the exaltation of the soul." (C28, 1) If they have value, it is because through them the soul is purified of its evil and imperfect habits and becomes perfect in love, and this love is the means by which God can most exalt it. "Since there is no way by which He can exalt her more than by making her equal to Himself, He is pleased only with her love. For the property of love is to make the lover equal to the object loved." (C28, 1) "A person, then, should live with great patience and constancy in all the tribulations and trials God places upon him, whether they are exterior or interior, spiritual or bodily, great or small, and he should accept them all as from God's hand as a good remedy and not flee from them, for they bring him health . . ." And as he shares in tribulations so will he share in the consolations of the kingdom. (F2, 30–31)

THE LIVING FLAME OF LOVE

*A commentary on the stanzas which treat of the very intimate and quali-
fied union and transformation of the soul in God, written at the request
of Doña Ana de Peñalosa by the author of the stanzas.*

PROLOGUE

1. I have felt, very noble and devout lady, somewhat reluctant to explain these four stanzas as you asked. Since they deal with matters so
interior and spiritual, for which words are usually lacking—in that the
spiritual surpasses sense—I find it difficult to say something of their content; also, one speaks badly of the intimate depths of the spirit if one
does not do so with a deeply recollected soul. Because of my want of
such recollection, I have deferred this commentary until now, a period
in which the Lord seems to have uncovered some knowledge and bestowed some fervor. This must be the result of your holy desire; perhaps,
since I have composed the stanzas for you, His Majesty wants me to
explain them for you.

I have been encouraged in knowing certainly that through my own
ability I shall say nothing worthwhile, especially in matters so sublime
and vital, and thus only the faults and mistakes of this commentary will
be mine. Submitting it to the judgment and better opinion of our Holy
Mother the Roman Catholic Church, by whose rule no one errs, depending upon Sacred Scripture, and knowing the reader understands that
everything I say is as far from the reality as is a painting from the living
object represented, I shall venture to declare what I know.

2. There is no reason to marvel at God's granting such sublime and
strange gifts to souls He determines to favor. If we consider that He is
God and that He bestows them as God, with infinite love and goodness,
it does not seem unreasonable. For He declared that the Father, the Son,
and the Holy Spirit would take up their abode in anyone who loved Him.
[Jn. 14:23] He takes up His abode in a man by making him live the life
of God and dwell in the Father, the Son, and the Holy Spirit, as the soul
points out in these stanzas.

3. Although in the stanzas we have already commented on, we speak of the highest degree of perfection one can reach in this life (transformation in God), these stanzas treat of a love within this very state of transformation that has a deeper quality and is more perfect. Even though it is true that what these and the other stanzas describe is all one state of transformation, and that as such one cannot pass beyond it; yet, with time and practice, love can receive added quality, as I say, and become more intensified. We have an example of this in the activity of fire: Although the fire has penetrated the wood, transformed it, and united it with itself, yet as this fire grows hotter and continues to burn, the wood becomes much more incandescent and inflamed, even to the point of flaring up and shooting out flames from itself.

4. It should be understood that the soul now speaking has reached this enkindled degree, and is so inwardly transformed in the fire of love and has received such quality from it that it is not merely united to this fire but produces within it a living flame. The soul feels this and speaks of it thus in these stanzas with intimate and delicate sweetness of love, burning in love's flame, and stressing in these stanzas some of its effects.

I shall use in this commentary the method I have used before: First I shall quote all the stanzas together, and then, after recording each stanza separately, I will present a brief explanation of it; finally, I will quote each verse and comment upon it.

Fray Juan de la Cruz, Discalced Carmelite.
Granada

STANZAS WHICH THE SOUL RECITES

In the intimate union with God, its beloved Bridegroom

1. O living flame of love
   That tenderly wounds my soul
   In its deepest center! Since
   Now You are not oppressive,
   Now Consummate! if it be Your will:
   Tear through the veil of this sweet encounter!

2. O sweet cautery,
   O delightful wound!
   O gentle hand! O delicate touch

That tastes of eternal life
And pays every debt!
In killing You changed death to life.

3. O lamps of fire!
In whose splendors
The deep caverns of feeling,
Once obscure and blind,
Now give forth, so rarely, so exquisitely,
Both warmth and light to their Beloved.

4. How gently and lovingly
You wake in my heart,
Where in secret You dwell alone;
And in Your sweet breathing,
Filled with good and glory,
How tenderly You swell my heart with love.

STANZA 1

O living flame of love
That tenderly wounds my soul
In its deepest center! Since
Now You are not oppressive,
Now Consummate! if it be Your will:
Tear through the veil of this sweet encounter!

Commentary

1. The soul now feels that it is all inflamed in the divine union, and that its palate is all bathed in glory and love, that in the most intimate part of its substance it is flooded with no less than rivers of glory, abounding in delights, and that from its bosom flow rivers of living waters [Jn. 7:38], which the Son of God declared will rise up in such souls. Accordingly it seems, because it is so vigorously transformed in God, so sublimely possessed by Him, and arrayed with such rich gifts and virtues, that it is singularly close to beatitude—so close that only a thin veil separates it.

And the soul sees that every time that delicate flame of love, burning within, assails it, it does so as though glorifying it with gentle and powerful glory. Such is the glory this flame of love imparts that each time it absorbs and attacks, it seems that it is about to give eternal life and tear the veil of mortal life, that very little is lacking, and that because of this lack the soul does not receive eternal glory completely. Hence with ardent desire the soul tells the flame, the Holy Spirit, to tear now the veil of mortal life by that sweet encounter in which He truly communicates entirely what He is seemingly about to give each time He encounters it, that is, complete and perfect glory.

And thus it says:

2.   O living flame of love

To lay stress on the sentiment and esteem with which it speaks in these four stanzas, the soul uses in all of them the exclamations, "O" and "how," which stress affection. Each time they are uttered, they reveal more about the interior than the tongue expresses. "O" serves to express intense desire and to use persuasion in petitioning. The soul uses this expression for both reasons in this stanza because it intimates and stresses its immense desire, persuading love to loose it.

3. This flame of love is the Spirit of its Bridegroom, which is the Holy Spirit. The soul feels Him within itself not only as a fire which has consumed and transformed it, but as a fire that burns and flares within it, as I mentioned. And that flame, every time it flares up, bathes the soul in glory and refreshes it with the quality of divine life. Such is the activity of the Holy Spirit in the soul transformed in love: the interior acts He produces shoot up flames for they are acts of inflamed love, in which the will of the soul united with that flame, made one with it, loves most sublimely.

Thus these acts of love are most precious; one of them is more meritorious and valuable than all the deeds a person may have performed in his whole life without this transformation, however great they may have been.

The same difference that lies between a habit and an act lies between the transformation in love and the flame of love; it is like the difference between the wood that is on fire and the flame that leaps up from it, for the flame is the effect of the fire that is present there.

4. Hence we can compare the soul in its ordinary condition in this state of transformation of love to the log of wood that is ever immersed in fire, and the acts of this soul to the flame that blazes up from the fire of love. The more intense the fire of union, the more vehemently does this fire burst into flames. The acts of the will are united to this flame and ascend, carried away and absorbed in the flame of the Holy Spirit, just as the angel mounted to God in the flame of Manue's sacrifice. [Jgs. 13:20]

Thus in this state the soul cannot make acts because the Holy Spirit makes them all and moves it toward them. As a result all the acts of the soul are divine, since the movement toward these acts and their execution stems from God. Hence it seems to a person that every time this flame shoots up, making him love with delight and divine quality, it is giving him eternal life, since it raises him up to the activity of God in God.

5. This is the language and these the words God speaks in souls that are purged, cleansed, and all enkindled; as David exclaimed: *Your word is exceedingly enkindled* [Ps. 118:140], and the prophet: *Are not my words, perchance, like a fire?* [Jer. 23:29] As God Himself says through St. John, these words are spirit and life. [Jn. 6:64] This spirit and life is perceived by souls who have ears to hear it, those souls, as I say, that are cleansed and enamored. Those who do not have a sound palate, but seek other tastes, cannot taste the spirit and life of His words; His words, rather, are distasteful to them.

Hence the loftier were the words of the Son of God, the more tasteless they were to the impure, as happened when He preached the sovereign and loving doctrine of the Holy Eucharist; for many turned away. [Jn. 6: 60–61, 67]

6. Those who do not relish this language God speaks within them must not think on this account that others do not taste it; St. Peter tasted it in his soul when he said to Christ: *Lord, where shall we go; You have the words of eternal life.* [Jn. 6:69] And the Samaritan woman forgot the water and the water pot because of the sweetness of God's words. [Jn. 4:28]

Since this soul is so close to God that it is transformed into a flame of love, in which the Father, the Son, and the Holy Spirit are communicated to it, how can it be thought unbelievable that it enjoy a foretaste of eternal life? Yet, it does not enjoy this perfectly since the conditions of this life do not allow for it. But the delight which that flaring of the Holy Spirit generates in the soul is so sublime that it makes it know that which savors of eternal life. Thus it refers to this flame as living, not because the flame is not always living, but because of this effect; it makes the soul live in God spiritually and experience the life of God in the manner David mentions: *My heart and my flesh rejoiced in the living God.* [Ps. 83:3] David did not refer to God as living because of a necessity to do so, for God is always living, but in order to manifest that the spirit and the senses, transformed in God, enjoy Him in a living way, which is to taste the living God—that is, God's life, eternal life. Nor did David call Him the living God other than because he enjoyed Him in a living way, although not perfectly, but as though by a glimpse of eternal life. Thus in this flame the soul experiences God so vividly and tastes Him with such delight and sweetness that it exclaims: O living flame of love!

7.   That tenderly wounds my soul

That is: O living flame of love that with your ardor tenderly touches me. Since this flame is a flame of divine life, it wounds the soul with the tenderness of God's life, and it wounds and stirs it so deeply as to make it dissolve in love. What the bride affirmed in the Canticle is fulfilled in the soul. She was so moved that her soul melted, and thus she says: *As soon as He spoke my soul melted.* [Ct. 5:6] For God's speech is the effect He produces in the soul.

8. But how can one claim that the flame wounds the soul since there is nothing left in it to wound now that it is all cauterized with the fire of love? It is something splendid that since love is never idle, but in continual motion, it is always emitting flames everywhere like a blazing fire, and, since its duty is to wound in order to cause love and delight, and it is present in this soul as a living flame, it dispatches its wounds like most tender flares of delicate love. Joyfully and festively it practices the arts and games of love, as though in the palace of its nuptials, as Assuerus did with Esther. [Est. 2:17] God shows His graces there, manifests His riches and the glory of His grandeur that in this soul might be fulfilled what He asserted in Proverbs: *I was delighted every day, playing before Him all the time, playing in the world. And my delights were to be with the children of men* [Prv. 8:30–31], that is, by bestowing delights on them. Hence these wounds (His games) are flames of tender touches; arising from the fire of love, which is not idle, they suddenly touch the soul. These, it says, occur inwardly and wound the soul

9.   In its deepest center!

This feast takes place in the substance of the soul, where neither the center of the senses nor the devil can reach. Therefore, it is the more secure, substantial, and delightful the more interior it is, because the more interior it is, the purer it is. And the greater the purity, the more abundantly, frequently, and generously God communicates Himself. Thus the delight and joy of the soul is so much the more intense because God is the doer of all without the soul's doing anything. Since the soul cannot do any work of its own save by the means and aid of the corporal senses, from which in this event it is very free and far removed, its sole occupation now is to receive from God, Who alone can move the soul and do His work in its depths. Thus all the movements of this soul are divine. Although they belong to it, they belong to it because God works them in it and with it, for it wills and consents to them.

Since saying that the flame wounds in the deepest center of the soul indicates that the soul has other centers less profound, we ought to explain what is meant by these words.

10. First it should be known that, being a spirit, the soul does not

possess in its being the high or the low, the more profound or the less profound as do quantitative bodies. Since it has no parts, there is no difference as to the inward and the outward; it is all of one kind and does not have degrees of quantitative depth. It cannot receive greater illumination in one part than in the other like physical bodies, but all of it is illumined equally in a degree of greater or lesser intensity, like the air that is illumined or not illumined according to degrees.

11. The deepest center of an object we take to signify the farthest point attainable by that object's being and power and force of operation and movement. So fire or a rock have the natural power and motion necessary to reach their center, but they cannot pass beyond it, nor fail to reach it and remain there, unless on account of a powerful impediment contrary to their movement.

Accordingly, we assert that when a rock is in the earth, it is after a fashion in its center, even though it is not in its deepest center, for it is within the sphere of its center, activity, and movement; yet we do not assert that it has reached its deepest center, which is the middle of the earth. Thus it always possesses the power, strength, and inclination to go deeper and reach the ultimate and deepest center; and this it would do if the hindrance were removed. When once it arrives and has no longer any power or inclination toward further movement, we declare that it is in its deepest center.

12. The soul's center is God. When it has reached God with all the capacity of its being and the strength of its operation and inclination, it will have attained to its final and deepest center in God, it will know, love, and enjoy God with all its might. When it has not reached this point (as happens in this mortal life, in which the soul cannot reach God with all its strength, even though in its center—which is God and His communion with it), it still has movement and strength for advancing further and is not satisfied. Although it is in its center, it is not yet in its deepest center, for it can go deeper in God.

13. It is noteworthy, then, that love is the soul's inclination, strength, and power in making its way to God, for love unites it with God. The more degrees of love it has, the more deeply it enters into God and centers itself in Him. We can say that there are as many centers in God possible to the soul, each one deeper than the other, as there are degrees of love of God possible to it. A stronger love is a more unitive love, and we can understand in this manner the many mansions the Son of God declared were in His Father's house. [Jn. 14:2]

Hence, that the soul be in its center—which is God, as we have said— it is sufficient for it to possess one degree of love, for by one degree alone it is united with Him through grace. Should it have two degrees, it will have become united and concentrated in God in another deeper center. Should it reach three, it will have centered itself in a third. But once it has attained the final degree, God's love will have arrived at wounding the soul in its ultimate and deepest center, which is to transform and clarify it in its whole being, power, and strength, and according to its capacity, until it appears to be God.

When light shines upon a clean and pure crystal, we find that the more intense the degree of light, the more light the crystal has concentrated within it and the brighter it becomes; it can become so brilliant due to the abundance of light it receives that it seems to be all light. And then the crystal is undistinguishable from the light, since it is illumined according to its full capacity, which is to appear to be light.

14. When the soul asserts that the flame of love wounds it in its deepest center, it means that insofar as the Holy Spirit reaches its substance, power, and strength, He assails and wounds it. It does not make such an assertion to indicate that this wounding is as essential and integral as in the beatific vision of the next life. Although a person attains to as lofty a state of perfection in this mortal life as that which we are discussing, he neither does nor can reach the perfect state of glory; although perhaps in a passing way God might grant Him some similar favor. Yet the soul says this in order to manifest the fullness and abundance of delight and glory it feels in this kind of communication from the Holy Spirit. This delight is so much more intense and tender the stronger and more substantially the soul is transformed and concentrated in God. Since this center is the furthest attainable in the present life—although not as perfectly attainable as in the next—it refers to it as the deepest center.

Even though the soul can perhaps possess in this life a habit of charity as perfect as in the next, yet the operation and fruition of charity in this life will not be so perfect; although the operation and fruition of love increase to such a degree in this state that it greatly resembles the beatific state. Such is the similarity that the soul dares to affirm only what it would dare affirm about the next life, that is: in the deepest center of my soul.

15. Since these rare experiences (which are what we ascribe to the soul in this state) are more remarkable than credible, I do not doubt that some persons, not understanding them through their own knowledge or knowing of them through experience, will either fail to believe them or consider the account of them an exaggeration, or will think they are less than what they really are.

Yet I reply to all these persons that the Father of lights [Jas. 1:17], who is not closefisted but diffuses Himself abundantly, as the sun does its rays, without being a respecter of persons [Acts 10:34], wherever there is room—always showing Himself gladly along the highways and byways—does not hesitate or consider it of little import to find His delights with the children of men at a common table in the world. [Prv. 8:31]

And it should not be held as incredible in a soul now examined, purged, and tried in the fire of tribulations, trials, and many kinds of temptations, and found faithful in love, that the promise of the Son of God be fulfilled, the promise that the Most Blessed Trinity will come and dwell within anyone who loves Him. [Jn. 14:23] The Blessed Trinity inhabits the soul by divinely illumining its intellect with the wisdom of the Son, delighting its will in the Holy Spirit, and by absorbing it powerfully and mightily in the delightful embrace of the Father's sweetness.

16. If He acts thus in some souls, as it is true He does, it should be believed that this soul we are speaking of will not be left behind in regard to receiving these favors from God. For what we are explaining about the activity of the Holy Spirit within it is something far greater than what occurs in the communication and transformation of love. This latter resembles the glowing embers, whereas the former is similar to embers not merely glowing but embers that have become so hot they shoot forth a living flame.

And thus these two kinds of union (union of love alone, and union with an inflaming of love) are somehow comparable to the fire of God, which Isaias says, is on Sion, and to His furnace which is in Jerusalem. [Is. 31:9] The one signifies the Church Militant, in which the fire of charity is not enkindled to an extreme; the other signifies the vision of peace, which is the Church Triumphant [Hymn. 1st Vesp. Dedication of a Church. *Coelestis urbs Jerusalem, beata pacis visio*], where this fire is like a furnace blazing in the perfection of love.

Although, as we said, the soul has not attained such great perfection as this vision of peace, yet, in comparison with the other common union, this union resembles a blazing furnace in which there is a vision so much more peaceful and glorious and tender, just as the flame is clearer and more resplendent than the burning coal.

17. Wherefore the soul, feeling that this living flame of love is vividly communicating to it every good, since this divine love carries all things with it, exclaims: "O living flame of love that tenderly wounds my soul." This is like saying: O enkindled love, with your loving movements you are pleasantly glorifying me according to the greater capacity and strength of my soul, bestowing divine knowledge according to all the ability and capacity of my intellect, and communicating love according to the greater power of my will, and rejoicing the substance of my soul

with the torrent of your delight by your divine contact and substantial union, in harmony with the greater purity of my substance and the capacity and breadth of my memory!

And this is what happens, in an indescribable way, at the time this flame of love rises up within the soul. Since the soul is completely purged in its substance and faculties (memory, intellect, and will), the divine substance which, because of its purity, as the Wise Man says, touches everywhere profoundly, subtly, and sublimely [Wis. 7:24], absorbs the soul in itself with its divine flame. And in that immersion of the soul in wisdom, the Holy Spirit sets in motion the glorious flickerings of His flame. Since the flame is so gentle the soul adds:

18.   Since now You are not oppressive,

This means: since You no longer afflict nor distress nor weary me as you did before. It should be recalled that when the soul was in the state of spiritual purgation, which was at the time of the beginning of contemplation, this flame of God was not so friendly and gentle toward it as now in this state of union. In order to explain this we shall have to delay somewhat.

19. Before the divine fire is introduced into and united to the substance of the soul through a person's perfect and complete purgation and purity, its flame, which is the Holy Spirit, wounds it by destroying and consuming the imperfections of its bad habits. And this is the work of the Holy Spirit, in which He disposes it for the divine union and transformation in God through love.

The very fire of love which afterwards is united with the soul, glorifying it, is that which previously assails it by purging it, just as the fire that penetrates a log of wood is the same that first makes an assault upon it, wounding it with its flame, drying it out, and stripping it of its unsightly qualities until it is so disposed that it can be penetrated and transformed into the fire.

Spiritual writers call this activity the purgative way. In it a person suffers great deprivation and feels heavy afflictions in his spirit, which ordinarily overflow into the senses, for this flame is extremely oppressive.

In this preparatory purgation the flame is not bright for a person, but dark. If it does shed some light, the only reason is that the soul may see its miseries and defects. It is not gentle, but afflictive. Even though it sometimes imparts the warmth of love, it does so with torment and pain. And it is not delightful, but dry. Although sometimes out of His goodness, God accords some delight in order to strengthen and encourage it, the soul suffers for this before and afterwards with another trial. Neither is the flame refreshing and peaceful, but it is consuming and contentious, making a person faint and suffer with self-knowledge. Thus it is not glorious for the soul, but rather makes it feel wretched and distressed in the spiritual light of self-knowledge which it bestows. As Jeremias declares, God sends fire into its bones and instructs it [Lam. 1:13]; and as David also asserts, He tries it with fire. [Ps. 16:3]

20. At this stage a person suffers from sharp trials in his intellect, severe dryness and distress in his will, and from the burdensome knowledge of his own miseries in his memory, for his spiritual eye gives him a very clear picture of himself. In the substance of his soul he suffers abandonment, supreme poverty, dryness, cold, and sometimes heat. He finds relief in nothing, nor is there a thought that consoles him, nor can he even raise his heart to God, so oppressed is he by this flame. This purgation resembles what Job said God did to him: *You are changed to be cruel toward me.* [Jb. 30:21] For when the soul suffers all these things jointly, it truly seems that God has become displeased with it and cruel.

21. A person's sufferings at this time cannot be exaggerated; they are but little less than the sufferings of purgatory. I do not know how to explain the severity of this oppression and the intensity of the suffering felt in it, save by what Jeremias says of it in these words: *I am the man that sees my poverty in the rod of His indignation. He has led me and brought me into darkness and not into light. Only against me He has turned and turned again His hand. He has made my skin and my flesh old, and He has broken my bones. He has surrounded me and compassed me with gall and labor. He has set me in dark places as those who are dead forever. He has built around me that I might not get out. He made my fetters heavy. And besides this when I have cried out and prayed, He has shut out my prayer. He shut up my ways with square rocks and turned my steps and paths upside down.* [Lam. 3:1–9] Jeremias laments all this and goes on to say much more.

Since in this fashion God mediates and heals the soul of its many infirmities, bringing it to health, it must necessarily suffer according to its sickness from this purge and cure. Tobias here places the heart upon the coals to release and drive out every kind of demon. [Tb. 6:8] All the soul's infirmities are brought to light; they are set before its eyes to be felt and healed.

22. Now with the light and heat of the divine fire, it sees and feels those weaknesses and miseries which previously resided within it, hidden and unfelt, just as the dampness of the log of wood was unknown until the fire being applied to it made it sweat and smoke and sputter. And this is what the flame does to the imperfect soul.

For (O wonderful thing!) contraries rise up at this time against contraries—those of the soul against those of God which assail it. And as the philosophers say: One contrary when close to the other makes it more manifest. They war within the soul, striving to expel one another in order to reign. That is: The virtues and properties of God, extremely perfect, war against the habits and properties of the soul, extremely imperfect; and the soul suffers these two contraries within itself.

When this flame, since its light is excessively brilliant, shines upon the soul, it shines within the darknesses of the soul, which are also excessive. A person then feels his natural and vicious darknesses, which are contrary to the supernatural light; and he fails to experience the supernatural light because he does not have it within himself as he does his darknesses—and the darknesses do not comprehend the light. [Jn. 1:5] He will feel these darknesses inasmuch as the light shines upon them, for no one can perceive his darknesses without the divine light focusing upon them. Once they are driven out, he is illumined and, being transformed, beholds the light within himself, since his spiritual eye was cleansed and fortified by the divine light. An immense light will cause total darkness in a weak and impure eye, for a highly sensible object deprives the faculty. And thus this flame was oppressive to the intellectual eye.

23. This flame of itself is extremely loving, and the will of itself is excessively dry and hard. When the flame tenderly and lovingly assails the will, hardness is felt beside the tenderness, and dryness beside the love. The will does not feel the love and tenderness of the flame, for, on account of its contrary hardness and dryness, it is unprepared for this, until the love and tenderness expel the dryness and hardness, and reign within it. Accordingly, this flame was oppressive to the will, making it feel and suffer its hardness and dryness.

Because this flame is immense and far-reaching, and the will is narrow and restricted, the will feels its confinement and narrowness in the measure that the flame attacks it. It feels this until the flame, penetrating within it, enlarges, widens, and makes it capable of receiving the flame itself.

Because this flame is savory and sweet, and the will possesses a spiritual palate disturbed by the humors of inordinate affections, the flame is unpleasant and bitter to it; and the will cannot taste the sweet food of God's love. And in this fashion it feels distress and distastefulness beside so ample and delightful a flame. The will does not experience the savor of the flame because it does not feel this flame within itself; it only feels that which it does have within itself—its own misery.

And finally, because this flame contains immense riches and delights, and the soul of itself is extraordinarily poor, without any goods or any satisfaction, the soul knows and feels clearly beside this goodness and these riches and delights its own misery, poverty, and evil. For evil cannot comprehend goodness, nor poverty riches, etc., until this flame purifies a man completely and by this transformation enriches, glorifies, and delights him.

This flame previously oppressed the soul in an indescribable way, since contraries were battling contraries: God, Who is all perfect, against all the imperfections of the soul. God does this that, by transforming the soul into Himself, He might soften, pacify, and clarify it, as does fire when it penetrates the wood.

24. Not many people undergo so strong a purgation. Only those whom God wishes to elevate to the highest degree of union. For He prepares each one by a purification more or less severe in accordance with the degree to which He wishes to raise him, and also according to that person's impurity and imperfection.

This suffering resembles that of purgatory. Just as the spirits suffer purgation there so as to be able to see God through clear vision in the next life, souls in their own way suffer purgation here on earth so as to be able to be transformed in Him through love in this life.

25. In *The Dark Night* of *The Ascent of Mount Carmel* we dealt with the intensity of this purgation, how it is greater and how less, and when it is in the intellect, and when in the will, and how it is in the memory, and when and how it is also in the soul's substance, and also when it involves the whole soul; we discussed, too, the purgation of the sensory part, and how it can be discerned when this purgation is of the sensory part and when of the spiritual part, and the time or stage along the spiritual road in which it begins. Since we have already explained all of this, and such is not our aim here, I will not go into it again. Let it suffice to know that the very God who desires to enter within the soul through the union and transformation of love is He who first assails and purges it with the light and heat of His divine flame, just as the fire that penetrates the wood is the same that first prepares it for this, as we said. Hence the very flame that is now gentle, since it has entered within the soul, is that which was formerly oppressive, assailing it from without.

26. Such is the meaning of the present verse, "Now You are not oppressive." It is in sum like saying: Not only now are You no longer dark as You were before, but You are the divine light of my intellect by which I can look at You; and You not only have ceased making me faint in my weakness, but are rather the strength of my will, by which I can love and enjoy You, being wholly converted into divine love; and You are no longer heavy and constringent to the substance of my soul, but rather its glory and delight and amplitude, for the words of the divine Canticle can be spoken of me: *Who is this that comes up from*

*the desert, flowing with delights, leaning upon her Beloved, diffusing
love everywhere?* [Ct. 8:5]

Since this is true,

27.   Now Consummate! if it be Your will:

That is, consummate the spiritual marriage with me perfectly by means
of the beatific vision. This is the soul's petition, for although it is true
that in this high state it is as conformed to the will of God and satisfied
as it is transformed in love (it wants nothing for itself, nor dares ask for
anything, but everything for its Beloved, since as St. Paul says, charity
seeks not things for self [1 Cor. 13:5], but for the Beloved), its sigh
nevertheless is as great as what it lacks for the perfect possession of
the adoption of the sons of God [Rom. 8:23]; for it still lives in hope, in
which one cannot fail to feel emptiness. When the soul's glory is consummated, its appetite will cease. However intimate may be a man's union
with God, he will never have satisfaction and rest until God's glory
appears [Ps. 16:15], especially since he now experiences its savor and
sweetness. This experience is so intense that if God had not favored the
flesh, by fortifying the sensory part with His right hand, as He did Moses
in the rock, enabling him to behold His glory without dying [Ex. 33:
22], nature would be torn apart and death would ensue, since the lower
part is unequipped to suffer so much and such a sublime fire of glory.

28. Affliction, then, does not accompany this desire and petition, for
the soul is no longer capable of such affliction, but with a gentle and
delightful desire it seeks this in the conformity of both spirit and sense
to God's will. As a result it says in this verse, "Now Consummate! if it
be Your will," for its will and appetite are so united with God that it
considers the fulfillment of God's will to be its glory.

Yet the sudden flashes of glory and love which appear vaguely in
these touches at the door of entry into the soul, and which are unable
to fit into it because of the narrowness of the earthly house, are so sublime
that it would rather be a sign of little love not to try to enter into that
perfection and completion of love.

Moreover, a soul is conscious that in that vigor of the Bridegroom's
delightful communication, the Holy Spirit rouses and invites it by the
immense glory He marvelously and with gentle affection places before
its eyes, telling it what He told the bride in the Canticles. The bride
thus refers to this: *Behold what my Spouse is saying to me: Arise and
make haste, my love, my dove, my beautiful one, and come; for winter
is now passed, and the rains are over and gone, and the flowers have
appeared in our land; the fig tree has put forth her fruits; the vines in
flower have given their fragrance. Arise my love, my fair one, and come;
my dove in the clefts of the rock, in the hollow of the wall, show me
your face, let your voice sound in my ears, because your voice is sweet*

and your face beautiful. [Ct. 2:10–14] The soul in a sublime experience of glory feels and understands most distinctly all these things which the Holy Spirit, desiring to introduce it into that glory, shows it in this gentle and tender blaze. Consequently, the soul thus roused answers: "Now Consummate! if it be Your will." It makes the two requests of the Bridegroom which He taught us in the Gospel: *Adveniat regnum tuum; fiat voluntas tua.* [Mt. 6:10] It is like saying: Now Consummate, give me this kingdom, if it be Your will, according to Your will. And that this may be true:

29.   Tear through the veil of this sweet encounter!

The veil is what impedes so singular an event. It is easy to reach God when all the impediments are removed and the veils that separate the soul from union with Him are torn. We can say there are three veils which constitute a hindrance to this union with God, and which must be torn if the union is to be effected and possessed perfectly by the soul, that is: the temporal veil, comprising all creatures; the natural, embodying the purely natural inclinations and operations; and the sensitive, which consists only of the union of the soul with the body, that is, the sensitive and animal life of which St. Paul speaks: *We know that if this our earthly house is dissolved, we have a building of God in heaven.* [2 Cor. 5:1]

The first two veils must necessarily be torn in order to obtain this union with God in which all the things of the world are renounced, all the natural appetites and affections mortified, and the natural operations of the soul divinized.

All of this was accomplished, and these veils were torn by means of the oppressive encounters of this flame. Through the spiritual purgation we referred to above, the soul tears these two veils completely and is united with God, as it here is; only the third veil of this sensitive life remains to be torn. As a result it mentions a veil and not veils, since there is only this one to tear. Because the veil is now so tenuous, thin, and spiritualized through this union with God, the flame is not harsh in its encounter as it was with the other two, but savory and sweet. The soul hence calls it a "sweet encounter"; so much the sweeter and more savory, the more it seems about to tear through the veil of mortal life.

30. It should be known that the death of persons who have reached this state is far different in its cause and mode than the death of others, even though it is similar in natural circumstances. If the death of other people is caused by sickness or old age, the death of these persons is not so induced, in spite of their being sick or old; their soul is not wrested from them unless by some impetus and encounter of love, far more sublime than previous ones, of greater power, and more valiant,

since it tears through this veil and carries off the jewel, which is the soul.

The death of such persons is very gentle and very sweet, sweeter and more gentle than was their whole spiritual life on earth. For they die with the most sublime impulses and delightful encounters of love, resembling the swan whose song is much sweeter at the moment of death. Accordingly, David affirmed that the death of the saints is precious in the sight of the Lord. [Ps. 115:15] The soul's riches gather together here, and its rivers of love move on to enter the sea, for these rivers, because they are blocked, become so vast that they themselves resemble seas. The just man's first treasures, and his last, are heaped together to accompany him when he departs and goes off to his kingdom, while praises are heard from the ends of the earth, which, as Isaias says, are the glory of the just man. [Is. 24:16]

31. The soul, then, conscious of the abundance of its enrichment, feels at the time of these glorious encounters to be almost at the point of departing for the complete and perfect possession of its kingdom, for it knows that it is pure, rich, full of virtues, and prepared for such a kingdom. God permits it in this state to discern its beauty and He entrusts to it the gifts and virtues He has bestowed, for everything is converted into love and praises, and it has no touch of presumption or vanity, since it no longer bears the leaven of imperfection which corrupts the mass. [1 Cor. 5:6; Gal. 5:9] Since it is aware that nothing is wanting other than to tear the weak veil of this natural life, in which it feels the entanglement, hindrance, and captivity of its freedom, and since it desires to be dissolved and to be with Christ [Phil. 1:23], it laments that a life so weak and base impedes another so mighty and sublime and asks that the veil be torn, saying: "Tear through the veil of this sweet encounter!"

32. There are three reasons for the term "veil": first, because of the union between the spirit and the flesh; second, because this union separates the soul from God; third, because a veil is not so thick and opaque that a brilliant light cannot shine through it; and in this state the bond seems to be so tenuous a veil, since it is now very spiritual, thin, and luminous, that it does not prevent the divinity from vaguely appearing through it. Since the soul perceives the power of the other life, it is conscious of the weakness of this one and that the veil is of delicate fabric, as thin as a spider's web; in David's words: *our years shall be considered as the spider.* [Ps. 89:9] And this life is even much less in the eyes of a person thus exalted, for, since he has God's view of things, he regards them as God does, in whose sight, as David also declares, a thousand years are as yesterday, which is past [Ps. 89:4], and according to Isaias, all nations are as though they were not. [Is. 40:17] These things

carry the same weight in the soul's view: All things are nothing to it, and it is nothing in its own eyes; God alone is its all.

33. The reason it begs that the veil be torn and not cut or destroyed is noteworthy, for there does not seem to be much difference. We can offer four reasons.

First, we use this term for the sake of speaking more appropriately, since tearing is more proper to this encounter than cutting or destroying.

Second, because love is the friend of the power of love and of the strong and impetuous touch, exercised more in tearing, than in cutting or destroying.

Third, because love desires the act to be very brief and quick. The strength and power of the act is commensurate with its brevity and spirituality, for virtue when united is stronger than when scattered. And love is introduced as form is introduced into matter; it is done in an instant, and until then there is no act but only the dispositions toward it. Spiritual acts are produced instantaneously in the soul, because God infuses them. But those the soul makes of itself can better be referred to as dispositive acts by means of successive desires and affections, which never become perfect acts of love or contemplation, unless, as I say, when God sometimes forms and perfects them very quickly in the spirit. As a result the Wise Man affirmed that the end of prayer is better than the beginning [Eccl. 7:9], and it is commonly quoted that the short prayer penetrates the heavens. A person already disposed can make many and far more intense acts in a short time than someone undisposed can in a long time; and, by reason of his being so fully disposed, he usually remains for a long time in an act of love or contemplation. With one who is not disposed, all is spent in preparing the spirit, and even then the fire usually holds back without entering the wood, either because of the excessive dampness of the wood or because of the lack of sufficient heat to dispose it, or for both reasons. But in the prepared soul, the act of love enters immediately, for at each touch the spark catches fire in the dry tinder, and thus the enamored soul desires the brevity of tearing more than the delay involved in cutting or destroying.

The fourth reason is that the veil of this life is done away with more quickly, and cutting or destroying requires greater care, since one must wait for the object to be prepared or ready, or for some other reason; whereas if one tears it there is no waiting, it seems to me, for this readiness or for anything of the sort.

34. The enamored soul desires this tearing so that it may suffer no delay by waiting for its life to be destroyed naturally, or cut off at such and such a time. The force of love and the disposition the soul sees in itself make it desire and beg that the veil of life be torn immediately by a supernatural encounter and impetus of love.

A person having reached this stage knows full well that it is characteristic of God to take to Himself, before their time, souls that love Him ardently, perfecting them in a short while by means of that love, which in any event they would have gained at their own pace. This is what the Wise Man said: *He pleased God and was loved; and living among sinners he was translated and carried away lest evil should change his understanding or affection deceive his soul. Perfected in a short time, he fulfilled a long time. Because his soul was pleasing to God, He therefore made haste to take him out of the midst,* etc. [Wis. 4:10–11, 13–14] These are the words of the Wise Man in which it will be seen how rightly and adequately the soul uses the expression "tear through," for the Holy Spirit uses the words "carry away" and "make haste," which indicate something apart from all delay. God's making haste signifies the haste by which He perfected in a short time the love of the just man, and "carry away" refers to a premature death.

It is vital for a person to make acts of love in this life so that in being perfected in a short time he may not be detained long, either here on earth or in the next life, before seeing God.

35. Let us see now why it calls this inner assault of the Spirit an encounter rather than something else. The reason is that when the soul feels in God an infinite longing, as we said, for the ending of its life and that this wish goes unfulfilled, since the time of its perfection has not arrived, it is aware that He produces these divine and glorious assaults in the manner of encounters so as to perfect it and raise it out of the flesh. Since their purpose is to purify it and draw it out of the flesh, they are indeed encounters, by which He ever penetrates and deifies the substance of the soul, absorbing it above all being into His own being. And the cause of this absorption is that He vigorously encountered and transported it in the Holy Spirit, whose communications are impetuous when they are fervent, as is this encounter.

Because the soul tastes God in a living way in this encounter, it calls it sweet; not because many other touches and encounters received in this state are not sweet, but because of its eminence over all others. God grants this, as we said, in order soon to loose and glorify it. Whereupon it acquires the courage to entreat: "Tear through the veil," etc.

36. To sum up the entire stanza now, it is like saying: O flame of the Holy Spirit that so intimately and tenderly pierces the substance of my soul and cauterizes it with Your glorious ardor! Previously, my requests did not reach Your ears, when, in the anxieties and weariness of love in which my sense and my spirit suffered because of considerable weakness, impurity, and lack of strong love, I was praying that You loose me and bring me to Yourself, because my soul longed for You, and impatient love did not allow me to be so conformed to the conditions of this life in

which You desired me still to live. The previous impulses of love were not enough, because they did not have sufficient quality for the attainment of my desire; now I am so fortified in love that not only do my sense and spirit no longer faint in You, but my heart and my flesh, reinforced in You, rejoice in the living God [Ps. 83:3], with great conformity between the sensory and spiritual parts. What you desire me to ask for, I ask for; and what you do not desire, I do not desire, nor can I, nor does it even enter my mind to desire it. My petitions are now more valuable and estimable in Your sight, since they come from You, and You move me to make them, and I make them in the delight and joy of the Holy Spirit, my judgment now issuing from Your countenance [Ps. 16:2], that is, when You esteem and hear my prayer. Tear then the thin veil of this life and do not let old age cut it naturally, that from now on I may love You with plenitude and fullness my soul desires forever and ever.

STANZA 2

O sweet cautery,
O delightful wound!
O gentle hand! O delicate touch
That tastes of eternal life
And pays every debt!
In killing You changed death to life.

Commentary

1. In this stanza the soul proclaims how the three Persons of the Most Blessed Trinity, the Father, the Son, and the Holy Ghost, are they Who effect in it this divine work of union. Thus the hand, the cautery, and the touch are substantially the same. The soul applies these terms to the Persons of the Trinity because of the effect each of the Persons produces. The cautery is the Holy Spirit; the hand is the Father; and the touch is the Son. The soul here magnifies the Father, the Son, and the Holy Ghost, stressing the three admirable favors and blessings they produce in it, having changed its death to life, transforming it in the Trinity.

The first is the delightful wound. This it attributes to the Holy Spirit, and hence calls Him a sweet cautery.

The second is the taste of eternal life. This it attributes to the Son, and thus calls Him a delicate touch.

The third is transformation, a gift by which all debts are fully paid. This it attributes to the Father, and hence calls it a gentle hand.

Although it names the three, according to the properties of their effects, it speaks only to one, saying, "You changed death to life," because all of them work together; and accordingly it attributes everything to one, and everything to all.

The verse is as follows:

2.   O sweet cautery,

This cautery, as we mentioned, is the Holy Spirit. For as Moses declares in Deuteronomy, *Our Lord God is a consuming fire* [Dt. 4:24], that is, a fire of love, which being of infinite power, can inestimably consume and transform into itself the soul it touches. Yet He burns each soul according to its preparation: He will burn one more, another less, and this He does insofar as He desires, and how and when He desires. When He wills to touch somewhat vehemently, the soul's burning reaches such a high degree of love that it seems to surpass that of all the fires of the world; for He is an infinite fire of love. As a result, in this union, the soul calls the Holy Spirit a cautery. Since the heat of a cautery is more intense and violent and produces a more singular effect than do other fires, the soul calls the act of this union a cautery in comparison with the others, for it is the outcome of a fire so much more aflame than all the others. Because the soul in this case is entirely transformed by the divine flame, it not only feels a cautery, but has become a cautery of blazing fire.

3. It is a wonderful thing and worth relating that, since this fire of God is so mighty it would consume a thousand worlds more easily than the fire of this earth would burn up a straw, it does not consume and destroy the soul in which it so burns. And it does not afflict it; rather, commensurate with the strength of the love, it divinizes and delights it, burning gently.

And this is so on account of the purity and perfection with which the spirit burns in the Holy Ghost. Similarly, as told in the Acts of the Apostles, this fire came with great vehemence and enkindled the disciples [Acts 2:3], who, as St. Gregory affirms, burned interiorly and gently with love. [*Homilia 30 in Evang.*: PL 76, 1220] This is the Church's meaning when, as regards the same subject, it says: *Fire came from heaven, not burning but emitting light; not consuming but giving illumination.* [Roman Breviary, Thursday within the Octave of Pentecost (First Response of Matins)] Since God's purpose in granting these communications is to exalt the soul, He does not weary and restrict it, but enlarges and delights it; He does not blacken it and convert it to ashes as fire does to coal, but He brightens and enriches it. Hence it calls Him a sweet cautery.

4. The happy soul that by great fortune reaches this cautery knows all things, tastes all things, does all it wishes, and prospers; no one

prevails before it and nothing touches it. This is the soul of which the Apostle speaks: *The spiritual man judges all things and he is judged by no one.* [1 Cor. 2:15] And again: *The spirit searches out all things, unto the deep things of God.* [1 Cor. 2:10] This is love's trait: to examine all the goods of the Beloved.

5. Oh, the great glory of you who have merited this supreme fire! It is certain that, though it does not destroy you (for it has the infinite force to consume and annihilate you), it does consume you immensely in glory. Do not wonder that God brings some souls to this high peak. The sun is distinguished by some of its marvelous effects; as the Holy Spirit says, it burns the mountains (that is, the saints) in three ways. [Ecclus. 43:4]

Since this cautery is sweet, then, how delighted will be the soul it touches! The soul, desiring to speak of it, does not do so, but keeps the esteem in its heart and only expresses exclamation vocally through the use of "O," saying: "O sweet cautery,"

6.   O delightful wound!

Having addressed the cautery, the soul now speaks to the wound caused by the cautery. The cautery was sweet, and the wound must logically conform to the cautery. Thus the wound issuing from a sweet cautery is a delightful wound. Since the cautery is a cautery of love, the wound is a wound of sweet love and is both delightful and sweet.

7. To understand the nature of this wound the soul is addressing, it should be known that the cautery of material fire always leaves a wound where it is applied. And it possesses this property: If applied to a wound not made by fire, it converts it into a wound caused by fire. Whether a soul is wounded by other wounds of miseries and sins or whether it is healthy, this cautery of love immediately effects a wound of love in the one it touches, and those wounds due to other causes become wounds of love.

Yet there is a difference between this loving cautery and the one generated by material fire. The wound left by material fire is only curable by other medicines, whereas the wound effected by the cautery of love is incurable through medicine; for the very cautery that causes it, cures it, and by curing it, causes it. As often as the cautery of love touches the wound of love, it causes a deeper wound of love, and thus the more it wounds, the more it cures and heals. The more wounded the lover, the healthier he is, and the cure love causes is to wound and inflict wound upon wound, to such an extent that the entire soul is dissolved into a wound of love. And now all cauterized and made one wound of love, it is completely healthy in love, for it is transformed in love.

This is what is understood by the wound of which the soul (all wounded and all healthy) speaks. Even though the soul is all wounded and all healthy, the cautery of love does not fail to fulfill its task, which is to touch and wound with love. Since it is wholly delightful and completely sound, the wound brings delight, just as a good doctor usually does. As a result the soul says: "O delightful wound!"

Oh, then, wound, so much the more delightful the higher and more sublime is the fire of love which causes it! The Holy Spirit produces it only for the sake of giving delight, and since His will to delight the soul is great, this wound will be great, for it will be extremely delightful.

8. O happy wound, wrought by one who knows only how to heal! O fortunate and choicest wound; you were made only for delight, and the quality of your affliction is delight and gratification for the wounded soul! You are great, O delightful wound, because He who caused you is great! And your delight is great, because the fire of love is infinite and makes you delightful according to your capacity and greatness. O, then, delightful wound, so much more sublimely delightful the more the cautery touched the intimate center of the substance of the soul, burning all that was burnable in order to give delight to all that could be delighted!

It is understandable that this cautery and this wound is of the highest degree possible in this state. For there are many other ways God cauterizes the soul that are unlike this one and fail to reach such a degree. For this cautery is a touch only of the divinity in the soul, without any intellectual or imaginative form or figure.

9. There is another way of cauterizing the soul by an intellectual form, usually very sublime, which is as follows. It will happen that while the soul is inflamed with the love of God, although not with a love of as deep a quality as that we mentioned (yet it is fitting that it be so for what I want to say), it will feel that a seraphim is assailing it by means of an arrow or dart which is all afire with love. And the seraphim pierces and cauterizes this soul which, like a red-hot coal, or better a flame, is already enkindled. And then in this cauterization, when the soul is transpierced with that dart, the flame gushes forth, vehemently and with a sudden ascent, like the fire in a furnace or an oven when someone uses a poker or bellows to stir and excite it. And being wounded by this fiery dart, the soul feels the wound with unsurpassable delight. Besides being fully stirred in great sweetness by the blowing or impetuous motion of the seraphim, in which it feels in its intense ardor to be dissolving in love, it is aware of the delicate wound and the herb (which serves as a keen temper to the dart) as though it were a sharp point in the substance of the spirit, in the heart of the pierced soul.

10. Who can fittingly speak of this intimate point of the wound, which seems to be in the middle of the heart of the spirit, there where the soul experiences the excellence of the delight? The soul feels that that point is like a tiny mustard seed, very much alive and enkindled, sending into its surroundings a living and enkindled fire of love. The fire issuing from the substance and power of that living point, which contains the substance and power of the herb, is felt to be subtly diffused through all the spiritual and substantial veins of the soul in the measure of the soul's power and strength. The soul feels its ardor strengthen and increase and its love become so refined in this ardor that seemingly there are seas of loving fire within it, reaching to the heights and depths of the earthly and heavenly spheres, imbuing all with love. It seems to it that the entire universe is a sea of love in which it is engulfed, for, conscious of the living point or center of love within itself, it is unable to catch sight of the boundaries of this love.

11. There is nothing else to say about the soul's enjoyment here except that it realizes how appropriately the kingdom of heaven was compared in the Gospel to a grain of mustard seed which, by reason of its intense heat, grows into a large tree, despite its being so small. [Mt. 13:31–32] For the soul is converted into the immense fire of love which emanates from that enkindled point at the heart of the spirit.

12. Few persons have reached these heights. Some have, however; especially those whose virtue and spirit was to be diffused among their children. For God accords to founders, with respect to the first fruits of the spirit, wealth and value commensurate with the greater or lesser following they will have in their doctrine and spirituality.

13. Let us return to the work of that seraphim, for he truly inflicts a sore and wounds inwardly in the spirit. Thus, if God sometimes permits an effect to extend to the bodily senses in the fashion in which it existed interiorly, the wound and sore appears outwardly, as happened when the seraphim wounded St. Francis. When the soul is wounded with love by the five wounds, the effect extends to the body and these wounds are impressed on the body and it is wounded, just as the soul is wounded with love. God usually does not bestow a favor upon the body without bestowing it first and principally upon the soul. Thus the greater the delight and strength of love the wound produces in the soul, so much the greater is that produced by the wound outside on the body, and when there is an increase in one there is an increase in the other. This so happens because these souls are purified and established in God, and that which is a cause of pain and torment to their corruptible flesh is sweet and delectable to their strong and healthy spirit. It is, then, a wonderful experience to feel the pain augment with the delight.

Job, with his wounds, clearly beheld this marvel when he said to God: *Returning to me, You torment me wondrously.* [Jb. 10:16] This is an unspeakable marvel and worthy of the abundance and sweetness God has hidden for them that fear Him [Ps. 30:20]: to cause a person to enjoy so much the more savor and sweetness the more pain and torment he experiences.

Nevertheless, when the wound is made only in the soul without being communicated outwardly, the delight can be more intense and sublime. The spirit has the flesh curbed in this state, but when the goods of the spirit are communicated also to the flesh, the flesh pulls the reins, bridles the mouth of this swift horse of the spirit, and restrains its great impetuosity; for if the spirit makes use of its power, the reins will break. Yet until the reins are broken, the flesh does not fail to oppress the spirit's freedom, as the Wise Man asserts: *The corruptible body is a load upon the soul, and the earthly dwelling oppresses the spiritual mind which of itself comprehends many things.* [Wis. 9:15]

14. I say this in order to make it clear that he who would go to God relying upon natural ability and reasoning will not be very spiritual. There are some who think that by pure force and the activity of the senses, which of itself is lowly and no more than natural, they can reach the strength and height of the supernatural spirit. One does not attain to this peak without suppressing and leaving aside the activity of the senses.

Yet it is something quite different when an effect of the spirit overflows in the senses. When this is true, the effect in the senses proceeds from an abundance of spirit, as in the event of the wounds which proceed from the inner strength and appear outwardly. This happened with St. Paul, whose immense compassion for the sufferings of Christ redounded into the body, as he explains to the Galatians: *I bear the wounds of the Lord Jesus in my body.* [Gal. 6:17]

15. What we have expounded concerning the cautery and the wound is sufficient. If the picture we have painted of them is true, what, do you think, will be the hand which produces this cautery, and what the touch? The soul reveals this in the subsequent verse more through interjection than by explanation, saying:

16.   O gentle hand! O delicate touch

This hand is, as we said, the merciful and omnipotent Father. We should understand that, since it is as generous and bountiful as it is powerful and rich, it gives, when opened to favor the soul, rich and powerful presents. For this reason the soul calls it a gentle hand. It is like saying: O hand, You are as gentle to my soul, which You touch by resting gently, as You would be powerful enough to submerge the entire world if You rested somewhat heavily, for by Your look alone the earth trembles [Ps. 103:32], the nations melt and faint, and the mountains crumble! [Hb. 3:6] Oh, then again, great hand, by touching Job somewhat roughly, You were as hard and rigorous with him [Jb. 19:21] as You are friendly and gentle with me; how much more lovingly, graciously, and gently do You permanently touch my soul! You cause death, and You give life, and no one flees from Your hand. For You, O divine life, never kill unless to give life, never wound unless to heal. When You chastise, Your touch is gentle, but it is enough to destroy the world. When You give delight, You rest very firmly, and thus the delight of Your sweetness is immeasurable. You have wounded me in order to cure me, O divine hand, and You have put to death in me what made me lifeless, deprived me of God's life in which I now see myself live. You granted this with the liberality of Your generous grace, which You used in contacting me with the touch of the splendor of Your glory and the figure of Your substance [Heb. 1:3], which is Your only begotten Son, through Whom, being Your substance, You touch mightily from one end to the other. [Wis. 8:1] And Your only begotten Son, O merciful hand of the Father, is the delicate touch by which You touched me with the force of Your cautery and wounded me.

17. O You, then, delicate touch, the Word, the Son of God, through the delicacy of Your divine being, You subtly penetrate the substance of my soul and, lightly touching it all, absorb it entirely in Yourself in divine modes of delights and sweetnesses unheard of in the land of Canaan and never before seen in Theman! [Bar. 3:22] O, then, very delicate, exceedingly delicate, touch of the Word, so much the more delicate for me insofar as, after overthrowing the mountains and smashing the rocks to pieces on Mount Horeb with the shadow of might and power that went before You, You gave the prophet the sweetest and strongest experience of Yourself in the gentle breeze! [3 Kgs. 19:11–12] O gentle breeze, since You are a delicate and mild breeze, tell us: How do You, the Word, the Son of God, touch mildly and gently, since You are so awesome and mighty? Oh, happy is the soul that You, being terrible and strong, gently and lightly touch! Proclaim this to the world! But You are unwilling to proclaim this to the world because it does not know of a mild breeze and will not experience You, for it can neither receive nor see You. [Jn. 14:17] But they, O my God and my life, will see and experience Your mild touch, who withdraw from the world and become mild, bringing the mild into harmony with the mild, thus enabling themselves to experience and enjoy You. You touch them the more gently the more You dwell permanently hidden within them, for the substance of their soul is now refined, cleansed, and purified, withdrawn from every creature and every touch and trace of creature. As a result, *You hide*

them in the secret of Your face, which is the Word, *from the disturbance of men.* [Ps. 30:21]

18. O, then again, repeatedly delicate touch, so much the stronger and mightier the more You are delicate, since You detach and withdraw the soul from all the other touches of created things by the might of Your delicacy, and reserve it for and unite it to Yourself alone, so mild an effect do You leave in the soul that every other touch of all things both high and low seems coarse and spurious. It displeases the soul to look at these things, and to deal with them is a heavy pain and torment to it.

19. It should be known that the breadth and capacity of an object corresponds to its refinement, and that the more diffuse and communicative it is the more it is subtle and delicate. The Word is immensely subtle and delicate, for He is the touch which comes into contact with the soul. The soul is the vessel having breadth and capacity because of its remarkable purity and refinement in this state.

O, then, delicate touch, the more abundantly You pervade my soul, the more substantial You are and the purer is my soul!

20. It should also be known that the more subtle and delicate the touch, and the more delight and gratification it communicates there where it touches, the less volume and bulk it has. This divine touch has no bulk or volume, because the Word who grants it is alien to every mode and manner, and free from all the volume of form, figure, and accident which usually encircles and imposes boundaries or limits to the substance. This touch we are discussing is indescribable insofar as it is substantial, that is from the divine substance. Finally, then, O Word, indescribably delicate touch, produced in the soul only by Your most simple being, which, since it is infinite, is infinitely delicate and hence touches so subtly, lovingly, eminently, and delicately!

21.   That tastes of eternal life

Although that which the soul tastes in this touch of God is not perfect, it does in fact have a certain savor of eternal life, as was mentioned. And this is not incredible if we believe, as we should, that this is a touch of substances, that is, of the substance of God in the substance of the soul. Many saints have attained to this substantial touch during their lives on earth.

The delicateness of delight felt in this contact is inexpressible. I would desire not to speak of it so as to avoid giving the impression that it is no more than what I describe. There is no way to catch in words the sublime things of God which happen in these souls. The appropriate language for the person receiving these favors is that he understand them, experience them within himself, enjoy them, and be silent. One is conscious in this state that these things are in a certain way like the white pebble that St. John said would be given to him who conquers: *and on that pebble a new name written which no one knows, but he who receives it.* [Ap. 2:17]

Thus one can only say, and truthfully, "that tastes of eternal life." Although one does not have perfect fruition in this life as in glory, this touch, nevertheless, since it is a touch, tastes of eternal life. As a result the soul tastes here all the things of God, since God communicates to it fortitude, wisdom, love, beauty, grace, and goodness, etc. Because God is all these things, a person enjoys them in only one touch of God, and the soul rejoices within its faculties and within its substance.

22. Sometimes the unction of the Holy Spirit overflows into the body and all the sensory substance, all the members and bones and marrow rejoice, not in so slight a fashion as is customary, but with the feeling of great delight and glory, even in the outermost joints of the hands and feet. The body experiences so much glory in that of the soul that in its own way it magnifies God, feeling in its bones something similar to what David declares: *All my bones shall say: God, who is like to You?* [Ps. 34:10] And because everything that can be said of this unction is less than what it is, it is sufficient to say in reference to both the bodily and the spiritual experience, "that tastes of eternal life."

23.   And pays every debt!
The soul affirms this because in the taste of eternal life, which it here enjoys, it feels the reward for the trials it passed through in order to reach this state. It feels not only that it has been compensated and satisfied justly but that it has been rewarded exceedingly. It thoroughly understands the truth of the Bridegroom's promise in the Gospel, that He would repay a hundredfold. [Mt. 19:29] It has endured no tribulation, or penance, or trial to which there does not correspond a hundredfold of consolation and delight in this life, and it can truly say: "and pays all debts."

24. In order to know the nature of these debts for which the soul feels compensated here, it should be noted that ordinarily no one can reach this high state and kingdom of espousal without first undergoing many tribulations and trials. As is said in the Acts of the Apostles: *through many tribulations we must enter the kingdom of heaven.* [Acts 14:21] In this state these tribulations are now ended, for the soul being purified suffers no more.

25. The trials that those who are to reach this state suffer are three-fold: trials, discomforts, fears, and temptations from the world, and these in many ways; temptations, aridities, and afflictions in the senses; and tribulations, darknesses, distress, abandonment, temptations, and

other trials in the spirit. In this fashion a soul is purified in its sensory and spiritual parts, as we mentioned in discussing the fourth verse of the first stanza.

The reason these trials are necessary in order to reach this state is that this highest union cannot be wrought in a soul that is not fortified by trials and temptations and purified by tribulations, darknesses, and distress, just as a superior quality liqueur is poured only into a sturdy flask which is prepared and purified. By these trials the sensory part of the soul is purified and strengthened and the spiritual part is refined, purged, and disposed. Since unpurified souls must undergo the sufferings of fire in the next life to attain union with God in glory, so in this life they must undergo the fire of these sufferings to reach the union of perfection. This fire acts upon some more vigorously than upon others, and upon some for a longer time than upon others, according to the degree of union to which God wishes to raise them, and according to what must be purged in them.

26. Through these trials, in which God places the spirit and the senses, the soul in bitterness acquires virtues, strength, and perfection, for virtue is made perfect in weakness [2 Cor. 12:9], and is refined through the endurance of suffering. Iron cannot serve for the artificer's plan, nor be adapted to it, without fire and the hammer; as Jeremias says of the fire that gave him knowledge: *You have sent fire into my bones and have instructed me.* [Lam. 1:13] And Jeremias also says of the hammer: *You have chastised me, Lord, and I was instructed.* [Jer. 31:18] Hence Ecclesiasticus says: *What can he know who is not tried? And he that has no experience knows little.* [Ecclus. 34:9-10]

27. And here it ought to be pointed out why there are so few who reach this high state of perfect union with God. It should be known that the reason is not because God wishes that there be only a few of these spirits so elevated; He would rather want all to be perfect, but He finds few vessels that will endure so lofty and sublime a work. Since He tries them in little things and finds them so weak that they immediately flee from work, unwilling to be subject to the least discomfort and mortification, it follows that, not finding them strong and faithful in that little [Mt. 25:21, 23], in which He favored them by beginning to hew and polish them, He realizes that they will be much less strong in these greater trials. As a result He proceeds no further in purifying them and raising them from the dust of the earth through the toil of mortification. They were in need of greater constancy and fortitude than they showed.

There are many who desire to advance and persistently beseech God to bring them to this state of perfection. Yet when God wills to conduct them through the initial trials and mortifications, as is necessary, they are unwilling to suffer them, and they shun them, flee from the narrow road of life, and seek the broad road of their own consolation, which is that of their own perdition; thus they do not allow God to begin to grant their petition. They are like useless containers, for although they desire to reach the state of the perfect, they do not want to be guided by the path of trials which leads to it. They hardly even begin to walk along this road by submitting to what is least, that is, to ordinary sufferings.

We can answer them in Jeremias's words: *If you have grown weary running with footmen, how will you contend with horses? And if you have had quiet in the land of peace, what will you do in the swelling of the Jordan?* [Jer. 12:5] This is like saying: If by the common trials (on foot), which form a part of human life, it seemed to you that you were running because there were so many, and you take such short steps, how will you keep up with the horse's stride, which signifies the more than ordinary trials, for which human strength and speed is not enough? And if you have not wanted to forego the peace and pleasure of your earth, which is your sensuality, or contradict it in anything, or stir up a war, I do not know how you will desire to enter the impetuous waters of spiritual tribulations and trials, which are deeper.

28. O souls who in spiritual matters desire to walk in security and consolation! If you but knew how much it behooves you to suffer in order to reach this security and consolation, and how, without suffering, you cannot attain to your desire, but rather turn back, in nowise would you look for comfort either from God or from creatures. You would instead carry the cross and, placed upon it, desire to drink the pure gall and vinegar. You would consider it good fortune that, upon dying to this world and to yourselves, you would live to God in the delights of the spirit, and that patiently and faithfully suffering exterior trials, which are small, you would merit that God fix His eyes on you and purge you more profoundly through deeper spiritual trials in order to give you more interior blessings.

Those to whom God grants so signal a favor as to tempt them more interiorly must have performed many services for Him, have had admirable patience and constancy for His sake, and in their life and works have been very acceptable to Him. For He tries them in this way so as to make them advance in gifts and merits, as He did with holy Tobias to whom St. Raphael said: *Since you were acceptable to God, He favored you by sending you temptation that He might try you more in order to exalt you more.* [Tb. 12:13] After that temptation, all the rest of his life was in joy, as Sacred Scripture says. [Tb. 14:4] We also see in the life of holy Job that once God accepted his works in the sight of the good and evil spirits, He immediately favored him by sending those great trials so that subsequently He could extol him much more. And this He did multiplying his goods, both spiritual and temporal. [Jb. 1–2; 42:10, 12]

29. God acts similarly with those He wishes to lead on by means of what is most beneficial for them. He allows them to be tempted in order to elevate them as high as possible, that is, to union with the divine wisdom, which, as David says, is silver examined in the fire, tried in the earth—that is, of our flesh—and purged seven times, which is all the purgation possible. [Ps. 11:7] There is no reason to be detained any longer in order to describe the nature of each of these seven purgations necessary to reach wisdom, or of how the seven degrees of love correspond to them. To the soul, this wisdom is still like the silver of which David speaks, however great may be the union, but in the other life it will be like gold to it.

30. A person, then, should live with great patience and constancy in all the tribulations and trials God places upon him, whether they are exterior or interior, spiritual or bodily, great or small, and he should accept them all as from God's hand as a good remedy and not flee from them, for they bring him health. In this matter let him take the counsel of the Wise Man: *If the spirit of Him who has power descends upon you, do not abandon your place* (the place and site of your probation which is the trial He sends you), *for the cure will make great sins cease* [Eccl. 10:4]; that is, it will cut the roots of your sins and imperfections—your evil habits. The combat of trials, distress, and temptations deadens the evil and imperfect habits of the soul and purifies and strengthens it. A man should hold in esteem the interior and exterior trials God sends him, realizing that there are few who merit to be brought to perfection through suffering and to undergo trials for the sake of so high a state.

31. Returning to our explanation, the soul knows in this state that everything has ended well and that now *sicut tenebrae ejus ita et lumen ejus*[1] [Ps. 138:12], and that, as it was a sharer of tribulations, it is now a sharer of consolations and of the kingdom. [2 Cor. 1:7] For God repays the interior and exterior trials very well with divine goods for the soul and body, so that there is not a trial which does not have a corresponding and considerable reward. It proclaims this by saying with full satisfaction: "and pays every debt." It thanks God in this verse for having withdrawn it from trials, as David also did in his psalm: *What great tribulations You have shown me, many and difficult, and You have freed me from them all, and have brought me back again from the abyss of the earth.*

[1] as is its darkness, so is its light

You have multiplied Your magnificence and turning to me You have comforted me. [Ps. 70:20–21]

Before attaining to this state, the soul was like Mardochai who sat at the gates of the palace, wept in the square of Susan over the danger of his life, wore sackcloth, and was unwilling to receive a garment from Queen Esther [Est. 4:1–2, 4] because he had not obtained any reward for the services he had rendered the king or for his fidelity in defending the king's honor and life. [Est. 6:3] One day, just as with Mardochai, the soul is repaid for all its trials and services [Est. 6:10, 11], and not only made to enter the palace and stand, clothed in royal garments, before the king, but also accorded the royal crown, scepter, and throne, and possession of the royal ring, so that it might do anything it likes and omit anything it does not like in the kingdom of its Spouse. [Est. 3: 10–13] Those who are in this state obtain everything they want. Thus they are not merely paid, but even the Jews, their enemies, the inordinate appetites, are dead, for these were eliminating the spiritual life in which it now lives through its faculties and appetites. Hence it subsequently says:

32.   In killing You changed death to life.

For death is nothing else than the privation of life, because when life comes no vestige of death remains. Spiritually speaking, there are two kinds of life:

One is beatific, consisting in the vision of God, which must be attained by natural death, as St. Paul says: *We know that if this our clay house is dissolved, we have a dwelling place of God in heaven.* [2 Cor. 5:1]

The other is the perfect spiritual life, the possession of God through union of love. This is acquired through complete mortification of all the vices and appetites and of one's own nature. Until this is achieved, one cannot reach the perfection of the spiritual life of union with God; as the Apostle also declares in these words: *If you live according to the flesh you shall die; yet if with the spirit you mortify the deeds of the flesh you shall live.* [Rom. 8:13]

33. Let it be known that what the soul calls death is all that goes to make up the old man: the entire engagement of the faculties (memory, intellect, and will) in the things of the world, and the indulgence of the appetites in the pleasures of creatures. All this is the activity of the old life, which is the death of the new spiritual life. The soul is unable to live perfectly in this new life, if the old man does not die completely. The Apostle warns: *take off the old man and put on the new man who according to God is created in justice and holiness.* [Eph. 4:22–24] In this new life, which the soul lives when it has arrived at the perfect union with God, here being discussed, all the inclinations and activity of

the appetites and faculties, which of their own were the operation of death and the privation of the spiritual life, become divine.

34. Since every living being lives by its operation, as the philosophers say, and the soul's operations are in God through its union with Him, it lives the life of God. Thus it changed its death to life, its animal life to spiritual life.

The intellect, which before this union understood naturally by the vigor of its natural light, by means of the natural senses, is now moved and informed by another higher principle of supernatural divine light, and the senses are bypassed. Accordingly, the intellect becomes divine, because through its union with God's intellect both become one.

And the will, which previously loved in a base and death-like fashion, only with its natural affection, is now changed into the life of divine love, for it loves in a lofty way, with divine affection, moved by the strength of the Holy Spirit in which it now lives the life of love. By means of this union, God's will and the soul's will are now one.

And the memory, which by itself perceived only the figures and phantasms of creatures, is changed through this union so as to have in its mind the eternal years mentioned by David. [Ps. 76:6]

And the natural appetite, which only had the ability and strength to relish creatures (which causes death), is changed now so that its taste and savor is divine, and it is moved and satisfied by another principle: the delight of God, in which it is more alive. And because it is united with Him, it is no longer anything else than the appetite of God.

Finally all the movements, operations, and inclinations the soul had previously from the principle and strength of its natural life are now in this union dead to what they formerly were, changed into divine movements, and alive to God. For the soul, like a true daughter of God, is moved in all by the Spirit of God, as St. Paul teaches in saying that those who are moved by the Spirit of God are sons of God Himself. [Rom. 8:14]

Accordingly, the intellect of this soul is God's intellect; its will is God's will; its memory is the memory of God; and its delight is God's delight; and although the substance of this soul is not the substance of God, since it cannot undergo a substantial conversion into Him, it has become God through participation in God, being united to and absorbed in Him, as it is in this state. Such a union is wrought in this perfect state of the spiritual life, yet not as perfectly as in the next life. Consequently the soul is dead to all that it was in itself, which was death to it, and alive to what God is in Himself.

Speaking of itself, the soul declares in this verse: "In killing You changed death to life." The soul can well repeat the words of St. Paul: *I live, now not I, but Christ lives in me.* [Gal. 2:20] The death of this soul is changed to the life of God. We can also apply the words of the Apostle, *absorpta est mors in victoria*[2] [1 Cor. 15:54], as well as those the prophet Osee speaks in the person of God: *O death, I will be your death.* [Os. 13:14] In other words: Since I am life, being the death of death, death will be absorbed in life.

35. The soul, then, is absorbed in divine life, withdrawn from its natural appetites and from all that is secular and temporal; it is brought into the king's cellars, where it rejoices in its Beloved, remembering His breasts more than wine, saying: *Although I am black I am beautiful, daughters of Jerusalem* [Ct. 1:3-4], for my natural black color was changed into the beauty of the heavenly king.

36. In this state of life so perfect, the soul always walks in festivity, inwardly and outwardly, and it frequently bears on its spiritual tongue a new song of great jubilation in God, a song always new, enfolded in a gladness and love arising from the knowledge the soul has of its happy state. Sometimes it walks in joy and fruition, expressing in its spirit those words of Job: *My glory will ever be renewed, and I shall multiply my days as a palm tree.* [Jb. 29:20, 18] This is equivalent to declaring that God Himself, always remaining the same, renews all things. As the Wise Man states: *Being ever one in my glory, I will ever renew my glory* [Wis. 7:27] that is, I will not let it grow old as it was before. And I will multiply my days as the palm tree, that is, raise my merits heavenward as the palm tree lifts its branches.

The merits of a person in this state are usually remarkable in number and quality, and ordinarily this person also sings in his spirit all that David proclaims in the Psalm which begins: *Exaltabo te, Domine, quoniam suscepisti me,* and especially in the last two lines: *Convertisti planctum meum in gaudium mihi,* etc., *conscidisti saccum meum, et circumdedisti me laetitia,* to the end that my glory may sing to you and I may not regret; my Lord, God, I will praise You forever. [Ps. 29:2, 12, 13]

There is no need to be amazed that the soul so frequently walks amid this joy, jubilance, fruition, and praise of God. Besides the knowledge it has of the favors received, it feels in this state that God is so solicitous in regaling it with precious, delicate, and enhancing words, and in extolling it by various favors, that He has no one else in the world to favor nor anything else to do, that everything is for the soul alone. With this feeling it proclaims like the bride in the Canticle: *Dilectus meus mihi et ego illi.*[3] [Ct. 2:16]

---

[2] death is swallowed up in victory
[3] My Beloved belongs to me and I to Him.

STANZA 3

O lamps of fire!
In whose splendors
The deep caverns of feeling,
Once obscure and blind,
Now give forth, so rarely, so exquisitely,
Both warmth and light to their Beloved.

Commentary

1. May God be pleased to help me here, for I certainly need His help to explain the deep meaning of this stanza. He who reads this commentary should do so attentively, for if he has no experience, it will seem somewhat obscure and prolix; if he is experienced, however, he will probably find it clear and pleasant to read.

The soul exalts and thanks its Spouse in this stanza for the admirable favors it receives from its union with Him. It states that by means of this union it receives abundant and lofty knowledge of God, which is all loving, and which communicates light and love to its faculties and feeling. That which was once obscure and blind can now receive illumination and the warmth of love, as it does, so as to be able to give forth light and love to the one who illumined it and filled it with love. The true lover is only content when he employs all that he is in himself, is worth, has, and receives in the beloved, and the greater all this is, the more satisfaction he receives in giving it. The soul rejoices on this account because, from the splendors and love it receives, it can shine brightly in the presence of its Spouse and give Him love. The verse follows:

2.   O lamps of fire!
First of all it should be known that lamps possess two properties: they transmit both light and heat. To understand the nature of these lamps and how they shine and burn within the soul, it ought to be known that God in His unique and simple being is all the powers and grandeurs of His attributes. He is almighty, wise, and good; and He is merciful, just, powerful, and loving, etc.; and He is the other infinite attributes and powers of which we have no knowledge. Since He is all of this in His simple being, the soul views distinctly in Him, when He is united with it and deigns to disclose this knowledge, all these powers and grandeurs, that is: omnipotence, wisdom, goodness, and mercy, etc. Since each of these attributes is the very being of God in His one and

only *suppositum*, which is the Father, the Son, and the Holy Spirit, and since each one is God Himself, Who is infinite light or divine fire, we deduce that the soul, like God, gives forth light and warmth through each of these innumerable attributes. Each of these attributes is a lamp which enlightens it and transmits the warmth of love.

3. Insofar as the soul receives the knowledge of these attributes in only one act of this union, God Himself is for it many lamps together, which illumine and impart warmth to it individually, for it has clear knowledge of each, and through this knowledge is inflamed in love. By means of all the lamps the soul loves each individually, inflamed by each one and by all together, because all these attributes are one being as we said. All these lamps are one lamp which, according to its powers and attributes, shines and burns like many lamps. Hence the soul in one act of knowledge of these lamps loves through each one and, in so doing, loves through them all together, bearing in that act the quality of love for each one and from each one, and from all together and for all together.

The splendor this lamp of God's being, insofar as He is omnipotent, imparts light to the soul and the warmth of love of Him according to His omnipotence. God is then to the soul a lamp of omnipotence which shines and bestows all knowledge in respect to this attribute. And the splendor of this lamp of God's being insofar as He is wisdom grants the soul light and the warmth of the love of God according to His wisdom. God is then a lamp of wisdom to it. And the splendor of this lamp insofar as it is goodness imparts to the soul light and the warmth of love according to His goodness. God is then a lamp of goodness to it. He is also to the soul a lamp of justice, fortitude, and mercy, and of all the other attributes which are represented to it together in God. The light communicated to it from all these attributes together is enveloped in the warmth of love of God by which it loves Him because He is all these things. In this communication and manifestation of Himself to the soul, which in my opinion is the greatest possible in this life, He is to it innumerable lamps giving forth knowledge and love of Himself.

4. Moses beheld these lamps on Mt. Sinai where, when God passed by, he prostrated himself on the ground and began to call out and enumerate some of them: *Emperor, Lord, God, merciful, clement, patient, of much compassion, true, who keeps mercy unto thousands, who takes away iniquities and sins, no one is of himself innocent before You.* [Ex. 34: 6-7] In this passage it is clear that the greatest attributes and powers Moses knew there in God were those of God's omnipotence, dominion, deity, mercy, justice, truth, and righteousness, which was the highest knowledge of God. Because love was communicated to him in

accord with the knowledge, the delight of love and fruition he enjoyed there was most sublime.

5. It is noteworthy that the delight the soul receives in the rapture of love, communicated by the fire of the light of these lamps, is wonderful and immense, for it is as abundant as it would be if it came from many lamps. Each lamp burns in love, and the warmth from each furthers the warmth of the other, and the flame of one, the flame of the other, just as the light of one sheds light on the other, because through each attribute the other is known. Thus all of them are one light and one fire, and each of them is one light and one fire.

Immensely absorbed in delicate flames, subtly wounded with love through each of them, and more wounded by all of them together, more alive in the love of the life of God, the soul perceives clearly that that love is proper to eternal life. Eternal life is the aggregation of all goods, and the soul somehow experiences this here and fully understands the truth of the Bridegroom's assertion in the Canticle, that the lamps of love are lamps of fire and of flames. [Ct. 8:6]

You are beautiful in your steps and shoes, prince's daughter. [Ct. 7:1] Who can relate the magnificence and rareness of your delight and majesty in the admirable splendor and love of your lamps?

6. Sacred Scripture recounts that in times long past one of these lamps went by Abraham and caused him a dark and terrible horror, for the lamp was from the rigorous justice which was to be exercised later upon the Canaanites. [Gn. 15:12, 17] Since all these lamps of the knowledge of God illumine you in a friendly and loving way, O enriched soul, how much more light and happiness of love will they, that produced that darkness and horror in Abraham, beget in you! How remarkable, how advantageous, and how multifaceted will be your delight, for in all and from all you receive fruition and love, since God communicates Himself to your faculties according to His attributes and powers!

When one loves and does good to another, he loves and does good to him in the measure of his own nature and properties. Thus your Bridegroom, dwelling within you, grants you favors according to His nature. Since He is omnipotent, He omnipotently loves and does good to you; since He is wise, you feel that He loves and does good to you with wisdom; since He is infinitely good, you feel that He loves you with goodness; since He is holy, you feel that with holiness He loves and favors you; since He is just, you feel that in justice He loves and favors you; since He is merciful, mild, and clement, you feel His mercy, mildness, and clemency; since He is a strong, sublime, and delicate being, you feel that His love for you is strong, sublime, and delicate; since He is pure and undefiled, you feel that He loves you in a pure and undefiled way; since He is truth, you feel that He loves you in truthfulness; since He is liberal, you feel that He liberally loves and favors you, without any personal profit, only in order to do good to you; since He is the virtue of supreme humility, He loves you with supreme humility and esteem and makes you His equal, gladly revealing Himself to you in these ways of knowledge, in this His countenance filled with graces, and telling you in this His union, not without great rejoicing: "I am yours and for you and delighted to be what I am so as to be yours and give myself to you."

7. Who, then, will be able to express your experience, O happy soul, since you know that you are so loved and with such esteem exalted? Your bosom, which is your will, is like the bride's, similar to a bundle of wheat, covered and surrounded with lilies. [Ct. 7:2] For while you are enjoying together the grains of the bread of life, the lilies, or virtues, surrounding you provide you with delight. These are the king's daughters mentioned by David, who will delight you with myrrh, stacte, and other aromatic spices [Ps. 44:9–10]; for the knowledge of His graces and virtues, which the Beloved communicates to you, are His daughter. You so overflow with these and are so engulfed in them that you are likewise the well of living waters which flow impetuously from Mount Libanus [Ct. 4:15], that is, from God. You were made wonderfully joyful according to the whole harmonious composite of your soul and even your body, converted completely into a paradise divinely irrigated, that the psalmist's affirmation might also be fulfilled in you: *the impetus of the river makes the city of God joyful.* [Ps. 45:5]

8. O marvelous thing, that the soul at this time is flooded with divine waters, abounding in them like a plentiful fount overflowing on all sides! Although it is true that this communication under discussion is the light and fire from these lamps of God, yet this fire here is so gentle that, being an immense fire, it is like the waters of life, which satisfy the thirst of the spirit with that impetus the spirit desires. Hence these lamps of fire are living waters of the spirit, like those that descended upon the Apostles [Acts 2:3]; although they were lamps of fire, they were clear and pure waters as well. The prophet Ezechiel referred to them in this fashion when he prophesied the coming of the Holy Spirit: *I will pour out upon you,* God says there, *clean waters and will put my spirit in the midst of you.* [Ez. 36:25, 27] Although it is fire, it is also water. For this fire is represented by the fire of the sacrifice which Jeremias hid in the cistern: While it was hidden it was water, and when they drew it out for the sacrifice it was fire. [2 Mc. 1:20–23] Thus the spirit of God insofar as it is hidden in the veins of the soul is like soft refreshing water, which satisfies the thirst of the spirit, and insofar as it is exercised in the sacrifice of loving God, it is like living flames of fire. These flames of fire are the lamps of the act of

love and of flames, which we ascribed above to the Bridegroom according to the Canticle: *Your lamps are lamps of fire and of flames.* [Ct. 8: 6] The soul calls them flames here, because it not only tastes them like water within itself, but also makes them active, like flames, in the love of God. Since in the communication of the spirit of these lamps, the soul is inflamed and put in the activity of love, in the act of love, it calls them lamps rather than waters, saying: "O lamps of fire!"

All that can be said of this stanza is less than the reality, for the transformation of the soul in God is indescribable. Everything can be expressed in this statement: The soul becomes God from God through participation in Him and in His attributes, which it terms the "lamps of fire."

9.   In whose splendors

To understand what these splendors of the lamps are, and how the soul is resplendent in them, it should be known that they are the loving knowledge which the lamps of God's attributes give forth from themselves to the soul. United with them in its faculties, the soul is also resplendent like them, transformed in loving splendors.

This illumination from the splendors, in which the soul shines brightly with the warmth of love, is not like that produced by material lamps, which through their flames shed light round about them, but like the illumination that is within the very flames, for the soul is within these splendors. As a result it says: in whose splendors, that is, within the splendors; and it does not merely say within them, but, as we pointed out, it says transformed in them. It is like the air within the flame, enkindled and transformed in the flame, for the flame is nothing but enkindled air. The movements and splendors of the flame are not from the air alone, nor from the fire of which the flame is composed, but from both the air and the fire. And the fire causes the air, which it has enkindled, to produce these same movements and splendors.

10. We can consequently understand how the soul with its faculties is illumined within the splendors of God. The movements of these divine flames, which are the flickering and flaring up we have mentioned, are not alone produced by the soul that is transformed in the flames of the Holy Spirit, nor does the Holy Spirit produce them alone, but they are the work of both the soul and Him, since He moves it in the manner that fire moves the enkindled air. Thus these movements of both God and the soul are not only splendors, but also glorifications of the soul.

This activity of the flames and these flares are the happy festivals and games which, as we said in the commentary on verse 2 of the first stanza, the Holy Spirit inspires in the soul. It seems in these that

He is always wanting to bestow eternal life and transport it completely to perfect glory by bringing it into Himself. All the gifts, first and last, great and small, which God grants to the soul, He always grants in order to lead it to eternal life. In the same way the flame flickers and flares together with the enkindled air in order to bring the air with itself to the center of its sphere, and it produces all these movements in order to persist in bringing the air nearer itself. As the flame does not carry the air away, because the air is in its own sphere, so too, although these movements of the Holy Spirit are most efficacious in absorbing the soul in sublime glory, they do not do so completely until the time comes for it to depart from the sphere of the air of this carnal life and enter into the center of the spirit of the perfect life in Christ.

11. Let it be known that these motions are motions of the soul more than of God, for God does not move. These glimpses of glory given to the soul are in God stable, perfect, continuous, and constantly serene. Afterwards this will also be true of the soul: There will be no change as to more or less and no intrusion of these movements; it will see distinctly how, although here below God seemingly moved within it, He does not in Himself move, just as fire does not move when in its center; and it will see how it experienced this wavering of the flame because it was not perfect in glory.

12. By what was said and what we shall now say it will be more plainly understood how excellent the splendors of these lamps are, for by another name they are called "overshadowings." To understand this expression, it should be known that an overshadowing is the equivalent of casting a shadow, and casting a shadow is similar to protecting, favoring, and granting graces. For when a person is covered by a shadow, it is a sign that someone else is nearby to protect and favor him. As a result the Angel Gabriel called the conception of the Son of God, that favor granted to the Virgin Mary, an overshadowing of the Holy Spirit: *The Holy Spirit will come upon you and the power of the Most High will overshadow you.* [Lk. 1:35]

13. For a clear understanding of the nature of this casting of the shadow of God, or these overshadowings of great splendor, which is all the same, it should be remarked that everything has and makes a shadow according to it size and its properties. If an object is opaque and dark, it makes a dark shadow; if it is transparent and delicate, its shadow is transparent and delicate. Thus the shadow of a dark object amounts to another darkness in the measure of the darkness of the object, and the shadow of something bright amounts to something else that is bright according to the brightness of the object.

14. Since these virtues and attributes of God are enkindled and re-splendent lamps, they cannot but touch the soul by their shadows, since, as we said, they are so close to it. These shadows must also be enkindled and resplendent in the measure of the splendor of the lamps that make them, and thus they will be splendors. As a result the shadow that the lamp of God's beauty casts over the soul will be another beauty according to the measure and property of God's beauty; and the shadow that fortitude casts over it will amount to another fortitude commensurate with God's; and the shadow of God's wisdom upon it will be another wisdom corresponding to God's wisdom; and so on with the other lamps. To express it better: it will be the very wisdom, and the very beauty, and the very fortitude of God in shadow, because the soul here cannot comprehend God perfectly. Since the shadow is so formed by God's size and properties that it is God Himself in shadow, the soul clearly knows God's excellence.

15. What, then, will be the shadows of the grandeurs of His virtues and attributes which the Holy Spirit casts upon the soul? For He is so close to it that His shadows not only touch it, but unite it with these grandeurs in their shadows and splendors, so that it understands and enjoys God according to His property and measure in each of the shadows. For it understands and enjoys the divine power in the shadow of omnipotence; and it understands and enjoys the divine wisdom in the shadow of divine wisdom; and it understands and enjoys the infinite goodness in the shadow of infinite goodness which surrounds it, etc. Finally, it enjoys God's glory in the shadow of His glory, which gives knowledge of the measure and property of God's glory. All this occurs in the clear and enkindled shadows of those clear and enkindled lamps. And these lamps are within the one lamp of the undivided and simple being of God, which is actually resplendent in all these ways.

16. Oh, then, what will be the soul's experience in the knowledge and communication of that figure which Ezechiel beheld in the animal with four faces and in the wheel with four wheels? [Ez. 1:5, 15] He saw how it resembled lamps and burning coal [Ez. 1:13]; and he beheld the wheel which is God's wisdom, full of eyes, within and without, which represent the divine knowledge and the splendors of its powers [Ez. 1:18]; and he heard in his spirit the sound it made in passing, which was like the sound of a multitude, like an army, which signifies God's countless grandeurs, which the soul knows distinctly here through the sound of His passing by it only once [Ez. 1:24]; and finally the prophet enjoyed that sound of the beating of its wings, which he asserted was like the sound of many waters and of the most high God, meaning here the impetus of the divine waters. [Ez. 1:24] These waters assail the soul by the fluttering of the Holy Spirit in the flame of love, gladdening it so that

it enjoys the glory of God's glory in likeness and shadow. For this prophet also said that the vision of that animal and wheel was a likeness of the Lord's glory. [Ez. 2:1]

Who can express how elevated this happy soul feels here, how exalted, how much admired in holy beauty? Conscious of being so abundantly assailed by the waters of these divine splendors, it realizes that the eternal Father has generously granted it the upper and lower watery land, as did Axa's father in response to her sigh. [Jos. 15:17–19] For these waters irrigate both the soul and the body, that is, the higher and lower part of the soul.

17. O wonderful excellence of God! Since these lamps of the divine attributes are a simple being and are enjoyed only in Him, they are seen and enjoyed distinctly, each one as enkindled as the other, and each substantially the other. O abyss of delights! You are so much the more abundant the more Your riches are concentrated in the infinite unity and simplicity of Your unique being, where one attribute is so known and enjoyed as not to hinder the perfect knowledge and enjoyment of the other; rather, each grace and virtue within You is a light for each of Your other grandeurs. By Your purity, O divine Wisdom, many things are beheld in You through one. For You are the deposit of the Father's treasures, the splendor of the eternal light, the unspotted mirror and image of His goodness [Wis. 7:26], in whose splendors

18.   The deep caverns of feeling,

These caverns are the soul's faculties: memory, intellect, and will. They are as deep as are the boundless goods of which they are capable, since anything less than the infinite fails to fill them. From what they suffer when they are empty, we can gain some knowledge of their enjoyment and delight when they are filled with God, since one contrary sheds light on the other.

In the first place, it is noteworthy that when these caverns of the faculties are not emptied, purged, and cleansed of every affection for creature, they do not feel the vast emptiness of their deep capacity. Any little thing that adheres to them in this life is sufficient to so burden and bewitch them that they do not perceive the harm, nor note the lack of their immense goods, nor know their own capacity.

It is an amazing thing that the least of these goods is enough so to encumber these faculties, capable of infinite goods, that they cannot receive these infinite goods until they are completely empty, as we shall see. Yet when these caverns are empty and pure, the thirst, hunger, and yearning of the spiritual feeling is intolerable. Since they have deep cavities they suffer profoundly, for the food they lack, which as I say is God, is also profound.

And this feeling which is so intense commonly occurs toward the end of a man's illumination and purification, just before he reaches union, where he is then satisfied. Since the spiritual appetite is emptied and purged of every creature and affection for creatures, and since it has lost its natural quality and is adapted to the divine, and since its void is disposed, and the divine is not communicated to it in union with God, the pain of this void and the thirst is worse than death, especially when a divine ray appears vaguely as though through some crevices and is not communicated to the soul. These are the ones who suffer with impatient love, for they cannot remain long without either receiving or dying.

19. In regard to the first cavern—the intellect—its void is thirst for God. This thirst is so intense when the intellect is disposed that David compares it to the thirst of the hart. Such thirst, they say, is so vehement David could find none greater for his comparison: *As the hart pants for the fountain of waters, so does my soul long for You, O God.* [Ps. 41:2] This thirst is for the waters of God's wisdom, the object of the intellect.

20. The second cavern is the will, and the hunger of the will for God is so immense that it makes the soul faint, as David also affirms: *My soul longs and faints for the courts of the Lord.* [Ps. 83:3] This hunger is for the perfection of love after which the soul aims.

21. The third cavern is the memory, and the void of the memory is a yearning and melting away of the soul for the possession of God, as Jeremias notes: *Memoria memor ero et tabescet in me anima mea,* that is: *With the memory I will be mindful and will remember Him often, and my soul will melt within me. Thinking these things over in my heart I shall live in the hope of God.* [Lam. 3:20–21]

22. The capacity of these caverns is deep, because the object of this capacity, namely God, is profound and infinite. Thus in a certain fashion their capacity is infinite, their thirst is infinite, their hunger is also deep and infinite, and their languishing and suffering are infinite death. Although its suffering is not as intense as is the suffering of the next life, yet it is a living image of that infinite privation, since it is in a certain way disposed to receive its plenitude. This suffering, however, is of another quality because it lies within the recesses of the will's love, and love is not that which alleviates the pain, since the greater a person's love so much the more impatient he is for the possession of God, for Whom he hopes at times with intense longing.

23. Yet—may the Lord help me—since it is true that when the soul desires God fully, it then possesses Him Whom it loves, as St. Gregory affirms in commenting on St. John [*Hom. 30 in Evang.*: PL 76, 1220], how does it suffer the want of what it already possesses? In the desire which St. Peter says the angels have for the vision of the Son of God

[1 Pt. 1:12] there is no pain or anxiety because they already possess Him. The more the soul desires God the more it possesses Him, and the possession of God delights and satisfies it. Similarly the angels, in satisfying their desire, delight in possession, for their spirit is ever being filled by the object of their desire without the disgust of satiety. Since there is no disgust, they are always desiring, and they do not suffer for they have possession. As a result it seems the greater the soul's desire the greater will be its satisfaction and delight rather than its suffering and pain.

24. In this matter it is worth noting the difference between the possession of God through grace in itself and the possession of Him through union, for the one lies in loving, and the other also includes communication. The difference resembles that between betrothal and marriage.

In the espousal there is only a mutual agreement and willingness between the two, and the bridegroom graciously gives jewels and ornaments to his espoused. But in marriage there is also a communication and union between the persons. Although the bridegroom sometimes visits the bride in the espousal and brings her presents, as we said, there is no union of persons, nor does this fall within the scope of the espousal. Likewise, when the soul has reached such purity in itself and its faculties that the will is very pure and purged of other alien satisfactions and appetites in the inferior and superior parts, and has rendered its "yes" to God concerning all of this, since now God's will and the soul's are one through their own free consent, then the soul has attained the possession of God insofar as this is possible by way of the will and grace. And this means that in the "yes" of the soul, God has given the true and complete "yes" of His grace. This is a high state of spiritual espousal between the soul and the Word, in which the Bridegroom favors it and frequently pays it loving visits by which it receives intense delight.

25. Yet these delights are not comparable to those of marriage, for these are preparations for the union of marriage. Although it is true that this espousal occurs in the soul that is greatly purified of every affection for creatures—for the spiritual espousal is not wrought until this comes to pass—the soul still needs other positive preparations from God. It needs His visits and gifts by which He purifies, beautifies, and refines it further that it might be suitably prepared for so lofty a union.

This preparation takes time, for some more than for others, since God carries out this work according to the mode of the soul. This is typified in those young maidens chosen by King Assuerus. Although he had already brought them out of their countries and the house of their fathers, they had still to wait a year, even in the palace, before approaching the king's bed. For half of the year they were prepared by means of certain ointments of myrrh and other spices, and for the remaining half by other more precious ointments. After this they went to the king's bed. [Est. 2:3, 12]

26. When, during this time of the espousal and expectation of marriage, and of the anointings of the Holy Spirit, the ointments preparatory for the union with God are more sublime, the anxieties of the caverns of the soul are usually extreme and delicate. Since these ointments are a more proximate preparation for union with God (for they are more closely related to God and consequently lure the soul and make it relish Him more delicately), the desire for Him is more refined and profound —and the desire for God is the preparation for union with Him.

27. Oh, what an excellent place this is to advise souls on whom God bestows these delicate unctions to watch what they are doing, and into Whose hands they are committing themselves, that they might not turn back! This does not pertain to our subject, yet the compassion and grief that comes to my heart in seeing souls fall back (not only by hindering the anointings so that there can be no progress in these unctions, but even by losing their effects) is so great that I do not think it improper here to warn them about what they should do to avoid such harm. Even though we may be somewhat detained before returning to our subject, for I plan to return to it soon, this will all help toward an understanding of the property of these caverns. Since this advice is very necessary, not only for all those who advance so prosperously, but also for all others who seek their Beloved, I want to discuss it.

28. In the first place it should be known that if a person is seeking God, his Beloved is seeking him much more. And if a soul directs to God its loving desires, which are as fragrant to Him as the pillar of smoke rising from the aromatic spices of myrrh and incense [Ct. 3:6], God sends it the fragrance of His ointments by which He draws it and makes it run after Him [Ct. 1:3], and these are His divine inspirations and touches. As often as these inspirations and touches are His, they are always bound and regulated by the perfection of His law and of faith. It is by means of this perfection that a person must always draw closer to Him. Thus it should be understood that the desire for Himself which God grants in all His favors of unguents and fragrant anointings is a preparation for other more precious and delicate ointments, made more according to the quality of God, until the soul is so delicately and purely prepared that it merits union with Him and substantial transformation in all its faculties.

29. The soul, then, should advert that God is the principal agent in this matter, and that He acts as the blind man's guide who must lead it by the hand to the place it does not know how to reach (to supernatural things of which neither its intellect, will, nor memory can know the

nature). It should use all its principal care in watching so as not to place any obstacle in the way of its guide on this road that God has ordained for it according to the perfection of His law and of the faith, as we said.

And it can cause this obstacle by allowing itself to be guided by another blind man. There are three blind men who can draw it off the road: the spiritual director, the devil, and the soul itself. That the soul may understand how this happens, we shall briefly discuss each of these blind men.

30. As regards the first, it is very important that a person, desiring to advance in recollection and perfection, take care into whose hands he entrusts himself, for the disciple will become like the master, and as is the father so will be the son. Let him realize that for this journey, especially its most sublime parts (and even for the intermediate parts), he will hardly find a guide accomplished as to all his needs, for besides being learned and discreet, a director should have experience. Although the foundation for guiding a soul to spirit is knowledge and discretion, the director will not succeed in leading the soul onward in it, when God bestows it, nor will he even understand it, if he has no experience of what true and pure spirit is.

31. As a result, many spiritual directors cause great harm to a number of souls, because, in not understanding the ways and properties of the spirit, they ordinarily make them lose the unction of these delicate ointments, with which the Holy Spirit anoints and prepares them for Himself, and they instruct them in other baser ways, serviceable only to beginners, which they themselves have used or read of somewhere. Knowing no more than what pertains to beginners—and please God they would even know this much—they do not wish to permit souls to pass beyond these beginnings and these discursive and imaginative ways (even though God may desire to lead them on). Thus they do not let them go beyond their natural capacity, but through their natural capacity souls cannot make much progress.

32. For a better understanding of this beginners' stage, it should be known that the practice of beginners is to meditate and make acts and discursive reflection with the imagination. A person in this state should be given matter for meditation and discursive reflection, and he should by himself make interior acts and profit in spiritual things from the delight and satisfaction of the senses. For by being fed with the relish of spiritual things, the appetite is torn away from sensual things and weakened in regard to the things of the world.

But when the appetite has been fed somewhat, and has become in a certain fashion accustomed to spiritual things, and has acquired some fortitude and constancy, God begins to wean the soul, as they say, and place it in the state of contemplation. This occurs in some persons after a very short time, especially with religious, for in denying the things of the world more quickly, they accommodate their senses and appetites to God and, in their activity, pass on to the spirit which God works in them. This happens when the soul's discursive acts and meditations cease, as well as its initial sensible satisfaction and fervor, and it is unable to practice discursive meditation as before, or find any support for the senses. The sensory part is left in dryness because its riches are transferred to the spirit, which does not pertain to the senses.

Since the soul cannot function naturally except by means of the senses, it is God who in this state is the agent, and the soul is the receiver. The soul conducts itself only as the receiver and as one in whom something is being done; God is the giver and the one Who works in it, by according spiritual goods in contemplation (which is knowledge and love together, that is, loving knowledge), without the soul's natural acts and discursive reflections, for it can no longer engage in these acts as before.

33. Hence a person at this time should be guided in a manner entirely contrary to the former. If, prior to this, directors suggested matter for meditation, and he meditated, now they should instead withhold this matter, and he should not meditate. For, as I say, he is unable to do so even though he may want to, and were he to try he would be distracted instead of recollected. If previously he sought satisfaction, love, and devotion, and found it, now he should neither desire nor seek it, for not only does he fail to procure it through his own diligence, but on the contrary he procures dryness. Through the activity he desires to carry on with the senses, he diverts himself from the peaceful and quiet good secretly being given to his spirit. In losing the one good, he does not gain the other, for these goods are no longer accorded through the senses as before.

Therefore directors should not impose meditation upon persons in this state, nor should they oblige them to make acts or strive for satisfaction and fervor. Such activity would place an obstacle in the path of the principal agent Who, as I say, is God, Who secretly and quietly inserts in the soul loving wisdom and knowledge, without specified acts; although sometimes He makes specific ones in the soul for a certain length of time. Thus the individual also should proceed only with a loving attention to God, without making specific acts. He should conduct himself passively, as we have said, without efforts of his own, but with the simple, loving awareness, as a person who opens his eyes with loving attention.

34. Since God, then, as the giver communes with him through a simple, loving knowledge, the individual also, as the receiver, communes with

God, through a simple and loving knowledge or attention, so that knowledge is thus joined with knowledge and love with love. The receiver should act according to the mode of what is received, and not otherwise, in order to receive and keep it in the way it is given. For as the philosophers say: Whatever is received is received according to the mode of the receiver.

It is obvious that if a person does not lay aside his natural active manner, he will not receive that good except in a natural manner, and thus he will not receive it but will remain only with his natural act. For the supernatural does not fit into the natural, nor does it have anything to do with it. If a person should, then, desire to act on his own through an attitude different from the passive loving attention we mentioned, in which he would remain very passive and tranquil without making any act, unless God would unite Himself with him in some act, he would utterly hinder the goods God communicates supernaturally to him in the loving knowledge. This loving knowledge is communicated in the beginning through the exercise of interior purgation, in which the individual suffers, as we said, and afterwards in the delight of love.

If as I say—and it is true—this loving knowledge is received passively in the soul according to the supernatural mode of God, and not according to the natural mode of the soul, a person, if he wants to receive it, should be very annihilated in his natural operations, unhampered, idle, quiet, peaceful, and serene, according to the mode of God. The more the air is cleansed of vapors, and the quieter and more simple it is, the more the sun illumines and warms it. A person should not bear attachment to anything, neither to the practice of meditation, nor to any savor, whether sensory or spiritual, nor to any other apprehensions. He should be very free and annihilated regarding all things, because any thought or discursive reflection or satisfaction upon which he may want to lean would impede and disquiet him, and make noise in the profound silence of his senses and his spirit, which he possesses for the sake of this deep and delicate listening. God speaks to the heart in this solitude, which he mentioned through Osee [Os. 2:14], in supreme peace and tranquillity, while the soul listens, like David, to what the Lord God speaks to it [Ps. 84:9], for He speaks this peace in this solitude.

35. When it happens, therefore, that a person is conscious in this manner of being placed in solitude and in the state of listening, he should even forget the practice of loving attentiveness I mentioned so as to remain free for what the Lord then desires of him. He should make use of that loving awareness only when he does not feel himself placed in this solitude, or inner idleness or oblivion or spiritual listening. That he may recognize it, it always comes to pass with a certain peace and calm and inward absorption.

36. Once a person has begun to enter this simple and idle state of contemplation, which comes about when he can no longer meditate, he should not at any time or season engage in meditations or look for support in spiritual savor or satisfaction, but stand upright on his own feet, with his spirit completely detached from everything, as Habacuc declared he was obliged to do in order to hear what God spoke to him: *I will stand on my watch and fix my foot upon my fortress, and I will contemplate what is said to me.* [Hb. 2:1] This is like saying: I will raise my mind above all activity and knowledge belonging to my senses and what they can retain, leaving all below, and will fix the foot of the fortress (my faculties), not allowing these faculties to advance a step as regards their own operation that they may receive through contemplation what God communicates to me; for we have already asserted that pure contemplation lies in receiving.

37. It is impossible for this highest wisdom and language of God, which is contemplation, to be received in anything less than a spirit that is silent and detached from discursive knowledge and gratification. Isaias speaks of it in these words: *Whom shall he teach knowledge and whom will God make understand the hearing?* And Isaias replies: *Them that are weaned from the milk* (that is from satisfaction) *and drawn away from the breasts* (from particular knowledge and apprehensions). [Is. 28:9]

38. Wipe away, O spiritual soul, the dust, the hairs, and the stains, and cleanse your eye, and the bright sun will illumine you, and you will see clearly. Pacify the soul, draw it out and liberate it from the yoke and slavery of its own weak operation, which is the captivity of Egypt (amounting to not much more than the gathering of straws for the baking of bricks). And, O spiritual master, guide it to the land of promise flowing with milk and honey. Behold that for this holy liberty and idleness of the sons of God, God calls the soul to the desert, in which it journeys festively clothed and adorned with gold and silver jewels, since it has now left Egypt and been despoiled of its riches, which is the sensory part. Not only this, but the Egyptians are drowned in the sea of contemplation, where the Egyptian of sense, not finding a foothold or some support, drowns and thereby frees the son of God, which is the spirit that has emerged from the narrow limits and slavery of the operation of the senses, from its little understanding, its base feeling, and its poor way of loving and being satisfied, that God may give it the sweet manna. Although this manna has all these tastes and savors with which you desire the soul to be occupied through its own labor, nonetheless, since it is so delicate it melts in one's mouth, it will not be tasted if mingled with some other taste or some other thing.

When a person approaches this state, strive that he become detached from all satisfaction, relish, pleasure, and spiritual meditations, and do not disquiet him with cares or solicitude concerning heavenly things, and still less earthly things. Bring him to as complete a withdrawal and solitude as possible, for the more solitude he obtains and the nearer he approaches this idle tranquillity, the more abundantly will the spirit of divine wisdom be infused into his soul. This wisdom is loving, tranquil, solitary, peaceful, mild, and an inebriator of the spirit, by which the soul feels tenderly and gently wounded and carried away, without knowing by whom, nor from where, nor how. The reason is that this wisdom is communicated without the soul's own activity.

39. And a little of this that God works in the soul in this holy idleness and solitude is an inestimable good, a good much greater at times than a person or his director can imagine. And although one is not always so clearly conscious of it, it will in due time shed its light. The least that a person can manage to feel is a withdrawal and an estrangement as to all things, sometimes more than at other times, accompanied by an inclination toward solitude and a weariness with all creatures and with the world, in the gentle breathing of love and life in the spirit. Wherefore everything unincluded in this estrangement becomes distasteful, for, as they say, once the spirit has tasted, all flesh becomes bitter.

40. Yet the blessings this silent communication and contemplation impresses on the soul, without its then experiencing them, are, as I say, inestimable. For they are most hidden unctions of the Holy Spirit and hence most delicate, and they secretly fill the soul with spiritual riches, gifts, and graces; since it is God who grants them, He does so in no other manner than as God.

41. Because of the refined quality and purity of these delicate and sublime anointings and shadings of the Holy Spirit, neither the soul nor its director understand them; only He who bestows them in order to be more pleased with the soul comprehends them. A person can with the greatest ease disturb and hinder these anointings by no more than the least act he may desire of his memory, intellect, or will, or by making use of his senses, appetite, knowledge, or his own satisfaction and pleasure. This is all seriously harmful and a great sorrow and pity.

42. Oh, it is a serious and regrettable situation that even though this interference with these holy unctions seems to cause hardly any damage at all, the harm done is greater and worthy of deeper sorrow and compassion than the harm done in the disturbance and ruin of many other ordinary souls, not in the position to receive such sublime adornment and shading! Were a portrait of extremely delicate workmanship touched over with dull and harsh colors by an unpolished hand, the destruction would be worse, more noticeable, and a greater pity than if many other

portraits of less artistry were effaced. Who will succeed in repairing that delicate painting of the Holy Spirit once it is marred by a coarse hand?

43. Although this damage is beyond anything imaginable, it is so common and frequent that scarcely any spiritual director will be found who does not cause it in souls God is beginning to recollect in this manner of contemplation. How often is God anointing a contemplative with some very delicate unguent of loving knowledge, serene, peaceful, solitary, and far withdrawn from the senses and what is imaginable, as a result of which this person cannot meditate, nor reflect on anything, nor enjoy anything heavenly or earthly (since God has engaged him in that lonely idleness and given him the inclination to solitude), when a spiritual director will happen along who, like a blacksmith, knows no more than how to hammer and pound with the faculties. Since hammering with the faculties is this director's only teaching, and he knows no more than how to meditate, he will say: "Come, now, lay aside these rest periods, which amount to idleness and a waste of time; take and meditate and make interior acts, for it is necessary that you do your part; this other method is the way of illusions and typical of fools."

44. Thus, not understanding the stages of prayer nor the ways of the spirit, these directors are not aware that those acts they say the soul should make, and the discursive reflection they want it to practice, are already accomplished, since the soul has already reached the negation and silence of the senses and of meditation and has come to the way of the spirit, which is contemplation. In contemplation the activity of the senses and of discursive reflection terminates, and God alone is the agent and one Who then speaks secretly to the solitary and silent soul. These directors fail to observe that if they want to make a person, who in this fashion has attained to spirit, still walk the path of the senses, that person will turn back and become distracted. If anyone who has reached the end of his journey continues to walk in order to reach the end, he will necessarily move away from that end, besides doing something ridiculous.

Once an individual, through the activity of his faculties, has reached the quiet recollection which every spiritual person pursues, in which the functioning of these faculties ceases, it would not merely be useless to repeat the acts of these same faculties in order to attain to this recollection, but it would be harmful, for, in abandoning the recollection he already possesses, he would become distracted.

45. Since these spiritual directors do not understand what recollection and spiritual solitude is, nor its properties (in which solitude God infixes these sublime unctions in the soul), they superpose or interpose anointings from a lower spiritual exercise, which is the soul's activity, as we

said. There is as much difference between what the soul does itself and
what it receives from God as there is between a human work and a divine
work, between the natural and the supernatural. In the one, God works
supernaturally in the soul, and in the other, the soul only works naturally.
What is worse is that by the activity of his natural operations a person
loses inner solitude and recollection and, consequently, the sublime image
God was painting within him. Thus all his efforts are like hammering the
horseshoe instead of the nail, and on the one hand he does harm, and on
the other hand he receives no profit.

46. These directors should reflect that they themselves are not the chief
agent, guide, and mover of souls in this matter, but that the principal
guide is the Holy Spirit, Who is never neglectful of souls, and that they
are instruments for directing them to perfection through faith and the
law of God, according to the spirit God gives each one.

Thus the director's whole concern should not be to accommodate souls
to his own method and condition, but he should observe the road along
which God is leading them, and if he does not recognize it, he should
leave them alone and not bother them. And in harmony with the path
and spirit along which God leads them, the spiritual director should
strive to conduct them into greater solitude, tranquillity, and freedom of
spirit. He should give them latitude so that when God introduces them
into this solitude they do not bind their corporal or spiritual faculties
to some particular object, interior or exterior, and do not become anxious
or afflicted with the thought that nothing is being done. Even though the
soul is not then doing anything, God is doing something in it.

Directors should strive to disencumber the soul and bring it into solitude and idleness so that it may not be tied to any particular knowledge,
earthly or heavenly, or to any covetousness for some satisfaction or
pleasure, or to any other apprehension, in such a way that it may be
empty, through the pure negation of every creature, and placed in spiritual poverty. This is what the soul must do of itself, as the Son of God
counsels: *He who does not renounce all that he possesses cannot be my
disciple.* [Lk. 14:33] This counsel refers not only to the renunciation according to the will of all corporal and temporal things, but also to the
dispossession of spiritual things, which includes spiritual poverty, to
which the Son of God ascribes beatitude. [Mt. 5:3]

When the soul frees itself of all things and attains to emptiness and
dispossession concerning them, which is equivalent to what it can do of
itself, it is impossible that God fail to do His part by communicating Himself to it, at least silently and secretly. It is more impossible than it
would be for the sun not to shine on clear and uncluttered ground. As the
sun rises in the morning and shines upon your house so that its light
may enter if you open the shutters, so God, who in watching over Israel

does not doze [Ps. 120:4], nor still less sleep, will enter the soul that is empty, and fill it with divine goods.

47. God, like the sun, stands above souls ready to communicate Himself. Let directors be content with disposing them for this according to evangelical perfection, which lies in nakedness and emptiness of sense and spirit; and let them not desire to go any further than this in building, since that function belongs only to the Father of lights from whom descends every good and perfect gift. [Jas. 1:17] *If the Lord,* as David says, *does not build the house, he labors in vain who builds it.* [Ps. 126:1] And since He is the supernatural artificer, He will construct supernaturally in each soul the edifice He desires, if you, director, will prepare it by striving to annihilate it in its natural operations and affections, which have neither the ability nor strength to build the supernatural edifice. The natural operations and affections at this time rather impede than help. It is your duty to prepare the soul, and God's office, as the Wise Man says, is to direct its path [Prv. 16:1, 9], that is, toward supernatural goods, through modes and ways understandable to neither you nor the soul.

Do not say, therefore: "Oh, the soul does not advance, because it is not doing anything." For if it is true that it is not doing anything, I shall prove to you that it is accomplishing a great deal by doing nothing. If the intellect empties itself of particular knowledge, natural or spiritual, it advances, and the freer it becomes of particular knowledge and acts of understanding, the further it advances in its journey toward the supreme, supernatural Good.

48. "Oh," you will say, "it doesn't understand anything in particular, and thus will be unable to make progress."

I reply that, quite the contrary, if it would have particular knowledge, it would not advance. The reason is that God transcends the intellect and is incomprehensible and inaccessible to it. Hence while the intellect is understanding, it is not approaching God but withdrawing from Him. It must withdraw from itself and from its knowledge so as to journey to God in faith, by believing and not understanding. In this way it reaches perfection, because it is joined to God by faith and not by any other means, and it reaches God more by not understanding than by understanding.

Do not be disturbed on this account; if the intellect does not turn back (which it would do if it were to desire to be occupied with particular knowledge and other discursive reflections), but desires to remain in idleness, it advances. It thereby empties itself of everything comprehensible to it, because none of that is God; as we have said, God does not fit in an occupied heart. In this matter of striving for perfection, not to turn back is to go forward, and the intellect goes forward by establishing itself more in faith, and thus advances by darkening itself, for faith is darkness to the intellect. Since the intellect cannot understand the nature of God, it must journey in submission to Him rather than by understanding, and thus it advances by not understanding. For its own well-being, the intellect should be doing what you condemn, that is, it should avoid busying itself with particular knowledge, for it cannot reach God through this knowledge, which would rather hinder it in its advance toward Him.

49. "Oh," you will say, "when the intellect does not understand particular things, the will is idle and does not love (something that must always be avoided on the spiritual road), because the will can only love what the intellect understands."

This is true, especially in the natural operations and acts of the soul, in which the will does not love except what the intellect understands distinctly. But in the contemplation we are discussing (by which God infuses Himself into the soul), particular knowledge as well as acts made by the soul are unnecessary, because God in one act is communicating light and love together, which is loving supernatural knowledge. We can assert that this knowledge is like light which transmits heat, for that light also enkindles love. This knowledge is general and dark to the intellect because it is contemplative knowledge, which is a ray of darkness for the intellect, as St. Dionysius teaches. [Pseudo-Dionysius Areopagita, *De Mystica Theologia*, c. 1: PL 3, 999]

Love is therefore present in the will in the manner that knowledge is present in the intellect. Just as this knowledge God infuses in the intellect is general and dark, devoid of particular understanding, the love in the will is also general, without any clarity arising from particular understanding. Since God is divine light and love in His communication of Himself to the soul, He equally informs these two faculties (intellect and will) with knowledge and love. Since God is unintelligible in this life, knowledge of Him is dark, as I say, and the love present in the will is fashioned after this knowledge.

Yet sometimes in this delicate communication, God wounds and communicates Himself to one faculty more than to the other; sometimes more knowledge is experienced than love, and at other times more love than knowledge, and likewise at times all knowledge is felt without any love, or all love without any knowledge.

Wherefore, I say that when the soul makes natural acts with the intellect, it cannot love without understanding. But in the acts God produces and infuses in it, as He does in these souls, there is a difference; God can communicate to one faculty and not to the other. He can inflame the will with a touch of the warmth of His love even though the intellect does not understand, just as a man can feel warmth from a fire without seeing it.

50. The will often feels enkindled or tenderly moved or captivated without knowing how or understanding anything more particularly than before, since God is ordaining love in it; as the bride declares in the Canticle: *The king brought me into the wine cellar and set in order charity in me.* [Ct. 2:4]

There is no reason to fear idleness of the will in this situation. If the will stops making acts of love on its own and in regard to particular knowledge, God makes them in it, inebriating it secretly with infused love, either by means of the knowledge of contemplation or without it, as we just said. These acts are much more delightful and meritorious than the acts the soul makes on its own, just as God, Who moves it and infuses this love, is much better.

51. God infuses this love in the will when it is empty and detached from other particular, earthly or heavenly pleasures and affections. Take care, then, to empty the will of its affections and detach it from them. If it does not retrogress through the desire for some satisfaction or pleasure, it advances, even though it experiences nothing particular in God, by ascending above all things to Him. Although it does not enjoy God very particularly and distinctly, nor love Him in so clear an act, it does enjoy Him obscurely and secretly in that general infusion more than it does all particular things, for it then sees clearly that nothing satisfies it as much as that solitary quietude. And it loves Him above all lovable things, since it has rejected all the gratifications and pleasures of these things, and they have become distasteful to it.

One, therefore, should not be disturbed, for if the will cannot dwell upon the satisfactions and pleasures of particular acts, it makes progress. For by not turning back in the embrace of something sensible, it goes forward to the inaccessible, which is God; and so it is no wonder if it does not feel Him.

To journey to God, the will must walk in detachment from every pleasant thing, rather than in attachment to it. It thus carries out well the commandment of love, which is to love God above all things; this cannot be done without nakedness and emptiness concerning them all.

52. Neither should there be any fear because the memory is void of forms and figures. Since God is formless and figureless, the memory walks safely when empty of form and figure, and it draws closer to God. The more it leans on the imagination, the farther away it moves from God and the more serious is its danger; for in being what He is—unimaginable—God cannot be grasped by the imagination.

53. These spiritual directors, not understanding souls that tread the path of quiet and solitary contemplation, since they themselves have

not reached it and do not know what it is to part with discursive meditation, think these souls are idle. They hinder them and hamper the peace
of restful and quiet contemplation, which God of His own was according
them, by making them walk along the path of meditation and imaginative
reflection and perform interior acts. In doing this, these souls find great
repugnance, dryness, and distraction; they would want to remain in their
holy idleness and quiet and peaceful recollection. Since the senses find
nothing to be attached to, to take pleasure in, or do in this recollection,
these directors also persuade souls to strive for satisfaction and feelings
of fervor when they should be counseling the opposite. When these persons cannot accomplish this as before, because the time for such activity
has passed and this is not their road, they grow doubly disquieted, thinking that they are lost. Their directors foster this belief in them, cause
them aridity of spirit, and deprive them of the precious anointings God
was bestowing on them in solitude and tranquillity. These directors do
them serious harm, as I said, bringing them grief and ruin, for on the
one hand such persons lose ground, and on the other hand they suffer a
useless affliction.

54. These directors do not know what spirit is. They do a great injury
to God and show disrespect toward Him by intruding with a rough hand
where He is working. It cost God a great deal to bring these souls to
this stage, and He highly values His work of having introduced them
into this solitude and emptiness regarding their faculties and activity so
that He might speak to their hearts, which is what He always desires.
Since He it is Who now reigns in the soul with an abundance of peace
and calm, He takes the initiative Himself by making the natural acts
of the faculties fail, by which the soul laboring the whole night accomplished nothing [Lk. 5:5]; and He feeds the spirit without the activity of
the senses because neither the sense nor its function is capable of spirit.

55. The extent to which He values this tranquillity and sleep or annihilation of sense, is clear in the entreaty, so notable and efficacious, which
He made in the Canticle: *I adjure you, daughters of Jerusalem, by the
roes and the harts of the fields that you stir not up nor awaken my beloved until she please.* [Ct. 3:5] He hereby indicates how much He loves
solitary sleep and forgetfulness, for He compares it to these animals that
are so retiring and withdrawn. Yet these directors do not want the soul
to rest and remain quiet, but want it always to labor and work, so that
consequently it does not allow room for God's work and ruins and ef-
faces through its own activity what He is doing. These operations of the
soul are like the little foxes that destroy the flourishing vineyard of the
soul [Ct. 2:15], and the Lord complains of them through Isaias: *You
have devoured My vineyard.* [Is. 3:14]

56. Perhaps in their zeal these directors err with good will because they do not know any better. Not for this reason, however, should they be excused for the counsels they give rashly, without first understanding the road and spirit a person may be following, and for rudely meddling in something they do not understand, instead of leaving the matter to one who does understand. It is no light matter or fault to cause a person to lose inestimable goods and sometimes to do him veritable harm through temerarious counsel.

Thus he who recklessly errs will not escape a punishment corresponding to the harm he caused, for he was obliged, as is everyone, to perform the duties of his office well and not be mistaken. The affairs of God must be handled with great tact and with open eyes, especially in so vital and sublime a matter as is that of these souls, where there is at stake almost an infinite gain in being right and almost an infinite loss in being wrong.

57. Since, however, you insist that you have some excuse, although I do not see it, at least you cannot hold that he has an excuse who in guiding a soul never lets it out of his hands on account of vain considerations of which he is aware. Such a director will not escape punishment for these considerations. For it is certain that since that soul must always advance along the spiritual road, on which God is always a help to it, it will have to change its style and mode of prayer and will need another doctrine more sublime than yours and another spirituality. Not everyone knows all the happenings and stages of the spiritual journey, nor is everyone spiritually so perfect as to know every state of the interior life in which a person must be conducted and guided. At least the director should not think that he has all the requirements, or that God will not want to lead the soul further on.

Not everyone capable of hewing the wood knows how to carve the statue, nor does everyone able to carve know how to perfect and polish the work, nor do all who know how to polish know how to paint it, nor do all who can paint it know how to put the finishing touches on it and bring the work to completion. No man can do more with the statue than what he knows how to do, and were he to try to do more than this, he would ruin it.

58. Let us see, then: If you are only a hewer, which lies in guiding the soul to contempt of the world and to mortification of its appetites, or a good carver, which consists in introducing it to holy meditations, and know no more, how can you lead this soul to the ultimate perfection of delicate painting, which no longer requires hewing or carving or even relievo work, but the work that God must do in it?

It is certain that if you ever bind it to your teaching, which is always of one kind, it will either backslide or fail to advance. What, I ask, will the statue look like if all you do is hammer and hew, which, in the case of the soul, is the active use of the faculties? When will the statue be complete? When or how will it be left for God to paint? Is it possible that all these functions are yours and that you are so perfect the soul will never need any other than you?

59. Granted that you may possess the requisites for the full direction of some soul (for perhaps it does not have the talent to make progress), it is impossible for you to have the qualities demanded for the guidance of all those you refuse to allow out of your hands. God leads each one along different paths so that hardly one spirit will be found like another in even half its method of procedure. For who is there who would think that, like St. Paul, he could make himself all things to all men so as to win them all? [1 Cor. 9:22] You tyrannize souls and deprive them of their freedom, and judge for yourself the breadth of the evangelical doctrine. Not only, therefore, do you endeavor to hold on to your penitents, but, what is worse, if by chance you learn that one of them has consulted another (for perhaps you were not the suitable one to consult, or God led him to this other person that he might learn what you did not teach), what is worse you treat him—and I am ashamed to say it—with the very jealous quarrelsomeness we find among married couples. And this is not jealousy for the glory of God, but a jealousy motivated by your own pride and presumption or some other imperfection, for you should not assume that in turning from you this person turned from God.

60. God becomes extremely indignant with such directors and in Ezechiel promises them chastisement: *You ate the milk of my flock and you covered yourself with their wool and did not feed my flock; I will,* He says, *seek my flock at your hand.* [Ez. 34:3, 10]

61. Spiritual directors, then, should give freedom to souls and encourage them in their desire to seek improvement. The director does not know the means by which God may wish to benefit a soul, especially if it is no longer satisfied with the director's teaching. This dissatisfaction in fact is a sign that the director is not helping it, either because God is making it advance by a road different from the one along which he is leading it, or because the director himself has changed his style. These directors should themselves counsel this change, and all the rest stems from foolish pride and presumption or some other ambition.

62. Let us leave aside our discussion of this attitude and speak of another more pestiferous trait of these directors or of other worse methods they use. It will happen that God is anointing some souls with the unctions of holy desires and motives for renouncing the world, changing their way of life, and serving Him, with contempt of the world (and God esteems this stage to which He has brought them, because worldly

things do not please Him), when these directors, by their human rationalizations or reflections, singularly contrary to the doctrine of Christ and His humility and contempt for all things, and by depending on their own interests or satisfactions, or out of fear where there is no reason to fear, either make matters difficult for these souls, or cause them to delay, or even worse try to make them put the thought from their minds. With a spirit not too devout, with little of Christ's meekness, and fully clothed in worldliness, since they do not enter by the narrow gate of life, these directors do not let others enter either. Our Lord threatens them through St. Luke: *Woe to you, for you have taken away the key of knowledge and you neither enter yourselves nor do you allow others to enter.* [Lk. 11:52]

These directors are indeed like barriers or obstacles at the gate of heaven, hindering those who seek their counsel from entering. They know that God has commanded them not only to allow and help souls enter but even to compel them to enter, when He says through St. Luke: *Compel them to enter that my house may be filled with guests.* [Lk. 14:23] But they, on the contrary, compel them to stay out.

The director may thus be an obstacle to the guidance of the Holy Spirit. We discover this to be the case with spiritual directors in the many ways we mentioned, in which some are aware of it and others are unaware. But both will be punished; since this is their duty, they are obliged to be careful and understand what they are doing.

63. The second blind man who, we said, was capable of thwarting the soul in this kind of recollection is the devil; being blind himself, he desires that the soul be blind too. When the soul is in the loftiest solitudes, receiving insofar as it is alone, despoiled, and withdrawn from every creature and trace of creature, the infusion of the delicate unctions of the Holy Spirit, the devil, with great sadness and envy, seeing that the soul is not only enriched but flying along at such a pace that he cannot catch it in anything, strives to intrude in this withdrawal with some clouds of knowledge and sensible satisfaction. This knowledge and satisfaction he gives is sometimes good, so that he may feed the soul more and make it revert to particular things and the work of the senses, and make it turn thus to this good knowledge and satisfaction, embrace it, and journey to God leaning upon it.

He consequently distracts it very easily and draws it out of that solitude and recollection in which, as we said, the Holy Spirit secretly produces those grandeurs. Since of himself a person is inclined toward feeling and tasting, especially if he is seeking something and does not understand the road he is traveling, he easily grows attached to the knowledge and satisfaction provided by the devil and loses the solitude God was providing. Since in that solitude and quiet of the faculties, the soul was doing nothing, it seems that this way is better because it is now doing something.

It is a great pity that, in not understanding itself, and for the sake of eating a morsel of particular knowledge and satisfaction, the soul impedes God from partaking of it entirely, which God does in that solitude where He places it, since He absorbs it in Himself by means of those solitary spiritual anointings.

64. With little more than nothing the devil causes the gravest harm. He makes the soul lose abundant riches by alluring it with a little bait —as one would allure a fish—out of the simple waters of the spirit, where it was engulfed and swallowed up in God without finding any bottom or foothold. And by this bait he provides it with a prop and drags it ashore so that it might find the ground and go on foot with great effort, rather than swim in the unctions of God, in the waters of Siloe that flow in silence. [Is. 8:6]

The devil considers this so important that it is worth noting that, since he accomplishes more through a little harm caused in these souls than by great damage effected in many others, as we have mentioned, there is hardly anyone walking this path upon whom he does not bring serious harm and loss. This evil one establishes himself cautiously at the passageway from sense to spirit, deceiving souls and feeding the sensory part itself, as we said, with sensible things. The soul does not think there is any loss in this, and thus fails to enter into the inner dwelling of the Spouse, and remains at the threshold to watch what is happening outside in the sensory part. *The devil sees every high thing,* says Job [Jb. 41:25], that is, every spiritual height of souls in order to combat them. If, possibly, some soul enters a sublime recollection in such fashion that the devil cannot distract it in the way we mentioned, he struggles to make it advert to sense at least through horrors, fears, or bodily pains, or exterior sounds and noises, and thereby draw it out and divert it from the interior spirit, until being able to do no more he leaves it.

But it is so easy for him to thwart and block the riches of these precious souls that even though he values this more than the downthrow of many others, he still does not esteem it highly because of the ease in which he accomplishes it and the little it costs him.

We can in this sense interpret God's words to Job about him: *He will absorb a river and not wonder and he trusts that the Jordan will run into his mouth,* which refers to the highest matters of perfection. *In his eyes as with a hook he will catch him and with awls pierce his nostrils* [Jb. 40:18–19], that is, with the points of the knowledge by which he is wounding it, he will divert the spirit; for the air that rushes out of the recollected nostrils that are pierced is scattered in many parts. And further on He says: *The rays of the sun will be under him and gold will be strewn under him like mire* [Jb. 41:21], for the devil causes illumined souls to lose wonderful rays of divine knowledge and seizes and scatters the precious gold of the divine embellishments.

65. Oh, then, souls, when God is according you such sovereign favors as to lead you by the state of solitude and recollection, withdrawing you from the labors of the senses, do not revert to the senses. Abandon your activity, for if this helped you, when you were beginners, to deny the world and yourselves, now that God favors you by being Himself the agent, it is a serious obstacle. God will feed you with heavenly refreshment since you do not apply your faculties to anything, nor encumber them, but detach them from everything, which is all you yourself have to do (besides the simple loving attentiveness in the way I mentioned above, that is, when you feel no aversion toward it). You should not use any force, except to detach the soul and liberate it, so as not to alter its peace and tranquillity.

66. The third blind man is the soul which, by not understanding itself, disturbs and harms itself. Since it only knows how to act by means of the senses and discursive reflection, it thinks it is doing nothing when God introduces it into that emptiness and solitude where it is unable to use the faculties and make acts, and as a result it strains to perform these acts. The soul, therefore, that was enjoying the idleness of spiritual peace and silence, in which God was secretly adorning it, is distracted and filled with dryness and displeasure.

It will happen that while God persists in keeping the soul in that silent quietude, it persists in its desire to act through its own efforts with the intellect and the imagination. It resembles a child who kicks and cries in order to walk when his mother wants to carry him, and thus neither allows his mother to make any headway nor makes any himself; or it resembles one who moves a painting back and forth while the artist is at work so that either nothing is accomplished or the painting is damaged.

67. A person should take note that even though he does not seem to be making any progress in this quietude or doing anything, he is advancing much faster than if he were treading along on foot, for God is carrying him. Although he is walking at God's pace, he does not feel this pace. Even though he does no work with his faculties, he achieves much more than if he did, for God is the agent.

It is no wonder if he does not advert to this, for the senses do not attain to what God effects in the soul at this time. As the Wise Man says: *The words of wisdom are heard in silence.* [Eccl. 9:17]

A soul, then, should abandon itself into God's hands and not its own, nor those of the other two blind men; for, insofar as it abandons itself to God and does not apply its faculties to anything, it will advance securely.

68. Let us return now to the subject of these deep caverns of the faculties of the soul, in which, we said, its suffering is usually intense when God is anointing and disposing it with the sublimest unctions of the Holy Spirit for union with Himself. These anointings are so subtle and delicate that, in penetrating the intimate substance of the soul's depths, they prepare it and give it such savor that the suffering and the fainting of desire in the tremendous void of these caverns is immense.

Hence, if the anointings which prepare these caverns of the soul for the union of the spiritual marriage with God are so sublime, what will be the possession of knowledge, love, and glory of the intellect, will, and memory in this union with God? Certainly the satisfaction, fullness, and delight of these caverns will then correspond to their former hunger and thirst. And the excellence of the soul's possession and the fruition of its senses will be in conformity with the delicacy of the preparations.

69. By the feeling of the soul, the verse refers to the power and strength that the substance of the soul has for feeling and enjoying the objects of the spiritual faculties; through these faculties a person tastes the wisdom and love and communication of God. The soul here calls these three faculties (memory, intellect, and will) the deep caverns of feeling because through them and in them it deeply experiences and enjoys the grandeurs of God's wisdom and excellence. It very appropriately calls them the deep caverns of feeling because, since it feels that the deep knowledge and splendors of the lamps of fire fit into them, it knows that its capacity and recesses correspond to the particular things it receives from the knowledge, savor, joy, delight, etc., of God. All these things are received and seated in this feeling of the soul which, as I say, is its power and capacity for experiencing, possessing, and tasting them all. And the caverns of the faculties administer them to it, just as the bodily senses go to assist the common sense of the phantasy with the forms of their objects, and this common sense becomes the receptacle and archives of these forms. Hence this common sense or feeling of the soul, which has become the receptacle or archives of God's grandeurs, is illumined and enriched according to what it attains of this high and enlightened possession.

70.   Once obscure and blind,
That is, before God enlightened and illumined it. To understand this it should be known that there are two reasons why the sense of sight loses its power of vision: either because of obscurity or because of blindness.

God is the light and the object of the soul, and when this light does not illumine it, the soul dwells in obscurity even though it may have very excellent vision. When it is in sin or occupies its appetites with other things, then it is blind. And even though God's light may shine upon it, it does not see its obscureness, which is its ignorance, because it is blind. Before God illumined it by means of this transformation, it was in obscurity and ignorant of so many of God's goods, as the Wise Man says he was before wisdom enlightened him: *He shed light on my ignorance.* [Ecclus. 51:26]

71. Spiritually speaking, it is one thing to be in obscurity and another to be in darkness. To be in darkness, as we have said, is to be blind in sin. Yet one can be in obscurity without being in sin, and this doubly: regarding the natural, not having light or knowledge about certain natural things; and regarding the supernatural, not having light or knowledge of supernatural things. And the soul says here that before reaching this precious union its feeling was in obscurity concerning both.

Until the Lord said, *fiat lux,* darkness was over the face of the abyss of the caverns of the soul's feeling. The more unfathomable and deep-caverned is the feeling, the more profound are its chasms and its darknesses, regarding the supernatural, when God Who is its light does not illumine it.

Thus it is impossible for it to lift its eyes to the divine light, or even think of doing so, for in never having seen it, it knows not what it is. Accordingly, it will be unable to desire this light; it will rather desire darkness because it knows what darkness is, and will go from darkness to darkness, guided by that darkness. One darkness cannot but lead to another. As David says: *The day overflows into the day and the night teaches knowledge to the night.* [Ps. 18:3] Thus one abyss calls to the other abyss [Ps. 41:8], that is: An abyss of light summons another abyss of light, and an abyss of darkness calls to another abyss of darkness, each like evoking its like and communicating itself to it.

The light of grace which God had previously accorded this soul (by which He had illumined the eye of the abyss of its spirit, opened its eye to the divine light, and made it pleasing to Himself) called to another abyss of grace, which is this divine transformation of the soul in God. In this transformation the eye of the soul's feeling is so illumined and agreeable to God that we can say God's light and that of the soul are one, since the natural light of the soul is united with the supernatural light of God, so that only the supernatural light is shining—just as the light God created was united to the light of the sun, and now only the sun shines even though the other light is not lacking.

72. It was also blind insofar as it was enjoying something else. The blindness of the rational and superior feeling is the appetite, which, like a cataract and cloud, interferes with and hangs over the eye of reason so

that things present cannot be seen. Insofar as the appetite proposed some satisfaction, the feeling was blind to the grandeurs of the divine riches and beauty on the other side of the cataract. Just as something in front of the eye, no matter how small, is sufficient to obstruct its vision of things before it, no matter how large, so a small appetite and idle act of the soul is enough to impede all these divine grandeurs, which stand behind the soul's appetites and gratifications.

73. Oh, who can tell how impossible it is for a man with appetites to judge the things of God as they are! If there is to be success in judging the things of God, the appetites and satisfactions must be totally rejected, and these things of God must be weighed apart from them. For otherwise one will infallibly come to consider the things of God as impertinent to God, and the things impertinent to God as belonging to God. Since that cataract shrouds the eye of judgment, only the cataract is seen, of one color sometimes, sometimes of another, according to the way the cataract appears to the eye. A person judges that the cataract is God because, as I say, he sees only the cataract which covers the faculty, and God cannot be grasped by the senses. Consequently the appetite and sensory gratifications impede the knowledge of high things. The Wise Man indicates this clearly with these words: *The deceitfulness of vanity obscures good things, and the inconstancy of concupiscence overturns the innocent mind* [Wis. 4:12], that is, good judgment.

74. Those who are not so spiritual as to be purged of appetites and satisfactions, but still keep in themselves something of the animal man, believe that things most vile and base to the spirit (those closest to the senses, according to which they are still living) are highly important; and those that are loftier and more precious to the spirit (those further withdrawn from the senses), they consider to be of little value and do not esteem them. They will even regard them sometimes as foolishness, as St. Paul clearly indicates: *The animal man does not perceive the things of God; they are foolishness to him and he cannot understand them.* [1 Cor. 2:14] By the animal man he means here the man who still lives with natural appetites and gratifications. Even though some satisfaction overflows from the spirit into the senses, a man has no more than natural appetites if he desires to become attached to it. It matters little that the object or cause is supernatural, if the appetite arises naturally and finds its roots and strength in nature. It does not thus cease being a natural appetite, for it has the very substance and nature it would have were it to deal with a natural object or cause.

75. You will say to me: "It therefore follows that when the soul desires God, it does not desire Him supernaturally, and thus its desire will be unmeritorious before God."

I reply that it is true that the soul's desire for God is not always supernatural, but only when God infuses it and Himself gives the strength for it. This is far different from the natural desire, and until God infuses the desire there is very little or no merit. Thus when you of your own power have the desire for God, your desire amounts to no more than a natural appetite, neither will it be anything more until God informs it supernaturally. When of yourself you become attached to spiritual things and bound to their savoriness, you exercise your natural appetite and thus you put cataracts before your eyes and become an animal man. You are then able neither to understand nor judge the spiritual man, who is above every natural feeling and appetite.

If you have any further doubts, I know not what to say, except that you reread this and perhaps you will understand. For the substance of the truth has been said, and this is not the place to enlarge upon it.

76. This feeling, then, of the soul which was once obscure, without this divine light, and blind through its appetites and affections, has now together with the deep caverns of its faculties not only become bright and clear, but like a resplendent light.

77.   Now give forth, so rarely, so exquisitely,
              Both warmth and light to their Beloved.

When these caverns of the faculties are so wonderfully and marvelously pervaded with the admirable splendors of those lamps which are burning within them, they give forth to God in God with loving glory, besides their surrender to Him, these very splendors they have received. Inclined in God toward God, having become enkindled lamps within the splendors of the divine lamps, they render the Beloved the same light and heat they receive. In the very manner they receive it, they return it to the one who gave it, and with the same beauty in which it was given; just as the window when the sun shines on it, for it then too reflects the splendors. Yet the soul reflects the divine light in a more excellent way because of the active intervention of its will.

78. "So rarely, so exquisitely," means: in a way rare or foreign to every common thought, every exaggeration, and every mode and manner.

Corresponding to the exquisiteness or to the excellence with which the intellect receives the divine wisdom, being made one with God's intellect, is the excellence with which the soul gives this wisdom, for it cannot give it save according to the mode in which it was given.

And corresponding to the excellence by which the will is united to goodness is the excellence by which it gives in God the same goodness to God, for it only receives it in order to give it.

And, no more nor less, according to the excellence by which it knows in the grandeur of God, being united to it, the soul shines and diffuses the warmth of love.

And according to the excellence of the divine attributes (fortitude, beauty, justice, etc.), which the Beloved communicates, is the excellence with which the soul's feeling gives joyfully to Him the very light and heat it receives from Him. Having been made one with God, the soul is somehow God through participation. Although it is not God as perfectly as it will be in the next life, it is like the shadow of God. Being the shadow of God through this substantial transformation, it performs in this measure in God and through God what He through Himself does in it. For the will of the two is one will, and thus God's operation and the soul's is one. Since God gives Himself with a free and gracious will, so too the soul (possessing a will the more generous and free the more it is united with God) gives to God, God Himself in God; and this is a true and complete gift of the soul to God.

It is conscious there that God is indeed its own and that it possesses Him by inheritance, with the right of ownership, as His adopted son, through the grace of His gift of Himself. Having Him for its own, it can give Him and communicate Him to whomever it wishes. Thus it gives Him to its Beloved, who is the very God who gave Himself to it. By this donation it repays God for all it owes Him, since it willingly gives as much as it receives from Him.

79. Because the soul in this gift to God offers Him the Holy Spirit, with voluntary surrender, as something of its own (so that God loves Himself in the Holy Spirit as He deserves), it enjoys inestimable delight and fruition, seeing that it gives God something of its own which is suited to Him according to His infinite being. Although it is true that the soul cannot give God again to Himself, since in Himself He is ever Himself, nevertheless it does this truly and perfectly, giving all that was given it by Him in order to repay love, which is to give as much as is given. And God, Who could not be considered paid with anything less, is considered paid with that gift of the soul, and He accepts it gratefully as something it gives Him of its own. In this very gift He loves it anew, and in this re-surrender of God to the soul, the soul also loves as though again.

A reciprocal love is thus actually formed between God and the soul, like the marriage union and surrender, in which the goods of both (the divine essence which each possesses freely by reason of the voluntary surrender between them) are possessed by both together. They say to each other what the Son of God spoke to the Father through St. John: *Omnia mea tua sunt et tua mea sunt et clarificatus sum in eis* (All my goods are yours and yours are mine, and I am glorified in them). [Jn. 17: 10] In the next life this will continue unintermittently in perfect fruition, but in this state of union it occurs, although not as perfectly as in the next, when God produces in the soul this act of the transformation.

Clearly the soul can give this gift, even though the gift has greater entity than the soul's own being and capacity, for if a person owns many nations and kingdoms, which have more entity than he does, he can give them to whomever he wills.

80. This is the soul's deep satisfaction and happiness: to see that it gives to God more than in itself it is worth; and this it does with that very divine light and divine heat and solitude. It does this in heaven by means of the light of glory and in this life by means of a highly illumined faith. Accordingly, the deep caverns of feeling give forth with rare excellence to their Beloved heat and light together.

It says "together," because the communication of the Father and of the Son and of the Holy Spirit in the soul is combined; it is the light and fire of love in it.

81. Yet we should note briefly the refinement with which the soul makes this surrender. In this respect it should be known that, since it enjoys a certain image of fruition caused by the union of the intellect and affection with God, and is delighted and obliged by this inestimable favor, it makes this surrender of God and of itself to God in marvelous ways. With regard to love, its bearing before God is of rare excellence, and so too in regard to this vestige of fruition, and also in regard to praise and to gratitude.

82. Concerning the first—its love—there are three chief qualities of excellence. The first is that the soul here loves God, not through itself but through Him. This is a remarkable quality, for it loves through the Holy Spirit, as the Father and Son love each other, according to what the Son Himself declares through St. John: *That the love with which You have loved Me be in them and I in them.* [Jn. 17:26] The second excellence is to love God in God, for in this union the soul is vehemently absorbed in love of God, and God in great vehemence surrenders Himself to the soul. The third excellence of love is to love Him on account of Who He is. The soul does not love Him only because He is generous, good, and glorious to it, but with greater force it loves Him because He is all this in Himself essentially.

83. In regard to this image of fruition, it has three other principal and precious qualities of excellence. The first is that it enjoys God, for it enjoys Him by means of Himself. Since it unites its intellect to the omnipotence, wisdom, goodness, etc., although not clearly as it will in the next life, it delights in all these things which are understood particularly, as we mentioned above. The second main excellence of this joy is that the soul delights with order in God alone, without any intermin-

gling of creature. The third delight is that it enjoys Him only on account of Who He is without any admixture of its own pleasure.

84. There are three excellent qualities of the praise the soul renders God in this union. The first is that it praises Him as its duty, for it sees that God created it for His own praise, as He asserts through Isaias: *This people I have formed for Myself; it will sing My praises.* [Is. 43:21] The second excellence of praise is that the soul praises God for the goods it receives and the delight it has in praising. The third excellence is that it praises God for what He is in Himself. Even though the soul would experience no delight, it would praise Him on account of Who He is.

85. As for gratitude, it has three other excellent qualities. The first is gratefulness for the natural and spiritual goods and benefices it has received. The second is the intense delight it has in praising God, for it is absorbed with extreme ardor in this praise. The third is praise only because of what God is, which is a much stronger and more delightful praise.

STANZA 4

How gently and lovingly
You wake in my heart,
Where in secret You dwell alone;
And in Your sweet breathing,
Filled with good and glory,
How tenderly You swell my heart with love!

Commentary

1. The soul here addresses its Bridegroom with deep love, esteeming Him and thanking Him for two admirable effects sometimes produced by Him through this union, noting also the manner in which each is wrought, as well as another effect which overflows in it from this union.

2. The first effect is an awakening of God in the soul, effected in gentleness and love. The second is the breathing of God within it, and this is effected through the good and glory communicated to it in this breathing. And that which overflows in it is its being tenderly and delicately inspired with love.

3. And thus it is as though the soul were to say: How gentle and loving (that is, extremely loving and gentle) is Your awakening, O Word, Spouse, in the center and depth of my soul, which is its pure and in-

timate substance, in which secretly and silently, as its only lord, You dwell alone, not only as in Your house, nor only as in Your bed, but also as in my own heart, intimately and closely united to it. And how delicately You captivate me and arouse my affections toward You in the sweet breathing You produce in this awakening, a breathing delightful to me and full of good and glory.

The soul uses this comparison because its experience here is similar to that of one who upon awakening breathes deeply.

The verses follow:

4.   How gently and lovingly
              You wake in my heart,

There are many kinds of awakening which God effects in the soul, so many that we would never finish explaining them all. Yet this awakening of the Son of God, which the soul wishes to refer to here, is one of the most elevated and most beneficial. For this awakening is a movement of the Word in the substance of the soul, containing such grandeur, dominion, and glory, and intimate sweetness that it seems to the soul that all the balsams and fragrant spices and flowers of the world are commingled, stirred, and shaken so as to yield their sweet odor, and that all the kingdoms and dominions of the world and all the powers and virtues of heaven are moved; and not only this, but it also seems that all the virtues and substances and perfections and graces of every created thing glow and make the same movement all at once.

Since, as St. John says, *all things in Him are life* [Jn. 1:3–4], and *in Him they live and are and move*, as the Apostle declares [Acts 17:28], it follows that when, within the soul, this great Emperor moves (Whose principality, as Isaias says, He bears upon His shoulders [Is. 9:6]—which consists of the three spheres, celestial, terrestrial, and infernal, and the things contained in them—upholding them all, as St. Paul says [Heb. 1:3], with the word of His power), all things seem to move in unison. This happens in the same manner as when at the movement of the earth all material things in it move as though they were nothing. So it is when this Prince moves, Who Himself carries His court, instead of His court carrying Him.

5. Even this comparison is most inadequate, for in this awakening they not only seem to move, but they all likewise disclose the beauties of their being, power, loveliness, and graces, and the root of their duration and life. For the soul is conscious of how all creatures, earthly and heavenly, have their life, duration, and strength in Him, and it clearly realizes what He says in the Book of Proverbs: *By Me kings reign and princes rule and the mighty exercise justice and understand it.* [Prv. 8:15–16] Although it is indeed aware that these things are distinct from God, insofar as they have created being, nonetheless that which it un-

derstands of God, by His being all these things with infinite eminence, is such that it knows these things better in God's being than in themselves.

And here lies the remarkable delight of this awakening: the soul knows creatures through God and not God through creatures. This amounts to knowing the effects through their cause and not the cause through its effects. The latter is knowledge *a posteriori,* and the former is essential knowledge.

6. How this movement takes place in the soul, since God is immovable, is a wonderful thing, for it seems to the soul that God indeed moves; yet He does not really move. For since it is the soul that is renewed and moved by God so that it might behold this supernatural sight, and since that divine life and the being and harmony of every creature in that life, with its movements in God, is revealed to it with such newness, it seems to the soul that it is God Who moves and that the cause assumes the name of the effect it produces. According to this effect, we can assert that God moves, as the Wise Man says: *For wisdom is more movable than all movable things.* [Wis. 7:24] And this is not because it moves but because it is the principle and root of all movement. *Remaining in itself the same,* as he goes on to say, *it renews all things.* [Wis. 7:27] Thus what he wishes to say in this passage is that wisdom is more active than all active things. We then ought to say that in this movement it is the soul that is moved and awakened from the sleep of natural vision to supernatural vision. Hence it very adequately uses the term "awakening."

7. Yet God always acts in this way—as the soul is able to see—moving, governing, bestowing being, power, graces, and gifts upon all creatures, bearing them all in Himself by His power, presence, and substance. And the soul sees what God is in Himself and what He is in His creatures in only one view, just as one who in opening the door of a palace beholds in one act the eminence of the person who dwells inside together with what he is doing.

That which I understand therefore as to how God effects this awakening and view of the soul (which is in Him substantially as is every creature) is that He removes some of the many veils and curtains hanging in front of it so that it might see Him as He is. And then that countenance of His, full of graces, becomes partially and vaguely discernible, for not all the veils are removed. Because all things are moving by His power, that which He is doing is evident as well, so that He seems to move in them and they in Him with continual movement. Hence it seems to the soul that, in being itself moved and awakened, it was God Who moved and awakened.

8. Such is the lowliness of our condition in this life, for we think others are like ourselves, and we judge others according to what we ourselves are, since our judgment arises from within us and not outside of us. Thus the thief thinks others also steal; and the lustful man thinks that others are lustful too; and the malicious person thinks that others also bear malice, his judgment stemming from his own malice; and a good person thinks well of others, for his judgment flows from the goodness of his own thoughts; and to him who is careless and asleep, it seems that others are too.

Hence it is that when we are careless and asleep in God's presence, it seems to us that it is God who is asleep and neglectful of us, as is seen in the psalm where David calls to Him: *Arise, Lord, why do You sleep? Arise.* [Ps. 43:23] He attributed to God what is characteristic of man, for since men are the ones who are fallen and asleep, he tells God to arise and awaken, although *He who watches over Israel never sleeps.* [Ps. 120:4]

9. Yet, since everything in man comes from God, and man of himself can do nothing good, it is rightly asserted that our awakening is an awakening of God and our rising is God's rising. It is as though David were to say: Let us arise and be awakened twice, because we are doubly asleep and fallen. Since the soul was in a sleep from which it could never awaken itself, and only God could open its eyes and cause this awakening, it very appropriately calls this an awakening of God, saying: "You wake in my heart."

Awaken and enlighten us, my Lord, that we might know and love the blessings which You ever propose to us, and that we might understand that You have moved to bestow favors on us and have remembered us.

10. That which a person knows and experiences of God in this awakening is entirely beyond words. Since this awakening is the communication of God's excellence to the substance of the soul, which is its heart, referred to in the verse, an immense, powerful voice sounds in it, the voice of a multitude of excellences, of thousands of virtues in God, infinite in number. The soul is established in them, terribly and solidly set in array in them like an army [Ct. 6:3], and made gentle and charming with all the gentleness and charm of creatures.

11. Yet a doubt will arise: How can a soul endure so forcible a communication in the weakness of the flesh? For in point of fact it does not have the capacity and strength to undergo so much without dying. Merely at the sight of King Assuerus clothed in royal garments and resplendent with gold and precious stones, seated awesomely upon his throne, Queen Esther feared so much that she fainted. She confesses there that she fainted because of the fear his great glory caused her, for

he appeared like an angel and his countenance was full of graces. [Est. 15:9–17] When glory does not glorify, it weighs heavily upon the one who beholds it. But what greater reason does the soul have to faint in this awakening, for it does not see an angel, but God, His countenance filled with the graces of all creatures, awesome in power and glory, and with the voice of a multitude of excellences. Job says of this communication: *When we have heard scarce a drop of His voice, who will be able to endure the greatness of His thunder?* [Jb. 26:14] And in another place he declares: *I do not desire that He commune and deal with me with much strength lest He overwhelm me by the weight of His grandeur.* [Jb. 23:6]

12. There are two reasons why a person does not faint or become afraid in this awakening which is so powerful and glorious.

First, the soul that is in this state of perfection, in which the lower part is highly purged and in conformity with the spirit, does not feel the pain and detriment commonly experienced by souls unpurged in their spirit and senses and undisposed to receive spiritual communications. Yet this is insufficient to prevent the suffering of some detriment in the presence of such grandeur and glory. Even though the sensory part may be very pure, nevertheless, this communication, still exceeding it, would overwhelm it, as would a highly sensible object overwhelm its respective faculty. The passage of Job we referred to has this meaning.

The second reason is the important one; it is what the soul mentions in the first verse, that is, that He shows Himself gently. As God shows the soul grandeur and glory in order to exalt and favor it, He aids it so that no detriment is done, fortifying the sensory part and unveiling His grandeur gently and with love, without using the senses, so that a person does not know whether this happens in the body or out of it. He Who with His right hand fortified Moses, so that His glory could be seen by him, can do this very easily. [Ex. 33:22]

Thus the soul experiences in Him as much gentleness and love as it does power and dominion and grandeur, for everything in God is one. The delight is strong; and the protection is powerful in gentleness and love, that the soul might endure the strong delight, and instead of fainting stand powerful and strong. If Esther fainted, it was because the king did not at first show himself to her favorably, but, as it says there, disclosed with burning eyes the furor of his heart. [Est. 15:10] Yet she came to herself after he favored her, held out his scepter and touched her with it, and embraced her and told her that he was her brother and not to fear. [Est. 15:11–12]

13. The soul no longer fears, since from henceforth the King of heaven acts in a friendly way toward it, as toward His brother and His equal. In revealing to it, in gentleness and not in furor, the might of His power

and the love of His goodness, He communicates to it from His heart strength and love, going out to it from His throne, which is the soul itself, like the Bridegroom from his bridal chamber [Ps. 18:6], where He was hidden and turned toward it, touching it with His scepter, and embracing it as a brother. There we find the royal garments and their fragrance, which are God's admirable virtues; there the splendor of gold, which is charity; there the glittering of the precious stones of knowledge of the higher and lower substances; there the face of the Word, full of graces, which shines upon the queen, which is the soul, and clothes it in such a fashion that, transformed in these attributes of the heavenly King, it is aware of having become a queen, and that what David says of the queen in the Psalm can indeed be said of it: *The queen stood at the right in garments of gold and surrounded with variety.* [Ps. 44:10] Since all this occurs in the intimate substance of the soul, it adds:

14.   Where in secret You dwell alone;

The soul says He dwells in its heart in secret because this sweet embrace is wrought in the depths of its substance.

It should be known that God dwells secretly in all souls and is hidden in their substance, for otherwise they would not last. Yet there is a difference, a great difference, in His dwelling in them. In some souls He dwells alone, and in others He does not dwell alone. Abiding in some, He is pleased; and in others, He is displeased. He lives in some as though in His own house, commanding and ruling everything; and in others as though a stranger in a strange house, where they do not permit Him to give orders, nor do anything.

It is in the soul in which less of its own appetites and pleasures dwell where He dwells more alone, more pleased, and more as though in His own house, ruling and governing it. And He dwells more in secret, the more He dwells alone. Thus in this soul in which neither any appetite nor other images or forms, nor any affections for created things, dwell, the Beloved dwells secretly with an embrace so much the closer, more intimate, and interior, the purer and more alone the soul is to everything other than God. His dwelling is in secret, then, because the devil cannot reach the area of this embrace, nor can man's intellect understand how it occurs.

Yet it is not secret to the soul itself that has attained this perfection, for within itself it has the experience of this intimate embrace. It does not, however, always experience these awakenings, for when the Beloved produces them, it seems to the soul that He is awakening in its heart, where before He remained as though asleep. Although it was experiencing and enjoying Him, this took place as though with a loved one who is asleep, for knowledge and love is not communicated mutually while one is still asleep.

15. Oh, how happy is this soul which ever experiences God resting and reposing within it! Oh, how fitting it is for it to withdraw from things, flee from business matters, and live in immense tranquillity, so that it may not even with the slightest mote or noise disturb or trouble its heart where the Beloved dwells.

He is usually there, in this embrace with His bride, as though asleep in the substance of the soul. And it is very well aware of Him and ordinarily enjoys Him. Were He always awake within it, communicating knowledge and love, it would already be in glory. For if, when He does waken, scarcely opening His eyes, He has such an effect on the soul, what would it be like were He ordinarily in it fully awake?

16. Although He is not displeased with other souls that have not reached this union, for after all they are in the state of grace, yet insofar as they are not well disposed, His dwelling is secret to them, even though He does dwell in them. They do not experience Him ordinarily, except when He grants them some delightful awakening. But such an awakening is not of this kind and high quality, nor is it comparable to these, nor as secret to the intellect and the devil, which are still able to understand something through the movements of the senses. For the senses are not fully annihilated until the soul reaches this union, and they still have some activity and movements concerning the spiritual, since they are not yet totally spiritual.

But in this awakening of the Bridegroom in the perfect soul, everything that occurs and is caused is perfect, for He is the cause of it all. And in that awakening, which is as though one were to awaken and breathe, the soul feels a strange delight in the breathing of the Holy Spirit in God, in which it is sovereignly glorified and taken with love. Hence it says in the subsequent verses:

17.   And in Your sweet breathing,
           Filled with good and glory,
           How tenderly You swell my heart with love!

I do not desire to speak of this spiration, filled for the soul with good and glory and delicate love of God, for I am aware of being incapable of so doing, and were I to try, it might seem less than it is. It is a spiration which God produces in the soul, in which, by that awakening of lofty knowledge of the Godhead, He breathes the Holy Spirit in it in the same proportion as its knowledge and understanding of Him, absorbing it most profoundly in the Holy Spirit, rousing its love with divine excellence and delicacy according to what it beholds in Him. Since the breathing is filled with good and glory, the Holy Spirit, through this breathing, filled the soul with good and glory, in which He enkindled it in love of Himself, indescribably and incomprehensibly, in the depths of God, to Whom be honor and glory forever and ever. Amen.

The Minor Works

INTRODUCTION TO THE MINOR WORKS

THE PRECAUTIONS

St. John of the Cross wrote *The Precautions*, it is commonly said, for the Carmelite nuns at Beas, while confessor to that community. This belief is based on the assertion of Madre Ana de Jesús that he gave the nuns some precautions against the enemies of the soul. However, since the masculine gender is used throughout instead of the feminine, there is reason for conjecturing that the *Precautions* which have reached us were destined for the friars of El Calvario. As their Prior, it was St. John's duty to have concern for their spiritual well-being and to give them conferences and instructions. In proposing that these precautions were written for the friars, we do not exclude the probability that the Saint also wrote similar precautions for the nuns, just as he made copies of the drawing of the Mount of Perfection for both friars and nuns. This little treatise, written sometime between November of 1578 and June of 1579, is perhaps the first of his didactic works.

COUNSELS TO A RELIGIOUS ON HOW TO REACH PERFECTION

These *Counsels* are similar in content and style to *The Precautions*. It seems from the use of the expression, "Your Charity," rather than, "Your Reverence," that they were written for either a lay brother or a student for the priesthood. They might have been written sometime between 1585–87; St. John's many occupations and travels at this time as Vicar Provincial would explain the lack of time and paper of which he speaks in the opening lines of these Counsels.

SAYINGS OF LIGHT AND LOVE

This collection of seventy-six maxims plus a fervent prayer enjoys a special authenticity because of the preservation of the original. From the time he was confessor at the Incarnation until the end of his life it was a common practice for St. John of the Cross to jot down spiritual maxims for souls under his direction; these maxims served as summaries and reminders of his instructions. Though the *Sayings* do not seem to point to any particular individual, but have a more general tone, it is probable, from the testimony of other manuscripts, that they were written for Madre Francisca de la Madre de Dios, one of the Carmelite nuns at Beas. The original is preserved in the parish church of Andújar in the province of Jaén. A photocopy of the work was published in Toledo (1913). Since the original is damaged both at the beginning and end, it lacks the prologue and suggests that there were more than seventy-six sayings. No definite date of composition has been established.

OTHER MAXIMS AND COUNSELS

The *Maxims on Love* (comprising eighty maxims), the *Degrees of Perfection* (with seventeen maxims), and the *Other Counsels* (with fourteen maxims) are similar to the *Sayings of Light and Love*. Many maxims and counsels have been attributed to St. John of the Cross, but great difficulty lies in determining whether he actually wrote them, or whether his disciples culled them from his sermons and conferences, or whether the maxims are simply spurious. We have included only those collections which are considered trustworthy. The counsels of Madre Magdalena have been omitted because they are repetitions of the counsels given in the *Ascent* (A1, 13), but not because of any doubt concerning their authenticity.

CENSURE AND OPINION ON THE SPIRIT AND THE ATTITUDE IN PRAYER OF A DISCALCED CARMELITE NUN

When Padre Nicolas Doria learned of the extraordinary experiences of this Carmelite nun and of how many other spiritual directors from various religious orders had examined and approved her spirit, he asked her to write a long and detailed account of her prayer and its effects. Padre Doria then passed on this written account to St. John of the Cross, asking him to study it and give his opinion of the nun's spirit. The saint wrote this censure while at Segovia, 1588–91.

THE LETTERS

The letters that have come down to us, some of them originals, others contained in the older and more reliable manuscripts, are unfortunately very few. We can surmise that a large number of them were destroyed during the persecution that was waged against the Saint at the end of his life. We know definitely, for example, that the nuns of Granada, those most persistently and infamously pestered by Padre Diego Evangelista, became frightened because of the perverse interpretation given to what was most holy; and they burned a whole sack filled with letters and writings of the Saint. St. John of the Cross's letters abound with admirable and solid spiritual teaching; they reflect, too, his singular gifts as a spiritual director.

THE PRECAUTIONS

Precautions for the use of anyone desiring to be a true religious and reach perfection quickly. Addressed to the Discalced Carmelite nuns of Beas.

1. The religious must practice the following instructions if he wishes to attain in a short time holy recollection and spiritual silence, nakedness, and poverty, where one enjoys the peaceful comfort of the Holy Spirit, reaches union with God, is freed of all the obstacles incurred from the creatures of this world, defended against the wiles and deceits of the devil, and liberated from one's own self.

2. It should be noted, then, that the evils which come upon a man are born of his enemies, those mentioned above: the world, the devil, and the flesh. The world is the enemy least difficult to conquer; the devil is the hardest to understand; the flesh is the most tenacious, and its attacks continue as long as the old man lasts.

3. To gain complete mastery over any of these three enemies, one must vanquish all three of them; and in the weakening of one, the other two are weakened also. When all three are overpowered, no further war remains for the soul.

Against the World

4. To free yourself from the harm the world can do you, you should practice three precautions.

The first precaution

5. The first is that you should have an equal love for and an equal forgetfulness of all persons, whether relatives or not, and withdraw your heart from relatives as much as from others, and in some ways even more for fear that flesh and blood might be quickened by the natural love which is ever alive among kin and which must always be mortified for the sake of spiritual perfection.

6. Regard all as strangers, and you will better fulfill your duty toward them than by giving them the affection you owe God.

Do not love one person more than another, for you will err; he is worthy of more love whom God loves more, and you do not know whom this is. But forgetting everyone alike, as is necessary for holy recollection, you will free yourself from this error of loving one person more or less than another.

Do not think about others, neither good things nor bad. Flee them inasmuch as possible. And if you do not observe this practice, you will not know how to be a religious, nor will you be able to reach holy recollection, or deliver yourself from the imperfections that thinking of others involves. And if you should wish to allow yourself some freedom in this matter, the devil will deceive you in one way or another, or you will deceive yourself under some color of good or of evil.

In doing what we said you will have security, for in no other way will you be capable of freeing yourself from the imperfections and harm derived from creatures.

The second precaution

7. The second precaution against the world concerns temporal goods. To free yourself truly of the harm stemming from this kind of good and to moderate the excess of your appetite, you should abhor all manner of possession and have no concern for these goods, neither for food, nor for clothing, nor for any other created thing, nor for tomorrow, and direct this care to something higher—to seeking the kingdom of God (seeking not to fail God); and the rest, as His Majesty says, will be added unto us [Mt. 6:33], for He who looks after the beasts will not be forgetful of you. By this practice you will attain silence and peace in the senses.

The third precaution

8. The third precaution is very necessary that you may know how to guard yourself in the community against all harm that may arise in regard to the religious. Many, by not observing it, not only have lost the peace and good of their soul, but have fallen and ordinarily continue to fall into many evils and sins.

It is that you very carefully guard yourself against thinking about what happens in the community, and even more against speaking of it, of anything in the past or present concerning a particular religious: nothing about his character or his conduct or his deeds no matter how serious any of this seems. Do not say anything under the color of zeal or of correcting a wrong, unless at the proper time to him whom by right you ought to tell. Never be scandalized or astonished at anything you happen to see or learn of, endeavoring to preserve your soul in forgetfulness of all that. For, should you desire to pay heed to things, many will seem wrong, even though you may live among angels, because of your not understanding the nature of them.

9. Take Lot's wife as an example: because she was troubled at the destruction of the Sodomites and turned her head to watch what was happening, God punished her by converting her into a pillar of salt. [Gn. 19:26] You are thus to understand God's will: that even though you live among devils you should not turn the head of your thoughts to their affairs, but forget these things entirely and strive to keep your soul occupied purely and entirely in God, and not let the thought of this thing or that hinder you from so doing.

And to achieve this be certain that in monasteries and communities there is never a lack of stumbling blocks, since there is never a lack of devils who seek to overthrow the saints; God permits this in order to prove and try religious.

And if you do not guard yourself, acting as though you were not in the house, you will be unable to be a religious no matter how much you do, nor will you attain holy denudation and recollection, nor free yourself of the harm arising from these thoughts. If you are not cautious in this manner, the devil will catch you in one way or another. And you are already fully captive when you allow yourself distractions of this sort.

Recall what the Apostle St. James asserts: *If any man thinks himself to be religious, not restraining his tongue, that man's religion is vain.* [Jas. 1:26] This applies to the interior as much as to the exterior tongue.

AGAINST THE DEVIL

10. He who aspires to perfection should use three precautions to deliver himself from the devil, his second enemy. It should be noted that among the many wiles of the devil to deceive spiritual persons, the most common is deceiving them under the appearance of good rather than of evil, for he already knows that they will scarcely choose a recognized evil. Thus you should always be suspicious of what appears good, especially when not obliged by obedience. To do the right thing, and be safe in such a matter, you ought to take the proper counsel.

The first precaution

11. Let, then, the first precaution be that, without the command of obedience, you never take upon yourself any work—apart from the obligations of your state—however good and full of charity it may seem, whether for yourself or for anyone else inside or outside the house. By such a practice you will win merit and security.

Renounce possessions and you will flee from the devil and from evils unknown to you, of which God will one day demand an account. If you do not observe this precaution in little things as well as big, you will be unable to avoid the devil's deceiving you, to a small or great degree, no matter how right you seem to be. Even if your negligence amounts to no more than not being governed by obedience in all things, you culpably err, since God wants obedience more than sacrifice. [1 Kgs. 15:22] The actions of a religious are not his own, but belong to obedience, and if you withdraw them from obedience, you will have to count them as lost.

The second precaution

12. Let the second precaution be that you always look upon the superior as though upon God, no matter who he happens to be, for he takes God's place. And note that the devil, humility's enemy, is a great and crafty meddler in this area. Much profit and gain comes from considering the superior in this light, but serious loss and harm lies in not doing so. Watch, therefore, with singular care that you study neither his character, his mode of behavior, his ability, or any of his other methods of procedure, for you will so harm yourself as to change your obedience from divine to human, being motivated only by the visible traits of the superior, and not by the invisible God Whom you serve through him.

Your obedience is vain and all the more fruitless in the measure that you allow the superior's unpleasant character to annoy you or his good and pleasing manners to make you happy. For I tell you that by inducing religious to consider these modes of conduct, the devil has ruined a vast number of them in their journey toward perfection. Their acts of obedience are worth little in God's sight, since they allow these considerations to interfere with obedience.

If you do not strive, with respect to your personal feelings, to be unconcerned about whether this one or another be superior, you will by no means be a spiritual person, nor will you keep your vows well.

The third precaution

13. The third precaution, directly against the devil, is that you ever seek with all your heart to humble yourself in word and in deed, rejoicing in the good of others as if it were your own, desiring that they be given precedence over you in all things; and this you should do wholeheartedly. You will thereby overcome evil with good, banish the devil, and possess a happy heart. Try to practice this more with' those who least attract you. Realize that if you do not train yourself in this way, you will not attain real charity nor make any progress in it. Prefer to be taught by all rather than desire to teach even the least of all.

Against the Flesh

14. The other three precautions to be practiced by him who wishes to conquer both himself and his senses, the third enemy.

The first precaution

15. The first precaution is to understand that you have come to the monastery so that all may fashion you and try you. Thus, to free yourself from the imperfections and disturbances that can be engendered by the mannerisms and attitudes of the religious and draw profit from every occurrence, you should think that all in the community are artisans— as indeed they are—present there in order to prove you; that some will fashion you with words, others by deeds, and others with thoughts against you; and that in all this you must be submissive as is the statue to the craftsman who molds it, to the artist who paints it, and to the gilder who embellishes it.

If you fail to observe this precaution, you will not know how to overcome your sensitiveness and feelings, nor will you get along well in the community with the religious, nor attain holy peace, nor free yourself from many stumbling blocks and evils.

The second precaution

16. The second precaution is that you should never give up your works because of a want of satisfaction and delight in them, if they are fitting for the service of God. Neither should you carry out these works merely because of the satisfaction or delight they accord you, but you should do

them just as you would the disagreeable ones. Otherwise it will be impossible for you to gain constancy and conquer your weakness.

The third precaution

17: The third precaution is that the interior man should never fix his eyes upon the pleasant feelings found in his spiritual exercises, becoming attached to them and carrying out these practices only for the sake of this satisfaction. Nor should he run from the bitterness he may find in them, but rather seek the arduous and distasteful and embrace it. By this practice the senses are held in check; without it, you will never lose self-love nor gain the love of God.

THE END

COUNSELS TO A RELIGIOUS
ON HOW TO REACH PERFECTION

JESUS MARIAE FILIUS

1. Your holy Charity with few words asked me for a great deal. An answer would require much time and paper. Seeing, then, that I lack both of these, I will try to be concise and jot down only certain points and counsels which in sum will contain much, so that whoever observes them perfectly will attain a high degree of perfection.

He who wishes to be a true religious and fulfill the promises which by his state he has professed, advance in virtue, and enjoy the consolations and the delight of the Holy Spirit, will be unable to do so if he does not try to practice with the greatest diligence the four following counsels concerning resignation, mortification, the practice of virtue, and bodily and spiritual solitude.

2. In order to practice the first counsel, concerning resignation, you should live in the monastery as though no one else were in it. And thus you should never, by word or by thought, meddle in things that happen in the community, nor with individuals in it, desiring not to notice their good or bad qualities or their conduct. And in order to preserve your tranquillity of soul, even if the whole world crumbles, you should not desire to advert to this or interfere, remembering Lot's wife who was changed into hard stone because she turned her head to look at those who in the midst of much clamor and noise were perishing. [Gn. 19: 26]

You should practice this with great fortitude, for you will thereby free yourself from many sins and imperfections and guard the tranquillity and quietude of your soul with much profit before God and man.

Ponder this often, because it is so important that many religious for not observing it not only failed to improve through their other works of virtue and religious observance, but ever slipped back from bad to worse.

3. To practice the second counsel, which concerns mortification, and profit by it, you should engrave this truth upon your heart. And it is that you have not come to the monastery for any other reason than to be worked and tried in virtue, that you are like the stone which must be chiseled and fashioned before being used in the building.

Thus you should understand that those who are in the monastery are craftsmen placed there by God to mortify you by working and chiseling at you. Some will chisel with words, telling you what you would rather not hear; others by deed, doing against you what you would rather not endure; others by their temperament, being in their person and in their actions a bother and annoyance to you; and others by their thoughts, neither esteeming nor feeling love for you.

You ought to suffer these mortifications and annoyances with inner patience, being silent for love of God and understanding that you did not enter the religious life for any other reason than that others work you in this way, and that you become worthy of heaven. If this was not your reason for entering the religious state, you should not have done so, but should have remained in the world to seek your comfort, honor, reputation, and ease.

4. This second counsel is wholly necessary for a religious, that he fulfill the obligations of his state and find genuine humility, inward quietude, and joy in the Holy Spirit. If you do not practice this, you will neither know how to be a religious nor even why you came to the religious life. Neither will you know how to seek Christ (but only yourself), nor find peace of soul, nor avoid sinning and often feeling troubled.

Trials will never be lacking in religious life, nor does God want them to be. Since He brings souls there to be proved and purified, like gold, with the hammer and the fire, it is fitting that they encounter trials and temptations from men and from devils, and the fire of anguish and affliction.

The religious must undergo these trials, and he should endeavor to bear them patiently and in conformity to God's will, and not so sustain them that instead of being approved by God in his affliction he be reproved for not carrying the cross of Christ in patience.

Since many religious do not understand that they have entered religious life to carry Christ's cross, they do not get along well with others. At the time of reckoning they will find themselves greatly confused and frustrated.

5. To practice the third counsel, which concerns the practice of virtue, you should be constant in your religious observance and in obedience, without any concern for the world, but only for God. In order to achieve this and avoid being deceived, you should never set your eyes upon the satisfaction or dissatisfaction of the work at hand as a motive for doing it or failing to do it, but upon doing it for God. Thus you must undertake all things, agreeable or disagreeable, for the sole purpose of pleasing God through them.

6. To do this with fortitude and constancy and acquire the virtues quickly, you should have care always to be inclined more to the difficult than to the easy, to what is rugged rather than to what is soft, to what is hard and distasteful in a work rather than to its delightful and pleasant aspects, and do not go about choosing what is less a cross, for that is a light burden, and the heavier a burden is, the lighter it becomes when borne for Christ.

You should try, too, by taking the lowest place always, that in things bringing comfort your brothers in religion be preferred to you. This you should do wholeheartedly, for it is the way to becoming greater in spiritual things, as God tells us in His Gospel: *Qui se humiliaverit exaltabitur.*[1] [Mt. 23:12]

7. To practice the fourth counsel, which concerns solitude, you should deem everything in the world as finished. Thus, when (for not being able to avoid it) you have to deal with some matter, do so in as detached a way as you would if it did not exist.

8. Pay no heed to the things out in the world, for God has already withdrawn and released you from them. Do not handle any business yourself that you can do through a third person. It is very fitting for you to desire to see no one and that no one see you.

And note carefully that if God will ask a strict account from all the faithful of every idle word, how much more will He ask it of the religious who has consecrated his entire life and all his works to Him. And God will demand all of this on the day of reckoning.

9. I do not mean here that you fail to fulfill the duties of your state with all necessary and possible care, and any others that obedience commands, but that you execute your tasks in such a way that no fault is committed, for neither God nor obedience wants you to commit a fault.

You should consequently strive to be incessant in prayer, and in the midst of your corporal practices do not abandon it. Whether you eat, or drink, or speak, or converse with lay people, or do anything else, you should always do so with the desire for God and with your heart fixed on Him. This is very necessary for inner solitude, which demands that the soul dismiss any thought that is not directed to God. And in forgetfulness of all the things that are and happen in this short and miserable life, do not desire to know anything in any way except how better to serve God and keep the observance of your institute.

---

[1] Whoever humbles himself shall be exalted.

10. If Your Charity observes these four counsels with care, you will reach perfection in a very short time. These counsels are so interdependent that if you are lacking in one of them, you will begin to lose the profit and gain you have from practicing the others.

SAYINGS OF LIGHT AND LOVE

PROLOGUE

O my God and my delight, for Your love I have also desired to give my soul to composing these sayings of light and love concerning You. Since, although I can express them in words, I do not have the works and virtues they imply (which is what pleases You more, O my Lord, than the words and wisdom they contain), may others, perhaps, moved by them, go forward in Your service and love—in which I am lacking. I will thereby find consolation, that these sayings prove an occasion that what I lack may be found in others.

Lord, You love discretion, You love light, You love love, these three You love above the other operations of the soul. Hence these will be sayings of discretion for the wayfarer, of light for the way, and of love in the wayfaring. May there be nothing of worldly rhetoric in them nor the long-winded and dry eloquence of weak and artificial human wisdom, which never pleases You. Let us speak to the heart words bathed in sweetness and love, which do indeed please You, removing obstacles and stumbling blocks from the paths of many souls who unknowingly trip and unconsciously walk in the path of error—poor souls who think they are right in what concerns the following of Your Beloved Son, our Lord Jesus Christ, and becoming like Him, imitating His life, actions, and virtues, and the form of His nakedness and purity of spirit. Father of mercies, come to our aid, for without You, Lord, we can do nothing.

1. The Lord has always revealed to men the treasures of His wisdom and His spirit, but now that the face of evil more and more bares itself, so does the Lord bare His treasures the more.

2. O Lord, My God, who will seek You with simple and pure love and not find You are all he desires, for You show Yourself first and go out to meet those who desire You?

3. Though the path is plain and smooth for men of good will, he who walks it will not travel far, and will do so only with difficulty if he does not have good feet, courage, and tenacity of spirit.

4. It is better to be burdened and in company with the strong than to be unburdened and with the weak. When you are burdened you are close to God, your strength, who abides with the afflicted. When you are relieved of the burden you are close to yourself, your own weakness; for virtue and strength of soul grow and are confirmed in the trials of patience.

5. He who wants to stand alone without the support of a master and guide, will be like the tree that stands alone in a field without a proprietor. No matter how much the tree bears, passers-by will pick the fruit before it ripens.

6. A tree that is cultivated and guarded through the care of its owner produces its fruit at the expected time.

7. The virtuous soul that is alone and without a master, is like a lone burning coal; it will grow colder rather than hotter.

8. He who falls alone remains alone in his fall, and he values his soul little since he entrusts it to himself alone.

9. If you do not fear falling alone, how do you presume that you will rise up alone? Consider how much more can be accomplished by two together than by one alone.

10. He who falls while heavily laden will find it difficult to rise under the burden.

11. The blind man who falls will not get up alone in his blindness, and if he does, he will take the wrong road.

12. God desires the least degree of purity of conscience in you more than all the works you can perform.

13. God desires the least degree of obedience and submissiveness more than all those services you think of rendering Him.

14. God values in you an inclination to aridity and suffering for love of Him more than all possible consolations, spiritual visions, and meditations.

15. Deny your desires and you will find what your heart longs for. For how do you know if any desire of yours is according to God?

16. O sweetest love of God, so little known, he who has found its veins is at rest!

17. Since a double measure of bitterness must follow the doing of your own will, do not do it even though you remain in single bitterness.

18. The soul that carries within itself the least appetite for worldly things bears more unseemliness and impurity in its journey to God than if it were troubled by all the hideous and annoying temptations and darknesses describable; for, so long as it does not consent to these, a soul thus tempted can approach God confidently, by doing the will of His Majesty, Who proclaims: *Come to Me all you who labor and are heavily burdened and I will refresh you.* [Mt. 11:28]

19. The person who in aridity and trial submits to the dictates of his reason is more pleasing to God than he who does everything with consolation, yet fails in this submission.

20. God is more pleased by one work, however small, done secretly, without desire that it be known, than a thousand done with desire that men know of them. The person who works for God with purest love not only cares nothing about whether men see him, but does not even seek that God Himself know of them. Such a person would not cease to render God the same services, with the same joy and purity of love, even if God were never to know of them.

21. He who does a pure and whole work for God merits a whole kingdom.

22. A bird caught in birdlime has a twofold task: it must free itself and cleanse itself. And he who satisfies his appetite suffers in a twofold way: he must detach himself and, after being detached, cleanse himself of what has clung to him.

23. He who does not allow his appetites to carry him away will soar in his spirit as swiftly as the bird that lacks no feathers.

24. The fly that clings to honey hinders its flight, and the soul that allows itself attachment to spiritual sweetness hinders its own liberty and contemplation.

25. Withdraw from creatures if you desire to preserve, clear and simple in your soul, the image of God. Empty your·spirit and withdraw far from them and you will walk in divine lights, for God is not like creatures.

PRAYER OF A SOUL TAKEN WITH LOVE

Lord God, my Beloved, if You remember still my sins in suchwise that you do not do what I beg of You, do Your will concerning them, my God, which is what I most desire, and exercise Your goodness and mercy, and You will be known through them. And if it is that You are waiting for my good works so as to hear my prayer through their means, grant them to me, and work them for me, and the sufferings You desire to accept, and let it be done. But if You are not waiting for my works, what is it that makes You wait, my most clement Lord? Why do You delay? For if, after all, I am to receive the grace and mercy which I entreat of You in Your Son, take my mite, since You desire it, and grant me this blessing, since You also desire that.

Who can free himself from lowly manners and limitations if You do not lift him to Yourself, my God, in purity of love? How will a man begotten and nurtured in lowliness rise up to You, Lord, if You do not raise him with Your hand which made Him?

You will not take from me, my God, what You once gave me in Your only Son, Jesus Christ, in Whom You gave me all I desire. Hence I rejoice that if I wait for You, You will not delay.

With what procrastinations do you wait, since from this very moment you can love God in your heart?

Mine are the heavens and mine is the earth. Mine are the nations, the just are mine, and mine the sinners. The angels are mine, and the Mother of God, and all things are mine; and God Himself is mine and for me, because Christ is mine and all for me.

What do you ask, then, and seek, my soul? Yours is all of this, and all is for you. Do not engage yourself in something less, nor pay heed to the crumbs which fall from your Father's table. Go forth and exult in your Glory! Hide yourself in It and rejoice, and you will obtain the supplications of your heart.

26. The very pure spirit does not meddle with exterior attachments or human respect, but it communes inwardly with God, alone and in solitude as to all forms, and with delightful tranquillity, for the knowledge of God is received in divine silence.

27. A soul enkindled with love is a gentle, meek, humble, and patient soul.

28. A soul that is hard because of its self-love grows harder. O good Jesus, if You do not soften it, it will ever continue in its natural hardness.

29. He who loses an opportunity is like the man who lets a bird fly from his hand, for he will never recover it.

30. I didn't know You, my Lord, because I still desired to know and relish things.

31. Well and good if all things change, Lord God, provided we are rooted in You.

32. One thought alone of man is worth more than the entire world, hence God alone is worthy of it.

33. For the insensible, what you do not feel; for the sensible, the senses; and for the spirit of God, thought.

34. Reflect that your guardian angel does not always move your desire for an action, but he does always enlighten your reason. Hence, in order to practice virtue do not wait until you feel like it, for your reason and intellect are sufficient.

35. Man's appetite when fixed on something else leaves no room for the angel to move it.

36. My spirit has become dry because it forgets to feed on You.

37. What you most seek and desire you will not find by this way of yours, nor through high contemplation, but in much humility and submission of heart.

38. Do not tire yourself, for you will not enter into the savor and sweetness of spirit if you do not apply yourself to the mortification of this that you desire.

39. Reflect that the most delicate flower loses its fragrance and withers fastest; therefore guard yourself against seeking to walk in a spirit of delight, for you will not be constant. Choose rather for yourself a robust spirit, detached from everything, and you will discover abundant peace and sweetness, for savory and durable fruit is gathered in a cold and dry climate.

40. Bear in mind that your flesh is weak and that no worldly thing can comfort or strengthen your spirit, for what is born of the world is world and what is born of the flesh is flesh. The good spirit is born only of the Spirit of God, Who communicates Himself neither through the world nor through the flesh.

41. Be attentive to your reason in order to do what it tells you concerning the way to God. It will be more valuable before your God than all the works you perform without this attentiveness and all the spiritual delights you seek.

42. Blessed is he who, setting aside his own liking and inclination, considers things according to reason and justice before doing them.

43. He who makes use of his reason is like one who eats substantial fruit, and he who is moved by the satisfaction of his will is like one who eats insipid fruit.

44. Lord, You return gladly and lovingly to lift up the one who offends You and I do not turn to raise and honor him who annoys me.

45. O mighty Lord, if a spark from the empire of Your justice effects so much in the mortal ruler who governs the nations, what will Your all-powerful justice do with the righteous and the sinner?

46. If you purify your soul of attachment to and desire for things, you will understand them spiritually. If you deny your appetite for them, you will enjoy their truth, understanding what is certain in them.

47. Lord, my God, You are not a stranger to him who does not estrange himself from You. How do they say that it is You who absent Yourself?

48. He has truly mastered all things who is not moved to joy by the satisfaction these things afford nor saddened by their insipidness.

49. If you wish to attain holy recollection, you will not do so by receiving but by denying.

50. Going everywhere, my God, with You, everywhere things will happen as I desire for You.

51. He will be unable to reach perfection who does not strive to be content with having nothing, in such fashion that his natural and spiritual desire is satisfied with emptiness; for this is necessary in order to reach the highest tranquillity and peace of spirit. Hence the love of God in the pure and simple soul is almost continually in act.

52. Since God is inaccessible, be careful not to concern yourself with all that your faculties can comprehend and your senses feel, so that you do not become satisfied with less and lose the lightness of soul suitable for going to Him.

53. The soul that journeys to God, but does not shake off its cares and quiet its appetites, is like one who drags a cart uphill.

54. It is not God's will that a man be disturbed by anything, or suffer trials, for if he suffers trials in the adversities of the world it is because of his weakness in virtue. The perfect man rejoices in what afflicts the imperfect man.

55. The way of life contains very little business and bustling and demands mortification of the will more than knowledge. The less one takes of things and pleasures the farther one advances along this way.

56. Think not that pleasing God lies so much in doing a great deal as in doing it with good will, without possessiveness and human respect.

57. At the evening of life, you will be examined in love. Learn to love as God desires to be loved and abandon your own ways of acting.

58. See that you do not interfere in the affairs of others, nor even allow them to pass through your memory, for perhaps you will be unable to accomplish your own task.

59. Do not think that, because the virtues you have in mind do not shine in your neighbor, he will not be precious in God's sight for something of which you are not thinking.

60. Man knows neither how to rejoice properly nor how to grieve properly, for he does not understand the distance between good and evil.

61. See that you are not suddenly saddened by the adversities of this world, for you do not know the good they bring, being ordained in the judgments of God for the everlasting joy of the elect.

62. Do not rejoice in temporal prosperity, since you do not know if it gives you assurance of eternal life.

63. In tribulation, immediately draw near to God with confidence, and you will receive strength, enlightenment, and instruction.

64. In joys and pleasures, immediately draw near to God in fear and truth, and you will neither be deceived nor involved in vanity.

65. Take God for your spouse and friend and walk with Him continually, and you will not sin and will learn to love, and the things you must do will work out prosperously for you.

66. You will without labor subject the nations and bring things to serve you if you forget them and yourself as well.

67. Abide in peace, banish cares, take no account of all that happens, and you will serve God according to His good pleasure, and rest in Him.

68. Consider that God reigns only in the peaceful and disinterested soul.

69. Although you perform many works, if you do not deny your will and submit yourself, losing all solicitude about yourself and your affairs, you will not make progress.

70. What does it profit you to give God one thing if He asks of you another? Consider what it is God wants, and then do it. You will as a result better satisfy your heart than with that toward which you yourself are inclined.

71. How is it you dare to relax so fearlessly, since you must appear before God to render an account of the least word and thought?

72. Reflect that many are called but few chosen and that, if you are not careful, your perdition is more certain than your salvation, especially since the path to eternal life is so narrow.

73. Do not rejoice vainly, for you know how many sins you have committed and you do not know how you stand before God, but have fear together with confidence.

74. Since, when the hour of reckoning comes, you will be sorry for not having used this time in the service of God, why do you not arrange and use it now as you would wish to have done were you dying?

75. If you desire that devotion be born in your spirit and that the love of God and the desire for divine things increase, cleanse your soul of every desire and attachment and ambition in suchwise that you have no concern about anything. Just as a sick man is immediately aware of good health once the bad humor has been thrown off and a desire to eat is felt, so will you recover your health, in God, if you cure yourself as was said. Without doing this, you will not advance no matter how much you do.

76. If you desire to discover peace and consolation for your soul and serve God truly, do not be content in this that you have left behind (because in that which now concerns you, you may be as impeded as you were before, or even more), but also leave all these other things and attend to one thing alone, which brings all these with it, namely, holy solitude, together with prayer and spiritual and divine reading, and persevere there in forgetfulness of all things. For if these things are not incumbent upon you, you will be more pleasing to God in knowing how to guard and perfect yourself than by gaining all other things together, for what does it profit a man if he gains the whole world and suffers the loss of his soul? [Mt. 16:26]

MAXIMS AND COUNSELS

MAXIMS ON LOVE

1. Bridle your tongue and your thoughts very much, direct your affection habitually toward God, and your spirit will be divinely enkindled.

2. Feed not your spirit on anything but God. Cast off concern about things, and bear peace and recollection in your heart.

3. Keep spiritually tranquil in a loving attentiveness to God, and when it is necessary to speak, let it be with the same calm and peace.

4. Preserve a habitual remembrance of eternal life, recalling that those who hold themselves the lowest and poorest and least of all will enjoy the highest dominion and glory in God.

5. Rejoice habitually in God, Who is your salvation, and reflect that it is good to suffer in any way for Him Who is good.

6. Let them reflect how necessary it is to be enemies of self and to walk to perfection by the path of holy rigor, and let them understand that every word spoken without the order of obedience is laid to their account by God.

7. Have an intimate desire that His Majesty grant you what He knows you lack for His honor.

8. Crucified inwardly and outwardly with Christ, you will live in this life with fullness and satisfaction of soul, and possess your soul in patience.

9. Preserve a loving attentiveness to God with no desire to feel or understand any particular thing concerning Him.

10. Habitual confidence in God, esteeming in yourself and in your sisters those things which God most values, which are spiritual goods.

11. Enter within yourself and work in the presence of your Spouse, Who is ever present loving you.

12. Be hostile to admitting into your soul things that of themselves have no spiritual substance, lest they make you lose your liking for devotion and recollection.

13. Let Christ crucified be enough for you, and with Him suffer and take your rest, and hence annihilate yourself in all inward and outward things.

14. Endeavor always that things be not for you, nor you for them, but forgetful of all, abide in recollection with your Spouse.

15. Have great love for trials and think of them as but a small way of pleasing your Spouse, Who did not hesitate to die for you.

16. Bear fortitude in your heart against all things that move you to that which is not God, and be a friend of the passion of Christ.

17. Be interiorly detached from all things and do not seek pleasure in any temporal thing, and your soul will concentrate on goods you do not know.

18. The soul that walks in love neither rests nor grows tired.

19. The poor man who is naked will be clothed, and the soul that is naked of desires and whims will be clothed by God with His purity, satisfaction, and will.

20. There are souls that wallow in the mire like animals, and there are others that soar like birds, which purify and cleanse themselves in the air.

21. The Father spoke one Word, which was His Son, and this Word He always speaks in eternal silence, and in silence must It be heard by the soul.

22. We must adjust our trials to ourselves, and not ourselves to our trials.

23. He who seeks not the cross of Christ seeks not the glory of Christ.

24. To be taken with love for a soul, God does not look upon its greatness, but upon the greatness of its humility.

25. "He who is ashamed to confess Me before men, I shall be ashamed to confess him before My Father," says the Lord. [Mt. 10:32; Lk. 9:26]

26. Frequent combing gives the hair more luster and makes it easier to comb; a soul that frequently examines its thoughts, words, and deeds, which are its hair, doing all things for the love of God, will have lustrous hair. Then the Spouse will look upon the neck of the bride and thereby be captivated, and will be wounded by one of her eyes, that is, by the purity of intention she has in all she does. If in combing hair one wants it to have luster, one begins from the crown. All our works must begin from the crown (the love of God) if we wish them to be pure and lustrous.

27. Heaven is stable and is not subject to generation, and souls of a heavenly nature are stable and not subject to the engendering of desires or of anything else, for in their way they resemble God Who does not move forever.

28. Eat not in forbidden pastures (those of this life), because blessed are they who hunger and thirst for justice sake, for they shall be filled. [Mt. 5:6] What God seeks, He being Himself God by nature, is to make us gods through participation, just as fire converts all things into fire.

29. All the goodness we possess is lent to us, and God considers it His own work. God and His work is God.

30. Wisdom enters through love, silence, and mortification. It is great wisdom to know how to be silent and to look at neither the remarks, nor the deeds, nor the lives of others.

31. All for me and nothing for You.

32. All for You and nothing for me.

33. Allow yourself to be taught, allow yourself to receive orders, allow yourself to be subjected and despised, and you will be perfect.

34. Any appetite causes five kinds of harm in the soul: first, disquiet; second, turbidity; third, defilement; fourth, weakness; fifth, obscurity.

35. Perfection does not lie in the virtues which the soul knows it has, but in the virtues which Our Lord sees in it. Thus is a closed book, and hence one has no reason for presumption, but must remain prostrate on the ground with respect to self.

36. Love consists not in feeling great things but in having great detachment and in suffering for the Beloved.

37. The entire world is not worthy of a man's thought, for this belongs to God alone; any thought, therefore, not centered on God is stolen from Him.

38. Not all the faculties and senses have to be employed in things, but only those which are required; as for the others leave them unoccupied for God.

39. Not observing the imperfections of others, preserving silence and a continual communion with God will eradicate great imperfections from the soul and make it the possessor of great virtues.

40. There are three signs of inner recollection: first, a lack of satisfaction in passing things; second, a liking for solitude and silence and an attentiveness to all that is more perfect; third, the considerations, medi-

tations, and acts which formerly helped the soul now hinder it, and it brings to prayer no other support than faith, hope, and love.

41. If a person has more patience in suffering and more forbearance in going without satisfaction, it is a sign that he is more proficient in virtue.

42. The traits of the solitary bird are five: first, it seeks the highest place; second, it withstands no company; third, it holds its beak in the air; fourth, it has no definite color; fifth, it sings sweetly. These traits must be possessed by the contemplative soul. It must rise above passing things, paying no more heed to them than if they did not exist. It must likewise be so fond of silence and solitude that it does not tolerate the company of another creature. It must hold its beak in the air of the Holy Spirit, responding to His inspirations, that by so doing it may become worthy of His company. It must have no definite color, desiring to do nothing definite other than the will of God. It must sing sweetly in the contemplation and love of its Spouse.

43. Habitual voluntary imperfections which are never completely overcome not only hinder the divine union, but also the attainment of perfection. Such imperfections are: the habit of much talking; some small unconquered attachment, such as to a person, an article of clothing, a cell, a book, or some kind of food, or other conversations and little satisfactions in tasting things, and knowing, and hearing, and the like.

44. If you wish to glory in yourself, but do not wish to appear ignorant and foolish, discard the things that are not yours and you will have glory in what remains. But certainly if you discard all that is not yours, nothing will be left, since you must not glory in anything if you do not want to fall into vanity. But let us descend now especially to those graces, the gifts of which make men pleasing in God's sight. It is certain that you must not glory in these gifts, for you do not even know if you possess them.

45. Oh, how sweet Your presence will be to me, You Who are the supreme good! I must draw near You in silence and uncover my feet before You that You may be pleased to unite me to You in marriage [Ru. 3:7], and I will not rest until I rejoice in Your arms. Now I ask You, Lord, not to abandon me at any time in my recollection, for I am a squanderer of my soul.

46. Detached from the exterior, dispossessed of the interior, disappropriated of the things of God—neither will prosperity detain you nor adversity hinder you.

47. The devil fears a soul united to God as he does God Himself.

48. The purest suffering produces the purest understanding.

49. The soul that desires God to surrender Himself to it entirely must surrender itself entirely to Him without keeping anything for itself.

50. The soul that has reached the union of love does not even experience the first motions of sin.

51. Old friends of God scarcely ever fail Him, for they stand above all that can make them fail.

52. My Beloved, all that is rugged and toilsome I desire for myself, and all that is sweet and delightful I desire for You.

53. What we need most in order to make progress is to be silent before this great God with our appetites and our tongue, for the language He best hears is silent love.

54. Simple faith is necessary in seeking God. In outward things, light helps to prevent one from falling; but in the things of God just the opposite is true: it is better for the soul not to see if it is to be more secure.

55. More is gained in one hour from God's good things than in a whole lifetime from our own.

56. Love to be unknown both by yourself and by others. Never look at the good or evil of others.

57. Walk in solitude with God; act according to the just measure; hide the blessings of God.

58. To lose always and let everyone else win is a trait of valiant souls, generous spirits, and unselfish hearts; it is their manner to give rather than receive even to the extent of giving themselves. They consider it a heavy burden to possess themselves and it pleases them more to be possessed by others and withdrawn from themselves, since we belong more to that infinite Good than we do to ourselves.

59. It is a serious evil to have more regard for God's blessings than for God Himself: prayer and detachment.

60. Look at that infinite knowledge and that hidden secret. What peace, what love, what silence is in that divine bosom! How lofty the science God teaches there, which is what we call the anagogical acts that so enkindle the heart.

61. Secrecy of conscience is considerably harmed and damaged as often as a person manifests its fruit to men, for then he receives as his reward the fruit of fleeting fame.

62. Speak little and do not meddle in matters about which you are not asked.

63. Strive always to keep God present and to preserve within yourself the purity He teaches you.

64. Do not excuse yourself nor refuse to be corrected by all; listen to every reproof with a serene countenance; think that God utters it.

65. Live as though only God and yourself were in this world so that your heart may not be detained by anything human.

66. Consider it the mercy of God that someone occasionally speak a good word to you, for you deserve none.

67. Never allow yourself to pour out your heart, even though it be but for the space of a creed.

68. Never listen to talk about the faults of others, and if someone complains of another, you can tell him humbly to say nothing of it to you.

69. Do not complain about anyone, nor ask for anything; and if it is necessary for you to ask, let it be with few words.

70. Do not refuse work even though it seems that you cannot do it. Let all find compassion in you.

71. Do not contradict; in no manner speak words that are not pure.

72. Let your speech be such that no one may be offended, and let it concern things which would not cause you regret were all to know of them.

73. Do not refuse anything you possess, even though you may need it.

74. Be silent concerning what God may have given you and recall that saying of the bride: *My secret for myself.* [Is. 24:16]

75. Strive to preserve your heart in peace and let no event of this world disturb it. Reflect that all must come to an end.

76. Take neither great nor little notice of who is with you or against you and try always to please God. Ask Him that His will be done in you. Love Him intensely, as He deserves to be loved.

77. Twelve stars for reaching the highest perfection: love of God, love of neighbor, obedience, chastity, poverty, attendance at choir, penance, humility, mortification, prayer, silence, peace.

78. Never take a man for your example in the tasks you have to perform, however holy he may be, for the devil will set his imperfection

before you. But imitate Christ, who is supremely perfect and supremely holy, and you will never err.

79. Seek in reading and you will find in meditation; knock in prayer and it will be opened to you in contemplation.

80. Once being asked how one becomes enraptured, the Venerable Father Fray John of the Cross, replied: by denying one's own will and doing the will of God; for an ecstasy is nothing else than going out of self and being caught up in God; and this is what he who obeys does; he leaves himself and his desire, and thus unburdened plunges himself in God.

Degrees of Perfection

1. Do not commit a mortal sin for all there is in the world, nor any deliberate venial sin, nor any known imperfection.

2. Endeavor to remain always in the presence of God, either real, imaginative, or unitive insofar as is permitted by your works.

3. Do nothing nor say any notable word that Christ would not have done or said were He in the state I am, as old as I, and with the same kind of health.

4. Strive for the greater honor and glory of God in all things.

5. Do not omit mental prayer for any occupation, for it is the sustenance of your soul.

6. Do not omit examination of conscience because of any of your occupations, and for every fault do some penance.

7. Be deeply sorry for any time that is lost or that passes without your loving God.

8. In all things, both high and low, let God be your goal, for in no other way will you grow in merit and perfection.

9. Never give up prayer, and should you find dryness and difficulty, persevere in it for this very reason. God often desires to see what love your soul has, and love is not tried by ease and satisfaction.

10. In heaven and on earth, always the lowest and the last place and office.

11. Never interfere in what you are not ordered to do, nor be obstinate about anything, even though you may be right. And if, as the

saying goes, they give you an inch, do not take a mile. Some deceive themselves in such matters and think they have an obligation of doing that which—if they reflect upon it well—in no way obliges them.

12. Pay no attention to the affairs of others, whether they be good or bad, for besides the danger of sin, this is a cause of distractions and the lack of spirit.

13. Strive always to confess your sins with a deep knowledge of your own wretchedness and with clarity and purity.

14. Even though your obligations and duties are difficult and disagreeable to you, you should not become dismayed, for this will not always be so. And God, Who proves the soul by a precept under the guise of a trial, will after a time accord it the experience of its own blessing and gain.

15. Remember always that everything that happens to you, whether prosperous or adverse, comes from God, so that you neither become puffed up in prosperity nor discouraged in adversity.

16. Remember always that you came here for no other reason than to be a saint; thus let nothing reign in your soul which does not lead you to sanctity.

17. Always be more disposed toward giving to others than giving to yourself, and thus you will not be envious of nor selfish toward your neighbor. This is to be understood from the viewpoint of perfection, for God is angered with those who do not give precedence to His good pleasure over that of men.

OTHER COUNSELS

1. The further you withdraw from earthly things the closer you approach heavenly things and the more you find in God.

2. Whoever knows how to die in all will have life in all.

3. Abandon evil, do good, and seek peace.

4. Anyone who complains or grumbles is not perfect, nor is he even a good Christian.

5. He is humble who hides in his own nothingness and knows how to abandon himself to God.

6. He is meek who knows how to suffer his neighbor and himself.

7. If you desire to be perfect, sell your will, give it to the poor in spirit, come to Christ in meekness and humility, and follow Him to Calvary and the sepulcher.

8. Anyone who trusts in himself is worse than the devil.

9. Anyone who does not love his neighbor abhors God.

10. Anyone who is lukewarm in his work is close to falling.

11. Whoever flees prayer flees all that is good.

12. Conquering the tongue is better than fasting on bread and water.

13. Suffering for God is better than working miracles.

14. Oh, what blessings we will enjoy in the vision of the Most Blessed Trinity!

CENSURE AND OPINION ON THE SPIRIT AND THE ATTITUDE IN PRAYER OF A DISCALCED CARMELITE NUN
[Probably written in Segovia between 1588–89]

In the affective attitude this religious bears there appear to be five defects which reveal that hers is not a good spirit.

First, it seems she has within her spirit a great attachment to possessing things, whereas the good spirit is always very detached in its appetites.

Second, she is too secure in her spirit and has little fear of being inwardly mistaken. Where this fear is absent, the spirit of God is never present to preserve the soul from harm, as the Wise Man says. [Prv. 15:27]

Third, it seems she has the desire to persuade others that her experiences are good and manifold. A person with a genuine spirit does not desire to do this, but, on the contrary, desires that his experiences be considered of little value and despised, and this he does himself.

Fourth—and this is the main fault—the effects of humility do not appear in her attitude. When favors are genuine, as she says here that hers are, they are ordinarily never communicated to a soul without first undoing and annihilating it in the inner abasement of humility. And if these favors had produced this effect in her, she would not have failed to say something about it here, and even a great deal. For the first thing the soul esteems and is eager to speak of are the effects of humility, which, certainly, are so strong that they cannot be disguised. For Although they may not be so noticeable in all the apprehensions of God, still, these apprehensions which she here calls union are never present without them: *Quoniam exaltetur anima, humiliatur*[2] [Prv. 18:12], and, *Bonum mihi quia humiliasti me.*[3] [Ps. 118:71]

Fifth, the style and language she uses doesn't seem to come from the spirit she claims, for the good spirit itself teaches a simpler style, one without the affectation or exaggeration she uses. And all this about what she said to God and God said to her seems to be nonsense.

I would advise that they should not command or allow her to write anything about this, and that her confessor should not show willingness to hear of it, other than to hold it in little esteem and contradict it. Let

[2] Before the soul is exalted, it is humbled.
[3] It is good for me that You have humbled me.

them try her in the practice of sheer virtue, especially in self-contempt, humility, and obedience; and by the sound of the metal when tapped, the quality of soul caused by so many favors will show itself. And the trials must be good ones, for there is no devil that will not suffer something for his honor.

LETTERS

1. [To Madre Catalina de Jesús

Baeza, July 6, 1581]

Jesus be in your soul, my daughter Catalina.

Although I know not where you are, I want to write these lines trusting that our *Madre* will send them on to you if you are not with her. And if it is so—that you are not with her—be consoled with the thought that you are not as abandoned and alone as I am down here. For after that whale swallowed me up [A biblical allusion to his imprisonment in Toledo.] and vomited me out upon this alien port, I have never merited to see her again nor the saints up there.

God has done well, for, after all, abandonment is a file and the endurance of darkness leads to great light. May it please God that we do not walk in darkness!

Oh, how many things I should like to say! But I am writing in darkness as to whether you will receive this or not. Thus I shall stop here without finishing.

Commend me to God. I do not want to say any more about matters down here, for I have no desire to do so.

From Baeza, July 6, 1581

Your servant in Christ,
Fray Juan de la Cruz

2. [To Madre Ana de San Alberto, Prioress of Caravaca

Granada, 1582]

. . . since you say nothing to me, I tell you not to be foolish and not to walk with fears that intimidate your soul. Return to God what He has given you and gives you each day. It seems you want to measure God by the measure of your own capacity, but it will not be so. Prepare yourself, for God desires to grant you a great favor.

3. [To the same Ana de San Alberto

Granada, 1582]

. . . How long, daughter, do you think you will be carried in the arms of others? Now I desire to see you so greatly despoiled of and detached from creatures that all hell would not be enough to disturb you. What tears are these, so trifling, which you are shedding these days? How much good time do you think you have lost with these scruples? Should you desire to let me know of your trials, go to that Spotless Mirror of the Eternal Father, that is, His Son, for there I see your soul every day, and doubtless you will be consoled and not find it necessary to beg at the doors of poor people.

4. [To Madre Ana de San Alberto, Prioress of Caravaca
Sevilla, June 1586]
Jesús be in your soul.

At the time I left Granada for the foundation in Córdoba, I wrote to you in haste. And afterwards, while in Córdoba, I received your letters and those of the gentlemen who were going to Madrid and who must have thought they would meet me while I was at the meeting of definitors. But you know this meeting never took place because we were waiting for the completion of the foundations and the visitations. The Lord gives us so much to do these days that we can hardly keep up with it all. The foundation for the friars in Córdoba was completed with greater applause and solemnity throughout the entire city than was ever given there to any other religious order. All the clergy and confraternities of Córdoba gathered, and the Most Blessed Sacrament was brought in great solemnity from the Cathedral. All the streets were beautifully decorated, and the people acted as though it were the feast of Corpus Christi. This took place on the Sunday after Ascension Thursday. The Bishop came and preached, praising us highly. The house is situated in the best district of the city, in the neighborhood of the Cathedral.

I am now in Sevilla for the transference of our nuns, who have bought some very fine houses. Although they cost around fourteen thousand ducats, they are worth more than twenty thousand. The nuns are now settled in them, and on the feast of San Bernabé, the Cardinal will reserve the Most Blessed Sacrament with great solemnity. I intend to leave another monastery of friars here before departing, so that there will then be two monasteries of friars here in Sevilla. Between now and the feast of San Juan I shall depart for Ecija, where, with God's help, we shall make another foundation, then to Málaga, and from there to the meeting.

Would that I had the commission for this foundation as I have had for the others and could avoid these many delays. But I hope in God that it will be accomplished, and in the meeting I shall do all I can. Tell this to these gentlemen to whom I am writing.

I am sorry you did not immediately sign the deed regarding the matter with the Fathers of the Society, for from what I observe they are not people who keep to their word. Thus I not only think they will deviate partly, but, if the matter is deferred, and if it is expedient to them, they will turn back completely. Hence take careful note of what I say: without mentioning anything to them or to anyone, discuss with Señor Gonzalo Muñoz the purchase of the other house in that other locale, and sign the deed. For since they see that they have you by the hook, they are in no hurry. It matters little if afterwards it be known that we bought only with the intention of being freed from our annoyance. Thus they will agree without so much breaking of heads, and we will even oblige them to agree to whatever we desire. Tell this to only a few, and do it, for sometimes you cannot surmount one ruse without using another.

I should like you to send me the small book of the *Stanzas of the Bride*, for surely by now Sister Francisca de la Madre de Dios is finished copying them.

This definitory meeting is being greatly delayed, and I am sorry on account of my desire that Doña Catalina enter, for I want to give . . .

Your servant,

Fray Juan de la Cruz

Be sure to give my heartiest greetings to Señor Gonzalo Muñoz. I am not writing to him because I do not want to tire him and because Your Reverence can tell him what I have said here.

5. [To a Discalced Carmelite Nun

1586, on journey from Granada to Madrid]

Daughter, God will try those who are strong soldiers in dryness and emptiness concerning all things that they might be victorious in battle, for they know how to drink water from their hands while standing (not bending over to the ground), like the soldiers of Gedeon, who conquered through the dry clay jars which had lighted candles within [Jgs. 7:5–7, 16–23]; these jars signify the dryness of sense outside and the good and enkindled spirit within.

6. [To the Discalced Carmelite Nuns of Beas

Málaga, November 18, 1586]

Jesus be in your souls, my daughters.

Do you think that, since you see me so silent, I have lost sight of you and have ceased considering how with great ease you can become saints and walk in the joy of your beloved Bridegroom with great delight and sure protection? I am coming to Beas, and you will see how I have not forgotten. And we shall see the riches gained in pure love and in the paths of eternal life and the beautiful steps you are making in Christ, whose brides are His delight and crown. It is unworthy of the crown that it roll along the ground, for it should be taken in the hands of the angels and seraphim and placed with reverence and esteem upon the head of its Lord.

When the heart walks along the ground among base things, the crown rolls and is kicked by every base thing. But when man attains to a lofty heart, as David says, then God is exalted [Ps. 63:7–8] with the crown of His bride's lofty heart, with which they crowned Him on the day of the joy of His heart [Ct. 3:11], that day in which His delights were to be with the children of men. [Prv. 8:31] These waters of inward delights do not spring from the earth. One must open toward heaven the mouth of desire, empty of all other fullness, that thus it may not be reduced or restricted by some mouthful of another pleasure, but truly empty and open toward Him who says: *Open your mouth wide and I shall fill it.* [Ps. 80:11]

Accordingly, he who seeks his satisfaction in something no longer keeps himself empty that God might fill him with His ineffable delight. And thus just as he goes to God so does he return, for his hands are encumbered and cannot receive what God is giving. May God deliver us from these evil obstacles which hinder such sweet and delightful freedom.

Serve God, my beloved daughters in Christ, following in His footsteps of mortification, in utter patience, in total silence, and with every desire to suffer, becoming executioners of your own satisfactions, mortifying yourselves, if perhaps something remains that must die and something still impedes the inner resurrection of the Spirit Who dwells within your souls. Amen.

From Málaga, November 18, 1586

> Your servant,
> Fray Juan de la Cruz

7. [To the Discalced Carmelite Nuns of Beas
>   Granada, November 22, 1587]

[Address:] To Ana de Jesús and the other Discalced Carmelite Nuns of the Convent of Beas

Jesus and Mary be in your souls, my daughters in Christ.

Your letter was a great comfort to me. May Our Lord repay you. My failure to write was not due to any unwillingness, for indeed I desire your great good, but to my belief that enough has already been said and written for doing that which is important; and that what is wanting, if anything is wanting, is not writing or speaking—rather these usually superabound—but silence and work. Furthermore, speaking distracts one, while silence and work recollects and strengthens the spirit. Once a person knows what has been told him for his benefit, he no longer needs to hear or speak, but to put it into practice, silently and carefully and in humility and charity and contempt of self. He must not then go in search of new things that serve only to satisfy the appetite outwardly— although they are not able to satisfy it—and leave the spirit weak and empty without interior virtue. Hence it follows that neither the former nor the latter is of profit. We can compare this situation to the man who eats before digesting what he previously ate; for since the natural heat is divided between the two portions, it has not the strength to convert it all into substance, and the man becomes sick.

It is very necessary, my daughters, to hide the spirit from the devil and from our senses, for if we do not, we shall, without realizing it, find ourselves very backward and far from the virtues of Christ. Afterwards we shall awaken only to find our labor and work done in the wrong way, and thinking that we were carrying a lighted lamp, we shall discover that it has gone out. Because by blowing, in our opinion to keep it lighted, we perhaps did more to extinguish it. I say, then, so that this might not happen, and that the spirit be preserved, that there is no better remedy than to suffer, to do, and to be silent, and to close the senses through the inclination toward and practice of solitude and the forgetfulness of all creatures and happenings, even though the whole world crumbles. Never, whether in adversity or in prosperity, cease to quiet your heart with deep love so as to suffer whatever comes along. For perfection is so singularly important and the delight of the spirit is so high-priced that all of this is hardly enough to obtain it. It is impossible to advance without doing and suffering virtuously, all enveloped in silence.

Keep this in mind, daughters: the soul that is quick to turn to speaking and conversing is slow to turn to God. For when it is turned toward God, it is then strongly and inwardly drawn toward silence and flight from all conversation. For God desires a soul to rejoice with Him more than with any other person, however advanced and helpful the person may be.

I commend myself to your prayers; and be assured that although my charity is little, it is so directed toward you that I do not forget those whom I owe so much in the Lord. May He be with you all. Amen.

From Granada, November 22, 1587

Fray Juan de la Cruz

Our greatest need is to be silent before this great God with the appetite and with the tongue, for the only language He hears is the silent language of love.

8. [To Madre Leonor Bautista, Discalced Carmelite in Beas

Granada, February 8, 1588]

Jesus be in Your Reverence.

Do not think, daughter in Christ, that I have ceased to grieve for you in your trials and for the others who share in them. Yet, in recalling that, since God called you to live an apostolic life, which is a life of contempt, He is leading you along its road, I am consoled. After all, God wishes a religious to be a religious—in such a way that he be done with all and that all be done to him. For it is God Himself who wishes to be the riches, comfort, and delightful glory of the religious. God has granted you a great favor, because in having forgotten all things you will be able to enjoy His good in solitude, and for love of Him have no care that they do to you what they will, since you do not belong to yourself but to God.

Let me know if your departure for Madrid is certain and if the Mother Prioress is going, and give my best regard to my daughters Magdalena and Ana and to all the others, for I have not time to write them.

From Granada, February 8, 1588

Fray Juan de la Cruz

9. [To Padre Ambrosio Mariano, Discalced Carmelite, Prior of Madrid
Segovia, November 9, 1588]

Jesus be in Your Reverence.

Because of the many foundations, the need for religious, as Your Reverence knows, is very great. Thus Your Reverence must be patient for Fray Miguel has to go to await Padre Provincial in Pastrana and then finish the foundation of that monastery in Molina.

Also, the fathers thought it would be expedient to give Your Reverence a subprior at once. And so they have given you Padre Fray Angel, thinking that he will get along well with his prior, something that is most desirable in a monastery. Your Reverence may give his patent letter to each one. You should be careful that no priest or other religious interfere with the novices, for as Your Reverence knows there is nothing more harmful than that the novices pass through many hands and that others be disturbing them. Since he has so many novices, it is right to help and and assist Padre Fray Angel and even give him the authority of subprior (which he has now been given) so that he might receive more respect in the house.

It seems that now there was not much need for Padre Fray Miguel here and that he can better serve the Order elsewhere.

There is nothing new concerning Padre Gracián, except that Padre Fray Antonio is already here.

From Segovia, November 9, 1588

Fray Juan de la Cruz

10. [To Doña Juana de Pedraza, in Granada
Segovia, January 28, 1589]

Jesus be in your soul.

A few days ago I wrote to you through Padre Fray Juan in answer to your last letter, which, as was your hope, I prized. I have answered you in that letter, since I believe I have received all your letters. An I have felt your grief, afflictions, and loneliness. These, in silence, ever tell me so much that the pen cannot declare it. They are all comparable to knocks and rappings at the door of your soul that it might love more, for they cause more prayer and spiritual sighs to God that He might fulfill the soul's petition. I have already told you that there is no reason . . . , but do what they have ordered you to do, and when they impede it, be obedient and let me know of it, for God will provide what is best. God watches over the affairs of those who truly love Him without their worrying about them.

In what concerns the soul, it is safest not to lean on anything nor desire anything. A soul should find its support wholly and entirely in its director, for not to do so would amount to no longer wanting a director. And when one director is sufficient and suitable, all the others are useless or a hindrance. Let not the soul be attached to anything, for since prayer is not wanting, God will take care of His possessions; they belong to no other owner, nor should they. I see this with myself: the more that things are mine, the more I set my heart and soul and care on them. The loved object becomes one with the lover, and so does God with him who loves Him. Hence one cannot forget the loved object without forgetting one's own soul; and a person even forgets his own soul for the object loved, because he lives in the thing he loves more than in himself.

O great God of love, and Lord! How many riches do You place in him who neither loves nor is satisfied save in You alone, for You give Yourself to him and become one with him through love. And consequently You give him for his enjoyment and love what his soul most desires in You and what brings it most profit. But because it behooves us not to go without the cross, just as our Beloved did not go without it, even to the death of love, He directs our sufferings in the love of what we most desire that we might make greater sacrifices and be worth more. But everything is brief, for it lasts only until the knife is raised; and then Isaac remains alive with the promise of a multiplied offspring.

Patience is necessary in this poverty, my daughter; it is helpful in truly departing from our land and entering into life where we have complete enjoyment of everything, which is . . . life.

Now I do not know when I shall leave. I am well, although my soul lags far behind. Commend me to God, and, when you can, give your letters to Fray Juan or to the nuns more often—and it would be better if they were not so short.

From Segovia, January 28, 1589

Fray Juan de la Cruz

11. [To a young lady from Narros del Castillo (Avila) aspiring to be a Discalced Carmelite.

Segovia, February 1589(?)]

Jesus be in your soul.

The messenger, arriving at a time when I was unable to answer, continued his journey, and now on his return is here awaiting my reply. May God ever give you, my daughter, His holy grace so that in all things you may employ yourself entirely in His holy love and service, as is your obligation, since this is why He created and redeemed you.

A great deal could be said about the three points you raised, more than my lack of time and paper now permits. But I shall speak to you of another three which you will find a help.

In regard to sins, which God so abhors that they obliged Him to die: you should, in order to weep truly over them and avoid falling into them, have as little to do with people as possible, flee from them, and never speak more than is necessary in each case. For conversing with people more than wholly necessary was never good for anyone, however holy he may have been. And together with this you should keep the law of God with great punctuality and love.

With regard to the Lord's passion: you should endeavor to treat your body with a discreet rigor, strive after self-contempt and mortification, and renounce the desire to do your own will or seek your own satisfaction, since that was the cause of His passion and death. And in all that you do let it be with your mother's counsel.

In regard to the third point, which is glory: to have the right idea of glory and to love it, you should consider all the riches of the world and its delights as mud and vanity and weariness, as they truly are, and do not esteem anything, however signal and precious, except being in God's grace. All that is best here below is ugly and bitter when compared to those eternal goods for which we were created. And however brief the ugliness and bitterness, it will last forever in the soul that esteems it.

I have not forgotten your business matter, but nothing more can be done now, although I have a great desire to do so. Entrust this earnestly to God and take our Lady and St. Joseph as your advocates in it.

Give my best regards to your mother and let this letter be for her too. Will you both pray for me and ask your friends also to do so out of charity.

May God grant you His Spirit.

From Segovia, February

Fray Juan de la Cruz

12. [To a Discalced Carmelite friar

Segovia, April 14, 1589]

May the peace of Jesus Christ, my son, be always in your soul. I received Your Reverence's letter in which you told me of the great desires our Lord gives you to occupy your will in Him alone by loving Him above all things, and in which you asked for some counsels to help you do this.

I am happy God has given you such holy desires, and I shall be much happier if you carry them out. In order to do so, you should observe how all pleasures, joys, and affections are ever caused in the soul by means of the desire and will for things which appear good, suitable, and delightful, being in a person's opinion satisfying and precious. And accordingly the appetite of the will inclines toward these things, hopes for them, rejoices in their possession, fears their loss, and grieves upon losing them. And thus according to its affection for and joy in things the soul is disturbed and restless.

In order to annihilate and mortify these attachments to pleasures in all that is not God, Your Reverence ought to note that every particular thing in which the will can rejoice is sweet and delightful, since it is in one's opinion satisfying; and nothing delightful and sweet in which one can rejoice is God. For, since God is inapprehensible to the faculties, He cannot be the object of the appetites and satisfactions of the will. Since the soul cannot in this life enjoy God essentially, all the sweetness and delight it tastes, however sublime, cannot be God. Likewise, any particular satisfaction and desire of the will derives from its knowledge of such and such an object. Since the will has never tasted God as He is, nor known Him through some gratification of the appetite, and consequently does not know what God is like, it cannot know what the pleasure of God is, nor can the appetite, and satisfaction of the will know how to desire God, for He transcends all its capacity. Thus it is obvious that none of all those particular things in which it can rejoice is God. In order to be united with Him, the will must consequently be emptied of and detached from all disordered appetite and satisfaction in every particular thing in which it can rejoice, whether earthly or heavenly, temporal or spiritual, so that purged and cleansed of all inordinate satisfactions, joys, and appetites it might be wholly occupied in loving God with its affections. For if in any way the will can comprehend God and be united with Him, it is through love, and not through any gratification of the appetite. And since the delight, sweetness, and satisfaction that can come to the will is not love, none of the delightful feelings can be an adequate means for the union of the will with God; it is the operation of the will which is the proportionate means for this union. The will's operation is quite distinct from the will's feeling: by its operation, which is love, the will is united with God and terminates in Him, and not by the feeling and gratification of its appetite which remains in the soul and goes no further. The feelings only serve as stimulants to love, if the will desires to pass beyond them, and they serve for no more. Thus the delightful feelings do not of themselves lead the soul to God, but rather cause it to become attached to them.

But the operation of the will, which is the love of God, concentrates the affection, joy, pleasure, satisfaction, and love of the soul only upon God, leaving aside all things and loving Him above them all. Hence if a person is moved to the love of God without dependence upon the sweetness he feels, he leaves aside this sweetness and centers his love on God Whom he cannot feel. Were he to love the sweetness and satisfaction, pausing and being detained in it, making an end and goal of the means, the work of the will would consequently be faulty. Since God is incomprehensible and inaccessible, the will, if it is to center its activity of love upon Him, must not set it upon that which it can touch and apprehend with the appetite, but on that which is incomprehensible and inaccessible to the appetite. Loving in this way, a soul loves truly and certainly according to the demands of faith, also in emptiness and darkness concerning its feelings, above all the sentiments it may experience in understanding its concepts, so that it believes and loves above everything it can understand.

Thus he would be very foolish who would think that God is failing him because of his lack of spiritual sweetness and delight, or would rejoice, thinking that he possesses God because of the presence of this sweetness. And he would be more foolish if he were to go in search of this sweetness in God and rejoice and be detained in it. With such an attitude he would no longer be seeking God with his will grounded in the emptiness of faith and charity, but he would be seeking spiritual satisfaction and sweetness, which are creatures, by following after his own pleasure and appetite. And thus he would no longer love God purely, above all things, which means centering all the strength of one's will on Him, for in binding and attaching itself to that creature by means of the appetite, the will does not rise above it to God, Who is inaccessible. It is impossible for the will to reach the sweetness and delight of the divine union and receive and feel the sweet and loving embraces of God without the nakedness and void of its appetite regarding every particular satisfaction, earthly and heavenly. This is what David meant when he said: *Dilata os tuum et implebo illud.*[4] [Ps. 80:11]

It is worth knowing, then, that the appetite is the mouth of the will. It is opened wide when it is not encumbered or occupied with any mouthful of pleasure. When the appetite is centered upon something, it becomes narrow by this very fact, since outside of God everything is narrow. That the soul have success in journeying to God and being joined to Him, it must have the mouth of its will opened only to God Himself, empty and dispossessed of every morsel of appetite, that God may fill it with His love and sweetness; and it must remain with this hunger and thirst for God alone, without desiring to be satisfied by

[4] Open wide your mouth and I will fill it.

any other thing, since here below it cannot enjoy God as He is in Himself. And what is enjoyable—if there is a desire for it, as I say—impedes this union. Isaias taught this when he said: *All you who thirst, come to the waters.* [Is. 55:1] He invites to the abundance of the divine waters of union with God only those who thirst for God alone and who have no other thirst, that is, other appetites.

It is very important and fitting for Your Reverence, if you desire to possess profound peace in your soul and attain perfection, that you surrender your whole will to God that it may thus be united with Him and that you do not let it be occupied with the vile and base things of earth.

May His Majesty make you as spiritual and holy as I desire you to be.

From Segovia, April 14
Fray Juan de la Cruz

13. [To Madre María de Jesús, Discalced Carmelite, Prioress of Córdoba

Segovia, June 7, 1589]

Jesus be in Your Reverence and make you as holy and poor in spirit as you desire, and may His Majesty also grant this to me.

Enclosed is the permission for the four novices. See that they be good servants of God.

Now I desire to answer all your questions briefly, for I have little time. I discussed them first with the Fathers here, because our Father Provincial is down there. May God bring him back to us safely.

1. The discipline of rods is no longer in use, even though the office may be from the ferial day. This practice expired with the Carmelite rite, for with that rite there were few ferial days and it was had only at certain times.

2. Second, neither give to all nor to anyone in particular, general permission to take the discipline three times a week as a recompense for this or anything else. In individual cases, as is the custom, you can make the decision. Keep to the common practice.

3. They should not ordinarily arise earlier in the morning than the Constitutions prescribe—that is, the community.

4. Permissions expire when the superior goes out of office. And so now as a result I am again sending you permission to allow the confessor, doctor, barber-surgeon, and laborers to enter the cloister in case of necessity.

5. Since you now have many empty places, we can discuss your question concerning Sister Aldonza when what you say is necessary. Give her my regards and commend me to God. Abide with Him. I cannot write at greater length.

From Segovia, June 7, 1589
Fray Juan de la Cruz

14. [To Madre Leonor de San Gabriel, Discalced Carmelite in Córdoba
Segovia, July 8, 1589]

Jesus be in your soul, my daughter in Christ.

Thank you for your letter. And I thank God for having desired to use you in this foundation, since His Majesty has done this in order to bring you greater profit. The more He wants to give, the more He makes us desire—even to the point of leaving us empty in order to fill us with goods. You will be repaid for the goods (the love of your sisters) which you leave behind in Sevilla. Since the immense blessings of God can only enter and fit in an empty and solitary heart, the Lord wants you to be alone. For He truly loves you with the desire of being Himself all your company. And Your Reverence will have to strive carefully to be content only with His companionship, that you might discover in it every happiness. Even though the soul may be in heaven, it will not be happy if it does not will this deliberately. And we will be unhappy with God, even though He is always with us, if our heart is not alone, but attached to something else.

I truly believe the nuns in Sevilla will feel lonely without Your Reverence. But perhaps you have done all you could there and God desires you to be of use here, for this foundation will be important. Endeavor to be a genuine help to the Mother Prioress, with great conformity and love in all things, although I clearly see that I do not have to make this recommendation, for since you are older and more experienced, you already know what usually happens in these foundations. On this account we chose Your Reverence. Were it simply a matter of nuns, there are so many here that there is hardly room for them all.

Best regards to Sister María de la Visitación and thank Sister Juana de San Gabriel for her greetings. May God give Your Reverence His Spirit.

From Segovia, July 8, 1589
Fray Juan de la Cruz

15. [To Madre Leonor de San Gabriel, Discalced Carmelite in Córdoba
Madrid, July 1589(?)]

Jesus be in your soul, my daughter in Christ.

In reading your letter I felt sorry for you in your affliction and I grieve over it because of the harm it can do your spirit and even your health. But you ought to know that I don't think you should be as afflicted as you are . . .

Do not be troubled nor pay any attention to this, for you have no reason to. I certainly believe it is a temptation the devil brings to your mind so that what should be employed in God is taken up with this. Be courageous, my daughter, and give yourself greatly to prayer, forgetting this thing and that, for after all we have no other good . . .

From Madrid, July

16. [To Madre María de Jesús, Prioress of the Discalced Carmelites in Córdoba

Segovia, July 18, 1589]

Jesus be in your soul.

You have the obligation of responding to the Lord in accordance with the acclaim with which you were received in Córdoba, for I was certainly consoled in reading the account. It was ordained by God that you enter such poor houses and in such heat so that you could give some edification and let them know what you profess, which is the naked Christ, that those who are inclined to join you may know with what spirit they ought to come.

Enclosed are all the permissions. Be very careful about whom you receive in the beginning, for upon them depends the spiritual well-being of all those who follow. See to it that they preserve the spirit of poverty and contempt for all things, with the desire to be content with God alone. If they don't, be assured that they will fall into a thousand spiritual and temporal necessities. And keep in mind that they will neither have nor feel any more needs than those to which they desire to submit their hearts. For he who is poor in spirit is happier and more constant in the midst of want, because he has placed his all in nothingness, and in all things he thus finds freedom of heart. O happy nothingness, and happy hiding place of the heart! For the heart has such power that it subjects all things to itself; this it does by desiring to be subject to nothing and losing all care so as to burn the more in love.

My greetings in the Lord to all the Sisters. Tell them that, since our Lord has chosen them as foundation stones, to consider what kind they ought to be, for the others should rest upon stronger ones. May they profit by this initial spirit which God gives in these beginnings so as to take up once again the way of perfection in all humility and detachment, interior and exterior, not with a childish spirit but with a robust will. Let them follow after mortification and penance, desiring that this Christ cost them something, and not be like those who seek their comfort and consolation either in God or outside of Him, but let them seek suffering both in God and outside of Him, for love of Him, in silence and hope and loving remembrance. Tell this to Gabriela and to her companions from Málaga, for I am writing to the others. May God give you His Spirit. Amen.

From Segovia, July 18, 1589
Fray Juan de la Cruz

Padre Fray Antonio and the other Fathers send their regards. Give my greetings to Padre Prior of Guadalcázar.

17. [To Magdalena del Espíritu Santo, Discalced Carmelite in Córdoba
Segovia, July 28, 1589]

Jesus be in your soul, my daughter in Christ.

I am happy to see the good resolutions shown in your letter. I praise
God that He provides in all things, for you will truly have need of these
resolutions at the beginning of the foundation because of the heat,
crowded quarters, poverty, and work that is everywhere; there will be so
much of all this that you will not notice whether you suffer or not.
Reflect that in these beginnings God does not want sluggish or cowardly
souls, nor still less those who love themselves. And to avoid this His
Majesty helps more at these times so that with a little diligence they can
advance in every virtue. And it has been fortunate for you and a sign
from God in that He has passed by others and chosen you. However
great was the cost in leaving behind what you did, it is nothing, because
soon you would have had to leave it anyhow. To possess God in all, you
should not possess anything in all. For how can the heart that belongs to
one belong completely to the other?

Tell the same to Sister Juana, and commend me to God. May He be in
your soul. Amen.

From Segovia, July 28, 1589
Fray Juan de la Cruz

18. [To Padre Nicolás de Jesús María (Doria), Vicar General of the
Discalced Carmelites
Segovia, September 21, 1589]

Jesus and Mary be with Your Reverence.

We were very glad to know that Your Reverence arrived in good
health and that everything is so well there, and that the Nuncio is well
too. I hope that God will look after His family; the religious here are in
good health and well-united. I shall try to carry out quickly what you
ordered, although the floods have not yet arrived.

Regarding the reception of aspirants in Genova without their having
studied the humanities, the Fathers say that this does not matter if they
understand enough Latin to comply with the decrees of the Council
(that they know how to construct sentences well) and that, if with this
alone they may be ordained there, they can be admitted. But the Fathers
think that, if the Ordinaries there are not content with this, it would seem
that these aspirants do not have the sufficient knowledge demanded by
the Council and that it would be burdensome to have to bring them here
to ordain or teach them. And, indeed, they would not want many
Italians to come here.

The letters will be sent to Padre Fray Nicolás as Your Reverence
says. May our Lord watch over you as He sees is necessary.

From Segovia, September 21, 1589
Fray Juan de la Cruz

19. [To Doña Juana de Pedraza, in Granada

Segovia, October 12, 1589]

[Address:] To Doña Juana de Pedraza, in the house of the archdeacon of Granada, in front of the College of the Abbots

Jesus be in your soul and thanks to Him that He has enabled me not to forget the poor, as you say, or be idle, as you say. For it greatly vexes me to think you believe what you say; this would be very bad after so many kindnesses on your part when I least deserved them. That's all I need now is to forget you! Look, how could this be so in the case of one who is in my soul as you are?

Since you walk in these darknesses and voids of spiritual poverty, you think that everyone and everything is failing you. It is no wonder that in this it also seems that God is failing you. But nothing is failing you, neither do you have to discuss anything, nor is there anything to discuss, nor do you know this, nor will you find it, because all of these are doubts without basis. He who desires nothing else than God walks not in darkness, however poor and dark he is in his own sight. And he who walks not presumptuously nor according to his own satisfactions, whether from God or from creatures, nor does his own will in anything has nothing to stumble over or discuss with anyone. You are making good progress. Do not worry, but rejoice! Who are you that you should guide yourself? Wouldn't that end up fine!

You were never better off than now, because you were never so humble nor so submissive, nor considered yourself and all worldly things to be so small, nor did you know that you were so evil, nor did you serve God so purely and so disinterestedly as now, nor do you follow after the imperfections of your own will and interests as perhaps you were accustomed to do. What is it you desire? What kind of life or method of procedure do you paint for yourself in this life? What do you think serving God involves other than avoiding evil, keeping His commandments, and being occupied with the things of God as best we can? When this is had, what need is there of other apprehensions or other lights and satisfactions from this source or that. In these there is hardly ever a lack of stumbling blocks and dangers for the soul, which by its understanding and appetites is deceived and charmed; and its own faculties cause it to err. And thus it is a great favor from God when He darkens them and impoverishes the soul in such a way that it cannot err with them. And if one does not err in this, what need is there in order to be right other than to walk along the level road of the law of God and of the Church and live only in dark and true faith and certain hope and complete charity, expecting all our blessings in heaven, living here below like pilgrims, the poor, the exiled, orphans, the thirsty, without a road and without anything, hoping for everything in heaven?

Rejoice and trust in God, for He has given you signs that you can very well do so, and in fact you must do so. If you do not, it will not be surprising if He becomes angry at seeing you walk so foolishly when He is leading you by a road most suitable for you and has brought you to so safe a place. Desire no other path than this and adjust your soul to it (for it is a good one) and receive communion as usual. Go to confession when you have something definite; you don't have to discuss these things with anyone. Should you have some problem, write to me about it. Write soon, and more frequently, for you can do so in care of Doña Ana when you are unable to do so through the nuns.

I have been somewhat ill. Now I am well, but Fray Juan Evangelista is sick. Commend him and me also to God, my daughter in the Lord.

From Segovia, October 12, 1589
Fray Juan de la Cruz

20. [To Madre María de Jesús, Prioress of the Discalced Carmelites of Córdoba

Madrid, June 20, 1590]

Jesus be in your soul, my daughter in Christ.

The reason for my not having written during all this time is due more to my having been in such an out-of-the-way place, as is Segovia, than because of a lack of desire. My will to write remains ever the same and I hope in God it will continue to be so. I have been sorry about your troubles.

I would desire that you be not so solicitous for the temporal things of this house, because God will gradually forget you and you will come to a state of great spiritual and temporal need, for it is our anxiety which creates our needs. Cast your care upon the Lord, daughter, and He will sustain you [Ps. 54:23], for He Who gives, and wants to give, the highest cannot fail to give the least. Be careful that you do not lack the desire to be poor and in want, for if you do, at that very hour devotion will fail you and you will gradually weaken in the practice of virtue. If previously you desired poverty, now that you are superior you ought to desire and love it much more. You ought to govern and provide the house with virtues and ardent desires for heaven rather than with worries and plans about temporal and earthly things. The Lord tells us not to be anxious about food or clothing or tomorrow. [Mt. 6:31, 34]

What you should do is endeavor to keep yourself and the nuns most perfectly and religiously united with God, in forgetfulness of all creatures and of any concern about them, wholly one with God, and happy with Him alone, for I assure you all the rest. I find it difficult to believe that the houses will help you out any longer, since you are in so good a locality and receiving nuns from such well-to-do families. However, if I see some chance anywhere of helping you, I shall not fail to do what I can.

I desire to send great comfort to Mother Subprioress. I hope in the Lord you will extend it to her, encouraging her to bear her pilgrimage and exile for love of Him. Enclosed is a letter for her. To my daughters Magdalena, San Gabriel, and María de San Pablo, María de la Visitación, San Francisco and all, many greetings in our Good. May He be ever in your spirit, my daughter. Amen.

From Madrid, June 20, 1590
Fray Juan de la Cruz

Soon, I believe, I shall return to Segovia.

21. [To a Discalced Carmelite nun suffering from scruples
Shortly before Pentecost, 1590]
Jesus, Mary.

In these days try to keep interiorly occupied with the desire for the coming of the Holy Spirit and on the feast and afterwards with His continual presence. Let your care and esteem for this be so great that nothing else will matter to you or receive your attention, whether it may concern some affliction or some other disturbing memories. And if there be faults in the house during these days, pass over them for love of the Holy Spirit and of what you owe to the peace and quietude of the soul in which He is pleased to dwell.

If you could put an end to your scruples, I think it would be better for your quietude of soul not to confess during these days. But when you do confess, you should do so in this manner:

With regard to thoughts and imaginings (whether they concern judgments, or other inordinate objects or representations, or any other motions) which occur without being desired or accepted or deliberately adverted to, do not confess them, nor pay attention to them, nor worry about them. It is better to forget them no matter how much they afflict the soul. At most you can mention in general any omission or remissness as regards the purity and perfection you ought to have in the interior faculties: memory, intellect, and will.

In regard to speaking: confess any want of caution in speaking with truthfulness and rectitude, with necessity, and with purity of intention.

Regarding your deeds: confess any lack of the proper and only motive —God alone without any other concern.

By such a confession you can be content and need not tell any other particular thing, however much it may battle against you. Receive communion on Pentecost in addition to those days on which you usually receive.

When something distasteful or unpleasant comes your way, remember Christ crucified and be silent.

Live in faith and hope, even though you are in darkness, because it is in these darknesses that God protects the soul. Cast your care upon

God, for He watches over you and will not forget you. Do not think that He leaves you alone; that would be an affront to Him.

Read, pray, rejoice in God, both your good and your salvation. May He grant you this good and this salvation and conserve it all until the day of eternity. Amen. Amen.

Fray Juan de la Cruz

22. [To Juan de Santa Ana, in Andalucía

Segovia, 1590]

. . . if at any time, my son, someone—whether he be a superior or not —should try to persuade you of any lax doctrine, do not believe in it or embrace it; even though he might confirm it with miracles. But believe in and embrace more penance and detachment from all things, and do not seek Christ without the cross.

23. [To Madre Ana de Jesús, in Segovia

Madrid, July 6, 1591]

Jesus be in your soul.

Thank you very much for your letter; this puts me under greater obligation than before. If things did not turn out as you desired, you ought rather to be consoled and thank God profusely. Since His Majesty has so arranged matters, it is what most suits everyone. All that remains for us is to accept it willingly so that since we believe He has arranged this we may show it by our actions. Things that do not please us seem to be evil and harmful, however good and fitting they may be. And it is obvious that this is not evil or harmful, neither for me nor for anyone. It is in my favor since, being freed and relieved from the care of souls, I can, if I want and with God's help, enjoy peace, solitude, and the delightful fruit of forgetfulness of self and of all things. It is also good for others that I be separated from them, for thus they will be freed of the faults they would have committed on account of my misery.

What I ask of you, daughter, are your prayers to the Lord that whatever happens He may continue to grant me this favor. I still fear they will make me go to Segovia and not leave me so free from all things, although I will do what I can to free myself from this too. But if this cannot be, still, Madre Ana de Jesús will not be left without my direction, as she fears, and thus she will not die of this sorrow that the opportunity, in her opinion, of being very holy has come to an end. Leaving or staying, wherever or however things may come to pass, I will neither forget nor neglect you, as you say, because truly I desire your good forever.

Now, until God gives us this good in heaven, pass the time in the virtues of mortification and patience, desiring to resemble somewhat in suffering this great God of ours, humbled and crucified. This life is not good if it is not an imitation of His life. May His Majesty preserve you and augment His love in you as in His holy beloved. Amen.

From Madrid, July 6, 1591
Fray Juan de la Cruz

24. [To María de la Encarnación, Prioress of the Discalced Carmelites in Segovia

July 6, 1591]

. . . do not let what is happening to me, daughter, cause you any grief, for it does not cause me any. What greatly grieves me is that he who is not at fault is blamed. Men do not do these things, but God, who knows what is suitable for us and arranges things for our good. Think nothing else but that God ordains all, and where there is no love, put love, and you will draw out love . . .

25. [To Padre Antonio de Jesús, Provincial of Andalucía

La Peñuela, August 1591]

. . . Father: I have become one of your subjects. Would Your Reverence consider what you would like me to do and where I should go?

26. [To the same Padre Antonio

La Peñuela, August 1591]

. . . Father: I am not coming to do my will nor to choose a house. Your Reverence could consider where you would like me to go, and I shall go . . .

27. [To a person under his direction

Of uncertain date]

Have you seen, daughter, how good it is not to have money, which only troubles us and is stolen from us, and that the treasures of the soul be hidden and at peace so that we cannot even know of or see them ourselves? For there is no worse thief than the one inside the house.

God deliver us from ourselves. May He give us what pleases Him and never show it to us until He wishes to do so. And, after all, he who out of love stores up treasures, stores them up for another. It is good that He guards and enjoys them, since they are all for Him, and that we neither see them nor enjoy them so not to deprive God of the joy He finds in the humility and the nakedness of our heart and in our contempt of worldy things for love of Him.

It is a very manifest treasure and it gives great joy to see that the soul continues to please God openly, paying no attention to the foolish ones of the world who know not how to keep anything for the next life.

The Masses will be said, and I shall go willingly unless they notify me to the contrary. May God keep you.

Fray Juan de la Cruz

28. [To Doña Ana del Mercado y Peñalosa
La Peñuela, August 19, 1591]

Jesus be in your soul!

Although I have sent a letter by way of Baeza concerning the outcome of my journey, I am happy that these two servants of Señor Don Francisco are passing because of the opportunity it affords of sending these lines which will reach you more surely.

I mentioned in the other letter how I desire to remain in this desert of La Peñuela, where I arrived about nine days ago and which is about six leagues north of Baeza. I like it very much, glory to God, and I am well. The vastness of the desert is a great help to the soul and body, although the soul fares very poorly. The Lord must be desiring that it have its spiritual desert. Well and good, for His Majesty already knows what we are of ourselves. I don't know how long this will last, for Padre Fray Antonio de Jesús threatens from Baeza that he will not leave me here for long. Be that as it may, for in the meanwhile I am well off without knowing anything, and the life of the desert is admirable.

This morning we have already returned from gathering our chick-peas, and so the mornings go by. On another day we shall thresh them. It is nice to handle these mute creatures, better than being badly handled by living ones. God grant that I may stay here. Pray for this, my daughter. But even though I am so happy here, I would not fail to come should you desire.

Take care of your soul and do not confess scruples or first motions or imaginings in which the soul does not desire to be detained. Look after your health and do not fail to pray when you can.

I already mentioned in the other letter, though this one will reach you first, that you can write to me by way of Baeza since they have mail service there. You can address the letters to the Discalced Fathers in Baeza; I have notified them to send the letters on to me.

Regards to Señor Don Luis and to my daughter Doña Inés. May God give you His Spirit as I desire. Amen.

From La Peñuela, August 19, 1591
Fray Juan de la Cruz

29. [To a person under his direction
La Peñuela, August 22, 1591]

. . . May God grant us the right intention in all these things and that we might not consent knowingly to sin, for in this way even though the battery of temptation be great and of many kinds, you will walk safely and everything will be converted into a crown. Give my greetings to your sister, and to Isabel de Soria my best regards in the Lord and tell her that I marveled that she is not in Jaén, since there is a monastery there.

The Lord be in your soul, daughter in Christ.

From La Peñuela, August 22, 1591
Fray Juan de la Cruz

30. [To Doña Ana del Mercado y Peñalosa
La Peñuela, September 21, 1591]
Jesus be in your soul, my daughter in Christ.

I received here in La Peñuela the packet of letters the servant brought me. I greatly appreciate your concern. Tomorrow I am going to Ubeda for the cure of a slight bout of fever. Since it has been returning each day now for more than a week and does not leave me, it seems I shall need the help of medicine. Yet I plan to return here immediately, for I am indeed very happy in this holy solitude. And thus in regard to what you said about being careful not to accompany Padre Fray Antonio, be sure that in this matter and in all else that may require it, I shall be as cautious as possible.

I am very happy to know that Señor Don Luis is now a priest of the Lord. May he be so for many years and may His Majesty fulfill the desires of his soul. Oh, how blessed a state this is for leaving aside cares and speedily enriching the soul! Congratulate him for me. I dare not ask him that he might some day remember me at the sacrifice of the Mass, and I as a debtor will ever remember him. Even though I am forgetful, I will not be able to forget him, since he is so close to his sister whom I always remember.

Greetings in the Lord to my daughter Doña Inés. And may both of you pray God to prepare me that He may bring me to Himself. I cannot think of any more to write now and I am also closing on account of the fever, for I would like to write at greater length.

From La Peñuela, September 21, 1591
Fray Juan de la Cruz

You say nothing about the lawsuit, whether it is being tried or still to come up.

31. [To Madre Ana de San Alberto, Prioress of the Discalced of Caravaca
La Peñuela, August–September 1591]
. . . you already know, daughter, the trials they are now suffering. God permits it to try His elect. *In silence and in hope shall our strength be.* [Is. 30:15] May God keep you and make you holy. Commend me to God.

32. [To Padre Juan de San Alberto, Discalced Carmelite in Málaga

Ubeda, October–November 1591]

. . . Son, do not let this grieve you, for they cannot take the habit from me save for being incorrigible or disobedient. I am very ready to amend all I may have done wrong and obey in whatever penance they may give me.

33. [To a Discalced Carmelite nun in Segovia

Ubeda, October–November 1591]

Have a great love for those who contradict and fail to love you, for in this way love is begotten in a heart that has no love. God so acts with us, for He loves us that we might love by means of the very love He bears toward us.

Poetry

INTRODUCTION TO THE POETRY

St. John of the Cross has received the title, "the loftiest poet of Spain," not on account of his books of poetry, but with some ten or twelve compositions. These compositions, however, display such variety that it can almost be affirmed that each of them represents a completely distinct poetic vision and technique, a singular accomplishment in Spanish literature.

Since the original copies of the poems have disappeared, the problem arises of determining the authentic from the unauthentic. The point of departure is the fortunate collection contained in the *Codex of Sanlucar*, which, having been corrected and approved by the saint himself, offers every desirable guarantee of authenticity. With this as our basis, we can designate the following poems as certainly authentic: *The Spiritual Canticle; The Dark Night; The Living Flame of Love; I Entered into Unknowing; I Live, but Not in Myself; I Went Out Seeking Love; A Lone Young Shepherd; For I Know Well the Spring; The Romances;* and *On the Psalm: "By the Waters of Babylon."* The authenticity of these works has also been strengthened by the testimony of contemporaries.

The genuineness of the other poems (*Without Support and with Support; Not for All of Beauty; Del Verbo Divino;* and *The Sum of Perfection*) is probable; only the guarantee of the manuscripts presents them as authentic.

Since we have already discussed those works which carry a commentary, nothing need be said of them here other than that as explained in the introduction to *The Spiritual Canticle*, we are presenting the first redaction of *The Spiritual Canticle*, which has only thirty nine stanzas, because of its superior literary quality.

I Entered into Unknowing. This poem was probably written in Granada (1582–84). It deals with the properties, both negative and positive, of a very high contemplation.

I Live, but Not in Myself. This work might possibly have been inspired by one of St. Teresa's poems, which has the same idea and even at times the same words. It was probably composed in Granada (1582–84). The poet laments in having to continue to live when he greatly desires to die and see God face to face.

I Went Out Seeking Love. The place and date of composition are also Granada (1582–84). In stating that these are stanzas applied to spiritual things, the introductory title indicates that they represent the adaptation of a popular love song to a spiritual theme, a common practice in the time of the Saint. Overtaking the prey is equivalent to obtaining possession of a loved one. Here the poet tells how through faith, hope, love, and humility he obtained possession of God.

A Lone Young Shepherd. The date and place of composition are uncertain, but the probability is Granada (1582–84). Here again we have an adaptation. St. John of the Cross recast a popular pastoral love song and applied the theme to Christ, the Good Shepherd. The discovery of the popular poem has enabled critics to observe St. John's genius in transforming a common song into a masterpiece.

For I Know Well the Spring. This poem was composed in the prison of Toledo (1577–78). It deals with the intimate life of God under the symbolism of a spring that flows and runs. This divine life is hidden in the bread of the Eucharist and is known only in darkness, or in faith.

The Romances. Since *The Romances* do not measure up to the superior quality of the other poems, some critics have denied their authenticity. There is, however, solid historic testimony that they were written in the prison of Toledo. The work as a whole, commenting on the Gospel of St. John read at the end of Mass, can be divided into two main parts: the first deals with the intimate life of God; the second, with the creation and the Incarnation, works of God *ad extra.*

On the Psalm: "By the Waters of Babylon." The prison of Toledo was the place of composition. But unlike the previous *Romances,* commenting on the gospel passage of St. John, this romance follows quite closely the scriptural text of Psalm 136.

Without Support and with Support. This was probably a popular poem that was taken and adapted by the Saint to a spiritual theme. It does not appear in the collection of the *Codex of Sanlucar,* which makes it difficult to determine anything about the date and place of composition. In it the poet rejoices that love, in spite of the darkness of faith, has detached him from every created thing and transformed him in itself.

Not for All of Beauty. This work is also absent from the collection of Sanlucar, and nothing certain can be said of the date or place of composition. It treats of the soul's turning from all created beauty to the uncreated beauty of God known through faith.

Del Verbo Divino. In all likelihood this is only the fragment of a longer hymn composed by the saint and sung by the friars during the Advent processions preparatory for Christmas.

The Sum of Perfection. Although nothing very definite can be said about the authenticity of this work, it is certainly an impressive little summary of sanjuanist teaching.

POETRY

NOCHE OSCURA	THE DARK NIGHT

1. En una Noche oscura
Con ansias en amores inflamada
—¡Oh dichosa ventura!—
Salí sin ser notada,
Estando ya mi casa sosegada.

2. A oscuras, y segura
Por la secreta escala disfrazada
—¡Oh dichosa ventura!—
A oscuras y en celada,
Estando ya mi casa sosegada.

3. En la noche dichosa
En secreto, que nadie me veía,
Ni yo miraba cosa,
Sin otra luz y guía
Sino la que en el corazón ardía.

4. Aquesta me guiaba
Más cierto que la luz del mediodía,
A donde me esperaba
—Quien yo bien me sabía—
En parte donde nadie parecía.

5. ¡Oh noche que guiaste!
¡Oh noche amable más que el
   alborada!
Oh noche que juntaste
Amado con amada,
Amada en el Amado transformada.

6. En mi pecho florido,
Que entero para él solo se guardaba,
Allí quedó dormido,
Y yo le regalaba,
Y el ventalle de cedros aire daba.

---

1. One dark night,
Fired with love's urgent longings
—Ah, the sheer grace!—
I went out unseen,
My house being now all stilled;

2. In darkness, and secure,
By the secret ladder, disguised,
—Ah, the sheer grace!—
In darkness and concealment,
My house being now all stilled;

3. On that glad night,
In secret, for no one saw me,
Nor did I look at anything,
With no other light or guide
Than the one that burned in my
   heart;

4. This guided me
More surely than the light of noon
To where He waited for me
—Him I knew so well—
In a place where no one else appeared.

5. O guiding night!
O night more lovely than the dawn!
O night that has united
The Lover with His beloved,
Transforming the beloved in her
   Lover.

6. Upon my flowering breast
Which I kept wholly for Him alone,
There He lay sleeping,
And I caressing Him
There in a breeze from the fanning
   cedars.

7. El aire de la almena,
Cuando ya sus cabellos esparcía,
Con su mano serena
En mi cuello hería,
Y todos mis sentidos suspendía.

7. When the breeze blew from the turret
Parting His hair,
He wounded my neck
With his gentle hand,
Suspending all my senses.

8. Quedéme y olvidéme,
El rostro recliné sobre el Amado,
Cesó todo, y dejéme,
Dejando me cuidado
Entre las azucenas olvidado.

8. I abandoned and forgot myself,
Laying my face on my Beloved;
All things ceased; I went out from myself,
Leaving my cares
Forgotten among the lilies.

CANTICO ESPIRITUAL

Esposa

1. ¿Adonde te escondiste,
Amado, y me dejaste con gemido?
Como el ciervo huiste
Habiéndome herido;
Salí tras ti clamando, y eras ido.

2. Pastores, los que fuerdes
Allá, por las majadas al otero,
Si por ventura vierdes
Aquel que yo más quiero,
Decilde que adolezco, peno y muero.

3. Buscando mis amores,
Iré por esos montes y riberas,
Ni cogeré las flores
Ni temeré las fieras,
Y pasaré los fuertes y fronteras.

4. ¡Oh bosques y espesuras,
Plantadas por la mano del Amado;
Oh prado de verduras,
De flores esmaltado,
Decid si por vosotros ha pasado!

5. Mil gracias derramando,
Pasó por estos sotos con presura,
Y yéndolos mirando,
Con sola su figura
Vestidos los dejó de hermosura.

THE SPIRITUAL CANTICLE

Bride

1. Where have You hidden,
Beloved, and left me moaning?
You fled like the stag
After wounding me;
I went out calling You, and You were gone.

2. Shepherds, you that go
Up through the sheepfolds to the hill,
If by chance you see
Him I love most,
Tell Him that I sicken, suffer, and die.

3. Seeking my Love
I will head for the mountains and for watersides,
I will not gather flowers,
Nor fear wild beasts;
I will go beyond strong men and frontiers.

4. O woods and thickets
Planted by the hand of my Beloved!
O green meadow,
Coated, bright, with flowers,
Tell me, has He passed by you?

5. Pouring out a thousand graces,
He passed these groves in haste;
And having looked at them,
With His image alone,
Clothed them in beauty.

6. Ay, ¿quién podrá sanarme?
Acaba de entregarte ya de vero,
No quieras enviarme
De hoy más ya mensajero,
Que no saben decirme lo que quiero.

7. Y todos cuantos vagan,
De ti me van mil gracias refiriendo,
Y todos más me llagan,
Y déjame muriendo
Un no sé qué que quedan balbuciendo.

8. Mas, ¿cómo perseveras,
Oh vida, no viviendo donde vives,
Y haciendo porque mueras,
Las flechas que recibes,
De lo que del Amado en ti concibes?

9. ¿Por qué, pues has llagado
Aqueste corazón, no le sanaste?
Y pues me le has robado,
¿Por qué así le dejaste
Y no tomas el robo que robaste?

10. Apaga mis enojos
Pues que ninguno basta a deshacellos,
Y véante mis ojos,
Pues eres lumbre de ellos,
Y sólo para ti quiero tenellos.

11. ¡Oh cristalina fuente,
Si en esos tus semblantes plateados,
Formases de repente
Los ojos deseados,
Que tengo en mis entrañas dibujados!

12. Apártalos, Amado,
Que voy de vuelo.
                Esposo
            Vuélvete, paloma,
Que el ciervo vulnerado
Por el otero asoma,
Al aire de tu vuelo, y fresco toma.

6. Ah, who has the power to heal me?
Now wholly surrender yourself!
Do not send me
Any more messengers,
They cannot tell me what I must hear.

7. All who are free
Tell me a thousand graceful things of
    You;
All wound me more
And leave me dying
Of, ah, I-don't-know-what behind
    their stammering.

8. How do you endure
O life, not living where you live?
And being brought near death
By the arrows you receive
From that which you conceive of your
    Beloved.

9. Why, since You wounded
This heart, don't You heal it?
And why, since You stole it from me,
Do You leave it so,
And fail to carry off what You have
    stolen?

10. Extinguish these miseries,
Since no one else can stamp them out;
And may my eyes behold You,
Because You are their light,
And I would open them to You alone.

11. O spring like crystal!
If only, on your silvered-over face,
You would suddenly form
The eyes I have desired,
Which I bear sketched deep within
    my heart.

12. Withdraw them, Beloved,
I am taking flight!
                Bridegroom
            Return, dove,
The wounded stag
Is in sight on the hill,
Cooled by the breeze of your flight.

Esposa	*Bride*
13. Mi Amado, las montañas,	13. My Beloved is the mountains,
Los valles solitarios nemorosos,	And lonely wooded valleys,
Las ínsulas extrañas,	Strange islands,
Los ríos sonorosos,	And resounding rivers,
El silbo de los aires amorosos.	The whistling of love-stirring breezes,
14. La noche sosegada	14. The tranquil night
En par de los levantes del aurora,	At the time of the rising dawn,
La música callada,	Silent music,
La soledad sonora,	Sounding solitude,
La cena que recrea y enamora.	The supper that refreshes, and deepens love.
15. Nuestro lecho florido	15. Our bed is in flower,
De cuevas de leones enlazado,	Bound round with linking dens of lions,
En púrpura tendido,	Hung with purple,
De paz edificado,	Built up in peace,
De mil escudos de oro coronado.	And crowned with a thousand shields of gold.
16. A zaga de tu huella	16. Following Your footprints
Las jóvenes discurren al camino	Maidens run along the way;
Al toque de centella,	The touch of a spark,
Al adobado vino,	The spiced wine,
Emisiones de bálsamo divino.	Cause flowings in them from the balsam of God.
17. En la interior bodega	17. In the inner wine cellar
De mi Amado bebí, y cuando salía	I drank of my Beloved, and, when I went abroad
Por toda aquesta vega,	Through all this valley
Ya cosa no sabía,	I no longer knew anything,
Y el ganado perdí que antes seguía.	And lost the herd which I was following.
18. Allí me dió su pecho,	18. There He gave me His breast;
Allí me enseñó ciencia muy sabrosa,	There He taught me a sweet and living knowledge;
Y yo le di de hecho	And I gave myself to Him,
A mí, sin dejar cosa,	Keeping nothing back;
Allí le prometí de ser su esposa.	There I promised to be His bride.
19. Me alma se ha empleado,	19. Now I occupy my soul
Y todo me caudal en su servicio;	And all my energy in His service;
Ya no guardo ganado,	I no longer tend the herd,
Ni ya tengo otro oficio,	Nor have I any other work
Que ya sólo en amar es mi ejercicio.	Now that my every act is love.

20. Pues ya si en el ejido
De hoy más no fuere vista ni hallada,
Diréis que me he perdido;
Que andando enamorada,
Me hice perdidiza, y fuí ganada.

21. De flores y esmeraldas,
En las frescas mañanas escogidas,
Haremos las guirnaldas,
En tu amor florecidas,
Y en un cabello mío entretejidas.

22. En solo aquel cabello
Que en mi cuello volar consideraste,
Mirástele en mi cuello,
Y en él preso quedaste,
Y en uno de mis ojos te llagaste.

23. Cuando tú me mirabas,
Su gracia en mí tus ojos imprimían:
Por eso me adamabas,
Y en eso merecían
Los míos adorar lo que en ti vían.

24. No quieras despreciarme,
Que si color moreno en mí hallaste,
Ya bien puedes mirarme,
Después que me miraste,
Que gracia y hermosura en mí dejaste.

25. Cazadnos las raposas,
Que está ya florecida nuestra viña,
En tanto que de rosas
Hacemos una piña,
Y no parezca nadie en la montiña.

26. Detente, cierzo muerto,
Ven, austro, que recuerdas los amores,
Aspira por mi huerto,
Y corran tus olores,
Y pacerá el Amado entre las flores.

Esposo
27. Entrado se ha la esposa
En el ameno huerto deseado,
Y a su sabor reposa,
El cuello reclinado
Sobre los dulces brazos del Amado.

20. If, then, I am no longer
Seen or found on the common,
You will say that I am lost;
That, stricken by love,
I lost myself, and was found.

21. With flowers and emeralds
Chosen on cool mornings
We shall weave garlands
Flowering in Your love,
And bound with one hair of mine.

22. You considered
That one hair fluttering at my neck;
You gazed at it upon my neck
And it captivated You;
And one of my eyes wounded You.

23. When You looked at me
Your eyes imprinted Your grace in
me;
For this You loved me ardently;
And thus my eyes deserved
To adore what they beheld in You.

24. Do not despise me;
For if, before, You found me dark,
Now truly You can look at me
Since You have looked
And left in me grace and beauty.

25. Catch us the foxes,
For our vineyard is now in flower,
While we fashion a cone of roses
Intricate as the pine's;
And let no one appear on the hill.

26. Be still, deadening north wind;
South wind come, you that waken
love,
Breathe through my garden,
Let its fragrance flow,
And the Beloved will feed amid the
flowers.

Bridegroom
27. The bride has entered
The sweet garden of her desire,
And she rests in delight,
Laying her neck
On the gentle arms of her Beloved.

28. Debajo del manzano,
Allí conmigo fuiste desposada,
Allí te dí la mano,
Y fuiste reparada,
Donde tu madre fuera vïolada.

29. A las aves ligeras,
Leones, ciervos, gamos saltadores,
Montes, valles, riberas,
Aguas, aires, ardores,
Y miedos de las noches veladores:

30. Por las amenas liras
Y canto de serenas os conjuro,
Que cesen vuestras iras,
Y no toquéis al muro,
Porque la Esposa duerma más seguro.

Esposc
31. ¡Oh ninfas de Judea!;
En tanto que en las flores y rosales
El ámbar perfumea,
Morá en los arrabales,
Y no queráis tocar nuestros umbrales.

32. Escóndete, Carillo,
Y mira con tu haz a las montañas,
Y no quieras decillo;
Mas mira las compañas
De la que va por ínsulas extrañas.

Esposo
33. La blanca palomica
Al arca con el ramo se ha tornado;
Y ya la tortolica
Al socio deseado
En las riberas verdes ha hallado.

34. En soledad vivía,
Y en soledad ha puesto ya su nido,
Y en soledad la guía
A solas su querido
También en soledad de amor herido.

28. Beneath the apple tree:
There I took you for My own,
There I offered you My hand,
And restored you,
Where your mother was corrupted.

29. Swift-winged birds,
Lions, stags, and leaping roes,
Mountains, lowlands, and river banks,
Waters, winds, and ardors,
Watching fears of night:

30. By the pleasant lyres
And the siren's song, I conjure you
To cease your anger
And not touch the wall,
That the bride may sleep in deeper
peace.

Bride
31. You girls of Judea,
While among flowers and roses
The amber spreads its perfume,
Stay away, there on the outskirts:
Do not so much as seek to touch our
thresholds.

32. Hide Yourself, my Love;
Turn Your face toward the mountains,
And do not speak;
But look at those companions
Going with her through strange
islands.

Bridegroom
33. The small white dove
Has returned to the ark with an olive
branch;
And now the turtledove
Has found its longed-for mate
By the green river banks.

34. She lived in solitude,
And now in solitude has built her
nest;
And in solitude He guides her,
He alone, who also bears
In solitude the wound of love.

Esposa	*Bride*
35. Gocémonos, Amado, Y vámonos a ver en tu hermosura Ai monte u al collado, Do mana el agua pura; Entremos más adentro en la espesura.	35. Let us rejoice, Beloved, And let us go forth to behold ourselves in Your beauty, To the mountain and to the hill, To where the pure water flows, And further, deep into the thicket.
36. Y luego a las subidas Cavernas de la piedra nos iremos, Que están bien escondidas, Y allí nos entraremos, Y el mosto de granadas gustaremos.	36. And then we will go on To the high caverns in the rock Which are so well concealed; There we shall enter And taste the fresh juice of the pomegranates.
37. Allí me mostrarías Aquello que mi alma pretendía, Y luego me darías Allí tú, vida mía, Aquello que me diste el otro día.	37. There You will show me What my soul has been seeking, And then You will give me, You, my Life, will give me there What You gave me on that other day:
38. El aspirar del aire, El canto de la dulce filomena, El soto y su donaire, En la noche serena Con llama que consume y no da pena.	38. The breathing of the air, The song of the sweet nightingale, The grove and its living beauty In the serene night, With a flame that is consuming and painless.
39. Que nadie lo miraba . . . Aminadab tampoco parecía, Y el cerco sosegaba, Y la caballería A vista de las aguas descendía.	39. No one looked at her, Nor did Aminadab appear; The siege was still; And the cavalry, At the sight of the waters, descended.

LLAMA DE AMOR VIVA

THE LIVING FLAME OF LOVE

1. ¡Oh llama de amor viva, Que tiernamente hieres De mi alma en el más profundo centro!; Pues ya no eres esquiva, Acaba ya, si quieres; Rompe la tela de este dulce encuentro.	1. O living flame of love That tenderly wounds my soul In its deepest center! Since Now You are not oppressive, Now Consummate! if it be Your will: Tear through the veil of this sweet encounter!
2. ¡Oh cauterio suave! ¡Oh regalada llaga! ¡Oh mano blanda! ¡Oh toque delicado, Que a vida eterna sabe,	2. O sweet cautery, O delightful wound! O gentle hand! O delicate touch That tastes of eternal life

Y toda deuda paga!
Matando, muerte en vida la has
    trocado.

And pays every debt!
In killing You changed death to life.

3. ¡Oh lámparas de fuego,
En cuyos resplandores
Las profundas cavernas del sentido,
Que estaba oscuro y ciego,
Con extraños primores
Calor y luz dan junto a su Querido!

3. O lamps of fire!
In whose splendors
The deep caverns of feeling,
Once obscure and blind,
Now give forth, so rarely, so
    exquisitely,
Both warmth and light to their
    Beloved.

4. ¡Cuán manso y amoroso
Recuerdas en mi seno
Donde secretamente solo moras,
Y en tu aspirar sabroso
De bien y gloria lleno
Cuán delicadamente me enamoras!

4. How gently and lovingly
You wake in my heart,
Where in secret You dwell alone;
And by Your sweet breathing,
Filled with good and glory,
How tenderly You swell my heart
    with love!

COPLAS DEL MISMO HECHAS SOBRE UN
EXTASIS DE HARTA CONTEMPLACION

STANZAS CONCERNING AN ECSTASY
EXPERIENCED IN HIGH CONTEMPLATION

Entréme donde no supe,
Y quedéme no sabiendo,
Toda ciencia trascendiendo.

I entered into unknowing,
And there I remained unknowing,
Transcending all knowledge.

1. Yo no supe dónde entraba,
Pero, cuando allí me vi,
Sin saber dónde me estaba,
Grandes cosas entendí;
No diré lo que sentí,
Que me quedé no sabiendo,
Toda ciencia trascendiendo.

1. I entered into unknowing
Yet when I saw myself there
Without knowing where I was
I understood great things;
I shall not say what I felt
For I remained in unknowing
Transcending all knowledge.

2. De paz y de pïedad
Era la ciencia perfecta,
En profunda soledad,
Entendida (vía recta);
Era cosa tan secreta,
Que me quedé balbuciendo,
Toda ciencia trascendiendo.

2. That perfect knowledge
Was of peace and holiness
Held at no remove
In profound solitude;
It was something so secret
That I was left stammering,
Transcending all knowledge.

3. Estaba tan embebido,
Tan absorto y ajenado,
Que se quedó mi sentido
De todo sentir privado,

3. I was so whelmed,
So absorbed and withdrawn,
That my senses were left
Deprived of all their sensing,

Y el espíritu dotado
De un entender no entendiendo,
Toda ciencia trascendiendo.

4. El que allí llega de vero,
De sí mismo desfallece;
Cuanto sabía primero,
Mucho bajo le parece;
Y su ciencia tanto crece,
Que se queda no sabiendo,
Toda ciencia trascendiendo.

5. Cuanto más alto se sube,
Tanto menos se entendía,
Que es la tenebrosa nube
Que a la noche esclarecía;
Por eso quien la sabía
Queda siempre no sabiendo
Toda ciencia trascendiendo.

6. Este saber no sabiendo
Es de tan alto poder,
Que los sabios arguyendo
Jamás le pueden vencer;
Que no llega su saber
A no entender entendiendo,
Toda ciencia trascendiendo.

7. Y es de tan alta excelencia
Aqueste sumo saber,
Que no hay facultad ni ciencia
Que le puedan emprender;
Quien se supiere vencer
Con un no saber sabiendo,
Irá siempre trascendiendo.

8. Y si lo queréis oir,
Consiste esta suma ciencia
En un subido sentir
De la divinal esencia;
Es obra de su clemencia
Hacer quedar no entendiendo,
Toda ciencia trascendiendo.

And my spirit was given
An understanding while not
    understanding,
Transcending all knowledge.

4. He who truly arrives there
Cuts free from himself;
All that he knew before
Now seems worthless,
And his knowledge so soars
That he is left in unknowing
Transcending all knowledge.

5. The higher he ascends
The less he understands,
Because the cloud is dark
Which lit up the night;
Whoever knows this
Remains always in unknowing
Transcending all knowledge.

6. This knowledge in unknowing
Is so overwhelming
That wise men disputing
Can never overthrow it,
For their knowledge does not reach
To the understanding of not-
    understanding,
Transcending all knowledge.

7. And this supreme knowledge
Is so exalted
That no power of man or learning
Can grasp it;
He who masters himself
Will, with knowledge in unknowing,
Always be transcending.

8. And if you should want to hear:
This highest knowledge lies
In the loftiest sense
Of the essence of God;
This is a work of His mercy,
To leave one without understanding,
Transcending all knowledge.

COPLAS DEL ALMA QUE PENA
POR VER A DIOS.

Vivo sin vivir en mí,
Y de tal manera espero,
Que muero porque no muero.

1. En mí yo no vivo ya,
Y sin Dios vivir no puedo;
Pues sin él y sin mí quedo,
Este vivir ¿qué será?
Mil muertes se me hará,
Pues mi misma vida espero,
Muriendo porque no muero.

2. Esta vida que yo vivo
Es privación de vivir;
Y así, es continuo morir
Hasta que viva contigo.
Oye, mi Dios, lo que digo,
Que esta vida no la quiero;
Que muero porque no muero.

3. Estando absente de ti,
¿Qué vida puedo tener,
Sino muerte padescer,
La mayor que nunca vi?
Lástima tengo de mí,
Pues de suerte persevero,
Que muero porque no muero.

4. El pez que del agua sale,
Aun de alivio no carece,
Que en la muerte que padece,
Al fin la muerte le vale.
¿Qué muerte habrá que se iguale
A mi vivir lastimero,
Pues si más vivo más muero?

5. Cuando me pienso aliviar
De verte en el Sacramento,
Háceme más sentimiento
El no poderte gozar.
Todo es para más penar,
Por no verte como quiero
Y muero porque no muero.

STANZAS OF THE SOUL THAT SUFFERS
WITH LONGING TO SEE GOD.

I live, but not in myself,
And I have such hope
That I die because I do not die.

1. I no longer live within myself
And I cannot live without God,
For if I have neither Him nor myself
What will life be?
It will be a thousand deaths,
Longing for my true life
And dying because I do not die.

2. This life that I live
Is no life at all,
And so I die continually
Until I live with You;
Hear me, my God:
I do not desire this life,
I am dying because I do not die.

3. When I am not with You
What life can I have
Except to endure
The bitterest death known?
I pity myself
For I go on and on living,
Dying because I do not die.

4. A fish that leaves the water
Has this relief:
The dying it endures
Ends at last in death.
What death can equal
My pitiable life?
For the longer I live, the more drawn
out is my dying.

5. When I try to find relief
Beholding You in the Sacrament
I find this greater sorrow:
I cannot enjoy You wholly.
All things are affliction
Since I do not see You as I desire,
And I die because I do not die.

6. Y si me gozo, Señor,
Con esperanza de verte,
En ver que puedo perderte
Se me dobla mi dolor;
Viviendo en tanto pavor
Y esperando como espero,
Muérome porque no muero.

6. And if I rejoice, Lord,
In the hope of seeing You,
Yet seeing I can lose You
Doubles my sorrow.
Living in such fear
And hoping as I hope,
I die because I do not die.

7. Sácame de aquesta muerte,
Mi Dios, y dame la vida;
No me tengas impedida
En este lazo tan fuerte;
Mira que peno por verte
Y mi mal es tan entero
Que muero porque no muero.

7. Lift me from this death,
My God, and give me life;
Do not hold me bound
With these so strong bonds;
See how I long to see You;
I am so wholly miserable
That I die because I do not die.

8. Lloraré mi muerte ya,
Y lamentaré mi vida
En tanto que detenida
Por mis pecados está.
¡Oh mi Dios!, ¿cuando será
Cuando yo diga de vero:
Vivo ya porque no muero?

8. I will cry out for death
And mourn my living
While I am held here
For my sins.
O my God, when will it be
That I can truly say:
Now I live because I do not die?

OTRAS DEL MISMO A LO DIVINO

MORE STANZAS APPLIED TO SPIRITUAL THINGS

Tras de un amoroso lance,
Y no de esperanza falto,
Volé tan alto, tan alto,
Que le di a la caza alcance.

I went out seeking love,
And with unfaltering hope
I flew so high, so high,
That I overtook the prey.

1. Para que yo alcance diese
A aqueste lance divino,
Tanto volar me convino
Que de vista me perdiese.
Y con todo, en este trance
En el vuelo quedé falto;
Mas el amor fué tan alto,
Que le di a la caza alcance.

1. That I might take the prey
Of this adventuring in God
I had to fly so high
That I was lost from sight;
And though in this adventure
I faltered in my flight,
Yet love had already flown so high
That I took the prey.

2. Cuando más alto subia,
Deslumbróseme la vista,
Y la más fuerte conquista
En oscuro se hacía;
Mas por ser de amor el lance
Di un ciego y oscuro salto,
Y fui tan alto, tan alto,
Que le di a la caza alcance.

2. When I ascended higher
My vision was dazzled,
And the most difficult conquest
Was achieved in darkness;
But since I was seeking love
The leap I made was blind and dark
And I rose so high, so high,
That I took the prey.

3. Cuanto más alto llegaba
De este lance tan subido,
Tanto más bajo y rendido
Y abatido me hallaba.
Dije: No habrá quien alcance.
Y abatíme tanto, tanto,
Que fui tan alto, tan alto,
Que le di a la caza alcance.

3. The higher I ascended
In this so lofty seeking
The lower and more subdued
And abased I became.
I said: No one can overtake it,
And sank, ah, so low,
That I was so high, so high,
That I took the prey.

4. Por una extraña manera
Mil vuelos pasé de un vuelo,
Porque esperanza de cielo
Tanto alcanza cuanto espera;
Esperé sólo este lance,
Y en esperar no fui falto,
Pues fui tan alto, tan alto,
Que le di a la caza alcance.

4. In a wonderful way
My one flight surpassed a thousand,
For the hope of heaven
Attains as much as it hopes for;
This seeking is my only hope
And I have not been disappointed,
Because I flew so high, so high,
That I took the prey.

OTRAS CANCIONES A LO DIVINO DE
CRISTO Y EL ALMA

MORE STANZAS APPLIED TO SPIRITUAL
THINGS ON CHRIST AND THE SOUL

1. Un pastorcico solo está penado
Ajeno de placer y de contento,
Y en su pastora puesto el pensamiento,
Y el pecho del amor muy lastimado.

1. A lone young shepherd lived in
pain
Withdrawn from pleasure and con-
tentment,
His thoughts fixed on a shepherd-girl
His heart an open wound with love.

2. No llora por haberle amor llagado,
Que no le pena verse así afligido,
Aunque en el corazón está herido;
Mas llora por pensar que está
olvidado.

2. He weeps, but not from the wound
of love,
There is no pain in such a wound
However deeply it opens the heart;
He weeps in knowing he's been for-
gotten.

3. Que sólo de pensar que está
olvidado
De su bella pastora, con gran pena
Se deja maltratar en tierra ajena,
El pecho del amor muy lastimado.

3. That one thought: his shining one
Has forgotten him, is such great pain
That he gives himself up to brutal
handling in a foreign land,
His heart an open wound with love.

4. Y dice el Pastorcico: ¡Ay,
desdichado
De aquel que de mi amor ha hecho
ausencia,
Y no quiere gozar la mi presencia,
Y el pecho por su amor muy
lastimado!

4. The shepherd says: I pity the one
Who draws himself back from my
love,
And does not seek the joy of my
presence,
Though my heart is an open wound
with love for him.

5. Y a cabo de un gran rato se ha encumbrado
Sobre un árbol do abrió sus brazos bellos,
Y muerto se ha quedado, asido de ellos,
El pecho del amor muy lastimado.

5. After a long time he climbed a tree,
And spread his shining arms,
And hung by them, and died,
His heart an open wound with love.

CANTAR DEL ALMA QUE SE HUELGA DE CONOCER A DIOS POR FE

Que bien sé yo la fuente que mana y corre
Aunque es de noche.

1. Aquella eterna fonte está escondida,
Que bien sé yo dó tiene su manida,
Aunque es de noche.

2. Su origen no lo sé, pues no le tiene,
Mas sé que todo origen de ella viene,
Aunque es de noche.

3. Sé que no puede ser cosa tan bella,
Y que cielos y tierra beben de ella,
Aunque es de noche.

4. Bien sé que suelo en ella no se halla,
Y que ninguno puede vadealla,
Aunque es de noche.

5. Su claridad nunca es oscurecida,
Y sé que toda luz de ella es venida,
Aunque es de noche.

6. Sé ser tan caudalosas sus corrientes,
Que infiernos, cielos riegan, y las gentes,
Aunque es de noche.

7. El corriente que nace de esta fuente,

SONG OF THE SOUL THAT REJOICES IN KNOWING GOD THROUGH FAITH

For I know well the spring that flows and runs,
Although it is night.

1. That eternal spring is hidden,
For I know well where it has its rise,
Although it is night.

2. I do not know its origin, for it hasn't one,
But I know that every origin has come from it.
Although it is night.

3. I know that nothing else is so beautiful,
And that the heavens and the earth drink there
Although it is night.

4. I know well that it is bottomless
And that no one is able to cross it
Although it is night.

5. Its clarity is never darkened,
And I know that every light has come from it
Although it is night.

6. I know that its streams are so brimming
They water the lands of hell, the heavens, and earth,
Although it is night.

7. I know well the stream that flows from this spring

Bien sé que es tan capaz y
omnipotente,
Aunque es de noche.

Is mighty in compass and power,
Although it is night.

8. El corriente que de estas dos
procede
Sé que ninguna de ellas le precede,
Aunque es de noche.

8. I know that the stream proceeding
from these two
Is preceded by neither of them,
Although it is night.

9. Aquesta eterna fonte está escondida
En este vivo pan por darnos vida,
Aunque es de noche.

9. This eternal spring is hidden
In this living bread for our life's sake,
Although it is night.

10. Aqui se está llamando a las
criaturas,
Y de esta agua se hartan, aunque a
oscuras,
Porque es de noche.

10. It is here to call to creatures: and
they
Are filled with this water, although
in darkness,
Because it is night.

11. Aquesta viva fuente, que deseo,
En este pan de vida yo la veo,
Aunque es de noche.

11. This living spring which I long
for,
I see in this bread of life,
Although it is night.

ROMANCES SOBRE EL EVANGELIO

"In principio erat Verbum"
ACERCA DE LA SSMA. TRINIDAD.

ROMANCES—FIRST ROMANCE: ON THE GOSPEL

"In Principio erat Verbum,"
REGARDING THE MOST BLESSED TRINITY.

1. En El Principio moraba
El Verbo, y en Dios vivía,
En quien su felicidad
Infinita poseía.

1. In the beginning the Word
Was; He lived in God
And possessed in Him
His infinite happiness.

2. El mismo Verbo Dios era,
Que El Principio se decía;
El moraba en el principio,
Y principio no tenía.

2. That same Word was God,
Who is the Beginning;
He was in the beginning
And had no beginning.

3. El era el mismo Principio,
Por eso, de él carecía;
El Verbo se llama Hijo,
Que del Principio nacía.

3. He was himself the Beginning
And therefore had no beginning.
The Word is called Son;
He was born of the Beginning

4. Hale siempre concebido
Y siempre le concebía,
Dale siempre su sustancia
Y siempre se la tenía.

4. Who had always conceived Him
And was always conceiving Him,
Giving of His substance always
Yet always possessing it.

5. Y así, la gloria del Hijo,
Es la que en el Padre había,
Y toda su gloria el Padre
En el Hijo poseía.

6. Como amante en el amado
Uno en otro residía,
Y aqueste amor que los une
En lo mismo convenía

7. Con el uno y con el otro
En igualdad y valía.
Tres Personas y un amado
Entre todos tres había,

8. Y un amor en todas ellas
Y un Amante las hacía;
Y el Amante es el Amado
En que cada cual vivía;

9. Que el Sér que los tres poseen,

Cada cual le poseía,
Y cada cual de ellos ama
A la que este Sér tenía.

10. Este Sér es cada una,
Y éste solo las unía
En un inefable nudo
Que decir no se sabía.

11. Por lo cual era infinito
El amor que las unía,
Porque un solo Amor Tres tienen,
Que su esencia se decía;
Que el amor cuanto más uno
Tanto más amor hacía.

5. And thus the glory of the Son
Was the Father's glory,
And the Father possessed
All His glory in the Son.

6. As the lover in the beloved
Each lived in the other,
And the Love that unites them
Is one with them,

7. Their equal, excellent as
The One and the Other:
Three Persons, and one Beloved
Among all three.

8. One love in them all
Makes of them one Lover,
And the Lover is the Beloved
In whom each one lives.

9. For the being that the three possess
Each of them possesses,
And each of them loves
Him who bears this being.

10. Each one is this being
Which alone unites them
Binding them deeply
One beyond words.

11. Thus it is a boundless
Love that unites them,
For the three have one love
Which is their essence;
And the more love is one
The more it is love.

ROMANCE 2.

De la comunicación de las tres Personas.

1. En aquel amor inmenso
Que de los dos procedía,
Palabras de gran regalo
El Padre al Hijo decía,

2. De tan profundo deleite
Que nadie las entendía;

ROMANCE 2.

On the communication among the three Persons.

1. In that immense love
Proceeding from the two
The Father spoke words
Of great affection to the Son,

2. Words of such profound delight
That no one understood them;

Sólo el Hijo lo gozaba,
Que es a quien pertenecía.

3. Pero aquello que se entiende
De esta manera decía:
—"Nada me contenta, Hijo,
Fuera de tu compañia,

4. Y si algo me contenta,
En ti mismo lo quería.
El que a ti más se parece,
A mí más satisfacía,

5. Y el que nada te semeja,
En mi nada hallaría.
En ti sólo me he agradado,
¡Oh Vida de Vida mia!

6. Eres lumbre de mi lumbre,
Eres mi sabiduría,
Figura de mi sustancia
En quien bien me complacía.

7. Al que a ti te amare, Hijo,
A mi mismo le daría,
Y el amor que yo en ti tengo,
Ese mismo en él pondría,
En razón de haber amado
A quien yo tanto quería."

ROMANCE 3. *De la creación*

1. —"Una esposa que te ame,
Mi Hijo, darte quería,
Que por tu valor merezca
Tener nuestra compañia,

2. Y comer pan a una mesa,
Del mismo que yo comía;
Porque conozca los bienes
Que en tal Hijo yo tenía,
Y se congracie conmigo
De tu gracia y lozanía."

3. —"Mucho lo agradezco, Padre,
(El Hijo le respondía)
A la esposa que me dieres
Yo mi claridad daría,

They were meant for the Son
And He alone rejoiced in them.

3. What He heard
Was this:
My Son, only your
Company contents Me,

4. And when something pleases Me
I love that thing in You;
He who resembles You most
Satisfies Me most,

5. And he who is like You in nothing
Will find nothing in Me.
I am pleased with You alone
O life of My life!

6. You are the light of My light,
You are My wisdom,
The image of My substance
In Whom I am well pleased.

7. My Son, I will give Myself
To him who loves You,
And I will love him
With the same love I have for You,
Because he has loved
You Whom I love so.

ROMANCE 3. *On Creation*

1. My Son, I wish to give You
A bride who will love You.
Because of You she will deserve
To share our company,

2. And eat bread at Our table,
The same bread I eat,
That she may know the good
I have in such a Son;
And rejoice with Me
In Your grace and fullness.

3. I am very grateful, Father,
The Son answered;
I will show My brightness
To the bride You give Me.

4. Para que por ella vea
Cuánto mi Padre valía,
Y cómo el Sér que poseo
De su Sér lo recibía.

5. Reclinarla he yo en mi brazo
Y en tu amor se abrasaría,
Y con eterno deleite
Tu bondad sublimaría."

ROMANCE 4. *Creación (prosigue)*

1. —"Hágase, pues—dijo el Padre—

Que tu amor lo merecía."
Y en este dicho que dijo,
El mundo criado había,

2. Palacio para la esposa,
Hecho en gran sabiduría,
El cual en dos aposentos,
Alto y bajo, dividía.

3. El bajo de diferencias
Infinitas componía,
Mas el alto hermoseaba
De admirable pedrería;

4. Porque conozca la esposa
El Esposo que tenía.
En el alto colocaba
La angélica jerarquía;

5. Pero la natura humana
En el bajo la ponía,
Por ser en su compostura
Algo de menor valía.

6. Y aunque el sér y los lugares
De esta suerte los partía,
Pero todos son un cuerpo
De la esposa que decía;

7. Que el amor de un mismo Esposo,
Una esposa los hacía.
Los de arriba poseían
El Esposo en alegría;

4. So that by it she may see
How great My Father is,
And how I have received
My being from Your being.

5. I will hold her in My arms
And she will burn with Your love,
And with eternal delight
She will exalt Your goodness.

ROMANCE 4. *Creation (continued)*

1. Let it be done, then, said the Father,
For Your love has deserved it;
And by these words
The world was created,

2. A palace for the bride
Made with great wisdom
And divided into rooms,
One above, the other below.

3. The lower was furnished
With infinite variety,
While the higher was made beautiful
With marvelous jewels,

4. That the bride might know
The Bridegroom she had.
The orders of angels
Were placed in the higher,

5. But man was given
The lower place
For he was, in his being,
A lesser thing.

6. And though beings and places
Were divided in this way,
Yet all form one
Who is called the bride;

7. For love of the same Bridegroom
Made one bride of them.
Those higher ones possessed
The Bridegroom in gladness,

8. Los de abajo en esperanza
De fe que les infundía,
Diciéndoles que algún tiempo,
El los engrandecería;

9. Y que aquella su bajeza
Él se la levantaría
De manera que ninguno
Ya la vituperaría,

10. Porque en todo semejante
El a ellos se haría,
Y se vendría con ellos,
Y con ellos moraría;

11. Y que Dios sería hombre,
Y que el hombre Dios sería,
Y trataría con ellos,
Comería y bebería.

12. Y que con ellos contino
El mismo se quedaría
Hasta que se consumase
Este siglo que corría,

13. Cuando se gozaran juntos
En eterna melodía.
Porque El era la Cabeza
De la esposa que tenía,

14. A la cual todos los miembros
De los justos juntaría,
Que son cuerpo de la esposa
A la cual El tomaría

15. En sus brazos tiernamente
Y allí su amor la daría.
Y que así juntos en uno
Al Padre la llevaría,

16. Donde del mismo deleite
Que Dios goza, gozaría.
Que como el Padre y el Hijo
—Y el que de ellos procedía—

17. El uno vive en el otro,
Así la esposa sería:
Que dentro de Dios absorta
Vida de Dios viviría.

8. The lower in hope, founded
On the faith which He infused in them,
Telling them: that one day
He would exalt them,

9. And that He would lift them
Up from their lowness
So that no one
Could mock it any more;

10. For He would make Himself
Wholly like them,
And He would come to them
And dwell with them;

11. And God would be man
And man would be God,
And He would talk with them
And eat and drink with them;

12. And He Himself would be
With them continually
Until the consummation
Of this world,

13. When, joined, they would rejoice
In eternal song;
For He was the Head
Of this bride of His

14. To Whom all the members
Of the just would be joined,
Who form the body of the bride.
He would take her

15. Tenderly in His arms
And there give her His love;
And when they were thus one,
He would lift her to the Father

16. Where God's very joy
Would be her joy.
For as the Father and the Son
And He who proceeds from them

17. Live in one another,
So it would be with the bride:
For, taken wholly into God,
She will live the life of God.

ROMANCE 5: *Creación* (*pros.*)	ROMANCE 5. *Creation* (*continued*)

1. Con esta buena esperanza
Que de arriba les venía,
El tedio de sus trabajos
Más leve se les hacía.

2. Pero la esperanza larga
Y el deseo que crecía
De gozarse con su Esposo
Continuo les afligía.

3. Por lo cual, con oraciones,
Con suspiros y agonía,
Con lágrimas y gemidos
Le rogaban noche y día,

4. Que ya se determinase
A les dar su compañia.
Unos decían:—"¡Oh, si fuese
En mi tiempo el alegría!"

5. Otros:—"¡Acaba, Señor;
Al que has de enviar, envía!"
Otros:—"¡Oh, si ya rompieses
Esos cielos y vería

6. Con mis ojos que bajases,
Y mi llanto cesaría!
Regad, nubes de la alto,

Que la tierra lo pedía,

7. Y ábrase ya la tierra
Que espinas nos producía,
Y produzca aquella flor
Con que ella florecería!"

8. Otros decían:—"¡Oh dichoso
El que en tal tiempo sería,
Que merezca ver a Dios
Con los ojos que tenía;

9. Y tratarle con sus manos,
Y andar en su compañia,
Y gozar de los misterios
Que entonces ordenaría!"

---

1. By this bright hope
Which came to them from above
Their wearying labors
Were lightened;

2. But the drawn out waiting
And their growing desire
To rejoice with their Bridegroom
Wore on them continually.

3. So, with prayers
And sighs and suffering,
With tears and moanings
They asked night and day

4. That now He would determine
To grant them His company.
Some said: If only
This joy would come in my time!

5. Others: Come, Lord,
Send Him Whom You will send!
And others: Oh, if only these heavens
Would break, and with my own eyes

6. I could see Him descending;
Then I would stop my crying out.
Oh clouds, rain down from your height,
Earth needs you,

7. And let the earth open
That has borne us thorns,
Let it bring forth that flower
That would be its flowering.

8. Others said: what gladness
For him who is living then,
Who will be able to see God
With his own eyes,

9. And touch Him with his hand
And walk with Him
And enjoy the mysteries
Which He will then ordain.

1. En aquestos y otros ruegos
Gran tiempo pasado había,
Pero en los postreros años,
El fervor mucho crecía;

2. Cuando el viejo Simeón
En deseo se encendía,
Rogando a Dios que quisiese
Dejalle ver este día.

3. Y así, el Espíritu Santo
Al buen viejo respondía,
Que le daba su palabra
Que la muerte no vería

4. Hasta que la Vida viese
Que de arriba descendía;
Y que él en sus mismas manos
Al mismo Dios tomaría,
Y le tendría en sus brazos,
Y consigo abrazaría.

1. In these and other prayers
A long time had passed;
But in the later years
Their fervor swelled and grew

2. When the aged Simeon
Burned with longing,
And begged God that he
Might see this day.

3. And so the Holy Spirit
Answering the good old man
Gave him His word
That he would not see death

4. Until he saw Life
Descending from the heights,
Until he took God Himself
Into his own hands
And holding Him in his arms,
Pressed Him to himself.

ROMANCE 7: *Encarnación.*

ROMANCE 7. *The Incarnation.*

1. Ya que el tiempo era llegado
En que hacerse convenía
El rescate de la esposa
(Que en duro yugo servía,

2. Debajo de aquella ley
Que Moisés dado le había)
El Padre, con amor tierno,
De esta manera decía:

3. —"Ya ves, Hijo, que a tu esposa
A tu imagen hecho había,
Y en lo que a ti se parece
Contigo bien convenía;

4. Pero difiere en la carne,
Que en tu simple Sér no había.
En los amores perfectos
Esta ley se requería:

1. Now that the time had come
When it would be good
To ransom the bride
Serving under the hard yoke

2. Of that law
Which Moses had given her,
The Father, with tender love,
Spoke in this way:

3. Now You see, Son, that Your bride
Was made in Your image,
And so far as she is like You
She will suit You well;

4. Yet she is different, in her flesh,
Which Your simple being does not
    have.
In perfect love
This law holds:

5. Que se haga semejante
El Amante a quien quería,
Que la mayor semejanza
Más deleite contenía.

6. El cual, sin duda, en tu esposa,
Grandemente crecería
Si te viese semejante
En la carne que tenía."

7. —"Mi voluntad es la tuya
(El Hijo le respondía)
Y la gloria que yo tengo
Es tu voluntad ser mía.

8. Y a mí me conviene, Padre,
Lo que tu Alteza decía,
Porque por esta manera
Tu bondad más se vería.

9. Veráse tu gran potencia,
Justicia y sabiduría;
Irélo a decir al mundo
Y noticia le daría
De tu belleza y dulzura
Y de tu soberanía.

10. Iré a buscar a mi esposa,
Y sobre mí tomaría
Sus fatigas y trabajos
En que tanto padecía.

11. Y porque ella vida tenga
Yo por ella moriría,
Y sacándola del lago
A ti te la volvería."

ROMANCE 8: *Encarnación* (pros.)

1. Entonces llamó a un Arcángel
Que San Gabriel se decía,
Y envióloa una doncella
Que se llamaba María,

2. De cuyo consentimiento
El misterio se hacía,
En la cual la Trinidad
De carne al Verbo vestía.

---

5. That the lover become
Like the one he loves;
For the greater their likeness
The greater their delight.

6. Surely Your bride's delight
Would greatly increase
Were she to see You like her,
In her own flesh.

7. My will is Yours,
The Son replied,
And My glory is
That Your will be Mine.

8. This is fitting, Father,
What You, the Most High, say;
For in this way
Your goodness will be the more seen,

9. Your great power will be seen
And Your justice and wisdom.
I will go and tell the world,
Spreading the word
Of Your beauty and sweetness
And of Your sovereignty.

10. I will go seek My bride
And take upon Myself
Her weariness and labors
In which she suffers so;

11. And that she may have life
I will die for her,
And, lifting her out of that deep,
I will restore her to You.

ROMANCE 8. *The Incarnation*
(*continued*)

1. Then He called
The archangel Gabriel
And sent him to
The virgin Mary,

2. At whose consent
The mystery was wrought,
In whom the Trinity
Clothed the Word with flesh.

3. Y aunque Tres hacen la obra,
En el Uno se hacía;
Y quedó el Verbo encarnado
En el vientre de María.

4. Y el que tenía sólo Padre
Ya también Madre tenía,
Aunque no como cualquiera
Que de varón concebía;

5. Que de las entrañas de ella
El su carne recibía,
Por lo cual, Hijo de Dios
Y del hombre se decía.

ROMANCE 9: *El Nacimiento.*

1. Ya que era llegado el tiempo
En que de nacer había,
Así como desposado
De su tálamo salía,

2. Abrazado con su esposa
Que en sus brazos la traía;
Al cual la graciosa Madre
En un pesebre ponía

3. Entre unos animales
Que a la sazón allí había.
Los hombres decían cantares,
Los ángeles melodía,

4. Festejando el desposorio
Que entre tales dos había.
Pero Dios en el pesebre
Allí lloraba y gemía;

5. Que eran joyas que la esposa
Al desposado traía.
Y la Madre estaba en pasmo
De que tal trueque veía:

6. El llanto del hombre en Dios
Y en el hombre la alegría;
Lo cual del uno y del otro
Tan ajeno ser solía.

FINIS.

3. And though Three work this,
It is wrought in the One:
And the Word lived incarnate
In the womb of Mary.

4. And He who had only a Father
Now had a Mother too,
But she was not like others
Who conceive by man.

5. From her own flesh
He received His flesh,
So He is called
Son of God and of man.

ROMANCE 9. *The Birth.*

1. When the time had come
For Him to be born
He went forth like the bridegroom
From his bridal chamber,

2. Embracing His bride,
Holding her in His arms,
Whom the gracious Mother
Laid in a manger

3. Among some animals
That were there at that time.
Men sang songs
And angels melodies

4. Celebrating the marriage
Of Two such as these.
But God there in the manger
Cried and moaned;

5. And these tears were jewels
The bride brought to the wedding.
The Mother gazed in sheer wonder
On such an exchange:

6. In God, man's weeping,
And in man, gladness,
To the one and the other
Things usually so strange.

FINIS.

ROMANCE QUE VA POR
"Super flumina Babylonis."
(*Ps. 136*)

1. Encima de las corrientes
Que en Babilonia hallaba,
Allí me senté llorando,
Allí la tierra regaba,

2. Acordándome de ti,
¡Oh Sión! a quien amaba.
Era dulce tu memoria
Y con ella más lloraba.

3. Dejé los trajes de fiesta,
Los de trabajo tomaba,
Y colgué en los verdes sauces
La música que llevaba,

4. Poniéndola en esperanza
De aquello que en ti esperaba.
Allí me hirió el amor,
Y el corazón se sacaba;

5. Díjele que me matase
Pues de tal suerte llagaba.
Yo me metía en su fuego
Sabiendo que me abrasaba,

6. Desculpando el avecica
Que en el fuego se acababa.
Estábame en mi muriendo
Y en ti sólo respiraba;

7. En mí por ti me moría
Y por ti resucitaba,
Que la memoria de ti
Daba vida y la quitaba.

8. Gozábanse los extraños
Entre quien cautivo estaba,
Preguntábanme cantares
De lo que en Sión cantaba:
—"Canta de Sión un himno
Veamos cómo sonaba."

9. —Decid: ¿cómo en tierra ajena,
Donde por Sión lloraba,
Cantaré yo la alegría

A ROMANCE ON THE PSALM
"By the Waters of Babylon."
(*Ps. 136*)

1. By the rivers
Of Babylon
I sat down weeping,
There on the ground,

2. And remembering you,
O Sion, whom I loved,
In that sweet memory
I wept even more.

3. I took off my feast-day clothes
And put on my working ones;
I hung on the green willows
All the joy I had in song,

4. Putting it aside for that
Which I hoped for in you.
There love wounded me
And took away my heart.

5. I begged love to kill me
Since it had so wounded me;
I threw myself in its fire
Knowing it burned,

6. Excusing now the young bird
That would die in the fire.
I was dying in myself,
Breathing in you alone.

7. I died within myself for you
And for you I revived,
Because the memory of you
Gave life and took it away.

8. The strangers among whom
I was captive rejoiced;
They asked me to sing
What I sang in Sion:
Sing us a song from Sion,
Let's hear how it sounds.

9. I said: How can I sing,
In a strange land where I weep
For Sion, sing of the happiness

Que en Sión se me quedaba?
Echaríala en olvido
Si en la ajena me gozaba.

10. Con mi paladar se junte
La lengua con que hablaba
Si de ti yo me olvidare
En la tierra do moraba.

11. Sión, por los verdes ramos
Que Babilonia me daba,
De mi se olvide mi diestra
(Que es lo que en ti más amaba)

12. Si de ti no me acordare
En lo que más me gozaba,
Y si yo tuviere fiesta
Y sin ti la festejaba.

13. ¡Oh hija de Babilonia
Mísera y desventurada!
Bienaventurado era
Aquel en quien confiaba,
Que te ha de dar el castigo
Que de tu mano llevaba.

14. Y juntará sus pequeños,
Y a mí, porque en ti lloraba,
A la piedra que era Cristo
Por el cual yo te dejaba.

GLOSA A LO DIVINO.

Sin arrimo y con arrimo,
Sin luz y a oscuras viviendo
Todo me voy consumiendo.

1. Mi alma está desasida
De toda cosa criada,
Y sobre sí levantada,
Y en una sabrosa vida,
Sólo en su Dios arrimada.
Por eso ya se dirá
La cosa que más estimo:
Que mi alma se ve ya
Sin arrimo y con arrimo.

That I had there?
I would be forgetting her
If I rejoiced in a strange land.

10. May the tongue I speak with
Cling to my palate
If I forget you
In this land where I am.

11. Sion, by the green branches
Babylon holds out to me,
May my right hand be forgotten
(That I so loved when home in you)

12. If I do not remember you,
My greatest joy,
Or celebrate one feast-day,
Or feast at all without you.

13. O Daughter of Babylon,
Miserable and wretched!
Blessed is He
In Whom I have trusted,
For He will punish you
As you have me;

14. And He will gather His little ones
And me, who wept because of you,
At the rock who is Christ
For Whom I abandoned you.

COMMENTARY APPLIED TO SPIRITUAL THINGS.

Without support and with support,
Living without light, in darkness,
I am wholly being consumed.

1. My soul is disentangled
From every created thing
And lifted above itself
In a life of delight
Supported only in God.
So now it can be said
That I most value this:
My soul now sees itself
Without support and with support.

2. Y aunque tinieblas padezco
En esta vida mortal,
No es tan crecido mi mal;
Porque, si de luz carezco,
Tengo vida celestial.
Porque el amor da tal vida,
Cuando más ciego va siendo,
Que tiene al alma rendida
Sin luz y a oscuras viviendo.

2. And though I suffer darknesses
In this mortal life,
That is not so hard a thing;
For though I have no light
I have the life of heaven.
For the blinder love is
The more it gives such life,
Holding the soul surrendered,
Living without light, in darkness.

3. Hace tal obra el amor,
Después que le conocí,
Que, si hay bien o mal en mí,
Todo lo hace de un sabor,
Y al alma trasforma en sí.
Y así, en su llama sabrosa,
La cual en mí estoy sintiendo,
Apriesa, sin quedar cosa,
Todo me voy consumiendo.

3. After I have known it
Love works so in me
That whether things go well or badly
Love turns all to one sweetness
Transforming the soul in itself.
And so in its delighting flame
Which I feel within me,
Swiftly, with nothing spared,
I am wholly being consumed.

GLOSA A LO DIVINO.

COMMENTARY APPLIED TO SPIRITUAL THINGS.

Por toda la hermosura
Nunca yo me perderé,
Sino por un no sé qué
Que se alcanza por ventura.

Not for all of beauty
Will I ever lose myself,
But for I-don't-know-what
Which is attained so gladly.

1. Sabor de bien que es finito
Lo más que puede llegar
Es cansar el apetito
Y estragar el paladar.
Y así, por toda dulzura
Nunca yo me perderé,
Sino por un no sé qué
Que se halla por ventura.

1. Delight in the world's good things
At the very most
Can only tire the appetite
And spoil the palate;
And so, not for all of sweetness
Will I ever lose myself,
But for I-don't-know-what
Which is so gladly found.

2. El corazón generoso
Nunca cura de parar
Donde se puede pasar
Sino en más dificultoso;
Nada le causa hartura,
Y sube tanto su fe
Que gusta de un no sé qué
Que se halla por ventura.

2. The generous heart
Never delays over easy things
But eagerly goes on
To more difficult ones.
Nothing satisfies it,
And its faith ascends so high
That it tastes I-don't-know-what
Which is so gladly found.

3. El que de amor adolece
Del divino Sér tocado

3. He who is sick with love,
Whom God Himself has touched,

Tiene el gusto tan trocado
Que a los gustos desfallece;
Como el que con calentura
Fastidia el manjar que ve,
Y apetece un no sé qué
Que se halla por ventura.

4. No os maravilléis de aquesto
(Que el gusto se quede tal)
Porque es la causa del mal
Ajena de todo el resto;
Y así (a) toda criatura
Enajenada se ve,
Y gusta de un no sé qué
Que se halla por ventura.

5. Que estando la voluntad
De Divinidad tocada,
No puede quedar pagada
Sino con Divinidad;
Mas, por ser tal su hermosura,
Que sólo se ve por fe,
Gústala en un no sé qué
Que se halla por ventura.

6. Pues de tal enamorado
Decidme si habréis dolor,
Pues que no tiene sabor
Entre todo lo criado;
Sólo, sin forma y figura,
Sin hallar arrimo y pié,
Gustando allá un no sé qué
Que se halla por ventura.

7. No penséis que el interior
(Que es de mucha más valía)
Halle gozo y alegría
En lo que acá da sabor
Mas sobre toda hermosura
Y lo que es y será y fué,
Gusta allá de un no sé qué,
Que se halla por ventura.

8. Más emplea su cuidado
Quien se quiere aventajar
En lo que está por ganar
Que en lo que tiene ganado.
Y así, para más altura
Yo siempre me inclinaré

Finds his tastes so changed
That they fall sway
Like a fevered man's
Who loathes any food he sees
And desires I-don't-know-what
Which is so gladly found.

4. Do not wonder
That the taste should be left like this,
For the cause of this sickness
Differs from all others;
And so he is withdrawn
From all creatures,
And tastes I-don't-know-what
Which is so gladly found.

5. For when once the will
Is touched by God Himself
It cannot be satisfied
Except by God;
But since His Beauty is open
To faith alone, the will
Tastes Him in I-don't-know-what
Which is so gladly found.

6. Tell me, then, would you pity
A man so in love,
For he takes no delight
In all of creation;
Alone, mind empty of form and
figure,
Finding no support or foothold,
He tastes there I-don't-know-what
Which is so gladly found.

7. Do not think that he who lives
The so precious inner life
Finds joy and gladness
In the sweetnesses of earth;
But there beyond all beauty
And what is and will be and was,
He tastes I-don't-know-what
Which is so gladly found.

8. The man who seeks to advance
Looks carefully to
What he has yet to gain
More than to what he has gained;
And so I will always tend
Toward greater heights;

Sobre todo a un no sé qué
Que se halla por ventura.

9. Por lo que por el sentido
Puede acá comprehenderse,
Y todo lo que entenderse,
Aunque sea muy subido,
Ni por gracia y hermosura
Yo nunca me perderé,
Sino por un no sé qué
Que se halla por ventura.

DEL VERBO DIVINO

Del Verbo divino
La Virgen preñada
Viene de camino:
Si le dais posada.

SUMA DE PERFECCION

Olvido de lo criado,
Memoria del Criador,
Atención a lo interior
Y estarse amando al Amado.

Beyond all things, to I-don't-know-
what
Which is so gladly found.

9. I will never lose myself
For that which the senses
Can take in here,
Nor for all the mind can hold,
No matter how lofty,
Nor for grace or beauty,
But only for I-don't-know-what
Which is so gladly found.

DEL VERBO DIVINO

The Virgin, weighed
With the Word of God,
Comes down the road:
If only you'll shelter her.

THE SUM OF PERFECTION

Forgetfulness of creation,
Remembrance of the Creator,
Attention to what is within,
And to be loving the Beloved.

NOTE ON THE INTRODUCTIONS

The following sanjuanist studies dealing with doctrinal and literary matters, as well as with problems concerning textual criticism, were particularly useful in the preparation of the introductions. I wish to acknowledge the debt I owe to these works of scholarship; and also to my collaborator, Father Otilio, for the information furnished on many historical and critical problems.

Amatus Van De H. Familie, O.C.D., "'La Fe Ilustradísima' A Propos D'Un Livre Récent," in *Ephemerides Carmeliticae,* Vol. 9, pp. 412–22 (1958).

——, "Le Méditation Chez Saint Jean De La Croix," in *Ephemerides Carmeliticae,* Vol. 11, pp. 176–96 (1960).

Dámaso Alonso, *La Poesía De San Juan De La Cruz* (Madrid: Aguilar, 1946).

Emeterio Del S. Corazon, O.C.D., "La Noche Pasiva Del Espíritu De San Juan De La Cruz," in *Revista de Espiritualidad,* Vol. 18, pp. 5–49; 187–228 (1959).

Eulogio de la Virgen del Carmen, O.C.D., *El "Prólogo" Y La Hermenéutica Del "Cántico Espiritual"* (Rome: Teresianum, 1958).

——, "La Clave Exegética Del Cántico Espiritual," in *Ephemerides Carmeliticae,* Vol. 9, pp. 307–37 (1958); Vol. 11, pp. 312–51 (1960).

——, "La Crítica Sanjuanista En Los Ultimos Veinte Años," in *Salmanticensis,* Vol. 8, pp. 195–246 (1961). For an account of the critical question on the two redactions of *The Spiritual Canticle,* cf. *ibid.,* "La Cuestión Crítica Del Cántico Espiritual," pp. 233–46.

Federico de San Juan de la Cruz, O.C.D., "Vida Teologal Durante La Purificación Interior En Los Escritos De San Juan De La Cruz," in *Revista de Espiritualidad,* Vol. 18, pp. 341–79 (1959).

Gabriel of the Bl. Denys and Redempt., O.C.D., "The Three Signs of Initial Contemplation," in *Ephemerides Carmeliticae,* Vol. 3, pp. 97–129 (1949).

Juan de Jesús María, O.C.D., "El Díptico Subida-Noche," in *Sanjuanistica,* pp. 27–83 (Rome: Teresianum, 1943).

——, "'Le Amará Tanto Como Es Amada' Estudio Positivo sobre 'la igualdad de amor' del alma con Dios, en las obras de San Juan de la Cruz," in *Ephemerides Carmeliticae,* Vol. 6, pp. 3–103 (1955).

Labourdette, M., O.P., "La Foi Théologale Et La Connaissance Mystique

D'Aprés S. Jean De La Croix," in *Revue Thomiste*, pp. 606–15 (1936); pp. 16–57; 191–229 (1937).

Ledrus, M., S.J., *Introductio in Doctrinam Theologicam Sancti Joannis a Cruce de Contemplatione* (*Argumenta lectionum*). Ad usum alumnorum (Rome: Gregorianum, 1955).

Pierluigi di S. Cristina, O.C.D., "Il Ritorno Alla Giustizia Originale," in *Sanjuanistica*, pp. 227–55 (Rome: Teresianum, 1943).

Urbano Barrientos, O.C.D., *Purificación y Purgatorio* (Madrid: Editorial de Espiritualidad, 1960).

Vilnet, Jean, "Bible Et Mystique Chez Saint Jean De La Croix," *Etudes Carmélitaines* (Desclée De Brouwer, 1949).

For an extensive bibliography of sanjuanist studies see: *San Juan de la Cruz, Vida y Obras*, completas de. Cuarta Edicion, pp. 1198–1215 (Madrid: Biblioteca De Autores Cristianos, 1960). See also: Archivum Bibliographicum Carmelitanum (Rome: 1956–).